Global Health 101

SECOND EDITION

Richard Skolnik, MPA

Lecturer
The George Washington University
Washington, DC

JONES & BARTLETT
LEARNING

World Headquarters
Jones & Bartlett Learning
5 Wall Street
Burlington, MA 01803
978-443-5000
info@jblearning.com
www.jblearning.com

Jones & Bartlett Learning books and products are available through most bookstores and online booksellers. To contact Jones & Bartlett Learning directly, call 800-832-0034, fax 978-443-8000, or visit our website, www.jblearning.com.

Substantial discounts on bulk quantities of Jones & Bartlett Learning publications are available to corporations, professional associations, and other qualified organizations. For details and specific discount information, contact the special sales department at Jones & Bartlett Learning via the above contact information or send an email to specialsales@jblearning.com.

Production Credits
Publisher: Michael Brown
Managing Editor: Maro Gartside
Editorial Assistant: Teresa Reilly
Editorial Assistant: Chloe Falivene
Production Manager: Carolyn F. Rogers
Marketing Manager: Grace Richards
Associate Marketing Manager: Jody Sullivan
Manufacturing and Inventory Control Supervisor: Amy Bacus
Composition: Publishers' Design and Production Services, Inc.
Illustrations: diacriTech
Cover Design: Kate Ternullo
Cover, Title Page, Section Opener, and Chapter Opener Image: A young girl receives the drug ivermectin
   (treatment for river blindness) from a community worker in Nigeria. © Kate Holt/Sightsavers
Printing and Binding: Malloy, Inc.
Cover Printing: Malloy, Inc.

Library of Congress Cataloging-in-Publication Data
Skolnik, Richard L.
   Global health 101 / Richard Skolnik. — 2nd ed.
         p. ; cm. — (Essential public health)
   Rev. ed. of: Essentials of global health. c2008.
   Includes bibliographical references and index.
   ISBN 978-0-7637-9751-5 (pbk.)
1. World health. 2. health—Developing countries. 3. Public health—International cooperation. I. Skolnik, Richard L. Essentials of global health. II. Title. III. Series: Essential public health.
   [DNLM: 1. World Health. 2. Health Services Accessibility. 3. Public Health. WA 530.1]
   RA441.S56 2012
   362.1—dc23
         2011014355

6048

Printed in the United States of America

15   14   13   12   10 9 8 7 6

Contents

Comprehensive Online Resources Available

go.jblearning.com/skolnik2e

A companion website with an exceptional array of valuable, current material, for faculty and students, to support the text.

FOR STUDENTS

Weblinks

Links to additional online resources, organized by chapter of the book, including global health videos; key journal articles and reports on important global health topics; presentations on critical issues in global health; interactive learning modules on topics central to the book; model policy briefs; and lists of work and study abroad opportunities.

Quizzes

Multiple choice quizzes for each chapter help reinforce material learned in the text.

Matching Questions

These exercises further emphasize key terms and topics in an interactive and fun way by having students match each term to its definition.

Animated Flashcards

These study tools provide a definition and ask for the key term—the student submits the answer.

Crossword Puzzles

Based on key terms and concepts in the text, crossword puzzles are an engaging way to reinforce information presented in the text.

Interactive Glossary

Allows you to search for key terms and their definitions alphabetically or by chapter.

FOR INSTRUCTORS

This text also offers a full suite of instructor resources to help facilitate in-class discussion and provide ideas for assignments and further study.

Visit http://www.jblearning.com to locate your sales representative and request these valuable resources.

Prologue

In the Prologue to the first edition, I wrote: "The issues of global health have finally arrived in the consciousness of the developed world through a unique union of efforts by former presidents, software pioneers, and rock stars. It is now time that students have a textbook . . . that systematically leads them through the issues of global health from basic principles, to the burden of disease, to examples of successful efforts to improve lives and livelihoods." The first edition of Richard Skolnik's book fulfilled these expectations and more.

What can you as students and as faculty expect from the second edition of *Global Health 101*? The second edition builds upon the strengths of the first edition, provides new and updated material, and links the book with one of the widest arrays of web-based global health materials available. Moreover, the second edition is part of the "101" approach to public health education, which fulfills the Recommendations for Undergraduate Public Health Education and learning outcomes published by the Association of American Colleges and Universities and the Association for Prevention Teaching and Research. These recommendations encourage the teaching of global health along with public health and epidemiology in all 4-year and 2-year colleges.

In terms of new and updated materials, you will find an increased emphasis on equity, the social determinants of health, and the use of the latest available data on the burden of specific diseases and their projected burden. This edition also includes many new materials on communicable diseases, including neglected tropical diseases, emerging and re-emerging infectious diseases, and anti-microbial resistance. The chapters on ethics and noncommunicable diseases have also been enhanced. The chapter on health systems has been substantially revised and 30 "Policy and Program Briefs" have been added to the book. Together these changes—and others—make the book the most up to date and comprehensive of the introductory texts available on global health.

In addition, the second edition is accompanied by a unique collection of ancillary materials for use by students and faculty. Try out the book's website at **go.jblearning.com/skolnik2e**.

As students you'll enjoy and learn from the engaging videos, expand your knowledge using the web links, and test your understandings using the interactive questions and answers. For faculty, the book's website provides an abundance of additional resources to help broaden and deepen students' understanding of global health.

The field of global health is fast becoming a cornerstone of public health education. Careers in global health are sought after options for many of today's college graduates. Richard Skolnik has captured the enthusiasm for global health in his book and capped it off with two chapters related to careers in global health. Whether you are taking a global health course as part of general education, a major or minor in public health or global health, your health professions education, or as part of your interest in international affairs, you will find the second edition an exhilarating experience that opens your mind and your heart to the world of global health.

Richard Riegelman, MD, MPH, PhD
Essential Public Health series editor

Foreword

Only a decade ago, a textbook on global health might have targeted students in the health sciences—public health, nursing, or medicine—without any thought that undergraduates might share an enthusiasm and engagement with this topic. Today, interest in global health has exploded and been embraced on campuses across America and around the world. Global Health has attracted the interest of students from many diverse fields—business, law, engineering, computer sciences, economics, and behavioral sciences—not just the health sciences. What has happened to bring about this extraordinary change? Why the tremendous growth in interest in the health of people in the far corners of the world and how does understanding their health affect others?

The end of the 20th century has brought about many changes that have emphasized the fact that we share a common destiny on a shrinking planet. Advances in information and communication technology have made global events instantaneously available, provided us electronic tools to interact with colleagues anywhere in the world at low cost and given us the power to access an incredible store of knowledge on the web. Modern travel makes no location on earth more than a day or so away. Similar advances in molecular biology and genomics have shortened the time between identifying problems and devising novel solutions for new drugs, vaccines, and interventions. These changes have not only opened the world to us but have changed our way of thinking about our fellow humans in this global village. We have been emboldened to want to work together to improve global health and reduce disparities among nations.

One shared and common goal of all humankind is the desire to have a long and healthy life for oneself, one's family, and one's community. The immediate metric that commands our attention is life expectancy at birth, understanding that a child born in many high-income countries today can expect to live about 80 years while a child born in Haiti or in Nigeria will be lucky to reach 40. Why should longevity be so dramatically determined by where we were born? These differences point to a central and motivating theme of global health: the issue of social equity and health disparities. These same inequities that exist globally, among countries, also exist locally, within countries. For example, in some inner cities in the United States, African American children can expect to live a decade or more less than a white child living a few blocks away. Throughout the developing world, these demographic and ethnic disparities apply as well. It is clear then, that while addressing these major disparities in the health of populations in low- and middle-income countries, high-income countries might also better understand and redress their own problems. In essence, global health and domestic health are not opposites but are part of the same continuum. Studies of one can certainly help us understand and find solutions for the other.

In the 20th century, life expectancy at birth, except for sub-Saharan Africa, has increased throughout the world, in part due to public health interventions, disease prevention, and economic development. In the United States, a child born at the turn of the 20th century could expect to live about 40 years and by the turn of the 21st century, this had increased to nearly 80 years. In China, life expectancy at birth was 39 years in 1960 and increased to 74 years by 2010, the most rapid prolongation of life expectancy in the history of humankind. Only in sub-Saharan Africa did life expectancy that was steadily increasing until 1990 fall off precipitously due to the combined impact of HIV/AIDS and tuberculosis—and it is just beginning to recover.

Global health in the 20th century focused primarily on the control of communicable diseases and diseases of children that were the major determinants of a short life span. As countries have addressed many of these problems and can now anticipate a life expectancy of 60 or more years, many of the problems they face are similar to those in high-income countries and noncommunicable diseases must become a new focus of attention for global health. In fact, in the world today, heart disease has become the number one cause of death, with cancer, stroke, diabetes, and accidents not far behind. Other disabling but nonfatal conditions, such as mental illness, Alzheimer's disease, obesity, and arthritis also diminish our quality of life. Global health in the 21st century will have to address not only the problems of communicable diseases and child survival that were predominant in the 20th century but also the second epidemic of noncommunicable diseases that affect much of the world's population today. We also see a third generation of new global health problems looming in our future—the obesity epidemic, addictions to drugs, alcohol, smoking, environmental hazards, and climate change—that will affect people everywhere and for which we do not have any obvious or simple solutions. These problems will require global solutions that can only be achieved by working together.

If the common aspiration of humankind is to achieve a long, healthy, and productive life for all, then the goal of global health is to create a path to achieve this. We now recognize that place of birth, social class, or ethnic group need not be the single determinant of life expectancy. We have learned a great deal about how to achieve a longer and healthier life—from interventions around clean water and sanitation to prevention programs to immunize children, stop smoking, and reduce obesity, as well as the organization of health systems to screen for disease and deliver care. Yet this huge body of knowledge gleaned over the past century has yet to be adapted and implemented in many parts of the world. The skill sets needed to understand and address these inequities in life expectancy are not the sole province of trained public health and medical specialists. Solutions must include the social scientists who understand and can help change human behavior, lawyers who can address public policies and ethical issues, economists who can identify priorities and economic incentives, business people who understand supply chains and marketing, communications and IT specialists who can link people to knowledge platforms, and engineers who can provide the innovations for change. Success in bringing about global improvements in health will require people with a diverse set of skills who are able to work in environments that are often different from their own and with people whose receptiveness to change may differ.

Ultimately, we may ask "Why should students be concerned about the health of others living with different beliefs in far off places?" The answer is, because it benefits us as much as them. We know that many contagious diseases can be spread rapidly by travel, so we are never more than a flight away from an imported infection. Global health research can be our first line of prevention and can help us identify problems and solutions where the problems are most urgent. Beyond this, the population of many countries is increasingly becoming a melting pot of people who have come from around the world—importing with them different genetic predisposition for diseases and environmental exposures from the past. By understanding global patterns of disease, we can identify hot spots for genetic or noncommunicable diseases or unusual environmental exposures that might provide clues to their origin and risk factors for prevention and cure. Through collaborations in global health research, we can extend our ability to address the most pressing health problems of mankind, combining forces to arrive at solutions faster than we could by working alone. We can also benefit from discoveries like oral rehydration therapy to treat diarrhea, new drugs like artemesin to treat malaria, and interventions like DOTs, directly observed treatment for tuberculosis that were developed through global collaborations in low income settings and are now the standard of care worldwide. Beyond these scientific rationales, global health plays upon the basic humanitarian instinct in all of us—to help those in need. And with this comes a political twist—"health diplomacy"—and the recognition that by working to improve the health of others, we can also improve their well-being, the progress of economic development of their country, and perhaps remove feelings of hopelessness that can lead to despair and terrorism. Indeed, investments in global health can bring many positive returns.

This remarkable volume provides a clear and cogent introduction to the essentials of global health. It lays out the complicated landscape of the field with examples, challenges, and approaches that should be engaging to students in a wide variety of fields of study. It demonstrates how difficult it has been to link ideas we know can improve health with their implementation in the field. And it challenges our morality to appreciate that people born a short flight away are dying at an early age of diseases long addressed in today's high-income societies with solutions that are known to be effective but which are not sufficiently being put in place. This book provides an entrée for students to begin to consider and perhaps engage in opportunities in global health that can address some of these most critical areas relevant to the future of humankind. The pursuit of health is an inherently global enterprise. It will be young people with energy, creativity, leadership, and drive who create the agenda and solutions to address and improve the health condition. Seize the opportunity. The need has never been greater nor the timing more urgent.

Roger I. Glass, MD, PhD
Director, Fogarty International Center
National Institutes of Health
Bethesda, Maryland, USA

Acknowledgments

THE FIRST EDITION

Many people graciously assisted me with the preparation of the first edition of this book, which could never have been completed without their help.

Four colleagues prepared initial chapter drafts and were the co-authors of the chapters indicated: Victor Barbiero for Communicable Diseases; Michael Doney for Unintentional Injuries; Heidi Larson for Child Health; and John Tharakan for Ethics and Human Rights. Vic also provided the Quotable Quotes at the beginning of the book.

A large number of individuals contributed case studies to the first edition. Florence Baingana prepared the case study on mental health in Uganda in Chapter 12. Sadia Chowdhury provided the case study on oral rehydration in Bangladesh in Chapter 5. Ambar Kulshreshtra prepared the case study of Kerala in Chapter 2. Nancy J. Haselow and Musa Obadiah, assisted by Julia Ross, prepared the case study on vitamin A and Ivermectin in Chapter 5. Peter J. Hotez, Ami Shah Brown, and Kari Stoever provided the case study on the Human Hookworm Vaccine Initiative in Chapter 16 of the first edition. Orin Levine prepared the case study on pneumococcal vaccine that is also in Chapter 16 of the first edition. Andrea Thoumi, a student at Tufts University, provided drafts of the case studies on fistula, the earthquake in Pakistan, refugees in Goma, motorcycle helmets in Taiwan, and speed bumps in Ghana. Andrea also prepared drafts of cases on cataract blindness in India and vitamin A in Nepal, based on *Case Studies in Global Health: Millions Saved.*

A large number of friends and colleagues also reviewed and commented on different book chapters, always adding great value as they did so. These people included: Ian Anderson, Alan Berg, Florence Baingana, Stephanie Calves, Roger-Mark de Souza, Wafaie Fawzi, Charlotte Feldman-Jacobs, Adrienne Germain, Reuben Granich, Robert Hecht, Judith Justice, James Levinson, Kseniya Lvovsky, Venkatesh Mannar, William McGreevey, Anthony Measham, Tom Merrick, Elaine Murphy, Rachel Nugent, Kris Olson, Ramanan Laxminarayanan, Rudy van Puymbroeck, Richard Southby, Ron Waldman, and Abdo Yazbeck.

Several of my former students at The George Washington University, including Yvonne Orji, Sapna Patel, David Schneider, and Melanie Vant, provided background information for the first edition and reviewed various book chapters. Pamela Sud, then a student at Stanford University, also reviewed a number of chapters.

Andrea Thoumi not only helped me to prepare cases, as noted above, but also provided background materials, help with citations, and reviewed a number of chapters.

Jessica Gottlieb, Molly Kinder, and Ruth Levine, then of the Center for Global Development, were especially helpful to the preparation of this book. I am very grateful to them and to the Center for agreeing to make *Case Studies in Global Health: Millions Saved* the companion reader to my book. In addition, my book includes abbreviated versions of 16 of the 20 cases in *Millions Saved*, 14 of which the Center graciously prepared for me. Jessica, Molly, and Ruth also reviewed many of the chapters of my book and Jessica Pickett, who then worked with the Center, also commented on a chapter.

Jessica Roeder, my former colleague at the Harvard School of Public Health, was kind enough to take on a second job at night to help me prepare tables and figures.

I am also especially grateful to my daughter, Rachel, who worked with me almost full time for many months and assisted in preparing background information, tables, figures, and citations and reviewing and editing each chapter of the first edition.

Barry Bloom, then Dean of the Harvard School of Public Health, was kind enough to prepare the preface for the first edition, for which I remain very appreciative.

I remain grateful, as well, to Sir George Alleyne, Dean Jamison, and Adrienne Germaine who very kindly wrote advance praise for the first edition. I am honored, of course, that three such distinguished people would do so.

The staff of Jones & Bartlett Learning, especially Katey Birtcher, Mike Brown, Sophie Fleck, and Rachel Rossi, were also immensely helpful to the preparation of the first edition.

THE SECOND EDITION

The second edition would also have been impossible without the extensive assistance of many people.

Roger Glass, the Director of the Fogarty International Center of the United States National Institutes of Health, has honored me by preparing the foreword for this edition.

Elizabeth H. Bradley, Professor of Public Health and Faculty Director, Global Health Leadership Institute at Yale University, and Prabhat Jha, Canada Research Chair in Health and Development and Director, Centre for Global Health Research at the Li Ka Shing Knowledge Institute, St. Michael's Hospital and Dalla Lana School of Public Health, University of Toronto, prepared advance praise for the book.

Joe Millum, of the United States National Institutes of Health, graciously co-authored the chapter on ethics and global health. Joe did marvelous work revising, expanding, and illuminating the text of the first edition to make the chapter more coherent, more enlightening, and more vibrant.

This edition of the book includes 30 new "Policy and Program Briefs," many of which were written with the assistance of friends and professional colleagues who provided drafts of the briefs or other major inputs to the brief writing process. These people included: Kate Acosta and Luzon Pahl of TOSTAN, Soji Adeyi of the Affordable Medicines Facility—malaria; Faruque Ahmed of BRAC; Lisa Beyer from the International AIDS Vaccine Initiative (IAVI); Aya Caldwell and Kris Olson of Massachusetts General Hospital; Susan Higman of the Global Health Council, Peg Willingham of Aeras; Dan Kammen, of the University of California, Berkeley and the World Bank, who prepared the draft of the brief on cookstoves; Linda Kupfer of the Fogarty International Center of the US National Institutes of Health; Anjana Padmanabhan of The Global Network on Neglected Tropical Diseases; Jennifer Staple-Clark of Unite for Sight; Eteena Tadjiogueu from the Human Hookworm Vaccine Initiative; and Karen Van der Westhuizen and Patrizia Carlevaro of the Eli Lilly Corporation. Josephine Francisco and her mentor, Tom Davis, allowed me to prepare a brief about breastfeeding in Burundi that was based on Josie's MPH research project. Josie also kindly reviewed the draft of the brief we prepared from her work.

Many former colleagues at the World Bank, WHO, and PRB, as well as other friends, helped me assemble data and other resources for the book. These included John Briscoe, Dave Gwatkin, Rob Hecht, Dean Jamison, Pete Kolsky, Joel Lamstein, Kseniya Lvovsky, Colin Mathers, Kris Olson, Eduardo Perez, David Peters, and Abdo Yazbeck.

A number of colleagues and friends were also kind enough to review sections of the book or whole book chapters, including Leslie Elder of the World Bank, Robert Hecht of the Results for Development Institute, Peter Hotez of The George Washington University, Susan Higman of the Global Health Council, and Rachel Nugent of the Center for Global Development.

I am also exceptionally grateful to the friends and colleagues for whom I have so much respect and who allowed me to prepare a profile of them for the chapter we have added to the second edition called "Profiles of Global Health Actors." These wonderful people gave much of their time and energy to help us develop a profile about them. Their names appear in Chapter 18.

It would have been impossible, over any time frame, to have prepared this edition without the many former students I was sensible enough to employ for this effort. Laura Chambers, Becky Crowder, Lindsay Gordon, and Emma Morse served as Principal Research Assistants for the second edition. Lindsay and Laura gathered research materials and data, prepared graphs and tables, and drafted countless policy and program briefs, with which Emma also helped. Lindsay and Laura also developed the initial drafts of most of the profiles in Chapter 18. Becky and Emma reviewed each chapter of the book at each stage of writing and production. Becky, Emma, Laura, and Lindsay were instrumental to the preparation of the book and a delight to work with at all times.

The same enjoyment and many valuable inputs came from working with another group of former students who put in a substantial number of hours on data collection; the review of draft chapters, copyedited chapters, and page proofs; and the preparation of materials for the website. These major contributors to the book included: Shannon Doyle, Elizabeth Gomes, Tae Min Kim, and Sara Walker.

A number of former students also assisted me with data collection for the book and the website including: Ahsan Butt, Tanvi Devi, Jenny Durina, David Hidalgo, and Mara Leff. Lisa Hendrickson commented on the brief on Calcutta Kids. Demitsa Rakitsa prepared the initial draft of the brief on HIV financing in Cambodia and South Africa. Candace Martin helped gather data, prepare references and materials for both the book and the website, and also helped to prepare the brief on sanitation in Indonesia.

My thanks also go to former students who allowed me to put on the book's website the policy briefs they wrote for my classes. Their names appear on their briefs on the website, unless they preferred to make their contributions anonymously.

Richard Riegelman, my former Dean at the George Washington University, friend, and editor of the series of which my book is a part, provided irreplaceable help throughout the preparation of the first and second editions.

The staff of Jones & Bartlett Learning was a delight to work with and immensely helpful, including Mike Brown, Sophie Fleck, Maro Gartside, Catie Heverling, Nicole LaLonde, Carolyn Rogers, and Teresa Reilly.

About the Author

Richard Skolnik has worked for more than 35 years in education, health, and development. Richard is now a half-time Lecturer in Global Health at The George Washington University (GWU) where he teaches two introductory global health courses for undergraduates each term and supervises Master of Public Health (MPH) student projects. Richard also works as an independent consultant on program design, monitoring, and evaluation activities in a number of global health areas.

Until November 2008, Richard was the Vice President for International Programs at the Population Reference Bureau. Earlier, he served as the Executive Director of the Harvard School of Public Health PEPFAR program for AIDS treatment in Botswana, Nigeria, and Tanzania. From 2001 to 2004, Richard was the Director of the Center for Global Health at The George Washington University, where he also taught undergraduate and graduate courses in global health.

Richard worked at the World Bank from 1976 to 2001, last serving as the Director for Health and Education for South Asia. His work at the World Bank focused on health systems development, family planning and reproductive health, child health, the control of communicable diseases, and nutrition in low-income countries. He was extensively engaged with TB, leprosy, and cataract blindness control projects in India that have been cited as important public health successes.

Richard has also participated extensively in policy-making and program development at the international level. Richard coordinated the World Bank's work on TB for 5 years, was deeply involved in the establishment of STOP TB, served on a number of WHO working groups on TB, and served three rounds on the Technical Review Panel of the Global Fund. Richard has led two evaluations of the International AIDS Vaccine Initiative and also led an evaluation of the Global Alliance to Eliminate Leprosy.

In addition, Richard has served on advisory groups and faculty for the Harvard Humanitarian Initiative, the development of a women's health program at Harvard University, and the Global Health Leadership Institute at Yale University. He was also a member of an expert panel that reviewed the Framework Program of the Fogarty Center of the United States National Institutes of Health. He is on the Advisory Board for the College of Health and Human Services at George Mason University. He has given numerous guest lectures.

Richard has been Undergraduate Public Health Teacher of the Year at The George Washington University and was asked in 2009 to deliver a lecture in the GWU "Last Lecture" series (http://gwired.gwu.edu/sac/LeadershipDevelopment/LastLecture/20092010LastLecture). In May 2011, Richard was the commencement speaker for the George Mason University College of Health and Human Services.

Richard received a BA from Yale University and an MPA from the Woodrow Wilson School of Princeton University. At Yale, he participated in the Experimental 5-Year BA Program, under which he spent 1 year teaching high school biology in Laoag City, Philippines, living with the same family with whom he had lived as an exchange student in 1966. Upon graduation from Yale, Richard was selected for a fellowship by the Yale–China Association and spent 2 years teaching at The Chinese University of Hong Kong. In between his 2 years at the Woodrow Wilson School, Richard was a Research Fellow at the Institute of Southeast Asian Studies in Singapore, where he authored a monograph on education and training in Singapore.

Richard has worked in health in Africa, Latin America and the Caribbean, the Middle East and North Africa, South Asia, and Southeast Asia. He has also studied and learned to varying degrees Cantonese, French, Ilocano, Mandarin, Spanish, and Tagalog.

Abbreviations

TERM	DEFINITION
ADB	Asian Development Bank
AfDB	African Development Bank
AIDS	acquired immune deficiency syndrome
APOC	African Programme for Onchocerciasis Control
ARI	acute respiratory infection
ART	antiretroviral therapy
AusAID	Australian Agency for International Development
BCG	Bacillus Calmette-Guérin (the tuberculosis vaccine)
BMI	body mass index
BOD	burden of disease
CDC	The U.S. Centers for Disease Control and Prevention
CFR	case fatality ratio
CHE	complex humanitarian emergency
CIDA	Canadian International Development Agency
CMR	crude mortality rate
CVD	cardiovascular disease
DALY	disability-adjusted life year
DANIDA	Danish International Development Agency
DFID	Department for International Development of the United Kingdom
DHS	Demographic and Health Survey
DPT	diphtheria, pertussis, and tetanus vaccine
EPI	Expanded Program on Immunization
EU	European Union
FAO	Food and Agriculture Organization of the United Nations
FSU	Former Soviet Union
GAVI	GAVI Alliance (formerly the Global Alliance for Vaccines and Immunisation)

GDP	gross domestic product
GNP	gross national product
GOBI	growth monitoring, oral rehydration, breastfeeding, and immunization
HALE	health-adjusted life expectancy
Hib	*Haemophilus influenzae* type b
HIV	human immunodeficiency virus
IAVI	International AIDS Vaccine Initiative
IBRD	International Bank for Reconstruction and Development (World Bank)
IDA	International Development Association (the "soft" lending window of the World Bank)
IDB	Inter-American Development Bank
IDD	iodine deficiency disorder
IDP	internally displaced person
IEC	information, education, and communication
IHD	ischemic heart disease
IMCI	integrated management of childhood illness
IMF	International Monetary Fund
IMR	infant mortality rate
IPT	intermittent preventive treatment
IPV	injectable polio vaccine
IQ	intelligence quotient
IRB	institutional review board
ITI	International Trachoma Initiative
ITN	insecticide-treated net
IUD	intrauterine device
LMICs	low- and middle-income countries
MCH	maternal and child health
MDG	Millennium Development Goal
MDT	multi-drug therapy
MI	The Micronutrient Initiative
MMR	maternal mortality rate
MSF	Doctors Without Borders (Médicins Sans Frontières in French)
NCD	noncommunicable disease
NGO	nongovernmental organization
NID	National Immunization Day
NNMR	neonatal mortality rate
OCP	Onchocerciasis Control Program
OPV	oral polio vaccine
ORS	oral rehydration solution
ORT	oral rehydration therapy
PAHO	Pan American Health Organization
PDP	product development partnership
PEPFAR	President's Emergency Plan for AIDS Relief
PHC	primary health care
PMTCT	prevention of mother-to-child transmission

PPP	public–private partnership
RBM	Roll Back Malaria
RTI	road traffic injury
SIDA	Swedish International Development Cooperation Agency
STI	sexually transmitted infection
SWAp	sector-wide approach
TB	tuberculosis
TBA	traditional birth attendant
TFR	total fertility rate
TRIPS	Agreement on Trade-Related Aspects of Intellectual Property Rights
TT	tetanus toxoid
UN	United Nations
UNAIDS	United Nations Program on HIV/AIDS
UNDP	United Nations Development Program
UNFPA	United Nations Family Planning Association
UNICEF	United Nations Children's Fund
USAID	U.S. Agency for International Development
WFP	World Food Program
WHA	World Health Assembly of the World Health Organization
WHO	World Health Organization
WHO/TDR	WHO Special Programme for Research and Training in Tropical Diseases
WTO	World Trade Organization
YLD	years lived with disability
YLL	years of life lost

Quotable Global Health Quotes

Health is a state of complete physical, mental and social well-being and not merely the absence of disease or infirmity. The enjoyment of the highest attainable standard of health is one of the fundamental rights of every human being without distinction of race, religion, political belief, economic or social condition.

World Health Organization

Public health . . . represents an organised response to the protection and promotion of human health and encompasses a concern with the environment, disease control, the provision of health care, health education and health promotion.

Research Unit in Health and Behavioural Change, University of Edinburgh

Public health is the science and art of promoting health. It does so based on the understanding that health is a process engaging social, mental, spiritual and physical well-being. Public health acts on the knowledge that health is a fundamental resource to the individual, to the community and to society as a whole and must be supported by soundly investing in living conditions that create, maintain and protect health.

Ilona Kickbusch

Prevention is better than cure.

Desiderius Erasmus

Every patient carries her or his own doctor inside.

Albert Schweitzer

The doctor of the future will give no medicine, but will interest his patients in the care of the human frame, in diet and in the cause and prevention of disease.

Thomas A. Edison

Of all forms of inequality, injustice in health care is the most shocking and inhumane.

Martin Luther King, Jr.

It is health that is real wealth and not pieces of gold and silver.

Mohandas K. (Mahatma) Gandhi

. . . class differences in health represent a double injustice: life is short where its quality is poor.

Richard G. Wilkinson

Where once it was the physician who waged bellum contra morbum, the war against disease, now it's the whole society.

Susan Sontag

Health consists of having the same diseases as one's neighbors.

Quentin Crisp

Be careful about reading health books. You may die of a misprint.

Mark Twain

Introduction

THE IMPORTANCE OF GLOBAL HEALTH

Why should we care about the health of other people, especially that of people in other countries? Why should global health matter to those who live in Australia, France, the United States, or other developed countries? Actually, for a number of critical reasons, the health of people everywhere must be a growing concern for all of us.

First, diseases do not respect boundaries. Human immunodeficiency virus (HIV) has spread worldwide. A person with tuberculosis can infect 15 people a year, wherever they are. The West Nile Virus came from Egypt but occurs today in many countries. In addition, there is an important risk of a worldwide epidemic of influenza. Clearly, the health of each of us increasingly depends on the health of others.

Second, there is an ethical dimension to the health and well-being of other people. Many children in poor countries get sick and die needlessly from malnutrition or from diseases that are preventable and curable. Many adults in poor countries die because they lack access to medicines that are customarily available to people in rich countries. Is this just? Are we prepared to accept such deaths without taking steps to prevent them?

Third, health is closely linked with economic and social development in an increasingly interdependent world. Children who suffer from malnutrition may not reach their full mental potential and may not enroll in or stay in school. Sick children from developing countries are less likely than healthy children to become productive adults who can contribute to the economic standing of their family, community, or country. Adults who suffer from AIDS, tuberculosis, malaria, and other diseases lose income while they are sick and out of work, which is a major contributor to keeping their families in an endless cycle of poverty.

Finally, the health and well-being of people everywhere have important implications for global security and freedom. High rates of HIV have had a destabilizing impact on some countries, as more teachers and health workers died than were being trained, and as there were increasingly insufficient numbers of rural workers to grow and harvest crops. Outbreaks of other diseases, such as cholera, the plague, and SARS (Severe Acute Respiratory Syndrome), for example, threaten people's ability to engage freely in economic pursuits. The 1991 outbreak of cholera in Peru cost that country about $1 billion, the plague in 1994 cost India about $2 billion, and SARS in Asia in 2003 cost the economies of Asia a staggering $18 billion in lost economic activity.

Indeed, these factors have caused an increasing interest in health within universities and a growing call for all university students to study health from a global perspective. The aim of this book is to examine the most critical global health topics in a clear and engaging manner. The book will provide the reader with an overview of the importance of global health in the context of development, an examination of the most important global health issues and their economic and social consequences, and a discussion of some of the steps that are being taken to address these concerns.

It will also provide numerous cases of "success stories" in dealing with important global health problems.

This book is intended to provide an introduction to global health for all students. This includes students who have never studied public health before and who will not take additional public health courses. It also includes those students, whether they have studied public health before or not, who may wish to pursue additional studies in public health later.

This book is largely based on an undergraduate course on global health that I have taught (with a 2-year break) since 2001 at The George Washington University in Washington, DC. The text seeks to "speak" to the reader in a manner one would find in an exciting and motivating classroom. In addition to covering key concepts in global health and frameworks for the analysis of global health issues, this book also contains numerous examples of on-the-ground experiences in addressing key global health problems. Those students who want to explore case studies in greater depth can read the companion volume to this textbook, *Case Studies in Global Health: Millions Saved*.

Very few introductory materials on global health are available to students or their professors. Hopefully, this book will help to close that gap by providing a foundation for enhanced studies in public health, global health, and economic and social development.

THE ORGANIZATION OF THE BOOK

This book is organized in several parts that closely follow the topics mentioned previously. Part I introduces the reader to the basic principles of global health, key measures of health, and the concepts of the health and the development link. Chapter 1 introduces readers to some key principles, themes, and goals of global health. Chapter 2 examines the determinants of health, how health is measured, and how health conditions change over time and as countries develop economically. Chapter 3 looks at the links between health and development, touching upon the connections between health and education, equity, and poverty.

Part II reviews cross-cutting themes in global health. Chapter 4 examines human rights and ethical issues in global health. Chapter 5 covers health systems. This chapter reviews the purpose and goals of health systems and how different countries have organized their health systems. The chapter also reviews the key challenges that health systems face, the costs and consequences of those challenges, and how some countries have addressed health system challenges. Culture plays an extremely important part in health, and Chapter 6 examines the links between culture and health. This chapter reviews the importance of culture to health, how health is perceived in different groups, the manner in which different culture groups seek health care and engage in health practices, and how one can promote change in health behavior.

Part III reviews the most important causes of illness, disability, and death, particularly in low- and middle-income countries. The chapters in this part of the book will examine environmental issues, nutrition, reproductive health, and child health. The book then looks at communicable diseases, noncommunicable diseases, and unintentional injuries.

Part IV examines how cooperative action can address global health issues. Chapter 14 reviews the impact on health of conflicts, natural disasters, and other health emergencies. Chapter 15 examines how different actors in the global health field work both individually and cooperatively to address key global health problems. Chapter 16 reviews how science and technology have helped to improve public health and how further advances in science and technology could help to address some of the most important global health challenges that remain.

A new Part V has been added to the second edition and focuses on careers in the global health field. Chapter 17 examines the types of careers in global health; the skills, knowledge, and experience needed to pursue these careers; and how you can get those skills, knowledge, and experience. The book ends with Chapter 18, which includes profiles of 18 actors in the global health field whose personal stories are meant to inspire you, as well as provide guidance about pursuing a career in global health if that is your interest.

Each chapter follows a similar outline. The chapters begin with vignettes that relate to the topic to be covered and which are intended to make the topic "real" for the reader. Some of these vignettes are not true in the literal sense. However, each of them is based on real events that occur regularly in the countries discussed in this book. Most chapters then explain key concepts, terms, and definitions. The chapters that deal with cross-cutting issues in the second and fourth parts of the book then examine the importance of the topic to enhancing global health, some key challenges in further improving global health, and what can be done to address those challenges.

The chapters that focus on health conditions look at the importance of the topic to the burden of disease; key issues related to this cause of illness, disability, and death; and the costs and consequences of these issues for individuals, communities, and the world. These chapters then examine what has been learned about how to deal with these health burdens in the most cost-effective ways, the future challenges in each of these areas, and some specific cases of successful efforts at addressing such challenges.

Most chapters contain several case studies. Some of these deal with well-known cases that have already proven to be models for global health efforts. Others, however, are based on experiences that show good promise, both for success and for providing lessons, but which have not yet proven themselves.

Many chapters also contain "policy and program briefs" that are meant to introduce you to important global health topics, actors, and organizations.

Each chapter concludes with a summary of the main messages in the chapter and a set of study questions that can assist the reader in reviewing the materials included in the chapter. Each chapter also contains endnotes with citations for the data that are used in the book. The book does not contain any additional lists of reference materials. Those wishing to explore topics in greater depth will find ample suggestions for additional reading in the endnotes, as well as on the book's website.

The reader should note that the chapters are not in order of importance. Nutrition, for example, is fundamental to all health concerns; however, it only makes sense to cover nutrition in this book after establishing the context for studying global health and after covering some cross-cutting global health issues. In addition, you will note that there is no chapter called "globalization and health." Rather, you will find that the relationships between globalization and health are integrated into all of the chapters. Some students may also wish to read Chapter 15 on global health policy, actors, and actions before they cover too many of the other chapters. This will help them understand at an earlier stage how the world has organized to address key global health issues.

THE PERSPECTIVE OF THE BOOK

The book will take a global perspective to all that it covers. Although the book includes many country case studies, topics will be examined from the perspective of the world as a whole. The book also pays particular attention to the links between poverty and health and the relationship between health and equity. Special attention will also be given to gender and ethnicity and their relation to health. Another theme that runs through the book is the connection between health and development.

The book follows the point of view that health is a human right. The book is written with the presumption that governments have an obligation to try to ensure that all of their people have access to an affordable package of healthcare services and that all people are protected from the costs of ill health. The book is also based on the premise, however, that the development of a health system by any country, as discussed further in Chapter 5, is inextricably linked to the value system and the political structure of that country.

The book covers key global health topics, including those that affect developed and developing countries; however, the book pays particular attention to low- and middle-income countries and to poor people within them. The rationale for this is that improving health status indicators within and across countries can only be accomplished if the health of the poor and other disadvantaged groups is improved. In addition, the idea of social justice is at the core of public health.

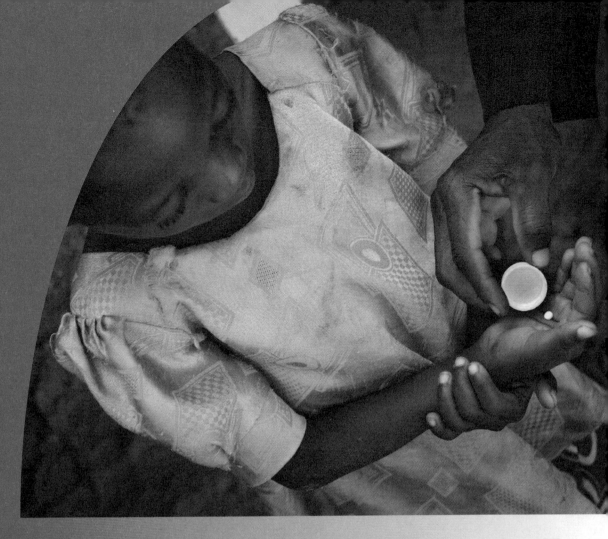

PART I

Principles, Measurements, and the Health–Development Link

CHAPTER 1

The Principles and Goals of Global Health

LEARNING OBJECTIVES

By the end of this chapter the reader will be able to:

- Define the terms *health, public health,* and *global health*
- Discuss some examples of public health efforts
- Discuss some examples of global health activities
- Describe some of the guiding principles of public health work
- Describe the Millennium Development Goals and their relation to global health
- Briefly discuss the global effort to eradicate smallpox

VIGNETTES

Laurie Smith lived in Portsmouth, Virginia, in the United States. She was 50 years old and had always been healthy. Last weekend, she woke up with a headache, a high fever, and a very stiff neck. Laurie was so sick that she went to the emergency room of the local hospital. The physicians diagnosed Laurie as having meningitis, an inflammation of the membrane around the brain and spinal cord,[1] that was caused by West Nile virus. This virus originated in Egypt in the 1930s and is transmitted by a mosquito. Over a number of decades, West Nile virus spread from Egypt to the Middle East, Africa, and Asia. In 1999, the first cases of West Nile appeared in the United States, and it is now found throughout the country, as shown in Figure 1-1.[2]

By 2005, polio was on the verge of being eradicated from every country. That year, however, rumors circulated in northern Nigeria that the polio vaccine was causing sterilization. In response to these rumors, some community leaders discouraged people from immunizing their children.

Within months, polio cases began to appear in the area. Shortly thereafter, polio cases spread from northern Nigeria to Sudan, Yemen, and Indonesia. The global campaign to eradicate polio had been dealt a major blow, stemming partly from rumors in one country about the alleged side effects of the vaccine.[3]

Getachew is a 20-year-old Ethiopian with HIV. His disease is advanced, but he receives no treatment for it. He has tuberculosis (TB) and much of his mouth is coated with a white, pasty yeast called thrush. He has lost more than 20 percent of his body weight. He stopped going to work some time ago, has no money, and is totally dependent on his family for care and day-to-day needs. Getachew is one of almost 1 million people in Ethiopia with HIV.[4] In fact, in 2008 about 33.4 million people were living with HIV worldwide.[5] There are countries in Africa, such as Botswana, Lesotho, and Swaziland,[6] in which about one-quarter of the people are HIV-positive.

Jim Smith is a high school student in London, England. Early in the school year, he had a fever and cough that would not go away. He did not feel like eating. He slept badly and woke up every morning in a sweat. Jim had TB. Although many people think that TB has been eliminated from high-income countries, it has not. Rather, the spread of HIV has triggered an increase in TB worldwide. In addition, immigration is helping to spread the disease from lower-income to higher-income countries. In fact, there are urban areas of the United Kingdom in which the rates of TB are higher than the rates in some low- and middle-income countries.[7]

FIGURE 1-1 West Nile Virus Activity in the United States, by State, 2010 (excluding Hawaii and Alaska)

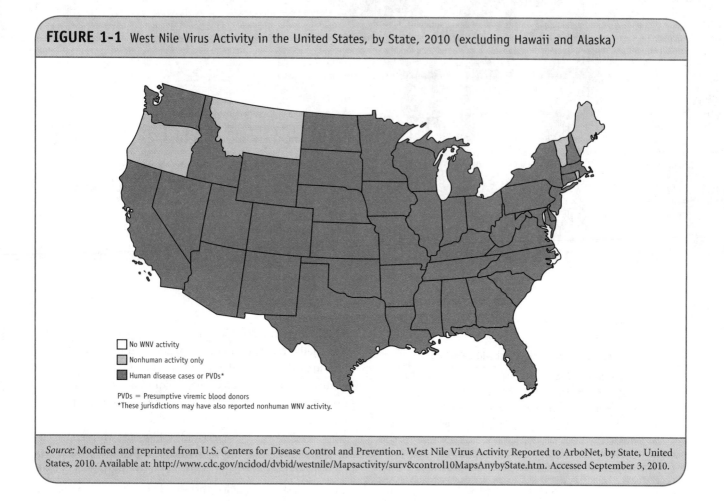

☐ No WNV activity
☐ Nonhuman activity only
■ Human disease cases or PVDs*

PVDs = Presumptive viremic blood donors
*These jurisdictions may have also reported nonhuman WNV activity.

Source: Modified and reprinted from U.S. Centers for Disease Control and Prevention. West Nile Virus Activity Reported to ArboNet, by State, United States, 2010. Available at: http://www.cdc.gov/ncidod/dvbid/westnile/Mapsactivity/surv&control10MapsAnybyState.htm. Accessed September 3, 2010.

WHY STUDY GLOBAL HEALTH

Over the last fifty years, the world has made significant progress in improving human health. Since 1950, for example, the death rate of children under 5 years has fallen from 148 deaths per 1000 children to fewer than 65 deaths per 1000 children.[8] During that same period, the average life expectancy in developing countries has increased from 40 years to 69 years.[9] Smallpox has been eradicated, polio has been nearly eliminated, and great progress has been made in reducing the burden of vaccine-preventable diseases in children and of parasitic infections, such as Guinea worm. One reason to study global health is to gain a better understanding of the progress made so far in addressing global health problems.

Another reason to study global health, however, is to better understand the most important global health challenges that remain and what must be done to address them most effectively. Despite the important progress in improving human health:

- There were 164,000 deaths from measles globally in 2008.[10]
- About 1.8 million people a year die of TB.[11]
- About 343,000 women died of maternal causes in 2008.[12]

In addition, the world is shrinking and the health of people everywhere must be of concern to all of us. This is particularly important because many diseases are not limited by national boundaries. Tuberculosis, HIV, and polio, for example, can spread from one country to the next. Dengue fever used to be concentrated in Southeast Asia but cases are now seen in many more countries, as shown in Figure 1-2.[13] The "avian flu" first appeared in East Asia but it, too, is spreading to other regions. Ten years ago, no one in the neighborhood of Laurie, mentioned in the vignette, ever thought of getting West Nile virus.

Besides the central global health challenges noted above, there are also exceptional disparities in the health of

FIGURE 1-2 Distribution of Dengue Fever, 2009

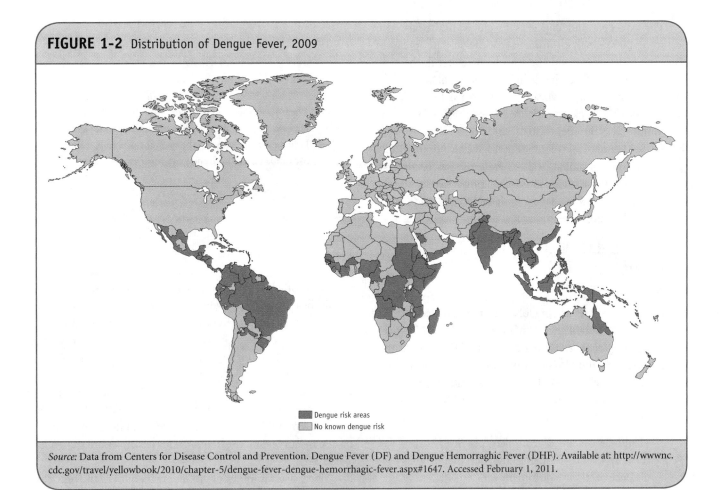

Dengue risk areas
No known dengue risk

Source: Data from Centers for Disease Control and Prevention. Dengue Fever (DF) and Dengue Hemorraghic Fever (DHF). Available at: http://wwwnc.cdc.gov/travel/yellowbook/2010/chapter-5/dengue-fever-dengue-hemorrhagic-fever.aspx#1647. Accessed February 1, 2011.

some groups compared to the health of others. Life expectancy in Japan, for example, is about 83 years,[14] but it is only 61 years in Haiti.[15] In addition, there are a number of life saving technologies that have been used in high-income countries for many years that are not yet in widespread use in low-income countries, such as the hepatitis B vaccine. In fact, the previous points raise important ethical and humanitarian questions about the extent to which people everywhere should be concerned about disparities in access to health services and in health status.

The important link between health and development is another reason to pay particular attention to global health. Poor health of mothers is linked to poor health of babies and the failure of children to reach their full mental and physical potential. In addition, ill health of children can delay their entry into school and can affect their attendance at school, their performance in school, and, therefore, their future economic prospects. Countries with major health problems, such as high rates of malaria or HIV, have difficulty attracting

the investments needed to develop their economy. Moreover, having large numbers of undernourished, unhealthy, and ill-educated people in any country is destabilizing and a health, economic, and security threat to all countries.

The nature of many global health concerns and the need for different actors to work together to address them are more reasons why we should be concerned with global health. Although locally relevant solutions are needed to address most health problems, some health issues can only be solved using a global approach. In addition, some problems, such as ensuring access to drugs to treat HIV, may require more financial resources than any individual country can provide. Still other global health issues require technical cooperation across countries because few countries themselves have the technical capacity to deal with them. Global cooperation might be needed, for example, to establish standards for drug safety, to set protocols for the treatment of certain health problems, such as malaria, or to develop an AIDS vaccine that could serve the needs of low-income countries.

The concepts and concerns of global health are also becoming increasingly prominent worldwide. The spread of HIV, the SARS scare, and the fear of the avian flu have all brought attention to global health. As you will read about later in the book, the advocacy efforts of Doctors Without Borders and the rock star Bono, the establishment of the Millennium Development Goals, and the philanthropy of the Bill & Melinda Gates Foundation have also dramatically raised attention to global health. The topic has become so important that there is a push in many universities throughout the world to ensure that all students have a basic understanding of key global health issues.

HEALTH, PUBLIC HEALTH, AND GLOBAL HEALTH

Health

Before starting our review of global health in greater detail, it will be helpful to establish a set of definitions for *health*, *public health*, and *global health* that can be used throughout this book. Most of us think of "health" from our individual perspective as "not being sick." The World Health Organization, however, set out a broader definition of health in 1948 that is still widely used:

> Health is a state of complete physical, mental and social well-being and not merely the absence of disease or infirmity.[16]

This is the definition of "health" used in this book.

Public Health

Although the World Health Organization (WHO) concept of "health" refers first to individuals, this book is mostly about "public health" and the health of populations. C.E.A Winslow, considered to be the founder of modern public health in the United States, formulated a definition of public health in 1923 that is still commonly used today. In his definition, public health is:

> . . . the science and the art of preventing disease, prolonging life, and promoting physical health and mental health and efficiency through organized community efforts toward a sanitary environment; the control of community infections; the education of the individual in principles of personal hygiene; the organization of medical and nursing service for the early diagnosis and treatment of disease; and the development of the social machinery to ensure to every individual in the community a standard of living adequate for the maintenance of health.[17]

TABLE 1-1 Selected Examples of Public Health Activities

- The promotion of hand washing
- The promotion of bicycle and motorcycle helmets
- The promotion of knowledge about HIV/AIDS
- Large scale screening for diabetes and hypertension
- Large scale screening of the eyesight of schoolchildren
- Mass dosing of children against worms
- The operation of a supplementary feeding program for poorly nourished young children

According to Winslow's definition, some examples of public health activities would include the development of a campaign to promote child immunization in a particular country, an effort to get people in a city to use seat belts when they drive, and actions to get people in a specific setting to eat healthier foods and to stop smoking. In addition, most levels of government also carry out certain public health functions. These include the management of public health clinics, the operation of public health laboratories, and the maintenance of disease surveillance systems. Other examples are shown in Table 1-1.

There are a number of guiding principles to the practice of public health that have been articulated, for example, by the American Public Health Association in its "Public Health Code of Ethics."[18] These principles focus on prevention of disease, respect for the rights of individuals, and a commitment to developing public health efforts in conjunction with communities. They also highlight the need to pay particular attention to disenfranchised people and communities and to working in public health on the basis of data and evidence. In addition, they note the importance of taking account of a wide range of disciplines and appreciation for the values, beliefs, and cultures of diverse groups. Finally, they put considerable emphasis on engaging in public health practice in a way that "enhances the physical and social environment" and that builds on collaborations across public health actors. These themes are at the foundation of this book and will recur throughout it.

Many people confuse "public health" and "medicine," although they have quite different approaches. Table 1-2 outlines these differences.[19] To a large extent, the biggest difference between the medical approach and the public health approach is the focus in public health on the health of populations rather than on the health of individuals. Exaggerating somewhat for effect, we could say, for example,

TABLE 1-2 Approaches of Public Health and Medicine

Differentiating Factors	Public Health	Medicine
Focus	Population	Individual
Ethical basis	Public service	Personal service
Emphasis	Disease prevention and health promotion for communities	Disease diagnosis, treatment, and care for individuals
Interventions	Broad spectrum that may target the environment, human behavior, lifestyle, and medical care	Emphasis on medical care

Source: Modified with permission from Harvard School of Public Health. About HSPH: Distinctions Between Public Health and Medicine. Available at: www.hsph.harvard.edu/about.html#publichealth. Accessed May 27, 2006.

that a physician cares for an individual patient whom he or she immunizes against a particular disease, whereas a public health specialist is likely to focus on how one ensures that the whole community gets vaccinated. A physician will counsel an individual patient on the need to exercise and avoid obesity; a public health specialist will work with a program meant to help a community stay sufficiently active to avoid obesity. In addition, there are branches of public health, such as epidemiology, that focus on studying patterns and causes of disease in specific populations and the application of this information to controlling health problems.[20] Finally, we should note the exceptional attention which public health approaches pay to prevention of health problems.

Global Health

What exactly is *global health*? The U.S. Institute of Medicine defined global health as "health problems, issues, and concerns that transcend national boundaries and may best be addressed by cooperative actions . . ."[21]

Another group defined what we would now call global health as "the application of the principles of public health to health problems and challenges that transcend national boundaries and to the complex array of global and local forces that affect them."[22]

The discussion of the definition of global health has continued. Two groups of distinguished public health scholars and practitioners recently offered additional commentaries on this matter. One group suggested that we should define global health as:

. . . an area for study, research, and practice that places a priority on improving health and

achieving equity in health for all people worldwide. Global health emphasizes transnational health issues, determinants, and solutions, involves many disciplines within and beyond the health sciences, and promotes interdisciplinary collaboration; and is a synthesis of population based prevention with individual-level clinical care.[23]

In response to the above suggestion, however, another panel suggested that one should not distinguish between global health and public health more broadly. They also suggested that the key principles of both are the same: a focus on the public good, belief in a global perspective, a scientific and interdisciplinary approach, the need for multi-level approaches to interventions, and the need for comprehensive frameworks for health policies and financing.[24]

The study and practice of global health today reflects many of the comments made above. *Global health* implies a global perspective on public health problems. It suggests issues that people face in common, such as the impact of a growing and aging worldwide population on health or the potential risks of climate change to health. The topic also relates in important ways to problems that require cooperative action. An important part of global health also covers the growing problem everywhere of noncommunicable diseases, as well as the "unfinished agenda" of the health needs of the poor in poor countries. In practical terms, as a new student to global health, it may be best not to worry much about the definition of *global health*, but rather, to see the topic as an important part of public health, which itself has many areas of critical importance.

Some examples of important global health concerns include the factors that contribute to women dying of pregnancy-related causes in so many countries; the exceptional amount of malnutrition among young children, especially in South Asia and Africa; the burden of different infectious and noncommunicable diseases worldwide and what can be done to control those diseases. The impact of the environment on health globally and the effects of natural disasters and conflicts are also important to global health. Other significant global health issues include how countries can organize and manage their health systems to enable the healthiest population they can attain with the resources available to them, the search for new technologies to improve important global health problems, and how different actors can work together to solve health problems, that are too significant for any country or actor to solve on their own. Another global health matter of importance is the relationship between globalization and the health of different communities. Some additional global health issues of importance are shown in Table 1-3.

CRITICAL GLOBAL HEALTH CONCEPTS

In order to understand and to help address key global health issues like those noted previously, there are a number of concepts concerning global health with which one must be familiar. Some of the most important include:

- The determinants of health
- The measurement of health status
- The importance of culture to health
- The global burden of disease
- The key risk factors for different health conditions
- The demographic and epidemiologic transitions
- The organization and functions of health systems

TABLE 1-3 Selected Examples of Global Health Issues

- Emerging and re-emerging infectious diseases
- Antimicrobial resistance
- Eradication of polio
- Diarrhea, measles, and pneumonia in young children
- Sexually transmitted infections in young women
- TB
- Malaria
- HIV/AIDS
- Parasitic infections, such as hookworm
- The increasing cases of diabetes and heart disease

It is also essential to understand the links among health, education, development, poverty, and equity.

Building on the previous concepts, those interested in global health also need to have an understanding of how key health issues affect different parts of the world and the world as a whole. These include:

- Environmental health
- Nutrition
- Reproductive health
- Child health
- Infectious diseases
- Noncommunicable diseases
- Injuries

Finally, it is important to understand global health issues that are generally addressed through cooperation. Some of these concern conflicts, natural disasters, and humanitarian emergencies. Others relate to the mechanisms by which different actors in global health activities work together to solve global health problems. Harnessing the power of science and technology to serve global health needs also requires cooperation.

SOME KEY TERMS

The book will sometimes speak of "developed countries" and "developing countries." These terms are not precise. *Developed countries* are those, such as the United States, France, Australia, and the United Kingdom, that have relatively high income per capita and that are often thought of as "industrialized." *Developing countries* are those, such as Haiti, Liberia, Laos, and Papua New Guinea, that have relatively low per capita incomes and that are not heavily industrialized.

Although the book will use the terms *developed* and *developing countries*, it will mostly use the terms *low-income*, *middle-income*, and *high-income* to refer to countries. These terms will follow the definitions used by the World Bank, which divides countries into four income groups, based on their gross national income per person (see Table 1-4):[25]

- $995 or less—low-income
- $996 to $3945—lower middle-income
- $3946 to $12,195—upper middle-income
- $12,196 or above—high-income

Much of the data discussed in this book will be broken down by the geographic regions used by the World Bank.

- East Asia and the Pacific
- Europe and Central Asia
- Latin America and the Caribbean

TABLE 1-4 Examples of Low-, Middle- and High-Income Countries, Following World Bank Classification

Low-Income	Lower Middle-Income	Upper Middle-Income	High-Income
Bangladesh	Angola	Botswana	Belgium
Cambodia	Bolivia	Costa Rica	Canada
Ethiopia	Egypt	Panama	Denmark
Haiti	Iraq	South Africa	Portugal
Mozambique	Morocco	Turkey	Italy
Zimbabwe	Philippines	Venezuela	Netherlands
	Swaziland		Singapore
	Tunisia		Switzerland

Source: Data from the World Bank. Country and Lending Groups. Available at: http://data.worldbank.org/about/country-classifications/country-and-lending-groups. Accessed September 4, 2010.

- Middle East and North Africa
- South Asia
- Sub-Saharan Africa

Occasionally, however, data will be discussed according to the regions that are used by the World Health Organization. For comparative purposes, data is sometimes also shown for high-income countries that belong to the Organization for Economic Cooperation and Development (OECD).

NOTE ON THE USE OF DATA

This is a book about global health that has a particular focus on the "health–development link," so data are organized wherever possible by World Bank region. However, where necessary, data are also organized by the regions of the World Health Organization.

Information included in this edition on the basic health status indicators is generally the latest data available from either the World Bank or the World Health Organization. However, it is sometimes supplemented with data from other sources.

The first edition of the book used a consistent data set on the global burden of disease that came from the 2006 *Global Burden of Disease and Risk Factors* and that used 2001 as its base year. The first edition of this book also made extensive use of data and information from *Disease Control Priorities in Developing Countries*, 2nd edition (DCP2). The information in DCP2 on the burden of disease was based on the *Global Burden of Disease and Risk Factors.*

Because the 2006 study contains the largest coherent published data set on the burden of disease and is linked to DCP2, this edition continues to use data extensively from both sources. However, the World Health Organization updated the global burden of disease data in 2008, with 2004 as the base year, and some of that data has been published in a manner consistent with the organization of data in the 2006 study. This edition generally uses information from the 2008 update when referring to projections of the burden of disease and when discussing risk factors that relate to the future burden of disease.

In addition, every effort has been made to use the latest available data that refer to particular health conditions in the individual chapters that cover those conditions. However, no effort has been made to reconcile those data with the 2001 or 2004 data on the global burden of disease.

THE MILLENNIUM DEVELOPMENT GOALS

This book will make continuous references to the Millennium Development Goals (MDGs). The MDGs were formulated in 2000 at the United Nations Millennium Summit and were articulated in the Millennium Declaration.[26] There are 8 MDGs and 15 core targets that relate to them. The countries that signed the declaration pledged to meet the MDGs by 2015. Keeping the MDGs in mind as you read this book is important because the MDGs are an explicit statement of the goals that many countries have set for an important part of their development efforts and, therefore, are an important part of the context for understanding global health issues. The MDGs and their related targets are noted in Table 1-5.

As you can see, all eight of the MDGs relate to health. The goals of reducing child mortality, improving maternal heath, and combating HIV/AIDS, malaria, and other diseases directly concern health. However, each of the other goals also relates to health. Hunger and poverty, referred to in goal 1,

TABLE 1-5 The Millennium Development Goals and Their Related Targets

Goal	Targets
Goal 1: Eradicate Extreme Hunger and Poverty	**Target 1.** Halve, between 1990 and 2015, the proportion of people whose income is less than $1 a day **Target 2.** Halve, between 1990 and 2015, the proportion of people who suffer from hunger
Goal 2: Achieve Universal Primary Education	**Target 3.** Ensure that, by 2015, children everywhere, boys and girls alike, will be able to complete a full course of primary schooling
Goal 3: Promote Gender Equality and Empower Women	**Target 4.** Eliminate gender disparity in primary and secondary education, preferably by 2005, and in all levels of education no later than 2015
Goal 4: Reduce Child Mortality	**Target 5.** Reduce by two thirds, between 1990 and 2015, the under-5 mortality rate
Goal 5: Improve Maternal Health	**Target 6.** Reduce by three quarters, between 1990 and 2015, the maternal mortality ratio
Goal 6: Combat HIV/AIDS, Malaria, and Other Diseases	**Target 7.** Have halted by 2015 and begun to reverse the spread of HIV/AIDS **Target 8.** Have halted by 2015 and begun to reverse the incidence of malaria and other major diseases
Goal 7: Ensure Environmental Sustainability	**Target 9.** Integrate the principles of sustainable development into country policies and programs and reverse the loss of environmental resources **Target 10.** Halve, by 2015, the proportion of people without sustainable access to safe drinking water and basic sanitation **Target 11.** Have achieved by 2020 a significant improvement in the lives of at least 100 million slum dwellers
Goal 8: Develop a Global Partnership for Development	**Target 12.** Develop further an open, rule-based, predictable, nondiscriminatory trading and financial system **Target 13.** Address the special needs of the Least Developed Countries **Target 14.** Address the special needs of landlocked developing countries and small island developing states **Target 15.** Deal comprehensively with the debt problems of developing countries through national and international measures in order to make debt sustainable in the long term

Source: Data from Millennium Project: Goals, Targets, and Indicators. Available at http://www.unmillenniumproject.org/goals/gti.htm. Accessed April 9, 2011.

are intimately linked with health status, both as causes of ill health and as consequences of ill health. The goal of universal primary education can only be met if children are well enough nourished and healthy enough to enroll in school, attend school, and have a good capacity to learn while they are there. As you will read throughout the book, the gender disparities referred to in goal 3 are central to the health issues that affect women globally, many of which relate to their lack of empowerment. Goal 7 is meant to address the need for safe water and sanitation, the lack of which is a major cause of ill health and death. Chapter 15 discusses how different actors in global health can work together to help countries improve health status, as indicated in goal 8 on partnerships for development.

THE CASE STUDIES

Many of the case studies in this book were provided by the Center for Global Development and are elaborated upon further in a companion piece to this book entitled *Case Studies in Global Health: Millions Saved*.[27] That book provides detailed case studies of 20 successful interventions in global health. The cases were carefully selected on the basis of five selection criteria: scale, importance, impact, duration, and cost-effectiveness. When considered together, the cases suggest a number of important lessons that will be reflected throughout this book:

- Success in addressing important health problems *is* possible, even in the poorest countries.
- Governments in poor countries *can* manage major public health successes and often can fund them, as well.
- Technology does enable progress in health; however, many successes stem from basic changes in people's behavior, such as filtering water, giving infants oral rehydration for diarrhea, and cessation of smoking.
- Cooperation among global health actors can make a major difference to the achievement of health aims.
- It is possible to find evidence of what works and does not work in global health efforts.
- Success comes in all shapes—different types of programs in different types of settings have been and can be successful.

SMALLPOX ERADICATION—THE MOST FAMOUS SUCCESS STORY

It is fitting to end this introductory chapter with a summary of the most famous public health success story of all, the case of smallpox eradication. This effort was not only a great triumph of public health, but also a great accomplishment for mankind. In addition, the history of smallpox eradication is well known to everyone who works in public health and it provides many lessons that can be applied to other public health efforts. The history of smallpox eradication and the lessons learned from dealing with it also remain very important because of the new threat of smallpox being used as a biological weapon.

Background

In 1966, smallpox ravaged over 50 countries, affecting 10 million to 15 million people, of whom almost 2 million died each year.[29] At the time, smallpox killed as many as 30 per-

cent of those infected. Those who survived might suffer deep pitted scars and blindness as a result of their illness.[30]

The Intervention

Although a vaccine against smallpox was created by Edward Jenner in 1798, eradication of smallpox became a practical goal only in the 1950s when the vaccine could be mass produced and stored without refrigeration. A later breakthrough came in the form of the bifurcated needle, a marvel of simple technology that dramatically reduced costs by allowing endless reuse after sterilization, and by requiring a far smaller amount of vaccine per patient. The needle also made vaccination easy, thereby reducing the time and effort required to train villagers in its use.

In 1959, WHO adopted a proposal to eradicate smallpox through compulsory vaccination, but the program languished until 1965, when the United States stepped in with technical and financial support. A Smallpox Eradication Unit was established at WHO, headed by Dr. D.A. Henderson of the Centers for Disease Control and Prevention (CDC) in the United States. As part of the smallpox eradication program, all WHO member countries were required to manage program funds effectively, report smallpox cases, encourage research on smallpox, and maintain flexibility in the implementation of the smallpox program to suit local conditions.

The Smallpox Eradication Unit proved to be a small but committed team, supplying vaccines and specimen kits to those countries that still had smallpox. Although wars and civil unrest caused disruptions in the program's progress, momentum was always regained with new methods and extra resources that focused on containing outbreaks by speeding with motorized teams to seek out new cases, isolate new cases, and vaccinate everyone in the vicinity of the new cases.

This military-style approach proved effective even in the most difficult circumstances. It also took practical account of the facts that: (1) it would have been extraordinarily difficult to immunize the whole world against smallpox, and (2) the transmission of the smallpox virus could be stopped by focusing vaccination efforts around new cases.

The Impact

In 1977, the last endemic case of smallpox in the world was recorded in Somalia. In 1980, after two years of surveillance and searching, WHO declared smallpox the first disease in history to have been eradicated. Smallpox had previously been eradicated in Latin America in 1971 and in Asia in 1975.[31]

Costs and Benefits

The annual cost of the eradication campaign between 1967 and 1979 was $23 million. For the whole campaign, international donors provided $98 million, while $200 million came from the endemic countries.[26] The United States saves the total of all its contributions every 26 days because it no longer needs to spend money on vaccination or treatment, making smallpox eradication one of the best values in health interventions ever achieved.[27] Estimates for economic loss due to smallpox in a developing country are available only for India. Based on these, it has been estimated that developing countries as a whole suffered economic losses related to smallpox of about $1 billion each year at the start of the intensified campaign.[32]

Lessons Learned

The success of the program can be attributed to the political commitment and leadership exemplified in the partnership between WHO and the US Centers for Disease Control and Prevention. Success in individual countries hinged on having someone who was responsible, preferably solely, for the eradication effort. In addition, small WHO teams made frequent field trips to review progress, and a small number of committed people working in the program were able to motivate large numbers of staff. Moreover, in the days before the Internet and email, the program managers held a monthly meeting in which they exchanged information about the progress of the campaign and the lessons learned from working on it in different countries.

No two national campaigns were alike, which makes flexibility essential in program design. The plan for eradicating smallpox used existing healthcare systems, and it also forced many countries to improve their health services. This benefited immunization programs more generally and offset the cost of the initial smallpox campaign.

Monitoring standards were established across the program to constantly evaluate the progress of the program against agreed benchmarks. The participation of communities provided strategic lessons for later community-based projects. The value of publicity about the program was highlighted when news about the program's progress triggered large donations in 1974 to complete eradication in five remaining countries. An important discovery made during the campaign was that immunization programs could vaccinate people with more than one vaccination at a time. This helped to pave the way for later programs of routine immunization, about which you will read later.

The eradication of smallpox continues to inspire efforts against other diseases, but it must be remembered that the particular features of smallpox made it a prime candidate for eradication. The disease was passed directly between people, without an intervening carrier, so there were no reservoirs; the distinctive rash of smallpox made diagnosis easy; survivors gained lifetime immunity; and the severity of symptoms, once the disease became infectious, made patients take to their beds and infect few others. Good vaccination coverage could therefore disrupt transmission entirely. Unfortunately, almost 30 years after eradication, funds are still allocated to precautionary measures against the disease because of the continuing threat of smallpox being used as an agent of bio-terrorism.

CENTRAL MESSAGES OF THE BOOK

Because this is the introductory chapter of the book, it will not end with a summary, as the other chapters do. Rather, it will be most valuable to end this chapter by highlighting some of the central messages of the book as a whole. They are listed below, without citations or recitation of the evidence behind them. That evidence will be provided and cited in the chapters that follow. It will be very important to keep these messages in mind as you go through the book.

- There are strong links among health, human development, labor productivity, and economic development.
- Health status is determined by a variety of factors, including age, culture, income, education, knowledge of healthy behaviors, social status, sex, genetic makeup, and access to health services. The economic and social conditions under which people live and government policies also have an important influence on people's health.
- There has been enormous progress in improving health status over the last 50 years in many countries. This is reflected in the substantial increases these countries have witnessed in that period, for example, in life expectancy.
- Some of this progress has come about as a result of overall economic development and improvements in income. However, much of it is due to improvements in public hygiene, better water supply and sanitation, and better education. Increased nutritional status has also had a large impact on improvements in health status. Technical progress in some areas, such as the development of vaccines against childhood diseases and the development of antibiotics, has also improved human health.

- The progress in health status, however, has been very uneven. Hundreds of millions of people, especially poorer people in low- and middle-income countries, continue to get sick, be disabled by, or die from preventable causes of disease. In many countries, nutritional status and health status of lower-income people have improved only slowly. In addition, HIV/AIDS has caused a decline in health and nutritional status and life expectancy in a number of countries in sub-Saharan Africa.

- There are enormous disparities in health status and access to health services both within and across countries. Wealthier people in most countries have better health status and better access to health services than poorer people. In general, urban dwellers and ethnic majorities enjoy better health status than rural people and disadvantaged ethnic minorities. In addition, women face a number of unique challenges to their health.

- Countries do not need to be high-income to enjoy good health status. By contrast, there are a number of examples, such as China, Costa Rica, Cuba, Kerala state in India, and Sri Lanka, that make clear that low-income countries or low-income areas within countries can help their people to achieve good health, even in the absence of extensive financial resources to invest in health. However, this requires strong political will and a focus on public hygiene, education, and investing in low-cost but high-yielding investments in nutrition and health.

- The burden of disease is evolving in light of economic and social changes, the aging of populations, and scientific and technical progress, among other things. The burden of disease is predominantly communicable only in sub-Saharan Africa. In all of other regions, the burden of disease is predominantly noncommunicable. In the absence of new communicable disease threats of major importance, the burden of disease is expected to shift universally toward noncommunicable disease.

- Some global health issues can only be solved through the cooperation of various actors in global health. This could include, for example, the development of an AIDS vaccine.

- An important part of health status is determined by an individual's and families' own knowledge of health and hygiene. People and communities have tremendous abilities to enhance their own health status.

- The world continues to shrink at a very rapid pace. For health, security, and humanitarian reasons, each of us should be concerned about the health of everyone else.

Study Questions

1. What has been some of the most important progress in health worldwide over the last 50 years?

2. What are some of the global health challenges that remain to be addressed?

3. How might one define *health*, *public health*, and *global health*?

4. What are some examples of public health activities?

5. What are some examples of global health issues?

6. What are the key differences between the approach of medicine and the approach of public health?

7. What are some of the most important challenges to health globally?

8. Why should everyone be concerned about critical global health issues?

9. What are the Millennium Development Goals, and how do they relate to health?

10. What were some of the keys to the eradication of smallpox? What lessons does the smallpox eradication program suggest for other global health programs?

REFERENCES

1. Centers for Disease Control and Prevention. Meningococcal Disease. October 12, 2005; Available at: http://www.cdc.gov/ncidod/dbmd/diseaseinfo/meningococcal_g.htm. Accessed May 27, 2006.

2. Mayo Clinic. Infectious Disease: West Nile Virus. Available at: http://www.mayoclinic.com/health/west-nile-virus/DS00438. Accessed May 28, 2006.

3. New Polio Cases Confirmed in Guinea, Mali and the Sudan. Available at: http://www.who.int/mediacentre/news/releases/2004/pr57/en. Accessed June 10, 2006.

4. UNAIDS. Country Responses—Ethiopia. Available at: http://www.unaids.org/en/CountryResponses/Countries/ethiopia.asp. Accessed September 4, 2010.

5. UNAIDS. AIDS Epidemic Update. Available at: http://data.unaids.org:80/pub/Report/2009/JC1700_Epi_Update_2009_en.pdf. Accessed September 4, 2010.

6. UNAIDS. 2010: A Global View of HIV Infection. Available at: http://www.unaids.org/documents/20101123_2010_HIV_Prevalence_Map_em.pdf. Accessed September 4, 2010.

7. Health Protection Agency of the United Kingdom. Focus on Tuberculosis. Available at: http://www.hpa.org.uk/publications/2006/tb_report/pdfs/introduction.pdf. Accessed January 2, 2007.

8. World Health Organization. World Health Statistics. Available at: http://www.who.int/whosis/whostat/EN_WHS10_Full.pdf. Accessed September 3, 2010.

9. The World Bank Data. Health. Available at http://data.worldbank.org/topic/health. Accessed September 3, 2010.

10. World Health Organization. Measles: Key Facts. Available at: http://www.who.int/mediacentre/factsheets/fs286/en. Accessed September 8, 2010.

11. World Health Organization. 2009 Update: Tuberculosis Facts. Available at: http://www.stoptb.org/assets/documents/resources/factsheets/tbfactsheet_2009update_one_page.pdf. Accessed September 8, 2010.

12. Hogan MC, Foreman KJ, Naghavi M, et al. Maternal mortality for 181 countries, 1980–2008: a systematic analysis of progress towards Millennium Development Goal 5. *Lancet.* 2010;375(9726):1609-1623.

13. Centers for Disease Control and Prevention. World Distribution of Dengue—2003. Available at: http://www.cdc.gov/ncidod/dvbid/dengue/map-distribution-2003.htm. Accessed June 8, 2006.

14. The World Bank. Japan. Available at: http://data.worldbank.org/country/japan. Accessed September 8, 2010.

15. The World Bank. Haiti. Available at: http://data.worldbank.org/country/haiti. Accessed September 8, 2010.

16. Preamble to the Constitution of the World Health Organization 1946, as adopted by the International Health Conference, New York, 19 June–22 July 1946.

17. Merson MH, Black RE, Mills A. *International Public Health: Diseases, Programs, Systems, and Policies.* Gaithersburg, MD: Aspen Publishers; 2001: xvii.

18. American Public Health Association. Code of Ethics. Available at: www.apha.org/codeofethics/ethics.htm. Accessed February 8, 2006.

19. Harvard School of Public Health. Distinctions Between Medicine and Public Health. Available at: http://www.hsph.harvard.edu/about.html#publichealth. Accessed February 8, 2006.

20. Last JM. *A Dictionary of Epidemiology.* 4th ed. New York: Oxford University Press; 2001.

21. Institute of Medicine. *America's Vital Interest in Global Health: Protecting Our People, Enhancing Our Economy, and Advancing Our International Interests.* Washington, DC: National Academy Press; 1998.

22. Merson MH, Black RE, Mills A. *International Public Health: Diseases, Programs, Systems, and Policies.* Gaithersburg, MD: Aspen Publishers; 2001: xix.

23. Koplan JP, Bond TC, Merson MH, et al. Towards a common definition of global health. *Lancet.* 2009;373(9679):1993-1995.

24. Fried LP, Bentley ME, Buekens P, et al. Global health is public health. *Lancet.* 2010;375(9714):535-537.

25. The World Bank. Country and Lending Groups. Available at: http://data.worldbank.org/about/country-classifications/country-and-lending-groups. Accessed September 4, 2010.

26. United Nations. 55/2. United Nations Millennium Declaration. Available at: http://www.un.org/millennium/declaration/ares552e.htm. Accessed May 16, 2006.

27. Levine R., and the What Works Working Group. *Case Studies in Global Health: Millions Saved.* Sudbury, MA: Jones and Bartlett Publishers; 2007.

28. World Health Organization. WHO Fact Sheet on Smallpox. Available at: http://www.who.int/mediacentre/factsheets/smallpox/en. Accessed August 6, 2004.

29. World Health Organization. Media Centre, Smallpox: Historical Significance. Available at: http://www.who.int/mediacentre/factsheets/smallpox/en. Accessed June 13, 2006.

30. Roberts M. How Doctors Killed Off Smallpox. July 3, 2005. Available at: http://news.bbc.co.uk/1/hi/health/4072392.stm. Accessed June 11, 2006.

31. Fenner F. *Smallpox and Its Eradication.* World Health Organization; 1988.

32. Brilliant LB. *The Management of Smallpox Eradication in India.* Ann Arbor: University of Michigan Press; 1985.

CHAPTER 2

Health Determinants, Measurements, and Trends

LEARNING OBJECTIVES

By the end of this chapter the reader will be able to:

- Describe the determinants of health
- Define the most important health indicators
- Discuss the differences between incidence and prevalence; morbidity, disability, and mortality; and noncommunicable and communicable diseases
- Discuss the concepts of health-adjusted life expectancy (HALE), disability-adjusted life years (DALYs), and the burden of disease
- Describe the leading causes of death in low-, middle-, and high-income countries
- Describe the demographic and epidemiologic transitions

VIGNETTES

Shawki is a 60-year-old Jordanian man who lives in Jordan's capital of Amman. Unfortunately, Shawki's health has deteriorated in the last year. His blood pressure and cholesterol are too high. He has developed diabetes. He is sometimes short of breath. What are the causes of his ill and declining health? Do these problems stem from any genetic issues? Could they come from a lack of understanding about a healthy lifestyle and diet? Could it be that Shawki lacks the income he needs to eat properly and to ensure that he gets health checkups when he needs them?

Life expectancy in Botswana prior to the spread of HIV/AIDS was about 65 years.[1] In 2009, life expectancy in Botswana was 49 years.[2] Life expectancy in Russia in 1985 was about 64 years for males and 74 years for females. By 2001, however, it had fallen to about 59 years for males

and 72 years for females, although by 2009 it had risen to 61 for males and 74 for females.[2] What does life expectancy measure? What are the factors contributing to its decline in both of these countries? What has happened to trends in life expectancy in other countries? Which countries have the longest and shortest life expectancies, and why?

In Cambodia in 2008, families had, on average, 2.9 children[3] and their life expectancy was about 61 years.[4] Thirty years ago, the demographic and epidemiologic profile of Thailand looked a lot like Cambodia looks today. Today, however, Thai families have on average about 1.8 children[3] and those children on average will live 69 years.[4] Children in Thailand rarely die, and when they do, 50 percent of them die from injury.[5] What causes these shifts in fertility and mortality? Do they occur consistently as countries develop economically? How long will it take before Cambodia has the same fertility and disease burden that Thailand has today?

In Peru, poor people tend to live in the mountains and be indigenous, less educated, and have worse health status than other people. In Eastern Europe, the same issues occur among their ethnic groups that are of lower socioeconomic status, such as the Roma people. In the United States, there are also enormous health disparities, as seen in the relative health status of African Americans and Native Americans. If one wants to understand and address differences in health status among different groups, then how do we have to measure health status? Do we measure it by age? By gender? By socioeconomic status? By level of education? By ethnicity? By location?

THE IMPORTANCE OF MEASURING HEALTH STATUS

If we want to understand the most important global health issues and what can be done to address them, then we must understand what factors have the most influence on health status, how health status is measured, and what key trends in health status have occurred historically. We must, in fact, be able to answer the questions that are posed in the narratives above.

This chapter, therefore, covers four distinct, but closely related topics. The first section concerns what are called "the determinants of health." That section examines the most important factors that relate to people's health status. The second section reviews some of the most important indicators of health status and how they are used. The third section discusses the burden of disease worldwide and how it varies across countries. The last section looks at how fertility and mortality change as countries become more developed and what this means for the types of health problems countries face.

THE DETERMINANTS OF HEALTH

Why are some people healthy and some people not healthy? When asked this question, many of us will respond that good health depends on access to health services. Yet, as you will learn, whether or not people are healthy depends on a large number of factors, many of which are interconnected, and most of which go considerably beyond access to health services.

There has been considerable writing about the "determinants of health," and one way of depicting these determinants is shown in Figure 2-1. The next section largely follows the approach to the determinants of health that is discussed in "What Determines Health" by the Public Health Agency of Canada.[6]

The first group of factors that helps to determine health relates to the personal and inborn features of individuals. These include genetic makeup, sex, and age. Our genetic makeup has much to do with what diseases we get and how healthy we live. One can inherit, for example, a genetic marker for a particular disease, such as Huntington's disease, which is a neurological disorder. One can also inherit the genetic component of a disease that has multiple causes, such as breast cancer. Sex also has an important relationship with health. Men and women are physically different, for example, and may get different diseases. Women face the risk of childbearing. They also get cervical and uterine cancers that men do not get. Women also have higher rates of certain health conditions, such as thyroid and breast cancers. For similar reasons, age is also an important determinant of

health. Young children in developing countries often die of diarrheal disease, whereas older people are much more likely to die of heart disease, to cite one of many examples of the relationship between health and age.

Social and cultural issues also play important roles in determining health. Social status is an important health determinant. There is good evidence that people of higher social status have more control over their lives than people of lower status, and people of higher social status also tend to have higher incomes and education, both of which are strongly correlated with better health.[7] In addition, the gender roles that are ascribed to women in many societies also have an important impact on health. In such environments, women may be less well treated than men and this, in turn, may mean that women have less income, less education, and fewer opportunities to engage in safe employment. All of these militate against their good health.

The extent to which people get social support from family, friends, and community has also been shown to have an important link with health.[7] The stronger the social networks and the stronger the support that people get from those networks, the healthier people will be. Of course, culture is also an extremely important determinant of health.[7] Culture helps to determine how one feels about health and illness, how one uses health services, and the health practices in which one engages.

The environment, both indoor and outdoor, is also a powerful determinant of health. Related to this is the safety of the environment in which people work. Although many people know about the importance of outdoor air pollution to health, few people are aware of the importance of indoor air pollution to health. In many developing countries, women cook indoors with very poor ventilation, thereby creating an indoor environment that is full of smoke and that encourages respiratory illness and asthma. The lack of safe drinking water and sanitation is a major contributor to ill health in poor countries. In addition, many people in those same countries work in environments that are very unhealthy. Because they lack skills, social status, and opportunities, they may work without sufficient protection with hazardous chemicals, in polluted air, or in circumstances that expose them to occupational accidents.

Education is a powerful determinant of health for several reasons. First, it brings with it knowledge of good health practices. Second, it provides opportunities for gaining skills, getting better employment, raising one's income, and enhancing one's social status, all of which are also related to health. Studies have shown, for example, that the single best predictor of the birth weight of a baby is the level of

FIGURE 2-1 Key Determinants of Health

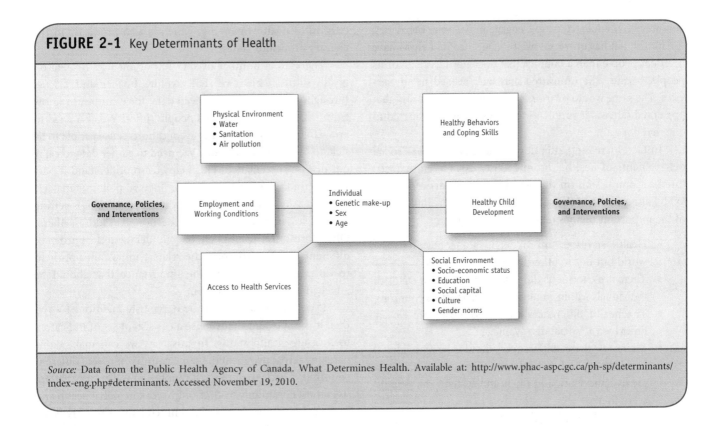

Source: Data from the Public Health Agency of Canada. What Determines Health. Available at: http://www.phac-aspc.gc.ca/ph-sp/determinants/index-eng.php#determinants. Accessed November 19, 2010.

educational attainment of the mother.[8] Most of us already know that throughout the world, there is an extremely strong and positive correlation between the level of education and all key health indicators. People who are better educated eat better, smoke less, are less obese, have fewer children, and take better care of their children's health than do people with less education. It is not a surprise, therefore, that they and their children live longer and healthier lives than do less well educated people and their children.

Of course, people's own health practices and behaviors are also critical determinants of their health. Being able to identify when you or a family member is ill and needs health care can be critical to good health. As noted previously, however, one's health also depends on how one eats, or if one smokes, drinks too much alcohol, or drives safely. We also know that being active physically and getting exercise regularly is better for one's health than is being sedentary.

Another important determinant of future health is the way in which families nourish and care for infants and young children. Being born premature or of low birthweight can have important negative consequences on health. There is a strong correlation between the nutritional status of infants and young children and the extent to which they meet their

biological potentials, enroll in school, or stay in school. In addition, poor nutritional status in infancy and young childhood may be linked with a number of noncommunicable diseases, including diabetes and heart disease.[9]

Of course, one's health does depend on access to appropriate healthcare services. Even if one is born healthy, raised healthy, and engages in good health behaviors, there will still be times when one has to call on a health system for help. The more likely you are to access services of appropriate quality, the more likely you are to stay healthy. To address the risk of dying from a complication of pregnancy, for example, one must have access to health services that can carry out an emergency cesarean section if necessary. Even if the mother has had the suggested level of prenatal care and has prepared well in all other respects for the pregnancy, in the end, certain complications can only be addressed in a healthcare setting.

The approach that governments take to different policies and programs in the health sector and in other sectors has an important bearing on people's health. People living in a country that promotes high educational attainment, for example, will be healthier than people in a country that does not promote widespread education of appropriate quality, because better educated people engage in healthier behaviors. A country that has universal health insurance is likely to have healthier people than a country that does not insure all of its people, because the uninsured may lack needed health services. The same would be true, for example, for a country that promoted safe water supply for all of its people, compared to one that does not.

In fact, increasing attention is being paid to the "social determinants of health." From 2005 to 2008 WHO constituted a Commission on the Social Determinants of Health. WHO also published the commission's report in 2008. Some of the important themes related to the report are:

- Health status is improving in some places in the world but not in others.
- There are enormous differences in the health status of individuals within countries, as well as across countries.
- The health differences within countries are closely linked with "social disadvantage."
- Many of these differences should be considered "avoidable," and they relate to the way in which people live and work and the health systems that should serve them.
- In the end, people's life circumstances, and therefore their health, are profoundly related to political, social, and economic forces.
- Countries need to ensure that these forces are oriented toward improving the life circumstances of the poor, thereby enabling them to enjoy a healthier life, as well. The global community should also work toward this end.[10]

The discussion of heath and equity later in the book will further touch on these points, which are also referred to throughout the book in a variety of ways.

KEY HEALTH INDICATORS

It is critical that we use data and evidence to understand and address key global health issues. Some types of health data concern the health status of people and communities, such as measures of life expectancy and infant and child mortality, as discussed further hereafter. Some concern health services, such as the number of nurses and doctors per capita in a country or the indicators of coverage for certain health services, such as immunization. This book will discuss health service data only briefly, mostly in Chapter 5 on health systems. Other data concern the financing of health, such as the amount of public expenditure on health or the share of national income represented by health expenditure. This book also provides only a limited dis-

cussion of health financing, which is also primarily in the chapter on health systems.

There are a number of very important uses of data on health status, which we shall explore further and discuss throughout the book.[11] We need data, for example, to know from what health conditions people suffer. We also need to know the extent to which these conditions cause people to be sick, to be disabled, or to die. We need to gather data to carry out disease surveillance. This helps us to understand if particular health problems such as influenza, polio, or malaria are occurring, where they are infecting people, who is getting these diseases, and what might be done to address them. Other forms of data also help us to understand the burden of different health conditions, the relative importance of them to different societies, and the importance that should be attached to dealing with them.

If we are to use data in the previously mentioned ways, then it is important that we use a consistent set of indicators to measure health status. In this way, we can make comparisons across people in the same country or across different countries. There are, in fact, a number of indicators that are used most commonly by those who work in global health and in development work, as well, as noted later. These are listed and defined in Table 2-1 and are discussed briefly below.

Among the most commonly used indicators of health status is *life expectancy at birth*. Life expectancy at birth is "the average number of additional years a newborn baby can be

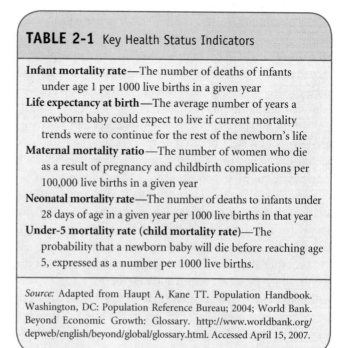

TABLE 2-1 Key Health Status Indicators

Infant mortality rate—The number of deaths of infants under age 1 per 1000 live births in a given year

Life expectancy at birth—The average number of years a newborn baby could expect to live if current mortality trends were to continue for the rest of the newborn's life

Maternal mortality ratio—The number of women who die as a result of pregnancy and childbirth complications per 100,000 live births in a given year

Neonatal mortality rate—The number of deaths to infants under 28 days of age in a given year per 1000 live births in that year

Under-5 mortality rate (child mortality rate)—The probability that a newborn baby will die before reaching age 5, expressed as a number per 1000 live births.

Source: Adapted from Haupt A, Kane TT. Population Handbook. Washington, DC: Population Reference Bureau; 2004; World Bank. Beyond Economic Growth: Glossary. http://www.worldbank.org/depweb/english/beyond/global/glossary.html. Accessed April 15, 2007.

expected to live if current mortality trends were to continue for the rest of that person's life."[12] In other words, it measures how long a person born today can expect to live, if there were no change in their lifetime in the present rate of death for people of different ages. The higher the life expectancy at birth, the better the health status of a country. In the United States, life expectancy at birth is about 78 years; in a middle-income country, such as Jordan, life expectancy is 73 years; in a very poor country, such as Mali, the life expectancy is 48 years. Figure 2-2 shows life expectancy at birth by region.[4]

Another important and widely used indicator is the *infant mortality rate*. The infant mortality rate is "the number of deaths of infants under age 1 per 1000 live births in a given year."[12] This rate is expressed in deaths per 1000 live births. In other words, it measures how many children younger than 1 year of age will die for every 1000 who were born alive that year. Each country seeks as low a rate of infant mortality as possible, but we will see that the rate varies largely with the income status of a country. Afghanistan, for example, has an infant mortality rate of 135 infant deaths for every 1000 live births, whereas in Sweden only about 2 infants die for every 1000 live births.[13] (See Figure 2-3.)

Although the infant mortality rate is a powerful indicator of health status of a country, most children younger than 1 year of age who die actually die in the first month of life. Thus, the *neonatal mortality rate* is also an important health status indicator. This rate measures "the number of deaths to infants younger than 28 days of age in a given year, per 1000 live births in that year."[12] Like the infant mortality rate, this rate will generally vary directly with the level of income of different countries. Poorer countries will have a much higher neonatal mortality rate than the richer countries. The neonatal mortality rate is about 40 per 1000 live births in sub-Saharan Africa but about 4 per 1000 live births in developed countries.[14] The neonatal mortality rate by region is portrayed in Figure 2-4.

The under-5 child mortality rate is also called the *child mortality rate*. This is "the probability that a newborn will die before reaching age five, expressed as a number per 1000 live births."[12] Like the infant mortality rate, this rate is also expressed per 1000 live births. Of course, this rate is very similar to the infant mortality rate, and here, too, the lower the rate the better. This rate also varies largely with the wealth of a country. In the developed countries the rate is generally about 3–5 per 1000 live births. However, in the poorest countries, the rate can be as high as 200 per 1000 live births.[15] The under-5 child mortality rate is depicted in Figure 2-5. As infant mortality declines, the under-5 child mortality rate becomes a more

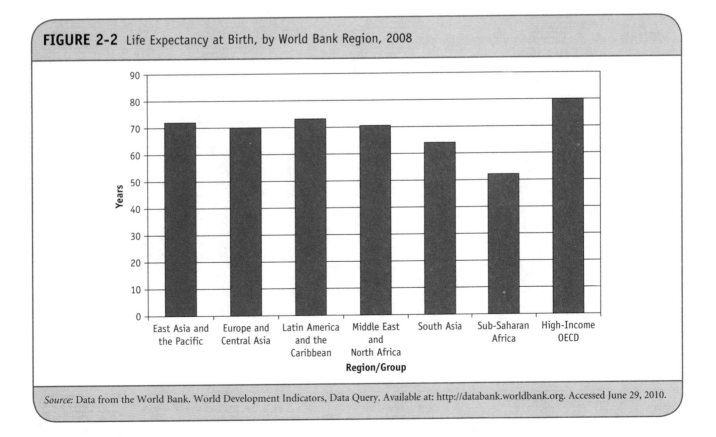

FIGURE 2-2 Life Expectancy at Birth, by World Bank Region, 2008

Source: Data from the World Bank. World Development Indicators, Data Query. Available at: http://databank.worldbank.org. Accessed June 29, 2010.

FIGURE 2-3 Infant Mortality Rate, by World Bank Region, 2008

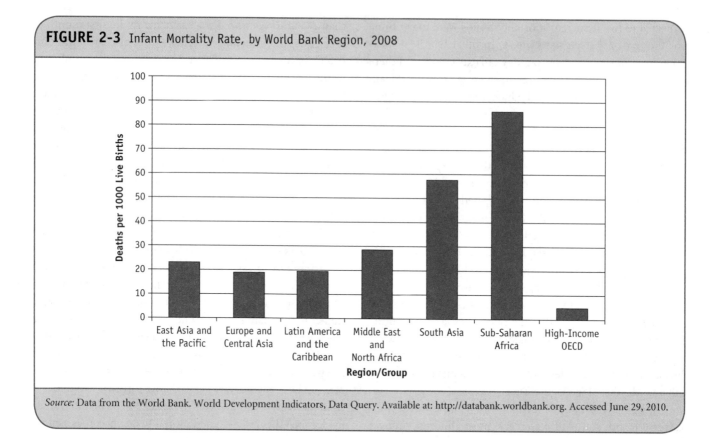

Source: Data from the World Bank. World Development Indicators, Data Query. Available at: http://databank.worldbank.org. Accessed June 29, 2010.

FIGURE 2-4 Neonatal Mortality Rate, by WHO Region, 2004

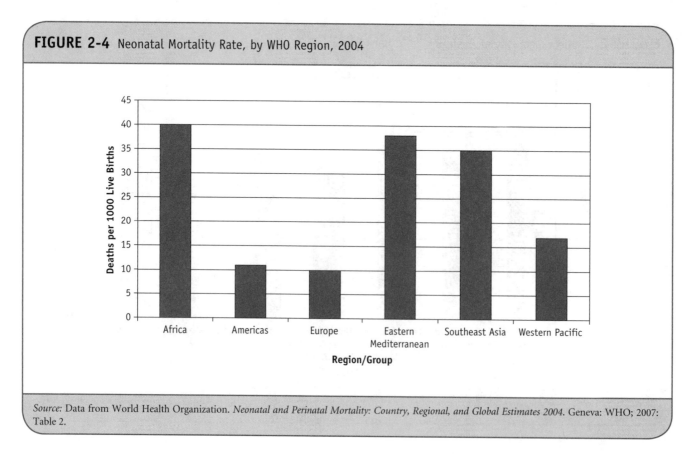

Source: Data from World Health Organization. *Neonatal and Perinatal Mortality: Country, Regional, and Global Estimates 2004.* Geneva: WHO; 2007: Table 2.

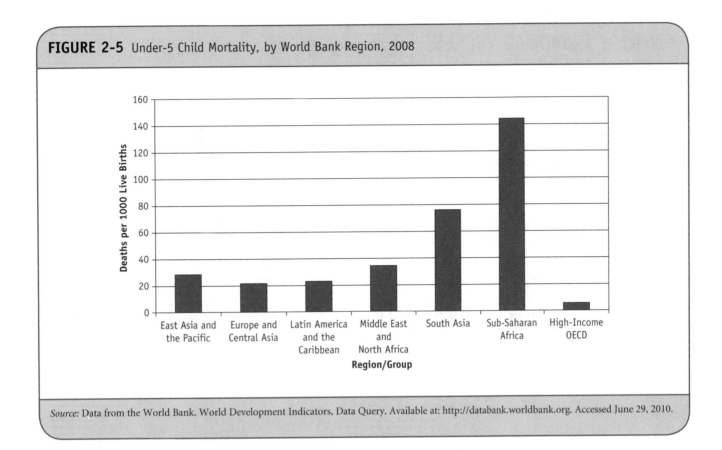

FIGURE 2-5 Under-5 Child Mortality, by World Bank Region, 2008

Source: Data from the World Bank. World Development Indicators, Data Query. Available at: http://databank.worldbank.org. Accessed June 29, 2010.

important health indicator. The relative standing of different regions in under-5 child mortality, as shown in Figure 2-5, looks very similar to that for infant mortality.

The maternal mortality ratio is a measure of the risk of death that is associated with childbirth. Because these deaths are more rare than infant and child deaths, the maternal mortality ratio is measured as "the number of women who die as a result of pregnancy and childbirth complications per 100,000 live births in a given year."[12] The rarity of maternal deaths and the fact that they largely occur in low-income settings also contributes to maternal mortality being quite difficult to measure. Very few women die in childbirth in rich countries; for example, the maternal mortality ratio in Sweden is 3 per 100,000 live births. On the other hand, in very poor countries, in which women have low status and there are few facilities for dealing with obstetric emergencies, the ratios can be over 1000 per 100,000 live births, as they are, for example, in Afghanistan, Angola, and Burundi.[16] As you can see in Figure 2-6, the maternal mortality ratio is also very strongly correlated with a country's income.

There are a few other concepts and definitions that are important to understand as we think about measuring health status. The first is *morbidity*. Essentially, this means sickness or any departure, subjective or objective, from a psychological or physiological state of well-being. Second is *mortality*, which refers to death. A *death rate* is the number of deaths per 1000 population in a given year.[12] The third is *disability*. Although some conditions cause people to get sick or die, they might also cause people to suffer the "temporary or long-term reduction in a person's capacity to function."[17]

There will also be considerable discussion in this book and most readings on global health of the *prevalence* of health conditions. This refers to the number of people suffering from a certain health condition over a specific time period. It measures the chances of having a disease. For global health work, one usually refers to "point prevalence" of a condition, which is "the proportion of the population that is diseased at a single point in time."[18] The point prevalence of HIV/AIDS among adults in South Africa, for example, is estimated to be about 18 percent. This means that today about 18 percent of

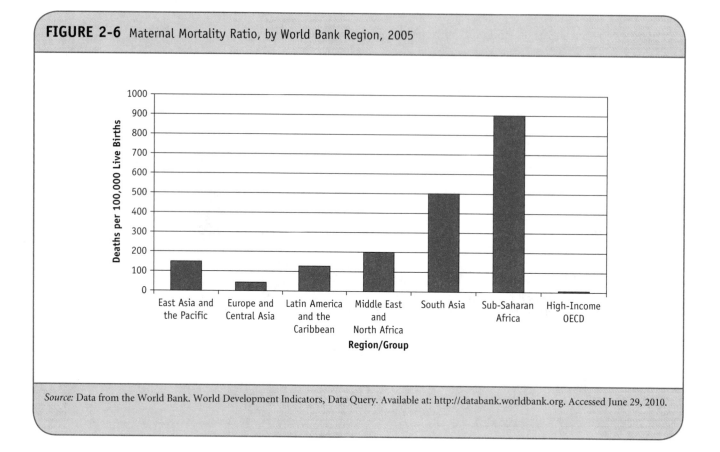

FIGURE 2-6 Maternal Mortality Ratio, by World Bank Region, 2005

Source: Data from the World Bank. World Development Indicators, Data Query. Available at: http://databank.worldbank.org. Accessed June 29, 2010.

all adults between the ages of 15 and 49 in South Africa are HIV-positive.[19]

The *incidence rate* is also a very commonly used term. This refers to the rate at which new cases of a disease occur in a population. Incidence measures the chances of getting a disease. An incidence rate is "the number of persons contracting a disease per 1000 population at risk, for a given period of time."[12] It is usually specified as the number of people getting the disease over a year, per 100,000 people at risk. In India, for example, the incidence rate for TB in 2007 was 168 per 100,000.[20] This means that for every 100,000 people in India, 168 got TB in 2007.

Many people confuse incidence rate and prevalence rate. It may be convenient to think of prevalence as the pool of people with a disease at a particular time and incidence as the flow of new cases of people with that disease each year into that pool. You should note, of course, that the size of the pool will vary as new cases flow into the pool and old cases flow out, as they die or are cured.

Finally, one needs to be familiar with how diseases get classified. When you read about health, there will be discussions of communicable diseases, noncommunicable diseases, and injuries. Communicable diseases are also called infectious diseases. These are illnesses that are caused by a particular infectious agent and that spread directly or indirectly from people to people, animals to people, or people to animals.[21] Examples of communicable diseases include influenza, measles, and HIV. Noncommunicable diseases are illnesses that are not spread by any infectious agent, such as hypertension, coronary heart disease, and diabetes. Injuries usually include, among other things, road traffic injuries, falls, self-inflicted injuries, and violence.[22]

VITAL REGISTRATION

The quality of data on population and health depends in many ways on the extent to which countries maintain a system of vital registration that can accurately record births, deaths, and the causes of death. Unfortunately, this is not the case in many low- and lower-middle-income countries.[23] They generally have only rudimentary systems for vital registration, which cannot fulfill either their statistical or their legal purposes. In addition, access to vital registration systems is highly inequitable, with higher income groups enjoying much better access than less well off people (Figure 2-7).

There are also cultural barriers to timely vital registration, because people in many countries wait until a child is a certain age before registering the birth. Coupled with the lack of access to vital registration, this means the existence of some children is never officially known, because they die before their births are registered. There are also enormous difficulties with accurate indications of causes of death in countries that have weak health systems and a limited number of well-trained physicians. This is especially so for causes of death of adults.

The former Director-General of WHO, Lee Jong-Wook, noted in a speech to his colleagues that: "To make people count, we first need to be able to count people."[23] To overcome the lack of effective vital registration systems in many developing countries, a number of tools, such as surveys and projection models, have been developed. Some, like the Demographic and Health Surveys, have become a backbone of information about health, population, and nutrition, and now HIV, in low-income countries.

In the longer term, however, the world would be better served by helping countries further develop their own vital registration systems. This would allow countries and their development partners to more accurately gauge the nature of key demographic and health issues and the progress made toward resolving them. Moving in this direction will require assessments of vital registration systems. It will also require programs to improve the organization and functioning of vital registration departments. This will have to include, among other things, strengthening their methods to improve the quality of vital statistics, including for the causes of death, and enhancing their approach to publishing data.[23]

MEASURING THE BURDEN OF DISEASE

We have already seen in Chapter 1 that the definition of health is "a state of complete physical, mental and social well-being and not merely the absence of disease or infirmity." Those who work on global health have attempted for a number of years to construct a single indicator that could be used to compare how far different countries are from the state of good health, as defined previously. Ideally, such an index would take account of morbidity, mortality, and disability; allow one to calculate the index by age, by gender, and by region; and allow one to make comparisons of health status across regions within a country and across countries.[24] This kind of index would measure what is generally referred to as "the burden of disease."

One such indicator is *health-adjusted life expectancy*, or HALE. It is a "health expectancy measure." The HALE "summarizes the expected number of years to be lived in what

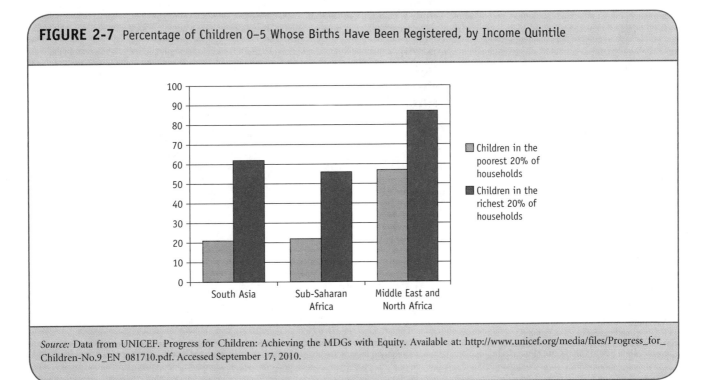

FIGURE 2-7 Percentage of Children 0–5 Whose Births Have Been Registered, by Income Quintile

Children in the poorest 20% of households

Children in the richest 20% of households

Source: Data from UNICEF. Progress for Children: Achieving the MDGs with Equity. Available at: http://www.unicef.org/media/files/Progress_for_Children-No.9_EN_081710.pdf. Accessed September 17, 2010.

might be termed the equivalent of good health."[25] This can also be seen as "the equivalent number of years in full health that a newborn can expect to live, based on current rates of ill health and mortality."[26] To calculate the HALE, "the years of ill health are weighted according to severity and subtracted from the overall life expectancy."[7]

WHO has calculated HALEs for most countries, using a standard methodology. Table 2-2 shows life expectancy at birth in 2004 for a number of low-, middle-, and high-income countries and how it compares with HALEs for those countries in the same year. As you can see from Table 2-2, the greater the number of years that people in any population are likely to spend in ill health or with disability, the greater the

difference will be between life expectancy at birth and health-adjusted life expectancy.

The composite indicator of health status that is most commonly used in global health work is called the *disability-adjusted life year*, or DALY. This indicator was first used in conjunction with the 1993 World Development Report of the World Bank, and is a "health gap measure." It is now used in burden of disease studies. In the simplest terms, a DALY is:

> . . . a unit for measuring the amount of health lost because of a particular disease or injury. It is calculated as the present value of future years

---

TABLE 2-2 Life Expectancy at Birth and Health-Adjusted Life Expectancy, Selected Countries, 2004

Country	Life Expectancy/Health-Adjusted Life Expectancy Males	Life Expectancy/Health-Adjusted Life Expectancy Females
Afghanistan	42/35.3	42/35.8
Bangladesh	62/55.3	63/53.3
Bolivia	63/53.6	66/55.2
Brazil	67/57.2	74/62.4
Cambodia	51/45.6	58/49.5
Cameroon	50/41.1	51/41.8
China	70/63.1	74/65.2
Costa Rica	75/65.2	80/69.3
Cuba	75/67.1	80/69.5
Denmark	75/68.6	80/71.1
Ethiopia	49/40.7	51/41.7
Ghana	56/49.2	58/50.3
India	61/53.3	63/53.6
Indonesia	65/57.4	68/58.9
Jordan	69/59.7	73/62.3
Malaysia	69/61.6	74/64.8
Nepal	61/52.5	61/51.1
Niger	42/35.8	41/35.2
Nigeria	45/41.3	46/41.8
Peru	69/59.6	73/62.4
Philippines	65/57.1	72/61.5
Sri Lanka	68/59.2	75/64.0
Turkey	69/61.2	73/62.8
United States of America	75/67.2	80/71.3
Vietnam	69/59.8	74/62.9

Source: Data from WHO. Core Health Indicators. Available at: http://www3.who.int/whosis/core/core_select_process.cfm. Accessed September 24, 2006.

of disability free life that are lost as the result of the premature deaths or causes of disability occurring in a particular year.[27]

The DALY is a measure of losses due to illnesses, disabilities, and premature death in a population. It does this by adding together the losses of healthy years of life that occur from illness, disability, and death. The calculation of losses from death take account of life expectancy at various ages, with life expectancy at birth set at the highest known at the time. The value of disability is based on values that have been established for the severity of different disabling conditions. The calculation of a DALY "discounts" losses so those from ill health, disability, and death in the future are worth less than losses that occur today, just as a dollar you get in the future will be worth less than one you would get today.[11, 28–30] This is why the DALY is referred to as a "present value."

For calculating DALYs, health conditions are generally broken down into three categories:[31]

Group 1—communicable, maternal, and perinatal conditions (meaning in the first week after birth), and nutritional disorders
Group 2—noncommunicable diseases
Group 3—injuries, including, among other things, road traffic accidents, falls, self-inflicted injuries, and violence

To get a better sense of the meaning of DALYs, it will be valuable to construct a few simple examples of what goes into their calculation and how they would be used. Consider, for example, that a male can expect under the standard used to live to be 80 years old. Now let us suppose that this person dies of a heart attack at 40 years of age. That person would have lost 40 years of life. The value of this loss, discounted to the present, would be part of the calculation of DALYs.

Let us also imagine that a woman, who is 40 years of age, has diabetes that has disabled her in a number of ways. Her life expectancy at 40 is 85. Let us also say that the person's disability is so severe that her quality of life is equal to only about half of what it would be if she were in a "disease free" state. Even if she were to live to be 80 years of age, therefore, she would have lost about half of the quality of her last 45 years due to disability. The value of this loss, discounted to the present, would also be part of the calculation of DALYs.

The DALYs for the society in which the two people are living would be a composite of the data calculated from the losses due to the premature death of the first person and the disability of the second.

In reality, of course, many health conditions produce both disability and premature death. Let us suppose that a man gets TB at 45 years of age. In the absence of treatment, let us say that he dies at 47 years of age. He suffered two years of disability and lost 33 years of life due to his illness, compared to his life expectancy of 80. A person who suffers a severe road traffic injury at age 50 may live, let us say, 10 years with severe disability due to his injuries and then at age 60 die due to those injuries. He would have lost quality of life years during the period of his disability and 25 years of life from premature death, compared to his life expectancy at 60 of 85.

A society that has more premature death, illness, and disability has more DALYs than a society that is healthier and has less illness, disability, and premature death. One of the goals of health policy is to avert these DALYS in the most cost-efficient manner possible. If, for example, a society is losing many hundreds of thousands of DALYs due to malaria that is not diagnosed and treated in a timely and proper manner, what steps can be taken to avert those DALYs at the lowest cost?

An important point to remember when considering DALYs, compared to measuring deaths, is that DALYs take account of periods in which people are living in ill health or with disability. By doing this, DALYs and other composite indicators try to give a better estimate than measuring deaths alone of the true "health" of a population. This is easy to understand. Most mental health problems, for example, are not associated with deaths. However, they cause an enormous amount of disability. Several parasitic infections, such as schistosomiasis (which is discussed in Chapter 11), also cause very few deaths, but enormous amounts of illness and disability. If we measured the health of a population with an important burden of schistosomiasis and mental illness only by measuring deaths, we would miss a major component of morbidity and disability and would seriously overestimate the health of that population. The next section on the global burden of disease will make the concept of DALYs clearer to you, especially as you see how DALYs compare to deaths for a number of health conditions. Other sections of the book will also make extensive use of the concept of DALYs.

Indeed, calculating DALYs requires information on disease prevalence and incidence that is not always available. In addition, the health expectancy measures are more widely used in high-income countries, given the health information available to them. A number of critiques of DALYs have been written.[32] Nonetheless, this book will repeatedly refer to DALYs because this measure is so extensively used in global health work. In addition, a considerable amount of important analysis has been carried out that is based on the use of DALYs for measuring overall health status and assessing the most cost-effective approaches to dealing with various health problems. These uses of the DALY will be discussed in Chapter 3.

THE GLOBAL BURDEN OF DISEASE

As you start a review of global health, it is important to get a clear picture of the leading causes of illness, disability, and death in the world. As noted earlier, it is also very important to understand how they vary by age, sex, ethnicity, and socioeconomic status, both within and across countries. It is also essential to understand how these causes have varied over time and how they might change in the future. These topics are examined briefly below and in much greater detail throughout the book.

As discussed earlier, it is important to note that the tables that follow on the burden of disease are based on a consistent set of 2001 data that was part of a study on the global burden of disease. The most up-to-date data on specific diseases is generally given in the chapters that review those diseases.

Table 2-3 shows the 10 leading causes of death and the 10 leading causes of DALYs lost for low- and middle-income countries and for high-income countries in 2001. Both deaths and DALYs are ranked in order of importance.

The table indicates that the leading causes of death in low- and middle-income countries are noncommunicable diseases, which account for about 54 percent of all deaths. This is followed by communicable diseases at about 36 percent of all deaths and then injuries at about 10 percent of all deaths.[33]

TABLE 2-3 The 10 Leading Causes of Death and DALYs, 2001

Low- and Middle-Income Countries		High-Income Countries	
Cause	**Percentage of Total Deaths**	**Cause**	**Percentage of Total Deaths**
1. Ischemic heart disease	11.8	1. Ischemic heart disease	17.3
2. Cerebrovascular disease	9.5	2. Cerebrovascular disease	9.9
3. Lower respiratory infections	7.0	3. Trachea, bronchus, and lung cancers	5.8
4. HIV/AIDS	5.3	4. Lower respiratory infections	4.4
5. Perinatal conditions	5.1	5. Chronic obstructive pulmonary disease	3.8
6. Chronic obstructive pulmonary disease	4.9	6. Colon and rectal cancers	3.3
7. Diarrheal diseases	3.7	7. Alzheimer's and other dementias	2.6
8. Tuberculosis	3.3	8. Diabetes mellitus	2.6
9. Malaria	2.5	9. Breast cancer	2.0
10. Road traffic accidents	2.2	10. Stomach cancer	1.9
Cause	**Percentage of Total DALYs**	**Cause**	**Percentage of Total DALYs**
1. Perinatal conditions	6.4	1. Ischemic heart disease	8.3
2. Lower respiratory infections	6.0	2. Cerebrovascular disease	6.3
3. Ischemic heart disease	5.2	3. Unipolar depressive disorders	5.6
4. HIV/AIDS	5.1	4. Alzheimer's and other dementias	5.0
5. Cerebrovascular disease	4.5	5. Trachea, bronchus, and lung cancers	3.6
6. Diarrheal diseases	4.2	6. Hearing loss, adult onset	3.6
7. Unipolar depressive disorders	3.1	7. Chronic obstructive pulmonary disease	3.5
8. Malaria	2.9	8. Diabetes mellitus	2.8
9. Tuberculosis	2.6	9. Alcohol use disorders	2.8
10. Chronic obstructive pulmonary disease	2.4	10. Osteoarthritis	2.5

Source: Adapted with permission from Lopez AD, Mathers CD, Murray CJL. The burden of disease and mortality by condition: data, methods, and results for 2001. In: Lopez AD, Mathers CD, Ezzati M, Jamison DT, Murray CJL, eds. *Global Burden of Disease and Risk Factors*. Washington, DC and New York: The World Bank and Oxford University Press; 2006.

In order of rank, ischemic heart disease and cerebrovascular disease are the two leading causes of death in low- and middle-income countries. However, all but one of the next leading causes of death in these countries is communicable. The third leading cause of death is lower respiratory conditions, related to pneumonia, often in children. The fourth leading cause is HIV/AIDS. The next are perinatal conditions, linked with the death of newborns. TB, diarrheal disease, and malaria are also major killers. Road traffic accidents are the 10th leading cause of death in low- and middle-income countries.[31]

Noncommunicable diseases are also the leading causes of deaths in high-income countries. However, in other respects, the picture of deaths that emerges in high-income countries is quite different from that in low- and middle-income countries. In high-income countries almost 87 percent of the deaths are from noncommunicable causes, 7.5 percent are from injuries, and only 5.7 percent are from communicable causes. In high-income countries, the first three leading causes of death are heart disease, stroke, and lung and related cancers. The fourth, and the only communicable cause among the leading causes of death, is lower respiratory infections, which is associated in high-income countries mostly with death from pneumonia of older people. Chronic obstructive pulmonary disease is the fifth leading cause of death and colon and rectal cancers are the sixth.[31]

If we look at DALYs, rather than deaths, for low- and middle-income countries, communicable diseases and injuries become slightly more important and noncommunicable diseases somewhat less important in percentage terms than they were for deaths. In terms of individual conditions, diarrheal disease, malaria, and perinatal conditions become more important percentages than they were for deaths. However, the most significant difference is for unipolar depressive disorders (depression), which were not in the 10 leading causes of death, but which are in the 10 leading causes of DALYs. This stems from the fact that mental illness, which is discussed more in Chapter 12, is not associated with many deaths but is associated with an exceptional amount of disability in almost all countries. In fact, when we look at DALYs compared to deaths for high-income countries, the relative shares of DALYs by cause group is generally not very different than it is for deaths. However, for high-income countries, as well as low- and middle-income countries, unipolar depressive disorders become very important, as do Alzheimer's disease and other dementias. As noted earlier and in the chapter on communicable diseases (Chapter 11), DALYs are also an important measure for understanding the impact of the neglected tropical diseases.

Causes of Death by Region

As you would expect, the burden of disease varies by region, as shown in Table 2-4. In general, the higher the level of income within the region, the more likely it is that the leading causes of the burden of disease will be noncommunicable. The lower the level of income, the more likely it is that the leading causes of the burden of disease will be communicable. What is most important to note is the extent to which the burden of disease in the Africa region remains dominated by communicable diseases and the relative importance of communicable diseases in the South Asia region. Of course, these are in the face of a growing burden, even in these regions, of noncommunicable diseases.[34]

Causes of Death by Age

Tables 2-5 and 2-6 show the leading causes of death by age group for both low- and middle-income countries and high-income countries.

It is clear from Table 2-5 that children in low- and middle-income countries often die of communicable diseases that are no longer problems in the more developed countries. You can also see that HIV/AIDS and TB are among the leading causes of death in low- and middle-income countries among adults, whereas no communicable disease is among the 10 leading causes of death in the high-income countries.

Causes of Death by Gender

It is also important to examine deaths by gender. Table 2-7 shows deaths by gender for low- and middle-income countries.

For this group of countries, the causes of death among men and women are largely alike. However, it is important to note that, even in these countries, heart disease and stroke are the leading causes of death among both genders, that men die much more than women of road traffic accidents, and that diabetes has become the 10th leading cause of death among women.

The Burden of Deaths and Disease Within Countries

As you consider causes of death and the burden of disease globally and by region, age, and sex, it is also important to consider how deaths and DALYs would vary within countries, by gender, ethnicity, and socioeconomic status. In most low- and middle-income countries, the answer to this is relatively simple:

- Rural people will be less healthy than urban people.
- Disadvantaged ethnic minorities will be less healthy than majority populations.

- Women will suffer a number of conditions that relate to their relatively weak social positions.
- Poor people will be less healthy than better-off people.
- Uneducated people will be less healthy than better educated people.

In addition, people of lower socioeconomic status will have higher rates of communicable diseases, illness, and death related to maternal causes and malnutrition than will people of higher status. Lower socioeconomic status people will also suffer from a larger burden of disease related to

TABLE 2-4 The 10 Leading Causes of the Burden of Disease in Low- and Middle-Income Countries by Region, 2001

East Asia and Pacific	Percentage of Total DALYs	Europe and Central Asia	Percentage of Total DALYs
1. Cerebrovascular disease	7.5	1. Ischemic heart disease	15.9
2. Perinatal conditions	5.4	2. Cerebrovascular disease	10.8
3. Chronic obstructive pulmonary disease	5.0	3. Unipolar depressive disorders	3.7
4. Ischemic heart disease	4.1	4. Self-inflicted injuries	2.3
5. Unipolar depressive disorders	4.1	5. Hearing loss, adult onset	2.2
6. Tuberculosis	3.1	6. Chronic obstructive pulmonary disease	2.0
7. Lower respiratory infections	3.1	7. Trachea, bronchus, and lung cancers	2.0
8. Road traffic accidents	3.0	8. Osteoarthritis	2.0
9. Cataracts	2.8	9. Road traffic accidents	1.9
10. Diarrheal diseases	2.5	10. Poisonings	1.9

Latin America and the Caribbean	Percentage of Total DALYs	Middle East and North Africa	Percentage of Total DALYs
1. Perinatal conditions	6.0	1. Ischemic heart disease	6.6
2. Unipolar depressive disorders	5.0	2. Perinatal conditions	6.3
3. Violence	4.9	3. Road traffic accidents	4.6
4. Ischemic heart disease	4.2	4. Lower respiratory infections	4.5
5. Cerebrovascular disease	3.8	5. Diarrheal diseases	3.9
6. Endocrine disorders	3.0	6. Unipolar depressive disorders	3.1
7. Lower respiratory infections	2.9	7. Congenital anomalies	3.1
8. Alcohol use disorders	2.8	8. Cerebrovascular disease	3.0
9. Diabetes mellitus	2.7	9. Vision disorders, age-related	2.7
10. Road traffic accidents	2.6	10. Cataracts	2.3

South Asia	Percentage of Total DALYs	Sub-Saharan Africa	Percentage of Total DALYs
1. Perinatal conditions	9.2	1. HIV/AIDS	16.5
2. Lower respiratory infections	8.4	2. Malaria	10.3
3. Ischemic heart disease	6.3	3. Lower respiratory infections	8.8
4. Diarrheal diseases	5.4	4. Diarrheal diseases	6.4
5. Unipolar depressive disorders	3.6	5. Perinatal conditions	5.8
6. Tuberculosis	3.4	6. Measles	3.9
7. Cerebrovascular disease	3.2	7. Tuberculosis	2.3
8. Cataracts	2.3	8. Road traffic accidents	1.8
9. Chronic obstructive pulmonary disease	2.3	9. Pertussis	1.8
10. Hearing loss, adult onset	2.0	10. Protein-energy malnutrition	1.5

Source: Reprinted with permission from Lopez AD, Mathers CD, Murray CJL. The burden of disease and mortality by condition: data, methods, and results for 2001. In: Lopez AD, Mathers CD, Ezzati M, Jamison DT, Murray CJL, eds. *Global Burden of Disease and Risk Factors.* Washington, DC and New York: The World Bank and Oxford University Press; 2006:91.

TABLE 2-5 The 10 Leading Causes of Death in Children Ages 0–14, by Broad Income Group, 2001

Low- and Middle-Income Countries		High-Income Countries	
Cause	Percentage of Total Deaths	Cause	Percentage of Total Deaths
1. Perinatal conditions	20.7	1. Perinatal conditions	33.9
2. Lower respiratory infections	17.0	2. Congenital anomalies	20.0
3. Diarrheal diseases	13.4	3. Road traffic accidents	5.9
4. Malaria	9.2	4. Lower respiratory infections	2.5
5. Measles	6.2	5. Endocrine disorders	2.4
6. HIV/AIDS	3.7	6. Drownings	2.4
7. Congenital anomalies	3.7	7. Leukemia	1.9
8. Whooping cough	2.5	8. Violence	1.8
9. Tetanus	1.9	9. Fires	1.2
10. Road traffic accidents	1.5	10. Meningitis	1.2

Source: Adapted with permission from Lopez A, Begg S, Bos E. Demographic and epidemiological characteristics of major regions, 1990–2001. In: Lopez A, Mathers C, Ezzati M, Jamison D, Murray C, eds. *Global Burden of Disease and Risk Factors*. Washington, DC and New York: The World Bank and Oxford University Press; 2006:70.

TABLE 2-6 The 10 Leading Causes of Death in Adults 15–59, by Broad Income Group, 2001

Low- and Middle-Income Countries		High-Income Countries	
Cause	Percentage of Total Deaths	Cause	Percentage of Total Deaths
1. HIV/AIDS	14.1	1. Ischemic heart disease	10.8
2. Ischemic heart disease	8.1	2. Self-inflicted injuries	7.2
3. Tuberculosis	7.1	3. Road traffic accidents	6.9
4. Road traffic accidents	5.0	4. Trachea, bronchus, and lung cancers	6.8
5. Cerebrovascular disease	4.9	5. Cerebrovascular disease	4.4
6. Self-inflicted injuries	4.0	6. Cirrhosis of the liver	4.4
7. Violence	3.1	7. Breast cancer	4.0
8. Lower respiratory infections	2.3	8. Colon and rectal cancers	3.1
9. Cirrhosis of the liver	2.2	9. Diabetes mellitus	2.1
10. Chronic obstructive pulmonary disease	2.2	10. Stomach cancer	2.0

Source: Adapted with permission from Lopez A, Begg S, Bos E. Demographic and epidemiological characteristics of major regions, 1990–2001. In: Lopez A, Mathers C, Ezzati M, Jamison D, Murray C, eds. *Global Burden of Disease and Risk Factors*. Washington, DC and New York: The World Bank and Oxford University Press; 2006:70.

smoking, alcohol, and diet than would be the case for better-off people. These points are fundamental to understanding global health and will also be highlighted throughout the book.

RISK FACTORS

As we discuss the determinants of health and how health status is measured, there will be many references to *risk factors* for various health conditions. A risk factor is "an aspect or

TABLE 2-7 The 10 Leading Causes of Death Ordered by Sex, in Low- and Middle-Income Countries, 2001

Males		Females	
Cause	Percentage of Total Deaths	Cause	Percentage of Total Deaths
1. Ischemic heart disease	11.8	1. Ischemic heart disease	10.8
2. Cerebrovascular disease	8.5	2. Cerebrovascular disease	7.2
3. Lower respiratory infections	6.7	3. Lower respiratory infections	6.9
4. Perinatal conditions	5.4	4. HIV/AIDS	6.8
5. HIV/AIDS	5.4	5. Chronic obstructive pulmonary disease	4.4
6. Chronic obstructive pulmonary disease	4.7	6. Perinatal conditions	4.4
7. Tuberculosis	4.1	7. Diarrheal diseases	4.0
8. Diarrheal diseases	3.6	8. Malaria	3.1
9. Road traffic accidents	3.1	9. Tuberculosis	2.1
10. Malaria	2.3	10. Diabetes mellitus	2.0

Source: Data from Lopez A, Begg S, Bos E. Demographic and epidemiological characteristics of major regions, 1990–2001. In: Lopez A, Mathers C, Ezzati M, Jamison D, Murray C, eds. *Global Burden of Disease and Risk Factors.* Washington, DC and New York: The World Bank and Oxford University Press; 2006:70.

personal behavior or life-style, an environmental exposure, or an inborn or inherited characteristic, that, on the basis of epidemiologic evidence, is known to be associated with health-related condition(s) considered important to prevent."[35] Risks that relate to health can also be thought of as "a probability of an adverse outcome, or a factor that raises this probability."[36] We are all familiar with the notion of risk factors from our own lives and from encounters with health services. When we answer questions about our health history, for example, we are essentially helping to identify the most important risk factors that we face ourselves. Do our parents suffer from any health conditions that might affect our own health? Are we eating in a way that is conducive to good health? Do we get enough exercise and enough sleep? Do we smoke or drink alcohol excessively? Are there any special stresses in our life? Do we wear seat belts when we drive?

If we extend the idea of risk factors to poor people in low- and middle-income countries, then we might add some other questions that relate more to the ways that they live. Does the family have safe water to drink? Do their house and community have appropriate sanitation? Does the family cook indoors in a way that makes the house smoky? Do the father and mother work in places that are safe environmentally? We might also have to ask if there is war or conflict in the country, because they are also important risk factors for illness, death, and disability.

If we are to understand how the health status of people can be enhanced, particularly poor people in low- and middle-income countries, then it is very important that we understand the risk factors to which their health problems relate. Table 2-8 shows the relative importance of different risk factors to deaths and DALYs in low- and middle-income countries, compared to high-income countries. These are shown in the table in order of their importance by category of risk.

When we consider low- and middle-income countries, the most striking factor is the extent to which malnutrition is a risk factor. Another important point is the extent to which other nutrition-related risk factors are important for deaths and DALYs, such as high blood pressure and high cholesterol. Deaths and DALYs attributable to the risks of smoking and unsafe sex make up the other most significant risk factors in low- and middle-income countries.[37]

In high-income countries, there is little undernutrition but a considerable amount of overweight and obesity. It is not surprising, therefore, that three of the most important risk factors for both deaths and DALYs in high-income countries are high blood pressure, high cholesterol, and overweight and obesity. Nor is it surprising that, despite important progress in reducing the prevalence of smoking in some countries, tobacco remains the leading risk factor for both deaths and DALYs in high-income countries.[37]

TABLE 2-8 The Leading Risk Factors for the Burden of Disease, 2001, Low- and Middle-Income and High-Income Countries, Ranked in Order of Percent of Total DALY

Low- and Middle-Income Countries		High-Income Countries	
Deaths	**DALYs**	**Deaths**	**DALYs**
High blood pressure (12.9)	Childhood underweight (8.7)	Smoking (12.7)	Smoking (12.7)
Childhood underweight (7.5)	Unsafe sex (5.8)	High blood pressure (17.6)	High blood pressure (9.3)
Smoking (6.9)	High blood pressure (5.6)	High cholesterol (10.7)	Overweight and obesity (7.2)
High cholesterol (6.3)	Smoking (3.9)	Overweight and obesity (7.8)	High cholesterol (6.3)
Unsafe sex (5.8)	Unsafe water, sanitation, and hygiene (3.7)	Physical inactivity (4.8)	Alcohol use (4.4)
Low fruit and vegetable intake (4.8)	Alcohol use (3.6)	Low fruit and vegetable intake (4.2)	Physical inactivity (3.2)
Alcohol use (3.9)	High cholesterol (3.1)	Urban air pollution (1.0)	Low fruit and vegetable intake (2.7)
Indoor smoke from household use of solid fuels (3.7)	Indoor smoke from household use of solid fuels (3.0)	Illicit drug use (0.5)	Unsafe sex (0.6)
Overweight and obesity (3.6)	Low fruit and vegetable intake (2.4)	Unsafe sex (0.4)	Iron-deficiency anemia (0.5)
Unsafe water, sanitation, and hygiene (3.2)	Overweight and obesity (2.3)	Alcohol use (0.3)	Child sexual abuse (0.5)

Source: Data used with permission from Lopez A, et al. *Global Burden of Disease and Risk Factors.* Washington, DC and New York: The World Bank and Oxford University Press; 2006:10.

DEMOGRAPHY AND HEALTH

There are a number of points related to population that are extremely important to people's health. Among the most important of these are:

- Population growth
- Population aging
- Urbanization
- The "demographic divide"
- The demographic transition

These are briefly discussed below, along with their implications for health. Other important matters related to population, such as the relationship between fertility and the health of women and children, are discussed in other chapters.

Population Growth

The population of the world is about 6.9 billion[38] and is still growing. As shown in Figure 2-8, it is estimated that by 2050 the population of the world will be about 9.2 billion. As also shown in the figure, the overwhelming majority of population growth in the future will occur in low- and middle-income countries. This reflects the fact that fertility is falling only slowly in many countries that have had high fertility rates historically, while many of the high-income countries have very low fertility. At a minimum, we should expect that increasing population growth in low-income countries will put substantial pressure on the environment, with its attendant risks for health. It will also mean that infrastructure, such as water supply and sanitation, will have to be provided to an increasing number of people—in the countries that have the largest service gaps, can least afford to expand such services, and will face substantial impacts on health as a result. Increasing population will also make it more difficult for low-income countries to provide education and health services, with additional consequences for the health of their people in the future.

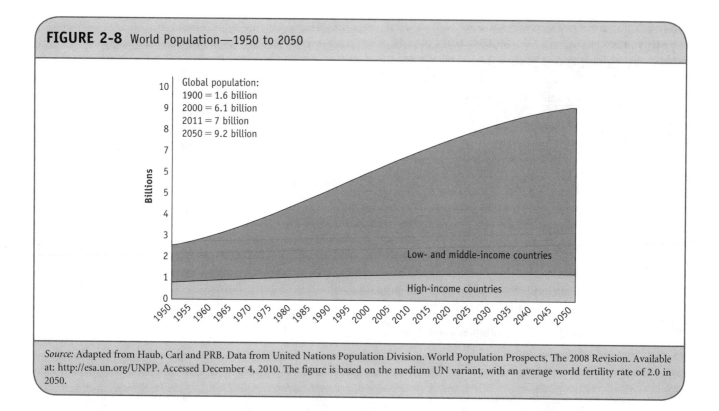

FIGURE 2-8 World Population—1950 to 2050

Global population:
1900 = 1.6 billion
2000 = 6.1 billion
2011 = 7 billion
2050 = 9.2 billion

Low- and middle-income countries

High-income countries

Source: Adapted from Haub, Carl and PRB. Data from United Nations Population Division. World Population Prospects, The 2008 Revision. Available at: http://esa.un.org/UNPP. Accessed December 4, 2010. The figure is based on the medium UN variant, with an average world fertility rate of 2.0 in 2050.

Population Aging

As shown in Table 2-9, the population of the world is aging. This is especially true in high-income countries that have low fertility, but this is occurring in other countries, as well. One impact of population aging is that it changes the ratio between the share of the population that is working and the share of the population that is 65 years of age or more. This is called the *elderly support ratio*. Whereas this ratio is 19 in

TABLE 2-9 Percentage of the Population Projected to Be Over 65 Years of Age

	2010	2050
High-income countries	15.9	26.2
Low- and middle-income countries	5.8	14.6

Source: Adapted from Haub, Carl and PRB. Data from United Nations Population Division. World Population Prospects. The 2008 Revision. Available at: http://esa.un.org/UNPP. Accessed December 4, 2010. Data is shown only for the medium population variant of the UN.

Niger, for example, it is already approaching 1 in Japan.[38] Population aging and the shift in the elderly support ratio have profound implications for the burden of disease and for health expenditures and how they will be financed. In the simplest terms, people will live longer and spend more years with morbidities and disabilities related to noncommunicable diseases. This will raise the costs of health care. In addition, the large numbers of older adults for every working person will make it difficult for countries to finance that health care.

Urbanization

In the last decade, the majority of the world's population has lived in urban areas for the first time in world history. People are continuing to move from rural to urban areas, especially in low- and middle-income countries, in which important shares of the population have continued to live in rural areas until recently. Continuing urbanization will also put enormous pressure on urban infrastructure, such as water and sanitation, schools, and health services, which are already in short supply in many countries. Gaps in such infrastructure, as well as the development of crowded and low-standard housing, for example, could have substantial negative consequences for health.

The Demographic Divide

There is an exceptional difference in the demographic indicators and future demographic paths of the best-off and the least-well-off countries, as suggested in the two sections above. The highest income countries generally have very low fertility, declining populations, and aging populations. By contrast, fertility in the lowest income countries is generally still high, although it is declining slowly. In addition, the population is still growing in these countries and will continue to grow for some time. As will be discussed throughout the book, and related to the demographic divide, there is also an enormous difference in the health circumstances of the high- and low-income countries. Table 2-10 portrays the demographic divide.

The Demographic Transition[39]

One important demographic trend of importance is called the *demographic transition*. This is the shift from a pattern of high fertility and high mortality to low fertility and low mortality, with population growth occurring in between.

When we look back historically at the countries that are now high-income, we can see that they had long periods historically when fertility was high, mortality was high, and population growth was, therefore, relatively slow, or which might even have declined in the face of epidemics. Beginning around the turn of the nineteenth century, however, mortality in those countries began to decline as hygiene and nutrition improved and the burden of infectious diseases became less. In most cases, this decline in mortality went before much decline in fertility. As mortality declined, the population increased and the share of the population that was of younger ages also increased. Later, fertility began to decline and, as births and deaths became more equal, population growth slowed. As births and deaths stayed more equal, the share of the population that was of older ages increased.

The demographic transition is shown graphically in Figure 2-9.

The first population pyramid reflects a country with high fertility and high mortality. The second population pyramid is indicative of a country in which mortality has begun to decline but fertility remains high. This would be similar to the demographics one would find, for example, in a number of countries in sub-Saharan Africa that are undergoing demographic transition. The third pyramid looks more like a cylinder than a pyramid. This reflects a population in which fertility has been reduced and in which there is a larger share of older people in the population than in the first and second pyramids. This would be similar to the demographics that one would find in a number of low-fertility, aging populations in Western Europe.

The Epidemiologic Transition[40]

The epidemiologic transition is closely related to the demographic transition, as suggested throughout the previous discussion. Historically there has been a shift in the patterns of disease that follows the trends noted below:

- First, high and fluctuating mortality, related to very poor health conditions, epidemics, and famine

TABLE 2-10 The Demographic Divide: The Example of Nigeria and Japan

	Nigeria	Japan
Population 2009 (millions)	153	128
Population 2050 (millions)	285	95
Lifetime births per woman	5.7	1.4
Annual number of births (millions)	6.2	1.1
Percentage of population below age 15	45	13
Percentage of population age 65+	3	23
Life expectancy at birth	47	83
Infant deaths per 1000 births	75	2.6
Annual number of infant deaths	465,000	2900
Percentage of adults with HIV/AIDS	3.1	—

Source: Data from Population Reference Bureau. 2009 World Population Data Sheet. Available at: http://www.prb.org/Publications/Datasheets/2009/2009wpds.aspx. Accessed November 24, 2010.

FIGURE 2-9 The Demographic Transition: (A) High Fertility/High Mortality, (B) Declining Mortality/High Fertility, (C) Reduced Fertility/Reduced Mortality

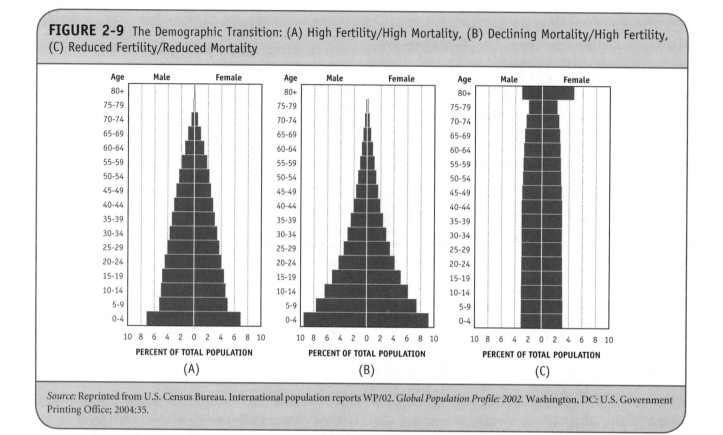

Source: Reprinted from U.S. Census Bureau. International population reports WP/02. *Global Population Profile: 2002.* Washington, DC: U.S. Government Printing Office; 2004:35.

- Then, progressive declines in mortality, as epidemics become less frequent
- Finally, further declines in mortality, increases in life expectancy, and the predominance of noncommunicable diseases

Figure 2-10 shows examples of two sets of countries. The first has a burden of disease profile that is pretransition. The second is of a developed country that has completed its epidemiologic transition.

You can see in Figure 2-10 how the pattern of disease differs between the two types of countries. You can also see the changes that will occur over time, as the low-income country develops and the burden of disease moves from one that is dominated by communicable diseases to one that is dominated by noncommunicable diseases.

The pace of the epidemiologic transition in different societies depends on a number of factors related to the determinants of health that were discussed earlier. In its early stages, the transition appears to depend primarily on improvements in hygiene, nutrition, education, and socioeconomic status. Some improvements also stem from advances in public health

and in medicine, such as the development of new vaccines and antibiotics.[41]

Most of the countries that are now high-income went through epidemiologic transitions that were relatively slow, with the exception of Japan. Most developing countries have already begun their transition; however, it is still far from complete in most of them.

In fact, most low-income countries are in an ongoing epidemiologic transition and many of them, therefore, face significant burdens of communicable and noncommunicable diseases, and injuries at the same time. This strains the capacity of the health system of many of these countries. It is also expensive for countries that are resource poor to address a substantial burden of all three of these types of conditions simultaneously.

PROGRESS IN HEALTH STATUS

As noted in the introductory chapter, there has been substantial progress in improving health and raising life expectancy in many parts of the world. However, as also noted, those gains have not been uniform across regions. Rather, life

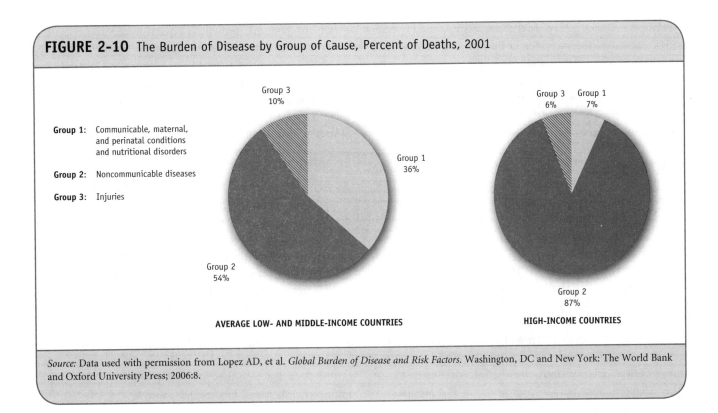

FIGURE 2-10 The Burden of Disease by Group of Cause, Percent of Deaths, 2001

Source: Data used with permission from Lopez AD, et al. *Global Burden of Disease and Risk Factors.* Washington, DC and New York: The World Bank and Oxford University Press; 2006:8.

expectancy in sub-Saharan Africa and South Asia continue to substantially lag that in other regions. In addition, for countries that had a life expectancy in 1960 of less than 50 years, the pace of improvements in life expectancy in sub-Saharan Africa has been much slower than in any other region.

Table 2-11 shows life expectancy in 1960, 1990, and 2008 by World Bank region, including for high-income countries. The table also shows the percentage gain in life expectancy over three different periods, 1960 to 2008, 1960 to 1990, and 1990 to 2008.

TABLE 2-11 Life Expectancy and Percentage Gain in Life Expectancy, 1960–2008, by World Bank Region

World Bank Region	Life Expectancy (Years)			Percentage Gain (1960–2008)	Percentage Gain (1960–1990)	Percentage Gain (1990–2008)
	1960	1990	2008			
East Asia and the Pacific	46	67	72	57%	46%	7%
Europe and Central Asia	—	69	70	—	—	1%
Latin America and the Caribbean	56	68	73	30%	21%	7%
Middle East and North Africa	47	64	71	51%	36%	11%
South Asia	43	58	64	49%	35%	10%
Sub-Saharan Africa	41	50	52	27%	22%	4%
High-income OECD	69	76	80	16%	10%	5%

Source: Data from the World Bank. World Development Indicators, Data Query. Available at: http://databank.worldbank.org. Accessed July 6, 2010.

No data for Europe and Central Asia for 1960.

Life expectancy grew over each successive period in each region; however, the increases in Europe and Central Asia were very small in the period 1990–2008, largely reflecting the social and economic consequences of the break-up of the former Soviet Union and the impact of changes on the health system, as well. The slow progress in improving life expectancy in sub-Saharan Africa between 1990 and 2008 mostly reflects the negative impact on life expectancy of the HIV/AIDS epidemic, as well as slow economic progress in some countries and political conflict. By contrast, the dramatic increases in life expectancy from 1960 to 2008 in the East Asia and the Pacific region suggest the rapid pace of economic development in that region, usually accompanied by substantial investments in improving nutrition, education, and health. The region was also relatively free of conflict.

The factors that lead to improvements in health are complex, as suggested by the determinants of health that you reviewed earlier in this chapter. Additional comments are made at the end of this chapter and in Chapter 3 about these factors, including the role, for example, of nutrition, education, political stability, and scientific improvements. Many other chapters also include comments on the progress in improving the health of women and children and in addressing particular causes of illness, disability, and death.

THE BURDEN OF DISEASE: LOOKING FORWARD

The burden of disease in the future will be influenced by a number of factors that will continue to change. Some of these will relate to the determinants of health discussed earlier in the chapter. Some will relate to the demographic forces just discussed, including population growth, population aging, and migration. The burden of disease in the future will also be driven, among other things, by:

- Economic development
- Scientific and technological change
- Climate change
- Political stability
- Emerging and re-emerging infectious diseases

These are discussed very briefly in the following sections. Chapter 12 offers additional comments on emerging and re-emerging infectious diseases.

Economic Development

The economies of low-income countries will need to grow if those countries are to generate the income they need to invest in improving people's health. The impact of economic development on health will depend partly on the extent to which economic growth is equitable across population groups. It will also depend on the extent to which countries are able—or choose—to use their increased income to invest in other areas that improve health, such as water, sanitation, hygiene, and education. The extent and appropriateness of their investments in health, such as in low-cost, high-yielding efforts in health, will also be critical.

Scientific and Technological Change

As you will read about further throughout the book and in Chapter 16, scientific and technological change have had an enormous impact on health and will continue to do so in the future. This is easy to understand, as one considers the development of vaccines or new drugs, such as antibiotics or antiretroviral therapy. The development of new diagnostics for TB, for example, would have an enormous impact on the health of the world, as would the development of a vaccine against HIV or malaria. As also discussed in Chapter 16, the impact of scientific and technological change on the low-income countries of today will depend to a large extent on the pace at which they are able to effectively adopt any improvements when they are developed.

Climate Change

The impact of climate change on health is not clear; however, it is anticipated that climate change and its attendant impact on weather and rising sea levels could directly and indirectly have an important impact on health. On the indirect side, climate change could alter the nature of the food crops that can be grown in different places and lead to migration from some places to others that are deemed more habitable. On the more direct side, climate change could lead to weather changes and adverse weather that harms people's health. It could also lead to the disappearance of disease vectors in some places as the weather is no longer hospitable to them, while allowing the emergence or re-emergence of disease vectors in other places.

Political Stability

In low-income countries, political stability appears to be necessary for achieving long-term gains in health. There is substantial evidence, for example, that the lack of political stability has been a major impediment to progress in achieving the MDGs in a number of countries. It is not hard to imagine, for example, how conflicts in Liberia, Sierra Leone, and the Democratic Republic of the Congo could set back health status for many years. These conflicts led directly to substantial illness, disability, and death. In addition, by causing a breakdown in infrastructure, such as water, sanitation, and electricity, as well as the erosion of health services, they also had enormous indirect impacts on health.

Emerging and Re-emerging Infectious Diseases

It is not possible to predict if and when new diseases will emerge or diseases already known will re-emerge. It is also not possible to know how well individual countries and the world will do in recognizing any such problems and addressing them quickly and effectively. What is clear is that pandemic flu, for example, could have a major impact on future disease patterns. It is also clear, for example, that if the growth of drug-resistance for, say, malaria, outpaced our ability to produce safe and effective drugs to fight malaria, this, too, could have a substantial impact on the burden of disease.

Projecting the Burden of Disease

Given the complex array of factors that influence health status and will drive future changes in the burden of disease, it is difficult to predict with any certainty how the burden of disease will evolve in different countries in the next two decades. Nonetheless, it is possible, using models, to project the future burden of disease, given assumptions about key health determinants and how they will evolve in different parts of the world. WHO has projected the burden of disease in 2030 by country income group.

Table 2-12 examines trends in the 10 leading causes of the burden of disease between 2004 and 2030, by country income group (low, lower-middle, upper-middle, and upper). In cases where there is very little difference between the tenth and eleventh leading cause of DALYs lost, the table also shows, in parentheses and without enumeration, an eleventh cause of disease.

The main message of the table is clear: over the period 2004 to 2030, it is projected that there will be substantial changes in the burden of disease in all country income groups. In the simplest of terms, we can see for low- and lower-middle-income countries there will be a substantial shift away from communicable diseases and toward non-communicable diseases and accidents and injuries. HIV/AIDS is projected to be the only communicable disease in the top 10 causes of DALYs lost in low-income countries, and no communicable diseases are predicted to be in the top 10 for lower-middle-income countries. Unipolar depressive disorders, ischemic heart disease, and cerebrovascular disease become more important causes of DALYs lost for both income groups. Some causes we associate with aging populations, such as hearing loss and refractive errors, also become more prominent, even in low-income countries. The projected growth of diabetes in all income groups is also evident in the table.

For the upper-middle-income countries, the burden would continue to shift in similar ways, as noted above. TB, which was the eleventh leading cause of DALYs lost, would decline in relative importance, and no communicable disease would be in the top 10. Adult-onset hearing loss and arthritis, however, would join the top 10 leading causes of DALYs lost, clearly reflecting the aging populations in these countries.

TABLE 2-12 Trends in the 10 Leading Causes of the Burden of Disease, by Income Group, 2004–2030

2004	Percentage of Total DALYs	Projected in 2030	Percentage of Total DALYs
Low-income countries			
1. Perinatal conditions	11.28%	1. Perinatal conditions	8.56%
2. Lower respiratory infections	9.30%	2. Unipolar depressive disorders	5.75%
3. Diarrheal diesease	7.15%	3. Road traffic accidents	5.53%
4. HIV/AIDS	5.18%	4. Ischemic heart disease	5.23%
5. Malaria	3.96%	5. Lower respiratory infections	4.95%
6. Unipolar depressive disorders	3.20%	6. Cerebrovascular disease	3.14%
7. Ischemic heart disease	3.14%	7. HIV/AIDS	3.13%
8. Other unintentional injuries	2.94%	8. Other unintentional injuries	3.09%
9. Tuberculosis	2.70%	9. Chronic obstructive pulmonary disease	3.08%
10. Road traffic accidents	2.02%	10. Hearing loss, adult onset	2.59%
(Cerebrovascular disease)	1.73%	(Refractive disorders)	2.56%

(continues)

TABLE 2-12 *(Continued)*

2004	Percentage of Total DALYs	Projected in 2030	Percentage of Total DALYs
Lower-middle-income countries			
1. Perinatal conditions	6.06%	1. Unipolar depressive disorders	6.43%
2. Unipolar depressive disorders	5.22%	2. Cerebrovascular disease	6.03%
3. Cerebrovascular disease	4.72%	3. Chronic obstructive pulmonary disease	5.90%
4. Other unintentional injuries	4.37%	4. Ischemic heart disease	5.16%
5. Ischemic heart disease	4.18%	5. Road traffic accidents	5.04%
6. Road traffic accidents	3.89%	6. Refractive errors	3.29%
7. Chronic obstructive pulmonary disease	3.25%	7. Hearing loss, adult onset	3.14%
8. Lower respiratory infections	3.13%	8. Perinatal conditions	2.93%
9. Refractive errors	2.72%	9. Diabetes mellitus	2.74%
10. Diarrheal disease	2.61%	10. Alcohol use disorders	2.72%
(Alcohol use disorders)	2.51%	(Other unintentional injuries)	2.66%
Upper-middle-income countries			
1. HIV/AIDS	8.32%	1. Ischemic heart disease	8.16%
2. Ischemic heart disease	8.23%	2. HIV/AIDS	6.20%
3. Cerebrovascular disease	5.13%	3. Unipolar depressive disorders	6.02%
4. Unipolar depressive disorders	4.46%	4. Cerebrovascular disease	5.57%
5. Other unintentional injuries	3.86%	5. Diabetes mellitus	4.20%
6. Perinatal conditions	3.21%	6. Violence	3.89%
7. Road traffic accidents	3.15%	7. Alcohol use disorders	3.08%
8. Violence	3.03%	8. Road traffic accidents	2.97%
9. Alcohol use disorders	2.91%	9. Hearing loss, adult onset	2.78%
10. Diabetes mellitus	2.08%	10. Osteoarthritis	2.32%
(Tuberculosis)	2.01%		
High-income countries			
1. Unipolar depressive disorders	8.19%	1. Unipolar depressive disorders	8.46%
2. Ischemic heart disease	6.34%	2. Ischemic heart disease	6.54%
3. Cerebrovascular disease	3.90%	3. Alzheimer's and other dementias	5.53%
4. Alzheimer's and other dementias	3.59%	4. Hearing loss, adult onset	4.07%
5. Alcohol use disorders	3.45%	5. Cerebrovascular disease	3.76%
6. Hearing loss, adult onset	3.44%	6. Alcohol use disorders	3.32%
7. Chronic obstructive pulmonary disease	3.00%	7. Osteoarthritis	2.75%
8. Diabetes mellitus	2.97%	8. Trachea/bronchus/lung cancers	2.74%
9. Trachea/bronchus/lung cancers	2.96%	9. Refractive errors	2.40%
10. Road traffic accidents	2.56%	10. Self-inflicted intentional injuries	2.39%

Source: Data from World Health Organization. Global Burden of Disease (GBD). Available at: http://www.who.int/healthinfo/global_burden_disease/en. Accessed September 14, 2010.

The projected burden of disease in high-income countries also suggests an increase in burdens associated with aging, such as dementias, hearing loss, and refractive disorders.

Mental health issues are projected to increase in importance in all income groups over the period 2004 to 2030. The largest percentage increases will occur in low-income countries, probably reflecting the extent to which these issues arise as people lose connections with their families and their culture group, as often occurs in modernizing and globalizing economies in which people leave their native places to migrate to cities in search of employment. As noted earlier, the neglected tropical diseases are not treated as a group in the burden of disease data, like those shown in Tables 2-3 to 2-8. We should anticipate that the burden of these diseases will remain substantial for many years to come, but that their burden will decline consistently between 2004 and 2030.

THE DEVELOPMENT CHALLENGE OF IMPROVING HEALTH

One of the key development challenges facing policy makers in low-income countries is how they can speed the demographic and epidemiologic transitions at the lowest possible cost. How can Niger, for example, improve its health status as rapidly as possible and at the least possible cost? Will it be possible for the people of Niger to enjoy the health status of a middle-income country, even if Niger remains a low-income country?

Figure 2-11 shows national income of a sample of countries, plotted against life expectancy at birth for females in those countries.

From this figure, one can see that, generally, the health of a country does increase as national income rises. However, one can also see that there are some countries, such as China,

Costa Rica, Cuba, and Sri Lanka, that have achieved higher average life expectancies at birth than one would have predicted for countries at their level of income.

To a large extent, countries like those above achieved these important health gains as a result of:

- Focusing on investing in nutrition, health, and education, particularly of their poor people
- Improving people's knowledge of good hygiene
- Making selected investments in health services that at low cost could have a high impact on health status, such as vaccination programs for children and TB control

These themes will also be discussed throughout this book.

Indeed, in the long run, economic progress *will* help to bring down fertility, reduce mortality from communi-

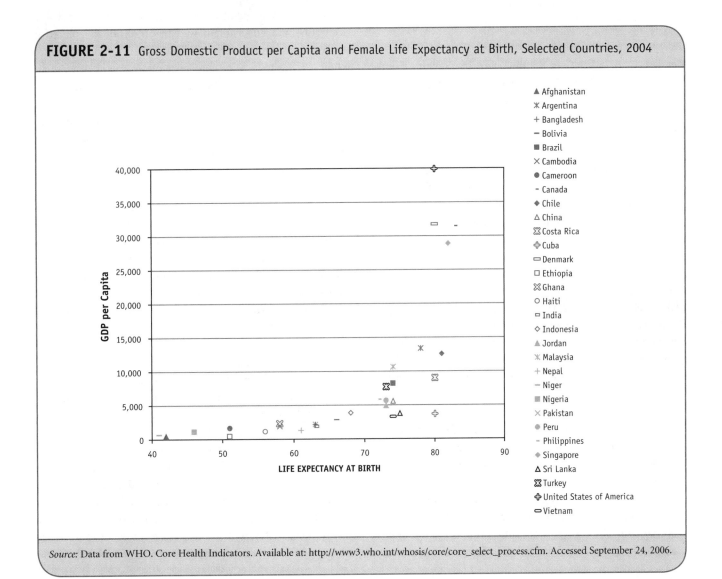

FIGURE 2-11 Gross Domestic Product per Capita and Female Life Expectancy at Birth, Selected Countries, 2004

Source: Data from WHO. Core Health Indicators. Available at: http://www3.who.int/whosis/core/core_select_process.cfm. Accessed September 24, 2006.

cable diseases, and help to produce a healthier population. However, at the present rates of progress in improving health in most low-income countries, these changes will take a very long time to occur. One great public policy challenge for these countries and their governments, therefore, is how they can "short-circuit" this process and reach reduced levels of fertility, lower mortality, and better health for their people, even as they remain relatively poor.

CASE STUDY

The State of Kerala

Having begun to review health status and how countries can speed improvements in health, it will be valuable to end this chapter by examining a well-known case of a place that improved health status considerably, even at relatively low levels of income. One of the best known of such success stories concerns Kerala State in India.

Introduction

Kerala is a coastal state in Southwestern India with a population of more than 31 million people.[42] Despite having only slow rates of economic growth and a state per capita income lower than that of many other states in India, the health indicators for Kerala are the best in India and rival those in developed countries. What approach did Kerala take historically to produce such high levels of health, even in the face of relatively low income? What factors contributed to improvements in health status? What lessons does the Kerala experience suggest for other countries and for other states within India?

The Kerala Approach

One of the primary reasons why people in Kerala have such high levels of health has been the emphasis that the state put on education and the exceptionally widespread access to education in Kerala. The state introduced free primary and secondary education in the early part of 20th century.[43] In addition, Kerala has always put important emphasis on the education of females.

Kerala also made an early commitment to widespread health services for its people. The state created, for example, an extensive network of primary healthcare centers. This provided its citizens, throughout the state, with access to free basic health care and free family planning services. This was coupled with programs to promote exclusive breastfeeding and the improved nutrition of infants, children, and pregnant women. The central government supported the family planning program, the maternal and child health program,

and the universal immunization program in all of India, but they were implemented far more effectively and efficiently in Kerala than in other states of India.[44]

The place of women in Kerala society also contributed to the uptake of education by females and improvements throughout Kerala in nutrition and health status. The role of women in many communities in Kerala differs from the roles ascribed to women in many other parts of India. In much of the rest of India, especially in parts of North India, women are regarded by families as liabilities rather than as assets. In most of India, this is partly represented in cultural terms by the fact that the family of a bride must pay a dowry to the family of the groom. In Kerala, however, women have been treated differently for over a century. They have been seen culturally much more as assets to families and they could inherit and own land, giving them a financial independence and power which was unrivalled among women elsewhere in India.[45]

It is also important to note that Kerala has historically been run by a government that has traditionally placed a premium on community mobilization on important social issues, such as education, greater empowerment of women, health, nutrition, and land reform. Many of these efforts were carried out in ways that raised social awareness about health and nutrition. In 1989, Kerala launched a total literacy campaign, for example, and by the start of the World Literacy Year in 1990, Ernakulam district in Kerala was declared India's first totally literate district.[46]

Given widespread education in Kerala and the place of women in society, it is not surprising that Kerala went through the demographic transition quite early and well before other places in India. Women with more education are more likely to work and marry later and thus have wider choice in economic and social pursuits. They also have a better knowledge of and easier access to family planning methods and lower fertility than do women with less education.[47]

The Impact

What were the impacts on health status of the emphasis that Kerala placed on education, health, nutrition, and the empowerment of women? Although it is not possible to scientifically indicate which policy contributed what share of better health, we can say that for many years the people of Kerala have enjoyed the best educational attainment of any group within India. In the 2001 census, the literacy rates of people aged 7 years and above for India were about 65 percent on average, with about 76 percent for males and 54 percent for females. Kerala, however, had the highest literacy rate in the country, with about 91 percent overall and about 94 percent for males and 88 percent for females.[48] Kerala also boasts one of the highest newspaper readerships in the world, another feature that promotes the value of women, education, nutrition, and health. It also helps to raise political awareness and the demands of people for participation in and solutions to their concerns, such as education, health, and water.

Linked with this high level of education, especially of women, and the promotion of nutrition and health, infant mortality in Kerala in 2001 was 14 per 1000, compared with 91 per 1000 for low-income countries generally and 68 per 1000 on average for India.[48] The national under-5 mortality rate for 1998–1999 was around 87 per 1000 live births with a wide variation between states. In Kerala, however, the mortality of children under 5 years was the best in India with an impressive rate of only 19 such deaths per 1000 births in 1998–1999.[49] In addition, maternal deaths in Kerala were much less common, at 87 per 100,000, than the Indian average of 407 per 100,000.[50] This partly reflects the extent to which deliveries take place in hospitals in Kerala. Indeed, Kerala's healthcare system garnered international acclaim when UNICEF and WHO designated it as the world's first "baby-friendly state." This was in recognition of the fact that more than 95 percent of Keralite births are hospital-delivered.[51]

Finally, one should note that life expectancy for men and women in Kerala at the time of the 2001 census was 73 years. This was close to life expectancy in many developed countries.[52]

Lessons Learned

Kerala has long been cited, along with China, Costa Rica, Cuba, and Sri Lanka, as a model of a country or state within a country that has achieved high levels of education and health for its people, before achieving high levels of income. It appears that Kerala has achieved these impacts by politically supporting widespread access to education, nutrition, and health; mobilizing communities around the importance of these areas and of women's empowerment; and investing in low-cost but high-yielding areas of education, nutrition, and health. In a manner much like Sri Lanka, Kerala has also managed to achieve high levels of health status at relatively low cost.

Have the high levels of health and education in Kerala, however, been associated with high levels of growth of income in the state? The answer to that question, at least until recently, was no. The annual per capita gross domestic product (GDP) for the state in year 2001 was $469. This was close to the Indian average of $460.[53] It appears that the economic policies held by the state government over time in Kerala

have not yielded high rates of economic growth or produced an environment in which domestic and foreign investors were prepared to work. Rather, the overall income of the state remains quite dependent on the money that workers from Kerala living abroad, especially in the Middle East, send back to their families in Kerala.[54]

What, then, are the messages to take away from Kerala in terms of the link between health and development? First, it is possible, even in the absence of high levels of income, to achieve high levels of health through political commitment, sound investments, and social mobilization. Second, however, in the absence of sound economic policies, the presence of a literate and healthy population alone will not be sufficient to promote rapid economic growth.

MAIN MESSAGES

To understand the most important global health issues, we must be able to understand the determinants of health, how health status is measured, and the meaning of the demographic and epidemiologic transitions. There are a number of factors that influence health status, including genetic makeup, sex, and age. Social and cultural issues and health behaviors are also closely linked to health status. The determinants of health also include education, nutritional status, and socioeconomic status. The environment is also a powerful determinant of health, as is access to health services, and the policy approaches that countries take to their health sectors and to investments that could influence the health of their people. Increasing attention is being paid to the social determinants of health.

It is also important to understand the most important risk factors that lead to ill health. In the low-income countries on which this book focuses considerable attention, some of the most important risk factors include nutritional status, the lack of safe water or appropriate sanitation, and tobacco smoking. Poor diets that relate to obesity, high blood pressure, high cholesterol, and cardiovascular disease are becoming increasingly important problems as well, even in low-income countries.

There are a number of uses of health data including measuring health status, carrying out disease surveillance, making decisions about investments in health, and assessing the performance of health programs. Those working in health use a common set of indicators to measure health status, including life expectancy, infant and neonatal mortality, under-5 child mortality, and the maternal mortality ratio. They also use composite indices, such as DALYs, to measure the burden of disease. Vital registration systems are weak in low-income countries and need to be strengthened to improve the quality of health data.

Poorer countries have a relatively larger burden of disease from communicable diseases than from noncommunicable diseases, compared to richer countries. As these poorer countries develop, fertility and mortality will decline, the population will age, and the burden of disease will shift toward the noncommunicable diseases. These phenomena occur as countries go through what are referred to as the demographic transition and the epidemiologic transition.

Life expectancy has improved in all regions of the world since 1990, but at a slower pace in sub-Saharan Africa than elsewhere. The leading cause of death worldwide has now become cardiovascular disease. However, communicable diseases remain relatively more important in South Asia and sub-Saharan Africa than in the rest of the world. Projections of the burden of disease to 2030 suggest a continuing trend toward noncommunicable diseases, even in the low-income countries.

Study Questions

1. What are the main factors that determine your health?

2. What are the main factors that would determine the health of a poor person in a poor country?

3. If you could only pick one indicator to describe the health status of a poor country, which indicator would you use and why?

4. Why is it valuable to have composite indicators like DALYs to measure the burden of disease?

5. What is a HALE, and how does it differ from just measuring life expectancy at birth?

6. As countries develop economically, what are the most important changes that occur in their burden of disease?

7. Why do these changes occur?

8. In your own country, what population groups have the best health indicators and why?

9. In your country, what population groups have the worst health status and why?

10. How would the population pyramid of Italy differ from that of Nigeria and why?

11. How does the burden of disease differ from one region to another?

12. How will the burden of disease evolve in different regions over the next 20 years?

REFERENCES

1. A global emergency: a combined response. *The World Health Report 2004—Changing History*. Geneva: World Health Organization; 2004:6.

2. Population Reference Bureau. 2009 World Population Data Sheet. Available at: http://www.prb.org/pdf09/09wpds_eng.pdf. Accessed April 9, 2011.

3. World Bank. Data. Fertility Rate, Total (Births per Woman). Available at: http://data.worldbank.org/indicator/SP.DYN.TFRT.IN/countries. Accessed November 19, 2010.

4. World Bank. Life Expectancy at Birth, Total (Years). Available at: http://data.worldbank.org/indicator/SP.DYN.LE00.IN. Accessed November 19, 2010.

5. Kozik CA, Suntayakorn S, Vaughn DW, Suntayakorn C, Snitbhan R, Innis BL. Causes of death and unintentional injury among schoolchildren in Thailand. *Southeast Asian J Trop Med Public Health*. 1999;30(1):129-135.

6. Public Health Agency of Canada. What Determines Health. Available at: http://www.phac-aspc.gc.ca/ph-sp/determinants/index-eng.php#determinants. Accessed November 19, 2010.

7. World Health Organization. WHO Issues New Healthy Life Expectancy Rankings: Japan Number One in New "Healthy Life" System. Available at: http://www.who.int/inf-pr-2000/en/pr2000-life.html. Accessed January 3, 2006.

8. Hobcraft J. Women's education, child welfare and child survival: a review of the evidence. *Health Transition Rev*. 1993;3(2):159-173.

9. World Bank. *Repositioning Nutrition as Central to Development—A Strategy for Large-Scale Action*. Washington, DC: The World Bank; 2006.

10. World Health Organization. Commission on Social Determinants of Health. Closing the Gap in a Generation. Available at: http://www.who.int/social_determinants/thecommission/finalreport/en/index.html. Accessed November 18, 2010.

11. Basch P. *Textbook of International Health*. 2nd ed. New York: Oxford University Press; 2001:73-113.

12. Haupt, A, Kane, TT. *Population Handbook*. Washington, DC: Population Reference Bureau; 2004.

13. World Bank. Data. Mortality Rate, Infant (per 1000 Live Births). Available at: http://data.worldbank.org/indicator/SP.DYN.IMRT.IN. Accessed November 18, 2010.

14. World Health Organization. Neonatal and Perinatal Mortality, Country, Regional and Global Estimates, 2004. Available at: http://whqlibdoc.who.int/publications/2007/9789241596145_eng.pdf. Accessed November 18, 2010.

15. World Bank. Data. Mortality Rate, Under-5 (per 1000). Available at: http://data.worldbank.org/indicator/SH.DYN.MORT. Accessed November 18, 2010.

16. World Bank. Data. Maternal Mortality Ratio (Modeled Estimate per 100,000 Live Births). Available at: http://data.worldbank.org/indicator/SH.STA.MMRT. Accessed November 20, 2010.

17. Last JM. *A Dictionary of Epidemiology*. 4th ed. New York: Oxford University Press; 2001:51.

18. Haupt, A, Kane, TT. *Population Handbook*. Washington, DC: Population Reference Bureau; 2004.

19. World Bank. Data. Prevalence of HIV, Total (% of Adult Population Ages 15-49). Available at: http://data.worldbank.org/indicator/SH.DYN.AIDS.ZS. Accessed November 10, 2010.

20. WHO. Global Tuberculosis Control WHO Report 2009. India. Available at: http://www.stoptb.org/assets/documents/countries/GlobalReport2009/ind.pdf. Accessed November 10, 2010.

21. Last JM. *A Dictionary of Epidemiology*. 4th ed. New York: Oxford University Press; 2001:35.

22. Lopez AD, Mathers CD, Murray CJL. The burden of disease and mortality by condition: data, methods, and results for 2001. In: Lopez AD,

Mathers CD, Ezzati M, Jamison DT, Murray CJL, eds. *Global Burden of Disease and Risk Factors*. New York: Oxford University Press; 2006:126-129.

23. Setel PW, Macfarlane SB, Szreter S, et al. A scandal of invisibility: making everyone count by counting everyone. *Lancet*. 2007;370(9398):1569-1577.

24. Merson MH, Black RE, Mills AJ. *International Public Health: Diseases, Programs, Systems, and Policies*. Gaithersburg, MD: Aspen Publishers; 2000:28.

25. Health Adjusted Life Expectancy: Statistics Canada. Available at: www.statcan.ca/english/fav/hale. Accessed May 25, 2006.

26. Global Burden of Disease. Available at: www.who.int/trade/glossary/story036/en/. Accessed May 25, 2006.

27. Jamison DT, Brennan J, Measham A, et al, eds. *Priorities in Health*. New York: Oxford University Press; 2006.

28. *World Development Report 1993*. New York: Oxford University Press; 1993:25-29.

29. Lopez AD, Mathers CD, Ezzati M, Jamison DT, Murray CJL. Measuring the global burden of disease and risk factors, 1990-2001. In: *Global Burden of Disease and Risk Factors*. New York: Oxford University Press; 2006:1-15.

30. Basch P. *Textbook of International Health*. 2nd ed. New York: Oxford University Press; 2001:108-112.

31. Lopez AD, Mathers CD, Ezzati M, Jamison DT, Murray CJL. Measuring the global burden of disease and risk factors, 1990-2001. In: Lopez AD, Mathers CD, Ezzati M, Jamison DT, Murray CJL, eds. *Global Burden of Disease and Risk Factors*. New York: Oxford University Press; 2006:8.

32. Lopez AD, Mathers CD, Ezzati M, Jamison DT, Murray CJL. Measuring the global burden of disease and risk factors, 1990-2001. In: Lopez AD, Mathers CD, Ezzati M, Jamison DT, Murray CJL, eds. *Global Burden of Disease and Risk Factors*. New York: Oxford University Press; 2006:3.

33. Lopez AD, Mathers CD, Murray CJL. The burden of disease and mortality by condition: data, methods, and results for 2001. In: Lopez AD, Mathers CD, Ezzati M, Jamison DT, Murray CJL, eds. *Global Burden of Disease and Risk Factors*. New York: Oxford University Press; 2006:228-231.

34. Lopez A, Begg S, Bos E. Demographic and epidemiological characteristics of major regions, 1990-2001. In: Lopez A, Mathers C, Ezzati M, Jamison D, Murray C, eds. *Global Burden of Disease and Risk Factors*. New York: Oxford University Press; 2006:15-44.

35. Last JM. *A Dictionary of Epidemiology*. 4th ed. New York: Oxford University Press; 2001:160.

36. Beaglehole R, Irwin A, Prentice T. The World Health Report 2004: Changing History. Available at: http://www.who.int/whr/2004/download/en/print.html. Accessed June 25, 2006.

37. Lopez AD, Mathers CD, Ezzati M, Jamison DT, Murray CJL. Measuring the global burden of disease and risk factors, 1990-2001. In: Lopez AD, Mathers CD, Ezzati M, Jamison DT, Murray CJL, eds. *Global Burden of Disease and Risk Factors*. New York: Oxford University Press; 2006:9.

38. Population Reference Bureau. 2010. World Population Data Sheet. Available at: http://www.prb.org/Publications/Datasheets/2010/2010wpds.aspx. Accessed November 23, 2010.

39. Lee R. The demographic transition: three centuries of fundamental change. *J Econ Perspect*. 2003;17(4):167-190.

40. Omran AR. The epidemiologic transition: a theory of the epidemiology of population change. *Milbank Q*. 2005;83(4):731.

41. Jamison DT. Investing in health. In: Jamison DT, Breman JG, Measham AR, et al, eds. *Disease Control Priorities in Developing Countries*. New York: Oxford University Press; 2006:3-34.

42. Registrar General & Census Commissioner. *Census of India 2001, Provisional Population Totals.* New Delhi: Government of India, New Delhi; 2001.

43. Black JA. Kerala's demographic transition: determinants and consequences. *BMJ.* 1999;318(7200):1771.

44. Zachariah K. *The Anomaly of the Fertility Decline in India's Kerala State.* Washington, DC: The World Bank; 1984.

45. Black JA. Family planning and Kerala. *Nat Med J Kerala.* 1989;3:187-197.

46. Tharakan P, Navaneetham K. *Population Projection and Policy Implications for Education: A Discussion with Reference to Kerala.* Centre for Development Studies (Thiruvananthapuram); 1999.

47. Ratcliffe J. Social justice and the demographic transition: lessons from India's Kerala State. *Int J Health Serv.* 1978;8(1):123-144.

48. United Nations Development Programme. Kerala—Human Development Fact Sheet. Available at: http://www.undp.org.in/programme/undpini/factsheet/kerala.pdf. Accessed July 21, 2006.

49. International Institute for Population Sciences and OrcMacro. *National Family Health Survey (NFHS-2) 1998-1999.* Mumbai: International Institute for Population Sciences and OrcMacro; 2000.

50. United Nations Economic and Social Commission for Asia and the Pacific. India: National Population Policy. Available at: http://www.unescap.org/esid/psis/population/database/poplaws/law_india/indiaappend3.htm. Accessed July 21, 2006.

51. Kutty VR. Historical analysis of the development of health care facilities in Kerala State, India. *Health Policy Plan.* 2000;15(1):103-109.

52. Centers for Disease Control and Prevention. Life Expectancy. Available at: http://www.cdc.gov/nchs/fastats/lifexpec.htm. Accessed January 3, 2007.

53. Tsai KS. Debating decentralized development: a reconsideration of the Wenzhou and Kerala models. *India J Econ Business, Special Issue China & India*; 2006.

54. Joseph K. *Migration and Economic Development of Kerala.* New Delhi: Mittal; 1988.

CHAPTER 3

Health, Education, Poverty, and the Economy

By the end of this chapter the reader will be able to:

- Describe the links between health and education
- Discuss the connections among health, productivity, and earnings
- Describe key relationships among health, the costs of illness, and the impact of health expenditure on poverty
- Discuss critical connections between health and equity
- Describe some relationships between expenditure on health and health outcomes
- Differentiate between public and private expenditures on health
- Understand the use of cost-effectiveness analysis as one tool for making investment choices in health
- Discuss the two-way relationship between health and development

VIGNETTES

Savitha lived in a poor village in north India. When she first became sick, she visited an unlicensed "doctor." She did not recover and then went to a practitioner of Indian Systems of Medicine. After another two weeks of illness, she went to the outpatient clinic of the main hospital. By the time Savitha had begun to recover, she had spent the equivalent of $20 on health services and transportation to get to them. She had also missed 2 weeks of work, during which she lost another $20 of income. The total cost of this illness was about 10 percent of Savitha's annual earnings.

Mohammed was in first grade in a small town in northern Nigeria. Mohammed's family was poor. Mohammed was very small for his age, was very thin, and got sick more often than most children. Because of his poor health, Mohammed

was unable to attend school regularly and was forced to quit school after only 1 year. Unfortunately, he could not read or write, had little knowledge of how to work with figures, and was most likely destined for a life of limited job prospects at very low pay.

Birte was born in Denmark to a middle class family. She was exclusively breastfed until she was 6 months old, when appropriate complementary foods were introduced. Her family took her regularly for "well baby" check-ups and she received all of her scheduled childhood immunizations. Her hearing and her eyesight were checked before she enrolled in school. Birte attended school regularly, was attentive in class, and performed well there. She was able to complete high school and medical school and today is a physician.

ABC company was looking for investments in forest products and examined in detail the possibility of investing in Africa. After carefully considering the potential costs and returns to such an investment, the company decided, however, not to invest in Africa but to invest instead in Asia. In the end, the company believed that they were unlikely to make an acceptable profit on any business in Africa because so many of their workers would be infected with HIV and malaria.

INTRODUCTION

Health and economic matters are intimately linked in a number of ways. First, health is an important contributor to people's ability to be productive and to accumulate the knowledge and skills they need to be productive, known as "human capital." Second, health status is also a major determinant of one's enrollment in and success in school, which itself is an important contributor to future earnings. Third, the costs of health care are also extremely important to individuals, especially to poor people, because large out-of-pocket expenditures can have a major impact on their financial status and can push them into poverty. Fourth, the costs of health care are also very important because health is a major item of national expenditure in all countries. Finally, the approach that different countries take to the financing and carrying out of health services raises important issues of equity.[1]

The objective of this chapter is to help you gain an introductory understanding of the two-way relationship between health and development. The chapter examines the connection between health and education. It then reviews the link between health and poverty and health and equity. Lastly, the chapter explores the link between health and income at the level of individuals and the connections between health and development more broadly. As it reviews these themes, the chapter will introduce you to some of the basic concepts of both global health and health economics.

HEALTH, EDUCATION, PRODUCTIVITY, AND POVERTY

Health and Education

Essentially, health and education are connected in three ways. First, there are intergenerational links; the health and education of parents affects the health and education of their children. Second, malnutrition and disease affect the cognitive development and school performance of children. Lastly, education contributes to the prevention of illness.

The AIDS epidemic worldwide shows how the poor health of one generation can affect the schooling prospects and future earnings of the next generation. When mothers die of HIV, for example, children are more likely to be poorly fed, malnourished, and in ill health. As a result, they are also less likely to attend school or to perform well there. During the period that a mother is sick with AIDS, it is also likely that one or more of her children will stay out of school to attend to the mother's health and the chores that the mother is no longer able to do.

Malnutrition and illness can limit schooling and school performance in a number of ways. First, families sometimes delay the enrollment in school of a sick or malnourished child. In addition, malnutrition and illness can reduce attendance at school, and thereby reduce an individual's performance in school. Malnutrition and illness can also decrease mental ability. All of these factors ultimately constrain children's ability to learn in school, decrease the number of

years of schooling they complete, and thereby reduce future earnings.

However, there is also a powerful connection between health and education in the other direction—the impact of education on health. We already know that education and knowledge of appropriate health behaviors are important determinants of health and, indeed, that the education of a child's mother is an important predictor of the health of a child. Numerous studies have consistently shown, in fact, that the higher the level of education of a mother, the more likely she is to immunize her child, as further reflected in Figure 3-1 for a number of countries.[2]

Another study done in the Philippines illustrated how better educated mothers are able to keep their children healthy, even in locations without a safe water supply.[3] In a study of a large number of developing countries, it was shown that every 10 percent increase in the level of education of mothers led to a reduction in the infant mortality rate by 4.1 deaths for every 1000 live births.[3] In addition, education affects the extent to which people make use of health services, and better education discourages people from engaging in unhealthy behaviors.

The most extensive studies of the links between education and health show that the education of women has a powerful impact on child survival. One key study showed that each additional year of schooling of a woman was associated with a 7–9 percent reduction in the mortality of her children under 5 years of age. That same study concluded that the mortality rate of children under 5 years of age was almost 60 percent lower for the children of mothers with at least 7 years of schooling, compared to the children of mothers with no schooling.[4]

A systematic analysis was recently carried out to assess the impact of the education of women on the mortality of children under 5 years of age over the period 1970 to 2009. That study also examined how the impact of a mother's education on child mortality compared with the impact of economic development on child mortality. The study focused on examining how many children died, compared to how many children would have died, if education and economic levels had stayed the same as they were in 1970. The study concluded that a little more than half of the 8.2 million deaths of children under 5 years of age that were averted over this period were attributable to higher educational attainment of women of reproductive age (15 to 44 years old). The study also concluded that economic development had an important association with averting child deaths. However, the association of increased educational attainment of women of reproductive ages with averting child deaths was greater than that of economic development.[5]

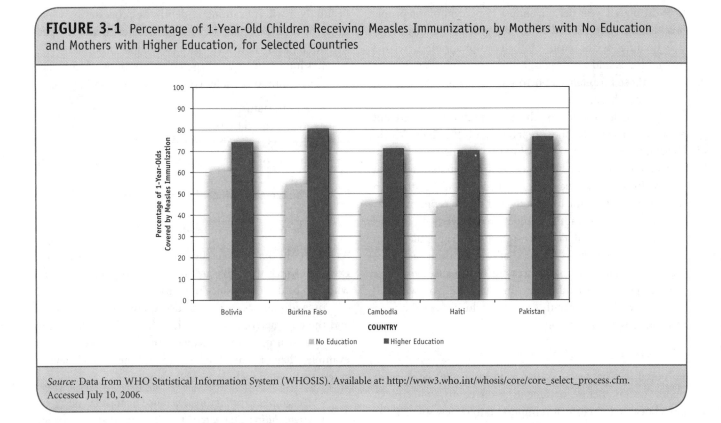

FIGURE 3-1 Percentage of 1-Year-Old Children Receiving Measles Immunization, by Mothers with No Education and Mothers with Higher Education, for Selected Countries

Source: Data from WHO Statistical Information System (WHOSIS). Available at: http://www3.who.int/whosis/core/core_select_process.cfm. Accessed July 10, 2006.

Health, Productivity, and Earnings

Health has an important impact on labor productivity and earnings, separate from its link with education. First, good health increases longevity and the longer one lives, the longer one can earn, and the higher one's lifetime earnings. Second, a number of studies have shown that healthy workers are more productive than unhealthy workers. Among the most cited of such studies was one done on men who tapped rubber trees in Indonesia, many of whom were anemic due to hookworm infection. When the workers were treated for their infections, they became less anemic and their productivity increased by about 20 percent.[6] Third, many people when ill cannot go to work, and when they are absent from work, they often do not earn.

Health, the Costs of Illness, and Poverty

The costs of illness to individuals and their families can be high, can force them to lose or dispose of assets, and can cause them to fall into poverty. When people become ill in poor countries, as noted in the vignette about Savitha at the start of this chapter, they usually do seek health care and they often seek care of different types. They frequently have to pay for treatment and for drugs, the costs of which can be a very substantial share of their income. In addition, illness often leads to a decline in earnings, because people miss work. There are also other indirect costs that people bear when they are ill, such as the costs of transportation to and from a health service provider.

Beyond the costs of either a short-term or a chronic illness, we must also remember the cost to individuals of living with the disability that comes from different health conditions. Measles or meningitis, for example, could lead to severe disability. Polio can lead to paralysis, and leprosy can lead to deformity. A number of mental health conditions are associated with long-term disability, as discussed further in Chapter 12. There is an increasing number of people with diabetes in rich and poor countries alike, and diabetes is often associated with a variety of disabilities. Long-lasting disabilities generally require considerable expenditure on health services. In addition, they usually lead to a significant decline in the earnings of the disabled person, compared to what they could earn if they were not disabled.

The costs of illness can be devastating for poor families. A study done in Bangladesh, for example, showed that a Bangladeshi lost the equivalent of 4 months of income from getting TB.[7] Surveys done in India showed that hospitalization was a major contributor to people and families falling into poverty. Of the patients who were hospitalized at some time during a 1-year period, almost 25 percent of the people hospitalized were pushed below the official Indian poverty line because of the costs of their hospitalization, related expenditures, and lost wages. Moreover, more than 40 percent of those hospitalized borrowed money or sold assets to pay for their health care.[8]

Indeed, in a study of the poor that was carried out as a background to the preparation of the 2000 World Development Report of the World Bank, the poor consistently noted the importance to them of maintaining good health. In addition, that report noted that ill health is an important contributor to poverty and to the economic vulnerability that is also at the foundation of poverty problems.[9] Indeed, we know that a certain segment of the population in many countries that do not have adequate health insurance are at risk that catastrophic costs of health care will drive them to poverty or bankruptcy. In Chapter 5, you will read about how different health systems try to protect the poor from the costs of health care.

HEALTH AND EQUITY

As noted in Chapter 1, equity is an important concern of public health. Before commenting on equity concerns in global health, therefore, it is important to review some of the most important ways in which the term *equity* is used in the global health field.

The Nobel Laureate in Economics, Amartya Sen, has suggested that we should see health equity as being multidimensional:

> It includes concerns about achievement of health and the capability to achieve good health, not just the distribution of health care. But it also includes the fairness of processes and thus must attach importance to non-discrimination in the delivery of health care.[10]

Amartya Sen also suggested that health equity must be seen in the broader context of social justice issues, social arrangements within countries, and how countries choose to allocate their resources.[10]

A well-known British scholar of public health and the determinants of health, Margaret Whitehead, suggested another definition of equity that has been commonly used: "differences in health that are not only unnecessary and avoidable, but also unfair and unjust."[11]

Equity is a theme that will run throughout this book. The treatment of equity will incorporate these thoughts of both Amartya Sen and Margaret Whitehead; however, the book will not examine in depth the political economy of health. Nor will it examine in depth the processes by which different societies reach decisions about health and the participation of different social groups in those processes.

It is important as you begin—and continue—your study of global health to consider equity as you deal with:

- Health status
- Access to health services
- Coverage of health services
- Protection from financial risks because of health costs
- The extent to which the approach to financing health is fair
- The distribution of health benefits

As you think about these issues, you will want to consider the extent to which they vary across groups, why they vary, and what can be done to reduce inequity.

In addition, as you consider questions of access to and the coverage of health services, it will be important to consider such questions broadly. It has been suggested, for example, that one must take a multidimensional view of access that would include:

- *Geographic availability:* Distance or travel time
- *Availability:* The extent to which needed services are offered in a convenient manner, by staff who are properly trained to deliver them
- *Financial accessibility:* The extent to which people are able or willing to pay for services and not fall into financial distress by doing so
- *Acceptablity:* The extent to which services are in line with local cultural norms and expectations[12]

It is also very important as you take "an equity lens" to global health concerns and the above matters that you consider how they vary with:

- Socioeconomic status
- Ethnicity
- Gender
- Religion
- Location
- Occupation
- Social capital

You will also want to keep in mind differences in key health issues both *across* countries and *within* countries.

You should understand as you go through the book that there is an enormous amount of variance and inequity in all of the areas noted above. To a large extent, the pattern of inequity can be summarized relatively easily:

- Less well off people, with less social and political power, will generally enjoy less good health, poorer health services, and less financial fairness and protection in the financing of health services than those who are better off.
- These less well off groups will generally include women, indigenous people, ethnic and religious minorities, the poor, those living in rural areas, those working in the informal sector of the economy, those with limited education, and those who have relatively lower levels of social capital.

The following section examines some examples of the most critical equity concerns.

Equity Across Countries

Figures 2-2 through 2-6 in Chapter 2 presented data by World Bank region on some of the basic indicators of health status, including life expectancy, maternal mortality, and neonatal, infant, and under-5 child mortality.

The graphs clearly portray the enormous variance across regions and countries. Life expectancy in the high-income countries is about 60 percent higher than in sub-Saharan Africa. The maternal mortality ratio in the poorest district in Afghanistan, at about 1800 per 100,000 live births, is about 300 times the maternal mortality ratio in some of the Scandinavian countries. Infant mortality in South Asia is more than 2 times that in East Asia and the Pacific and more than 10 times that in the high-income countries.

Some people see these differences largely as *a reflection* of the status of economic development in different parts of the world. However, it is important to note that others believe that inequitable relationships among countries are at least partly *the cause* of weak economic development in the poorer countries. These people would see differences in health status at least partly as a reflection of inequity and injustice.

Equity Within Countries

Some countries have relatively little variance in health indicators across different population groups. This would generally be the case, for example, in Scandinavia and some of the other high-income countries of Europe. There are other countries, however, that have substantial variance in health indicators across population groups. These will tend to be high-income countries with significant ethnic minorities, such as the United States and Australia, or they will be low- and middle-income countries. Life expectancy for a white American male in 2006, for example, was 75.7 years, whereas that for a black American male was 69.7 years. This is a difference of about 10 percent.[13] Life expectancy for an aboriginal

Australian female born between 1996 and 2001 is 64.8 years, about 16–17 years or about 25 percent less than that for a white Australian female born in the same period.[14]

Figure 3-2 shows the under-5 child mortality rate for a sample of five Indian states, including the state with the lowest rate and the state with the highest rate. Figure 3-3 shows the infant mortality rate for five provinces of Brazil, including the best and worst performing. As you can see in

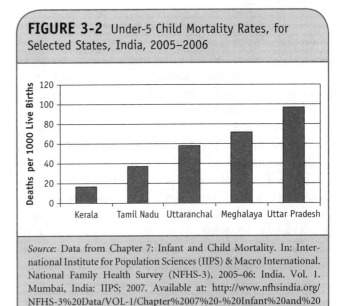

FIGURE 3-2 Under-5 Child Mortality Rates, for Selected States, India, 2005–2006

Source: Data from Chapter 7: Infant and Child Mortality. In: International Institute for Population Sciences (IIPS) & Macro International. National Family Health Survey (NFHS-3), 2005–06: India. Vol. 1. Mumbai, India: IIPS; 2007. Available at: http://www.nfhsindia.org/NFHS-3%20Data/VOL-1/Chapter%2007%20-%20Infant%20and%20Child%20Mortality%20(313K).pdf. Accessed November 26, 2010.

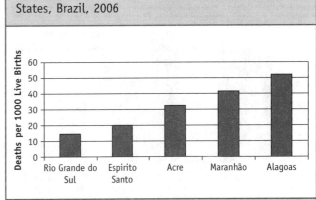

FIGURE 3-3 Infant Mortality Rates, for Selected States, Brazil, 2006

Source: Data from Instituto Brasileiro de Geografia e Estatística (IBGE). Complete Mortality Tables 2006: In 2006, Life Expectancy at Birth of Brazilians Was 72.3 Years. Rio de Janeiro, Brazil: IBGE; 2007. Available at: http://www.ibge.gov.br/english/presidencia/noticias/noticia_impressao.php?id_noticia=1043. Accessed November 27, 2010.

the graphs, the worst performing Indian state had a child mortality rate six times that of the best performing state. The worst performing Brazilian state had an infant mortality rate almost four times that in Brazil's best performing state. These data are critical reminders of how important it is to look beyond *average* or *national* rates in all countries if one is to understand the health status of a country's people, particularly its poorer and more marginalized people.

Equity and Location

We should expect basic health indicators to vary by location, with urban dwellers generally enjoying better access to health services, coverage, and status than rural dwellers. We would also expect the variance between urban and rural dwellers to be greater in low-income countries than in middle- and high-income countries.

Figure 3-4 shows how the rate of stunting varies by location in three regions, Latin America and the Caribbean, South Asia, and sub-Saharan Africa. The gaps are most severe in Latin America and the Caribbean, with stunting of children under 5 years of age being almost 2.5 times greater in rural areas than in urban ones. Rural children are about 33 percent more likely to be stunted in sub-Saharan Africa than urban children. In South Asia, rural children are about 25 percent more likely to be stunted than urban children. Although dif-

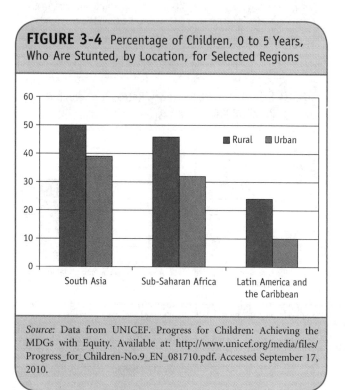

FIGURE 3-4 Percentage of Children, 0 to 5 Years, Who Are Stunted, by Location, for Selected Regions

Source: Data from UNICEF. Progress for Children: Achieving the MDGs with Equity. Available at: http://www.unicef.org/media/files/Progress_for_Children-No.9_EN_081710.pdf. Accessed September 17, 2010.

ferences in health indicators between the lowest and highest income quintiles are often greater in poorer countries, it is important to note that the differences between the lowest and highest income quintiles for some health indicators will be greater in Latin America than elsewhere. This reflects the enormous gaps in some Latin American countries between the incomes of richer and poorer people. These variances also reflect some of the substantial gaps in the way indigenous people live and the way nonindigenous people live in Central America and the Andean countries.

Figure 3-5 shows, in ascending order by region, how contraceptive use varies between rural and urban areas. In the East Asia and the Pacific region, contraceptive prevalence rates are very high and about the same for urban and rural dwellers. In all other regions shown, however, there is a substantial gap in contraceptive prevalence between rural and urban dwellers, ranging from a more than 70 percent difference in sub-Saharan Africa to about a 10 percent difference in Latin America and the Caribbean.

We should expect there to be substantial variance in access, coverage, and health status between rural and urban dwellers. Although many cities do contain large numbers of poor and slum-dwelling people, rural people generally will have lower incomes, less education, less access to health services and other health-related infrastructure, and a weaker political voice than those who live in urban areas. Many ethnic minorities and indigenous people are also more likely to live in rural than in urban settings.

Equity and Income

Much of the literature on equity and global health has focused on the relationship between equity and income. This literature has highlighted the sharp gaps in access, coverage, health status, fairness of financing, and health benefits between the less well off and the better off.[15] Much of this work has been based on examining the variance of different health indicators by income quintiles, meaning divisions of the population into five equal income groups from the least well off to the best off.

Figure 3-6 examines the extent to which births are attended by a skilled attendant in South Asia and sub-Saharan Africa. The figure reflects enormous gaps in both regions between the richest and the poorest income groups. In South Asia, the richest 20 percent of the population is more than four times more likely to have a birth attended by skilled personnel than the poorest 20 percent. In sub-Saharan Africa, the richest are more than three times more likely than the poorest to have their birth attended by skilled personnel.

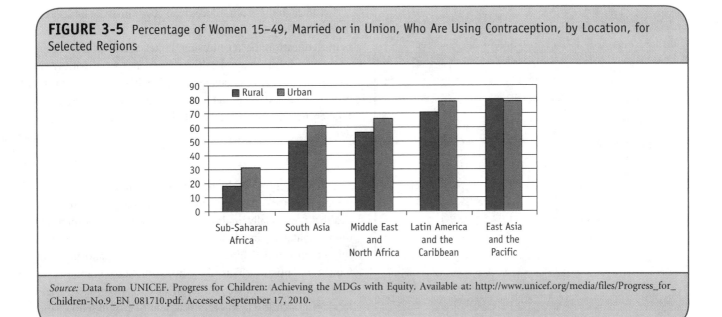

FIGURE 3-5 Percentage of Women 15–49, Married or in Union, Who Are Using Contraception, by Location, for Selected Regions

Source: Data from UNICEF. Progress for Children: Achieving the MDGs with Equity. Available at: http://www.unicef.org/media/files/Progress_for_Children-No.9_EN_081710.pdf. Accessed September 17, 2010.

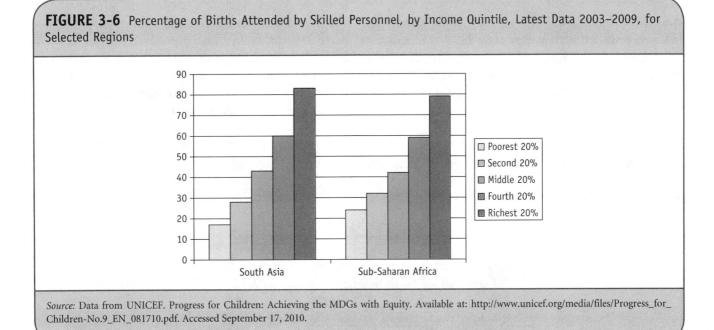

FIGURE 3-6 Percentage of Births Attended by Skilled Personnel, by Income Quintile, Latest Data 2003–2009, for Selected Regions

Source: Data from UNICEF. Progress for Children: Achieving the MDGs with Equity. Available at: http://www.unicef.org/media/files/Progress_for_Children-No.9_EN_081710.pdf. Accessed September 17, 2010.

Figure 3-7 looks at the percentage of children who are underweight by income group for South Asia and sub-Saharan Africa. This figure reflects almost the same level of variances between the better off and the least well off as in the previous figure. Children under 5 from the lowest income group in South Asia are almost three times more likely to be underweight than children from the highest income group. Children under 5 from the lowest income group in sub-

Saharan Africa are more than two times more likely to be underweight than those from the highest income group.

Figure 3-8 shows data from UNICEF on the coverage of measles immunization by income group in the UNICEF West and Central Africa and South Asia country groups. The rates of coverage in West and Central Africa are lower for each income group than in South Asia and the gaps in immunization coverage between groups are also greater in

FIGURE 3-7 Percentage of Underweight Children, 0 to 5 Years of Age, by Income Quintile, Selected Regions

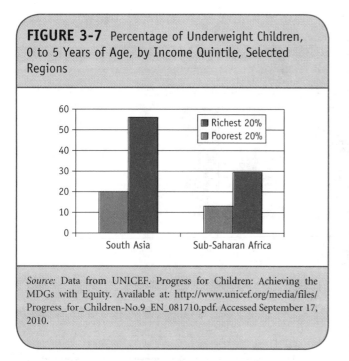

Source: Data from UNICEF. Progress for Children: Achieving the MDGs with Equity. Available at: http://www.unicef.org/media/files/Progress_for_Children-No.9_EN_081710.pdf. Accessed September 17, 2010.

Although these differences by income may not be acceptable to us, they are not surprising. Income is associated with better education; better housing; better access to safe water, sanitation, hygiene, and health services; and safer work environments. It is also associated mostly with dominant ethnic groups, rather than indigenous people, as in the Americas. Higher incomes are also associated with more political power and voice.

Equity and Gender

Chapter 7 focuses on the health of women. One of its basic premises is that "being born female is dangerous to your health,"[16] especially in low-income countries. Women are discriminated against in many settings in ways that are harmful to their health. This starts with sex-selective abortion and female infanticide. This discrimination also manifests in some settings in shorter duration of breastfeeding and less food for girl children, lower enrollment of girls in school, and less attention to the healthcare needs of girls. There is also an exceptional amount of violence against women and neglect of the healthcare needs of adult women. In most settings women will also have less power and voice than men. These points are explored in greater depth in the chapter on women's health. The main point to note here is the importance of keeping in mind throughout your study of global health the health concerns of women that relate to their diminished place and power in some societies.

West and Central Africa. In West and Central Africa, the children of the richest 20 percent of the families are immunized against measles at more than two times the rate of the children from the poorest 20 percent of the families. In South Asia, the gap between the richest and poorest groups is a bit less than two times.

FIGURE 3-8 Coverage of Measles Immunization by Income Quintile, for Selected Regions, 2008

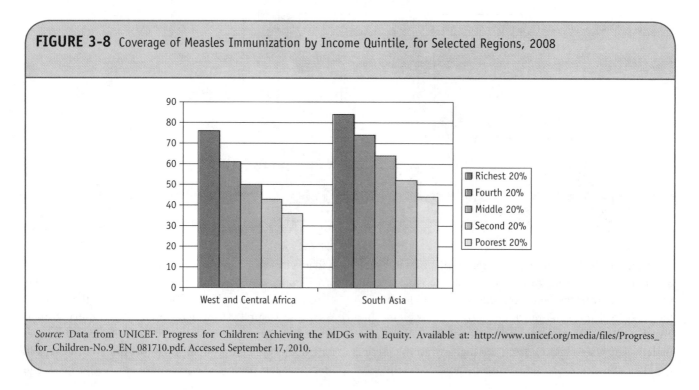

Source: Data from UNICEF. Progress for Children: Achieving the MDGs with Equity. Available at: http://www.unicef.org/media/files/Progress_for_Children-No.9_EN_081710.pdf. Accessed September 17, 2010.

Equity and Ethnicity

There is a strong association in most countries between ethnicity and health status, access, and coverage. Examples were given above of the large gaps between white people and black people in the United States and white people and aboriginal people in Australia.

Figure 3-9 shows how maternal mortality ratios vary in Bolivia and Honduras between indigenous people and nonindigenous people, which is the most important ethnic difference in Central and South America that is associated with health. In Honduras, the maternal mortality ratio is about 60 percent higher among indigenous women than the national average. Indigenous women in Bolivia have a maternal mortality ratio that is more than twice the national average.[17]

Given the strong association among ethnicity and power, education, and income, it is not surprising to find such a strong association between ethnicity and health status.

Equity and Financial Fairness

All high-income countries, except the United States, have some type of mandatory and universal health insurance system that is meant to ensure that access to health services is not dependent on income. The United States has recently adopted legislation moving in this direction. Many middle-income countries also have such insurance systems. However, most low-income countries do not have formalized health insurance systems, outside of the free or low-cost provision of some health services by the public sector or nongovernmental sectors. Thus, the poor in many countries must bear substantial out-of-pocket costs for health, as discussed later. In addition, many low-income countries fail to protect their poor from potentially catastrophic health costs that higher income individuals could afford. Moreover, the relative cost of those health services is much greater for the poor than for better off people, which also raises important equity issues.

Another set of important equity concerns deals with the extent to which different income groups benefit from public subsidies for health services. This can be a complicated issue to assess.[8] Nonetheless, it is clear that there are many countries in which public subsidies for health are disproportionately received by better off people, as shown in Figure 3-10, for India.

It is easy to imagine, for example, a country in which poor people use basic health services that are financed by the public sector which are relatively inexpensive, while better off people in the urban areas disproportionately use publicly supported hospital services that are relatively expensive. Under these circumstances, better off people, who will have higher rates of noncommunicable disease, will get most of the expensive surgeries. Those surgeries will cost hundreds of times what basic health care costs, and the country would be providing a disproportionate share of

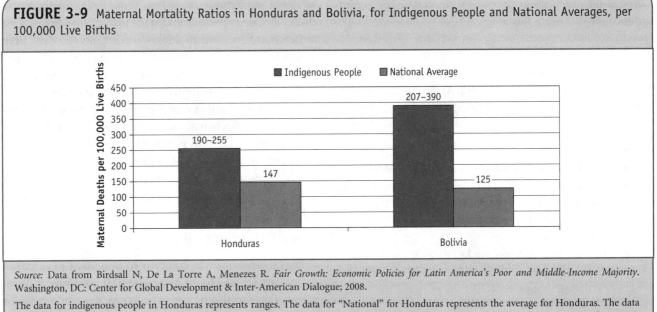

FIGURE 3-9 Maternal Mortality Ratios in Honduras and Bolivia, for Indigenous People and National Averages, per 100,000 Live Births

Source: Data from Birdsall N, De La Torre A, Menezes R. *Fair Growth: Economic Policies for Latin America's Poor and Middle-Income Majority.* Washington, DC: Center for Global Development & Inter-American Dialogue; 2008.

The data for indigenous people in Honduras represents ranges. The data for "National" for Honduras represents the average for Honduras. The data for indigenous people in Bolivia represents ranges for indigenous people in Bolivia and Peru. The data for "National" for Bolivia represents the average for Peru and Bolivia.

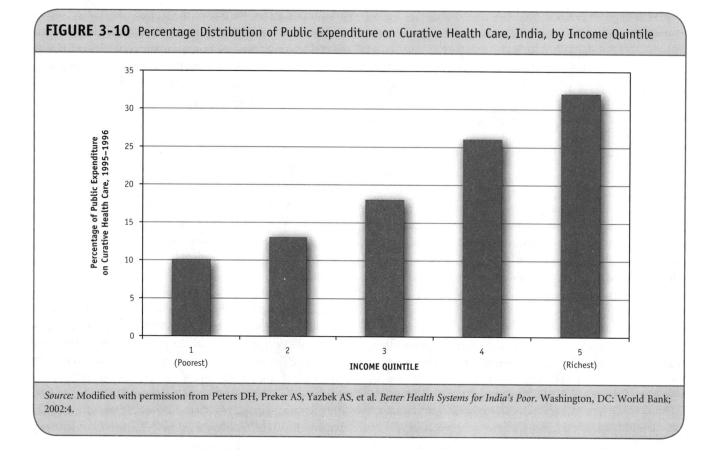

FIGURE 3-10 Percentage Distribution of Public Expenditure on Curative Health Care, India, by Income Quintile

Source: Modified with permission from Peters DH, Preker AS, Yazbek AS, et al. *Better Health Systems for India's Poor*. Washington, DC: World Bank; 2002:4.

public subsidies to the better off, rather than to the poor. There is no justification on clinical, economic, or equity grounds for this being the case.

Concluding Comments on Equity

This section has only introduced you to the many dimensions of equity issues in global health. As you review the rest of the book and engage in global health activities, it is critical that you:

- Keep equity issues in mind at all times.
- Always consider the various dimensions to equity.
- Be careful how you use numbers that reflect averages concerning any health indicators, because they may hide more about variance across and within groups than they reveal.
- Examine how each piece of key data on health status, access, coverage, and financing relates to different population groups, especially the poor and marginalized.

As noted earlier, much of this book is oriented toward addressing the health concerns of the poor, especially in low-

and middle-income countries. Different parts of the book will offer suggestions about how those health needs can be met as quickly as possible and at the lowest possible cost. One critical point in efforts to do this, which emerges partly from concerns for equity, is to ensure that the poor and other marginalized groups are involved in the design, development, monitoring, and evaluation of such efforts. It is also crucial to ensure that such activities pay particular attention to monitoring the benefits that accrue to them and the distribution of those benefits to various population groups. Without paying sufficient attention to these points, it is highly unlikely that equity issues will be addressed satisfactorily or that one will know the extent to which the desired benefits go to those intended.[12]

HEALTH EXPENDITURE AND HEALTH OUTCOMES

One of the reasons why health is so important to countries is that they spend a lot of money on it. In addition, as noted earlier, they are also trying, in principle, to get the most for the money they spend, consistent with national values. Figure 3-11 shows the relationship between gross domestic product (GDP) per capita and health expenditure as a share of GDP.

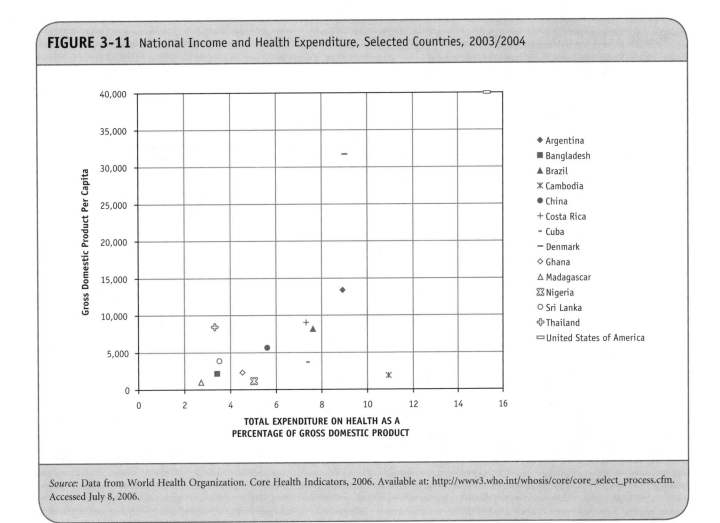

FIGURE 3-11 National Income and Health Expenditure, Selected Countries, 2003/2004

Source: Data from World Health Organization. Core Health Indicators, 2006. Available at: http://www3.who.int/whosis/core/core_select_process.cfm. Accessed July 8, 2006.

The main themes that emerge from this figure are clear:

- The higher a country's income per person, the more money it is likely to spend per person on health.
- Most high-income countries cluster around an expenditure of 9–12 percent of their national income on health.
- Most countries that are low-income cluster around an expenditure of 3–6 percent of their national income on health. This can be seen in the figure in Bangladesh, Ghana, and Nigeria.
- Despite the clustering, there are countries that are outliers and that sit significantly away from the general relationship between income per capita and percentage of national income spent on health. The United States spends more than any other country on health as a share of GDP. Cambodia and Cuba spend relatively more than one would expect for countries with their income.

Having seen what countries spend on health, it is now important to ask what they get in return for that expenditure. Do countries that spend higher shares of their national income on health have better health outcomes? Figure 3-12 plots health expenditure as a share of GDP against life expectancy for selected countries.

We can see from this figure that:

- Many low-income countries spend a relatively low share of their GDP on health and also have low life expectancy. This is seen in Ghana, Kenya, and Mali.
- Most high-income countries spend a relatively high share of their GDP on health and have high life expectancy. This can be seen from Germany and Iceland.
- Some low-income countries spend relatively little on health but still have relatively higher life expectancy than many countries that spend a higher share of GDP on health. This can be seen in Cuba, Costa Rica, China, and Sri Lanka.

FIGURE 3-12 Expenditure on Health as a Share of GDP, Compared to Life Expectancy, Selected Countries, 2003/2004

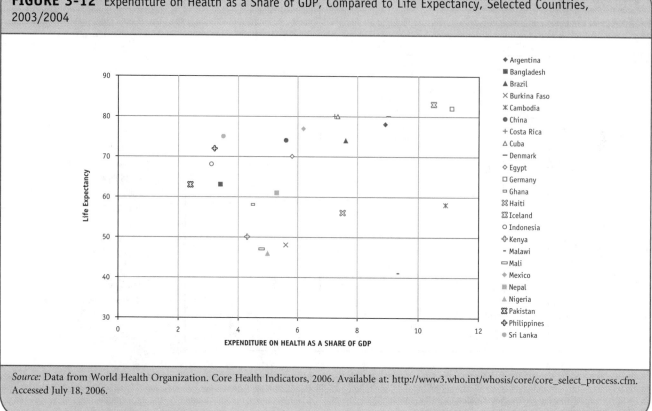

Source: Data from World Health Organization. Core Health Indicators, 2006. Available at: http://www3.who.int/whosis/core/core_select_process.cfm. Accessed July 18, 2006.

- Some high-income countries spend relatively high shares of GDP on health but still have lower life expectancy than countries that spend a lower share of GDP on health than they do. This is best shown by the United States, which is an outlier on this figure as well as on Figure 3-11, which portrays public expenditure on health as a share of GDP.

Why is it that some countries are outliers when considering their health outcomes related to health expenditure? First, we know that health status depends on a number of genetic, social, and economic factors and those factors vary across countries. Second, however, health outcomes depend not only on how much expenditure countries make per capita on health, but also on the particular investments they make with that money. In colloquial terms we could say, "It is not just how much money per capita they spend on health, but it is also how they spend it that is important." This theme will also be explored throughout this book.

PUBLIC AND PRIVATE EXPENDITURE ON HEALTH

Another important concept is the distinction between public and private expenditures on health. Public expenditure refers to expenditure by any level of government or of a government agency. Expenditure by a city government, a state government, or a national government would be public expenditure. Expenditure on health by government agencies such as a social security system, as in many countries in Latin America; the national insurance agency, as in most countries in Western Europe; or of a specialized agency, such as a National Commission on HIV/AIDS, would also be considered public expenditure.

Private expenditure is that expenditure that comes from sources other than governments. One such source is the money that individuals spend on health. When this money is not covered or reimbursed by an insurance program, it is also called out-of-pocket expenditures on health. Other sources of private expenditure on health include expenditure by nongovernmental organizations, such as by BRAC or the Self Employed Women's Association (SEWA) in India. In addition, private expenditure on health includes expenditure by the private for-profit sector. Private sector firms, for example, might contribute to the cost of health insurance or health services for their employees. They might also make contributions to the health work of other organizations.

There is some debate about what are legitimate focuses of public expenditure on health.[18] However, there is widespread agreement that public expenditure on health is warranted when the investment benefits society as a whole, such as an immunization program; when health investments promote equity; and when such expenditure provides financial protection to the poor from expenditures on health that they cannot afford.[18]

THE COST-EFFECTIVENESS OF HEALTH INTERVENTIONS

Most governments have a limited amount of money for health, and that money is rarely enough to finance all of the health interventions that a country would like to carry out. Thus, governments have to decide what share of their total budget will go to health and how much of the health budget will be allocated to different health interventions. All governments have to set priorities for expenditure on health, just as they have to set priorities for expenditure in other sectors.

One important tool for setting priorities for public expenditure on health is cost-effectiveness analysis. This is a method for comparing the cost of an investment with the amount of health that can be purchased with that investment. The cost of the investment can be thought of as the price of the investment. The amount of health that can be purchased could be measured in life years saved or DALYs. The cost-effectiveness of an investment in health will depend, among other things, on the incidence and prevalence of the health condition being considered, the cost of the intervention, the extent to which it can reduce morbidity, mortality, and disability, and how effectively it can be implemented.

One important example of the use of cost-effectiveness analysis is to set priorities among different ways of achieving the same health goal. Important studies were conducted, for example, on the cost-effectiveness of alternative approaches to treating tuberculosis. These studies examined the cost-effectiveness of 6 months of treatment with direct supervision of people taking their medicines, compared to treatment that was not supervised. The supervised method led to a

higher rate of people taking all of their medicine and being cured than the unsupervised approach. As a result, it proved to be more cost-effective than the traditional approach that had been used. These studies strengthened the case for the World Health Organization recommending the supervised approach to therapy, which continues to be the global standard of TB treatment.[19]

It is easy to imagine how important this type of cost-effectiveness analysis can be when considering different ways of delivering the same health services. In fact, there are many important issues in delivering health services in low-income countries in which such questions remain critical. In Haiti, for example, there is a program operated by Partners in Health. Those carrying out the program had to assess whether the services could be delivered as effectively by volunteer workers as they could be by workers who were paid for their efforts. Although it cost more to deliver the program when the workers were paid, the outcomes were superior to those when the workers were not paid, and Partners in Health has continued to use the approach of paid workers.[20] Another issue of great importance today is the extent to which antiretroviral drugs for HIV/AIDS can be delivered effectively by nurses and community health workers, instead of physicians, because physicians are in such short supply in many countries that have high rates of prevalence of HIV/AIDS. This question is one of many concerning the delivery of services for HIV/AIDS that is in need of careful cost-effectiveness analysis.

The second manner in which cost-effectiveness analysis is used is to compare the costs and the gains of different health interventions so that investment choices can be made among them. For every $100, for example, that a government has to spend on health, what allocation of government expenditure on health will buy the most DALYs averted? What is the cost per disability-adjusted life year saved from different interventions? In a relatively poor country, with a high burden of communicable diseases, such as TB and malaria, is it more cost-effective to invest in infectious disease control or in coronary bypass surgery? In a richer country with little TB, will it be cost-effective to invest in vaccination against TB?

Even if we examine the first question above in a somewhat exaggerated and simplistic manner, it will still help us to understand some of the value of cost-effectiveness analysis. Let us say, for example, that the cost of coronary bypass surgery in a low-income country is about $5000. Let us also say that the costs of such surgery are covered completely by the public sector. This surgery would benefit one individual, who will live an additional 20 years in perfectly good health because of the surgery. In the same country, we can assume an entire course of treatment for TB costs about $100. In addition, we can assume that people who get TB will all be 40 years of age and that they will live an additional 20 years in perfectly good health if they are treated for TB. What this means, in principle, is that if these were the only choices for the investment of $5000 in health that a country faced and if this were the only type of analysis that would be done to assess investment choices, then the choice would be between saving one life or saving 50 lives. In addition, the choices would be between saving 20 additional years of healthy life of the coronary bypass patient or 2000 additional healthy years of life of TB patients. Figure 3-13 illustrates the cost-effectiveness of a selected number of health interventions.

The cost of avoiding ill health caused by TB, malaria, and hookworms, for example, is low, whereas the cost of saving a life through cancer treatment is high. It is very cost-effective to get people to use seat belts in cars, but much less cost-effective to save the lives of people after they have had car accidents. As discussed further in Chapter 8, it is cost-effective to enhance the nutritional and health status of young children through supplementation with vitamin A. However, it is much less cost-effective to deal in health centers and hospitals with the additional morbidity and mortality that occur from measles and pneumonia for children who are deficient in vitamin A.[21]

It is important to note that cost-effectiveness analysis is rarely the sole means for determining choices among investments and generally should not be used in that way.[22] However, it is one valuable tool in making such choices. It will always be important, however, to consider such analyses in light of a number of other factors, including:

- Equity considerations
- The burden of disease
- The extent to which the investment serves society as a whole

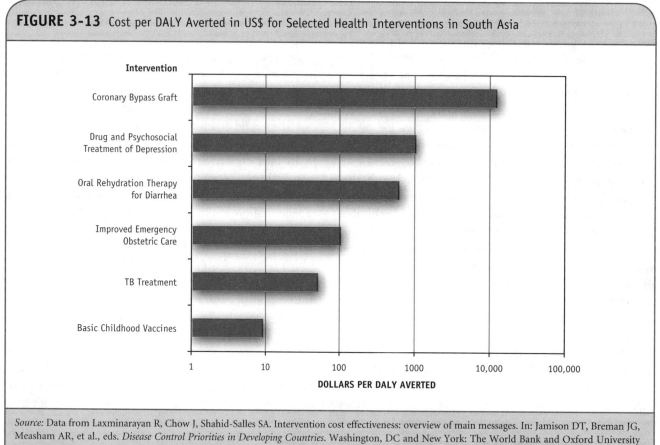

FIGURE 3-13 Cost per DALY Averted in US$ for Selected Health Interventions in South Asia

Source: Data from Laxminarayan R, Chow J, Shahid-Salles SA. Intervention cost effectiveness: overview of main messages. In: Jamison DT, Breman JG, Measham AR, et al., eds. *Disease Control Priorities in Developing Countries.* Washington, DC and New York: The World Bank and Oxford University Press; 2006:51.

- The extent to which the investment produces benefits that are additional to its usual ones
- The impact of the intervention on the provision of insurance

In addition, those who set priorities for health investments will also have to take account of:

- The capacity to deliver the proposed services
- The links between the proposed services and other important services
- The ability to change budget priorities in favor of the proposed investment
- Any transitional costs associated with making the proposed changes in priorities[22]

In this book, most of the assessments of cost-effectiveness will relate to DALYs averted. This is because examining the cost of life years saved from death would fail to capture the morbidity and disability that are also important aims of health interventions. In addition, it is important to note that there is no unique cut-off, below which interventions are "cost-effective" and above which they are not. Rather, it is preferable to group the cost-effectiveness of different interventions into ranges and to use cost-effectiveness analysis to explore the relative extent to which various interventions will lead to DALYs averted. In other words, it is not so important to think of TB control as cost-effective, *per se*, as it is to understand that in a county with a high prevalence of TB, control of TB using directly observed therapy will be one of the most cost-effective investments in health that can be made.[23]

HEALTH AND DEVELOPMENT

An important question at the core of thinking about global health concerns the links between health and development, at the individual, community, and society levels. Does individual health produce more individual wealth and higher levels of economic development at the community and societal levels? Or, are the effects in the opposite direction: Does more economic development at the level of society produce better health for individuals, communities, and societies? What we find when we examine these questions is that the effects of health and development go in both directions.

There is no question that good health promotes economic development at the level of societies. First, we know that when countries have to spend money to address health problems, they cannot use that money for other purposes. Countries that have to spend substantial resources to treat malaria, for example, have less money to spend not only on other areas of health, but also on schools, roads, and other investments outside of the health sector that could spur economic growth.

In addition, investment in economic activities, by local and foreign investors, is an essential ingredient to the economic growth prospects of low-income countries. Yet, as seen in one of the vignettes that opened this chapter, countries that have high burdens of communicable diseases do not appear to be good investment choices. In fact, in a study of the impact of malaria on economic development that is frequently cited, it was found that "a high prevalence of malaria is associated with a reduction of economic growth of 1% per year or more."[24]

There is also growing evidence of the importance of health to economic development from a number of other studies done by economists. Some have shown that higher life expectancy at birth is associated with faster economic growth rates. These studies suggest that a country with a life expectancy at birth of 77 years would be expected to grow economically 1.6 percent faster each year than a country with a life expectancy at birth of 49 years.[25] Another study showed that poor health was an important contributor to the slow pace of economic growth of countries in Africa, compared to other countries with better health.[26] Another series of studies showed that improvements in nutritional status and related health status improvements were very important historically in boosting labor productivity and spurring economic growth in the United Kingdom and Europe.[21, 27–29]

It is also true that higher levels of economic development do promote better health at the level of both individuals and society. In fact, studies that have been done on the impact of income on the health of different societies suggest that higher income is associated with better health and longer life expectancy.[30] However, more recent analyses of this question suggest that although income growth is associated with better health indicators for a country, the effect of income alone on health indicators is less significant than previously thought. Rather, these analyses suggest that a considerable share of the improvements in health indicators stem, as noted earlier, from progress in education; from technical progress such as the development of new vaccines or new drugs; or from simple life saving approaches, such as the use of oral rehydration for young children with diarrhea.[31]

In this light, we should ask: Is income growth necessary or sufficient for enhancing health status at the individual, community, or societal levels? Over the long run, increases in income will improve health. However, they will not improve it fast enough in most settings to achieve the health status objectives that many countries have set for themselves or that are necessary to achieve the MDGs in the time that has been set for them. What low- and middle-income countries must do, therefore, is adopt public policy choices that will allow them to speed the achievement of their health aims, even in the face of constrained income, as Kerala did. As indicated earlier, and as will be repeated throughout the book, this is the approach that has been taken by the small number of countries that have been particularly successful in meeting their health aims, even at relatively low levels of income per capita.

CASE STUDY

Having read about the high returns to some investments in health and the need to prioritize investments in health, it will be valuable to end this chapter with a case study of another public health success story. This one concerns Guinea worm. Those interested in more detail in the case should consult *Case Studies in Global Health: Millions Saved.*

The Challenge of Guinea Worm in Asia and Sub-Saharan Africa

Background

Dracunculiasis, or Guinea worm disease, is an ancient scourge that once afflicted much of the world. Today, it is truly a disease of the poor, persisting only in some of the world's most remote and disadvantaged regions with limited access to potable water, despite being one of the most preventable parasitic diseases. In the 1980s, an estimated 3.5 million people in 20 countries in Africa and Asia were infected with Guinea worm disease, and an estimated 120 million were at risk of becoming infected.[32]

The disease is contracted by drinking stagnant water from a well or pond that is contaminated with tiny fleas that carry Guinea worm larvae. Once inside the human, the larvae can grow up to 3 feet long. After a year, the grown female worm rises to the skin in search of a water source to release her larvae. A painful blister forms, usually in the person's lower limbs. To ease the burning pain, infected individuals frequently submerge the blister in water, causing the blister's rupture and the release of more larvae into the water. This contaminated water, when it is drunk, perpetuates the cycle of reinfection. Worms, usually as wide as a match, can take up to 12 weeks to emerge from the blister. They are coaxed out by being slowly wound around a stick a few centimeters each day. Debilitating pain from this process can linger for as long as 18 months.

Although rarely fatal, the disease takes a heavy toll by causing low productivity that makes it both a symptom and perpetrator of poverty—in Mali, it is called the "disease of the empty granary." Because water in contaminated ponds is widely consumed during peak periods of cyclical harvesting and planting, an entire community can be left debilitated and unable to work during the busiest agricultural seasons. The economic damage is severe: annual economic loss in three rice-growing states in Nigeria was calculated at $20 million.[33] Although the disease afflicts all age groups, it particularly harms children.[33] School absenteeism rises when infected children are unable to walk to school and when children forego school to take on the agricultural and household work of sick adults. The likelihood of a child in Sudan being malnourished is more than three times higher when the adults in the child's home are infected with the disease.

The Intervention

In 1980, when the U.S. Centers for Disease Control and Prevention (CDC) first proposed an eradication campaign, the three interventions that would be required to address the disease effectively did not seem feasible: construction of expensive water sources; controlling the vector that spreads the disease through the use of larvicides in water sources; and health education campaigns promoting the filtration of water with a cloth filter, self-reporting of infestations, and avoidance of recontamination of public water sources. The absence of a vaccine or cure made success seem even more improbable.

The International Drinking Water Supply and Sanitation Decade was launched the following year, however, and the CDC's Dr. Donald Henderson seized the opportunity to include the eradication of Guinea worm disease as a subgoal of the Water Decade program. Nonetheless, progress against Guinea worm disease remained slow until 1986, when three key events occurred: WHO declared eradication of Guinea worm disease a goal, public health ministers from 14 African nations met to affirm their commitment to the eradication effort, and U.S. President Jimmy Carter became a powerful advocate, personally persuading many leaders to launch national eradication efforts. He also recruited the help in the eradication program of two former popular heads of state of Mali and Nigeria, General Touré and General Gowon, respectively, thereby consolidating political commitment in Africa.

Meanwhile, technical and financial resources of the donor community were marshaled, and by 1995, eradication programs had been established in 20 countries. Water sources were provided, mainly through the construction of wells; in southeast Nigeria alone, village volunteers hand-dug more than 400 wells.[34] Larvicide was added to water sources to kill the fleas. People were taught to filter drinking water using a simple cloth filter. However, these filters were found to clog up and were used as decoration items instead.[33] A newly developed nylon cloth was then donated by the Carter Center, Precision Fabrics, and DuPont. Public education campaigns, including intensive efforts during so-called worm weeks, encouraged people to use the nylon filters, avoid recontaminating ponds, and report infestations.[35] Most of the eradication staff were volunteers trained by the ministries of health, but they pioneered a monthly reporting system for tracking and monitoring that is now hailed as a model for disease surveillance.[36]

The Impact

The campaign led to a 99 percent drop in Guinea worm disease prevalence. In 2005, fewer than 11,000 cases were reported, compared with an estimated 3.5 million infected people in 1986. Most remaining cases were then in Sudan where civil conflict impeded progress against the disease over many years. By 1988, the campaign had already prevented between 9 million and 13 million cases of Guinea worm disease.[37] The Asian countries that were targeted, India, Pakistan, and Yemen, are now free of the disease.

Costs and Benefits

The total cost of the program between 1986 and 1998 was $87.5 million, with an estimated cost per case averted of $5 to $8.[37] The World Bank determined that the campaign has been highly cost-effective and cost-beneficial. In addition, the program had a very high economic rate of return, even when basing the calculation of economic benefits only on increases in agricultural productivity that accrued from people having avoided the disease.[37]

Lessons Learned

Success of the program has been attributed to three factors. The first is the exemplary coordination between major partners and donors. The second is the power of data, gathered through the monthly reporting system, to monitor national programs and to help keep countries focused and motivated on the program goals. The third is the high-level advocacy and political leadership from current and former heads of state, especially President Jimmy Carter and General Gowon, who visited and revisited villages in Nigeria to check on progress. The program drew on a truly global partnership among the CDC, UNICEF, WHO, the Carter Center, governments, NGOs, the private sector, and volunteers that was able to motivate changes in individual and community behaviors and successfully control a disease.

MAIN MESSAGES

The aim of this chapter was to introduce you to some of the basic concepts of economics as they relate to the global health arena. One important message of the chapter is that education and health are closely linked. Good health encourages the enrollment of students in school at the appropriate age, enhanced student attendance at school, better cognitive performance of students, and more completed years of schooling. Education and knowledge are consistently correlated with people's engagement in more appropriate health behaviors and living healthier lives than those with less schooling. Important progress in reducing child mortality, for example, is associated with increased educational attainment for women. In addition, education promotes greater opportunities for income earning, which itself is an important determinant of health.

We also learned that health is strongly associated with productivity and earnings. Healthier people can work harder, work more hours, and work over a longer lifetime than can those who are less healthy. Related to this in many ways, we also saw that health has an important relationship with poverty. If people work fewer hours because of ill health, then there is a risk that their income status will decline, perhaps below the poverty line. In addition, there is evidence from many countries that the direct and indirect costs to people of getting health services can push people into poverty.

Equity is an important concern of public health. It is essential to consider equity as one deals with health status, access to health services, coverage of services, protection from financial risk, the fairness of financing health, and the distribution of health benefits.

Health is an important subject for all countries for many reasons, among the most important of which is the amount of money they spend on health. High-income countries spend more money on health than do low-income countries. However, health outcomes depend not just on how much money is spent, but also on how the money is used. One way that countries set priorities for health expenditure is by using cost-effectiveness analysis, a tool that is used in the health sector to compare how much health one can buy for a given level of expenditure. All countries, of course, face the question of how they can maximize the health of their population for the minimum cost.

There are also many strong relationships between the health of a population and the economic development of the society in which they live. Better health does promote wealth in a variety of ways, including enhancing labor productivity, reducing the amount countries have to spend on health, and enabling a more attractive investment climate. In addition, the negative impact of some diseases on economic development, such as TB, HIV/AIDS, and malaria, can be very significant. Economic development does improve health; however, many gains in health stem from educational and technological progress, such as on vaccines. Low-income countries have to develop approaches to improving population health faster than economic development alone will do.

Study Questions

1. How does poor health status impact a person's income?

2. What is the relationship between health and the productivity of individuals?

3. What part does health play in promoting the education of a child?

4. What part does the education of a mother play in promoting the health of her children?

5. Why might the health of some culture groups be different from the health of others?

6. What is the relationship between a country's expenditure on health as a share of national income and its health status?

7. In your country, is expenditure on health from the public sector, private sector, or both?

8. In using cost-effectiveness analysis, why should you also take into account issues such as equity?

9. How could you ensure that public subsidies on health care appropriately benefit the poor?

10. Does "health make wealth," or does "wealth make health"?

11. What impact would the health status of a country have on the likelihood that people will invest in economic activity in that country?

12. Why did Guinea worm disease remain so prevalent for so long?

REFERENCES

1. Ruger JP, Jamison DT, Bloom DE. Health and the economy. In: Merson MH, Black RE, Mills AJ, eds. *International Public Health, Diseases, Programs, Systems, and Policies*. Gaithersburg, MD: Aspen; 2001:617-666.

2. Pebley A, Goldman N, Rodriguez G. Prenatal and delivery care and childhood immunization in Guatemala: do family and community matter? *Demography*. 1996;33:197-210.

3. Glewwe P. *How Does Schooling of Mothers Improve Child Health? Evidence from Morocco*. Washington, DC: World Bank; 1997.

4. Hobcraft J. Women's education, child welfare and child survival: a review of the evidence. *Health Transition Review*. 1993;3(2):159-175.

5. Gakidou E, Cowling K, Lozana R, Murray CJL. Increased educational attainment and its effect on child mortality in 175 countries between 1970 and 2009: a systematic analysis. *Lancet*. 2010;376(9745):959-974.

6. Basta SS, Soekirman, Karyadi D, Scrimshaw NS. Iron deficiency anemia and the productivity of adult males in Indonesia. *Am J Clin Nutr*. 1979;32(4):916-925.

7. Croft RA, Croft RP. Expenditure and loss of income incurred by tuberculosis patients before reaching effective treatment in Bangladesh. *Int J Tuberc Lung Dis*. 1998;2(3):252-254.

8. Peters DH, Preker AS, Yazbek AS, et al. *Better Health Systems for India's Poor*. Washington, DC: The World Bank; 2002.

9. Bank W. *World Development Report 2000/2001: Attacking Poverty*. New York: Oxford University Press; 2001.

10. Sen A. Why health equity? *Health Econ*. 2002;11(8):659-666.

11. Whitehead M. The concepts and principles of equity in health. *Int J Health Serv*. 1992;22:429-445.

12. Peters DH, Garg A, Bloom G, Walker DG, Brieger WR, Rahman MH. Poverty and access to health care in developing countries. *Ann NY Acad Sci*. June 2008;1136:161-171.

13. U.S. Census Bureau. Statistical Abstract of the United States: 2010 (129th edition). Washington, DC: 2009. Available at: http://www.census.gov/statab/www. Accessed November 27, 2010.

14. Australian Institute of Health and Welfare. Indigenous Life Expectancy. Available at: http://www.aihw.gov.au/mortality/life_expectancy/indig.cfm. Accessed November 26, 2010.

15. Gwatkin DR, Rutstein S, Johnson K, Suliman E, Wagstaff A, Amouzou A. *Socio-Economic Differences in Health, Nutrition, and Population Within Developing Countries*. Washington, DC: The World Bank; September 2007.

16. Murphy EM. Being born female is dangerous to your health. *Am Psychol*. 2003;58(3):205-210.

17. Birdsall N, De La Torre A, Menezes R. *Fair Growth: Economic Policies for Latin America's Poor and Middle-Income Majority*. Washington, DC: Center for Global Development & Inter-American Dialogue; 2008.

18. Preker AS, Harding A. *The Economics of Public and Private Roles in Health Care*. Washington, DC: The World Bank; 2000.

19. Murray CJ, DeJonghe E, Chum HJ, Nyangulu DS, Salomao A, Styblo K. Cost effectiveness of chemotherapy for pulmonary tuberculosis in three sub-Saharan African countries. *Lancet*. 1991;338(8778):1305-1308.

20. Walton DA, Farmer PE, Lambert W, Leandre F, Koenig SP, Mukherjee JS. Integrated HIV prevention and care strengthens primary health care: lessons from rural Haiti. *J Public Health Policy*. 2004;25(2):137-158.

21. Laxminarayan R, Chow J, Shahid-Salles SA. Intervention cost effectiveness: overview of main messages. In: Jamison DT, Breman JG, Measham AR, et al, eds. *Disease Control Priorities in Developing Countries*. New York: Oxford University Press; 2006.

22. Yazbek AS. *An Idiot's Guide to Prioritization in the Health Sector*. Washington, DC: The World Bank; 2002.

23. Public Health Agency of Canada. Population Health Approach, What Determines Health? Available at: http://www.phac-aspc.gc.ca/ph-sp/phdd/determinants/index.html. Accessed October 6, 2005.

24. Comission on Macroeconomics and Health. *Macroeconomics and Health: Investing in Health for Economic Development*. Geneva: World Health Organization; 2001.

25. Comission on Macroeconomics and Health. *Macroeconomics and Health: Investing in Health for Economic Development*. Geneva: World Health Organization; 2001.

26. Bloom DE, Sachs J. Geography, demography, and economic growth in Africa. *Brookings Papers Econ Activity*. 1998;2:207-295.

27. Fogel R. *New Sources and New Techniques for the Study of Secular Trends in Nutritional Status, Health, Mortality and the Process of Aging* 1991.

28. Fogel R. New findings on secular trends in nutrition and mortality: some implications for population theory. In: Rosenzweig M, Stark O, eds. *Handbook of Population and Family Economics*. Vol. 1a. Amsterdam: Elsevier Science; 1997:433-481.

29. Fogel R. *The Fourth Great Awakening and the Future of Egalitarianism*. Chicago and London: The University of Chicago Press; 2000.

30. Pritchett LH, Summers LH. Wealthier is healthier. *Human Resources*. 1996;31(4):841-868.

31. Jamison DT, Sandbu M, Wang J. *Why Has Infant Mortality Decreased at Such Different Rates in Different Countries?* Bethesda, MD: Disease Control Priorities Project; 2004.

32. Carter J. The power of partnership: the eradication of Guinea worm disease. *Cooperation South*. 1999;2:140-147.

33. Cairncross S, Muller R, Zagaria N. Dracunculiasis (Guinea worm disease) and the eradication initiative. *Clin Microbiol Rev*. 2002;15(2):223-246.

34. Hopkins DR. Perspectives from the dracunculiasis eradication programme. *Bull World Health Organ*. 1998;76 Suppl 2:38-41.

35. Hopkins DR, Ruiz-Tiben E, Diallo N, Withers PC, Jr., Maguire JH. Dracunculiasis eradication: and now, Sudan. *Am J Trop Med Hyg*. 2002;67(4):415-422.

36. Hopkins DR. The Guinea worm eradication effort: lessons for the future. *Emerg Infect Dis*. 1998;4(3):414-415.

37. Kim A, Tandon A, Ruiz-Tiben E. *Cost-Benefit Analysis of the Global Dracunculiasis Eradication Campaign*. Washington, DC: World Bank; 1997.

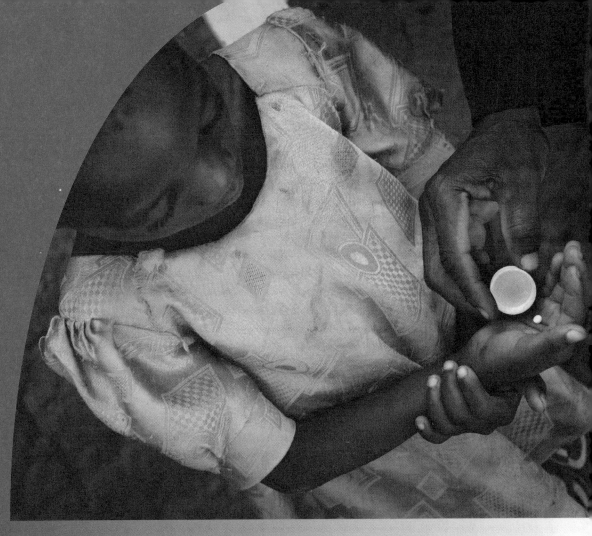

PART II

Cross-Cutting Global Health Themes

CHAPTER 4

Ethical and Human Rights Concerns in Global Health[1]

VIGNETTES

Suraiya was a 21-year-old woman in Kabul, Afghanistan. Her sister recently died in childbirth at the age of 16. Suraiya took her sister to a health center when she had trouble with her labor. However, the health center was 50 miles away from their house. In addition, partly because of the neglect of the last government and its discrimination against women, the health center was dilapidated. It had no equipment and the midwife there was unable to save Suraiya's sister. The baby died a few days later.

John Williams was a 32-year-old office clerk in a small country in sub-Saharan Africa. For 3 months he had experienced weight loss, continuous fever, and chronic fatigue. He finally got up the strength to visit the local hospital. When he got there, the staff were not welcoming. They did not treat him kindly. They did not offer to help him. They did not arrange for him to be seen by a doctor. They knew that he had HIV and did not want to treat him in their hospital.

A research team was conducting a study of malaria in villages in West Africa. When the doctors working for the study diagnosed children with severe malaria, they would provide treatment free of charge. However, sometimes the children in the study had other medical problems that needed attention. For example, many children presented with diarrheal diseases, parasitic infections, or pneumonia. Some of the doctors wanted to treat all these children, too. Other members of the team worried that their budget would not cover these extra costs. In any case, they said, the purpose of the study was to learn about malaria, not to provide clinical care.

The newly elected government of an Indian state won election on a pledge to increase investment in health care. The government plans to build new primary health clinics, but with the limited money available only a few can be built and staffed. Some members of the government argue that the clinics should be located in the countryside. People there are poorer than in the cities and have less access to medical facilities. Others argue that the cities should get priority. A clinic in the slums serves more people than a rural clinic and it is easier to staff and supply urban clinics. Besides, they say, the party's electoral base is in the city, and if they want to be re-elected to continue their good work, it is important to keep their voters happy.

THE IMPORTANCE OF ETHICAL AND HUMAN RIGHTS ISSUES IN GLOBAL HEALTH

Painful ethical dilemmas arise in the pursuit of global health, whether planning healthcare provision, implementing public health measures, or conducting health research. It is important to address these issues, both for their own sake and because there is a strong complementarity between good ethical and human rights practices on the one hand and good health outcomes on the other.[2]

One set of important ethical issues that relate to global health concerns human rights. International conventions and treaties recognize access to health services and health information as human rights. Yet, there are remarkable gaps in many countries in access to health services. The poor and the disenfranchised suffer from those gaps the most.

The failure to respect human rights is often associated with harm to human health. This has often been the case, for example, with diseases that are highly stigmatized, such as leprosy, TB, and HIV. If leprosy patients are not provided with the best care because some health workers are afraid to work with them, the leprosy patients cannot stop the progression of their disease. If TB patients are shunned by health workers, they may die, usually after infecting many other people.

Efforts to maintain public health while dealing with new and emerging diseases, such as SARS or a potential avian influenza, raise another array of ethical and human rights issues. When we face a potential health threat, for example, what are the rights of individuals compared to the rights of society to protect its members from illness? Is it acceptable to quarantine a city? Is it fair to ban travel to and from certain places? Should patients with TB who refuse to take their medicines be kept in a hospital and forced to take them? These are real issues with which health practitioners and policy makers must wrestle.

Another set of ethical issues is associated with research with human subjects. Health research involving people is generally considered ethically challenging because, in contrast to clinical care, participants in research are put at risk for the sake of other people's health, rather than their own. A great deal of the research that takes place in the pursuit of global health must also deal with further ethical concerns that arise when research is conducted with poor people who do not have access to satisfactory levels of health care outside of a research study.

Finally, it is important to ensure that health investments are fair, and are made in fair ways. Even in high-income countries, the resources available for health care are limited. In low- and middle-income countries, where there are fewer resources and greater needs, difficult decisions about which populations and disease groups should get priority must constantly be made.

This chapter provides an overview of some of the most important ethical issues pertaining to global health. It briefly reviews the most important charters and conventions that set the foundation for health-related human rights and shows

some of the contexts in which human rights concerns arise. It summarizes some important cases and guidance documents pertaining to the ethics of international medical research and discusses how to evaluate the ethics of clinical research. It then lays out the principles that are often thought to underlie fair allocation decisions and some of the difficulties in applying them. The chapter concludes with comments on key challenges concerning ethics and human rights in global health activities.

THE FOUNDATIONS FOR HEALTH AND HUMAN RIGHTS

The cornerstone of human rights is the International Bill of Human Rights, which is made up of the Universal Declaration of Human Rights, the International Covenant on Civil and Political Rights, and the International Covenant on Economic, Social, and Cultural Rights. These documents place obligations on governments to *respect*, *protect*, and *fulfill* the rights they state; that is, to refrain from violating people's rights, to prevent others from violating them, and to actively promote the realization of people's rights.

The most significant international declaration on human rights is the Universal Declaration of Human Rights (UDHR), which was promulgated in 1948. The UDHR is generally regarded as the basis for most of the later treaties and documents pertaining to human rights. As a declaration, the UDHR does not have the force of law. However, it has moral force, it has influenced the development of a number of national constitutions, and its invocation by states over the last 50 years has led some to argue that it has the status of customary international law—unwritten law that is nonetheless reflected in the practice of states.[3] With respect to health, the UDHR states in Article 25:

> (1) Everyone has the right to a standard of living adequate for the health and well-being of himself and of his family, including food, clothing, housing and medical care and necessary social services, and the right to security in the event of unemployment, sickness, disability, widowhood, old age or other lack of livelihood in circumstances beyond his control.
>
> (2) Motherhood and childhood are entitled to special care and assistance. All children, whether born in or out of wedlock, shall enjoy the same social protection.[4]

Since 1948, more than 20 multilateral treaties that relate to health have been formulated that are legally binding. In 1966, two important treaties were adopted—the International

Covenant on Economic, Social, and Cultural Rights (ICESCR) and the International Covenant on Civil and Political Rights (ICCPR).[5,6] These two covenants are legally binding on those states that have ratified them (155 countries in the case of the ICESCR and 160 in the case of the ICCPR). The ICCPR discusses rights of equality, liberty, and security, and freedom of movement, religion, expression, and association.[6] The ICESCR focuses on the well-being of individuals, including their right to work in safe conditions, receive fair wages, be free from hunger, get an education, and enjoy the highest attainable standard of physical and mental health.[5]

Although increasing attention is being paid to the links between health and human rights, there is no mechanism for holding countries accountable for ensuring that they honor or even try to honor the right to health. The international mechanism now in place for reviewing compliance with treaties and conventions that include the right to health is voluntary reporting by national governments. There are also provisions in human rights treaties and conventions that recognize that resource-poor countries will not be able to help all of their people to "achieve the highest standard of health possible."[7] Instead, states are only required to "take steps" toward the progressive realization of positive rights. There is also no clear definition of the meaning of the right to health or agreed indicators for measuring progress toward fulfilling it.[8] Although considerable attention is paid to the MDGs and progress toward meeting them, the discussion about the MDGs frequently does not take human rights explicitly into account.

At least 115 countries have written a right to health or health care into their constitutions.[9] In recent years, several countries have seen successful litigation for access to health care as a result. For example, in Brazil there are thousands of court cases each year in which individual patients sue the government to receive drugs that they are not receiving through the public health system.[10] In South Africa, the Treatment Action Campaign successfully sued the national government over its failure to make the drug nevirapine widely available for HIV-infected pregnant women to prevent mother-to-child transmission.[11] In 1999, a court in Venezuela held that the Venezuelan government violated the constitutional right of its people to health by failing to guarantee access to antiretroviral therapy for people living with HIV/AIDS. The court ruled that this right is *both* part of the Venezuelan constitution and a part of the ICESCR, to which Venezuela is party.[12]

As discussed further in Chapters 8 and 9, women and children are especially vulnerable groups in many countries, and enhancing their health is central to improving the well-being of the poor. For these reasons, a number of international conventions focus on women and children.

The Convention on the Elimination of All Forms of Discrimination Against Women was adopted in 1979 by the United Nations General Assembly. It has been ratified by 83 countries. The Convention commits states to legally promote equality between men and women and to eliminate discriminatory practices against women, and it affirms women's reproductive rights.[13]

Many international human rights documents, including the ICCPR, have specific clauses for protecting the rights of children. Most articles in the general human rights instruments also apply equally to both adults and children. The 1989 Convention on the Rights of the Child (CRC), however, is the first human rights document that focuses specifically on children. This document accords children—defined as "every human being below the age of 18 years"—rights to be free of discrimination, to health, and to education. In addition, it states that children must have a say in decisions affecting their lives, and puts the rights of children on the same plane as the rights of adults.[14]

The CRC says the following concerning health:

> States Parties recognize the right of the child to the enjoyment of the highest attainable standard of health and to facilities for the treatment of illness and rehabilitation of health. States Parties shall strive to ensure that no child is deprived of his or her right of access to such health care services.[14]

SELECTED HUMAN RIGHTS ISSUES

There are many human rights issues relating to health that could be considered here. This section examines two overarching issues—the rights-based approach to health and limits to human rights—and then discusses some human rights issues related to HIV/AIDS, which illustrate many of the points previously made.

The Rights-Based Approach

Some scholars and global health advocates argue that we should adopt a human rights approach to global health. This approach builds upon the insight that the fulfillment of people's human rights is conducive to their health (and the violation of human rights tends to be detrimental to health). For some human rights—such as the right to health or the right to an adequate standard of living—this is obvious. However, the importance of the social determinants of health, including relative social status, discrimination, and social exclusion, suggests that the fulfillment of civil and political rights may have an important relationship with population health.[15] Health and human rights are therefore inextricably linked.[1]

In simple terms, if we were to apply the health and human rights approach to global health, this would mean that we would:

- Assess health policies, programs, and practices in terms of their impact on human rights
- Analyze and address the health impacts resulting from violations of human rights when considering ways to improve population health
- Prioritize the fulfillment of human rights

The health and human rights approach reminds us to take an inclusive view of what is needed to promote health: it is not just a matter of having sufficient doctors and drugs, but of addressing poverty, homelessness, education, discrimination, violence, and civil and political inclusion. Moreover, in the design and implementation of global health efforts, we should pay particular attention to factors such as the participation in program design of affected people and communities, equity across groups, and the empowerment of individuals over their own lives.

Limits to Human Rights

The importance of protecting human rights related to health is widely acknowledged. Yet, there are exceptional circumstances in which someone's rights may be temporarily suspended. For instance, in order to protect the interest of the public during an influenza epidemic, a government might suspend for a certain time the right of people to leave their homes, to go to work, to travel, or to participate in mass gatherings, such as sporting events. Few people would deny the obligation of governments to make laws that permit urgent action to protect public health. However, few would also deny the tendency of autocratic governments to use the excuse of public order or the public interest in order to consolidate power and quash political opposition. Consequently, any suspension of people's rights should be as narrow as possible, so that only those aspects of their rights that must be suspended in order for the government to achieve its legitimate goals are suspended. Furthermore, the suspension should be carried out with due process, rights should be monitored during the suspension period, and all efforts should be made to reinstate them as soon as possible.[16]

Human Rights and HIV/AIDS

As much as any health condition in history, HIV/AIDS, which is discussed in Chapter 11, raises a host of human rights issues. One reason for this is that HIV/AIDS is a health condition that is stigmatized and discriminated against in most cultures. For example, many people see HIV/AIDS as a disease that people bring on themselves by engaging in what they consider promiscuous behavior. This could be homosexual sex, injection drug use, having multiple sex partners, or commercial sex work. In addition, in places where people are not familiar with how the disease is spread, there is often great fear of catching the disease.

An important question that has arisen in many societies is how to protect the rights of people who are HIV-positive to employment, schooling, and participation in social activities. When the epidemic was first recognized, there was considerable discrimination in a number of countries against HIV-positive people, some of whom lost their jobs or were not allowed to enroll in school. Such discrimination continues in many places.

Another matter, as we saw in the opening vignette with John Williams, is the access of people with HIV to health care. At least at the early stages of an HIV epidemic in a country, most health workers are poorly informed about HIV, not aware of how it is spread, and are afraid to care for people who are HIV-positive. People living with HIV/AIDS have frequently been denied care or treated with discrimination when they did receive it.

HIV testing raises further questions related to protecting people's well-being while respecting human rights. For many years, a cardinal principle of work on HIV has been that testing for it should be voluntary and confidential. This is to ensure that people are not forced to get tested and then discriminated against if people find out that they are HIV-positive. Recently, however, an increasing number of people involved in HIV work have come to believe that in settings with high HIV prevalence, every adult should be tested. People promoting this approach want to encourage much greater testing for HIV because it is spread largely by people who do not know their status and have unprotected sex with multiple partners.

In line with this, Botswana was the first country to institute an HIV testing policy based on people "opting out" of testing, rather than volunteering to be tested ("opting in"). In Botswana, any adult who has contact with the health system is asked to take an HIV test. He or she has to opt out by asking not to get a test or one will be given. Although this type of approach has become more widespread, there remains concern among some people engaged in HIV work that even a well-organized country will not be able to implement such a program without people being coerced into being tested.[17]

Issues of confidentiality also arise in the context of HIV/AIDS. HIV information about patients should be kept confidential to ensure that those who are HIV-positive are not discriminated against. Yet, the clinical settings in many resource-poor countries with high HIV prevalence are poorly organized, inefficient, and not accustomed to treating patients and patient records confidentially. They also may not have the physical space to treat people privately and confidentially.

Related to concerns about privacy are important questions about the disclosure of HIV status. Should the health-care system notify spouses or sexual partners of the HIV status of patients? Should the patients do that? What are the risks, for example, if a husband is notified about the status of his wife that he may harm her, reject her, or that his family will throw her out of the house?

As mentioned already, a constitutional right to health has been successfully invoked in several countries in order to get access to HIV/AIDS treatment. One of the reasons why this strategy has been adopted is the high price of antiretroviral therapy (ART). At present, patients with HIV/AIDS in low- and middle-income countries must be put on ART when their immune systems have deteriorated to a certain point, and must then remain on ART for the rest of their lives. The majority of people living in these countries cannot afford the thousands of dollars that this costs.

The high price of ART is, in part, a function of the patent system. Patents are intellectual property rights that allow the inventors of novel pharmaceutical products and medical technologies the right to exclude others from making, selling, or importing the invention for a fixed period (usually 20 years). The quasi-monopoly granted to the patent holder allows the setting of prices without regard to ordinary market forces and, therefore, allows higher prices than would be the case in the event of competition. Some countries historically refused to grant patents or granted only process patents on what they regarded as "essential drugs," because they believed that their people have a right to these drugs at affordable prices. However, recent international agreements have changed this picture. The World Trade Organization's (WTO's) 1994 Agreement on Trade-Related Aspects of Intellectual Property Rights (TRIPS), once fully implemented, will standardize intellectual property rights across WTO member states. Its impact is already apparent: India, an important source of generic pharmaceuticals for developing countries, recently substantially tightened its patent laws.[18]

The basic principle behind granting intellectual property rights is to provide incentives for research, development, and use of new technologies. Some people believe that the possibility of getting a patent is essential to ensuring the continued search for new drugs. On the other hand, only 16 out of the 1393 new chemical entities marketed between 1975 and 1999 were to treat tropical diseases and tuberculosis,[19] a picture that does not appear to have greatly changed in the last decade.[20] This suggests that patents are not sufficient to encourage the development of drugs for low- and middle-income countries.[21] In the case of HIV/AIDS, the cost of antiretrovirals has dropped dramatically over the last decade or so, partly because of competition from generic manufacturers and partly because of extensive international activism and diplomacy.

In certain cases, intellectual property rights seem to be an impediment to the fulfillment of human rights, such as the right to health. The challenge with respect to patents for medicines is how to encourage scientific discovery of diagnostics, drugs, and vaccines while ensuring the affordability of medicines by poor people in poor countries. This challenge is examined in detail in Chapter 16. Those advocating a human rights approach to health, as well as others concerned about the price of medicines, insist on safeguard mechanisms to ensure access to medicines by all who need them, and on exceptions to intellectual property rights for least developed countries.[22]

Although these rights-related questions are particularly prominent when thinking about HIV/AIDS, many of them are relevant to global health more generally. For example, many vulnerable populations and disease groups are stigmatized or discriminated against. Likewise, all patients ought to be treated with respect and their medical records kept confidential. Finally, questions about the appropriate limits that can be placed on people's rights arise even more dramatically with other, more contagious diseases. For example, the isolation or quarantine of people who have drug-resistant tuberculosis forcefully raises the question of how to balance individual liberty with the safety of the public.

RESEARCH ON HUMAN SUBJECTS

Research is essential for improving global health. Not only do new health interventions need to be developed to address the world's diseases, but ways to deliver existing interventions also need to be improved. However, health research generates some distinctive ethical problems. Eventually all new healthcare interventions must be tested with human beings, but most research studies are not designed to benefit the people who participate in them. Instead, they are designed to create knowledge that can help patients in the future. Medical research therefore raises special ethical concerns because research participants are put at risk for the sake of other people's health.

This section outlines some historically important cases in research ethics and surveys some of the ethical guidelines that emerged from them. It describes the current global system of review for research ethics. Finally, it considers how to go about the ethical evaluation of clinical research.

Key Human Research Cases

A number of historical cases of research on human subjects have raised ethical concerns and encouraged the development of guidelines for carrying out research ethically. Among the best known of these are the Nazi medical experiments, the Tuskegee Study in the United States, and the "short-course" trials for the drug zidovudine (AZT) in Africa and Asia.

The Nazi Medical Experiments

In 1931 the Reich Circular on Human Experimentation laid out German regulations for the conduct of research with human beings. With a strict requirement for the consent of the subject (or the subject's legal representative) and restrictions on the risks to which children could be exposed, these regulations were ahead of their time. But, just a few years later, German physicians and scientists perpetrated some of the worst medical atrocities in history.

Hitler's accession to the Chancellorship in 1933 began a process of Nazification of the German state and German society. This included research institutions, universities, and the medical profession. It coincided with the rise in popularity of eugenics in many countries. With the Nazi emphasis on racial purity, this eventually led to widespread forced sterilization of "undesirable groups," such as the disabled, people with inherited mental and physical anomalies, and ethnic minorities, and eventually the "euthanasia" of hundreds of thousands of "incurables."[23] The views that justified these acts were supported by the research of anthropologists and geneticists.

German medical researchers conducted many experiments on euthanasia victims, prisoners of war, and the occupants of concentration camps. In support of the war effort, prisoners were deliberately infected with diseases like tuberculosis and malaria. Josef Mengele, as camp doctor at Auschwitz, studied around 900 children in his twin camp, where he conducted operations without anesthetic, killed children's siblings, and injected children with infective agents. Anthropologists collected body parts from prisoners of war and concentration camps for the study of comparative anatomy.

Following the end of the Second World War, amid widespread evidence of medical research abuses by the Nazis, the Allies set up an International Scientific Commission to investigate and document these abuses. Subsequently, 23 Nazi scientists were charged with war crimes and crimes against humanity at the Nuremberg Doctors' Trial. Sixteen were convicted, of whom seven were sentenced to death and hanged.

Most of the researchers who took part in medical research under the Nazis were not prosecuted. Indeed, many of them went on to scientific careers in post-war Germany, and until the 1990s, specimens taken from Holocaust and "euthanasia" victims were preserved in German medical institutes.[23] Debate continues over the use of the results of the Nazi medical research. Some commentators argue that most of the experiments were poorly designed and so the data are valueless. Others contend that the research does contain valuable data, but there is disagreement over whether it would be ethical to use it.[24]

The Tuskegee Study

In 1932, the U.S. Public Health Service (PHS), in collaboration with the Tuskegee Institute, began a study of syphilis in Macon County, Alabama. One of the study's original aims was to justify the creation of syphilis treatment programs for African Americans at a time of considerable racial discrimination.

Six hundred African American men took part in the study, 399 with syphilis and 201 without. The men were told by researchers that they were being treated for "bad blood," a term that was used locally to describe a number of ailments, including syphilis, anemia, and fatigue. Those participating in the study received aspirin and iron tonics to make them think that they were being treated, and their families were offered burial stipends if they agreed to autopsies.[25] In fact, the men were not being treated at all: the study's aim was simply to document the natural history of syphilis.

The Tuskegee Study of Untreated Syphilis in the Negro Male, though originally planned to last 6 months, went on for 40 years.[26] In its early years, the infected participants would not have received treatment outside of the study, anyway, given the limited treatment options available for syphilis and their limited contact with doctors. However, during the late 1930s and the 1940s the PHS repeatedly intervened to prevent them from receiving effective treatment, even when penicillin became widely available after World War II.

In July 1972, a front-page article in the *New York Times* broke the story of the Tuskegee study. In response to the ensuing public outcry, the U.S. Assistant Secretary for Health and Scientific Affairs appointed an advisory panel to review the study, and it was swiftly brought to a close. In the summer of 1973, the National Association for the Advancement of Colored People (NAACP) filed a class-action lawsuit on behalf of the Tuskegee subjects. It was settled out of court. As part of the $9 million settlement, the U.S. government promised to give free medical and burial services to all living participants, as well as health services for wives, widows, and children who had been infected because of the study.

The impact of Tuskegee on human subjects research was profound. U.S. Senate hearings on human experimentation in 1973 focused further attention on the study. These hearings were followed by the creation of the National Commission for the Protection of Human Subjects of Biomedical and Behavioral Research, whose recommendations would eventually result in the U.S. regulations for the protection of human research subjects.[25]

The "Short-Course" AZT Trials

In 1994, a study conducted by the AIDS Clinical Trials Group demonstrated the effectiveness of the antiretroviral drug zidovudine (AZT) in preventing mother-to-child transmission of HIV. The complex "076 regimen," which started administering AZT in the second trimester of pregnancy and continued through to treatment of the infant, reduced HIV infection by two thirds.[27] It immediately became the standard of care in developed countries. In most developing countries, however, the 076 regimen was too complicated and too expensive to implement. Such countries were exactly the places where the HIV/AIDS epidemic was worst, and where an effective preventive was needed. Consequently, there was great interest in developing a cheaper intervention that would be easier to implement.

Following a meeting organized by WHO, 15 trials were planned to take place in developing countries, mostly in sub-Saharan Africa, including tests of simpler "short-course" AZT regimens. The trials provoked fierce criticism. Opponents of the trials noted that they would not be permitted to take place in developed countries, where the 076 regimen was the standard of care. They therefore accused the sponsors of the short-course AZT trials of ethical double standards. Moreover, they claimed that the studies violated the restrictions on placebo use stated in the Declaration of Helsinki (which is discussed later in this chapter).[28] In 1997, Peter Lurie and Sidney Wolfe wrote in the *New England Journal of Medicine*:

Residents of impoverished, postcolonial countries, the majority of whom are people of color, must be protected from potential exploitation in research. Otherwise, the abominable state of health care in these countries can be used to justify studies that could never pass ethical muster in the sponsoring country.[29]

Proponents of the trials defended their design. They noted that the results of the trials were likely to be valuable to the communities from which the participants were drawn. The trials were therefore not exploiting poor people for the gain of people in developed countries. The 076 regimen would not, in any case, be available to the women enrolling in these trials, and so they were not being deprived of treatment. Finally, they argued that there were methodological reasons for using a placebo-controlled design. A study using the 076 regimen as an active control was quite likely to show that the short-course regimen was inferior. However, it would not show whether the short-course regimen was better than nothing at all. Furthermore, the background rate of mother-to-child transmission of HIV varied between populations, which meant that a comparison to placebo would be scientifically necessary.[30]

Unlike the Nazi experiments and the Tuskegee study, which were clearly unethical, the ethics of the short-course AZT trials remain controversial. Although some commentators remain convinced that they were unethical, many people think that trials like these are essential if we are to develop interventions that can help large numbers of people in low- and middle-income countries. The debate over these trials did highlight the existence of additional ethical issues concerning research conducted in developing countries. Along with a framework for evaluating the ethics of human subjects research, these additional issues are outlined below.

RESEARCH ETHICS GUIDELINES
The Nuremberg Code

At the close of the Nuremberg Trial, the three presiding U.S. judges issued the Nuremberg Code (see Table 4-1). It was the first document to specify the ethical principles that should guide physicians engaged in human subjects research.[31] Among other principles, it states that the "voluntary consent of the human subject is absolutely essential," emphasizes that human subjects should only be involved in research if it is necessary for an important social good, and requires limits on and safeguards against risks to participants. The Nuremberg Code was foundational for later research ethics guidelines and national regulations.

TABLE 4-1 The Standards of the Nuremberg Code

- Those who participate in the study must freely give their consent to do so. They must be given information on the "nature, duration, and purpose of the experiment." They should know how it will be conducted. They must not be forced or coerced in any way to participate in the experiment.
- The experiment must produce valuable benefits that can not be gotten in other ways.
- The experiment should be based on animal studies and a knowledge of the natural history of the disease or condition being studied.
- The conduct of the research should avoid all unnecessary physical and mental suffering and injury.
- The degree of risk of the research should never exceed that related to the nature of the problem to be addressed.
- The research should be conducted in appropriate facilities that can protect research subjects from harm.
- The research must be conducted by a qualified team of researchers.
- The research subject should be able to end participation at any time.
- The study will be promptly stopped if adverse effects are seen.

Source: Regulations and Ethical Guidelines—Directives for Human Experimentation—Nuremberg Code. Available at: http://ohsr. od.nih.gov/guidelines/nuremberg.html. Accessed June 2, 2011.

TABLE 4-2 The Declaration of Helsinki: Key Principles

Scientific Validity
- Medical research involving human subjects must conform to generally accepted scientific principles and be based on a thorough knowledge of the scientific literature.

Fairness
- Populations that are underrepresented in medical research should be provided appropriate access to participation.
- Medical research involving a disadvantaged or vulnerable population or community is only justified if the research is responsive to the health needs and priorities of this population or community and if there is a reasonable likelihood that it stands to benefit from the results of the research.
- Study participants are entitled to be informed of the study's outcome and to share benefits that result from it, such as access to interventions identified as beneficial in the study.

Risks and Benefits
- The well-being of the individual research subject must take precedence over all other interests.
- The importance of the objective of a study must outweigh the risks to the research subjects.
- Physical, mental, and social risks must be minimized.

Placebos
- A new intervention must be tested against the best current proven intervention, except when:
  - No current proven intervention exists; or
  - Where for methodological reasons the use of placebo is necessary and subjects who receive placebo will not be subject to any risk of serious or irreversible harm.

Consent
- Potential subjects must give voluntary, informed consent.
- For a potential research subject who is incompetent, the physician must seek informed consent from a legally authorized representative.
- Where possible, the physician must seek the assent and respect the dissent of an incompetent potential research subject.

Oversight and Accountability
- The research protocol must be submitted to an independent research ethics committee before the study begins.
- Every clinical trial must be registered in a publicly accessible database before recruitment begins.
- Authors have a duty to make publicly available the results of their research, including negative and inconclusive results.

Source: Adapted from World Medical Association. Declaration of Helsinki. Available at: http://www.wma.net/en/30publications/10policies/b3/index.html. Accessed August 16, 2010.

The Declaration of Helsinki

In 1964, the World Medical Association (WMA) developed a set of ethical principles to guide physicians conducting biomedical research with human subjects. Though the declaration targets physicians (the members of the WMA), its principles are supposed to apply equally to nonphysicians. It is the most influential and most cited set of international research ethics guidelines. The Declaration of Helsinki was revised in 1975, 1983, 1989, 1996, 2000, and 2008.[32]

Some key principles from the Declaration of Helsinki are summarized in Table 4-2.

The Belmont Report

On July 12, 1974, the U.S. National Commission for the Protection of Human Subjects of Biomedical and Behavioral Research was created via the U.S. National Research Act. The commission's mandate was to identify basic ethical principles

TABLE 4-3 The Belmont Report

Basic Ethical Principle	Application of the Principle
Respect for Persons: • Treat individuals as autonomous persons. • Protect individuals with diminished autonomy.	Informed Consent: • Individuals should be allowed to make an informed, voluntary decision about what happens to them. • Individuals whose capacity is limited should be given the opportunity to choose to the extent that they are able.
Beneficence: • Maximize possible benefits. • Minimize possible harms.	Assessment of Risks and Benefits: • A data-based risk/benefit assessment should be made. • Risks to subjects should be outweighed by the sum of the benefits to subjects and the benefit to society. The interests of the subjects should be given priority. • Risks should be reduced to those necessary to achieve the research objective.
Justice: • The benefits and burdens of research must be distributed fairly.	Selection of Subjects: • There must be fair procedures and outcomes in the selection of those participating in the research.

Source: U.S. National Institutes of Health, Office of Human Subjects Research. The Belmont Report: Ethical Principles and Guidelines for the Protection of Human Subjects of Research. Available at: http://ohsr.od.nih.gov/guidelines/belmont.html. Accessed September 9, 2010.

for the conduct of biomedical and behavioral research with human subjects, and to develop guidelines for researchers so that all human research would conform to the principles identified. The commission prepared what has come to be known as the Belmont Report.[33] The ethical principles and their applications are outlined in Table 4-3.

EVALUATING THE ETHICS OF HUMAN SUBJECTS RESEARCH

The Nuremberg Code, the Declaration of Helsinki, and the Belmont Report all provide ethical principles that should be used to evaluate research protocols. But how should one carry out this evaluation? A simple framework, derived from the general principles enunciated in the Belmont Report, can help us systematically think through the ethics of many proposed clinical research studies. According to this framework, a clinical research protocol must satisfy at least six conditions: (1) social value, (2) scientific validity, (3) fair subject selection, (4) acceptable risk/benefit ratio, (5) informed consent, and (6) respect for enrolled subjects.[34]

In general, research is only ethically justified if it is socially beneficial; that is, if it generates knowledge that can help people. Otherwise, it exposes participants to risks and burdens for no good reason. A study can fail to be socially beneficial in two ways. First, if the scientific questions that the study seeks to answer are not important questions; for

example, if the results of the study are known beforehand, then its data are not important. This gives rise to the requirement that research must have *social value*. Second, a study can fail to be socially beneficial, even if it is trying to answer important questions, if the study methodology is inadequate to answer those questions. For example, if a study will not enroll enough participants to generate a statistically significant result, then the methodology is inadequate. If a study cannot test its hypotheses, then no matter how important they are, it cannot result in social benefit. This gives rise to the requirement that research must be *scientifically valid*.

The third requirement, *fair subject selection*, concerns the equitable distribution of the benefits and burdens of research. When considering who will be asked to enroll in a study, researchers should make sure they do not enroll members of vulnerable populations in risky studies simply for reasons of convenience. Similarly, privileged people should not be preferred for participation in research that promises to be beneficial. Sometimes enrollment criteria are explicit; for example, a study may exclude children or people with certain comorbidities. Other times they are more subtle; for example, a study that requires extended visits to a hospital may exclude people who cannot take time away from work or family responsibilities, and a study that advertises for participants online will exclude people who do not have access to the Internet.

The requirement for an *acceptable risk/benefit ratio* combines several concerns. First, the risks to participants should be minimized as far as possible consistent with meeting the scientific objectives of the study. Second, there is a limit to the level of risk to which participants may be exposed. We do not, for example, think that people should be asked to risk their lives for the cause of science. Finally, the risks to participants must be balanced by the possible benefits to the participants and to society. Thus, the social value of a study is a vital part of the assessment of whether the risk/benefit ratio is acceptable.

Obtaining competent people's *informed consent* to research participation respects them by letting them choose what happens to them. Valid informed consent consists of several elements, including that potential participants must understand key elements of the research, and that they must make a voluntary choice to participate. Some individuals, such as children, are unable to give their own consent. They are respected by having a surrogate decision maker give permission for research enrollment on their behalf, and by being involved in the decision as far as they are able.

In some cultures, there are people with the authority to make decisions on behalf of other competent adults. For example, it may be considered normal for a village elder to make decisions on behalf of the people living in the village, or for a husband to make decisions on behalf of his wife. It is important that research be conducted in culturally sensitive ways. However, this does not imply that any competent adult may be enrolled in research against his or her will. The individual's informed consent should always be obtained.

Researchers still have a number of ethical duties once participants are enrolled. For example, they must respect participants' rights to withdraw from research, protect their confidentiality, and so on. These duties fall under the umbrella of *respect for enrolled subjects*.

Going through these principles in order is a helpful way to systematically evaluate the ethics of a proposed research study. However, they are not the only considerations that are ethically relevant, and the framework does not tell us how to balance conflicting principles against one another. For example, how should we decide when it is permissible to use a study design that exposes subjects to a slightly greater risk of harm in order to collect more valuable data? Thus, the framework does not constitute a checklist, but simply a guide to some of the most important ethical considerations and an order in which to consider them.

Research in Low- and Middle-Income Countries

The short-course AZT trials controversy put a spotlight on the ethics of clinical research conducted in low- and middle-income countries. Such research is frequently sponsored by institutions or companies based in high-income countries, and draws on a pool of potential participants who are likely to be poor, undereducated, and without access to good quality medical care outside of research participation. Consequently, some ethical issues arise much more frequently in this research. Three of the most important issues are summarized here: (1) the standard of care, (2) post-trial benefits, and (3) ancillary care.

The "standard of care" discussion centers on questions concerning what level of medical care should be provided to participants in controlled clinical trials. These trials give an experimental intervention, say a new drug, to members of one group of participants and compare their symptoms with a similar group of people who do not receive the intervention. Sometimes the comparison group, or *arm*, receives an established treatment, sometimes an inactive substance (placebo), and sometimes nothing at all. A lot of debate has focused on when it is permissible to give participants a placebo when there already exists an effective treatment for the condition being studied. This was the question at the heart of the dispute over the short-course AZT trials. However, similar questions can arise whenever the standard of care offered in any arm of the trial is less than the standard available to patients in high-income countries with universal health care.[30] At present, there is some consensus that a lower standard of care may be offered when this is both scientifically necessary to answer a socially valuable question and participants receiving a lower standard of care will not be at risk of serious harm. Other cases remain controversial.

The issue of post-trial benefits arises both with respect to participants and with respect to the community or society they come from. When research participants are also patients they may receive treatment during a trial. But at the end of the trial their condition may not be cured. For example, participants in HIV/AIDS treatment trials may be treated with antiretroviral therapy during the trial. However, if they do not continue this treatment after the trial, their condition will start to deteriorate again. In high-income countries with universal health care this is not a problem, because participants will leave the trial and then receive continuing treatment in their communities. In low- and middle-income countries this may not be an option for the majority of participants. It is widely recognized that post-trial benefits to participants is an important ethical issue. What benefits should be provided and by whom, however, is not well worked out.[35]

Concerns have also been raised about whether other members of the communities hosting research will benefit. For example, a pharmaceutical company might test a new drug for schizophrenia on patients in Peru, but either not market the drug in Peru or price it out of the reach of most of Peru's population. To some commentators, such trials seem exploitative. They argue that research should not be permitted unless the communities that host it will have access to successful interventions that result.[36,37] Other commentators argue for a broader understanding of how exploitation can be avoided. They think that communities that host research should receive a fair level of benefits from the research, but this need not be in the form of post-trial access to interventions.[38] So, for example, the provision of other medical care or investment into healthcare facilities might be acceptable community benefits.

Ancillary care is medical care that is given to study participants but that is not required by the scientific design of the study. In the vignette at the beginning of this chapter, malaria researchers were conflicted about whether they should provide ancillary care to the children in their study, including treatment for malaria, diarrhea, parasitic infections, and pneumonia. Such dilemmas are common for researchers who are working in environments where many people lack access to health care. The researchers may be trained clinicians who could provide much-needed care. However, time and resources spent on medical care take away from those that can be spent on conducting research. There is no established way to work out how much ancillary care researchers ought to provide to participants. However, there is agreement that researchers have *at least* the following duties:

- First, researchers, like other people, have a duty to provide life-saving medical care when they can do so at a relatively low cost.
- Second, if participants are harmed by research procedures, and do not have access to health care outside the trial, they should be treated for those harms.
- Third, thinking about ancillary care should be incorporated into the planning for research studies conducted in poor populations.

Some bioethicists have also tried to work out further ancillary care responsibilities on the basis of the contribution participants make and the relationship that develops between researchers and participants.[39]

Human Subjects Research Oversight Today

In the majority of countries today, it is a legal requirement for most clinical research with human subjects to undergo independent ethical review by a research ethics committee (REC). Also called a research ethics board, an institutional review board, or an independent ethics committee, the REC is intended to provide a safeguard against the exploitation

of human subjects in research. Many countries also have a national ethics committee, which may oversee the local RECs, review certain studies, or promulgate guidelines for research.

The regulations that govern REC review of research vary from country to country. Some RECs are regionally based, so they are responsible for all the human subjects research taking place in a particular area of the country. For example, Sweden has six regional boards for research ethics. Others are institutionally based, so they review research that is conducted by that particular institution, as well as research by other bodies who do not have their own REC. This is the situation in South Africa, for example. The U.S. system requires ethical review for research that is funded by the federal government or regulated by the U.S. Food and Drug Administration (FDA). This is important when research sponsored by the U.S. government is carried out in another country, because the research is then subject to both the U.S. and the host country regulations.

ETHICAL ISSUES IN MAKING INVESTMENT CHOICES IN HEALTH

As noted earlier, one central issue in global health is the need to make choices among investments that can enhance the health of a population. This is necessary, especially in low- and middle-income countries, because resources will always be fewer than needed to meet everyone's health needs. Sometimes a single type of scarce resource needs to be distributed. For example, there may be a limited number of kidneys, or a limited amount of blood for transfusion. More commonly, government ministries have tight budgets and must decide how to allocate their funds among many options, ranging from the purchase of medicines to investments in infrastructure. These investment choices will get made, one way or another. It is better that they be made according to explicit, publicly justified criteria, than in secret or without serious consideration of the ethical reasons for different distributions.

Cost-effectiveness analysis, as discussed in Chapter 3, is one important tool for making decisions about health investments; however, it is rarely sufficient in order to decide what to do. Decision makers must still make value judgments about what use to make of a cost-effectiveness analysis. Consider the vignette about the Indian state discussed at the beginning of this chapter. Investing in urban clinics would likely have the greatest total impact on health—it would avert the most DALYs. But the poorer people in the countryside might still, quite reasonably, think that they were being unfairly treated. After all, they were already worse off than the city folks, so why should they lose out again? Health economics, though indispensable for making health investment choices, cannot replace hard decisions about what is fair.

Principles for Distributing Scarce Resources

Various ways to distribute scarce resources have been suggested. Take the problem of allocating live organs for transplant. One way to allocate organs is to have a waiting list, so that those people who are diagnosed as needing a transplant first are also the people who receive an organ first. This would be a "first come, first served" principle. Alternatively, some sort of lottery might seem fair, so that everyone diagnosed as needing an organ would have the same chance of receiving one. Lotteries need not be equal in this way, however. It might be thought that someone whose lifestyle choices made her illness more likely is less deserving of a transplant, such as an alcoholic who develops liver failure. It might alternatively be thought that people who have better prognoses should receive some sort of priority. A weighted lottery could incorporate these considerations, giving smaller or larger chances to members of particular populations. Similar, but more complex, systems could be developed for allocating different types of resources within a healthcare system.

Some ways to allocate scarce resources are obviously unfair. Preferring certain people's health needs over others because they are of a particular ethnic group or sexual orientation is unethical. But there are various alternative ways to allocate resources that may seem more reasonable. The justification underlying most plausible allocation proposals is one or more of four basic ethical principles:

- Health maximization
- Equality
- Priority to the worst off
- Personal responsibility

Methods for allocating resources, like lotteries or queues, are ways to put these principles into practice. Decision makers should be aware of possible unintended effects, where the method for allocating resources does not result in the desired pattern of allocation. For example, the "first come, first served" system might accidentally favor the well-connected or people who already have access to good quality medical care and so are likely to get an early diagnosis.[40]

The principle of *health maximization* tells us that we should allocate healthcare resources in such a way that the total beneficial impact on health is as large as possible. For example, if someone proposed allocating kidneys based on the criterion of best prognosis for the recipient, this would be a form of health maximization. If health maximization

were the only principle used, then people making health investments might simply look at the DALYs averted by different allocations of interventions and choose the most cost-effective way to avert DALYs.

Health maximization has obvious appeal: it means producing the greatest benefit that we can. However, it also has drawbacks. One important drawback is illustrated by the vignette at the beginning of this chapter. Sometimes a given amount of money could do the greatest good if it is spent helping people who are already well off. For example, if a government wants a new clinic to vaccinate the greatest number of children possible, it should locate the clinic in a city, not in the countryside. But people living in cities are usually better off already than people living in the country—they are likely to make more money, have better education, and have improved water supplies and sanitation. So, just focusing on helping people in cities looks unfair. The principles of equality and priority to the worst-off seek to address this unfairness.

There are several ways to interpret the principle of *equality*. One interpretation is that we should try to ensure that everyone has an equal chance at receiving a scarce resource or having access to health care. In this case, people are treated equally by treating them the same. Giving *priority to the worst off* takes existing health disparities even more seriously. When we adopt this principle we make decisions about providing health care on the basis of who is already badly off, rather than on the basis of who would benefit the most (as maximization would dictate). This principle works well when the worst off can be helped relatively easily. It works less well when helping the worst off would be a severe drain on resources, for example, when terminally ill patients require continuous expensive therapies. There is also the question of how to identify the worst off. Are they the people who are sickest now? Those who have the worst health over a lifetime? Those who are poorest, even if their health is not the worst?

Each of these three principles has some plausibility. In general, if each is taken to an extreme, it would justify allocations of resources that seem unfair. Most people therefore think that some balance of maximizing benefits, giving equal chances, and prioritizing the worst off is the best way to decide how to invest resources into health. Exactly how to balance these principles in any particular case is difficult.

Finally, some people cite *personal responsibility* as a principle that can be used in combination with other principles to make decisions about health investments. Those who think that personal responsibility can be a basis for allocation decisions argue that when spending society's resources, lower priority should be given to people whose health problems may relate to their own health behaviors. Why, they may ask, should the tax money of responsible citizens be spent treating lung cancer in smokers, providing methadone and clean needles to heroin addicts, or providing ICU beds to motorcycle riders who refuse to wear helmets? Alternatively, it may be proposed that people who contribute to society should be thanked by giving them greater priority. For example, organ donors might be given greater priority to be organ recipients.

Doctors' decisions about whether to treat are traditionally based only on need and not on actions that have led to that need. Generally, those analyzing these decisions believe that it would only be fair to give a lower priority to the care of people whose behaviors appear to have caused the need for care under the following conditions:

> [T]he needs must have been caused by the behavior; the behavior must have been voluntary; the persons must have known that the behavior would cause the health needs and that if they engaged in it their health needs would receive lower priority.[41]

At present, these conditions are rarely, if ever, met.

Fair Processes

Whatever the content of a decision about health investments, there are better and worse ways to make the decision. If an unelected civil servant in a Ministry of Health were to unilaterally decide which medicines would be provided in the public healthcare system, this would be troubling. Justice is not just a matter of the result, but of the process, too. The idea of fair process is accorded great importance in contemporary democracies. For example, people accused of crimes are supposed to get a fair trial, and political leaders are supposed to be fairly elected. The proper processes for making health investment decisions have not been completely worked out. However, it seems clear that a fair process will involve at least transparency about how decisions are made, and representation from stakeholders affected by the results of the process. The National Institute for Health and Clinical Excellence (NICE) in the United Kingdom, which makes recommendations about which treatments and procedures should be provided by the National Health Service, is one example of an institution that has attempted to combine fair processes for making recommendations about health spending with an appropriate use of scientific data and medical experts.[42]

In cases where disagreement about principles of distribution seems intractable, the introduction of a fair process has been proposed as a way to resolve the disagreement.[43] The idea here is that even if people cannot agree, for example, on how their state should spend its tax revenue on health and welfare, they may still be able to agree on a process for making such decisions. By analogy, a divorcing couple might not be able to agree between themselves how to divide up their possessions; however, they might be able to agree on a process of mediation by a third party, which would lead to a division that they would both accept. This may be one solution to disagreements. However, it has its own potential problems. First, there may be similarly intractable disagreement about what counts as a fair process. Second, the fact that people agree on a process does not guarantee that either the process or its results are fair.

This overview has only scratched the surface of the ethical problems involved in deciding how to allocate resources for health. Many other questions arise when considering investment choices in health and the use of cost-effectiveness analysis. One concerns the way that cost-effectiveness analyses are conducted; for example, measuring health benefits in DALYs may seem to discriminate against disabled people, because the methodology for DALYs inherently values a condition of disability less highly than a condition of good health. Another important question is how to balance present benefits against future benefits. Should governments give greater priority to giving people vital medications now, or should they equally focus on training doctors, building infrastructure, and conducting medical research to help future patients? One could consider these and other related issues at great length. The important point of this section, however, is that, when considering investment choices and the tools one will use to make decisions about them, it is necessary to critically assess the value judgments that are implicit in them.

KEY CHALLENGES FOR THE FUTURE

Efforts to incorporate ethical and human rights concerns into global health work face a number of challenges. Some of these are briefly explained here.

First, many students of public health and global health get insufficient exposure in their training to ethical and human rights issues. Normally, they do have to understand the core concepts of research on human subjects and how an institutional review board functions. However, they may have few opportunities to take courses that cover broader issues of human rights and health or give them the tools to think systematically through the ethical aspects of research and policy making. This chapter is a small attempt to correct that gap.

Second, there are deficits in implementation. As noted earlier, compliance with human rights norms is self-reported by countries. There are really no indicators for measuring such compliance, and no enforcement mechanisms either. Perhaps the movement to focus attention on global health needs, which is discussed in greater detail in Chapter 15, can serve as a platform for having civil society hold countries more accountable for fulfilling the right of their people to health.

The governance of human subjects research has been more successful. In most countries there are systems for ethics review. However, these remain patchy—there is still a shortage of trained personnel for reviewing research; research ethics committees are understaffed, underfunded, and often undervalued; and it is not known how effective even established review systems are at protecting research participants.

There is a lack of explicit review of the fairness of many of the investment choices that are made, both by countries and by the development assistance agencies with which they work. If one reviews the documents that relate to investments in health in low- and middle-income countries, attention is generally paid to ensuring that project benefits go to disad-

vantaged people. However, it is rare that there are explicit reviews or articulation of how investment choices are made and the ethical choices that are a part of them. With respect to HIV/AIDS, for example, what criteria will be used to allocate drugs if there are more people clinically eligible for drugs than the amount of drugs available? Will it be access to the health center, so that there is a greater likelihood that the person will comply with treatment? Will it be pregnancy, so that one can reduce mother-to-child transmission?[44] If there were greater pressure to articulate these choices openly, then these decisions might be made more fairly.

Third, there are many unsolved ethical problems for people working in global health. For example, if human rights are going to guide decisions about global health interventions, we need to know exactly what those rights include. How do we work out what is included in the right to health and what is not? The discussion of the ethics of research in developing countries indicated a number of unanswered questions about what is owed to research participants and poor communities in which researchers work.

The readers of this book are encouraged to think carefully about their answers to the ethical questions that this chapter has left open, and to articulate the reasons that justify their answers.

Study Questions

1. The chapter begins with four vignettes. Briefly explain what ethical or human rights issue each vignette reveals.

2. What do the human rights documents mentioned in this chapter say about health?

3. Consider a disease other than HIV/AIDS, such as tuberculosis. How might public health efforts with respect to this disease raise human rights concerns?

4. How do intellectual property laws affect the development and pricing of medicines?

5. Explain the three ethical principles stated in the Belmont Report. Give an example of a research study and show how the three principles apply to it.

6. What are the most important ethical concerns that arise when research is conducted with people in developing countries?

7. Do you think the short-course AZT trials were ethical? Give reasons why or why not.

8. What principles might be used to justify a decision about how to allocate scarce resources for health care?

9. Why should we pay attention to the process by which health investment decisions are made?

10. How do you think cost-effectiveness analysis should be used by a government making an ethical decision about allocating a scarce healthcare resource, such as antiretroviral therapy for HIV/AIDS?

REFERENCES

1. This chapter is coauthored by Joseph Millum and Richard Skolnik. Joseph Millum is a bioethicist who serves as a Research Fellow at the Clinical Center Department of Bioethics/Fogarty International Center, United States National Institutes of Health. The opinions expressed are the authors' own. They do not reflect any position or policy of the National Institutes of Health, U.S. Public Health Service, or Department of Health and Human Services.

2. Mann J, Gostin L, Gruskin S, Brennan T, Lazzarini Z, Fineberg H. Health and human rights. *Health Hum Rights*. 1994;1(1):6-23.

3. Hannum H. The UDHR in national and international law. *Health Hum Rights*. 1998;3(2):144-158.

4. United Nations General Assembly. Universal Declaration of Human Rights. Available at: http://www.un.org/Overview/rights.html. Accessed September 10, 2006.

5. Office of the United Nations High Commissioner for Human Rights. International Covenant on Economic, Social and Cultural Rights New York, 16 December 1966. Available at: http://www2.ohchr.org/english/law/cescr.htm. Accessed September 8, 2010.

6. Office of the United Nations High Commissioner for Human Rights. International Covenant on Civil and Political Rights New York, 16 December 1966. Available at: http://www2.ohchr.org/english/law/ccpr.htm. Accessed September 8, 2010.

7. Gruskin S, Tarantola D. Health and human rights. In: Gruskin S, Grodin MA, Annas GJ, Marks SP, eds. *Perspectives on Health and Human Rights*. New York: Routledge; 2005:3-58.

8. Mokhiber CG. Toward a measure of dignity: indicators for rights-based development. In: Gruskin S, Grodin MA, Annas GJ, Marks SP, eds. *Perspectives on Health and Human Rights*. New York: Routledge; 2005: 383-392.

9. Office of the United Nations High Commissioner for Human Rights, World Health Organization. The Right to Health: Fact Sheet No 31. June 2008. http://www.ohchr.org/documents/publications/factsheet31.pdf. Accessed August 20, 2010.

10. Biehl J et al. Judicialisation of the right to health in Brazil. *Lancet*. 2009;373(9682):2182-2184.

11. Annas GJ. The right to health and the nevirapine case in South Africa. *N Engl J Med*. 2003;348(24):2470-2471.

12. Torres MA. The human right to health, national courts, and access to HIV/AIDS treatment: a case study from Venezuela. In: Gruskin S, Grodin MA, Annas GJ, Marks SP, eds. *Perspectives on Health and Human Rights*. New York: Routledge; 2005:507-516.

13. United Nations. Convention on the Elimination of All Forms of Discrimination Against Women. Available at: http://www.un.org/womenwatch/daw/cedaw/text/econvention.htm. Accessed September 8, 2010.

14. Office of the United Nations High Commissioner for Human Rights. Convention on the Rights of the Child. Available at: http://www2.ohchr.org/english/law/crc.htm. Accessed September 8, 2010.

15. Wilkinson R, Marmot M. Social Determinants of Health: The Solid Facts. World Health Organization, 2003. Available at: http://www.euro.who.int/__data/assets/pdf_file/0005/98438/e81384.pdf. Accessed September 10, 2010.

16. Easley CE, Marks SP, Morgan Jr. RE. The challenge and place of international human rights in public health. In: Gruskin S, Grodin MA, Annas GJ, Marks SP, eds. *Perspectives on Health and Human Rights*. New York: Routledge; 2005:519-526.

17. Steinbrook R. The AIDS epidemic in 2004. *N Engl J Med*. 2004;351(2):115-117.

18. 2005 Indian Patents Act.

19. Trouiller P, Olliaro P, Torreele E, et al. Drug development for neglected diseases: a deficient market and a public-health policy failure. *Lancet*. 2002;359(9324):2188-2194.

20. Cohen J, Dibner MS, Wilson A. Development of and access to products for neglected diseases. *PLoS ONE* 2010;5(5):e10610.

21. World Health Organization. Public Health, Innovation, and Intellectual Property Rights. 2006. Available at: http://www.who.int/intellectual property/documents/thereport/ENPublicHealthReport.pdf. Accessed September 8, 2010.

22. Cullet P. Patents and medicines: the relationship between TRIPS and the human right to health. In: Gruskin S, Grodin MA, Annas GJ, Marks SP, eds. *Perspectives on Health and Human Rights*. New York: Routledge; 2005:179-202.

23. Weindling PJ. The Nazi medical experiments. In Emanuel E, Grady C, Crouch RA, et al, eds. *The Oxford Textbook of Clinical Research Ethics*. Oxford: Oxford University Press; 2008:18-30.

24. Moe K. Should the Nazi research data be cited? *Hastings Cent Rep*. 1984 Dec;14(6):5-7.

25. Jones JH. The Tuskegee syphilis experiment. In Emanuel E, Grady C, Crouch RA, et al, eds. *The Oxford Textbook of Clinical Research Ethics*. Oxford: Oxford University Press; 2008:86-96.

26. Centers for Disease Control and Prevention. The Tuskegee Timeline. Available at: http://www.cdc.gov/nchstp/od/tuskegee/time.htm. Accessed September 8, 2010.

27. Connor EM, Sperling RS, Gelber R, et al. Reduction of maternal-infant transmission of human immunodeficiency virus type 1 with zidovudine treatment. *N Engl J Med*. 1994;331:1173-1180.

28. Angell, M. The ethics of clinical research in the third world. *New Engl J Med*. 1997;337:847-849.

29. Lurie P, Wolfe SM. Unethical trials of interventions to reduce perinatal transmission of the human immunodeficiency virus in developing countries. *N Engl J Med*. 1997;337(12):853-856.

30. Wendler D, Emanuel E, Lie R. The standard of care debate: can research in developing countries be both ethical and responsive to those countries' health needs? *Am J Public Health*. 2004;94(6):923-928.

31. U.S. National Institutes of Health Office of Human Subjects Research. The Nuremberg Code. Available at: http://ohsr.od.nih.gov/guidelines/nuremberg.html. Accessed September 9, 2010.

32. World Medical Association. Declaration of Helsinki. Available at: http://www.wma.net/en/30publications/10policies/b3/index.html. Accessed August 16, 2010.

33. U.S. National Institutes of Health Office of Human Subjects Research. The Belmont Report. Available at: http://ohsr.od.nih.gov/guidelines/belmont.html. Accessed September 9, 2010.

34. Emanuel EJ, Wendler D, Grady C. What makes clinical research ethical? *JAMA*. 2000;283(20):2701-2711.

35. Millum J. Post-trial access to antiretrovirals: who owes what to whom? *Bioethics*. 2011;25(3):145-154.

36. Glantz, LH, Annas GJ, Grodin MA, et al. Research in developing countries: taking "benefit" seriously. *Hastings Center Rep*. 1998;28(6):38-42.

37. Council for International Organizations of Medical Sciences. *International Ethical Guidelines for Biomedical Research Involving Human Subjects*. 2nd ed. Geneva: CIOMS; 2002.

38. Participants in the 2001 Conference on Ethical Aspects of Research in Developing Countries. Moral standards for research in developing countries: from "reasonable availability" to "fair benefits." *Hastings Center Rep*. 2004;34(3):17-27.

39. Richardson HS, Belsky L. The ancillary-care responsibilities of medical researchers: an ethical framework for thinking about the clinical care that researchers owe their subjects. *Hastings Center Rep*. 2004;34(1):25-33.

40. Persad G, Wertheimer A, Emanuel EJ. Principles for allocation of scarce medical interventions. *Lancet*. 2009;373(9661):423-431.

41. Brock D, Wikler D. Ethical issues in research allocation, research and new product development. In: Jamison DT, Breman JG, Measham AR, et al., eds. *Disease Control Priorities in Developing Countries*. 2nd ed. New York: Oxford University Press; 2006:259-270.

42. National Institute for Health and Clinical Excellence. How We Work. 2009. Available at: http://www.nice.org.uk/HowWeWork. Accessed September 9, 2010.

43. Daniels N, Sabin JE. *Setting Limits Fairly: Can We Learn to Share Medical Resources?* New York: Oxford University Press; 2002.

44. Macklin R. *Ethics and Equity in Access to HIV Treatment—3 by 5 Initiative*. Geneva: World Health Organization; 2004.

CHAPTER 5

An Introduction to Health Systems

VIGNETTES

Uchenna lived in Nigeria. She had a high fever and suspected she had malaria. Her family took her to the local health clinic. When they arrived at 11:00 in the morning, the clinic was not open. In addition, the community health worker who staffed the clinic was nowhere to be found. Uchenna's family knew that the clinic rarely operated as it was supposed to and took her instead to the district hospital. She waited 6 hours to be seen, but was finally examined by a doctor and given medicine for malaria.

Sajitha lived in a small village in northern India. She woke up with a rash that covered the upper half of her body. Her family lived quite far from the government health center and had little faith in the quality of the staff there. Thus, they took Sajitha to a local medical practitioner. He came from the village, was always polite to people, could be paid in cash or in kind, and seemed to have a good record in curing people of their ills. He examined Sajitha, gave her an injection of vitamin B_1, and told her she would be fine. He used the same needle on Sajitha that he had used on several other people that day.

Melissa lived in the state of Virginia in the United States. She had been unemployed for some time, had little money, and had no health insurance. She also had cancer. She was thousands of dollars in debt to doctors and hospitals for the tests and treatment she had received so far; however, she needed more treatment, more drugs, and additional surgery. Several physicians would not take her as a patient because she had no health insurance. Eventually, after she became sicker, she found a physician who would do the surgery for very low cost. Unfortunately, she was so ill by the time she got the operation that she died a few months later from the cancer.

Cesar lived in San Jose, the capital of Costa Rica, and had been ill for some time. He visited his local health center, where he was referred to the national hospital because it appeared that he might have cancer. The hospital confirmed the diagnosis of cancer and then treated him with drugs and surgery. He stayed several weeks in the hospital during his recovery. The cost of Cesar's care was covered by the national health insurance program of Costa Rica.

INTRODUCTION

This chapter is about health systems. It will introduce you to the definition of a health system, the functions of a health system, and how health systems are organized. The chapter will also examine some aspects of how health systems are financed. The chapter will briefly review some examples of health systems in different countries, before turning to critical issues that health systems in low- and middle-income countries face and how they are being addressed. The chapter concludes with policy and program briefs on contracting out health services, universalizing insurance coverage in Thailand, and results-based financing. Those briefs are followed with case studies on controlling diarrheal disease in Bangladesh, integrating vitamin A supplements into the onchocerciasis program in Africa, and improving the effectiveness and efficiency of health spending in Tanzania.

It is especially important for several reasons to learn about health systems early in one's study of global health:

- Health systems are the vehicle through which health services are delivered.
- The health of individuals has an important relationship with the effectiveness of health systems.
- Most countries spend a substantial share of national income on their health system, often with major gaps in effectiveness and efficiency.
- Individuals in many countries spend an important share of their family income on health.
- Global forces such as population aging are exerting pressure on the costs of health systems.
- Achieving the best population health at the lowest possible cost is an important goal for individual countries.
- Developing and sustaining an effective and efficient health system is a goal for every country, and an especially challenging one for countries with limited financial and human resources.

You should note that this chapter focuses mainly on health services, which is only one important aspect of a health system. As you go through the chapter you will want to keep in mind a number of questions, including:

- What values do different health systems reflect about the "right to health"?
- What is the role in various health systems of individuals, and of the public, private, and nongovernmental organization (NGO) sectors?
- What is the extent to which different actors in the system are engaged in the financing and provision of health services?
- How are different health systems organized and managed?
- What are key issues constraining the effectiveness and efficiency of health systems in different settings?
- How can those constraints best be addressed?

WHAT IS A HEALTH SYSTEM?

The World Health Organization defines a health system as "all actors, institutions and resources that undertake health actions—where a health action is one where the primary intent is to improve health."[1] A related definition of a health system is "the combination of resources, organization, and management that culminate in the delivery of health services to the population."[2]

Another way to put this would be to see the health system as:

- Agencies that plan, fund, and regulate health care
- The money that finances health care
- Those who provide preventive health services
- Those who provide clinical services
- Those who provide specialized inputs into health care, such as the education of healthcare professionals and the production of drugs and medical devices[3]

It is important to remember when considering health systems that they are composed of a set of interdependent parts. The organizations, money, and people that comprise health systems may be public, private, for-profit, or private, not-for-profit.

THE FUNCTIONS OF A HEALTH SYSTEM

The World Health Organization produces a report each year on a special topic of interest; the *World Health Report 2000* focused entirely on health systems.[4] That report has been widely read and has been the basis for considerable analysis of the goals of health systems, their functions, how they are organized, and how well they perform.

The World Health Report 2000 suggests that there are three goals for every health system:

- Good health
- Responsiveness to the expectations of the population
- Fairness of financial contribution[5]

The report further suggests that if these are the goals of health systems, then each health system has four functions to play:

- Provide health services
- Raise money that can be spent on health, referred to as "resource generation"
- Pay for health services, referred to as "financing"
- Govern and regulate the health system, referred to as "stewardship"[5]

Elaborating somewhat on those ideas, one could say that all health systems should do the following:

- Provide access to a comprehensive range of health services, including prevention, diagnosis, treatment, and rehabilitation

- Protect the sick and their families against the financial costs of ill health and disability through the establishment and operation of some type of insurance scheme
- Improve the health of populations through appropriate governance of the health system, regulation of that system, promotion of good health, and the carrying out of key public health functions, such as surveillance, the operation of public health laboratories, and food and drug administration[6]

The World Health Organization has also developed a framework for considering the different parts of health systems and the roles they play in health system performance.[7] This framework includes six building blocks of a health system, depicted in Figure 5-1.

WHO defines the health system building blocks in the following ways:

- *Good health services* deliver safe and effective health interventions to people where and when they need them, in an efficient manner.
- A *health workforce* performs well when it has the right number of trained staff, in the right fields, in the places they are needed, and they perform their work as effectively and efficiently as possible.

- A *health information system* functions well when it delivers the information needed for monitoring health status and health system performance in a reliable and timely manner.
- To function well, a health system has to ensure that it provides equitable access to *medical products, vaccines, and technologies* that are safe, of appropriate quality, have been procured at the best available prices, and can be used in cost-effective ways.
- An effective *health financing system* is one that raises enough money to fund an agreed-upon health program and protect individuals from financial harm due to the costs of health services.
- *Leadership and governance* concern the management, oversight, and regulation of health systems in open, participatory, and accountable ways, that seek to maximize health for the money spent.

The WHO framework suggests that if countries combine these building blocks with attention to ensuring quality, safety, and universality of coverage, then the services are most likely to improve health in equitable ways that are responsive to the needs of individuals, protect them from financial risk, and get as much value in better health for the money spent as possible.

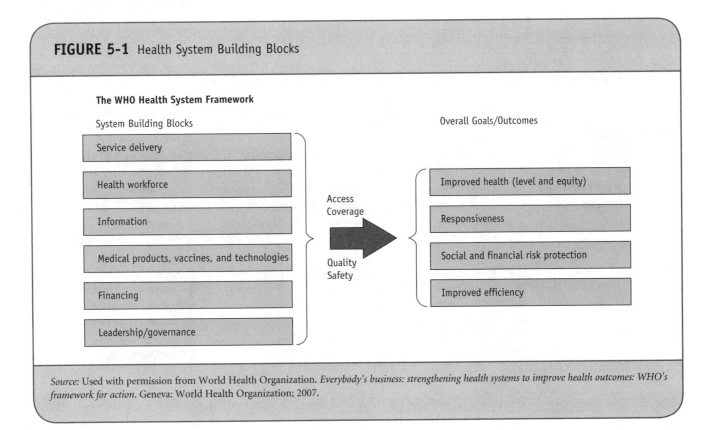

FIGURE 5-1 Health System Building Blocks

Source: Used with permission from World Health Organization. *Everybody's business: strengthening health systems to improve health outcomes: WHO's framework for action.* Geneva: World Health Organization; 2007.

HOW ARE HEALTH SERVICES ORGANIZED?

Categorizing Health Services

The manner in which health systems are organized has much to do with the history, politics, and values of individual countries. To a large extent, as discussed partly in Chapter 3, countries spend more money on health as their incomes rise. At the same time, as countries become better-off, they generally focus greater attention on trying to ensure universal access to a basic package of health services and universal coverage of health insurance. As they develop economically, they also pay increasing attention to improving the effectiveness, efficiency, and equity of their health systems. Of course, as also discussed earlier in the book, one goal of low- and middle-income countries must be to address these aims, as far as possible, even before their incomes have risen to substantially higher levels.

There is no ideal way of categorizing healthcare systems because they are so varied and so complex. However, Table 5-1 reflects one way of thinking about how health systems are organized to address several key health sector issues.[8] Nonetheless, as you examine this table and consider the comments on it, you need to keep in mind that the table represents a dramatic oversimplification of a very complicated matter.

In this table, health systems are organized into three types:

- Systems that include a national health insurance scheme, such as in Canada, France, Germany, and Japan. These systems, in principle, offer health insurance to all people for an agreed package of services. Some systems include a number of different insurance providers who cover the same service package. In other systems, insurance is generally provided through government entities, as in Canada.
- The system focusing on a national health service, in which, outside of a relatively small private health sector, the government is the sole payer for health care and owns most of the healthcare facilities. This is the case, for example, in the constituent parts of the United Kingdom. In this case, some, but not all, healthcare providers are essentially state employees.
- Pluralistic systems, such as that in the United States, in which the public sector, private, for-profit sector, and private, not-for-profit sectors play important roles. In some of these systems, the private sector has a predominant place in the system. In all of them it plays a large role.
- It is also worth noting that in Cuba today, all health services, facilities, and personnel are part of a govern-

TABLE 5-1 Simplified Categorization of Approaches to Selected Health System Issues

	National Health Insurance	National Health Service	Pluralistic
Health as a Right	Fundamental	Fundamental	Health as a personal good
Ownership of Facilities	Vast majority public and private, not-for-profit	Overwhelmingly public	Public, private, for-profit, and private, not-for-profit
Employment of Providers	Largely private	The health service and private	Largely private
Form of Insurance	Largely government single payers and firms working with government schemes	Overwhelmingly public insurance linked to the health service	Public insurance and private, for-profit and private, not-for-profit insurers, with substantial numbers lacking insurance
Financing of Insurance	Some based on individual premiums; others based on employee and employer payroll taxes; some are tax-based	Overwhelmingly tax-based	Taxes, employer and employee insurance contributions, individual purchase out of insurance, and out-of-pocket
Country Examples	France, Canada, Japan, Germany	United Kingdom	India, Nigeria, Philippines, United States

Source: Adapted from Birn A-E, Pillay Y, Holtz TH. *Textbook of International Health.* New York: Oxford University Press; 2009.

ment-operated healthcare system. Such systems were also the case in the former Soviet Union.

Table 5-1 first examines the approach of each type of health system to providing universal coverage of an insured basic package of health services as a "right." Most high-income countries do have such an approach, except the United States, which has recently taken some steps in that direction. Most middle-income countries have accepted the principle of "universal health care" as a right, but not all of them have attained it. A few low-income countries, such as Rwanda, are striving to implement universal health care as a right. However, most low-income countries have not yet moved very far toward implementing such an approach, even if it is sometimes enshrined in the laws of the country.

The table also examines who owns health facilities. In the health systems of most high-income countries, facilities are generally owned by the public sector or by private, not-for-profit organizations. In more pluralistic systems, however, including both the United States and many low and middle-income countries, facilities could be owned by the public sector, private, for-profit sector, or private, not-for-profit sector.

Table 5-1 also examines the manner in which insurance is operated in different healthcare systems. In the national health insurance models like those in most high-income countries, a number of private firms provide insurance for a package of services that is agreed upon with the government. The price of the insurance is the same across all insurers. In the United Kingdom model, the public insurance scheme is inherent to and linked with the National Health Service. In pluralistic systems, insurance can come in many forms and many people may lack insurance. The public sector may operate some insurance schemes. In addition, people may purchase insurance from private, for-profit insurers and from private, not-for-profit insurers.

Another dimension for examining health systems is the manner in which they finance their insurance schemes. The constituent parts of the National Health Service of the United Kingdom raise their funds through general taxes. The Canadian government and provincial governments also raise money for their health insurance schemes through general taxes. In some of the other countries with national insurance schemes, such as Germany, however, most of the funding for health insurance comes from payroll tax contributions from employers and employees. In national health insurance schemes, governments usually use funds from general taxes to purchase insurance for those who are not able to make contributions to the insurance scheme, such as the unemployed. In more pluralistic settings, the government may finance through general and earmarked taxes health insurance for special groups, such as the disabled, poor, and aged. In addition, individuals and employers generally contribute to the purchase of insurance. In these systems, significant numbers of people may be without insurance and such systems usually feature substantial out-of-pocket expenditures.

Most low-income countries have very fragmented and pluralistic health systems that include both public and private providers. Many of these countries have a publicly supported and provided health system and a range of private providers and facilities. They often have publically organized insurance programs for government employees and relatively small private insurance markets. They may also have a number of community-based insurance schemes. As you have seen and will examine further, private out-of-pocket payments represent a substantial share of the costs of health in low-income countries.

Many of the middle-income countries, particularly in Latin America, have organized a substantial part of their health system around a national health insurance scheme or schemes. Many of them, as well, are working to expand the schemes to be universal in coverage, as noted later in this chapter. Private out-of-pocket expenditures are generally much lower in these countries than in many low-income countries and are concentrated in those who are not covered by the insurance schemes.

Finally, it is valuable to keep the financing and provision of healthcare services conceptually separate and to examine whether the public or private sector delivers healthcare services in settings with varying financing arrangements. Again, the reader is reminded of the extent to which these comments are oversimplified.

- There is only one country today in which the public sector essentially finances and delivers all healthcare services, which is Cuba.
- In many low- and middle-income countries in which the private healthcare sector is not well developed, most formal healthcare services will be provided by the public sector. They will generally be financed through a combination of public funds and private payments for some services.
- The National Health Service (or its related entities) finances most healthcare services in the United Kingdom. It owns most healthcare facilities. The National Health Service can purchase services from providers it does not employ.

- There are many countries in which the private sector delivers services, but the public sector is responsible for health care financing, such as Canada, Thailand, and New Zealand.
- There are also countries in which most healthcare services are in the private sector, with some of those services being paid for through public financing schemes and some through privately financed schemes. Such countries usually also contain a substantial establishment of government owned healthcare services, which are generally financed through the public sector and through private payments for services. Such countries would include, for example, the United States and a number of low- and middle-income countries, such as India, the Philippines, and Nigeria.

Levels of Care

Health systems are generally organized into three levels of care that are referred to as primary, secondary, and tertiary. In most high-income countries, primary care is provided by a physician who is the first point of contact with the patient. Secondary care is usually provided by specialist physicians and

TABLE 5-2 Typical Health System Services in Low-Income Countries, By Level

Primary Level
 Well baby care
 Sick baby diagnosis
 Maternal health care
 Family Planning
 Diagnosis and treatment of TB
Secondary Level
 As above, plus:
 Treatment of sick children
 Emergency obstetric care
 Diagnosis and treatment of adult illness
 Basic surgical services
 Some emergency care
Tertiary Level
 As above, plus:
 Treatment of complicated pediatric cases
 Treatment of complicated adult cases
 Treatment of HIV
 Specialist surgical services
 Advanced emergency care

general hospitals, which are generally located in towns and cities. At these physician services and hospitals, one would get treatment for certain illnesses and conditions, including medical procedures and surgery that primary-level providers cannot do. Tertiary care is provided in specialized hospitals that are generally located only in cities. These specialized hospitals are staffed with a wide range of physicians and can address a diverse array of illnesses with high-level diagnostics, treatments, and surgeries.

Many low- and middle-income countries have established primary, secondary, and tertiary level facilities by geographic area, depending on the size of the population. These countries, for example, might have a primary healthcare center for every 5000 to 10,000 people, a secondary hospital in each district, and a tertiary hospital in large cities. In many low-income countries, medical assistants, nurses, or nurse-midwives would staff the lowest level of the system. The first level at which there might be a trained physician would be in large primary healthcare centers or district hospitals. Table 5-2 shows the types of services that one might typically expect to find at the different service levels in a low-income country.

PRIMARY HEALTH CARE

At the core of ideas about health systems in low- and middle-income countries is the notion of "primary health care," which springs partly from a historic conference in 1978 in Alma-Ata, in the former USSR. This was one of the most important meetings in the history of global health and it produced the Declaration of Alma-Ata.[9]

To a large extent, the declaration discusses two matters. First, it speaks of health as a human right. These parts of the declaration note the right to health, the unacceptable levels of health disparities, and the need for social and economic development to enable better health, as better health would promote social and economic development. It also speaks about people's right to participate in the planning and implementation of health care. In addition, it set a goal of ensuring that there would be "health for all" by the year 2000, in a manner that would help people to enjoy the health needed to fulfill their capabilities.

The document also outlines the content of "primary health care." It sees this as care that is essential and socially acceptable. It must also be based on evidence and made universally available. It would address the needs of the community and be affordable. It would provide preventive, promotive, curative, and rehabilitative services. Personnel who are sensitive to the needs of the community would staff primary healthcare services. Primary health care would be linked to other levels of health services through a referral system. It would also be linked to action on the key determinants of health, including health education, water supply and sanitation, and nutrition. The approach to primary health care would promote self-reliance in the community. It would pay particular attention to infectious diseases and other common causes of morbidity and mortality, family planning, immunization, and the provision of essential drugs.

This notion of primary health care remains an important one. Many countries—at all income levels, but especially low- and middle-income countries—continue to work toward a model of primary health care that is effective and efficient. It is important as you go through the book and study global health that you be familiar with this concept of primary health care, the efforts underway to achieve it, and that you not confuse it with "primary care," which is the first level of health services. Approaches to primary health care are discussed further later in this chapter and throughout the book.

THE ROLES OF THE PUBLIC, PRIVATE, AND NGO SECTORS

It is important to distinguish among the different actors that participate in health systems and the different functions they play. The public sector is the first actor in most health systems. The involvement of the public sector could be at the national, state, or municipal level, depending on the country. The public sector is responsible for the "stewardship" of the system, meaning its governance, policy setting, rulemaking, and enforcement of rules. The public sector is also responsible for raising the funds for the health system, making decisions about allocating those funds, and establishing approaches to health insurance—often referred to as financial protection from health costs. In addition, the public sector is responsible for managing and financing key public health functions, such as setting public health policies, enforcing regulations and laws related to health, disease surveillance, and food and drug administration. In some countries, as noted further hereafter, the public sector provides health services through facilities that it owns and operates. However, the public sector can also purchase health services from the private, for-profit or private, not-for-profit sectors.

Although some people believe that health is a right that should not be "for sale," the private, for-profit sector is involved in the provision and financing of health systems in many countries. As you will read about further in Chapter 6, Culture and Health, and elsewhere in the book, there are many types of health service providers that go beyond those involved in formal health services. Especially in low- and

middle-income countries, people often buy health services from medicine men, shamans, healers, and bonesetters. There is also a range of nonlicensed "medical practitioners" that operate in many settings, including traditional birth attendants. In addition, many people get medical advice from drug vendors that operate small kiosks or mobile "drug stores," or from pharmacists. When considering the ways in which health systems function and how they can be made more effective and efficient, it is essential to keep in mind where people get their health services, the role those providers play in the health system, and how people pay for these different kinds of services.[10]

In some countries, physicians operate in the private, for-profit sector. In some countries, the private sector may also operate health clinics, hospitals, and health services. Private sector health insurers are also involved in health in many countries. The private sector might also operate laboratories. The private, for-profit sector can operate on its own financing, it can sell selected services to the government, or it can operate under contract to the government for a range of services. The private, for-profit sector can play a very important role for those people who wish to make use of it and can either afford to make use of it or whose care is paid for by others, such as employers or by insurance.

When one thinks about the private, not-for-profit sector, particularly in low- and middle-income countries, one is often thinking about nongovernmental organizations, or NGOs. Broadly defined, an NGO is:

> A non-profit group or association organized outside of institutionalized political structures to realize particular social objectives, such as environmental protection, or serve particular constituencies, such as indigenous peoples. NGO activities range from research, information distribution, training, local organization, and community service to legal advocacy, lobbying for legislative change, and civil disobedience.[11]

NGOs may be large or small, may be local, national, or international, and may work in one area of activity or many. Some examples of NGOs are given in Table 5-3.

NGOs are actively involved in many areas of health in a large number of countries. Typical examples would be in community-based efforts to promote better health through health education and improved water supply and sanitation. NGOs are also very involved in carrying out selected health services. Like the private, for-profit sector, NGOs can operate with their own financing or they can work under contract

TABLE 5-3 Examples of NGOs Involved in Health in Selected Countries

BRAC—Bangladesh
PHILCAT—Philippine Coalition Against Tuberculosis
Profamilia—Dominican Republic
Tilganga Eye Center—Nepal
Voluntary Health Services—India

to the government, the private sector, or the philanthropic sector.

A critical issue in designing and operating health systems is the role in the health system that ought to be assigned to the public, private, for-profit, private, not-for-profit, and NGO sectors and how those roles should be paid for. It is particularly important to consider carefully the extent to which the public sector should provide services, compared to the extent to which it would be more cost-efficient for the public sector to buy certain services from the private, for-profit, private, not-for-profit, and NGO sectors. It could be the case that public sector health services at the primary level are not as effective and efficient as similar services operated by the NGO sector. As Afghanistan engaged in reconstruction after its civil war, for example, it contracted out a package of primary health care to the NGO sector.[12] In Bangladesh, BRAC, a large NGO with a presence throughout the country, is carrying out an array of nutrition programs under contract to the government of Bangladesh.[13] You will see many examples of this type of effort in this book. Contracting out for services is reviewed in one of the policy and program briefs at the end of the chapter.

HEALTH SECTOR EXPENDITURE

The health sector is an important part of the economy in all countries and a matter on which government and private individuals spend a substantial amount of resources. Table 5-4 shows the total expenditure on health as a share of GDP for selected countries organized by income group. The table also shows the share of total expenditure that is private.

Table 5-4 highlights a number of important points. First, total health expenditure as a share of GDP varies substantially across countries. It is as low as 2.4 percent in Indonesia, 2.6 percent in Pakistan, and 3.4 percent in Bangladesh. A number of lower- and middle-income countries spend from 4–7 percent of their GDP on health. Several middle-income

countries spend around 8 percent of GDP on health. Some of the high-income countries and Cuba spend more than 10 percent and the United States spends about 16 percent of its GDP on health.

We can also see a very wide range in the share of total expenditure on health that is private sector expenditure. Only about 10–25 percent of total expenditure on health is private sector expenditure in a number of high-income countries that have substantial health insurance programs, such as Denmark, France, and Ireland. On the other hand, in a number of relatively poor countries such as Sudan, Kenya, India, Bangladesh, and Vietnam, which lack a formal system of social insurance, private sector expenditure on health as a share of total expenditure on health is between 60 and 80 percent.[14]

In some respects, these data are contrary to what one might expect: poorer countries, in which people can least afford to spend for health out of pocket, have the highest private expenditure. Better-off countries, in which people can most afford out-of-pocket expenditure, spend relatively less out-of-pocket, because their insurance schemes are so well developed. Among high-income countries, only the United States has more than 50 percent of total expenditure in the private sector.[14]

SELECTED EXAMPLES OF HEALTH SYSTEMS

The section that follows provides very brief and stylized comments on the main features of a small number of health systems in low-, middle-, and high-income countries. It is important to note the common approaches of some of the countries to selected issues. However, it is also important to remember that each country has its own health system, built from its unique historical experience.

High-Income Countries

Germany

Germany was the first country in the world to have a universal program of health insurance, which started in the 1880s.[15] The German health system is organized largely around "sickness funds." These are insurance funds that are financed by equal contributions from employers and employees, based on the salary of the worker. The government makes contributions to the sickness funds for people who are unemployed and for people who are retired. The government also regulates the health system. There are more than 200 sickness funds, which are organized by region and by occupation. The sickness funds operate on a nonprofit basis. They do not provide services but rather serve as an intermediary to help organize and pay for health services.

TABLE 5-4 Total Health Expenditure as a Percentage of GDP and Private Expenditure on Health as a Percentage of Total Expenditure of Health, Selected Countries, 2009

Country	Health Expenditure as % of GDP	Private Health Expenditure as % of Total Health Expenditure
Indonesia	2.4	48.2
Pakistan	2.6	67.2
Bangladesh	3.4	68.3
Philippines	3.8	65.1
Sri Lanka	4.0	54.8
India	4.2	67.2
Thailand	4.3	24.2
Kenya	4.3	66.2
Peru	4.6	41.4
Egypt	5.0	58.9
Cameroon	5.6	72.1
Nepal	5.8	64.7
Cambodia	5.8	72.7
Nigeria	5.8	63.7
Dominican Republic	5.9	58.6
Haiti	6.1	77.9
Vietnam	7.2	61.3
Sudan	7.3	72.6
Afghanistan	7.4	78.5
Israel	7.6	41.1
Ghana	8.1	46.8
South Africa	8.5	59.9
Australia	8.5	32.3
Brazil	9.0	54.3
Jordan	9.3	35.4
Ireland	9.7	20.4
Costa Rica	10.5	32.6
Denmark	11.2	13.6
France	11.7	20.8
Cuba	11.8	6.9
United States of America	16.2	51.4

Source: Data from WHO. Global Health Observatory. Health expenditure ratios. Available at: http://apps.who.int/ghodata. Accessed June 6, 2011.

In the German healthcare system, associations of physicians get contracts from the sickness funds to provide care to people who do not require hospitalization. The sickness funds also make arrangements for hospital services for their insured people by entering into agreements with hospitals about how many services they will be able to render at a certain price that the sickness fund will pay. Many health services are free, but there are copayments for some services.[16,17] The sickness funds cover about 90 percent of the population. About 10 percent of the population has private

insurance. Most health systems in high-income countries are based on Germany's model, which is called a "social insurance scheme."[18]

The United Kingdom

The United Kingdom (UK) established a system of universal healthcare coverage in 1946, following World War II.[19] It aimed to provide a comprehensive set of health services to all people in the UK, without regard to their ability to pay for such services. The health services part of the UK healthcare system is called the National Health Service (NHS). Money for the NHS is raised from general taxes and used to make an annual NHS budget. The NHS purchases primary healthcare services for the population from groups of physicians who are trained as general practitioners and work as independent contractors to the NHS. Patient visits to these general practitioners are free. Hospitals are owned and managed by NHS Trusts, which receive a budget each year from the NHS for agreed amounts and types of healthcare services. Private health insurance and the private provision of health care in the UK comprised less than 17 percent of total health expenditure in the latest available estimates.[20]

The United States

The healthcare system of the United States is based on a combination of public and private financing, with overwhelmingly private provision of care. Close to 50 percent of healthcare financing relates to four publicly financed programs:

- Medicaid—for people below a certain income level
- Medicare—for people above a certain age
- The Veterans Administration—for people who served in the military
- Worker's Compensation—for illnesses and disabilities related to people's occupation

Another 50 percent of the financing of health care comes from individuals and their employers. Most people who are insured receive health insurance through their work, with both the employer and the employee contributing to the cost of that insurance. People who do not receive such insurance or who are self-employed or not employed can purchase insurance themselves. Most health insurance companies operate on a for-profit basis.

Health service providers work independently of the healthcare system, except for the Veterans Administration and some public health clinics. Some patients have insurance plans that allow them to visit any doctor. Others have plans that require that they use only doctors that have arranged to charge lower fees to those people in a particular insurance plan. Some people get their services from health maintenance organizations, which provide a set of agreed services to their members for an annual charge. Most insurance plans and health maintenance organizations have varying copayments for different types of services.

The United States is the only high-income country whose healthcare system has not been founded on the principle that everyone has a right to health care, without respect to their ability to pay. Linked to this, more than 40 million people, or about 15 percent of the population, until recently have been without health insurance.[21] In 2010, however, the United States enacted legislation, one aim of which is to move toward more universal coverage of health insurance.

Middle-Income Countries

Costa Rica

The health system of Costa Rica resembles the National Health Service of the United Kingdom in many ways. In Costa Rica, the federal government controls most of the health sector directly. The Costa Rican Social Security Administration (CCSS) owns most hospitals. Most doctors are employed by the public sector, even if they also have private practices. People who work in the formal sector of the economy are obliged to participate in the Social Security Administration, which derives its financing from taxes on wages and from funding from the government's general tax revenues. Salaried workers and their employers both contribute to the CCSS, as does the government. Informal sector workers may also join the CCSS, with fees that depend on their income. Participants in the CCSS receive most services for free but do have copayments for some services. The government has divided the country into Health Areas, each of which has nine health teams serving 4000 people each. The health teams focus on primary healthcare services.[22]

Brazil

The Brazilian healthcare system has three main parts. The first is services at the federal, state, and municipal level, as well as for the military, that are publicly owned and publicly financed. The second consists of private sector services that are contracted by the public sector. These two parts of the system operate under the auspices of the Unified Health System (Sistema Unico de Saude). The third part of the healthcare system is made up of private sector services that are paid for by individuals or corporate health insurance. The municipalities are responsible for primary and secondary care and the states for tertiary-level care. The municipalities offer a package of basic care. They also operate programs for particular health conditions, such as the infectious diseases.[23]

Low-Income Countries

India

India has a tiered network of health services in the public sector. At the lowest level is a health subcenter, which serves 3000 to 5000 people, depending on whether it is in a difficult geographic area or serves tribal people. Subcenters are staffed by one female and one male multipurpose worker. Primary health centers serve 20,000 to 30,000 people and are staffed with a physician, a nurse, a female multipurpose worker, a health educator, a laboratory technician, and assistant-level staff. Community health centers serve 80,000 to 120,000 people and are staffed with a physician, a pediatrician, a gynecologist, and a surgeon, as well as a number of paramedical staff. Each operates as a small hospital with 30 beds and a laboratory and X-ray facilities. At the top of the Indian publicly provided healthcare system are fully fledged hospitals of varying sizes and complexities. Most primary healthcare services are free in public facilities. There are charges on other services, although there are exemptions for people of limited incomes.

In addition to having an extensive array of public facilities, India also has a very large private healthcare sector. In fact, about 80 percent of all healthcare expenditures are private out-of-pocket expenditures. There are two large government insurance schemes. One serves federal government employees. The other is open to public and private sector organizations and both the employer and employee make contributions to the scheme.

India has a federal political system and state governments provide most of the financing of public services. However, the federal government contributes about 10 percent of total expenditure by the public sector on health. Federal financing focuses on "public goods," including family planning; maternal and child health, such as immunizations; and the prevention and control of infectious diseases.[24,25]

Tanzania

Like many low-income countries in Africa, Tanzania has a health system that is largely managed and provided by the public sector. This stems partly from the fact that after gaining independence, Tanzania prohibited the provision of for-profit health services.[26] It also stems from the relatively low number of healthcare workers per person and the relative lack of income of much of the population for expenditure on private health care.

The public healthcare system has several levels. At the lowest level, there are village health posts. These are staffed by two members of the community who are given short training courses and who focus on working with the community on prevention of disease and promotion of good health. Dispensaries are the next level of primary care and serve 6000 to 10,000 people. These are staffed by a clinical officer, nurse midwife, maternal and child health aide, nurse assistant, and laboratory assistant. Secondary care starts at the level of health centers, which are staffed by a number of physicians, clinical officers, nurse midwives, maternal and child health aides, a public health nurse, a nurse assistant, laboratory and pharmaceutical technicians, and a medical records clerk.

Each health center serves approximately 50,000 people. It is intended that each district should also have a district hospital. When possible, these are public; however, when there is no public hospital, the government assists in the financing of a hospital from the NGO sector that can serve the functions of a district hospital. Regional hospitals perform many of the same functions of district hospitals but have some additional physicians in areas such as pediatrics, obstetrics and gynecology, and surgery. Tanzania has four tertiary hospitals that provide the highest level of services available in the country. A basic package of primary healthcare services is provided free in Tanzania.[26] The health systems in many countries in sub-Saharan Africa are organized in a manner similar to the organization of the healthcare system in Tanzania.

KEY HEALTH SECTOR ISSUES

When we consider the extent to which various health systems meet the criteria WHO has set for measuring health system performance, it is clear that some health systems produce better outcomes than others. Table 5-5 indicates for a selected group of countries how they fared in the 2000 WHO ranking of health system performance.

The WHO ranking suggests that, in general, health systems in high-income countries perform better than do the health systems in low- and middle-income countries. However, the ranking also confirms a point noted earlier: the health systems of a small group of middle-income countries, such as Costa Rica and Morocco, rate higher in the WHO ranking than a number of countries with higher incomes. Cuba ranked almost as high as many countries with higher incomes.[27]

As we explore health systems in greater detail, however, it becomes clear that all systems wrestle with a variety of challenges and constraints, no matter how high they rank on the WHO scale. Some of the most important of such challenges have to do with how to address changing epidemiologic and demographic patterns, governance of the health sector, having an appropriate number and disposition of healthcare personnel, the financing of health care, and the role of the private sector in the overall health system. In addition, the quality of care poses many issues, as does providing financial cover for the poor from the cost of health services, and the extent to which people have access to and get covered by the most appropriate health services for their needs. As was discussed earlier and will be discussed further throughout the book, the health systems in many countries face critical issues of equity. Finally, health systems face a number of problems concerning their design and the overall achievement of health outcomes, some of which have been

TABLE 5-5 Overall Health System Performance Ranking, Selected Countries

Country	Overall Performance Ranking	Country	Overall Performance Ranking
Afghanistan	173	Haiti	138
Argentina	75	India	112
Bangladesh	88	Jordan	83
Bolivia	126	Mexico	61
Cambodia	174	Morocco	29
Cameroon	164	Nepal	150
Canada	30	Niger	170
China	144	Pakistan	122
Costa Rica	36	Peru	129
Cuba	39	Philippines	60
Denmark	34	South Africa	175
Dominican Republic	51	Sri Lanka	76
Egypt	63	Turkey	70
France	1	United States of America	37
Germany	25	Vietnam	160
Ghana	135	Zambia	182

Source: Data from WHO. *The World Health Report 2000.* Geneva: WHO; 2000:Annex Table 1.

the subject of "health sector reform" efforts. These themes are explored briefly here.

Demographic and Epidemiologic Change

Demographic and epidemiologic changes raise critical challenges for the health systems of most countries, as discussed in Chapter 3. In high-income countries, and in many low- and middle-income countries, people are living longer. As they do so, societies face higher burdens of noncommunicable diseases. Many of these conditions are chronic and the cost of treating these conditions is high compared to conditions that occur at younger ages or the cost of acute bouts of communicable diseases. As a result, relatively poor countries, with few resources to spend on health and weak institutions to address health issues, face a triple burden of disease simultaneously—the burdens of noncommunicable disease, communicable disease, and injuries.[28]

Stewardship

The quality of governance is an important determinant of outcomes in the health sector, as well as in many other sectors. In high-income countries, the health sector will tend to be governed in relatively open and transparent ways. These countries will tend to have clear rules and regulations for

the management and operation of the health sector, and high-income countries can enforce those regulations. There is usually relatively little corruption in the health sectors of high-income countries.

Unfortunately, however, there are major problems of governance in many low- and middle-income countries. These problems often affect the performance of the healthcare system and penalize poor people more than other people, because the poor have fewer choices about where they can go for their health care and less power in dealing with healthcare personnel. Governance in these settings will tend to be weak across all sectors and governments in low- and middle-income countries are often unable to enforce health sector rules and regulations. This may be especially true with respect to the inability of the health sector to oversee the work of the private healthcare sector.[29]

The management of human resource matters is often especially weak, with staff sometimes being recruited by virtue of their connections, rather than their merit or fit with existing hiring rules. In addition, some staff that are recruited have to "pay off" the people who are recruiting them by giving them an up-front payment for their post or a percentage of their salary each month. Healthcare personnel are often absent from their jobs without sanction. When health services procure goods or construct facilities, they frequently do not get the best prices available, because they are engaging in corrupt practices with the providers of those goods or construction or because they do not have the capacity to engage in sound procurement practices. In many countries, healthcare personnel arrange to get payments from patients for services that are intended to be free.[29]

Human Resource Issues

The most severe human resource issues in better-off countries will tend to be imbalances in the number of certain types of healthcare personnel. Some countries do not produce enough physicians. Others do not produce enough nurses, and they tend to make up these shortages through the recruitment of healthcare personnel from other countries, particularly low- and middle-income countries. This greatly contributes to the problem of "brain drain" in the healthcare sector of lower income countries, as discussed later in the chapter.[30]

The human resource issues in low-income countries are considerable and consistent. The very poorest countries, especially in sub-Saharan Africa, will not have enough healthcare personnel to operate a health system effectively. They will face shortages of physicians, nurse midwives, nurses, and laboratory and other technicians. Despite their needs for better stewardship, they will also face important gaps in qualified health service managers, both clinical and nonclinical. In addition, the quality of training, knowledge, and skills of many of their healthcare staff will be deficient. Those staff who are well-trained will usually be clustered in major cities, and there are often important shortages of appropriately trained healthcare personnel everywhere else in the country, especially in rural and poor areas. Public sector salaries of staff will be very low compared to salaries in the private sector. As a result, many staff members lack the incentive to perform their jobs properly; often practice in the private sector as well as in the public sector, even if this is not allowed; and are frequently absent from work. In the face of poor salaries and working conditions in which they often lack the facilities, equipment, and materials needed to perform their work well, many healthcare personnel move to other countries, particularly higher income countries, in which salaries and working conditions are much better.[29,31]

Quality of Care

The United States Institute of Medicine (IOM) defines quality as "the degree to which health services for individuals and populations increase the likelihood of desired health outcomes and are consistent with current professional knowledge." According to the IOM approach, health services need to be

- Safe
- Effective
- Patient-centered
- Timely
- Efficient
- Equitable[32]

There is good evidence from low-, middle-, and high-income countries that many health systems suffer from important problems of quality and that quality varies considerably within health systems. Studies in the United States, for example, showed that "physicians complied with evidence based guidelines for at least 80% of patients in only 8 of 306 hospital regions."[33] In a study in Papua New Guinea, a low-income country with rampant malaria, only 24 percent of health workers could indicate correct treatment for malaria.[34] In a similar study in another low-income country, Pakistan, only 35 percent of the health workers could indicate the proper treatment for a certain type of diarrhea.[35] In another study of clinical practices in seven developing countries, 75 percent of the cases were "not adequately diagnosed, treated, or monitored and . . . inappropriate treatment with antibiotics, fluids, feeding, or oxygen occurred in 61% of the patients."[36]

There are many causes of poor quality health services in low-income countries, including poor management, a lack of financial resources, poorly trained and inappropriately deployed staff, a failure of staff to do their work as intended, and unempowered patients, as discussed throughout this chapter. Many health systems also provide very little supervision of healthcare personnel and have only weak systems for monitoring the performance of their health system.[33]

The Financing of Health Systems

The health systems in many countries battle continuously for sufficient financing to meet their highest priorities in effective and efficient ways. Better-off countries face issues of rising costs because of aging populations and the ever-increasing demands for the use of new technologies and new drugs. All health systems ration services in some ways. In many high-income countries, a critical issue is how to find the funding that is needed, even with increased efficiency, to reduce the waiting times for certain medical procedures that are financed through the national insurance program. This has been a highlight of the healthcare debates, for example, in the United Kingdom and Canada. A few of the high-income countries, such as Switzerland and the United States, also face important economic questions about the share of their total GDP that they are devoting to health and the implications of this for the rest of the economy.

As you would expect, the financing issue in most low- and middle-income countries revolves around the absolute lack of public sector financial resources for health. It is true that many low-income countries do not spend effectively or efficiently the financial resources that they do have for health. However, it is also true that most low-income countries do not provide the health sector with the public funds needed to ensure that an appropriate basic package of health services is available to all people without respect to their ability to pay. The costs of such a basic package have been estimated to range in the low-income countries between the equivalent of $12 and $50.[37] We have already seen, however, that the very poorest countries allocate from public funds only between 1 and 3 percent of their GDP for health, which would give them only about $3 to $10 per year to finance such a basic package.[38]

Financial Protection and the Provision of Universal Coverage

As also discussed earlier, one measure of the performance of a health system is "fairness of financial contribution," as WHO calls it. This refers to financing health care in a way that does not cause people to be denied access to health care or to become impoverished because of their inability to pay for health services.[39]

The capacity of people to pay for health services *is* a barrier to their access to health care, and catastrophic health costs impoverish people in many settings. In most high-income countries, this is not a significant problem because they have social insurance schemes and essentially offer health insurance to all of their people. However, this is a common problem in poorer countries. Studies in India have shown that expenditure on health is a leading cause of families falling below the poverty line and a major cause of families selling assets to pay their bills for health care.[25] Other studies have shown a decline in the use of TB medicines and hospital deliveries of babies when charges were levied on these services.

Access and Equity

You read in Chapters 2 and 3 about the extent to which health disparities are an important feature of many health systems. You have also seen how important it is to always assess health status, the provision of health services, and health outcomes by sex, age, ethnicity, income, education, and location. In low- and middle-income countries, dispari-

ties in access to services and in equity are often reflected in the following ways, among others:

- A lack of coverage of basic health services in areas where poor, rural, and minority people live
- Service coverage with a lower level of inputs in the areas previously noted, compared to other areas, such as fewer trained personnel and less equipment and drugs
- Service coverage that varies, such as already illustrated for immunization programs, with income and education levels, as well as by location, with urban dwellers getting preference
- Better-off people getting access to relatively expensive services that are generally less available to the lower-income groups

It is very important as we assess the performance of health systems that we examine the coverage of health programs for different types of people. It is also important that we examine how services that are accessible to lower-income and other disadvantaged groups compare to the services available to higher-income groups.

ADDRESSING KEY HEALTH SECTOR CONCERNS

There are few easy answers to addressing effectively the most critical health sector issues, particularly in low-income countries. Nevertheless, there is an increasing body of evidence about measures that can be taken to deal with some of the specific problems noted above and to design and manage heath systems more effectively and efficiently. These are discussed briefly here.

Demographic and Epidemiologic Change

The very poorest countries can take only a limited number of steps to deal with the multiple burdens of communicable and noncommunicable diseases and injuries. Yet, most of these countries will face an increasing burden from non-communicable disease, particularly cardiovascular disease, as discussed in Chapter 12, and road traffic accidents, as discussed in Chapter 13.

Perhaps the single most important step that low- and middle-income countries can take today to reduce the burden of cardiovascular disease later will be to reduce the disease burden that is related to tobacco use. There is very good evidence that even in low-income settings, measures to make it harder and more expensive to buy cigarettes can reduce tobacco smoking.[40] Even with their limited financial resources and management capacity, low-income countries need to start now to take these steps. They can also take other measures including better engineering of roads, safer cars, and more traffic enforcement to reduce road traffic accidents.[41]

The health systems of low- and middle-income countries will need to be strengthened to address the growing burden of noncommunicable diseases related to economic, demographic, and epidemiologic change. Low- and middle-income countries will need to pay increasing attention to these problems, even as they continue to confront the problems of communicable diseases and undernutrition. To an important extent, countries will need to assess the six building blocks of health systems from the perspective of managing prevention, treatment, and care related to noncommunicable diseases. Addressing chronic noncommunicable diseases requires prolonged and frequent contacts with patients, unlike care for most communicable diseases, with the exception of HIV treatment. Countries will need to adapt such models of care that can sustain more frequent contacts with patients over a longer period of time than they have had to do thus far.[42]

Stewardship

It will also be difficult to improve the governance of the health system in countries in which overall governance is weak and corruption is high. Nonetheless, a number of measures are proving to be useful in addressing key governance issues in health. Corruption has been reduced, for example, in countries like Poland that have launched national anticorruption programs with strong political backing. In addition, reforming procurement systems and making them more open and transparent has been associated with reducing corruption in contracting in countries such as Chile and Argentina. Increasing audits of the health system and enforcing penalties to deal with adverse findings has assisted Madagascar in reducing corruption. There are an increasing number of efforts at reducing corruption and enhancing management through oversight by communities. In a number of cases, such as in Uganda, the Philippines, and Bolivia, community boards were provided more information about the money and services that the community should have received and the authority to provide oversight of these resources in a way that could lead to the firing of corrupt officials. Contracting out some services, carrying out customer satisfaction surveys among the users of the health system, and letting communities provide services with "citizen report cards" are also proving to be helpful to enhancing governance in some settings.[29]

Human Resources

The problems of human resources for health relate to a lack of staff, a maldistribution of staff, the inadequate training and quality of personnel, and the poor environment in which many of them have to carry out their work. An international group examining human resources for health has suggested that there needs to be more shared global responsibility for these resources, given the extent to which health workers migrate in search of better pay and working conditions. In addition, they suggested that countries need to have much more explicit strategies for workforce development that would focus on "coverage, motivation, and competence." They also highlighted the need for countries and their development partners to provide greater support for education and training of health personnel and to developing better policies and programs for retaining personnel.[43]

Even as they seek to address these problems in more comprehensive ways, some countries have taken steps to deal with human resource issues. Countries might be able to reduce the share of their health workers who are migrating, for example, by training them so they gain needed skills but do not get credentials for those skills that would be recognized by other countries.[44] Moreover, lower-level health personnel can be trained to carry out a number of functions often reserved for higher-level staff. In Malawi, which has an acute shortage of doctors, nurses were trained to perform cesarean sections.[45] As antiretroviral therapy is being scaled up for AIDS, community-based workers are being taught how to dispense drugs for patients who have been doing well on treatment and to recognize when the patients are having problems and need to be referred for other care. These are tasks reserved for doctors in some AIDS treatment programs.

Financial incentives are also very important to encourage better performance of healthcare personnel. These might include better salaries, additional payments for serving in hard to reach areas, providing housing for people who work in those areas, or special allowances for training. There is also good evidence that the productivity of health workers is higher when their pay is tied to services provided per patient that they actually perform, rather than just paying them a salary. The design of incentives and provider payment mechanisms, of course, has to take important account of what one is trying to achieve and of the local culture. Incentives might be different, for example, if one were trying to reduce migration, trying to get staff to serve in rural areas, or just trying to get staff to come to work in a timely way.[46] One of the policy and program briefs later in the chapter discusses results-based financing.

Financing Health Services

The scope for very low-income countries to raise additional resources for health is limited, given the overall scarcity of resources. Nevertheless, there is some scope for shifting resources from other areas of the economy in some countries, given the potentially high returns to investments in health. Many low-income countries, however, will probably require development assistance for health for some time in order to boost expenditure on health and more effectively address some of their key health goals.

As can be seen in the case study on Tanzania at the end of this chapter, however, there is also some scope for enhancing health outcomes by shifting expenditure within the health sector. By focusing expenditure on a selected group of low-cost investments that are known to be effective if managed properly, even very poor countries may be able to improve health outcomes of their poorest people.[38,47] To assist in raising and managing resources for health more effectively, many countries will need to enhance the data they have on health expenditure and also monitor health investments and expenditures more carefully.

Many countries also have substantial room for improving the efficiency of the resources they spend on health. WHO has estimated that between 20 and 40 percent of the expenditures on health in low-income countries are wasted. Improvements in the efficiency of expenditures could help to free resources for high priority expenditures. In addition, the better management of financial resources by ministries of health will strengthen any arguments they make to ministries of finance about the need for additional financing for health and their ability to use it wisely.[7]

Financial Protection and Universal Coverage

WHO has suggested that countries need to take a number of steps to enhance people's protection from the burden of health expenditure and to achieve universal coverage of a basic package of health services. These would include raising additional revenue for health, improving efficiency of health sector expenditure, reducing dependence on out-of-pocket expenditures, and enhancing equity. This will be related to the development of broad-based health insurance schemes, even in low-income countries. Although at one time such schemes were generally considered to be possible only in middle- and high-income countries, a number of low- and middle-income countries have recently made substantial progress in providing universal health insurance, including Brazil, Mexico, Rwanda, and Thailand.[7] The Thai example is discussed in one of the policy and program briefs later in this chapter.

In the meantime, countries can take a number of measures to reduce the dependence on direct payments by people when they need care. Greater financial protection would be offered to the poor, for example, if governments allocated a larger amount of funding to a basic package of free primary health care and targeted that to those places and people most in need. Governments could couple this with subsidies for selected hospital services for the poor, as well, although these schemes are often difficult to manage. Second, governments could also contract a package of primary healthcare services from NGOs and the private sector and subsidize that package for the poor. This has been done with some success in Afghanistan and Cambodia. Third, governments could encourage NGOs to provide services from their own resources, as selected local and international NGOs have the resources to do. BRAC, which will be discussed later, is one such NGO, with a long record of involvement in primary health care for the poor. Fourth, there is some evidence that schemes in which communities raise funds for an insurance pool and purchase health services with those funds might enhance the availability of health services to communities.[38,48,49]

Access and Equity

Improving access and equity of services is largely a question of political will and health systems planning. Many countries have not focused sufficient attention on the health of their disadvantaged people and have not been sufficiently aware of the kinds of gaps in health coverage and health status that these people face. There is increasing evidence, however, like that cited earlier, that the coverage of health services is inequitable and often leaves out those living in difficult regions and those with less income, less education, and less empowerment. Countries need to use the data they get from national surveys, such as the Demographic and Health Surveys,[50] to identify gaps in health status and health coverage. They then need to specifically target health resources to the places and people most in need. Very substantial gains could be had in health status within many countries, for example, if the coverage of effective programs for at least childhood vaccination, TB, and malaria were increased among the poor. The enhancements in health would be even greater if carried out in conjunction with improvements in water supply, sanitation, nutrition, and overall hygiene and health-caring behaviors. Some of this can be accomplished through improvements in knowledge that also need to be at the core of efforts to improve the health of the poor.

Quality

Low quality health services waste money and are dangerous to people's health. Although most of us probably believe that low quality is primarily a reflection of inadequate financial resources, there is good evidence that quality can be enhanced in a number of ways even in the absence of additional resources.

It is very important, first, that health systems carry out assessments that will help them to understand the quality gaps in their programs. Second, there is evidence that better professional oversight, supervision, and continuing training can enhance the quality of care provided by health service providers. Third, the use of clear guidelines, protocols, and algorithms for services can also improve quality, particularly where health workers are not well educated or trained. Fourth, when contracting services to the private and NGO sectors, governments can link their payments with performance against specific goals and can independently verify that they have been achieved. Finally, focusing some health staff, as noted earlier, on becoming very proficient at a small number of services they can perform very well is consistently associated with better quality of care.[51]

There is also evidence that "total quality management" approaches can enhance the quality of care, even in low-income countries. In this approach, which is a continuous one, groups of health providers define goals, measure how the system is doing in achieving them, get together to decide how they might best address the gaps in their program, and then test to see how their proposed improvements are working. Even in the poorest areas of North India, this kind of effort, coupled with standard guidelines for managing certain services, produced improvements in the quality of care. The safety of anesthesia has been enhanced in Malaysia in similar ways.[52]

Delivering Primary Health Care

In the end, of course, trying to enhance health outcomes for the poor through better health services in low- and middle-income countries is not just a question of addressing the specific issues discussed previously. Rather, it is also a question of the overall orientation of the health system and how it will carry out those services that can potentially have the biggest impact on improving health outcomes for disadvantaged groups.

There is a broad consensus that a number of measures are needed to achieve this aim. First, services should be focused on the main burdens of disease. Second, health outcomes can only be achieved if the health system is strengthened to deliver those services effectively and efficiently. Third, the core of activities to meet these goals should be through primary health care and the district hospital.[53]

There have been a number of very important declarations, studies, and reports that have suggested what the "basic healthcare package" should contain. The most important elements of what a primary healthcare package should contain are noted in Table 5-6.

Although there are some important differences in the exact content of the packages that have been suggested, most of the elements of such a package are agreed upon. To a large extent, it has been recommended that countries try to deliver the services noted in Table 5-7 as close to where people live as possible, through close work between primary healthcare and the district hospital. The hospital would help to supervise the work in primary health care as well as serve as the referral service for activities that cannot be handled adequately at the primary level, such as complications of pregnancy. Each of the components of the package is explored in greater detail in the chapters that follow, but they are outlined in Table 5-7.[53] It is important to note that services like those outlined in Table 5-7 need to be provided whether countries organize their health system along the lines of public or private provision of services.

Ideally, these services would be delivered in an integrated manner. You should be aware, however, that because of weaknesses in the health systems of many countries, some governments and their development partners have established some "vertical" programs. These have historically been used to address problems such as smallpox, malaria, and TB for which governments set up separate management, financing, procurement, staffing, and reporting, in parallel with the regular health programs of the government.

Although this vertical approach may not be the most efficient and effective manner in principle in which to operate health services, in practice it is sometimes seen as the only way to accomplish urgent goals in weak health systems. There is an increasing consensus that if such approaches are going to be taken, then they should be linked with efforts to improve related aspects of the health system. The polio eradication program, for example, can be used to strengthen laboratories, surveillance, and the management of the cold chain for some medicines and vaccines.

POLICY AND PROGRAM BRIEFS

Three policy and program briefs follow to illustrate some of the concepts that were discussed earlier in the chapter. The first discusses a review of efforts to improve access to and the effectiveness and efficiency of services by "contracting out" services to the private and NGO sectors. The second reviews the experience of Thailand in trying to achieve universal coverage of health services, in conjunction with the development of a national health insurance scheme. The third concerns results-based financing. This addresses efforts to improve the

TABLE 5-6 Model Primary Care Package of Essential Health Services Interventions

Maternity-related interventions	**Childhood disease-related interventions (treatment)**	**HIV/AIDS prevention**
Prenatal care	Acute respiratory infections	Youth-focused interventions
Treatment of complications during pregnancy	Diarrhea	Interventions with sex workers and clients
Skilled birth attendants	Causes of fever	Condom social marketing and distribution
Emergency obstetric care	Malnutrition	Workplace interventions
Postpartum care	Anemia	Strengthening of blood transfusion systems
Family planning	Feeding and breastfeeding counseling	Voluntary counseling and testing
Tetanus toxoid		Prevention of mother-to-child transmission
	Malaria prevention	Mass media campaigns
Childhood disease-related interventions (prevention)	Insecticide-treated nets	Treatment for sexually transmitted infections
Bacillus Calmette-Guerin	Residual indoor spraying	
Polio vaccination		**HIV/AIDS care**
Diphtheria-pertussis-tetanus vaccination	**Malaria treatment**	Palliative care
Measles vaccination		Clinical management of opportunistic illnesses
Hepatitis B vaccination	**Tuberculosis treatment**	Prevention of opportunistic illnesses
Haemophilus influenza type B vaccination	Directly Observed Therapy, Short-Course (DOTS) for smear-positive patients	Home-based care
Vitamin A supplementation	DOTS for smear-negative patients	HIV/AIDS highly active antiretroviral therapy (HAART) provision
Iodine supplementation		
TB vaccination		**Tobacco control program (taxes, legal action, information, nicotine replacement)**
Anthelminthic treatment		
School health program (incorporating micronutrient supplementation, school meals, antihelminthic treatment, and health education)		**Alcohol control program**

Source: Data used with permission from Tollman S, Doherty J, Mulligan J-A. General primary care. In: Jamison DT, Breman JG, Measham AR, et al, eds. *Disease Control Priorities in Developing Countries.* 2nd ed. Washington, DC and New York: The World Bank and Oxford University Press; 2006: 1193-1209.

demand for health services and the supply of better quality and more effective and efficient services by providing incentives at different parts of a health system.

Contracting Out Health Services

As noted earlier in this chapter, countries have taken a number of steps to try to improve access, coverage, effectiveness, and efficiency of their health systems. One approach has been to "contract out" services. This refers to governments making contracts with health service providers in the private and NGO sectors for them to deliver health services. In this case, the government becomes the purchaser and financer, rather than the provider, of services. Generally, it is recommended that the government finance services against a clearly defined set of achievements that the contracted party is to attain and that those achievements be independently verified before the government pays for such services.

The premise behind contracting out to the private or NGO sector is that they can provide the desired services more effectively and more efficiently than the government can, particularly in low-income countries with very weak health systems. Both Afghanistan and Cambodia, for example, made important use of contracting out as they sought to rebuild their health systems after periods of conflict, at a time when their health systems were barely functional.

TABLE 5-7 Selected Essential Healthcare Interventions by Level of Service in a "Close to the Client" System

Level of Care	TB	Malaria	HIV/AIDS	Childhood Diseases	Maternal/ Perinatal	Smoking
Outreach services		Epidemic planning and response Indoor residual spraying	Peer education for vulnerable groups; needle exchange	Specific immunization campaign Outreach integrated management of childhood illness (IMCI): home management of fever Outreach for micronutrients and deworming		
Health centre/ health post	DOTS	Treatment of uncomplicated malaria Intermittent treatment of pregnant women for malaria	Antiretrovirals plus breast-milk substitutes for mother-to-child transmission Prevention of opportunistic infections (OIs), and treatment of uncomplicated OIs Voluntary counseling and testing (VCT) Treatment of sexually transmitted infections (STIs)	IMCI Immunization Treatment of severe anemia	Skilled birth attendance Antenatal and postnatal care Family planning postpartum	Cessation advice; pharmacological therapies for smoking
Hospital	DOTS for complicated TB cases	Treatment of complicated malaria	Blood transfusion for HIV/AIDS HAART treatment of severe OI for AIDS Palliative care	IMCI: severe cases	Emergency obstetric care	

Source: Adapted with permission from Jha P, Mills A. *Improving Health Outcomes for the Poor: Report of Working Group 5 of the Commission on Macroeconomics and Health.* Geneva: WHO; 2002:52.

Individual evaluations have been conducted of many of the contracting-out schemes that have been put into place. However, questions remain about the extent to which such schemes have met their aims. In this light, two researchers conducted a study in 2008 of all of the evaluations of contracting out that had been done up to that point, to further understand if contracting out had been successful in increasing access to health services, improving equity in services, and enhancing the quality and efficiency of services.[54]

This review of 13 projects revealed that contracting out to private providers was associated with improved access to health services. The study further concluded that improvements in access to the services purchased by the government through contracting out did not lead to decreases in the use of other desirable services or have other negative consequences on the health system.[54]

Of the 13 projects the study reviewed, only two focused on improving the equity of health services for the poor. The first was a project in Bangladesh that targeted a poor urban slum population. The second was a project in Cambodia that resulted in a decrease in out-of-pocket expenditures by the poor. The researchers concluded that these two projects were associated with an increase in the access of the poor to health services, by reducing the costs of services to the poor. They also concluded that contracting-out projects does have the ability to increase equity in health care.[54]

The majority of the 13 projects that were studied focused on improving the quality of health care. However, it was difficult for the study authors to determine if contracted-out projects were able to increase the quality of services provided compared to the public sector, because of the manner in which quality was defined in the evaluations and their lack of clear indicators for measuring quality. The study highlighted the importance of clearly defining quality and indicators for measuring quality if rigorous assessments are to be made of the impact of contracting out on quality. This would also have to be coupled with an understanding of how much the contracted-out services are utilized. Additionally, indicators need to take into account how much providers are paid by the government for their services to see if there is a relationship between cost and quality.[54]

Five of the 13 studies addressed improved efficiency in health services. The researchers found that in some cases, healthcare costs were lower among contracted-out projects than public services, but in other cases, health-related costs were higher in contracted-out projects than in government schemes. The study acknowledged that contracted-out projects could lead to lower health costs; however, they were not able to conclude that these projects have increased the efficiency of health care systems.[54]

Overall, based on the assessments of contracting-out schemes carried out to date, the study concluded that contracted-out projects are able to increase access to services and equity in health care. However, the study also concluded that the effects of these projects on quality and efficiency are difficult to determine, and further research is necessary on these points.

Universalizing Insurance Coverage in Thailand

Very few low- and middle-income countries have been able to achieve universal health coverage. However, as discussed in this section, Thailand introduced a reform of its health system almost a decade ago with that goal in mind. The Thai experience has a number of useful lessons for other countries.

Despite increases in health expenditure in Thailand from 3.82 percent of GDP in 1980 to 6.21 percent in 1998, nearly 30 percent of the country's population remained uninsured. In addition, the cost of health care rose during that period, creating important financial constraints that impacted people's ability to access appropriate health care.

In 2001, the Thai Ministry of Public Health (MoPH) announced its desire to provide universal health care. The approach to universalizing health care would have four important objectives, each of which would seek to remedy a critical deficiency of the existing health system. First, they sought to promote equal sharing of health expenditure and equitable access to high quality services regardless of income. Second, the new system should facilitate the efficient allocation of resources by trained and experienced administrative and management officials. Third, the system should allow citizens to choose what health services they wish to receive, rather than distribute services uniformly. Finally, universal coverage was intended to promote "good health for all" through the provision of preventive and health-promoting services, as well as treatment and care.[55]

With these aims in mind, the Thai government introduced the "30 baht health policy" in 2001. The cornerstone of the policy was a public insurance scheme that provided services within a standardized benefit package for a small copayment of 30 baht (U.S. $0.80). Registered members of the health plan received a gold card permitting them access to treatment in their health district. Patients could also be referred to specialists from other districts for more complicated cases. Under this system, elderly people, children, and poor people were entitled to a free registration card for the insurance scheme. Prescription drugs under this plan were limited to those included on a national list, which later expanded to include antiretroviral therapy and other high cost drugs. Accident and emergency care was included in the basic benefit package.[56]

The 30 baht policy has had some important successes. Prior to the introduction of the policy, nearly a fifth of the population was covered under the health card scheme, which provided treatment for families within a defined benefit scheme for 500 baht (U.S. $13.30) per year. Public servants and the poor were also covered through several different government policies, although these programs collectively only provided coverage to 20 percent of the population. However, between 2001 and 2004, after the introduction of the 30 baht policy, Thailand's insured population increased from 25 million to more than 59 million. This 55.5 percent increase was predominantly due to the new scheme.[56]

Health reforms increased public health expenditure from 66.25 billion baht in 2000/2001 to 72.78 billion baht in 2001/2002. In order to efficiently coordinate this increased funding, the 30 baht program relied on two major changes in the existing system for allocating health resources. First, a "purchaser–provider" system was created that established the National Health Security Office (NHSO) as the primary purchasing agency for health services financed by the 30 baht scheme. In addition, the majority of the system's finances would be funneled through contracting units for primary care (CUPs), primary care providers responsible for managing the treatment of their registered population. The advantage of this approach was intended to be increased responsiveness of the provider due to the proximity of the CUP to the patient, as well as increased cost-control and accountability.[56] Second, a funding system was created that would reflect the demographics of the population and reduce geographic spending inequalities. Under this scheme, 1404 baht per capita per year was paid to healthcare facilities from government tax revenues.[55]

Despite having had some widely regarded successes, the 30 baht program has been criticized for several reasons. The quality of care under this scheme was initially viewed with skepticism. To some patients, the provision of services was seen as substandard and less good than the care they had been receiving. To address this concern, the government requested that all hospitals participate in the Hospital Accreditation Program to provide high and standardized quality of care.[55] Further criticism focused on the way finances were allocated within the local health systems. CUPs in rural areas were commonly pressured by the directors of community hospitals to distribute resources in the way they saw fit. This often led to funds being tied up in community hospital projects. Critics also noted that funding on a per-patient basis led to deficits among larger hospitals, which have to deal with health problems that are more complicated and expensive than other parts of the system face. This problem was addressed when the Ministry of Public Health introduced the central contingency fund in 2002, which guaranteed funding for hospitals by disbursing the salary budget at the national level.[56]

The establishment of universal healthcare insurance in Thailand suggests a number of lessons for other countries. First, it demonstrates that universal health insurance, a goal once viewed as unachievable for low- and middle-income countries, is within reach for many middle-income countries. Thailand's experience also demonstrates that although

reforms may quickly expand coverage, they require a sustained political and financial commitment on the part of the government in order to be successful in the long-term. Financing reforms take time and require the implementation of a series of changes that place large burdens on state funding.

Despite several shortcomings, the rapid increase in coverage and the importance of primary care in the financing system may also be instructive for other countries. Other valuable areas for assessment include the problems the Thais faced after the initial reforms, the purchaser–provider split, the creation of the CUPs, and the risks of creating competing responsibilities between agencies that can lead to tensions, as was seen with the National Health Security Office and the Ministry of Public Health in Thailand.[56] It will also be important to examine the functioning of the Thai hospitals to determine their effectiveness and efficiency in the face of Thailand's changing demographics, growing noncommunicable diseases, and relatively low expenditure on health.

Results-Based Financing (RBF)

Results-based financing (RBF), also known as performance-based incentives (PBI), is an umbrella term that encompasses many different financing approaches that create incentives for healthy outcomes. RBF can be defined as: "a cash payment or non-monetary transfer made to a national or subnational government, manager, provider, payer or consumer of health services after predefined results have been attained and verified. Payment is conditional on measurable actions being undertaken."[57] In simple terms, RBF is the provision of cash or in-kind incentives for measurable results, upon verification by a third party.

RBF tries to address health system problems through incentives. These rewards and penalties seek to improve health-related behaviors and, ultimately, health outcomes. The RBF approach reflects a move away from investing in inputs, such as drugs and equipment, and a renewed focus on outputs, such as deliveries in a facility, or outcomes, such as a decrease in maternal mortality.

In recent years, the development community has shown a growing interest in RBF for health because of its potential to increase the impact of health investments. RBF is now being used in a number of different countries to help carry out national health plans and try to accelerate progress toward achievement of the Millennium Development Goals (MDGs).

RBF can create incentives on the supply side, to improve the quantity and/or quality of health services delivered, or on the demand side, to increase utilization of health services.

RBF can also be applied at the same time to both the supply and demand side. RBF incentives can function at many levels, including at the "level of health facilities (or networks of facilities), the individual provider, the household decision makers, and the patients."[58]

In a supply-side scheme, for example, a health worker or facility may receive a cash incentive for every fully vaccinated child, a curative consultation, or an attended delivery. In a demand-side scheme, a woman might, for example, receive a transport voucher to deliver in a facility, or receive a cash transfer based on certain conditions, such as bringing her child in for growth monitoring. Ideally, barriers on both the supply and demand side will be addressed to ensure that the quantity and quality of health services can be improved and that there will be the desired demand for such services. To encourage institutional deliveries, for example, a project with an RBF approach might provide cash incentives to health workers attending deliveries, and transport vouchers to pregnant women who deliver in a facility.

At the core of RBF is a performance contract that "specifies what is to be paid for and under what conditions."[57] That contract can be written between many different parties. A few examples follow of how incentives might be structured in different RBF approaches, one concerning development assistance; a second, government efforts to improve the quality and quantity of services; and the third, with respect to government incentives to individuals to participate in selected health schemes.

- *Cash on delivery (COD):* Transfers are made from donor aid agencies to governments.
- *Performance-based contracting (PBC) and performance-based financing (PBF):* Transfers are made from payers to providers.
- *Conditional cash transfers (CCTs):* Transfers are made from governments to their citizens.[59]

RBF approaches can be categorized by the following key elements:

- Who gets paid the incentive?
- What are the actions, outputs, and outcomes for which they get paid?
- How are these things measured and verified?
- What is the nature of the incentive? How big is it? Is it monetary or nonmonetary? What can people do with it?[60]

RBF emphasizes transferring autonomy and flexibility to the local level, thereby encouraging local creativity and innovation in devising solutions to improve health. In addition, the necessity of monitoring results and payments and third-party verification means that RBF can strengthen health management information systems by "improving the timeliness, credibility and accuracy of national reporting and monitoring."[61]

Few rigorous impact evaluations have been done on RBF schemes. However, existing evidence shows that "positive effects have been demonstrated when only a modest sum was used as the reward (or penalty)." Thus, incentives do appear to be effective ways to achieve important improvements in health.[62]

Several CCT programs have been widely recognized for their innovative approach to poverty reduction and for their impressive results. Brazil's Bolsa Familia, for example, is a family stipend program aimed at reducing poverty in 11 million families. The program is showing positive results in child health, nutrition, and empowerment of women and is credited with helping achieve an 81 percent drop in poverty.[63] Mexico's Oportunidades CCT program resulted in households with more income, more children in school, and improved health and nutrition for participants of all ages.[64]

In addition, an RBF model in Rwanda, which provides supply-side incentives through a fee-for-service model that is conditional on quality of care at the health center level, is also showing promising results. According to a recently published evaluation, the scheme was associated with:

- A 21 percent increase in institutional deliveries
- A 64 percent increase in preventative visits for children less than 2 years of age
- A 133 percent increase in visits for children between ages 2 and 5
- Improved quality of prenatal care[65]

The impact evaluation also showed that these results would not have occurred if financing was not conditional on performance. It is important to note, however, that perverse effects can potentially occur if RBF programs are not carefully designed and implemented. These effects include corruption, trying to maximize benefits, and failure to carry out the necessary behaviors in the absence of incentives. In addition, paying for some services and not others may discourage the provision or use of some important services.[66]

Concerns about the sustainability of RBF are also being raised. RBF projects are complex and can take 12–18 months to design.[67] In addition, they require a substantial amount of technical expertise to get off of the ground and there are a limited number of global experts. Furthermore, financial sustainability must be considered. Although inputs and transaction costs vary depending on the approach, RBF can cost as much as $4.82 per capita, per year, as in the USAID Reach Project in Afghanistan.[68] This is a substantial sum in low-income countries that spend little per capita per year on health.

Limited studies have been carried out so far about the cost-effectiveness of RBF approaches, which has also been questioned.[69] A recent systematic review, for example, showed that although "the evidence suggests that conditional cash transfer programs are effective in increasing the use of preventive services and sometimes improving health status . . . further research is needed to clarify the cost effectiveness of conditional cash transfer programs and better understand which components play a critical role."[70] More information is needed on the cost-effectiveness of supply-side schemes, especially in comparison with demand-side approaches. In addition, more research must be done to assess the appropriate size of cash transfers.[71]

The RBF agenda faces a number of challenges besides cost-effectiveness and sustainability. Decentralizing public health systems so that health centers are given true financial autonomy to carry out RBF schemes is a major obstacle. To ensure autonomy, local capacity must be developed, including health management information systems (HMIS), financial management, and training.

CASE STUDIES

Many countries have undertaken efforts to address the key health sector challenges discussed earlier. One consistent theme that arises when looking at those efforts that have succeeded is the importance of community-based approaches to health services at the lowest level. Three cases are discussed below. The first is a very well-known case about the work of BRAC in helping Bangladesh to reduce mortality from diarrhea. This case is complemented in Chapter 10 by a case about Egypt's efforts at spreading the use of oral rehydration therapy. The intervention started by BRAC has been shown to be replicable in other countries and has provided the world with a number of very important lessons about improving health services for the poor in low- and middle-income countries. The second and third cases in this section discuss some interesting efforts in Africa to enhance the effectiveness and efficiency of health systems. They were small in size when the cases were prepared and had not been fully and independently evaluated. However, at the time, they did suggest opportunities for expansion of their approaches that could become important.

The case on Vitamin A and onchocerciasis reviews the attempts by a number of African countries to provide services in more effective and efficient ways by combining the delivery of several programs. This case is complemented by the case in Chapter 15 about the successes in reducing the burden of onchocerciasis in a large number of countries. The third case discusses a pilot project in Tanzania that sought to improve health outcomes by explicitly targeting a larger share of health expenditure on the diseases that most affect the poor.

Combating Diarrheal Disease in Bangladesh

Introduction

In Bangladesh, almost three out of every five infants who die during the first month of life die from diarrhea, pneumonia, and malnutrition, with diarrhea being the major cause. Children under the age of 5, and especially those under 2, have the highest rate of diarrhea and are prone to severe illness and mortality. Diarrhea results in the loss of water and electrolytes, which causes dehydration and subsequent morbidity and mortality. Therefore, it is essential that fluids and electrolytes be replaced.

The Intervention

BRAC is an important nongovernmental organization that is active in health and community development in Bangladesh. In 1980, BRAC began to implement a large-scale intervention to make oral rehydration therapy widely available and easy to administer by nonprofessionals without special equipment. As part of this effort, BRAC taught mothers to prepare oral saline and to treat their children with it. However, because about 80 percent of the population were illiterate, there was concern as this activity got underway that mothers would not be able to prepare the solution accurately and that this could result in their children having high blood sodium rather than overcoming their diarrhea.

Through its Oral Rehydration Teaching Program, BRAC communicated a 10-point health message, including how to prepare the oral rehydration solution (ORS) using local ingredients and accurate measurements. ORS was prepared with a three-finger pinch of common table salt and one fistful of unrefined brown sugar in half a local container (467 cc) of water, and was stirred well. The salt–sugar solution was simple to make, cheap, safe, effective, and the ingredients were readily available.[72]

Female health workers, or oral rehydration workers (ORWs) as they were called, were trained in the preparation of the solution. The ORWs worked in teams to visit every household in each village. One woman/mother in every household was taught 10 critical points using a flip chart with pictorial representations of ORS preparation and diarrhea management. Questions asked on each of the points ensured that the messages were understood before the workers left. Most importantly, the mother had to prepare the solution under the direct supervision of the ORW. The ORWs ensured that the women accurately measured the right amount of water. The process of accurate measurement was reviewed and the women were asked to repeat the preparation process. The team moved from one location to another approximately every 2 weeks.

The Impact

Oral rehydration workers visited all the villages in Bangladesh, except for a few tribal districts. Twelve million households received supervised teaching, and often more than one woman in a household was taught to prepare the ORS. When tested later, over 90 percent of the women knew of and could prepare the solution and about 90 percent of the solutions they prepared were safe and effective. In addition, prior to BRAC's initiation of this program, there was very little knowledge of oral rehydration in Bangladesh, and ORS packets were not available in rural Bangladesh. However, from the mid-1980s, the sale of these packets increased. If all types of diarrhea, mild or moderate, watery or nonwatery, are included, then about half the diarrhea episodes in the following decade were treated with oral rehydration therapy.[73] Furthermore, another study done in the mid-1990s showed that treatment of diarrhea by oral rehydration therapy was known to over 70 percent of children who were 11 to 12 years of age in Bangladesh, 10 to 15 years after their mothers were taught about this method.

The Costs and Benefits

In addition to using its own funds, BRAC also received financial support for this effort from Oxfam, the government of the United Kingdom, the Swedish Free Church Aid, the aid agency of the Swiss government, and the United Nations Children's Fund (UNICEF). The total value of this assistance was about $9.3 million. The cost of teaching one household about oral rehydration therapy was a one-time investment of $0.75.

Lessons Learned

BRAC's intervention in Bangladesh shows that mothers, regardless of their literacy level, can learn to improve health behaviors when provided with the right kind of training. When BRAC started the pilot, the general opinion was that illiterate women would not be able to learn how to measure and mix the ingredients. The strategy chosen by BRAC was not new or unknown to the women—BRAC simply built on their knowledge of cooking and feeding their children. The training was also done in familiar surroundings with ingredients that they use on a daily basis. The women were also taught in groups and found it easier to learn from each other than learning on one's own.

Evaluation of the program indicated some of the characteristics that made scaling up oral rehydration therapy possible. The intervention was relatively simple, requiring no assistance once the method was taught; it was inexpensive, requiring no household expenses, except for the purchase of the salt and sugar. The training and messages were built on existing knowledge and skills, such as childcare and cooking, and were also culturally acceptable. The performance of the ORWs was measured through the knowledge acquired by mothers. Though the program was large, an administrative structure of checks and balances could be put into place along with rigorous supervision. Lastly, there was a clear goal with a specific outcome and an institutional commitment to the process.[73]

NGOs often focus on small populations, which are not representative, and on pilot projects that do not get scaled up. BRAC's effort showed that NGOs are capable of taking to scale pilot or demonstration projects. To do so, however, required strong supervision, supervisor accountability, and local-level flexibility and autonomy. In addition, however, experience with the incentive salary system used by BRAC shows that this approach can only be used when employees who are not effective can be dismissed and not reassigned to any other position or job, as is usually the case for government workers. It is also important that there be tangible and quantifiable outcomes that are relatively easy to measure, and an independent monitoring unit is necessary. Finally, the strategic use of male and female workers allowed female workers to access households and gain the confidence of women, while male workers talked to the men in places where men congregate.

Integrating Services at the Grassroots Level

Introduction

All health systems face the question of how they can most effectively and efficiently provide health services, particularly in difficult to reach areas. Often these programs are carried out in vertical ways. In this case, the program is operated parallel to other programs and may have its own management, staff, financing, and procurement arrangements. It might even have its own facilities. In some settings, this way of operating is undertaken because of extreme weaknesses of the overall health system. However, it would be much more efficient if programs could be carried out in an integrated fashion like they are performed in the health systems of most high-income countries. This case study discusses efforts to integrate the delivery of vitamin A and drugs for onchocerciasis (river blindness) in a number of countries in Africa, in hopes of improving the effectiveness and efficiency of the vitamin A program, the onchocerciasis program, and the overall health system.

As will be discussed in much greater detail in Chapters 8 and 10, vitamin A deficiency is a leading risk factor for under-5 childhood mortality,[74] childhood blindness, and infectious disease in 95 developing countries worldwide. According to the World Health Organization in 2001, 140 million preschool children and more than 7 million pregnant women suffered from vitamin A deficiency. Vitamin A supplementation has proven effective in combating vitamin A deficiency and has therefore become a key intervention to improve child survival. At the time this program was begun, more than 40 percent of the children in sub-Saharan Africa were at risk for vitamin A deficiency. Estimates indicate that correcting vitamin A deficiency would avert more than 645,000 child deaths per year in sub-Saharan Africa.[75]

Onchocerciasis is the second leading infectious cause of blindness in the world and is endemic throughout much of sub-Saharan Africa. It is caused by a parasite, the filaria *Onchocerca volvulus*. The transmission of this parasite to humans takes place through the bite of the blackfly (*Simulium* genus). According to 2005 estimates,[76] about 37 million people were infected with the disease in Africa. Two hundred and seventy thousand people are blind due to onchocerciasis, but it is more than a blinding disease; it can also cause disfiguring skin changes, musculoskeletal problems, weight loss, immune system changes, and, in some cases, epilepsy and growth arrest. Onchocerciasis is commonly found in remote regions where government health services are unavailable.

Ivermectin is the front-line drug used to treat onchocerciasis and is usually delivered through "community-directed treatment." This strategy trains community volunteers to sensitize other community members about the disease and its treatment, and to organize campaigns to distribute ivermectin to eligible members of a community once a year for 15 to 20 years.

The Intervention

Because polio is no longer a threat in most of Africa, African governments are currently phasing out National Immunization Days (NID). This policy change leaves a gap in delivery of vitamin A supplementation to children younger than 5 years, which was previously included in NID campaigns. Nigeria and Cameroon sought, with the assistance of an NGO called Helen Keller International, to bridge this gap by combining vitamin A supplementation with community-directed treatment with ivermectin for river blindness. Both countries had high vitamin A deficiency among young children at the time this program was developed. In Nigeria, 25 percent of the children were vitamin A deficient,[77] and in Cameroon about 40 percent of the children were vitamin A deficient.[78]

Integrating the two treatments seemed logical for a number of reasons. First, both are relatively easy to deliver by trained community volunteers. Second, they target complementary beneficiary groups, thereby providing something for both young children and women who have recently delivered babies. In addition, both rely on similar supply systems and support from Ministries of Health. It was estimated that combining the treatments had the potential to supplement over 11 million children at least once per year with high doses of vitamin A.[74]

To test the integration, pilot studies were conducted in Nigeria, beginning in 2001, and in Cameroon, beginning in 2003, where community-directed treatment with ivermectin was well-established. Careful planning was undertaken with community representatives and Ministry of Health personnel, and training modules and materials were adapted to include vitamin A information and messages. Community volunteers were trained to discuss the practical aspects of how to integrate the two interventions in their village. Volunteers then explained to village residents the importance of vitamin A for child survival and that vitamin A doses would be given only to children from 6 to 59 months of age and to women who had given birth within the last 2 months, during the campaign period. They also discussed the need for a second vitamin A dose for children in 6 months, and the importance of exclusive breastfeeding to protect young children from malnutrition.

The Impact

A program evaluation of the Cameroon pilot showed good results, with high vitamin A supplementation and high ivermectin coverage maintained in all pilot communities. As the project was scaled up in a 2-month campaign, from 1 health district covering under 50,000 people to 15 health districts covering over 642,000 people, vitamin A supplementation coverage was 77 percent among children from 6 to 59 months of age and 90 percent among women who had given birth in the last 2 months. In addition, ivermectin coverage increased from 70.3 percent in 2003 to 74 percent in 2004.

In Nigeria, the integrated program was piloted in two states, reaching more than 300,000 children from 6 to 59 months of age and about 72,000 postpartum women. By 2003 and 2004, the strategy was replicated in an additional four states supported by the State Onchocerciasis Control Programs with assistance from UNICEF, Sight Savers International, and the Mission to Save the Helpless. During the scaling up phase, the pilot program provided supplements to about 950,000 children from 6 to 59 months of age with 80 percent coverage and to about 117,000 women within 6 weeks of giving birth, with 60 percent coverage. Ivermectin coverage did not decline in these areas, but rather was maintained at over 80 percent of the total population, indicating again that community volunteers are able to provide both interventions together.

Costs and Benefits

The cost to integrate vitamin A supplementation into community-directed treatment with ivermectin was minimal compared to implementing two separate interventions. The cost to undertake key community-directed treatment activities, including training, supervision, distribution, and reporting, was cost-shared among the Ministry of Health, nongovernmental organizations, communities, and donors including the African Program for Onchocerciasis Control. Ivermectin is donated by Merck and Co. Inc, through the Mectizan Donation Program to governments.

A World Health Organization cost study[79] found that the average cost of one ivermectin treatment is $0.58, without volunteer time included, and $0.78 if volunteer time was included. In Nigeria, the study found that integrating vitamin A supplementation and ivermectin treatment cost an extra $0.18 per vitamin A treatment but decreased to $0.15 per treatment when scaled up to six states. At the national level, the cost of integrating the two treatments would be $0.10 per vitamin A treatment.

Lessons Learned

Integration means expanding partnerships to include all stakeholders at each level. Advocacy is essential to ensure that governments are willing to bring in relevant partners and commit funding to an integrated approach. To scale up, a strategy must be fully tested and well planned. Ongoing supervision, monitoring, and evaluation are critical during scale-ups to improve program results across a more diverse cultural and geographic area. The vitamin A–ivermectin integrated treatment approach has been or was being adopted by other countries as well, including the Democratic Republic of Congo, Sierra Leone, and Sudan.

Enhancing Community Health Services in Tanzania[80]

Introduction

Tanzania is a low-income country in sub-Saharan Africa. Most people in Tanzania live in rural areas. The burden of disease in Tanzania is typical of that for a low-income African country, with high rates of infant and child mortality, maternal mortality, and high prevalence of malaria, TB, and HIV/AIDS. Until recently, the government of Tanzania was spending about $8 per person each year on health.

The Intervention

The International Development Research Center (IDRC) of Canada and the government of Tanzania established a joint program to determine if health outcomes of poor people in rural areas could be improved by aligning health expenditure more closely with the burden of disease and increasing expenditure on selected health conditions. This effort was called the Tanzania Essential Health Interventions Project and took place in two rural districts with a total population of about 700,000 people.

The program started by trying to map the burden of disease. Given the poor database with which they had to work, this was done by a door-to-door survey of the involved communities to see what people said were the causes of ill health, disability, and death. The program team then calculated the burden of disease and reviewed government expenditure to see if it was being allocated in accordance with that burden.

What they found was substantial gaps between the two. Only 5 percent of the budget went for malaria, although it caused 30 percent of the DALYs lost. Only 13 percent went to the leading causes of DALYs lost in children, despite the fact that they caused 28 percent of the disease burden. In addition, some diseases received more funding than seemed reasonable, given their contributions to the burden of disease and the cost of addressing them.

An additional $2 was allocated to the two pilot communities per person to spend on areas of high disease burden. In addition, the communities began to use simple algorithms for diagnosing and treating common diseases in a standard way, such as diarrhea, pneumonia, and malaria. The health districts also began to order drugs more in line with their needs, rather than just using a common package of drugs sent by the government that did not always meet their needs. Finally, health education was undertaken to get members of the community to use insecticide-treated bed nets when they slept to reduce the likelihood of contracting malaria.

The Outcome

Studies showed that the infant mortality rate decreased from 100 to 78 from the year 1999 to the year 2000 in one of the districts, which was a decrease of 22 percent. The under-5 child mortality rate decreased from 140 to 120 over the same period, which was a drop of 14 percent. It appears that the second district had similar results to the first. Comparable communities that did not participate in this pilot did not see drops in infant and child mortality like those that occurred in the pilot communities. People in the involved communities also decided to build their own health centers so that they do not have to travel so far for health services.

Costs

The communities did not use all of the $2 that was allocated for the program. Rather, to achieve the outcomes noted above, they used only about $0.80, which was equal to about a 10 percent increase in public expenditure per person on health in these two areas.

Lessons Learned

The success of this pilot program appears to have depended on a number of factors. First, the project was carefully planned. Second, the communities were involved in the planning, designing, and execution of the program. Third, the approach of the project was based on good data and evidence about the burden of disease. Fourth, the program focused on implementing low-cost interventions that are known to be highly effective and that targeted health conditions of importance. Finally, the program reflects a point noted in Chapters 2 and 3: The manner in which countries spend money on health is as important as how much they spend. These lessons are consistent with the lessons learned from a variety of other important health programs over the last several decades.

MAIN MESSAGES

A health system is "the combination of resources, organization, and management that culminate in the delivery of health services to the population."[7] The main functions of a health system are to raise money for health services, provide health services, pay for health services, and engage in gover-

nance and regulation of health activities. In line with this, health systems provide prevention, diagnosis, treatment, and rehabilitative services; protect the sick and their families against the cost of ill health; and carry out key public health functions, such as surveillance, the operation of public health laboratories, and food and drug administration. Health systems are important parts of all economies.

Health systems have three levels of health care: primary, secondary, and tertiary. Depending on the country, the public, private, and nongovernmental sectors participate in different parts of the health system. A critical issue in the design of health systems is the roles that each of these sectors should play. There is agreement that governments must regulate and provide oversight of the health system. However, there is also a growing view that the government does not need to provide all services but, instead, should consider how they might most effectively be provided, which could mean government contracting the private or NGO sectors for some services.

The notion of primary health care, as developed at the Alma Ata Conference in 1978, remains very important. Many countries continue to try to provide essential and socially acceptable health services close to the people who need them most. They also seek to embody preventive, promotive, curative, and rehabilitative services in their primary healthcare programs and to link them with higher levels of the health system. Achieving such programs, however, has remained a challenge for many countries, especially low-income countries.

Health systems reflect the unique history and culture of each country. They are also diverse, complex, and very difficult to categorize. One very simplified approach to thinking about health systems, however, considers those that have national health insurance programs, such as Canada, Japan, and Germany; those that are based on a national health service model, like the United Kingdom; and those that have pluralistic systems like that in the United States or India, Nigeria, or the Philippines. When thinking about different approaches to health systems, it is valuable to consider the roles different actors play in the regulation, financing, and provision of services. It is also important to consider the extent to which these systems offer financial protection through insurance, how such insurance is organized, and how insurance is financed.

Countries spend a wide range of their GDP on health, from about 2 percent in Indonesia to about 16 percent in the United States. Countries spend a larger share of their GDP on health as their income grows more developed. Most of the high-income countries have health systems that provide a universal package of insured health benefits. In low-income countries that lack national health insurance, most expenditure on health is private and out-of-pocket. In general, the health systems of high-income countries are more effective at meeting health system aims than are the systems in low- and middle-income countries.

The health systems of all countries, but especially those in low- and middle-income countries, face a number of important challenges, including:

- How to cope with an aging population and increasing amounts of noncommunicable disease
- The quality of governance
- The number, quality, and distribution of healthcare personnel
- The mobilization of sufficient financial resources for the health sector
- How to provide health care at an appropriate level of quality
- How to ensure access to and equitable provision of services
- The creation of mechanisms to provide the poor with protection from the costs of health services

Governance is a difficult issue to address because governance issues are generally problems across all sectors, and not just the health sector. Nonetheless, by giving communities more control over health sector resources, having them openly monitor their use, enhancing the capacity of the health sector to engage in procurement functions, and contracting out services that can most effectively and efficiently be delivered by the private or NGO sectors, governance can be improved.

Ensuring that countries have the right number of trained health personnel in the right places will continue to be difficult. However, there is evidence that different kinds of incentives, such as housing, additional pay, and greater access to training, can encourage health personnel to serve in underserved areas. The productivity of health providers can also be encouraged through appropriate incentives.

It will continue to be difficult for low-income countries to raise the resources they need to finance a cost-efficient package of health services. However, given the potential returns to investments in health, even very poor countries must consider allocating a larger share of their overall resources to health. In addition, existing expenditure on health is very inefficient in many countries and some financial savings can be generated from improving the efficiency of existing expenditure and by allocating a higher share of resources to areas that will yield the highest returns.

The quality of services can be improved, even in low-income settings. Accreditation of services is potentially promising, but not yet a proven way of improving health outcomes. Oversight by senior health staff in structured ways has improved outcomes in some settings. Providing health personnel with clear guidelines, protocols, and algorithms for treatment of patients can also improve the quality of care. There is also increasing evidence that total quality management activities can improve health outcomes, even in very low-income settings. Efforts at improving quality through results-based financing are also becoming more prominent.

Greater attention needs to be paid in most countries to enhancing the coverage by the health system of poor and marginalized populations. One way to do this is to engage these communities in the planning and design of health system interventions. Improving services for the poor and ensuring that these services do not hurt families financially will also require that greater attention be paid to various insurance schemes.

In addition, low- and middle-income countries can help to enhance the health of their poor by moving in the previously noted directions and then focusing expenditure on a package of services that at relatively low-cost will have the highest impact on preventing illness among the poor and on treating those illnesses that most affect them. As discussed further in other chapters, this would include:

- Promoting access to safe water and enhanced sanitation and encouraging improved hygiene
- Enhancing people's food habits and providing selective nutrition supplementation
- Providing a basic package of reproductive health services, including emergency obstetric care
- Providing a basic package of neonatal health services
- Vaccinating and deworming young children, providing oral rehydration for diarrhea, and treating of pneumonia and malaria
- Preventing and treating, as appropriate, HIV, TB, and malaria
- Preventing tobacco use and reducing salt consumption

Study Questions

1. What is a health system?

2. What are the primary functions of a health system?

3. What are primary, secondary, and tertiary health care and what services are generally rendered at each level?

4. How might one compare and contrast the organizational forms of healthcare systems of the United Kingdom, Germany, and the United States?

5. What is the range of public expenditure on health as a share of their GDP that countries spend on health? Why is there such a wide range?

6. Which types of countries tend to have a larger share of private expenditure on health than public expenditure on health? Why is this so, compared to countries that have health systems that are mostly publicly funded?

7. What are some of the significant issues that arise in trying to govern health systems in low- and middle-income countries?

8. What are some of the key human resource challenges that low- and middle-income countries face in staffing and operating their health systems?

9. What are the most important epidemiologic and demographic issues that face health systems and what are the implications of those issues for healthcare costs?

10. What are some of the most important steps that can be taken to improve the effectiveness and efficiency of weaker health systems in low- and middle-income countries?

REFERENCES

1. World Health Organization (WHO). HSP. Available at: http://www.who.int/health-systems-performance/about.htm. Accessed May 6, 2006.

2. Roemer M. *National Health Systems of the World.* Vol 1: The Countries. Oxford, England: Oxford University Press; 1991.

3. Roberts MJ, et al. *Getting Health Reform Right: A Guide to Improving Performance and Equity.* New York: Oxford University Press; 2004.

4. World Health Organization (WHO). *The World Health Report 2000.* Geneva: World Health Organization; 2000.

5. World Health Organization (WHO). Overview. *The World Health Report 2000.* Geneva: World Health Organization; 2000:1.

6. Southby R. Presentation. George Washington University; 2004.

7. World Health Organization. *Everybody's Business: Strengthening Health Systems to Improve Health Outcomes: WHO's Framework for Action.* Geneva: World Health Organization; 2007.

8. Birn A-E, Pillay Y, Holtz TH. *Textbook of International Health.* New York: Oxford University Press; 2009.

9. World Health Organization. *Declaration of Alma-Ata.* International Conference on Primary Health Care; September 6-12, 1978; Alma Ata, USSR. Geneva: World Health Organization; 1978.

10. Bloom G, Champion C, Lucas H, et al. Health markets and future health systems: innovation for equity. *Global Forum Update Res Health.* 5:30-33.

11. World Resources Institute. Biodiversity Glossary of Terms. Available at: www.edu.gov.nf.ca/curriculum/teched/resources/glos-biodiversity.html. Accessed September 22, 2006.

12. World Bank. *Afghanistan Health Sector and Emergency Reconstruction and Development Project.* Washington, DC: World Bank; 2003.

13. World Bank. *Bangladesh Integrated Nutrition Project.* Washington, DC: World Bank; 1995.

14. World Health Organization. Global Health Observatory. Health expenditure ratios. Available at: http://apps.who.int/ghodata. Accessed December 28, 2010.

15. Basch P. *Textbook of International Health.* 2nd ed. New York: Oxford University Press; 2001:376.

16. Brenner G, Rublee D. Germany. In: Fried BJ, Gaydos LM, eds. *World Health Systems: Challenges and Perspectives.* Chicago: Health Administration Press; 2002:121-135.

17. Basch P. *Textbook of International Health.* 2nd ed. New York: Oxford University Press; 2001:121-136.

18. Basch P. *Textbook of International Health.* 2nd ed. New York: Oxford University Press; 2001:376-578.

19. Basch P. *Textbook of International Health.* 2nd ed. New York: Oxford University Press; 2001:380.

20. Office for National Statistics. Expenditure on Health Care in the UK, April 2008. Available at: www.statistics.gov.uk/articles/nojournal/Expenditureonhealth08.pdf. Accessed April 14, 2011.

21. Upshaw VM, Deal KM. The United States of America. In: Fried BJ, Gaydos LM, eds. *World Health Systems: Challenges and Perspectives.* Chicago: Health Administration Press; 2002:67-82.

22. Dow WH, Sáenz LB. Costa Rica. In: Fried BJ, Gaydos LM, eds. *World Health Systems: Challenges and Perspectives.* Chicago: Health Administration Press; 2002:463-473.

23. Portugal R, Abrantes AV. Brazil. In: Fried BJ, Gaydos LM, eds. *World Health Systems: Challenges and Perspectives.* Chicago: Health Administration Press; 2002:404-419.

24. Shah ON. India. In: Fried BJ, Gaydos LM, eds. *World Health Systems: Challenges and Perspectives.* Chicago: Health Administration Press; 2002:495-506.

25. Peters DH, Preker AS, Yazbek AS, et al. *Better Health Systems for India's Poor.* Washington, DC: The World Bank; 2002.

26. Health. Available at: http://www.tanzania.go.tz/health.html. Accessed September 12, 2006.

27. World Health Organization (WHO). Statistical Annex. *The World Health Report 2000.* Geneva: World Health Organization; 2000.

28. Mathers CD, Lopez AD, Murray CJL. The burden of disease and mortality by condition: data, methods, and results for 2001. In: Lopez AD, Mathers CD, Ezzati M, Jamison DT, Murray CJL, eds. *Global Burden of Disease and Risk Factors.* New York: Oxford University Press; 2006:45-93.

29. Lewis M. *Tackling Healthcare Corruption and Governance Woes in Developing Countries.* Washington, DC: Center for Global Development; 2006. Working Paper 78.

30. Physicians for Human Rights. An Action Plan to Prevent Brain Drain: Building Equitable Health Systems in Africa. Available at: http://www.physiciansforhumanrights.org/library/report-2004-july.html. Accessed January 22, 2007.

31. Hongoro C, Normand C. Health workers: building and motivating the workforce. In: Jamison DT, Breman JG, Measham AR, et al, eds. *Disease Control Priorities in Developing Countries.* 2nd ed. New York: Oxford University Press; 2006:1309-1322.

32. Institute of Medicine. *Measuring the Quality of Health Care.* Washington, DC: IOM; 1999.

33. Peabody JW, Taguiwalo MM, Robalino DA, Frenk J. Improving the quality of care in developing countries. In: Jamison DT, Breman JG, Measham AR, et al, eds. *Disease Control Priorities in Developing Countries.* 2nd ed. New York: Oxford University Press; 2006:1293-1307.

34. Beracochea E, Dickenson R, Freemand P, Thomason J. Case management quality assessment in rural areas of Papua New Guinea. *Tropical Doctor.* 1995;25(2):69-74.

35. Thaver IH, Harpham T, McPake B, Garner P. Private practitioners in the slums of Karachi: what quality of care do they offer? *Soc Sci Med.* 1998;46(11):1441-1449.

36. Nolan T, Angos P, Cunha AJ, et al. Quality of hospital care for seriously ill children in less-developed countries. *Lancet.* 2001;357(9250):106-110.

37. Jamison DT, Breman JG, Measham AR, et al, eds. *Priorities in Health.* Washington, DC: World Bank; 2006.

38. Schieber G, Baeza C, Kress D, Maier M. Financing health systems in the 21st century. In: Jamison DT, Breman JG, Measham AR, et al, eds. *Disease Control Priorities in Developing Countries.* 2nd ed. New York: Oxford University Press; 2006:225-242.

39. World Health Organization (WHO). *The World Health Report 2000.* Geneva: World Health Organization; 2000:93-115.

40. Jha P, Chaloupka FJ, Moore J, et al. Tobacco addiction. In: Jamison DT, Breman JG, Measham AR, et al, eds. *Disease Control Priorities in Developing Countries.* 2nd ed. New York: Oxford University Press; 2006:869-885.

41. Norton R, Hyder AA, Bishai D, Peden M. Unintentional injuries. In: Jamison DT, Breman JG, Measham AR, et al, eds. *Disease Control Priorities in Developing Countries.* 2nd ed. New York: Oxford University Press; 2006:737-753.

42. Samb B, Desai N, Nishtar S, et al. Prevention and management of chronic disease: a litmus test for health-systems strengthening in low-income and middle-income countries. *Lancet.* 2010;376:1785-1797.

43. Joint Learning Initiative. *Human Resources for Health: Overcoming the Crisis.* Cambridge, MA: Joint Learning Intiative; 2004.

44. Hongoro C, Normand C. Health workers: building and motivating the workforce. In: Jamison DT, Breman JG, Measham AR, et al, eds. *Disease Control Priorities in Developing Countries.* 2nd ed. New York: Oxford University Press; 2006:1312.

45. Hongoro C, Normand C. Health workers: building and motivating the workforce. In: Jamison DT, Breman JG, Measham AR, et al, eds. *Disease Control Priorities in Developing Countries.* 2nd ed. New York: Oxford University Press; 2006:1313.

46. Hongoro C, Normand C. Health workers: building and motivating the workforce. In: Jamison DT, Breman JG, Measham AR, et al, eds.

Disease Control Priorities in Developing Countries. 2nd ed. New York: Oxford University Press; 2006:1316-1317.

47. World Health Organization (WHO). *The World Health Report 2000.* Geneva: World Health Organization; 2000:73-92.

48. Mills A, Rasheed F, Tollman S. Strengthening health systems. In: Jamison DT, Breman JG, Measham AR, et al, eds. *Disease Control Priorities in Developing Countries.* 2nd ed. New York: Oxford University Press; 2006:87-102.

49. World Health Organization (WHO). *The World Health Report 2000.* Geneva: World Health Organization; 2000:73-91.

50. USAID. Demographic and Health Surveys. Available at: http://www.measuredhs.com/. Accessed September 24, 2006.

51. Peabody JW, Taguiwalo MM, Robalino DA, Frenk J. Improving the quality of care in developing countries. In: Jamison DT, Breman JG, Measham AR, et al, eds. *Disease Control Priorities in Developing Countries.* 2nd ed. New York: Oxford University Press; 2006:1299.

52. Peabody JW, Taguiwalo MM, Robalino DA, Frenk J. Improving the quality of care in developing countries. In: Jamison DT, Breman JG, Measham AR, et al, eds. *Disease Control Priorities in Developing Countries.* 2nd ed. New York: Oxford University Press; 2006:1298.

53. Tollman S, Doherty J, Mulligan J-A. General primary care. In: Jamison DT, Breman JG, Measham AR, et al, eds. *Disease Control Priorities in Developing Countries.* 2nd ed. New York: Oxford University Press; 2006:1193-1210.

54. Liu X, Hotchkiss DR, Bose S. The effectiveness of contracting-out primary health care services in developing countries: a review of the evidence. *Health Policy Plan.* 2008;23:1-13.

55. Sreshthaputra N, Kawmthong I. The universal coverage policy of Thailand: an introduction. A paper prepared for Asia-Pacific Health Economics Network (APHEN). July 19, 2001. http://www.unescap.org/aphen/thailand_universal_coverage.htm.

56. Hughes D, Songkramachai L. Universal coverage in the land of smiles: lessons from Thailand's 30 baht reforms. *Health Aff.* 2007;26(4):999-1008.

57. Musgrove P. Results-Based Financing for Health (RBF). Financial and Other Rewards for Good Performance or Results: A Guided Tour of Concepts and Terms and a Short Glossary. Available at: http://www.rbfhealth.org/rbfhealth/system/files/RBF%20Glossary%20long.pdf. Accessed November 30, 2010.

58. Center for Global Development. Performance Incentives for Global Health: Potential and Pitfalls. 2009:6. Available at: http://www.cgdev.org/doc/books/PBI/01_CGD_Eichler_Levine-Ch1.pdf. Accessed January 4, 2010.

59. Glassman A. Comments presented at The Alphabet Soup of Results-Based Financing (RBF); September 14, 2010; Washington, DC; World Bank. Available at: http://www.rbfhealth.org/rbfhealth/library/doc/392/alphabet-soup-results-based-financing-rbf. Accessed January 4, 2010.

60. Loevinsohn B. Comments presented at The Alphabet Soup of Results-Based Financing (RBF); September 14, 2010; Washington, DC; World Bank. Available at: http://www.rbfhealth.org/rbfhealth/library/doc/392/alphabet-soup-results-based-financing-rbf. Accessed January 4, 2010.

61. The World Bank. Results-Based Financing for Health (RBF). About. Available at: http://www.rbfhealth.org/rbfhealth/about. Accessed January 4, 2010.

62. Center for Global Development. Performance Incentives for Global Health: Potential and Pitfalls. 2009:7. Available at: http://www.cgdev.org/doc/books/PBI/01_CGD_Eichler_Levine-Ch1.pdf. Accessed January 4, 2010.

63. The World Bank. Results-Based Financing for Health (RBF). Brazil: Results-Based Financing (RBF) Helps Achieve Decline in Family Poverty. Available at: http://www.rbfhealth.org/rbfhealth/news/item/320/brazil-results-based-financing-rbf-helps-achieve-decline-family-poverty. Accessed November 30, 2010.

64. The World Bank. Results-Based Financing for Health (RBF). Mexico's Model Conditional Cash Transfer (CCT) Program for Fighting Poverty. Available at: http://www.rbfhealth.org/rbfhealth/news/item/406/mexico%E2%80%99s-model-conditional-cash-transfer-cct-program-fighting-poverty. Accessed November 30, 2010.

65. The World Bank. Paying Primary Health Care Centers for Performance in Rwanda. January 2010. Available at: http://siteresources.worldbank.org/EXTDEVDIALOGUE/Images/537296-1238422761932/5968067-1269375819845/Rwanda_P4P.pdf. Accessed January 4, 2010.

66. The World Bank. Results-Based Financing (RBF) for Health. Cure, Curse, or Mixed Blessing? Available at: http://www.rbfhealth.org/rbfhealth/library/doc/cure-curse-or-mixed-blessing. Accessed January 4, 2010.

67. USAID. PBI Primer for USAID Missions. July 2010. Available at: http://www.healthsystems2020.org/content/resource/detail/2653. Accessed January 4, 2010.

68. KIT Development Policy and Practice. Performance Based Financing: An International Review of the Literature. Available at: http://www.kit.nl/net/KIT_Publicaties_output/ShowFile2.aspx?e=1533. Accessed November 30, 2010.

69. Brenzel L. Evaluating the Cost and Financial Impact of RBF Schemes. Presentation. October 2010. Available at: http://www.rbfhealth.org/rbfhealth/system/files/1_Tools%20for%20Impact%20Analysis%20Costing%20and%20Cost%20effectiveness_Brenzel_ENG.pdf. Accessed January 4, 2010.

70. Lagarde M, Haines A, Palmer N. Conditional cash transfers for improving uptake of health interventions in low- and middle-income countries: a systematic review. *JAMA.* 2007;298:1900-1910.

71. SUPPORT. Summary of a Systematic Review: Do Conditional Cash Transfers Improve the Uptake of Health Interventions in Low and Middle-Income Countries? August 2008. Available at: http://apps.who.int/rhl/effective_practice_and_organizing_care/SUPPORT_cash_transfers.pdf. Accessed January 4, 2010.

72. Chowdhury S. Educating Mothers for Health—Output Based Incentives for Teaching Oral Rehydration in Bangladesh. Available at: http://rru.worldbank.org/Documents/Other/11ch6.pdf. Accessed January 22, 2007.

73. Chowdhury A, Cash R. *A Simple Solution: Teaching Millions to Treat Diarrhea at Home.* Dhaka: University Press; 1996.

74. Beaton, GH, Martorell R, Aronson KJ, et al. *Effectiveness of VAS in the Control of Young Children Morbidity and Mortality in Developing Countries.* Geneva: World Health Organization; 1993. ACC/SSN nutrition policy discussion paper 13.

75. Aguayo V, Baker S. Vitamin A deficiency and child survival in sub-Saharan Africa: a reappraisal of challenges and opportunities. *Food Nutri Bull.* 2005;26(4):348-355.

76. World Health Organization. *Report of the Joint Action Forum of the African Program for Onchocerciasis Control.* Geneva: World Health Organization; December 2005.

77. Maziya-Dixon B, Akinyele IO, Oguntona EB, Nokoe S, Sanusi RA, Harris E. Nigeria Food Consumption and Nutrition Survey 2001–2003: Summary. Available at: http://old.iita.org/cms/details/NFC.pdf. Accessed May 20, 2011.

78. Haselow N, Obadiah M, Akame J. The Integration of Vitamin A Supplementation into Community-Directed Treatment with Ivermectin: A Practical Guide for Africa. Available at: http://www.hki.org/research/Guide_Integ_VitA_CDTI_Africa.pdf. Accessed May 20, 2011.

79. McFarland D, et al. *Study of Cost per Treatment with Ivermectin Using CDTI Strategy.* WHO/APOC; August 2005.

80. For 80 cents more: even a tiny health budget, if spent well, can make a difference. *Econ.* 2002(August 15). Available at: http://www.economist.com/node/1280587?story_id=1280587. Accessed May 20, 2011.

CHAPTER 6

Culture and Health

By the end of this chapter the reader will be able to:

- Define *culture*
- Describe the most important relationships between culture and health
- Outline some of the theories of how behavior change occurs in health
- Describe some key measures to promote behavior change for better health
- Discuss the importance of social assessments

VIGNETTES

Joshua was just older than 1 year of age and lived in eastern Zimbabwe. His mother could tell that he had a fever. She wondered what had caused it. Was it the food that he ate? Was it the mixing of the "hot" foods and the "cold" foods? Or was it possible that they had done something to offend local custom? If the fever did not get better tomorrow, then she would take Joshua to the local healer.

Siu-Hong was 80 years old and lived in Hong Kong. He had a severe toothache for more than a week. His children repeatedly encouraged him to go to the dentist, but he would not go. He did not like dentists or "Western medicine." In addition, he would have to wait in line to be seen at the dentist's office and would miss work at the clothes market. His children finally convinced him to go to the dentist by giving him a "present" of $25 and offering to take him to "dim sum," the traditional South Chinese "brunch."

Dorji lived in Bhutan, just outside the capital city of Thimpu. He felt tired, weak, and dizzy for some time but had no fever. After another week of feeling this way, Dorji went to visit his local health clinic. Each clinic in Bhutan had two medical practitioners, one who practiced the indigenous system of medicine and the other who practiced "Western biomedical medicine."[1] In light of Dorji's symptoms, he visited the indigenous practitioner inside the clinic. The "doctor" gave him some herbs that he thought would help his condition. However, he also thought Dorji had an underlying infection and took him across the hall to the "other doctor" who prescribed antibiotics for him.

Arathi was a young mother in southeast India. She and the other women in her village were participating in the Tamil Nadu Nutrition Project. They were all young mothers, many of whose babies were underweight for their age. Arathi nursed her baby as she had learned from her mother to do. She also gave the baby some other foods as she had learned from her mother and grandmother. Despite this, her baby was quite small for her age. As part of the project, the community nutrition workers taught all the women and children in the village songs about proper feeding and about the vitamins the children needed. They also sponsored weekly weighing parties, in which all of the babies of the village were weighed and the mothers together decided if the baby was growing properly and what could be done to make the baby healthier. They also helped the mothers to make a food supplement for the babies who were "too small."

THE IMPORTANCE OF CULTURE TO HEALTH

Culture is an important determinant of health in a number of ways, as discussed in Chapter 2. First, culture is related to health behaviors. People's attitudes toward foods and what they eat, for example, are closely related to culture. The food that pregnant women eat, birthing practices, and how long women breastfeed are also linked to their cultural backgrounds. Hygiene practices are closely tied to culture, as well. Second, culture is an important determinant of people's perceptions of illness. Different culture groups may have different beliefs about what constitutes good health and what constitutes illness. Third, the extent to which people use health services is also very closely linked with culture. Some groups may use health services as soon as they feel ill. Others, however, may visit health practitioners only when they are very sick. Fourth, different cultures have different practices concerning health and medical treatment. Chinese and Indian cultures have well-defined systems of medicine. There is a long history in many other societies, as well, of local systems of medicine that include notions of illness, various types of practitioners of medicine, and different kinds of medicines.

The purpose of this chapter is to introduce you to the most important links between health and culture, particularly as they relate to global health and people in low- and middle-income countries. The chapter begins by introducing you to the concept of "culture." It then examines how views of health, illness, the use of health services, and the role of different health providers vary by culture. The chapter also reviews some of the theories of behavior change that relate to enhancing people's health. The chapter concludes with four policy and program briefs that reflect some of the critical relationships between culture and health and how they need to be taken into account in efforts to improve health.

As you review this chapter, it is important to note that some cultural values enhance health. A culture, for example, that puts a strong emphasis on monogamy in marriage should have lower rates of HIV/AIDS than cultures in which having multiple sexual partners is more tolerated. However, some cultural values may not enhance health. A cultural emphasis on heaviness in people, for example, as a sign of prosperity or wealth, may be harmful to health, because it would encourage cardiovascular disease and diabetes. Some cultures have food taboos that prevent pregnant women from getting all of the nutrients they need in pregnancy. This chapter aims to help you to understand the relationship between culture and health, identify practices helpful and hurtful to good health, and learn about approaches to promoting healthier behaviors.

THE CONCEPT OF CULTURE

The concept of culture was developed at the end of the 19th century by anthropologists. There have been many defini-

tions of culture. An early definition suggested that culture was:

> that complex whole which includes knowledge, beliefs, art, law, morals, custom and any other capabilities and habits acquired by man as a member of society.[2]

A relatively modern definition states that culture is "a set of rules or standards shared by members of a society, which when acted upon by the members, produce behavior that falls within a range of variation the members consider proper and acceptable."[3] In the simplest terms, one may call culture "behavior and beliefs that are learned and shared."[4]

Cultures operate in a variety of domains, including:

- The family
- Social groups beyond the actor's family
- Individual growth and development
- Communication
- Religion
- Art
- Music
- Politics and law
- The economy[4]

As one thinks about the links between culture and health, it is also important to understand the term *society*, which refers to "a group of people who occupy a specific locality and share the same cultural traditions."[3] Societies have social structures that are the "relationships of groups within society that hold it together."[5] In addition, we must note that there is heterogeneity within all cultures. Sometimes this is reflected in what people call subcultures. There are many shared aspects, for example, of Chinese culture. However, China is a very large country, and even among the Han Chinese, there are important variations as one moves across China in language, food, wedding customs, and music, among other things. The same would be true of North India. People across North India have much in common. Yet, there are many variations of North Indian culture in different places, such as in the state of West Bengal, on the one hand, and Rajasthan, on the other. This can be seen, again, in language, music, art, and food.

When thinking about the links between culture and health, one also needs to consider that some cultural practices may be well adapted to some settings but poorly adapted to others. Alternatively, they may be well adapted to the way people have been living, but less well adapted to the way people live after important changes or developments in their communities.[6] The culture of nomadic people, for example, may be well suited to their nomadic lifestyle. However, their culture may be very ill equipped to deal with a lifestyle after societal change that would cause them to be more sedentary.

As we consider the relationship between culture and health, we should be aware of the ways in which a culture is viewed by people from outside that culture group. This helps us to understand when we are looking at something from our perspective, compared to looking at it from the perspective of those who live within that culture.

Especially in the early days of anthropology, those who studied cultures other than their own often viewed them solely through the prism of their own society and judged much of what they saw to be lacking. This view is called ethnocentrism. Contrary to this view is "cultural relativism," or the idea that "because cultures are unique, they can be evaluated only according to their own standards and values."[7]

The approach that will guide the rest of this chapter and, indeed, the book as a whole, is the question: "How well does a given culture satisfy the physical and psychological needs of those whose behavior it guides?"[7] For example, is female circumcision, also called female genital mutilation, a health-enhancing procedure or a harmful procedure? Is it good or bad for the health of a newborn to be given sugar water? How should one see cultural practices that discriminate against women and cause them to eat less well than men or that might lead to the disproportionate abortion of female fetuses, as in India and China? On the other hand, what about cultures that do encourage exclusive breastfeeding for 6 months? What about male circumcision, which is associated with reduced transmission of HIV?

You will realize as you make your way through the book that those responsible for guiding health policies and programs in different countries must have a good understanding of the cultures with which they are working if they are to be helpful in enhancing health for the members of those societies. This is also true of outsiders, including development assistance agencies. They must be very sensitive to local cultures, while simultaneously considering with their government partners and in conjunction with insiders to the culture, what behavior changes may be needed to enhance individual and population health in a particular setting.[8]

HEALTH BELIEFS AND PRACTICES

Different cultures vary in their perceptions of the body and their views of what is illness, what causes illness, and what should be done about it. They have different views on how to prevent health problems, what health care they should seek, and the types of remedies that health providers might offer.[4] This section will highlight selected aspects of belief systems about health that one would see most in low- and middle-income countries and in immigrant populations in high-income countries.

Perceptions of Illness

Perceptions of illness vary considerably across culture groups. What one culture may view as entirely normal, for example, another culture may see as an affliction. Worms are so common among children in some cultures that people do not see infection with worms as an illness. Malaria is so common in much of sub-Saharan Africa that many families see it as normal. In much of South Asia, back pain among women is very common and is also seen by women as just a normal part of being a woman.[9] Schistosomiasis is very common in Egypt. It causes blood in the urine, which is referred to in Egypt as "male menstruation" and seen as normal because it is so common.[10]

Perceptions of Disease

Medical anthropologists, among others, define disease as the "malfunctioning or maladaptation of biologic and psychophysiologic processes in the individual."[11] Pneumonia is a disease. HIV/AIDS is a disease. Polio is a disease. Illness, however, is different from disease. "Illness represents personal, interpersonal, and cultural reactions to disease or discomfort."[11] People may feel like they have an illness. They can describe it and its symptoms. They may have a name in their culture for this problem: However, they may not have a "disease," which is a physiological condition. This is a very important point, because different cultures may have very different perceptions of the causes of illness.

Most people in high-income countries follow the "Western medical paradigm" in explaining the causes of disease. This will be familiar to you. You get influenza and colds from viruses. You get diabetes as an adult from an inability to control your blood sugar, although there may be a genetic component to this. You get heart disease from smoking, from being obese, or from having cholesterol that is too high.

On the other hand, many people, especially those in or from low- and middle-income countries and more "traditional societies" often see illness as being caused by factors other than disease, as defined in the biomedical model. There are many cultures, for example, that believe that illness is brought on by the body being "out of balance." Among the most common of these concepts is the notion of "hot" and "cold." In this case, the body may get out of balance if one engages in certain unhealthy practices. In some cultures, some foods are regarded as "hot" and some foods are regarded as "cold" and people are supposed to achieve a balance between these foods to avoid illness.

Many people also believe that illness has supernatural causes. A study done among Americans of Caribbean and African descent living in the southern United States showed that many people believed that the symptoms of illness stem from supernatural causes.[12] There are many cultures in which people believe that illness comes from being affected by "the evil eye," being bewitched or possessed, losing their soul, or offending gods.[13] Some First Nations people in Canada have a belief that "illness is not necessarily a bad thing, but instead a sign sent by the Creator to help people re-evaluate their lives."[14] A study of the cultural perceptions of illness among Yoruba people in Nigeria found that illness could be "traced to enemies, including witchcraft, sorcery, gods, ancestors, natural illnesses, or hereditary illness."[15]

Emotional stresses are also seen in different cultures as causes of illness. This could come about as a result of being stressed or extremely frightened. Being too envious is also viewed as a cause of illness.[13] Sexual matters are seen as causes of illness in some cultures, as well. In several cultures, for example, frequent sexual relations is believed to weaken men, by taking away their blood.[13] These beliefs are quite common in parts of India.

Folk Illness

Many cultures also have what are called "folk illnesses." These are local cultural interpretations of physical states that people perceive to be illness, but that do not have a physiologic cause. "Empacho" is an illness that is commonly described in a number of Latin American cultures. This is often discussed as a condition caused by food that "gets stuck to the walls of the stomach or intestines, causing an obstruction."[16] It is said to be caused by any of a variety of inappropriate food practices, and in children it is said to produce a number of gastrointestinal symptoms, including bloating, diarrhea, and a stomachache.

To cure empacho, families may limit some foods, give abdominal massages with warm oil, or pop the skin on the small of the back. They will also often consult a local healer, such as the *santiguadora* in the Puerto Rican community and *sobadora* in the Mexican community. Some Mexican communities in both the United States and Mexico also treat this "illness" with powders.

To understand health problems in low- and middle-income countries, it is very important to understand the existence of folk illnesses such as empacho. It may be that the condition described by communities as empacho has no known or real biomedical basis. However, even if this condition has no biomedical basis, people believe this is an important illness, and any efforts to improve the health of the community will have to consider such beliefs.[16] Table 6-1 lists some of the culturally defined causes of illness.

The Prevention of Illness

Given the wide range of views of what causes illness, it is not surprising that there are many different cultural practices that concern avoiding illness. Many cultures, for example, have taboos, or things that they forbid people to do if they are to stay healthy. A large number of taboos concern what not to eat during pregnancy, as was suggested in a study of traditional beliefs in Western Malaysia, which indicated that pregnant women should avoid certain important sources of protein.[17] A study in southern Nigeria about traditional

TABLE 6-1 Selected Examples of Cultural Explanations of Disease

Body Balances	Emotional	Supernatural	Sexual
Temperature	Fright	Bewitching	Sex with forbidden
Energy	Sorrow	Demons	person
Blood	Envy	Spirit possession	Overindulgence in sex
Dislocation	Stress	Evil eye	
Problems with organs		Offending God or gods	
Incompatibility of horoscopes		Soul loss	

Source: Adapted from Scrimshaw SC. Culture, behavior, and health. In: Merson MH, Black RE, Mills A, eds. *International Public Health: Diseases, Programs, Systems, and Policies.* Sudbury, MA: Jones and Bartlett; 2006:53-78.

beliefs concerning eating in pregnancy found widespread belief that pregnant women must avoid:

- Sweet foods, so the baby would not be weak
- Eggs, so the baby would not grow up to be a thief
- Snails, so the baby would not be dull, salivate excessively, or not develop speech properly[18]

A study in Brazil suggested that women should not eat game meat and fish during pregnancy, although both could be good sources of protein.[19] A study of poor women in South India showed that "taboos affected the intake of fruits and legumes" and legumes are among the most important sources of protein for many Indian women.[20]

There is also a wide array of ritual practices that people undergo to avoid illness. Related to this, there are traditions in some cultures to get rid of bad spirits or evil forces to ensure that one does not fall ill. There are beliefs among the Yoruba people in Nigeria, for example, that charms, amulets, scarification, or some oral potions can prevent illness that is caused by one's enemies.[15] Some tribal groups in Rajasthan, India, put charms at certain crossings to inflict harm on others, to avoid harm to themselves, to appease an evil spirit, or to leave their affliction there with the spirit.[21] In rural Senegal, a special ritual is performed for women who have lost two children, or had two miscarriages, or appear to be infertile. The ritual is intended to prevent the causes of child death and infertility.[22]

The Diagnosis and Treatment of Illness and the Use of Health Services

In many cultures, when people are ill, it is common that they first try to care for the illness themselves with home remedies. This is often followed by a visit to some type of local healer and the use of indigenous medicines from that healer. Only if the illness does not resolve after that will families seek the help of a "Western doctor." Even then, it is quite common for people to use modern medicines and indigenous medicines at the same time.

Studies that were done on the treatment of diarrheal disease in Central America showed very clearly, for example, that people tried a variety of mechanisms for diagnosing and treating their illnesses.

The manner in which people and families care for illnesses is called "patterns of resort." People seek help from different healthcare providers at different times for a number of reasons.[23] One important concern is the cost of services, both direct, such as fees, and indirect, such as the cost of transportation, time en route, or waiting. Another concern

is the means of payment. People with little cash may prefer to visit a healer or doctor who takes payment in kind, rather than in cash. This could be in small gifts or payment in farm products such as fruits, vegetables, or poultry. People are also driven by the reputation of the provider. They will go to a provider that is reputed in their community to have good results over a provider who does not enjoy this type of reputation.

The manner in which the provider treats them socially is also an important determinant of the use of services. People generally prefer to go to a provider who is from their community, speaks their language, is known to them, and treats them with respect, rather than an outsider who may be disrespectful. It is interesting to note that people tend to treat folk illnesses at home and then go to a local healer. As a last resort, they may go to a physician, even if they understand that the physician "does not treat empacho."[16]

It is also very important to understand the extent to which a large share of the treatment of illness in most cultures takes place first at home. People in high-income countries may take some aspirin, drink plenty of water, eat a certain soup, and try to rest when they first develop symptoms. They may also take a variety of different types of herbal products or vitamins. Only if people do not feel better by a certain time will they try to see a health provider. People in more traditional societies have analogous patterns of behavior when they believe themselves to be ill. Understanding these patterns, of course, is central to any efforts to enhance their health through efforts such as maternal care, vaccination programs, or treatment of infectious diseases, such as AIDS, TB, or malaria.

Health Providers

There are a many different types of health service providers. Some of these are shown in Table 6-2. As you can see in the table, some of the providers are practitioners of indigenous systems of medicine, such as ayurvedic practitioners in India and practitioners of Chinese systems of medicine, such as herbalists and acupuncturists. Other practitioners will be part of a wide array of local health providers. These include, for example, traditional birth attendants, priests, herbalists, and bonesetters. The types of practitioners of Western medicine will depend on the size and location of the place in which they work and could include, for example, community health workers, nurses, midwives, nurse-midwives, physicians, and dentists. You should also be aware that in many low- and middle-income countries, pharmacists, or stores that sell drugs, also frequently dispense both drugs and medical advice. Although prescriptions for drugs may

TABLE 6-2 Selected Examples of Health Service Providers

Indigenous	Western Biomedical	Other Medical Systems
Midwives	Pharmacists	Chinese medical system
Shamans	Nurse-midwives	• Practitioners
Curers	Nurses	• Chemists/herbalists
Spirtualists	Nurse-practitioners	• Acupuncturists
Witches	Physicians	Ayurvedic practitioners
Sorcerers	Dentists	
Priests		
Diviners		
Herbalists		
Bonesetters		

Source: Adapted from Scrimshaw SC. Culture, behavior, and health. In: Merson MH, Black RE, Mills A, eds. *International Public Health: Diseases, Programs, Systems, and Policies.* Sudbury, MA: Jones and Bartlett; 2006:53-78.

be legally required, many low- and middle-income countries are unable or unwilling to enforce this requirement. It is also important to note that many healthcare providers will combine indigenous health practices with Western medicine.[24]

HEALTH BEHAVIORS AND BEHAVIOR CHANGE

As you saw in Chapter 2, the leading causes of death in low- and middle-income countries are ischemic heart disease, cerebrovascular disease, HIV, and pneumonia. Malaria, TB, and diarrhea are also among the top 10 causes of death in these countries.[25] The risk factors for these diseases and conditions include nutrition (both undernutrition and overnutrition), tobacco use, unsafe sex, and unsafe water and sanitation.[26] There are many behaviors that *are* conducive to good health. However, what is the extent to which behavior is a contributing factor to the leading risk factors for illness and premature death in low- and middle-income countries? A number of examples are discussed next.

An infant's being underweight for age is the most important risk factor for premature death in low-income countries. Although income and education are closely linked with nutritional status of both mother and child, cultural variables are also important determinants of their nutrition. As noted earlier, many cultures have food taboos for pregnant women that are not helpful to birth outcomes, and other cultures encourage pregnant women to eat less rather than more. In addition, the extent to which women breastfeed their babies is closely linked with culture, as is the timing for the introduction of complementary foods. Undernutrition also stems from other eating practices that are also closely

tied to culture. Can behaviors be changed so that pregnant women will eat the most nutritious foods they can, given their level of income, and exclusively breastfeed their babies for 6 months?

Unsafe sex is the major risk factor for HIV/AIDS in low-, middle-, and high-income countries. Some people, such as commercial sex workers, may not have the bargaining power with their clients to negotiate sex with a condom. The same will often be true of women who are forced into unsafe sex by their husbands and boyfriends or because of their own economic position, as you will read about in Chapters 9 and 11. However, many people who engage in unsafe sex do have control over whether or not to use a condom. What would it take to ensure that they do so?

Hygiene is another area that closely relates to health behaviors, and the lack of safe water and sanitation is a major risk factor for diarrheal disease. In many low- and middle-income countries hygiene may be low, and families need to learn to use water safely, dispose of human waste in sanitary ways, and wash their hands with soap after defecating. Behaviors regarding hygiene, of course, are intimately linked with culture. How can they be changed?

As you will read about later, indoor air pollution is a major risk factor for respiratory infections. This relates largely to the fact that families in many cultures cook indoors without appropriate ventilation. Some families may not be able to afford an improved stove. However, other families cook as they do because of tradition and the lack of knowledge of the health impacts of indoor air pollution. How could the way people cook be changed?

Cigarettes are the leading risk factor for cardiovascular disease and cancer, as you will read more about in Chapter 12. Most people who smoke cigarettes start smoking as adolescents. Are there measures that can be taken to change these behaviors? How would the efforts to change behavior have to differ if one tried to stop adolescents from taking up smoking, compared to helping adult smokers to quit?

Of course, behaviors are closely linked with culture and health not only in developing countries, but also in developed countries. Moreover, in developed, as well as in developing countries, there is a wide array of behaviors that do not promote good health. In the developed countries, for example, an increasing number of people are obese and have diabetes, associated, as you will read in Chapter 12, with poor diet and a sedentary lifestyle. Many people also continue to smoke, even though smoking is the single largest risk factor for both cardiovascular disease and cancer. Despite the widespread availability of seat belts in cars, some people still do not use them. What needs to be done to get people to change these behaviors to ones that are healthier?

Improving Health Behaviors

There are a number of models or theories that explain why people engage in certain health behaviors and what can be done to encourage changes in those behaviors. Those interested in greater detail in health behaviors can review *The Essentials of Health Behavior*, another book in this series.[27] Some of the most important concepts about health behavior and models about behavior change, however, are examined very briefly here.

The Ecological Perspective

As one considers the factors that influence behaviors that relate to health, it is important to take what is called an ecological perspective. This is a concept that suggests that the factors influencing health behaviors occur at several levels. These are noted in Table 6-3.

The basic precepts concerning the ecological approach are:

- "Health related behaviors are affected by, and affect, multiple levels of influence: intrapersonal or individual factors, interpersonal factors, institutional factors, community factors, and public policy factors."
- "Behavior both influences and is influenced by the social environments in which it occurs."[28]

You can try to imagine, for example, whether or not an adolescent male will take up smoking. This will depend on how he feels about smoking, what he thinks others think of his smoking, the setting in which he operates, how expensive

TABLE 6-3 The Ecological Perspective

Factors	Definition
Individual	Individual characteristics that influence behavior such as knowledge, attitudes, beliefs, and personality traits
Interpersonal	Interpersonal processes, and primary groups including family, friends, and peers
Institutional	Rules, regulations, policies, and informal structures
Community	Social networks and norms or standards that exist formally or informally among individuals, groups, and organizations
Public policy	Local, state, and federal policies and laws that regulate or support healthy actions and practices for disease prevention, early detection, control, and management

Source: Adapted with permission from Murphy E. *Promoting Healthy Behavior, Health Bulletin 2*. Washington, DC: Population Reference Bureau; 2005.

it is to buy cigarettes, and how easy it is to buy them. Of course, if he does start smoking, some of his own peer group may follow.

The Health Belief Model

The Health Belief model was the first effort to articulate a coherent understanding of the factors that enter into health behaviors. It was developed by the U.S. Public Health Services as they tried to understand why people did or did not avail themselves of the opportunity to get chest x-rays for tuberculosis.[29] The premises of this model are that people's health behaviors depend on their perceptions of:

- Their likelihood of getting the illness
- The severity of the illness if they get it
- The benefits of engaging in behavior that will prevent the illness
- The barriers to engaging in preventive behavior

In this model, people's health behavior also depends on whether or not people feel that they could actually carry out the appropriate behavior if they tried, which is called *self-efficacy*.[28]

One could think about how this model pertains to engaging in safe sex. The extent to which a young man uses a condom will be influenced by his fear of getting HIV/AIDS, how serious a disease he believes it to be, the extent to which a condom can prevent HIV/AIDS, and how easy it is to buy a condom and get a partner to agree to use it. The young man must also feel that he will buy the condom and use it.

Stages of Change Model

The Stages of Change model was developed in the 1990s in the United States in conjunction with work on alcohol and drug abuse.[28] The premise behind this model is that change in behavior is a process and that different people are at different stages of readiness for change. The stages of change are outlined in Table 6-4.

It is easy to see how this model might apply to alcohol and drug abuse. You can imagine an excessive drinker, as discussed in Chapter 12, who is not aware of his problem or who will not face it and needs help in doing so. Other people, who are aware of their problem and willing to do something about it, may need help to stop. Still others, who have already broken their addictions, need positive reinforcement to maintain their health.[28]

The Diffusion of Innovations Model

The Diffusion of Innovations model had its origins in work that was done on promoting agricultural change in the United States. In this model, "an innovation is an idea, practice, service, or other object that is perceived as new by the individual or group."[30] This model is based on the notion that communication is needed to promote social change and that "diffusion" is the process by which innovations are communicated over time among members of different groups and societies.[31] This model focuses on how people adopt and can be encouraged to adopt "innovations," but does not get involved with how they might maintain what they have adopted.

Table 6-5 outlines the stages that have to be undertaken to try to diffuse a health innovation.

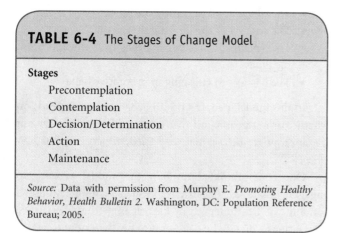

TABLE 6-4 The Stages of Change Model

Stages
  Precontemplation
  Contemplation
  Decision/Determination
  Action
  Maintenance

Source: Data with permission from Murphy E. *Promoting Healthy Behavior, Health Bulletin 2.* Washington, DC: Population Reference Bureau; 2005.

TABLE 6-5 Diffusions of Health Innovations Model

Stages of Diffusion
  Recognition of a problem or need
  Conduct of basic and applied research to address the specific problem
  Development of strategies and materials that will put the innovative concept into a form that will meet the needs of the target population
  Commercialization of the innovation, which will involve production, marketing, and distribution efforts
  Diffusion and adoption of the innovation
  Consequences associated with adoption of the innovation

Source: Adapted from Scrimshaw SC. Culture, behavior, and health. In: Merson MH, Black RE, Mills A, eds. *International Public Health: Diseases, Programs, Systems, and Policies.* Sudbury, MA: Jones and Bartlett; 2006:53-78.

This model also suggests that as the innovation begins to be diffused, people will fall into six groups:

- Innovators
- Early adopters
- Early majority
- Late majority
- Late adopters
- Laggards[30,31]

In addition, the model also indicates that the pace of adoption will be influenced by:

- The gains people think they will get by adopting the innovation
- How much the innovation fits in with their existing culture and values
- How easy it is to try out the innovation
- Whether or not there are role models who are already trying out the innovation
- The extent to which potential adopters see the innovation as cost-efficient and not taking too much of their time, energy, or money[30,31]

One can imagine how the Diffusion of Innovations model may apply to efforts to change diets in high-income countries away from certain fats and toward more fruits and vegetables, fewer processed foods, and more whole grains. Some people change their diets relatively quickly. Others in the community make these shifts only as they can overcome some of their long held dietary patterns. Some people shift as they learn more from their friends, some of whom become role models for change. The relatively high costs of some of the organic and other healthy foods may be a constraint to adoption of change by some people. Others may simply not be willing or able to change the way they and their families have always eaten.

UNDERSTANDING AND ENGENDERING BEHAVIOR CHANGE

As you can clearly see, in many instances, improving health requires that the behaviors of individuals, families, and communities be changed. You also see, however, that behaviors are intimately connected to culture, which is inherently not easy to change. Under these circumstances, what can be done, first to understand what behaviors need to be changed and, second, to change them? These questions are answered briefly here.

Understanding Behaviors

A first step in trying to promote behavior change must be to gain a good understanding of the behaviors that are taking place. This requires a careful assessment of:

- The behaviors that are taking place
- The extent to which they are helpful or harmful to health
- The underlying motivation for these behaviors
- The likely responses to different approaches to changing the unhealthy behaviors

By taking a look at breastfeeding, for example, we can get a sense of how one would carry out such an assessment. One can consider how infant deaths might be reduced. As part of this effort, it is important to get a better sense of the extent to which any nutritional issues are harmful to infant health and how they might be improved. One important part of this effort would be to examine breastfeeding practices. In doing so, we would try to answer the following questions, among others:

- When do women start breastfeeding?
- Do they feed on schedule or on demand?
- Do they feed male and female children the same way?
- For how long do they breastfeed exclusively?
- At what age do they introduce complementary foods?
- Until what age do they continue to breastfeed, even while the children are getting complementary foods?
- Why do they engage in these practices?
- Why do some women not breastfeed?
- Who breastfeeds and who does not?
- Who has influence over their breastfeeding practices?

The answers to these questions, of course, will vary by culture group; however, once we get answers to them, we can begin to formulate a plan for behavior change that is built on the cultural values and approaches of the people. Without understanding current practices, the rationale for them, and who has influence over them, it will be impossible to promote behavior change in the appropriate directions. When we do have a sense of the existing practices and why they take place, what can be done to change behaviors?

Changing Health Behaviors

There are many different approaches to changing health behaviors. Some operate at the level of the individual, some at the level of the community, and some at the level of society as a whole. Generally, they include some combination of communication through the mass media and more personal communication. Several approaches to behavior change are discussed briefly here.

Community Mobilization

One very important way to encourage change in health behaviors is to engage in community mobilization. In this case, the effort focuses on getting an entire community to engage in the effort of promoting more healthy behaviors. This requires considerable efforts aimed at helping people across the community to identify the problems that they face and potential solutions to them, and then working together to implement those solutions. Generally, it also requires that the leaders within the community are themselves mobilized, willing to be "champions" for the needed change, and then promote that change.[28] You will read more later, for example, about the Tamil Nadu Nutrition Project, which was noted in one of the vignettes at the opening of this chapter, and the manner in which the affected communities were involved in promoting a variety of innovations, including weighing babies together, identifying together the babies who were not thriving, and working together to make supplementary food for their children. In addition, all of the community was involved in learning about appropriate foods and about needed micronutrients. You will also read later about a variety of community-based activities, including efforts to address diarrheal disease through oral rehydration in Egypt and polio campaigns in Latin America.

Mass Media

The mass media is often used to promote change in health behaviors. Most people in low- and middle-income countries have access to radio, which is often used for this purpose.

Increasingly, however, those engaged in promoting better health are using a tool referred to as "entertainment-education." Many of these efforts have focused on soap opera series in which the characters bring out the main messages about healthy behaviors. The British Broadcasting Company has a group, for example, that works with developing countries to produce soap operas on health topics of importance such as HIV/AIDS. Such a series was done on HIV in India and Nigeria. The government of Myanmar had a soap opera about leprosy that featured Myanmar's best known actress. The aims of the soap opera were to help destigmatize leprosy, let people know how to diagnose leprosy, inform them that it could be treated completely if treated early, and get people to come forward for treatment at an early stage.

Social Marketing

Social marketing is the application of the tools of commercial marketing to try to promote behavior change and the uptake of important health actions or products. This has been used widely in family planning work. It is also being used in other fields, such as in selling bed nets for malaria control. In social marketing, a local brand of a product is often created, such as a condom, a contraceptive pill, or an insecticide-treated bed net. Mass media and other forms of communication are then used to promote the brand and the behaviors related to the product. Of course, successful marketing depends on very careful market research and a good understanding of the local culture, values, and behaviors. It also depends on what is called "the four Ps" in social marketing:

- Attractive product
- Affordable price
- Convenient places to buy the product
- Persuasive promotion[28]

Often the products being marketed through social marketing are sold through commercial channels but their price is subsidized by the government.

Health Education

Health education is something with which every reader of this book will be familiar. It comes in many forms, such as in the classroom, in the news media, on the radio and television, and on the Internet. Successful health education programs that were aimed at sex education have several features in common that hold lessons for other efforts at making health education effective.

- They focused on risky behaviors and were clear about abstinence and consistent condom use
- They provided accurate information
- They addressed how to deal with social pressures
- They selected teachers and peer educators who believed in the program
- They geared the content of the program to the age, sexual experience, and culture of the students[28]

Conditional Cash Transfers

A number of countries are turning increasingly to the use of economic incentives to encourage behavior change in health and help reduce poverty, as discussed in the case study on the *Oportunidades* (Opportunities) program in Mexico toward the end of this chapter. These incentives are called *conditional cash transfers*. In this case, a government program offers a payment to families on an agreed-upon time frame, provided that the family engages in agreed-upon nutrition, health, or education behaviors. The desired behaviors could include activities such as giving birth in a hospital; engaging in regular well-baby care, including immunizations; participating in a nutrition program that checks on the nutritional status of a child and offers food supplements, as needed; or sending female children to school on a regular basis. Conditional cash transfers are further discussed in Chapter 5 on health systems.

Achieving Success in Health Promotion

The previous section refers to specific types of health promotion that can be used to encourage a change in health behaviors or the adoption of healthy behaviors. There are a number of lessons that have emerged both about these approaches and when looking broadly at what constitutes an effective health promotion effort. These are noted in Table 6-6.

SOCIAL ASSESSMENT

There is one additional area that it is important to cover concerning the links between health and culture. This is *social assessment* or *social impact assessment*. A social impact assessment is "a process for assessing the social impacts of planned interventions or events and for developing strategies for the ongoing monitoring and management of those impacts."[32] In more expansive terms,

> Social impact assessment includes the processes of analyzing, monitoring, and managing the intended and unintended social consequences, both positive and negative, of planned interventions (policies, programs, plans, projects) and any social change processes invoked by those interventions. Its primary purpose is to bring about a more sustainable and equitable biophysical and human environment.[32]

TABLE 6-6 Selected Factors for Success in Health Promotion

Identify specific health problems, related behaviors, and key stakeholders.

Know and use sound behavioral theories.

Research motivations and constraints to change, considering biologic, environmental, cultural, and other contextual factors.

Use participatory assessment tools and include relevant stakeholders in the design, implementation, and evaluation of the intervention.

Plan and budget carefully.

Identify people who exhibit healthy behaviors that differ from the social norm.

Create an environment that enables behavior change through policy dialogue, advocacy, and capacity building.

Organize an intervention that addresses both specific behaviors and contextual factors.

Work to ensure sustainability.

Evaluate from the beginning.

Form partnerships to scale up and/or adapt the most successful interventions for implementation in other settings.

Source: Adapted with permission from Murphy E. *Promoting Healthy Behavior, Health Bulletin 2.* Washington, DC: Population Reference Bureau; 2005.

TABLE 6-7 Selected Focuses of Social Impact Assessment

Identifies interested and affected peoples

Facilitates and coordinates the participation of stakeholders

Analyzes the local setting of the planned intervention to assess likely impacts to it

Collects baseline data to allow for evaluation of the impact of the intervention

Gives a picture of the local cultural context, and develops an understanding of local community values, particularly how they relate to the planned intervention

Identifies and describes the activities that are likely to cause impacts

Predicts likely impacts and how different stakeholders are likely to respond

Assists in evaluating and selecting alternatives

Recommends measures to mitigate any likely negative impacts

Assists in the valuation process and provides suggestions about compensation for affected peoples

Describes potential conflicts between stakeholders and advises on resolution processes

Develops coping strategies for dealing with residual and non-mitigatable impacts

Contributes to skill development and capacity building in the community

Assists in devising and implementing monitoring and management programs

Source: Adapted with permission from Vanclay F. International principles for social impact assessment. *Impact Assess Proj Apprais.* 2003;21(1):5-11.

The social impact assessment looks at a variety of domains that go beyond health. These include impact, among other things, on historical artifacts and buildings, communities, demography, gender, minority groups, culture, and health. The assessment should be carried out in a way that builds on local processes, engages the community fully, and proactively tries to maximize the potential good that can come from the proposed investment. It "promotes community development and empowerment, builds capacity, and develops social capital."[32] The detailed approach of a social impact assessment is outlined in Table 6-7.

Many readers will be familiar with environmental assessment of proposed investment schemes, and many countries require such assessments be done before any major physical investment. In some respects, a social assessment is the social analogue to an environmental assessment. In this case, let us suppose that a development agency and a government are going to collaborate to develop a series of health centers in a particular region of a country. First, the country would carry out a social assessment to set the foundation project design. The affected communities should participate in this assess-

ment. The country would also ensure that the design took account of the needs of various groups in the community and was based on their culture and values, and it would keep in mind how programs need to be tailored to address them. The assessment would seek to identify any negative consequences that might emerge from the investment and how those consequences might be mitigated. The plan emerging from the assessment would also include a scheme for monitoring and evaluating the social impacts of the project and if the program design really is consistent with local values and the underlying needs of the community.

Some years ago, very little attention was paid in some development assistance agencies and in some governments to social assessment. Little effort was spent on examining the social and cultural issues involved in designing appropriate interventions in health. In addition, little attention was paid to the potential impact on health or on other social areas of investments in sectors outside of health. Although the quality of social assessment may vary both within and across some agencies and governments, social assessments are now done more frequently for major development projects.

POLICY AND PROGRAM BRIEFS

Four policy and program briefs follow. They are based on published reports and on literature from peer-reviewed journals. They are meant to illustrate some of the key issues concerning the relationship between culture and health and how some of those issues can be addressed in trying to engender better health through behavior change.

The first case examines breastfeeding practices in Burundi and the barriers to exclusive breastfeeding for 6 months, as recommended. The second case reviews some of the cultural issues related to efforts to eradicate polio in India and how communications programs have been enhanced to address them. The third reviews a program that was established in the Andean region of Peru to encourage women, by building on local cultural practices, to give birth in hospitals with trained birth attendants. The last case reviews the *Oportunidades* program in Mexico, which provides conditional cash transfers to the poor to promote better nutrition, health, and education behaviors.

Breastfeeding in Burundi[33]

There is substantial evidence that giving only breast milk to an infant for the first 6 months of life is a critical health-promoting practice, as you will read about further in Chapter 8 on nutrition and Chapter 10 on child health. This is called *exclusive breastfeeding (EBF)*. Nonetheless, the rate of exclusive breastfeeding is only about 25 percent in Africa, 31 percent in Latin America, and 45 percent in Asia.[34] In order to promote exclusive breastfeeding and enhance the health of young children, it is critical to understand why many women do not engage in EBF at higher rates.

An examination of this issue was carried out in December 2009 in Burundi, a low-income country in Africa. In Burundi, the rate of exclusive breastfeeding for the first 4 months is about 74 percent. However, many women stop this practice after the fourth month, and the rate of exclusive breastfeeding for 6 months is only 45 percent.

The study focused on breastfeeding practices in families in two provinces, Cancuzo and Ruyigi. Given the importance of cultural beliefs to health behaviors, the study aimed at understanding how certain beliefs affected whether a woman chose to breastfeed exclusively for 6 months. The goal of the study was to understand barriers to exclusive breastfeeding in order to develop an effective exclusive breastfeeding promotion program.

The study was based on an approach called *barrier analysis*, which focuses on trying to understand barriers to the adoption of positive health behaviors so that more effective behavior change communication messages and support activities can be developed.[35] This methodology has been used for work not only on breastfeeding, but also, for example, on other nutrition practices, use of latrines, and use of bed nets. With respect to exclusive breastfeeding, the study set out to gain a better understanding primarily of the extent to which a mother believes:

- People important to her would approve of EBF
- God would approve of EBF
- She has sufficient knowledge, capacities, and resources to successfully perform EBF
- Malnutrition is a serious problem
- Her child could become malnourished
- EBF is effective in preventing malnutrition
- She can remember to practice EBF
- In certain negative or positive attributes of practicing EBF

Following barrier analysis methods, 45 women with children under 1 year of age who had exclusively breastfed their children were interviewed. Forty-nine women who had not exclusively breastfed their children under 1 year of age were also interviewed. The questions they were asked included:

- Do you think that exclusive breastfeeding until the age of 6 months could help your child avoid becoming malnourished?
- Do you think that God approves of mothers exclusively breastfeeding their children until the age of 6 months?
- In your opinion, would most of the people you know approve of your exclusively breastfeeding your child?
- Who are the people who would approve of your breastfeeding your child?
- With your current knowledge and abilities, do you think you would be able to exclusively breastfeed your next child until the age of 6 months?
- What are the disadvantages of exclusively breastfeeding your child?
- If you wanted to exclusively breastfeed your child until the age of 6 months, would it be difficult to remember to not give your child other foods or liquids other than breast milk?

A number of statistically significant findings emerged from the research:

- Those who exclusively breastfed were 21 times more likely than those who did not to say that a child who does not exclusively breastfeed will become malnourished.
- Those who did not exclusively breastfeed were 17.6 times more likely than those who did to say that God does not approve of exclusive breastfeeding.
- Those who exclusively breastfed were many times (10.4, 6.5, 5.9, 3.8 times) more likely than those who did not to say that mothers-in-law, husbands, cousins, and mothers, respectively, approved of exclusive breastfeeding.
- Those who exclusively breastfed were 8 times more likely than those who did not to say that they had the knowledge and abilities to practice exclusive breastfeeding.
- Those who did not exclusively breastfeed were 7 times more likely than those who did to believe that exclusive breastfeeding would lead to babies always being hungry.
- Those who exclusively breastfed were 6.3 times more likely to say that it is not difficult at all to remember to practice EBF.

Among these findings, three stood out as especially significant in terms of designing a breastfeeding promotion program. These included the extent to which women believed: (1) that a child who is not exclusively breastfed can become malnourished, (2) God approved of exclusive breastfeeding, and (3) persons important to them approved of exclusive breastfeeding.

With these findings in mind, the study authors together with local staff made a number of recommendations for strengthening the promotion of breastfeeding in these two provinces. These included:

- Track and expose to the communities positive deviants who faithfully practice EBF and who also have healthy, well-nourished babies.
- Provide peer-based lactation counseling to help women understand the importance of EBF in combating malnutrition.
- Educate health promotion trainers on how to effectively demonstrate the link between EBF and good nutrition.
- Mobilize spiritual leaders to show support for EBF.
- Give pastors and priests sermon guidelines related to breastfeeding practices and good nutrition.

- Use radio broadcasts featuring mothers-in-law, husbands, cousins, and mothers who support EBF.
- Train some of these mothers-in-law, female cousins, and mothers to be "Leader Mothers," the community-level cadre of health promoters in the project.

Polio Vaccination in India

In 1988, India launched a Polio Eradication Initiative. India's polio eradication program is a part of the Global Polio Eradication Initiative and includes a "social mobilization and communication" component.[36] This is meant to encourage universal immunization by providing accurate information about the vaccine, mobilizing demand for vaccination, and countering popular beliefs and behaviors that might constrain vaccination against polio.

India's polio program is a collaborative effort of national and international partners. These include India's national and local governments, via the Ministries of Health and Family Welfare, UNICEF, the World Health Organization National Polio Surveillance Project, Rotary International, the United States Centers for Disease Control and Prevention, and numerous nongovernmental organizations.[37,38]

India is the second largest country in the world and has a population over 1 billion. The country is divided into 28 states and has a very diverse population.[39] As would be expected, health beliefs vary across India and among different social groups. Despite these challenges, India has made substantial progress toward eradicating polio.

Nonetheless, India remains one of four countries in the world in which polio is endemic.[40] In addition, there have been periodic outbreaks of polio in India in the last decade, with the annual number of cases jumping to 1600 in 2002 and 874 in 2007, from considerably lower levels in most other years.[40] The more recent polio outbreaks have occurred primarily in the states of Uttar Pradesh and Bihar.[41]

These outbreaks have been attributed to a variety of biological, social, political, and programmatic factors. Biological factors contributing to persistent polio outbreaks include high population density, poor sanitation, and pervasive poverty in certain regions. The primary social forces that have contributed to the outbreaks are resistance to immunization among minority communities, as well as difficulty in vaccinating the children of the great numbers of people who migrate for work. Political forces that may inhibit polio programs are rooted in tensions between Muslim minorities and the Hindu-dominated government. Programmatic challenges, such as low coverage of immunization activities and falsification of data, continue to affect certain regions of India.[41]

Certain communities and social groups, primarily marginalized Muslim minority groups, have been resistant to giving oral polio vaccine to their children. This has been attributed partly to a failure of the parents to understand the need for repeated vaccinations. It has also been due to misinformation that has circulated in some communities that the vaccine was ineffective, causes illness in children, causes infertility, or is part of a plot to curb the growth of Muslims.[42] The strength of these rumors may be exacerbated by the fact that most health professionals and community health workers tend to be Hindu.

In the face of these difficulties, public health leaders in India and from key international organizations have collaborated to enhance the health communication and social mobilization program associated with India's polio program. Greater focus has been put on reaching those resistant to vaccination and convincing them both to immunize their children and to continue vaccinating them with the appropriate number of doses.[42] In addition, efforts at communication and social mobilization have been decentralized to the district, block, and village level, which has allowed them to be more closely tailored to local mores. The program has also enlisted community members in communication efforts to a greater extent than earlier.[37,43] These measures are intended to ensure that families receive information about the program from respected community members with whom they already have a relationship and trust.[43]

Some of the major steps that have been taken to support this approach have included:

- The establishment of a social mobilization network that extended to the village level.
- The linking of the social mobilization network, including community mobilization coordinators, with vaccination teams. These teams work in booths on immunization days and then go house to house to immunize children who were missed on those days.
- Greater involvement of community and religious leaders in mobilizing members of their communities to be vaccinated.
- More use of intensive, house-to-house interpersonal communications to ensure families would vaccinate their children.
- Greater engagement of well-known celebrities for mass media advertisements to support the polio program.
- Greater involvement in the program of professional associations, such as the Pediatric Association.

The evidence suggests that communities in which the above social mobilization and communications activities have taken place have higher rates of immunization coverage than other communities.[42] This has also been associated recently with fewer new cases of polio in these areas. In the first 9 months of 2010, for example, India had 37 new cases of polio, compared to 367 during the same period in 2009.[40]

The implementation of the polio eradication program in India suggests that health communication efforts must pay particular attention to cultural context, as well as to epidemiologic factors and the political environment. The polio program in India has also highlighted the importance of:

- Engaging more effectively with marginalized communities
- Ensuring messages reach the village level
- The need in some settings for intensive interpersonal communications from respected people with influence who are seen as members of the community
- The power of involving religious leaders in programs, as well[42]

Birthing Services in Peru

As discussed earlier in the chapter, cultural values can have an immense bearing on where and how people give birth, who attends the delivery, and their willingness to address complications that do arise with emergency obstetric care, if available. As also noted, however, other factors, such as a lack of empowerment and discrimination, may also influence health-seeking behavior.

In the Andean region of Peru, both of these factors have been at play. Women in some settings have traditionally given birth at home, without the help of a skilled birth attendant. They have done this, however, not only for cultural reasons, but also because they did not always feel welcome in healthcare settings in which health providers do not speak their language, may not treat them respectfully, and often insist that they give birth in a manner different from their traditional ways.

These factors, combined with poverty and low educational levels, especially among women, contributed in the late 1990s to very high maternal mortality ratios in some places in the Peruvian Andes. In Ayacucho, for example, maternal mortality ratios were six times the rates in Lima, the capital of Peru.

If women are not comfortable with available birthing services, they are less likely to utilize them. This is of critical concern when most obstetric complications occur during or immediately after delivery and cannot be predicted. It is therefore crucial that women, especially high-risk groups such as the indigenous women around Ayacucho, deliver with a skilled birth attendant.[44] In an effort to address these concerns, the international nongovernmental organization Health Unlimited teamed up with Salud Sín Límites Perú (Health Without Limits Peru) to create a model for birthing services that is more responsive to the needs of indigenous communities in the Santillana district in Ayacucho.

The new model of care was planned in stages, with the participation of all key stakeholders.

- A survey was done to understand local birthing practices. Men and women in the community were surveyed, as well as traditional birth attendants and trained health professionals.
- The stakeholders then designed the new model over a series of meetings. The aim of these meetings was to design a model that would respect local beliefs and practices as much as possible, but still ensure better outcomes for pregnant women.
- The model was rolled out over a nearly 2-year period, and promoted through a variety of communication efforts in the local language, Quechua.
- The new model was then evaluated and refinements were made to the model, based on what was learned in the evaluation.
- A long-run evaluation of the model was set up on a continuous basis.[44]

During the planning stages of the program, a number of barriers were identified to women giving birth in government health centers, including:

- Health professionals speak only Spanish, although most indigenous women in this region speak Quechua.
- The husband, family, and traditional birth attendant are not permitted in the delivery room, although the women prefer their participation in the delivery.
- There is no option to utilize traditional medicines such as herbs and oils during the delivery process.
- Women are required to deliver in a horizontal position on a gynecological bed, although they prefer a traditional, vertical, squatting position.
- The umbilical cord cannot be cut by a family member according to tradition.
- The placenta is thrown away, so it cannot be buried according to tradition.

Solutions to these barriers, as well as others identified during the interviews, were proposed and incorporated into a new healthcare model for birthing services in the Santillana district. This new model combines certain aspects of Andean "traditional" medicine with "modern" medicine to ensure that indigenous women are comfortable but also receive high quality care.

Some features of the new model include Quechua language training for health professionals, the option to include the husband and traditional birth attendant in the labor and delivery process, utilization of traditional medicines, delivery in the vertical squatting position or on a normal bed, and return of the placenta to the family for proper burial. Although these and other aspects of traditional birthing were incorporated into the new model, there were certain things that the program managers felt could not be compromised if high quality care was to be ensured. For example, in the new model the umbilical cord must still be cut by a health professional, despite the tradition of having this done by a family member.

Women in the Ayacucho region appear to have been receptive to the new model for birthing services. Between 1999 and 2007, the proportion of deliveries in a health facility with a skilled birth attendant increased from 6 percent to 83 percent in the Santillana district in Ayacucho. Data are still being collected to allow for more extensive evaluation of the impact of the new model on maternal mortality.[44]

Programs such as this one highlight the importance of trying to improve the health of poor and marginalized people by understanding and building on their cultural practices, rather than asking them to change their behaviors in ways that may seem contrary to their traditions. This work in Peru also highlights the importance of careful planning, implementation, and evaluation of programs in ways that engage all key stakeholders and give them a stake in the program's success.

Conditional Cash Transfers in Mexico

The poor are often unable to purchase sufficient foods to ensure that their children are well nourished and healthy. In addition, the poor often have difficulty accessing health services, even when they are available in principle, because of the direct and indirect costs of services such as transportation, the time spent using these services, and payment for services. The poor also underinvest in the education of their children, not only because of their poverty, but also because the family may depend on income from working children.

As discussed in the chapter on health systems, one of the approaches that governments have adopted to try to reduce poverty and enhance the future prospects of poor families and their children is the conditional cash transfer (CCT). A CCT is a cash payment to a household for meeting specific requirements, primarily related to preventive health care and children's education. CCT programs generally try to enhance the income available to the poor so they can increase food consumption. They also try to increase the demand of the poor for health and education. The aim of CCTs in these efforts is to reduce short-term poverty and to improve family members' prospects of overcoming poverty and participating more fully in the economy in the long term.

One CCT program is *Oportunidades*, the Mexican government's social safety net program for poor households, which was previously known as *Progressa*. *Oportunidades* provides CCTs to poor households in an attempt to break the cycle of poverty, poor nutritional status and poor health, and limited educational attainment by enabling families to engage in better health and education practices. Like many CCT programs, *Oportunidades* selects its participants by targeting geographic areas with high levels of poverty. The program then targets only those with incomes below a certain level.[45]

In 2005, *Oportunidades* provided a monthly cash transfer to participating families that averaged about $20, which constituted about 23 percent of the amount needed to be above the poverty line in Mexico. The transfers included:

- $13 per household
- $8–17 per child of primary school age
- $25–32 per child of secondary school age
- $12–22 per child as a one-time grant for school supplies[45]

In exchange for the cash transfers, families must meet certain conditions, or "co-responsibilties." These include:

- Full immunization and participation in growth monitoring of children under 2 years of age
- Participation in growth monitoring of children 2 to 5 years of age three times a year
- Attendance at four prenatal visits by pregnant women
- Two postpartum care visits for breastfeeding women
- Once a year physical exams for adult family members
- Attendance at health education sessions by adult family members[45]

Oportunidades also aims to promote gender equality by creating social and economic opportunities specifically for women. For example, *Oportunidades* delivers CCTs to women, which contrasts with traditional social programs that are often geared toward economic empowerment of the head of household, who is usually a male. Moreover, *Oportunidades* provides larger CCTs for girls enrolled in secondary school than boys, to counter social norms that drive gender discrimination and cause girls to drop out of school. Finally, the visibility of women in the community is enhanced though the election of women to serve as liaisons between program beneficiaries and *Oportunidades* officials.

Oportunidades was the first national, government-run CCT program. The program incorporates unique approaches to target poor households, empower women, engage beneficiaries, and evaluate program outcomes. By 2006, the program reached more than 5 million beneficiaries.

Thus far, it appears that *Oportunidades* has been associated with significant gains in a number of areas. It has led to more than a 10 percent increase in household expenditure, a substantial increase in the number of health visits, and a 44 percent reduction in stunting. It has also led to a reduction in illness among its participants and a decrease in maternal mortality of between 2 percent and 11 percent. In addition, the enrollment in secondary schools increased by 20 percent for girls and 10 percent for boys.[45]

Partly based on the successes of *Oportunidades*, many other countries are developing similar programs in an effort to alleviate poverty and improve health, nutrition, and education. The first countries to engage in such efforts were in Latin America, with Brazil also having a large national program of importance. However countries in Asia and Africa have also used CCTs to achieve greater demand for health and education, such as a girls' secondary school scholarship scheme in Bangladesh and CCTs for hospital-based delivery in India.

An important research agenda is being carried out on CCTs that focuses, among other things, on their effectiveness, especially compared to transfers that are not conditional; the cost-effectiveness of CCT programs, including compared to interventions meant to alter supply rather than demand; and the impact of CCT programs on health outcomes. Research is also needed to examine the quality of the ongoing CCT programs to ensure that participation leads to impact.[45]

MAIN MESSAGES

Culture is a set of beliefs and behaviors that are learned and shared. Culture operates, among other areas, in the domains of the family, social groups beyond the family, religion, art, music, and law. Culture is an important determinant of health, in many ways. It relates to people's health behaviors, their perceptions of illness, the extent to which they use health services, and forms of medicine that they have practiced traditionally. This chapter examines the links between culture and health from the perspective of the extent to which a culture satisfies the physical and psychological needs of those who follow it.

Perceptions of illness vary considerably across cultures. What is seen as normal in some societies may be seen as illness in others. Different societies also have differing perceptions of the causes of illness and of disease. In addition to perceptions related to the "Western medical paradigm," diseases may be viewed, for example, as due to the body "being out of balance," supernatural causes, offending the gods, emotional stress, or witchcraft. Different cultures also take an array of steps, beyond the western medical paradigm, to prevent illness. Some of these include rituals, the wearing of charms, and the observance of certain food taboos.

When people believe themselves to be ill, they usually resort to trying "home remedies" first. Following that, people in traditional societies often visit some type of traditional healer. It may be some time before they consult a physician practicing "modern medicine," and often only when they are certain they are quite ill and other forms of treatment have not brought relief.

Many forms of traditional behavior are conducive to good health. This might include, for example, traditional practices that allow the mother to spend some time with her baby before she returns to her normal work and household chores. Male circumcision, as practiced in many cultures, reduces the transmission of HIV/AIDS. Other traditional practices, however, are not health promoting. Feeding sugar water to infants, for example, is not good for the health of the infants, who should be exclusively breastfed for 6 months. It is important to consider how healthy behaviors can be promoted.

There are a number of "models" of how behaviors can be changed, including the Health Belief model, the Diffusion of Innovations model, and the Stages of Change model. To encourage behavior change, of course, requires a good understanding of the behaviors that are taking place, how they relate to health, the underlying motivation for them, and the likely response to various approaches to changing them.

When thinking about trying to change behavior on a large scale, such as promoting an immunization program, the use of seat belts, or the willingness to seek treatment for leprosy, several approaches are important. One way to engender change is to engage in community mobilization. Promoting messages about desirable and undesirable health behaviors can also be done effectively using the mass media. Social marketing and health education efforts are also important. Conditional cash transfers are also being used increasingly to promote behavior change. An effective tool for setting the foundation for any efforts at investing in health or trying to change behaviors is to carry out a social assessment, which will identify the social basis of the health issues one is trying to influence, as well as the likely social impacts of the proposed activities.

Study Questions

1. What is culture? Give some examples of aspects of culture that vary across different societies.

2. Why is it important to assess the relationship between culture and health in specific societies by the extent to which cultural practices promote or discourage good physical and mental health?

3. Name three cultural practices that are health promoting. Name three cultural practices that are harmful to health.

4. How does culture relate to people's perceptions of illness? Why would some cultures regard some illnesses as "normal"?

5. What would low-income people in traditional societies likely see as possible causes of illness?

6. What is the difference between "illness" and "disease"?

7. When an infant is ill in a traditional society in a low-income country, from whom and in what order are the parents likely to seek help?

8. Why would members of the community seek treatment for illness from traditional healers?

9. If you wanted to encourage the large scale adoption of a healthy behavior, such as giving up cigarette smoking, what information would you want to know as you plan your effort?

10. Why are social assessments important? If they are done well, what gains would they produce that might not come if there were no such assessment?

REFERENCES

1. Scrimshaw SC. Culture, behavior, and health. In: Merson MH, Black RE, Mills A, eds. *International Public Health: Diseases, Programs, Systems, and Policies*. Gaithersburg, MD: Aspen Publishers; 2001:53-78.

2. Tylor E. *Primitive Culture*. London: J. Murray; 1871.

3. Haviland WA. The nature of culture. *Cultural Anthropology*. 6th ed. Fort Worth, TX: Holt, Rinehart & Winston, Inc.; 1990:30.

4. Miller B. *Culture and Health*. Presentation given at George Washington University, Washington DC; 2004.

5. Haviland WA. The nature of culture. *Cultural Anthropology*. 6th ed. Fort Worth, TX: Holt, Rinehart & Winston, Inc.; 1990:31.

6. Haviland WA. The nature of culture. *Cultural Anthropology*. 6th ed. Fort Worth, TX: Holt, Rinehart & Winston, Inc.; 1990:46.

7. Haviland WA. The nature of culture. *Cultural Anthropology*. 6th ed. Fort Worth, TX: Holt, Rinehart & Winston, Inc.; 1990:51.

8. Scrimshaw SC. Culture, behavior, and health. In: Merson MH, Black RE, Mills A, eds. *International Public Health: Diseases, Programs, Systems, and Policies*. Gaithersburg, MD: Aspen Publishers; 2001:56.

9. Murphy EM. Being born female is dangerous for your health. *Am Psychol*. 2003;58(3):205-210.

10. Scrimshaw SC. Culture, behavior, and health. In: Merson MH, Black RE, Mills A, eds. *International Public Health: Diseases, Programs, Systems, and Policies*. Gaithersburg, MD: Aspen Publishers; 2001:57.

11. Kleinman A, Eisenberg L, Good B. Culture, illness, and care: clinical lessons from anthropologic and cross-cultural research. *Ann Intern Med*. 1978;88(2):251-258.

12. Hopper S. The influence of ethnicity on the healthcare of older women. *Clin Geriatr Med*. 1993;9:231-259.

13. Scrimshaw SC. Culture, behavior, and health. In: Merson MH, Black RE, Mills A, eds. *International Public Health: Diseases, Programs, Systems, and Policies*. Gaithersburg, MD: Aspen Publishers; 2001:58.

14. Letendre AD. Aboriginal traditional medicine: where does it fit? *Crossing Boundaries*. 2002;1(2):78-87.

15. Jegede AS. The Yoruba cultural construction of health and illness. *Nordic J Afr Stud*. 2002;11(3):322-335.

16. Pachter LM. Culture and clinical care. Folk illness beliefs and behaviors and their implications for health care delivery. *JAMA*. 1994;271(9):693.

17. Bolton JM. Food taboos among the Orang Asli in West Malaysia: a potential nutritional hazard. *Am J Clin Nutr*. 1972;25(8):788-799.

18. Chiwuzie J, Okolocha C. Traditional belief systems and maternal mortality in a semi-urban community in Southern Nigeria. *Afri J Reprod Health*. 2001;5(1):75-82.

19. Trigo M, Roncada MJ, Stewien GT, Pereira IM. [Food taboos in the northern region of Brazil]. *Rev Saude Publica*. 1989;23(6):455-464.

20. Sundararaj R, Pereira SM. Dietary intakes and food taboos of lactating women in a South Indian community. *Trop Geogr Med*. 1975;27(2):189-193.

21. Bhasin V. Sickness and therapy among tribals of Rajasthan. *Stud Tribes Tribals*. 2003;1(1):77-83.

22. Fassin D, Badji I. Ritual buffoonery: a social preventive measure against childhood mortality in Senegal. *Lancet*. 1986;18(1):142-143.

23. Scrimshaw SC. Culture, behavior, and health. In: Merson MH, Black RE, Mills A, eds. *International Public Health: Diseases, Programs, Systems, and Policies*. Gaithersburg, MD: Aspen Publishers; 2001:62.

24. Scrimshaw SC. Culture, behavior, and health. In: Merson MH, Black RE, Mills A, eds. *International Public Health: Diseases, Programs, Systems, and Policies*. Gaithersburg, MD: Aspen Publishers; 2001:63.

25. Lopez AD, Mathers CD, Murray CJL. The burden of disease and mortality by condition: data, methods, and results for 2001. In: Lopez AD, Mathers CD, Ezzati M, Jamison DT, Murray CJL, eds. *Global Burden of Disease and Risk Factors*. New York: Oxford University Press; 2006:70.

26. Lopez AD, Mathers CD, Ezzati M, Jamison DT, Murray CJL. Measuring the global burden of disease and risk factors 1990–2001. In: Lopez AD, Mathers CD, Ezzati M, Jamison DT, Murray CJL, eds. *Global Burden of Disease and Risk Factors*. New York: Oxford University Press; 2006:10.

27. Edberg M. *Essentials of Health Behavior: An Introduction to Social and Behavioral Theory Applied to Public Health*. Sudbury, MA: Jones & Bartlett Publishers; 2007.

28. Murphy E. *Promoting Healthy Behavior, Health Bulletin 2*. Washington, DC: Population Reference Bureau; 2005.

29. Rosenstock IM, Strecher VJ, Becker MH. Social learning theory and the Health Belief Model. *Health Educ Q*. 1988;15(2):175-183.

30. Scrimshaw SC. Culture, behavior, and health. In: Merson MH, Black RE, Mills A, eds. *International Public Health: Diseases, Programs, Systems, and Policies*. Gaithersburg, MD: Aspen Publishers; 2001:66.

31. Rogers E. *Diffusion of Innovations*. 3rd ed. New York: Free Press; 1983.

32. Vanclay F. Social Impact Assessment: International Principles. Available at: http://www.iaia.org/Members/Publications/Guidelines_Principles/SP2.pdf. Accessed October 27, 2006.

33. This case is adapted with permission from a paper prepared in May 2010 by Josephine E.V. Francisco, entitled *Barrier Analysis of Exclusive Breastfeeding Practices in Ruyigi and Cancuzo Provinces, Burundi*. This paper was part of a Culminating Experience to meet the requirements for the Master of Public Health degree at The George Washington University.

34. Lauer J, Betrán AP, Victora CG, De Onís M, Barros AJ. Breastfeeding patterns and exposure to suboptimal breastfeeding among children in developing countries: review and analysis of nationally representative surveys. *BMC Med*. 2004;2(26):1-29.

35. Food for the Hungry. Barrier Analysis. Available at: http://barrieranalysis.fhi.net. Accessed April 23, 2011.

36. Centers for Disease Control and Prevention. Progress toward poliomyelitis eradication—India, 1998. *MMWR*. 1998;47(37):771-781.

37. The Communication Initiative Network. Social Mobilisation-Communication Polio Eradication Partnership—India. Available at: http://www.comminit.com/en/node/127845/292. Accessed April 23, 2011.

38. UNICEF. India Polio Eradication. Available at: http://www.unicef.org/india/health_3729.htm. Accessed April 23, 2011.

39. Central Intelligence Agency. India. The World Fact Book. Available at: https://www.cia.gov/library/publications/the-world-factbook/geos/in.html. Accessed April 23, 2011.

40. Global Polio Eradication Initiative. Monthly Situation Reports. Available at: http://www.polioeradication.org/Mediaroom/Monthlysituationreports.aspx. Accessed April 23, 2011.

41. Chaturvedi S, Dasgupta R, Adhish V, et al. Deconstructing social resistance to pulse polio campaign in two north Indian districts. *Indian Pediatr*. 2009;46(11):963-974.

42. Obregón R, Chitnis K, Morry C, et al. Achieving polio eradication: a review of health communication evidence and lessons learned in India and Pakistan. *Bull World Health Org*. August 2009;87(8):628.

43. Bhagat P. Vaccination campaign focuses on tackling social resistance to vaccine. Available at: http:www.unicef.org/infobycountry/india_25290.html. Accessed April 23, 2011.

44. Gabrysch S, Lema C, Bedrinana E, et al. Cultural adaptation of birthing services in rural Ayachucho, Peru. *Bull World Health Org*. 2009;87(9):724-729.

45. Eichler R, Levine R, Performance-Based Incentives Working Group. *Performance Incentives for Global Health*. Washington, DC: Center for Global Development; 2009.

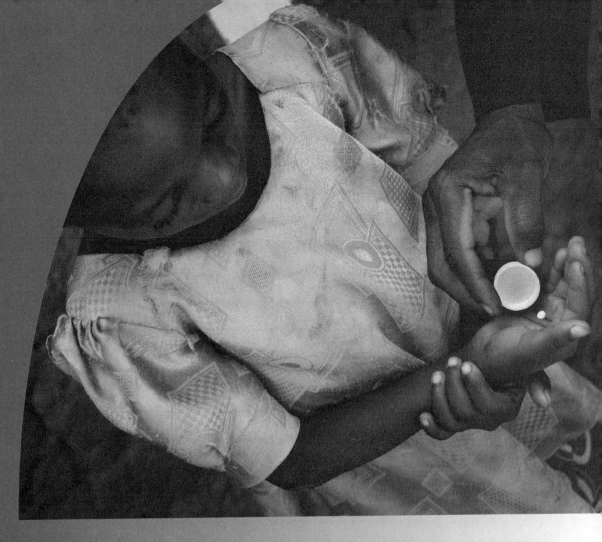

PART III

The Burden of Disease

CHAPTER 7

The Environment and Health

VIGNETTES

Rashmi lived in the eastern part of Nepal in a modest home. Rashmi often had difficulty breathing. This was linked to the way Rashmi cooked, with a stove inside the house that was not vented outside. She used cow dung or wood as fuel. She cooked two meals a day on the stove and she often held her new baby on her back as she did so. She heard about different stoves and about using kerosene for fuel. However, she lacked the money to buy a new stove or to fuel it with kerosene.

Sunisa was a young mother in a rural area in northern Laos. She had two children, a 1-year-old and a 3-year-old. Sunisa was not wealthy. Her house was simple and had no water supply. She collected water daily from the stream about half a mile from her house in containers she carried on her head. She stored the containers at the edge of her house, covered by cloth. Sunisa was not an educated woman and did nothing to purify the water. Her two daughters regularly had bouts of diarrhea, partly the result of drinking unsafe water.

Juan had lived in Mexico City his whole life and was now 70 years old. He remembered a time when the city was not so crowded, had few cars, and when the views from the city were magnificent. He lamented the fact that today the city was too crowded to enjoy, the traffic was overwhelming, and the air was often unbreathable. It was so polluted that on many days there was no view at all. Juan had a very hard time breathing, because he suffered from chronic obstructive pulmonary disease (COPD). Juan suspected that air pollution contributed to his illness.

Raj and his family lived in a slum at the edge of Patna, India. The slum was the size of a small city. Most of the houses were made of scrap wood with scrap metal roofing. The houses had no water connection and people had to walk to the edge of the slum to get their water from a standpipe or buy it from a tanker if the standpipe did not work. There were no private toilets either. There were a few communal toilets that were shared but they were always dirty. For this reason, many people in the slum, especially the women, waited until dark and then went to defecate in fields near the slum.

THE IMPORTANCE OF ENVIRONMENTAL HEALTH

Environmental health issues are major risk factors in the global burden of disease. Using a somewhat narrow definition of what is an "environmental" cause of disease, one study of the global burden of disease[1] suggests that about 8.4 percent of the total burden of disease in low- and middle-income countries is the result of three environmental conditions: unsafe water, hygiene, and excreta disposal; urban air pollution; and indoor smoke from household use of solid fuels. Another study, which took a broader view of "environmental" risk factors, concluded that between 25 and 33 percent of the global burden of disease can be attributed to environmental risk factors.[2]

The importance of environmental risk factors to the global burden of disease should not be a surprise. The third leading cause of death in low- and middle-income countries

---

TABLE 7-1 Key Links Between Environmental Health and the MDGs

Goal 1: Eradicate Poverty and Hunger
Link: Reducing environmental risk factors is central to eradicating poverty by reducing the burden, which falls largely on the poor, of environmentally related morbidity and mortality.

Goal 2: Achieve Universal Primary Education
Link: Children that do not have access to clean water and sanitation are more likely to suffer from undernutrition due to a vicious cycle of diarrheal disease and malnutrition. There is a correlation between nutritional status and learning. Children with poor nutritional status are not as likely to stay in school or learn as much as healthy children.

Goal 3: Promote Gender Equality and Empower Women
Link: Improving access to water can improve the lives of poor women in the developing world by reducing the amount of time required to get water. Reducing indoor air pollution can also substantially improve the lives of women because they suffer a disproportionate burden when they are cooking.

Goal 4: Reduce Child Mortality
Link: Addressing environmental risk factors can reduce the two leading causes of death in children—diarrheal diseases and pneumonia. Diarrheal disease is reduced through improved access to clean water and sanitation. Pneumonia can be reduced through improvements in indoor air quality.

Goal 5: Improve Maternal Health
Link: Diarrheal disease associated with poor sanitation and unsafe water can harm the nutritional status of the mother.

Goal 6: Combat HIV/AIDS, Malaria, and Other Diseases
Link: Environmental improvements can reduce the breeding grounds for malarial mosquitoes and vectors of some other disease, such as schistosomiasis and dengue fever.

Goal 7: Ensure Environmental Sustainability
Link: Measures to improve water supply, sanitation, and personal hygiene promote sustainability, especially when they are carried out in community-based ways.

Source: Adapted from United Nations. Millennium Development Goals. Available at: http://www.un.org/millenniumgoals/goals. Accessed July 11, 2006.

---

is lower respiratory infections, the sixth is chronic obstructive pulmonary disease, and the seventh is diarrheal disease. As you know, each of these is closely linked with environmental factors. In addition, environmental risk factors are even more important when considering the causes of death of children 0 to 14 years of age in low- and middle-income countries. Lower respiratory conditions are the second leading cause of death for them and diarrheal diseases third. Together, they account for about 30 percent of all deaths in this age group.[3]

Environmental health matters are also of special importance because addressing them effectively is central to the achievement of the MDGs, as shown in Table 7-1.

As you can see in the table, reducing environmental risk factors is critical to meeting the poverty and hunger goal, given the large share of ill health and resulting economic losses from these risk factors. Improving access to water can be a major improvement in the lives of poor women in low- and middle-income countries, given the amount of time they have to spend getting water. Enhancing sanitation produces important social gains for women, as well, because in the absence of improved sanitation, they face major discomforts, inconveniences, and sometimes illness. Addressing environmental risk factors can clearly make a major contribution to reducing child mortality by reducing two of the leading causes of death in children. As you will read about later, reducing indoor air pollution can also lead to major improvements in the health of women and children. Finally, environmental improvements can reduce the breeding grounds for malarial mosquitoes, and many measures that reduce the health risks of the environment will increase environmental sustainability.

This chapter aims to introduce you to some of the most important links between health and the environment. Environmental health is a very broad topic. Given the introductory nature of this book, this chapter will focus largely on only three of the most important risk factors in terms of the burden of environmentally related diseases in low- and middle-income countries. Following the 2001 burden of disease study, these will include unsafe water, sanitation, and hygiene; outdoor air pollution; and indoor air pollution that comes from the use of solid fuels.[3] These factors are also the focus of attention of this chapter because the risk factors that will be examined take a disproportionate toll on the health of low-income people in the developing world, and the enhancement of their health status will require important gains in environmental health.

The chapter begins by covering some of the most important terms and concepts that relate to environmental health. It then explores the burden of disease related to the three risk factors noted previously. After that, it briefly reviews the costs and consequences of the selected environmental risk factors.

The chapter concludes with the policy and program briefs that discuss some of the most cost-effective ways to address these risk factors in low- and middle-income settings. Much has been written about environmental health. Readers who wish to explore environmental health in greater detail are encouraged to pursue those writings. They might wish to begin with an introductory text on environmental health.[4,5]

KEY CONCEPTS

It is important to understand how the word *environment* will be used in this chapter. In some cases, the word *environment* in a health context is defined very broadly, meaning everything that is not genetic. In other cases, when considering health, the word *environment* includes only physical, chemical, or biological agents that directly affect health. For the purposes of this chapter, the environment will largely be defined as "external physical, chemical, and microbiological exposures and processes that impinge upon individuals and groups and are beyond the immediate control of individuals."[6] The chapter, however, also looks at some behavioral matters related to water and sanitation and indoor air pollution.

It is also valuable to understand the meaning of *environmental health*. This generally refers to a set of public health efforts that "is concerned with preventing disease, death, and disability by reducing exposure to adverse environmental conditions and promoting behavior change. It focuses on the direct and indirect causes of disease and injuries and taps resources inside and outside the healthcare system to help improve health outcomes."[7]

The World Health Organization takes a broad view of the environment and says,

> Environmental health comprises those aspects of human health, including quality of life, that are determined by physical, chemical, biological, social, and psychosocial factors in the environment. It also refers to the theory and practice of assessing, correcting, controlling, and preventing those factors in the environment that can potentially affect adversely the health of present and future generations.[8]

Table 7-2 highlights some examples of environmental health issues, their determinants, and their consequences. It organizes these examples by their level of impact: the household, the community, or global.

TABLE 7-2 Typical Environmental Health Issues: Determinants and Health Consequences

Underlying Determinants	Selected Adverse Health Consequences
Household	
Unsafe water, inadequate sanitation and solid waste disposal, improper hygiene	Diarrhea and vector-related diseases, such as malaria, schistosomiasis, and dengue
Crowded housing and poor ventilation of smoke	Respiratory diseases and lung cancer
Exposure to naturally occurring toxic substances	Poisoning from arsenic, manganese, and fluorides
Community	
Improper water resource management, including poor drainage	Vector-related diseases, such as malaria and schistosomisasis
Exposure to vehicle emissions and industrial air pollution	Respiratory diseases, some cancers, and reduced IQ in children
Global	
Climate change	Injury/death from extreme heat/cold, storms, floods, and fires Indirect effects: spread of vector-borne diseases
Ozone depletion	Aggravation of respiratory diseases, population dislocation, water pollution from sea level rise, etc. Skin cancer, cataracts Indirect effects: compromised food production, etc.

Source: Adapted with permission from The World Bank. Environmental Health. Available at: http://web.worldbank.org/WBSITE/EXTERNAL/TOPICS/EXTHEALTHNUTRITIONANDPOPULATION/EXTPHAAG/0,,contentMDK:20656146~menuPK:2175463~pagePK:64229817~piPK:64229743~theSitePK:672263,00.html. Accessed October 27, 2006.

KEY ENVIRONMENTAL HEALTH BURDENS

This section very briefly examines the most important health conditions that relate to the environmental issues that are discussed in this chapter. The section will then examine the burden of disease from those conditions.

Indoor Air Pollution

WHO estimates that about half of all of the people in the world depend on solid fuel for their cooking and heating. The indoor air pollution that is discussed here is related to these uses. Such fuels include the fossil fuel coal, and the biomass fuels of cow dung, wood, logging wastes, and crop waste.[9,10] In the cases that most concern us, cooking and heating are done on open stoves that are not vented to the outside. These are generally used by poorer segments of society, because people usually move to kerosene or gas for cooking and switch to improved stoves as their family income grows.

Biomass fuels and coal do not completely combust when they are burned. Instead, they leave behind breathable particles of a variety of gases and chemical products. The amount of these substances in a poorly ventilated home can exceed WHO norms by more than 20 times.[10] Smoke from burning biomass inside the home can produce conjunctivitis, upper respiratory irritation, and acute respiratory infection. The carbon monoxide produced can lead to acute poisoning. Other gases and smoke are associated over the long term with cardiovascular disease, chronic obstructive pulmonary disease, adverse reproductive outcomes, and cancer.[11] As discussed further later, women and children are especially vulnerable to the effects of indoor air pollution.

Outdoor Air Pollution

Many pollutants can be found in the urban air. The most common effects of outdoor air pollution are respiratory symptoms, including cough, irritation of the nose and throat, and shortness of breath.[12] Table 7-3 indicates some of the most common pollutants in the outdoor air, examples of their sources, and the most important health effects. Some preexisting health factors make some people susceptible to being harmed by air pollution. Older and younger people are generally most susceptible to the health effects of outdoor air pollution.

There have been a number of instances in which severe air pollution has been associated with considerable excess mortality in a very short time. Among the most famous cases was in London, England, in 1952. Because of what is called a temperature inversion, a dense fog, full of pollutants, hung over the city center for several days. The value of certain particulates in the air was 3 to 10 times the normal value. On December 13, 1952, the city administration reported a death rate per 100,000 people that was more than four times the normal daily death rate for that period.[13]

TABLE 7-3 Common Air Pollutants and Their Health Effects

Name of Pollutant	Example of Source	Health Effects
Carbon monoxide	Combustion of gasoline and fossil fuels; cars	Reduction in oxygen-carrying capacity of the blood
Lead	Leaded gasoline, paint, batteries	Brain/CNS damage; digestive problems
Nitrogen dioxide, nitrogen oxides	Combustion of gasoline and fossil fuels; cars	Damage to lungs and respiratory system
Ozone	Variety of oxygen formed by chemical reaction of pollutants	Breathing impairment; eye irritation
Particulate matter	Burning of wood and diesel fuels	Respiratory irritation; lung damage
Smog	Mixture of pollutants, esp. ozone; originates from petroleum-based fuels	Irritation of respiratory system, eyes
Sulfur dioxide	Burning of coal and oil	Breathing problems; lung damage
Volatile organic compounds (VOCs)	Burning fuels; released from certain chemicals (e.g., solvents)	Acute effects similar to those of smog; possible carcinogen

Source: Adapted from U.S. Environmental Protection Agency. The Plain English Guide to the Clean Air Act: The Common Air Pollutants. Available at: http://www.epa.gov/oar/oaqps/peg_caa/pegcaa11.html. Accessed March 28, 2005; and U.S. Environmental Protection Agency. The Plain English Guide to the Clean Air Act: Glossary. Available at: http://www.epa.gov/oar/oaqps/peg_caa/pegcaa10.html. Accessed January 28, 2007.

Sanitation, Water, and Hygiene

Only about 60 percent of the people in the world have access to improved sanitation. This ranges from about 80 percent in South America to only about 30 percent in sub-Saharan Africa.[14] Many of the large cities in Africa have no modern sanitation system, and in Asia large shares of the populations in some areas also have no access to sanitary disposal of human waste.

There is good evidence that improved disposal of human waste is associated with reductions in diarrheal disease, intestinal parasites, and trachoma. Failure to dispose properly of human waste contaminates water and food sources and leads to an increase in transmission of pathogens through the oral–fecal route. Failure to improve sanitation is also associated with the spread of parasitic worms, such as ascaris and hookworm.[15] Improved sanitation reduces the burden of trachoma, because the flies that are significantly involved in the spread of that disease breed, among other places, in human waste.[16]

More than 1 billion people, mostly in low- and middle-income countries, lack access to safe water sources within a reasonable distance of their home.[17] Access to improved water sources in 2004 was estimated to range from 56 percent in sub-Saharan Africa to about 70 percent in Asia to almost universal access in high-income countries.[18] It is estimated that about 400 million children lack access to safe water.[19] In addition, even the water that people do have access to and that is deemed safe in official statistics often contains important pathogens. Many diseases relate to water in a variety of ways.

Waterborne diseases are among the most important in terms of the burden of disease, and they are numerous in low- and middle-income countries. Table 7-4 indicates how water-related diseases may be classified. Some of the most important waterborne pathogens are shown in Table 7-5.

TABLE 7-5 Selected Waterborne Pathogens

Enteric protozoal parasites
- *Entamoeba histolytica*
- *Giardia intestinalis*
- *Cryptosporidium parvum*
- *Cryptosporidium cayetanensis*

Bacterial enteropathogens
- *Salmonella*
- *Shigella*
- *Escherichia coli*
- *Vibrio cholerae*
- *Campylobacter*

Viral pathogens
- Enteroviruses
- Adenoviruses
- Noroviruses

Source: Adapted from Friis RH. Water quality. *Essentials of Environmental Health.* Sudbury, MA: Jones and Bartlett; 2007:211.

These pathogens are associated with diarrhea and a host of other gastrointestinal problems. As you will read about further in the chapters on child health and infectious diseases, they can be deadly when they lead to severe diarrhea and dehydration. Such diseases are especially risky for the very young, the very old, and people who have compromised immune systems, such as people living with HIV/AIDS.

THE BURDEN OF ENVIRONMENTALLY RELATED DISEASES

As noted earlier, it is estimated that about 8.4 percent of the total burden of disease in low- and middle-income countries

---

TABLE 7-4 Classification of Water-Related Infections

Transmission	Water-Related infections
Waterborne	The pathogen is in water that is ingested
Water-washed (or water-scarce)	Person-to-person transmission because of a lack of water for hygiene
Water-based	Transmission via an aquatic intermediate host
Water-related insect vector	Transmission by insects that breed in water or bite near water

Source: Data with permission from Cairncross S, Valdmanis V. Water supply, sanitation, and hygiene promotion. In: Jamison DT, Breman JG, Measham AR, et al., eds. *Disease Control Priorities in Developing Countries.* 2nd ed. Washington, DC and New York: The World Bank and Oxford University Press; 2006:775.

is due to water, sanitation, and hygiene; urban air pollution; and indoor air pollution. The relative share of each of these factors is:

- Indoor smoke from household use of solid fuels—3.7 percent
- Unsafe water, sanitation, and hygiene—3.2 percent
- Urban air pollution—1.5 percent[3]

These are explored more fully later.

Many people believe that the most important environmental risk factor in low- and middle-income countries is outdoor air pollution; however, this is not true. Rather, indoor air pollution is the third most important risk factor in high mortality developing countries, exceeded only by malnutrition and unsafe sex, and similar in importance to water, sanitation, and hygiene.[9] It is estimated that indoor air pollution from the use of solid fuels is responsible for 1.6 million deaths annually from pneumonia, chronic respiratory disease, and lung cancer. It is thought, in fact, that indoor air pollution is responsible for about 700,000 of the 2.7 million annual deaths from chronic obstructive pulmonary disease (COPD) and about 15 percent of all deaths from lung cancer.[9]

These figures include only those diseases for which there is solid evidence of a link with indoor air pollution from the use of solid fuels. However, this may be an underestimate of the real burden of disease from indoor air pollution because there is some evidence that indoor air pollution of this type is also associated with asthma, cataracts, and TB. There is also tentative evidence of links with adverse pregnancy outcomes, especially low birthweight, ischemic heart disease, and two types of cancer other than lung cancer.[9]

Almost all the burden of disease from indoor air pollution from the use of solid fuels is in low- and middle-income countries. Women do most of the cooking in low- and middle-income countries and they are most subject to the health risks from indoor air pollution. Indeed, it is estimated that 59 percent of all of the deaths attributable to indoor air pollution are among females.[9] Young children in developing countries are often carried by their mothers on their backs as they attend to household and work chores, such as cooking. They also tend to spend long hours at home with their mothers. Therefore, they are also exposed more than others to indoor air pollution. It is estimated that 56 percent of all deaths attributable to indoor air pollution are among children younger than 5 years.[9]

Urban Outdoor Air Pollution

One study of the global burden of disease attributed 1.5 percent of annual deaths and 0.5 percent of the total burden of disease to outdoor air pollution.[20] The study further indicated that 81 percent of the deaths and 49 percent of the DALYs attributable to outdoor air pollution occur among people 60 years of age or older. Three percent of the deaths and 12 percent of the DALYs occur in children younger than 5 years.[20] It also has been estimated that outdoor air pollution by urban particulate matter causes about 5 percent of the global cases of lung cancer, 2 percent of the deaths from cardiovascular and respiratory conditions, and 1 percent of respiratory infections.[21]

India and China have major burdens of disease that relate to outdoor air pollution from particulate matter. In fact, about two thirds of the global burden of disease from outdoor air pollution is in the low- and middle-income countries of Asia.[22] A number of countries in Eastern Europe also face a high burden of disease from outdoor air pollution. In some countries of that region, between 0.6 and 1.4 percent of the burden of disease is attributable to outdoor air pollution from particulate matter.[22]

Sanitation, Water, and Hygiene

Unsafe disposal of human waste, unsafe water, and poor hygiene are associated with 3.2 percent of the total deaths in low- and middle-income countries and 3.7 percent of the DALYs.[3] Studies that have been done suggest that within the African region, about 85 percent of the DALYs from these risk factors are related to the oral–fecal route of disease transmission and to diarrheal disease, primarily among young children. These studies also suggest that schistosomiasis, in the water-based group, has the second largest loss of DALYs related to these risk factors in Africa.[3]

We should expect globally that the burden of disease related to these risk factors will fall disproportionately on children, who suffer such a large share of the global burden of disease from diarrhea. The burden of these risk factors will also fall overwhelmingly on poor and less well-educated people in the poorer countries of South Asia and of sub-Saharan Africa. They have less access than others to improved water supply and sanitation and to the knowledge of good hygiene they need to avoid illness in the face of unsafe water and sanitation.

It is very complicated to try to assess individually the relative contribution of unsafe sanitation, unsafe water, and poor hygienic practices to the burden of diarrheal disease, partly because they are all so closely linked with each other. Nonetheless, both historical experiences in what are now the high-income countries and a number of studies in low- and middle-income countries suggest that improving water supply alone will not reduce diarrheal disease as needed. This seems to stem from the large amount of diarrhea that is associated with food that is unsafe and poor personal hygiene. More will be said about these later.

Separate from any impact on the reduction of diarrheal disease, improvements in water supply are associated with important reductions in the burden of disease from dracunculiasis, schistosomiasis, and trachoma.[23]

THE COSTS AND CONSEQUENCES OF KEY ENVIRONMENTAL HEALTH PROBLEMS

The social and economic consequences of the key environmental health issues that have been discussed are enormous. First, they constitute 8.4 percent of the total deaths in low- and middle-income countries and 7.2 percent of their total burden of disease. Taken together, the burden of disease from these causes is about 25 percent more than unsafe sex and about twice as much as tobacco use.[3] The magnitude of their burden itself suggests substantial social and economic costs related to these issues.

Second, as indicated earlier, the burden of these causes falls disproportionately on relatively poorer people. It is the poorer people who cook with biomass fuels and coal, not the better-off people. These burdens also fall on low- and middle-income countries more than on high-income countries. People in high-income countries do not customarily cook with biomass fuel or coal and they do not have to contend with the problems of unsafe water and sanitation that people in lower- and middle-income countries face. Their knowledge of good hygiene practices is also superior to the level of knowledge of most people in developing countries.

Third, these environmental health burdens have very negative consequences on productivity. It is women who suffer the ill effects of indoor air pollution the most. The results of this are very costly to women in terms of morbidity and disability and days of reduced productivity from both acute and chronic illnesses. In addition, the economic and social consequences of ill health for women in many low- and middle-income countries go considerably beyond just women's health. Rather, they spill over onto the health of the rest of her family, especially young children, whose own health and survival depend in important ways on the health of the mother.

Young children are especially at risk from all three forms of the environmental issues discussed in this chapter. They are especially vulnerable to unsafe water, and diarrheal disease can put them into a cycle of infection and malnutrition, ultimately retard their growth and development, or be deadly. Indoor air pollution can also lead to a cycle of illness and respiratory infection, death from pneumonia, or disability from asthma. To a lesser extent, outdoor air pollution can do the same. The elderly face particular risks from outdoor air pollution. This can exacerbate chronic health problems they already have, leading to additional disability and its attendant reduction in productivity.

REDUCING THE BURDEN OF DISEASE

Important progress has been made in some settings in addressing the environmental health issues discussed here. The next section examines some of the lessons learned to date and some of the most cost-effective measures that can be taken to enhance health in low- and middle-income countries by addressing selected environmental health issues.

Outdoor Air Pollution

Outdoor air pollution is a very broad topic, and there is very little published data on the cost-effectiveness of approaches to addressing outdoor air pollution in low- and middle-income countries. The studies that have been done on high-income countries, however, suggest that high-income countries could take a number of cost-effective steps to reduce the health burden of outdoor air pollution.[24]

A number of cities, including Jakarta, Manila, Kathmandu, and Mumbai, participated in a World Bank–assisted effort to assess their outdoor air pollution and take measures to reduce it. They examined:

- The amount and type of pollution
- How it was being dispersed
- The health impacts of reductions in particulate matter
- Time and cost to implement reductions
- Health benefits
- The value of those health benefits
- How the benefits compared to the costs of the intervention[24]

Some of the first measures that these cities and some other large cities in low- and middle-income countries have taken to reduce outdoor air pollution have included:

- The introduction of unleaded gasoline
- Low-smoke lubricant for two-stroke engines
- The banning of two-stroke engines
- Shifting to natural gas to fuel public vehicles
- Tightening emissions inspections on vehicles
- Reducing the burning of garbage[24]

It would also be reasonable to ensure that governments use their regulatory authority to incorporate information about outdoor air pollution in their policies on transportation and industrial development.[24] In line with this, many of the low-income countries do not yet have a significant problem of outdoor air pollution. It will be much more cost-effective for those countries to put in place cost-effective approaches now to minimize outdoor air pollution and its health effects than it will be to try later to mitigate those effects. In doing so, they should take account of vehicular and industrial pollution.

Indoor Air Pollution

There are a number of areas in which actions could be taken to reduce indoor air pollution from the burning of solid fuels for cooking and heating. In terms of the source of pollution, cooking devices can be improved, less polluting fuels can be used, and families can reduce their need for these fuels by using solar cooking and heating. Some changes can also be made to the living environment. Mechanisms for venting smoke can be built into the house, for example, or the kitchen can be moved away from the main part of the house. People can also change their behaviors to reduce pollution or exposure to it by using dried fuels, properly maintaining their stoves and chimneys, and keeping children away from the cooking area.[25]

Public policy can also play a helpful or hurtful role in trying to reduce indoor air pollution. The public sector, for example, can promote information and education about indoor air pollution and how to reduce it in schools, in the media, and in communities. The government can also use tax policy to reduce the cost of cooking appliances and fuels that will reduce pollution. If necessary, it could subsidize the cost of improved fuels and appliances for those below a certain income level. Governments could also undertake surveillance of the problem and, if possible, set and enforce standards for indoor air pollution, although this will certainly be beyond the capacity of most low-income countries.[25]

Calculating the cost-effectiveness of different approaches to reducing the health effects of indoor air pollution is a very complicated matter and requires many assumptions. Nonetheless, the conclusions of the analyses that have been done are instructive. The main findings are that the most cost-effective approach to reducing indoor air pollution in sub-Saharan Africa and South Asia, where the needs are greatest, would be to promote the use of improved stoves. The most cost-effective approach in East Asia would be to promote the use of better fuels, such as kerosene and gas. Of course, these conclusions presume that the stoves get maintained and the fuels are of good quality, which may not always be the case and the failure of which would detract from the effectiveness of these approaches.[26]

In addition, a number of lessons have been learned about how to encourage the uptake of better stoves and better

fuels, some drawn from extensive experiences in China and India. These include:

- Involve end users, especially women, in helping to assess needs and design approaches.
- Promote demand for better stoves and fuels to encourage the development of competitive suppliers and market choice.
- Consider subsidies and microcredit for selected interventions to help defray the cost of improvements for the poor.
- Establish national and local policies that encourage the needed changes in stoves and fuels.[27]

Sanitation

There are a number of different levels of technology associated with excreta disposal, many different forms of toilets, and a wide array of costs associated with them. Sanitation could range from the simple technology of bucket latrines to modern urban sewage systems. Table 7-6 lists the different approaches to excreta disposal. Although we usually think of toilets as owned by individuals, they can also be public and shared by many individuals and families.

The cost per person for methods of sanitary removal of human waste varies considerably. At the bottom levels of service, it appears that pour-flush latrines, ventilation-improved latrines, and simple pit latrines can be constructed in low- and middle-income settings for about $60. Assuming that these last approximately 5 years, the annual cost per capita would be about $12. The construction cost of conventional sewage systems in some countries is more than 10 times that amount. In addition, they need water to function properly and water is often in short supply.[28] Work is ongoing to develop more cost-effective toilets, and in Bangladesh a simple pour-flush pan has been developed that costs only about $0.27 per household to construct.[28]

Contrary to what we might normally believe, all of these systems can be operated in a hygienic manner that addresses health concerns. A very important review that was done in the early 1980s, for example, concluded that from the point of view of health, pit latrines would be just as hygienic as modern sewage systems, even if they were considerably less convenient.[29]

Given the relatively low cost of simple methods of sanitation and their relative effectiveness, it might be surprising that such a small share of households in low- and middle-income countries have a sanitary means of excreta disposal. Yet, besides the cultural constraints to their use, there are some other important constraints, as well:

- *Lack of knowledge of options:* The poor in particular may not understand the options available to them and may believe that toilets cost more to install than they do.
- *Cost:* Even at relatively low prices, the poor may not have the money to pay for the up-front costs of a toilet.
- *Construction:* There may be a lack of skills to help install the toilets.
- *Local laws:* Particularly in urban areas, local laws may forbid low-cost sanitation, even if the area has no modern sewage system.[30]

In some countries the public sector leads the effort to build low-cost sanitation systems. In some places, the public sector also subsidizes the cost of toilets for the poorest families, given what can be seen as the benefits to society as a whole of toilets being used by individual families. In addition, the public sector can try to enforce regulations to require the use of toilets. Although such regulatory authority is weak in most low-income and many middle-income countries, one of the main cities in Burkina Faso was able to promote toilet construction by taking away the title of homes if their owners did not install a toilet within a specific period of time.[31]

It is also possible, if the private sector believes that there is a market for low-cost sanitation, for such efforts to be handled in the private sector. In this case, the public sector may confine its role to areas needed to encourage private sector involvement and public demand for the toilets. This would include, for example, promoting the use of toilets, encouraging private sector involvement, setting standards, and helping to train people in installation and maintenance techniques.[31]

Promotion of improved sanitation can also be done with a public and private partnership and led by NGOs. Two of the most successful cases of improving low-cost sanitation were led by NGOs in Zimbabwe and Bangladesh. In Zimbabwe, an NGO was able to help communities construct 3400 latrines for about $13 per unit, or only about $2.25 per person served.[32] In Bangladesh, an NGO has helped to make 100 villages free of open defecation for a cost of only about $1.50 per person served.[33] In both of these cases, the families in the communities served paid for the latrines themselves.

The largest impact of improved sanitation is in the reduction of diarrhea; studies suggest that this impact may be on the order of about 35 percent overall. Some studies, such as one in Brazil, suggested that children living in slum homes with a toilet suffered only one third the number of cases of diarrhea as children in homes without a toilet. It is very

important to note that having a toilet seems to also increase the handwashing habits of families, which itself brings benefits, as discussed later.

Finally, the benefits of sanitary excreta removal go beyond reducing diarrhea. Improving sanitation should reduce the prevalence of several worms, including ascaris, trichuris, and hookworm.[34] Given the low cost of some forms of latrines, they would be cost-effective approaches to reducing the prevalence of these worms. As noted earlier, the same would be true in terms of the positive impact and low costs of reducing trachoma through improved sanitation.[35]

Water Supply

There are many analogies between water supply and sanitation. For water, as well as for sanitation, there are many different levels of technology and the costs vary considerably according to the level of technology employed. One could get water, for example, from the following types of improved water sources:

- House connection
- Standpost
- Borehole
- Dug well
- Rainwater collection

This section examines the relative cost-effectiveness of different approaches to achieving health benefits from improved water supply. In considering these costs and benefits, reasonable access to water was considered to be access to at least 20 liters per day from one of these sources from not more than 1 kilometer distance.[36]

Improving water supply can lead to a variety of health benefits. The most important studies that have been done

TABLE 7-6 Selected Sanitation Technologies

- Simple pit latrine
- Small bore sewer
- Ventilation-improved latrine
- Pour-flush
- Septic tank
- Sewer connection

Source: Data with permission from Cairncross S, Valdmanis V. Water supply, sanitation, and hygiene promotion. In: Jamison DT, Breman JG, Measham AR, et al., eds. *Disease Control Priorities in Developing Countries.* 2nd ed. Washington, DC and New York: The World Bank and Oxford University Press; 2006:780.

have shown that providing a continuous supply of water with good bacteriological quality can reduce the morbidity of a number of diseases, as shown in Table 7-7. Studies showed a median reduction in trachoma, for example, of 27 percent, schistosomiasis of 77 percent, and dracunculiasis of 78 percent.[23]

Other studies have looked at the health benefits from different combinations of investments in water quantity, water quality, sanitation, and the promotion of hygiene. The results of these studies are somewhat surprising to those not involved in the environmental field. They suggest that the largest reductions in diarrhea morbidity—approximately 30 percent—come from investing in sanitation only, water and sanitation, or hygiene only. The lowest reductions, between 15 percent and 20 percent, came from investing in water quantity only, or a combination of water quality and quantity, all without complementary investments in hygiene or in sanitation.

As noted earlier, many of the pathogens that are waterborne are also carried on food. Thus, sanitation has a large potential impact on reducing those pathogens. However, water alone may not yield the results that sanitation would. For this, among other reasons, complementary investments for the promotion of hygiene are critical to realizing gains from water and sanitation.[37]

Another important lesson is that the greatest effect of investments in water on health are realized when people have water connections in their homes. Unfortunately, community standpipes, for example, do not produce the level of health gains of individual household water connections.[37] A review in New Guinea, for example, showed that there was

TABLE 7-7 Potential Morbidity Reduction from Excellent Water Supply

Condition	Percentage Reduction
Scabies	80
Typhoid fever	80
Trachoma	60
Most diarrheas and dysentery	50
Skin and subcutaneous infections	50
Paratyphoid, other *Salmonella*	40

Source: Adapted with permission from Cairncross S, Valdmanis V. Water supply, sanitation, and hygiene promotion. In: Jamison DT, Breman JG, Measham AR, et al., eds. *Disease Control Priorities in Developing Countries.* 2nd ed. Washington, DC and New York: The World Bank and Oxford University Press; 2006:776.

56 percent less diarrhea in homes with an individual connection than in homes that got their water from standpipes.[37] This may partly be the case because people with individual connections use considerably more water than those without such connections and much of the additional water may be used to engage in better hygiene.

Hygiene

Unfortunately, there have been relatively few studies of the impact of hygiene promotion on actual health behaviors and on related reductions in the burden of disease. The studies that have been done showed that investing in hygiene promotion led to a 33 percent reduction in diarrhea. They also found that to be successful and sustainable, hygiene promotion efforts need to focus on simple messages about handwashing and avoid trying to promote too many messages at once. It appears that the messages that families acquire through hygiene promotion do stay with them, and that retraining is necessary only once every 5 years.[38] Studies have also been done on the impact of handwashing on respiratory infections. Handwashing was associated in these studies with a significant reduction in acute respiratory infections.[38]

Integrating Investment Choices About Water, Sanitation, and Hygiene

When the information from the studies previously discussed is reviewed together, it appears that the promotion of hygiene, the promotion of sanitation, and the construction of standposts are all likely to be cost-effective in low- and middle-income countries. However, using public funds to provide individual household connections to water supply systems is likely to be above the cut-off for cost-effective investments. This is shown in Table 7-8.

The costs of hygiene and sanitation promotion compare favorably, for example, with the costs per DALY averted of oral rehydration. In addition, such investments might help to reduce the burden of diarrhea and decrease the need for oral rehydration.

On that basis, what would be a sensible approach to improving health through investments in water supply, sanitation, and hygiene in low- and middle-income countries? First would be to promote hygiene. This is necessary both for its own sake and to maximize the value that will accrue from investments in water supply and sanitation. Second, governments should promote low-cost sanitation schemes. In doing this, they should encourage the private sector to invest in this business, encourage demand from consumers, try to ensure that there are skills to install the latrines, and try to set and enforce standards to which they have to be built. Third, low-cost water supply schemes should also be developed. This can often be done best in conjunction with communities and with community-based approaches. Finally, the government should use its regulatory and other authority to be sure that it helps consumers meet the costs of these schemes and also encourages investment in water supply schemes with household connections that families pay for. Much has been written about approaches to water and sanitation. Those interested in how such schemes get designed, built, operated, and financed are encouraged to review some of the literature on those topics, which is beyond the scope of this book.

POLICY AND PROGRAM BRIEFS

Three policy and program briefs follow that reflect the importance of hygiene, sanitation, and indoor air pollution to health. They also suggest ways in which community-based approaches can be taken to address the failure to wash hands with soap and the problem of open defecation. The first case discusses a program for handwashing with soap in Senegal. The second concerns a campaign for "total sanitation" in East Java, Indonesia. Both cases were largely successful in meeting their goals and have valuable lessons for other countries trying to improve hygiene and sanitation. The third case comments on the increasing attention being paid to improved efficiency cookstoves and their potential health impact.

Handwashing with Soap in Senegal

Handwashing with soap is key to preventing the spread of disease because it kills various agents, such as harmful bacteria, that can cause infection. Nonetheless, the rate of handwashing with soap in Senegal is relatively low, as it is in many low- and middle-income countries. According to a study conducted in Senegal in 2004, for example, the rate of handwashing with soap was 18 percent after cleaning a child, 18 percent before handling food, and 23 percent after going to the toilet.[39] Distance between soap and a source of water, soap being controlled by people who don't want to share it, and the lack of a designated place for handwashing are all barriers to handwashing with soap in Senegal.

The Public-Private Partnership for Handwashing with Soap (PPPHW) was created in Senegal in 2003 with the mission to promote handwashing with soap. With technical assistance from an international partnership housed at the World Bank, the Water and Sanitation Program (WSP), PPPHW was originally sited within the Senegalese government unit that oversees sanitation within the Ministry of Health.

The PPPHW launched a communications campaign in 2004 with the goal of educating people about the importance of using soap when washing hands, in addition to the

TABLE 7-8 Cost per DALY of Selected Investments in Water, Sanitation, and Hygiene

Investment	US$/DALY
Hygiene promotion	3.35
Sanitation promotion only	11.15
Water sector regulation and advocacy	47.00
Hand pump or standpost	94.00
House connection	223.00
Construction and promotion	≤ 270.00

Source: Adapted with permission from Cairncross S, Valdmanis V. Water supply, sanitation, and hygiene promotion. In: Jamison DT, Breman JG, Measham AR, et al., eds. *Disease Control Priorities in Developing Countries.* 2nd ed. Washington, DC and New York: The World Bank and Oxford University Press; 2006:791.

most critical times for handwashing. "Water Rinses but Soap Cleans" was the main message of this first phase of communications efforts.

The campaign made use of a number of communications methods to send its message. Television and radio spots were aired nationally, especially during times when mothers were preparing meals. More than 87 percent of Senegalese own radios and 40.1 percent own televisions, explaining why mass media can be an effective tool for exposing the campaign's slogan and visual aspects. Billboards, which are prevalent in Senegal, were also used.

The campaign also hosted interactive local community events to extend its messages directly to the population. Local marketplaces and schools hosted live entertainment and demonstrations to educate women and children about the importance of handwashing with soap. In addition, small-group discussions were held at women's associations and waiting rooms of local health centers to facilitate communication among the people about the importance of using soap.

The PPPHW project introduced a second phase of activities to promote handwashing with soap in 2008 after being incorporated into the Water and Sanitation Program's Global Scaling Up Handwashing Project, which seeks to "apply innovative promotional approaches to behavior change to generate widespread and sustained improvements in handwashing with soap." The project expanded in this phase to reach 8 of the 11 regions in Senegal with a more defined target of women of reproductive age and primary school–aged children ages 5 to 9. The goal was to improve handwashing with soap practices of over 500,000 mothers and children.

Studies in 2008 identified which behavioral determinants were correlated with handwashing with soap in an attempt to incorporate a wider spectrum of behavioral determinants into the second phase of the behavior change program. At this point, the majority of the 2040 mothers who participated in the study understood the campaign message of the first phase, or the importance of using soap when handwashing. Fifty-two percent disagreed with the statement that "water alone is enough." Mothers also understood the link between handwashing with soap and disease prevention, with close to 80 percent agreeing or strongly agreeing that removing dirt and invisible germs requires handwashing with soap. However, research suggested that access to and availability of soap and water in the household is a key determinant for handwashing with soap and had to be planned for.

Based on the assumption that most mothers now understood the importance of handwashing with soap, the second phase of the program aimed to "awaken, fortify, and support" intentions to wash hands with soap. The campaign encouraged mothers to act upon intentions by planning for handwashing, such as designating a certain place for handwashing with soap. The campaign message was delivered through the same communications channels used in the first phase. With technical assistance and guidance from WSP, local communications and consulting firms and NGOs designed, planned, and carried out different components of the project.

New billboards and radio and television spots were created with the intention of positively reinforcing mothers' and children's commitment to washing hands with soap. From June to December 2009, 92 television and 1496 radio spots aired. At local soccer games and other community locations, respected community members gave handwashing demonstrations and testimonials of their pledge to wash hands with soap. The 161 events that were held through December 2009 reached an estimated 140,000 people.

Workers from local NGOs also visited homes to discuss with mothers tangible ways of turning into action the intention of washing hands with soap. The 150 trained workers helped mothers plan the necessary steps for setting up a designated handwashing station, including making sure that water and soap were available and accessible.

Of course, the program has faced a number of challenges. Engaging local partners, while still ensuring that campaign messages were communicated effectively and consistently, presented some initial challenges. At first, local advertising agencies created negative messages that emphasized germs and disease, rather than positive messages of healthy outcomes from handwashing with soap, as instructed. As a result, WSP worked closely with local agencies to coordinate advertisements.

Another challenge has been making sure that outreach workers who visit homes go beyond offering information, by discussing mothers' obstacles to handwashing with soap and devising practical solutions through careful planning and building of handwashing stations. Performance monitoring and coaching of workers has helped to ensure they do their job effectively. A lesson learned for changing behavior is that the use or demonstration of a tangible product that facilitates behavior change, such as a sample handwashing station, can be a powerful tool for turning intention into action.

This project also exemplifies the importance of continually revising campaign strategy to account for the project's past successes or failures. In addition to reevaluating the entire campaign message to launch the second phase, throughout this phase certain program elements will be further revised to reflect current evaluations. The 2008 campaign advertisements originally portrayed men merely as social supporters; however, recent monitoring of the program suggests that a man's role in the family as provider, protector, and role model gives him tremendous influence in promoting handwashing with soap. In fact, half of women surveyed consider their husbands the decision makers in purchasing soap. Thus, program planners are realizing the significant role that men play in overcoming barriers to accessibility and availability of soap, and they are adjusting the campaign to engage men more in "selling" the importance of handwashing with soap. Modified communication materials portray men as committed to handwashing with soap, thus fortifying men's intentions to do so and increasing the visibility of their influential role.[40]

The second phase of the project is currently being monitored to examine the extent to which people do engage in handwashing with soap and the impact of this practice on the health of the involved communities.

Total Sanitation and Sanitation Marketing: East Java, Indonesia[41]

The Water and Sanitation Program is an international partnership housed at the World Bank that supports poor people in acquiring affordable, safe, and sustainable access to water and sanitation services.[42] One part of this program has been Total Sanitation and Sanitation Marketing (TSSM) projects in a number of countries. These are based on a three-pronged approach to rapidly increasing the number of people who use sanitary means of disposing of human waste:

- The development of a strategy for changing behaviors, based on consumer research
- The development of an approach to increasing the market for latrines, based on market research
- A community-led campaign for "total sanitation"—an approach that seeks to make a community completely free of open defecation

TSSM projects also pay particular attention to the monitoring of progress, continuous evaluation of results, and "learning as you go." Special emphasis is also placed on creating an "enabling environment" for the project to meet its goals, by working to enhance the policy, institutional, and financial frameworks within which a sanitation program has to be carried out.

In 2007, a TSSM project was launched in East Java, Indonesia. At the time the project was launched, sanitation coverage was just below 70 percent in urban areas and only about 55 percent in rural areas. The intended project outcome was to provide access to sustainable sanitation services for 1.4 million people, in one of the most densely populated places in the world.[43]

This project paid greater attention than many earlier projects to involving the community in the design and development of the project, having the community participate financially in the project, increasing the community's demand for toilets, and ensuring that there would be a sufficient supply of appropriate toilets to meet that demand.[44]

Demand Creation

Districts had to volunteer to participate in the program. One of the first steps in the implementation of the project in East Java, therefore, was to create community-based and household-level demand for improved sanitation.

In order to garner government support of the behavior change program, discussions were held with local and district officials about the economic impact of poor sanitation at the country and district levels and the social and economic returns from investing in sanitation improvements.[43]

To create demand for improved sanitation, the project utilized the Community-Led Total Sanitation (CLTS) methodology, which mobilizes communities to completely eliminate open defecation. This approach focuses on community-wide sustainable behavioral change, rather than toilet construction for individual households. CLTS efforts try to help communities understand that, regardless of the number of toilets constructed, there is still a risk of disease if even one person continues to defecate in the open. As part of the CLTS approach, communities develop their own solutions to obtain improved sanitation and become open defecation free.[43] An initial step in this process is mapping village boundaries and indicating where people defecate in the open.[45]

In addition, the program used marketing techniques to improve the demand for sanitation-related products and services, which included advertisements for desirable hygienic behaviors.[45] The program created and marketed, for example, a communication campaign with a character, "Lik Telek," or "Uncle Shit" in the local language, which personifies the open defecation habit. With flies dancing around his head, and a smug smile, Lik Telek goes behind a tree to defecate in the open, while onlookers advise him to use improved sanitation facilities.[46] The districts fund the campaign, which includes a series of posters, radio commercials, and an 8-minute video drama.

Improvements in the Supply of Sanitation

The project conducted market research for 18 months to better understand the sanitation market, as well as the demand for sanitation services. Market research revealed that there was no common definition of what is the "ideal" sanitation facility among consumers, sanitation suppliers, and engineers. Standards varied greatly and generated an impression that a good sanitation facility was unaffordable. In addition, open defecation into water was considered socially acceptable, convenient, safe, and clean because the feces are considered invisible, carried away by water or eaten by fish.

In light of these findings, the project worked with designers and suppliers to ensure that there would be a common definition of improved sanitation and that various sanitation options would be available, at a range of prices. To popularize a common definition of an "ideal" sanitation facility, the program created a "WC-ku Sehat," or "my latrine is healthy/hygienic," thumbs-up sign to identify facilities that meet the "improved sanitation" criteria. The program also prepared an Informed Choice Catalogue of improved WC-ku Sehat sanitation options at varying prices, which displays all possible combinations of belowground, on the ground, and aboveground sections of latrines.[43]

To further strengthen the quantity, quality, and appropriateness of the supply of sanitation, a technological training institute in East Java holds a mason training and accreditation program. This aims to ensure that a qualified mason will be available in every district to work on improved sanitation facilities. As of June 2009, a total of 600 artisans in 10 districts were trained in this way, and an additional 1110 artisans were to receive training after that.[44]

Achievement of Project Goals

Overall, the program appears to have produced larger benefits than more conventional approaches to sanitation that had less community involvement, market- and community-based research, or research-based strategies for increasing both demand and supply. The community-led approach in East Java yielded a 49 percent increase in access to improved sanitation within an 18-month period. More conventional approaches generally yield increases of only about 10–15 percent over such a period. Moreover, between November 2007 and May 2009, more than 325,000 persons gained access to improved sanitation facilities in 21 districts of East Java. As important, again in contrast to the conventional approach, the poorest households in East Java established 715 open defecation–free villages and gained access to improved sanitation at higher rates than nonpoor households.

It is also anticipated that the TSSM approach taken in East Java will be more sustainable than less community-based approaches, because it involves active participation and community investment, and is not dependent on external funding. Community households finance their own projects or collaborate with credit groups. Local governments co-fund project interventions. TSSM approaches are integrated into local governments' budgeting, planning, implementation, and monitoring systems, which should also make them more sustainable.[43] One year of the subsidy-free approach taken in this project led to 10 to 15 times more toilets being constructed than in conventional subsidized schemes.

Nonetheless, the TSSM program in Indonesia still faces a number of challenges. New interventions such as sanitation marketing, although effective, require significant inputs from skilled staff that are in short supply. They are also resource-intensive and may be beyond the financial means of local governments. In addition, because Indonesia did not have a national sanitation program at the time the East Java program was launched, the government would need sustained political commitment and help from TSSM to scale up total sanitation efforts to other Indonesian provinces.[44]

Improved Efficiency Cookstoves

Increasing attention is being paid to improved efficiency cookstoves for their potential to reduce the health burden associated with indoor air pollution, the emission of greenhouse gases, the economic and social burden of collecting or purchasing fuel, and, in some locations, the environmental stress of excessive biomass harvesting for fuel. When com-

bined with programs to access sustainable fuels, the use of these devices could potentially significantly reduce the global burden of disease at a very low cost.

Smoke exposure from biomass combustion in stoves, often inside small, unventilated homes, is a significant cause of respiratory infections, which globally rank as a leading cause of both morbidity and mortality. Recent studies reveal the exposure–response relationship between particulate smoke, which can be reduced by improved efficiency cookstoves, and acute respiratory illness (ARI). For example, when 500 people on an isolated ranch in Kenya were monitored for fuel and stove use, indoor pollution levels, and subsequent health outcomes, it was determined that the transition from the least efficient stoves and fuels, such as those using dung or agricultural wastes burned on a "three stone fire," to the most efficient stoves and fuels, such as the improved wood or charcoal stoves, could cut the incidence of ARIs by half.[47-49] Since that initial field study, several other efforts have emerged with similar findings, and different stoves and stove/fuel combinations yield different degrees of health benefits.

If implemented effectively, a regionally tailored but globally coordinated stove program could significantly reduce the total global burden of disease. Furthermore, improved efficiency stoves can reduce both CO_2 and non-CO_2 emissions from stoves, also significantly reducing greenhouse gases around the world. Thus, improved efficiency stoves are of interest to the global climate, global health, and development communities.

In addition, the cost effectiveness of programs to disseminate improved stoves was found to be superior to many of the public health programs in use around the globe. This was demonstrated by an analysis that followed the initial identification of the health benefits of improved, pollution reducing, stoves.[48] On a per-DALY basis, for example, improved stoves can reduce illness as cheaply—as low as $1 per DALY—as the programs for childhood immunization and vitamin supplementation.

As demonstrated in a longitudinal study of a rural community in Kenya, and in an increasingly diverse set of pilot projects, improved stoves can be effectively introduced in communities throughout Africa, Asia, and Latin America. Stove programs have been proven to work if the design phase, the testing and feedback phase, and the dissemination efforts are coordinated and involve true partnerships between those who develop the stove program and those who implement it, even though this is often difficult. Outreach efforts must ensure that the stoves are adapted to local customer needs and preferences. Additionally, the support of local market forces, including local entrepreneurs, is necessary to bring these stoves to markets throughout the developing world at the lowest possible cost. In the future, it is hoped that a range of new and improved stove designs could invigorate community groups, the public health sector, and end users to work together to implement these programs around the globe.

As communities, nations, and the global community explore avenues to connect local needs for increased energy services to regional development efforts,[50] it is likely that attention will continue to be paid to improved efficiency cookstoves. This would be in line with their potential for direct health and economic benefits for end users, impact on forest management, and reduction of global greenhouse gas emissions.[51]

FUTURE CHALLENGES

Many challenges will be associated with reducing the burden of disease that is related to hygiene, water supply, and sanitation; indoor air pollution; and outdoor air pollution. One important challenge has to do with population growth. The population is continuing to grow in many developing countries and will do so for some time. As the population grows, and as increasing numbers of people move to cities, for example, will low- and middle-income countries be able to provide the infrastructure needed for improved water supply and sanitation when they already face such substantial gaps in this provision?

At the same time, as the economies of low- and middle-income countries hopefully grow at a relatively rapid and sustained pace, how will they manage the pollution that is related, for example, to increased use of energy and greater use by better-off people of automobiles? In addition, will relatively poorly governed societies be able to manage and regulate industrial forms of pollution that could further harm air and water quality?

Many of the more difficult problems of indoor air pollution and health impacts of unsafe water and sanitation exact a larger toll on rural people than urban people, on the poor rather than the better-off, and on women and children. In this light, many countries will need to explore ways to reduce indoor air pollution and improve the safety of the water supply through community-based approaches. Such approaches will often have to link the public, private, and NGO sectors with communities and that will have to explicitly focus on women and children.

Reducing the burden of environmentally related health problems will also require that people be better informed about that burden. At the societal level, people and communities will need to understand more about the links between their health and the environment. At national,

regional, local, and family levels, people will also need to be more aware of the solutions to these problems that might be available to them. The need for better and more information about issues and options for addressing them will be especially important among the poor, the poorly educated, the rural, and women.

Another challenge of addressing environmental health issues is that efforts to address them generally require action outside the health sector. Urban water supply systems are usually under the control of public or private companies. Urban sanitation is usually managed by individual cities. In rural areas, water supply and sanitation are most likely to be controlled by communities and individuals. Indoor air pollution is an issue that can best be addressed by working with families and communities to change the way they cook and the fuel they use for cooking. Outdoor air pollution comes, among other things, from industrial plants and vehicles, the control of which depends on an array of economic and policy matters beyond the scope of the health ministry.

MAIN MESSAGES

Environmental health issues have a large impact on the global burden of disease. These impacts occur at the individual, household, community, and global level. Broadly speaking, about one third of the total global burden of disease is related to environmental factors.[52] About 8 percent of the global burden of disease is associated with the environmental factors discussed in this chapter, including outdoor air pollution, indoor air pollution from the use of sold fuels, and water, sanitation, and hygiene.[3]

The risks of these environmental factors are greatest for poor women and their children due to their exposure to indoor air pollution from the burning of solid fuel and to poor quality water. The risks of environmental impacts on health are greatest in the low-income countries of Africa and Asia. Environmental risk factors are especially important causes of illness and death from diarrhea and acute respiratory infections among young children. They also have a large impact on the burden of disease from certain parasitic infections, such as worms. Given the prominence of these risk factors, it is essential that improvements be made in water, sanitation, and hygiene if the MDGs are to be met.

The burden of indoor air pollution stems largely from cooking on unventilated stoves with solid biomass fuels or coal, as done by a large share of poor people in the world. The sources of outdoor air pollution are many, and vehicle emission is among the most important in most cities. Poor sanitation allows pathogens in human waste to spread, but only about 60 percent of the people in the world have access to improved sanitation. Unsafe water carries pathogens. The lack of water prevents people from engaging in appropriate hygiene practices. Poor hygiene practices, including open defecation and the failure to engage in handwashing, are common in low- and middle-income countries, especially among people who lack education.

Data are weak on cost-effective approaches to reducing outdoor air pollution in low- and middle-income countries. However, it appears that a number of measures could be taken to reduce pollution and enhance health, including eliminating leaded gasoline, eliminating two-stroke engines, strengthening emissions standards, and shifting vehicle fuel to natural gas. In Africa and South Asia, the most cost-effective approach to reducing indoor air pollution will be to promote the use of improved stoves. In East Asia, the most cost-effective approach would be to encourage a shift from biomass fuels and coal to kerosene or gas.

The most cost-effective approach to reducing the burden of water-related diseases, especially diarrhea, is to invest in low-cost sanitation and standposts for water and to promote handwashing. Investments in water can have numerous benefits, including saving the time of women who are usually charged with getting water and often have to expend large amounts of energy to do so. The provision of water can also contribute to reduction in certain parasitic diseases. However, in the absence of improved hygiene, the provision of improved access to water alone still fails to address an important share of the burden of diarrheal disease.

Study Questions

1. Why are environmental health issues important in global health? Which of them are the most important and why?

2. Why would the burden of disease from indoor air pollution in low- and middle-income countries be larger than that from outdoor air pollution?

3. In what regions of the world would the burden from indoor air pollution be the greatest? Why?

4. What are the different ways in which unsafe water is related to the spread of disease? Give some examples of specific diseases that are spread in various water-related ways.

5. What are some of the health problems associated with outdoor air pollution?

6. Why is it important to promote handwashing?

7. What approach would you take in a low-income African country to enhance the access of the poor to better water supplies? Why?

8. How would you try to expand access to low-cost sanitation in Nepal? Why?

9. What would constrain poor people in Nepal from investing their own resources in improved low-cost sanitation? How could those constraints be overcome?

10. How would you help people in Guatemala to adopt the use of better stoves?

REFERENCES

1. Lopez AD, Mathers CD, Murray CJL. *Global Burden of Disease and Risk Factors*. New York: Oxford University Press; 2006.

2. Smith KR, Corvalan CF, Kjellstrom T. How much global ill health is attributable to environmental factors? *Epidemiology*. 1999;10(5):573.

3. Lopez AD, Mathers CD, Ezzati M, Jamison DT, Murray CJL. Measuring the global burden of disease and risk factors 1990–2001. In: Lopez AD, Mathers CD, Ezzati M, Jamison DT, Murray CJL, eds. *Global Burden of Disease and Risk Factors*. New York: Oxford University Press; 2006:10.

4. Friis RH. *Essentials on Environmental Health*. Sudbury, MA: Jones and Bartlett Publishers; 2007.

5. Yassi A, Kjellstrom T, de Kok T, Guidotti TL. *Basic Environmental Health*. New York: Oxford University Press; 2001.

6. McMichael AJ, Kjellstrom T, Smith KR. Environmental health. In: Merson MH, Black RE, Mills A, eds. *International Public Health: Diseases, Programs, Systems, and Policies*. Gaithersburg, MD: Aspen Publishers; 2001:379.

7. The World Bank. Environmental Health. Available at: http://web.worldbank.org/WBSITE/EXTERNAL/TOPICS/EXTHEALTHNUTRITIONANDPOPULATION/EXTPHAAG/0,,contentMDK:20656146~menuPK:2175463~pagePK:64229817~piPK:64229743~theSitePK:672263,00.html. Accessed October 27, 2006.

8. World Health Organization. Protection of the Human Environment. Available at: http://www.who.int/phe/en. Accessed May 19, 2005.

9. World Health Organization. Indoor Air Pollution and Health: Fact Sheet No. 292. Available at: http://www.who.int/mediacentre/factsheets/fs292/en/index.html. Accessed October 29, 2006.

10. Yassi A, Kjellstrom T, de Kok T, Guidotti TL. Health and energy use. *Basic Environmental Health*. New York: Oxford University Press; 2001:315.

11. Yassi A, Kjellstrom T, de Kok T, Guidotti TL. Health and energy use. *Basic Environmental Health*. New York: Oxford University Press; 2001:317.

12. Yassi A, Kjellstrom T, de Kok T, Guidotti TL. Air. *Basic Environmental Health*. New York: Oxford University Press; 2001:188.

13. Yassi A, Kjellstrom T, de Kok T, Guidotti TL. Air. *Basic Environmental Health*. New York: Oxford University Press; 2001:193-194.

14. World Resources Institute. Sanitation: Access and Health. Available at: http://earthtrends.wri.org/updates/Node/359. Accessed November 6, 2010.

15. Cairncross S, Valdmanis V. Water supply, sanitation, and hygiene promotion. In: Jamison DT, Breman JG, Measham AR, et al., eds. *Disease Control Priorities in Developing Countries*. 2nd ed. New York: Oxford University Press; 2006:776.

16. Cairncross S, Valdmanis V. Water supply, sanitation, and hygiene promotion. In: Jamison DT, Breman JG, Measham AR, et al., eds. *Disease Control Priorities in Developing Countries*. 2nd ed. New York: Oxford University Press; 2006:784.

17. World Bank. Access to Safe Water. Available at: http://www.worldbank.org/depweb/english/modules/environm/water. Accessed November 3, 2006.

18. Pacific Institute. The World's Water. MDG Progress on Access to Safe Drinking Water by Region. Available at: http://www.worldwater.org/data.html. Accessed November 6, 2010.

19. UNICEF. Press Release: 400 Million Children Deprived of Safe Water. Available at: http://www.unicef.org/media/media_31772.html. Accessed November 3, 2006.

20. Ostro B. Outdoor Air Pollution: Assessing the Environmental Burden of Disease at National and Local Levels. Available at: http://www.who.int/quantifying_ehimpacts/publications/ebd5.pdf. Accessed November 3, 2006.

21. Kjellstrom T, Lodh M, McMichael AJ, Ranmuthugala G, Shrestha R, Kingsland S. Air and water pollution: burden and strategies for control. In: Jamison DT, Breman JG, Measham AR, et al., eds. *Disease Control Priorities in Developing Countries*. 2nd ed. New York: Oxford University Press; 2006:820.

22. Cohen AJ, Ross Anderson H, Ostro B, et al. The global burden of disease due to outdoor air pollution. *J Toxicol Environ Health Part A*. 2005;68(13-14):1301-1307.

23. Cairncross S, Valdmanis V. Water supply, sanitation, and hygiene promotion. In: Jamison DT, Breman JG, Measham AR, et al., eds. *Disease Control Priorities in Developing Countries*. 2nd ed. New York: Oxford University Press; 2006:778.

24. Kjellstrom T, Lodh M, McMichael AJ, Ranmuthugala G, Shrestha R, Kingsland S. Air and water pollution: burden and strategies for control. In: Jamison DT, Breman JG, Measham AR, et al., eds. *Disease Control Priorities in Developing Countries*. 2nd ed. New York: Oxford University Press; 2006:825-826.

25. Bruce N, Rehfuess E, Mehta S, Hutton G, Smith K. Indoor air pollution. In: Jamison DT, Breman JG, Measham AR, et al., eds. *Disease Control Priorities in Developing Countries*. 2nd ed. New York: Oxford University Press; 2006:800.

26. Bruce N, Rehfuess E, Mehta S, Hutton G, Smith K. Indoor air pollution. In: Jamison DT, Breman JG, Measham AR, et al., eds. *Disease Control Priorities in Developing Countries*. 2nd ed. New York: Oxford University Press; 2006:802-808.

27. Bruce N, Rehfuess E, Mehta S, Hutton G, Smith K. Indoor air pollution. In: Jamison DT, Breman JG, Measham AR, et al., eds. *Disease Control Priorities in Developing Countries*. 2nd ed. New York: Oxford University Press; 2006:808-811.

28. Cairncross S, Valdmanis V. Water supply, sanitation, and hygiene promotion. In: Jamison DT, Breman JG, Measham AR, et al., eds. *Disease Control Priorities in Developing Countries*. 2nd ed. New York: Oxford University Press; 2006:780.

29. Feachem R, Bradley D, Garelick H, Mara D. *Sanitation and Disease: Health Aspects of Excreta and Wastewater Management*. Chichester, U.K.: John Wiley & Sons; 1983.

30. Cairncross S, Valdmanis V. Water supply, sanitation, and hygiene promotion. In: Jamison DT, Breman JG, Measham AR, et al., eds. *Disease Control Priorities in Developing Countries*. 2nd ed. New York: Oxford University Press; 2006:780-782.

31. Cairncross S, Valdmanis V. Water supply, sanitation, and hygiene promotion. In: Jamison DT, Breman JG, Measham AR, et al., eds. *Disease Control Priorities in Developing Countries*. 2nd ed. New York: Oxford University Press; 2006:781.

32. Waterkeyn J. Cost-Effective Health Promotion: Community Health Clubs. Abuja, Nigeria: Paper presented at the 29th WEDC Conference; 2003.

33. Allan S. *The WaterAid Bangladesh/VERC 100% Sanitation Approach; Cost, Motivation and Subsidy*. [M.Sc. dissertation]. London School of Hygiene; 2003.

34. Cairncross S, Valdmanis V. Water supply, sanitation, and hygiene promotion. In: Jamison DT, Breman JG, Measham AR, et al., eds. *Disease Control Priorities in Developing Countries*. 2nd ed. New York: Oxford University Press; 2006:783-784.

35. Emerson PM, Lindsay SW, Alexander N, et al. Role of flies and provision of latrines in trachoma control: cluster-randomised controlled trial. *Lancet*. 2004;363(9415):1093-1098.

36. Cairncross S, Valdmanis V. Water supply, sanitation, and hygiene promotion. In: Jamison DT, Breman JG, Measham AR, et al., eds. *Disease Control Priorities in Developing Countries*. 2nd ed. New York: Oxford University Press; 2006:772.

37. Cairncross S, Valdmanis V. Water supply, sanitation, and hygiene promotion. In: Jamison DT, Breman JG, Measham AR, et al., eds. *Disease Control Priorities in Developing Countries*. 2nd ed. New York: Oxford University Press; 2006:777.

38. Cairncross S, Valdmanis V. Water supply, sanitation, and hygiene promotion. In: Jamison DT, Breman JG, Measham AR, et al., eds. *Disease Control Priorities in Developing Countries*. 2nd ed. New York: Oxford University Press; 2006:784-785.

39. This brief is based on: Water and Sanitation Program. Senegal: A Handwashing Behavior Change Journey. September 2010. Available at: http://www.wsp.org/wsp/sites/wsp.org/files/publications/WSP_SenegalBCJourney_HWWS.pdf. Accessed October 20, 2010.

40. Water and Sanitation Program. Involving Men in Handwashing Behavior Change in Senegal. June 2010. Available at: http://www.wsp.org/wsp/sites/wsp.org/files/publications/WSP_InvolvingMen_HWWS.pdf. Accessed October 26, 2010.

41. This brief is based largely on: Water and Sanitation Program. Total Sanitation and Sanitation Marketing Project: Indonesia Country Update June 2009. Learning at Scale. Available at: http://www.wsp.org/wsp/sites/wsp.org/files/publications/learning_at_scale.pdf. Accessed October 11, 2010.

42. Water and Sanitation Program. Website. Available at: http://www.wsp.org/wsp. Accessed October 12, 2010.

43. Water and Sanitation Program. Total Sanitation and Sanitation Marketing Project: Indonesia Country Update June 2009. Learning at Scale. Available at: http://www.wsp.org/wsp/sites/wsp.org/files/publications/learning_at_scale.pdf. Accessed October 11, 2010.

44. Water and Sanitation Program. Annual Report 2009. Available at: http://www.wsp.org/wsp/global-initiatives/Global-Scaling-Up-Handwashing-Project/Annual-Progress-Report-2009. Accessed October 12, 2010.

45. Water and Sanitation Program. Sanitation Core Components. Available at: http://www.wsp.org/wsp/global-initiatives/global-scaling-sanitation-project/Sanitation-core-components#applying_total_sanitation. Accessed October 12, 2010.

46. The Bill & Melinda Gates Foundation. Communications: A Creative Poster Campaign Promotes Sanitation in Indonesia. Available at: http://www.gatesfoundation.org/global-development/Pages/communications-creative-poster-campaign-promotes-sanitation-indonesia-podcast.aspx#. Accessed October 12, 2010.

47. Kammen DM. Cookstoves for the developing world. *Sci Am*. 1995; 273:72-75.

48. Ezzati M, Kammen DM. Evaluating the health benefits of transitions in household energy technologies in Kenya. *Energy Policy*. 2001;30:815-826.

49. Ezzati M, Kammen D. Indoor air pollution from biomass combustion and acute respiratory infections in Kenya: an exposure–response study. *Lancet*. 2001;358:619-624.

50. Casillas C, Kammen DM. The energy-poverty-climate nexus. *Science*. 2010;330(6008):1182.

51. Bailis R, Ezzati M, Kammen DM. Mortality and greenhouse gas impacts of biomass and petroleum energy futures in Africa. *Science*. 2005; 308(5718):98-103.

52. Smith KR, Corvalan CF, Kjellstrom T. How much global ill health is attributable to environmental factors? *Epidemiology*. 1999;10(5):573-584.

CHAPTER 8

Nutrition and Global Health

By the end of this chapter, the reader will be able to:

- Define key terms related to nutrition
- Describe the determinants of nutritional status
- Discuss nutrition needs at different stages of the life cycle
- Discuss the burden of undernutrition problems globally
- Review the costs and consequences of the burden of undernutrition problems
- Discuss measures that can be taken to address key undernutrition problems
- Discuss important successes that countries have had in dealing with issues of undernutrition

VIGNETTES

Shireen was 1 year old and lived in Dhaka, the capital of Bangladesh. Shireen was born with low birthweight. In addition, her family lacked the income needed to provide her with adequate food after she was no longer breastfeeding. Shireen had also repeatedly been ill with respiratory infections and diarrhea and she was now hospitalized with pneumonia. Despite the best efforts of the hospital, Shireen died after 2 days there.

Ruth lived in Liberia and was pregnant with her first child. Ruth had been anemic for all of her adult life, partly from hookworm infection and partly from not having enough iron-rich foods in her diet. She also had no access during pregnancy to iron and folic acid tablets or to foods that were fortified with vitamins and minerals. Ruth went into labor one evening and delivered the baby with the help of a traditional birth attendant. After the baby was born, however, Ruth began to bleed severely.

Her family was not able to get her to a hospital and Ruth died.

Dorji was 15 years old and lived in the mountains of northern India. Dorji was very short and had severe intellectual disabilities. Dorji was not the only one in his village with these problems. Dorji lived in an area in which the soils had little iodine. Although the government of India was encouraging the fortification of salt with iodine, such salt was not sold in Dorji's region of the country.

Rachel and her mother lived in Mombassa, a port city in Kenya. Rachel had already received her first polio vaccine and she was soon to get another. When the children participated in "polio days" not only did they get polio vaccine, but they also got a dose of vitamin A. Until recently, there were many young children who were blind due to the lack of vitamin A. Since the polio campaign started and children got extra vitamin A as part of that campaign, almost no children had become blind.

THE IMPORTANCE OF NUTRITION

Some things really are more important than others, and the role of nutrition in health is one of them. As noted in Table 8-1, and elaborated on throughout this chapter, nutritional status has a profound impact on and relationship with health status.

Nutritional status is fundamental to the growth of young children, their proper mental and physical development, and their health as adults. In addition, because of the impact of nutrition on health, nutritional status is intimately linked with whether or not children enroll in school, perform effectively while there, or complete their schooling. Nutritional

TABLE 8-1 Selected Links Between Nutrition and the Health of Mothers and Children

Good maternal nutrition is essential for good outcomes of pregnancy for the mother.

Exclusive breastfeeding for 6 months promotes better health for infants than mixing breastfeeding with other foods during that period.

Nutritional deficits in fetuses and in children under 2 years of age may produce growth and development deficits in infants and young children that can never be overcome.

About 35 percent of all deaths in children under five years worldwide are associated with nutritional deficits.

Underweight and micronutrient deficiencies in children make those children more susceptible to illness, cause illnesses to last longer, and can lead to deaths from diarrhea, measles, pneumonia, and malaria that might have been preventable.

status, therefore, has a profound effect on labor productivity and people's prospects for earning income.

Despite the importance of nutrition to health, an exceptional number of people in the world are malnourished. This is especially the case for poor women and children in low-income countries, and particularly in South Asia and sub-Saharan Africa. Nutrition is the leading risk factor for the loss of health in low- and middle-income countries.[1] In addition, UNICEF has estimated that about 26 percent of the children under 5 in low- and middle-income countries were underweight in 2008.[2] Moreover, it is estimated that about 30 percent of the children in these countries are stunted.[3] The latest WHO update of the global burden of disease suggested that about 35 percent of all child deaths, or 3 million child deaths each year, are attributable to nutrition-related causes.[3] Remarkably, that would be the equivalent of more than 8000 nutrition-related child deaths in the world every day.

These nutritional issues are even more difficult to accept because there are a number of low cost, but highly effective, nutrition interventions that can dramatically improve nutrition status, which are not being implemented sufficiently. Many improvements in nutrition can be enabled largely by communication efforts, such as the promotion of breastfeeding, the introduction of appropriate complementary foods, and the eating of foods that are rich in certain micronutrients. Such communication efforts, however, are not put in place frequently enough. The fortification of salt with iodine

has been carried out in high-income countries for more than 50 years but un-iodized salt is still sold in many low-income countries. The importance of iron and folic acid to successful outcomes of pregnancy has also been well-known for decades,[4] yet most women in low-income countries, like Ruth in the vignette, do not get supplements of iron and folic acid or eat food that is fortified with iron and folate.

Nutrition is also central to the achievement of the MDGs. Directly or indirectly, nutrition is related to almost all of these goals, as noted in Table 8-2. In fact, this table makes clear that there are *no* prospects for meeting the MDGs without substantial improvements in nutrition. The hunger goal is completely linked with nutrition, and nutrition deficits are intimately connected to whether or not people are poor. The large number of children who are poorly nourished will challenge the realization of the education goal. In addition, if about 35 percent of all child deaths are related to nutrition, then how can the child mortality goal be met unless nutrition problems are tackled more effectively? The nutritional concerns that are particular to women will constrain their productivity, limit improvements in their economic and social status, and preclude gains in the reduction of maternal mortality.

In light of the exceptional importance of nutrition to human health, this chapter will provide an overview of the most critical matters concerning nutrition globally. First, it will introduce you to the most important terms used in discussing nutrition. It will then examine the determinants of nutritional status. After that, the chapter will explore the most important nutritional needs of people at different stages in their life cycle. It will then review the nutritional state of the world and the costs and consequences of key nutrition problems. This will be followed by two policy and program briefs and two case studies that illustrate key themes covered in this chapter. The chapter will conclude by examining some of the challenges of trying to further improve nutritional status worldwide.

This chapter will deal almost exclusively with undernutrition. Chapter 12 discusses the relationship between diet and noncommunicable diseases, examines obesity, and reviews measures to reduce the burden of disease associated with being overweight and obese. Nutritional problems related to famine, drought, and civil conflict are touched on in Chapter 14.

DEFINITIONS AND KEY TERMS

A number of terms related to nutrition will be used throughout this chapter and in other sections of the book, as well. These terms are defined in Table 8-3.

The term *malnutrition* should be used to refer to those who do not get proper nutrition, whether too little, too much, or of the wrong kind. This is the way that this book will use malnutrition. In addition, people who lack sufficient energy and nutrients will be referred to as *undernourished*. People who have low weight for their age will be called *underweight*. People who are nourished to the point of being too heavy for their height will be called *overweight* or *obese*, depending on how overweight they are.

THE DETERMINANTS OF NUTRITIONAL STATUS

Nutritional status depends on a number of factors, as shown in Figure 8-1, which follows the UNICEF framework.[5]

In line with that, we can consider first the "immediate causes" of malnutrition. The two most important are inadequate dietary intake and illness. People may get an insufficient amount of food or not enough of some of the nutrients they need. These factors weaken the body, open the person to illness and infection, and lead to longer and more frequent illness than would otherwise be the case. Inadequate dietary intake becomes part of a vicious cycle with illness and infection, because they make it harder for people to eat, more difficult for them to absorb what they do take in, and actually raise the need for some nutrients. The relationship between infection and nutritional status is very important to keep in mind, especially when considering how to improve the nutritional status of poor children in low- and middle-income countries.

The UNICEF framework also includes a set of "underlying causes" to inadequate dietary intake and infectious disease that include "inadequate access to food in a household; insufficient health services and an unhealthful environment; and, inadequate care for children and women."[5] Whether people get enough food within a household depends on a number of factors, including access to land and the ability to produce food for those living in rural areas. They also include having access to food and the money to purchase it. In addition, the amount and type of food one gets depends in many families on social position, with girls and women sometimes getting less food or less nutritious food than men and boys get. It is also important to note that in rural areas in low-income countries, there may be a "hungry season," in which families have exhausted the food from their last harvest, have not yet produced the food for this year, and do not have the income to buy food, even if a market is accessible to them.

As discussed in Chapter 7, the lack of safe water and sanitation are extremely important causes of diarrheal disease and, therefore, greatly contribute to the cycle of infection and malnutrition. This is made worse when people

TABLE 8-2 Key Links Between Nutrition and the MDGs

Goal 1: Eradicate Poverty and Hunger
Link: Poor nutritional status is both a cause and a consequence of poverty. Improving income and nutritional status will improve health status.

Goal 2: Achieve Universal Primary Education
Link: Children who are properly nourished enroll in school at higher rates than undernourished children, attend school for more years, and perform better while they are there than undernourished children.

Goal 3: Promote Gender Equality and Empower Women
Link: Women suffer very high rates of some nutritional deficiencies, such as iron deficiency anemia, that constrain their health and their productivity. Improving the nutritional status of women will enhance their income earning potential and ability to be more productive in all of their work.

Goal 4: Reduce Child Mortality
Link: About 35 percent of all child deaths worldwide are associated with malnutrition. It will not be possible to make major strides in reducing child mortality without significant improvements in the nutritional status of young children.

Goal 5: Improve Maternal Health
Link: Maternal health and pregnancy outcomes are intimately connected to the nutritional status of the pregnant women.

Goal 6: Combat HIV/AIDS, Malaria, and Other Diseases
Link: Poor nutritional status makes people more susceptible to illness and to being sick for longer periods of time. Good nutrition is especially important for people suffering from some health conditions, such as TB and HIV/AIDS. Supplementation with some micronutrients, even in the absence of antiretroviral therapy, can lengthen the time that HIV-positive people can go without progressing to full-blown AIDS.

Source: Adapted from United Nations. Millennium Development Goals. Available at: http://www.un.org/millenniumgoals/goals. Accessed July 11, 2006.

live in generally unhygienic circumstances, in which food is often handled in unhygienic ways. These are also the circumstances under which people, especially children, are likely to get parasitic infections, such as worms, about which you will read in Chapters 10 and 11. These parasites sap the energy of children and make it harder for them to absorb what they do eat.

TABLE 8-3 Key Terms and Definitions

Anemia—Low level of hemoglobin in the blood, as evidenced by a reduced quality or quantity of red blood cells.

Body mass index (BMI)—Body weight in kilograms divided by height in meters squared (kg/m^2).

Iodine deficiency disorders (IDDs)—The spectrum of IDDs includes goiter, hypothyroidism, impaired mental function, stillbirths, abortions, congenital anomalies, and neurological cretinism.

Low birthweight—Birthweight less than 2500 grams.

Malnutrition—Various forms of poor nutrition. Underweight or stunting and overweight, as well as micronutrient deficiencies, are forms of malnutrition.

Obesity—Excessive body fat content; commonly measured by BMI. The international reference for classifying an individual as obese is a BMI greater than 30.

Overweight—Excess weight relative to height; commonly measured by BMI among adults. The international reference for adults is as follows:
- 25–29.99 for grade I (overweight)
- 30–39.99 for grade II (obese)
- > 40 for grade III

For children, overweight is measured as weight-for-height two z-scores above the international reference.

Stunting—Failure to reach linear growth potential because of inadequate nutrition or poor health. Stunting is measured as height-for-age two z-scores below the international reference.

Undernutrition—Poor nutrition. The three most commonly used indexes for child undernutrition are height-for-age, weight-for-age, and weight-for-height. For adults, undernutrition is measured by a BMI less than 18.5.

Underweight—Low weight-for-age; that is, two z-scores below the international reference for weight-for-age. It implies stunting or wasting and is an indicator of undernutrition.

Vitamin A deficiency—Tissue concentrations of vitamin A low enough to have adverse health consequences such as increased morbidity and mortality, poor reproductive health, and slowed growth and development, even if there is no clinical deficiency.

Wasting—Weight, measured in kilograms, divided by height in meters squared, that is two z-scores below the international reference.

Z-score—A statistical term, meaning the deviation of an individual's value from the median value of a reference population, divided by the standard deviation of the reference population.

Source: Adapted with permission from The World Bank. *Repositioning Nutrition as Central to Development.* Washington, DC: The World Bank; 2006:xvii.

Child caring practices affect the nutritional status of children in similar ways to the manner in which they impact children's health status. If a child is exclusively breastfed for 6 months, if complementary foods are introduced that are of sufficient quality and quantity, and if food and water are handled in hygienic ways, then the nutritional status of young children will be enhanced. In addition, as discussed earlier, the nutrition and health status of the mother is an exceptionally important determinant of whether the child will be born with low birthweight and will thrive thereafter.

Access to appropriate health services is also very important to nutritional status, in a manner similar to its importance for health status. Receiving basic childhood immunizations is an important way to avoid illness and infection. The same is true for vitamin A supplements that are provided by many health services. Medicines to rid children of worms can also be very important to their nutritional status. Unfortunately, as noted in Chapters 5 and 10, there are still too many health systems that are not capable of effectively providing even these basic services.

Of course, at the root of nutritional status are the factors that UNICEF calls "basic causes." These relate to the social determinants of health, which are discussed in Chapters 2 and 3. In a manner similar to the factors that determine health, the root causes of nutritional status also have to do with socioeconomic status, family income, the level of knowledge people have of appropriate health and nutritional practices, and the amount of control that people have over their lives. Governmental and global policies that affect agricultural production, marketing, and distribution, and that impact education, health, and nutrition programs can also have a profound effect on the nutritional status of individuals, communities, and societies.

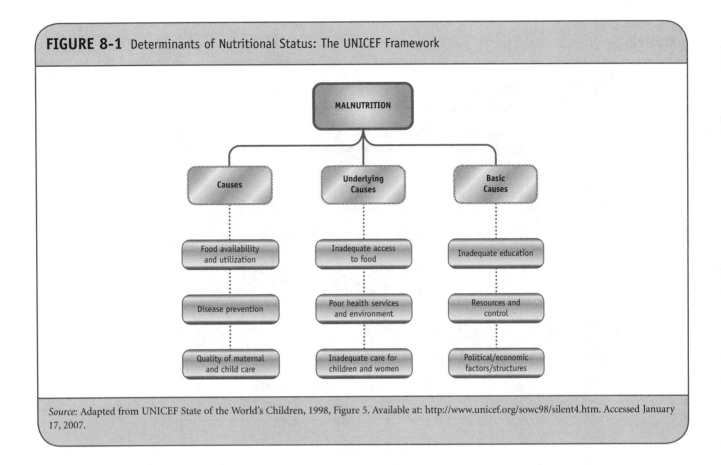

FIGURE 8-1 Determinants of Nutritional Status: The UNICEF Framework

Source: Adapted from UNICEF State of the World's Children, 1998, Figure 5. Available at: http://www.unicef.org/sowc98/silent4.htm. Accessed January 17, 2007.

GAUGING NUTRITIONAL STATUS

The nutritional status of infants and children is largely gauged by measuring and weighing these children and then plotting their weight and height on growth charts, like the one shown in Figure 8-2.

These growth charts have been standardized. The place of the child on the growth curves indicates whether the child is growing normally or not. The nutritional status of adults is generally determined on the basis of the person's weight in relation to the person's height, while also taking account of his or her age.

We usually think of deficits in nutrition as being large and evident; however, it is extremely important to note that this is not necessarily the case. Rather, a very large share of the nutritional deficits that exist globally are "mild" or "moderate" and may not be very obvious. Nonetheless, even mild and moderate malnutrition can have very negative consequences on the biological development of people, on their health, and on their productivity, and some of these negative effects will be irreversible.

KEY NUTRITIONAL NEEDS

Many nutrients are important; however, from the point of view of global health, several are of paramount importance. These include protein, energy, and the four micronutrients: vitamin A, iron, iodine, and zinc. This section briefly examines each of these topics, and Table 8-4 summarizes the sources of these nutrients and their key impacts.

Undernutrition

In order to thrive, people have to take in enough energy and micronutrients to fulfill their physiological needs. When this does not happen, undernutrition results. According to UNICEF, undernutrition is defined as "the outcome of insufficient food intake (hunger) and repeated infectious diseases. Undernutrition includes being underweight for one's age, too short for one's age (stunted), dangerously thin for one's height (wasted), and deficient in vitamins and minerals (micronutrient malnutrition)."[6]

Stunting or chronic undernutrition is the result of cumulative deficiencies in dietary intake (inadequate amounts of

FIGURE 8-2 Model Growth Chart

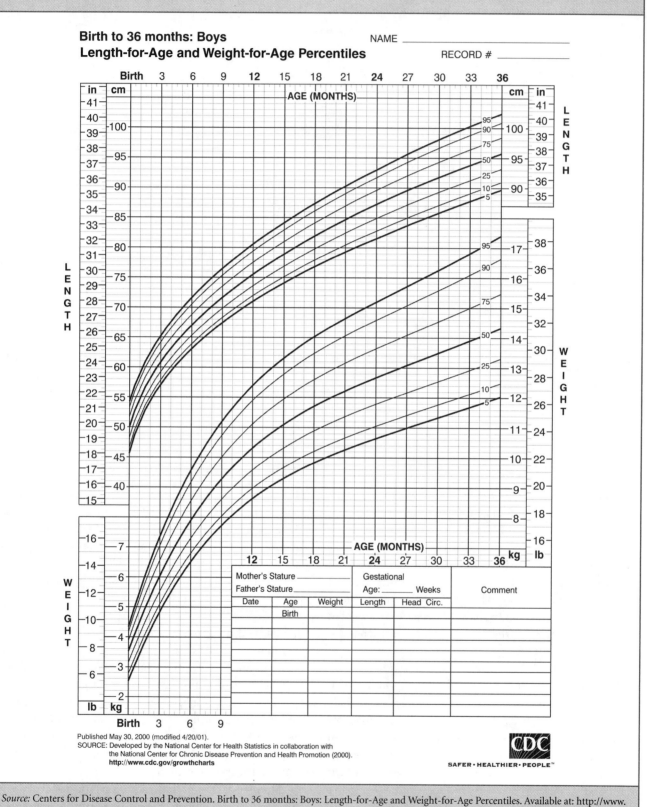

Source: Centers for Disease Control and Prevention. Birth to 36 months: Boys: Length-for-Age and Weight-for-Age Percentiles. Available at: http://www.cdc.gov/nchs/data/nhanes/growthcharts/set1clinical/cj411017.pdf. Accessed January 31, 2007.

TABLE 8-4 Key Nutritional Needs, Sources, and Selected Functions

Key Nutritional Needs	Sources	Selected Functions
Protein	Milk, eggs, chicken, and beans	Proper growth of children and immune functions
Vitamin A	Liver, eggs, green leafy vegetables, orange and red fruits and vegetables	Proper immune function and prevention of xerophthalmia
Iodine	Selected seafoods and plants grown in iodine-containing soil	Growth and neurological development
Iron	Fish, meat, poultry, grains, vegetables, and legumes	Prevent iron deficiency anemia, prevent low birthweight and premature babies
Zinc	Red and white meat and shellfish	Promote growth, immune function, and cognitive development

Source: Data from *The Journal of Nutrition.* Nutrient Information. Available at: http://jn.nutrition.org/nutinfo/. Accessed February 8, 2007.

energy and micronutrients) and recurrent bouts of infectious diseases.[6] This causes linear growth failure resulting in low height for age. Stunting is defined as height-for-age that is below minus 2 standard deviations of the median WHO growth standards.[7]

Underweight or low weight for age is a composite measure of being too thin (wasted) and too short (stunted). It is the indicator used in Millennium Goal 1 (eradicate extreme poverty and hunger) to measure progress in addressing undernutrition at the individual level.

Wasting is the outcome of weight loss that is often associated with acute shortages of food and infection. Wasting is defined as being below minus 2 standard deviations of the median WHO growth standards. Sometimes wasting is related to shocks such as drought or famine. However, wasting can also be a result of substantial acute energy deficits related to other factors that are discussed in this chapter and that help to determine nutritional status.

"Severe acute malnutrition" is generally defined by a very low weight-for-height measurement of below minus 3 standard deviations of the median WHO growth standards. Severe acute malnutrition is an extreme form of undernutrition. Wasting, including that associated with severe acute malnutrition, needs to be treated as an emergency.

Undernourishment greatly raises the risk of illness, especially for children. In addition, being malnourished in childhood is also associated with decreased intellectual capacity. Somewhat ironically, young children who are malnourished but who rapidly gain weight later in childhood and adolescence are at high risk as adults of nutrition-related chronic diseases such as diabetes, high blood pressure, and high cholesterol.[8]

In addition, undernourished women of short stature have greatly increased risks of dying of pregnancy-related causes. Furthermore, undernourished women have a greatly increased risk of delivering premature or low birthweight babies. Such babies are, in turn, at much greater risk than full-term babies or babies with a birthweight of over 5.5 pounds of growing poorly, not developing properly, or dying.[7]

Vitamin A

Vitamin A is found in a variety of plants but mostly in green leafy vegetables, yellow and orange fruits that are not citrus, and carrots. It is also found in some animal products, including liver, milk, and eggs.[7] The lack of vitamin A is associated with the development of a condition known as xeropthalmia. The person with this condition first gets "night blindness." Later, the eye dries out, which can lead to permanent blindness.[9]

What is less well known, however, is that vitamin A is extremely important to the proper functioning of the immune system and to a child's growth. Trials of vitamin A supplements on newborns reduced the risk of deaths from infections by 25 percent and from prematurity by about 66 percent.[3] Deficiency in vitamin A has a profound impact on the severity of certain illnesses and whether a child will survive a bout of pneumonia, malaria, measles, or diarrhea.[7]

Iodine

Iodine is generally found in some types of seafood and in plants that are grown in soil that naturally contains iodine.[10] People who live in mountainous areas often do not get enough iodine in their diets, because they do not consume much seafood and mountainous soils often lack iodine. This was the case, for example, for Dorji, in the vignette at the start of this chapter. The lack of iodine is most often associated with a growth on the thyroid, called a goiter, and the failure to develop full intellectual potential.[10] However, iodine deficiency disorders "can also include fetal loss, stillbirth, congenital anomalies, and hearing impairment."[11] In fact, iodine deficiency most often manifests itself in mild intellectual disabilities,[11] and people with cretinism have an IQ that is on average 10 to 15 points below that of people who do not suffer this deficit.[12] In extreme forms, iodine deficiency may also lead to severe mental retardation and being both deaf and mute. Iodine deficiency "is the most common form of preventable mental illness in the world."[13]

Iron

The most easily absorbable form of iron is found in fish, meat, and poultry. Less absorbable forms can be found in fruits, grains, vegetables, nuts, and dried beans. The lack of iron is most often associated with iron deficiency anemia, which we usually associate with weakness and fatigue. This is especially a problem for adolescent women and pregnant women, because women who are iron deficient have an increased risk of giving birth to a premature or low birthweight baby or of hemorrhaging and dying in childbirth.[14] Iron deficiency is also associated with poor mental development and reduced immune function.[11] In addition, iron is a critical requirement for children in the 6- to 24-month age group to ensure optimal development of their cognitive and motor skills.

Zinc

The best sources of zinc are red and white meat and shellfish.[15] Severe deficiency in zinc is associated with "growth retardation, impaired immune function, skin disorders, hypogonadism, and cognitive dysfuncion."[11] Mild to moderate deficiency increases susceptibility to infecion.[11] Indeed, children who receive zinc supplementation when they have diarrhea recover more rapidly than those who do not,[16] and zinc deficiency is a major risk factor for morbidity and mortality from diarrhea, pneumonia, and malaria, as discussed later.[3,11]

NUTRITIONAL NEEDS THROUGHOUT THE LIFE CYCLE

Nutritional needs vary with one's place in the life cycle. Having outlined the most important nutritional needs that concern global health issues, therefore, it will now be valuable to examine how those needs change from pregnancy, through infancy, childhood, adolescence, adulthood, and old age. This will assist us in getting a better understanding of the nature of the nutrition problems globally, the burden of disease related to nutrition, and how this burden might be addressed.

Pregnancy and Birthweight

The nutritional status of a pregnant woman is especially important to the outcome that she will have in pregnancy, both for herself and for her newborn. It is critical that a pregnant woman stay well-nourished and healthy. During pregnancy, the woman will need to get a sufficient amount of protein and energy from the food she eats, and it is generally recommended that she consume 300 calories more per day than when she is not pregnant. In addition, iron, iodine, folate, zinc, and calcium will be very important to the health of the woman and her newborn.[17]

The birthweight of a baby is an extremely important determinant of the extent to which a child will thrive and become a healthy adult. Fetuses that do not get sufficient and appropriate nutrition from the mother may suffer a number of problems, including stillbirth, mental impairment, or a variety of severe birth defects. They could also undergo a general failure to grow properly, referred to as intrauterine growth retardation. Babies who are born at term but who are low birthweight have a much greater risk of getting diarrhea and pneumonia. Those born with a birthweight from 1500 to 1999 grams are 8 times more likely to die from birth asphyxia and infections than those born with a birthweight of 2000 to 2499 grams.[3]

Infancy and Young Childhood

An important share of a child's biological development takes place between conception and 2 years of age. It is essential to understand that nutritional gaps that arise during that period may produce problems in stature or mental development that can never be overcome. They may also lead to more frequent infection and infections that last longer than would be the case in a better-nourished child. Thus, it is extraordinarily important that infants and young children get a sufficient amount of protein, energy, and fat from their foods. They also need sufficient amounts of iodine, iron, vitamin A, and zinc.

There is very strong evidence worldwide that infants will grow best and stay healthiest if they are exclusively breastfed for the first 6 months of their lives. In fact, the latest estimates suggest that about 1.4 million deaths a year and about 10 percent of the burden of disease in children are associated with "suboptimal breastfeeding."[3] Children will also thrive best if foods other than breast milk or infant formula begin to be introduced in hygienic ways around 6 months of age, while breastfeeding continues.[18] Especially in low-income countries in which nutritional deficits are likely to be considerable, such foods will be especially valuable if they are fortified with key vitamins and minerals.

The nutrition needs of the infant continue into young childhood, but the nutritional status of many children faces risks as the child stops breastfeeding, as noted earlier. At this stage, the child's nutritional status depends on the ability of the family to provide an adequate diet and to help the child avoid illnesses and infections. Among the most critical issues concerning childhood nutrition is that stunted children have very little chance to catch up in their growth and that most of the damage done to their development, both physical and mental, cannot be changed.[19]

This fact has enormous implications for public policy aimed at enhancing nutrition status. It means that the focus of attention in addressing undernutrition and its consequences must be on children under 2 years of age, and it must start by trying to ensure that pregnant women are well nourished and healthy enough to give birth to healthy babies of acceptable birthweight. As some have said, there is a "window of opportunity" for ensuring that children grow properly and reach their biological potential. This window opens at conception and closes, at least most of the way, around the time the child is 2 years of age.[20]

Adolescence

Adolescent girls who are well nourished grow faster than adolescent girls who are not well nourished. Adolescent girls who are poorly nourished, but still growing, are much more likely than well-nourished girls to give birth to an underweight baby. This may stem from the fact that the fetus and the girl are competing for nutrients in the adolescent who is still growing.[19] Poorly nourished and very small adolescent girls also have more complications of pregnancy than do older girls who are taller. This relates partly to the difficulties of very small women giving birth, because of their size. In addition, all adolescents go through a growth spurt, although children who are stunted are unable to make up in adolescence for their retarded growth. For adolescents to grow properly and become healthy adults, they need appropriate protein and energy. They also have particular needs for iodine, iron, and folic acid. Because of their growth during this period, calcium is also especially important for adolescents.[19]

Adulthood and Old Age

Adults need appropriate, well-balanced nutrition to stay healthy and productive. All people, including adults, also need to pay particular attention in their diets to foods that can be harmful to their health, such as foods that contain too much fat, cholesterol, sugar, or salt. Older adults have special nutritional needs that are very important, but often forgotten. The ability of older people to live on their own and to function effectively depends in many ways on their nutritional status; however, many older people lack the income or the support needed to eat properly. Like other adults, they need to get enough protein, energy, and iron and avoid obesity. They also have to pay particular attention to getting enough calcium to reduce the risk of osteoporosis, which is a condition in which bones become fragile and can break.[21]

THE NUTRITIONAL STATE OF THE WORLD
Overview

Before you continue, it will be important to note some matters related to the data that are used in this section. The tables that follow are based on 2001 data that were developed in conjunction with the 2001 study on the global burden of disease. As noted earlier, these data are used here, despite their age, because they are still the most recent estimates of such data done consistently, by World Bank region. These data are also consistent with data on other areas of the burden of disease.

In addition to the data referred to above, some data are taken from a partial update of the 2001 global burden of disease study WHO carried out in 2008 and that used 2004 data. Other data in the sections that follow are largely drawn from UNICEF and other organizations that work in nutrition, such as the Micronutrient Initiative.

There has been some important progress in reducing the burden of undernutrition over the last decade. According to recent UNICEF data, the rate of children younger than 5 years in developing countries who are underweight, for example, fell from 31 percent to 26 percent from 1990 to 2008.[2] In addition, there were a number of countries that were able to reduce levels of undernutrition in their under-5 children by 25 percent or more, including Bangladesh, China, Indonesia, Mexico, and Vietnam.[22] Important progress has been made in addressing micronutrient deficiency, as well. The number of households using iodized salt has increased from about 20 percent in 1990 to about 70 percent today.[22] There has also been a dramatic increase in the share of the world's children who receive vitamin A supplements, which now stands at about 72 percent.[4]

Despite this progress, however, the nutritional state of the world is, in many respects, deplorable. About 800 million people worldwide are malnourished to at least some degree.[23] About 30 percent of the children under 5 in low- and middle-income countries are moderately or severely stunted.[24] Many poor women in the world are also underweight. A large share of the poor women and children in the world also suffer from deficiencies in important micronutrients. Nutritional problems remain a fundamental cause of ill health and of premature death for infants, children, and pregnant women. The economic costs of undernutrition are great.

The section that follows examines the burden of nutrition disorders that relate to undernutrition and reviews undernutrition as a risk factor for ill health. For undernutrition and for deficiencies in vitamin A, iodine, iron, and zinc, it looks first at the prevalence of deficiencies and then examines the contribution of each issue to the global burden of disease. Table 8-5 summarizes the deaths that were directly attributable to these nutritional concerns in the 2001 study.

Undernutrition

Undernutrition remains disturbingly prevalent. It was estimated that in 2001 almost 130 million children, or about 23 percent of the children younger than 5 years of age, were underweight in low- and middle-income countries. The 2004 update of the global burden of disease study estimated that about 20 percent of those children were underweight.[3] The latest UNICEF estimates suggest that 26 percent of the under-5 children are underweight.[2] As shown in Table 8-6, the regional rates of underweight vary from 6 percent in Latin America to almost 50 percent in South Asia, with sub-Saharan Africa being the second worst-off region.

The share of under-5 children who are wasted in low- and middle-income countries was estimated as part of the 2004 global burden of disease update. These data suggested that about 10 percent of these children were wasted and about 3.5 percent of them were severely wasted. The percentage of these children who were severely wasted also varied considerably by region, with almost 6 percent severely wasted in parts of South Asia, again followed by parts of sub-Saharan Africa with about 5 percent severely wasted.[3]

The 2004 update estimated that 32 percent of the children under 5 in low- and middle-income countries were stunted. According to these data, the worst rates of stunting were found in several parts of Eastern and Central Africa, where almost half of the children were stunted, followed by South Asia. However, it is important to note the wide variation in the rates of stunting within India, for example. In some states in the north of India, between 50 and 60 percent of the young children were stunted.[25]

Only about 0.5 percent of the total deaths in low- and middle-income countries are directly due to undernutrition, referred to as "protein-energy malnutrition" in the studies on the global burden of disease.[26] About 1 percent of the DALYs lost are directly due to undernutrition.[27] However, undernutrition, as discussed earlier, is an exceptionally important risk factor for illness, disability, and death from other causes. It has been estimated, for example, that 5–16 percent of the illness from pneumonia, diarrhea, and malaria is directly attributable to undernutrition and the extent to which it increases the susceptibility to illness.[7] Moreover, it has also been estimated that 44–60 percent of the deaths due to measles, malaria, pneumonia, and diarrhea are also attributable to undernutrition, and 53 percent of these deaths could be

TABLE 8-5 Nutrition-Related Deaths in Children Under 5 Years, by Region, 2001, in Thousands

Region	Undernutrition	Vitamin A	Iron Deficiency Anemia	Zinc Deficiency
East Asia & Pacific	125	11	18	15
Europe & Central Asia	14	0	3	4
Latin America & the Caribbean	22	5	10	15
Middle East & North Africa	305	70	10	94
South Asia	870	157	66	252
Sub-Saharan Africa	1334	383	21	400

Source: Adapted with permission from Caulfield LE, Richard SA, Rivera JA, Musgrove P, Black RE. Stunting, wasting, and micronutrient disorders. In: Jamison DT, Breman JG, Measham AR, et al., eds. *Disease Control Priorities in Developing Countries.* Washington, DC and New York: The World Bank and Oxford University Press; 2006:552.

eliminated if these children were not undernourished.[7] The 2004 update suggested that about 38 percent of young child deaths and about 45 percent of the DALYs in children under 5 in low- and middle-income countries were attributable to underweight, stunting, and wasting.[3]

Low Birthweight

The 2004 update of the global burden of disease examined babies who were born at term, meaning they completed 37 weeks of gestation but were still below 2500 grams at birth. This study referred to such babies as "intrauterine growth restriction—low birthweight."[3] The study estimated that about 11 percent of the babies born in low- and middle-income countries fit this group. Of these, about 1 percent weighed 1500 to 1999 grams and about 10 percent weighed 2000 to 2500 grams.

Given the extent of undernutrition in South Asia, it should not be a surprise that about 30 percent of the babies born in South Asia are born with low birthweight. The Middle East, North Africa, and sub-Saharan Africa have the next highest prevalence of low birthweight, at about 15 percent.[28] More than 20 million low birthweight babies are born each year in low- and middle-income countries.[28] Table 8-7 shows the prevalence of low birthweight by region.

About 2.5 percent of the total deaths in children under 5 years of age that occur in low- and middle-income countries are attributable to low birthweight, according to 2001 estimates. The 2004 estimates suggested that this figure was 3 percent.[3,26] Both the 2001 and the 2004 estimates indicate that about 3 percent of the DALYs lost in low- and middle-income countries are attributable to low birthweight.[3,27] The difference between the two figures for deaths and DALYs stems from the illness and disability that many low birthweight children will face, if they do survive.

Vitamin A

More than 250 million children worldwide suffer from vitamin A deficiency.[18] The prevalence of vitamin A deficiency among children younger than 72 months of age in the developing world varies from a low of about 20 percent in Central America and the Caribbean to more than 50 percent in South Asia. In India alone, more than 60 percent of the children younger than 72 months of age are vitamin A deficient.[29] As shown in Table 8-8, 32 percent of the children of this age in sub-Saharan Africa are vitamin A deficient.

Vitamin A deficiency has an enormous impact on morbidity, disability, and deaths in young children. The 2001 data indicated that 20–24 percent of the deaths from measles, diarrhea, and malaria, or 630,000 deaths each year, are attrib-

utable to vitamin A deficiency.[30] The 2004 data were very similar to the 2001 data and suggested that 6.5 percent of all deaths of children under 5 in low- and middle-income countries were attributable to vitamin A deficiency.[3] In addition, it is estimated that between 250,000 and 500,000 children each year are blinded due to vitamin A deficiency.[3]

TABLE 8-6 Prevalence of Underweight in Low- and Middle-Income Countries, by Region, Children Under 5 Years, 2001

Region	Prevalence Rate of Underweight
East Asia & Pacific	18
Europe & Central Asia	6
Latin America & the Caribbean	6
Middle East & North Africa	21
South Asia	48
Sub-Saharan Africa	32

Note: Underweight is weight for age less than 2 standard deviations

Source: Adapted with permission from Caulfield LE, Richard SA, Rivera JA, Musgrove P, Black RE. Stunting, wasting, and micronutrient disorders. In: Jamison DT, Breman JG, Measham AR, et al., eds. *Disease Control Priorities in Developing Countries.* Washington, DC and New York: The World Bank and Oxford University Press; 2006:552.

TABLE 8-7 Prevalence of Low Birthweight, Low- and Middle-Income Countries, 2001

Region	Percentage of Babies Born with Low Birthweight
East Asia & Pacific	7
Europe & Central Asia	6
Latin America & the Caribbean	8
Middle East & North Africa	14
South Asia	28
Sub-Saharan Africa	13

Source: Adapted with permission from The World Bank. *Repositioning Nutrition as Central to Development.* Washington, DC: The World Bank; 2006:47.

TABLE 8-8 Prevalence of Vitamin A, Iron, and Zinc Deficiency in Children Under 5 Years, Low- and Middle-Income Countries, 2001, by Region

Region	Vitamin A	Iron	Zinc
East Asia & Pacific	11	40	7
Europe & Central Asia	< 1	22	10
Latin America & the Caribbean	15	46	33
Middle East & North Africa	18	63	46
South Asia	40	75	79
Sub-Saharan Africa	32	60	50

Source: Adapted with permission from Caulfield LE, Richard SA, Rivera JA, Musgrove P, Black RE. Stunting, wasting, and micronutrient disorders. In: Jamison DT, Breman JG, Measham AR, et al., eds. *Disease Control Priorities in Developing Countries.* Washington, DC and New York: The World Bank and Oxford University Press; 2006:552.

Iodine

Iodine deficiency disorders are estimated to affect more than 70 million people worldwide.[31] The highest rates of such disorders are found in the Eastern Mediterranean region and in Africa, where about 30 percent of the population suffers from goiter. This is followed by South Asia, where more than 20 percent of the population has goiter.[32]

Iodine deficiency is associated with only a small number of deaths. However, such deficiencies are associated with substantial DALYs lost in low- and middle-income countries, equal to about the same amount as chlamydia, syphilis, or intestinal worms.[33] The DALYs lost from iodine deficiency disorder are about 30 percent as many DALYs as are lost from iron deficiency anemia in low- and middle-income countries.[33]

Iron

The latest consistent data on the prevalence of anemia worldwide are from a WHO global database, based on surveys conducted between 1993 and 2005.[33] These data indicate that more than 1.6 billion people worldwide were affected by anemia. Almost 50 percent of children under 5 years of age, 25 percent of school-age children, 30 percent of nonpregnant women, and 42 percent of pregnant women suffered from anemia in the WHO surveys.

The highest rates among preschool-age children and pregnant women were found in the WHO Africa region, at almost 68 percent and 57 percent, respectively. This was followed very closely by the WHO Southeast Asia region, at about 66 percent for children under 5 and 48 percent for pregnant women. Rates of prevalence for both groups were also very high for the Eastern Mediterranean region of WHO. Based on the survey data, WHO concluded that iron deficiency anemia is a substantial public health problem for children under 5 and pregnant women throughout the world, especially in low- and middle-income countries.[34]

The 2001 global burden of disease study indicated that the number of deaths directly relating to iron deficiency anemia in low- and middle-income countries is about the same as the total number of deaths caused by a group of six tropical diseases. It is also similar to the deaths caused individually by prostate, bladder, and pancreatic cancer.[26] About 0.7 percent of the total DALYs lost in low- and middle-income countries is related to iron deficiency anemia. This is similar to the DALYs lost in these countries due to sexually transmitted diseases (not including HIV), stomach cancer, schizophrenia, or asthma.[33] The 2004 update suggested that 0.5 percent of the total DALYs for children under 5 was attributable to iron deficiency.[3]

Zinc

The data on zinc deficiency are not as well established as those on the other micronutrient deficiencies noted earlier; however, a study has estimated the prevalence rate of zinc deficiency by region for children younger than 5 years. Prevalence in low- and middle-income regions ranges from a low of 7 percent in the East Asia and the Pacific region to almost 80 percent of the children younger than 5 years in South Asia. In high-income countries, it is estimated that only about 5 percent of the children younger than 5 are zinc deficient.[7]

The 2004 update on the global burden of disease shows zinc to be the second most important of the micronutrients responsible for death and DALYs in children under 5, next to vitamin A. That study indicated that about 450,000 deaths of children under 5 years of age were attributable to zinc deficiency and that almost 4 percent of the DALYs in that group were linked to zinc deficiency, as well.[3]

NUTRITION, HEALTH, AND ECONOMIC DEVELOPMENT

Nutrition has an important bearing on the economic development prospects of people, communities, and countries. In some of the early thinking about economic development, many economists saw nutrition as something that people consumed, but they did not see it as a "productive" investment. However, as we will see later, nutrition is an extremely important contributor to human health, the development of human intellectual and biological potential, and therefore, has an extremely important link with what people learn, their strength and ability to use their own labor, and other factors relating to their potential productivity. The following comments follow the life cycle.

First, nutritional deficits can take an enormous toll on maternal health, with important economic consequences. Women are responsible for child care in most low- and middle-income countries. In addition, they often contribute to household income. The death of a woman in the prime of her life, in childbirth, due to undernutrition or deficiencies in iron or vitamin A, can leave poor families with needs for child care they cannot meet and with reduced income. It is common, in fact, in poor families in low-income countries for very young children to die not long after their mothers die.

In addition, we have seen that low birthweight is a powerful predictor of the future productivity of a child and that a number of forms of malnutrition contribute to the failure of infants and children to grow or to achieve their full mental potential. Children who are undernourished and small in stature enroll in schools at lower rates or later in age than students who are perceived by their parents to be normal in size. Children who are undernourished have IQs that are lower than students who are properly nourished. These undernourished students are less attentive in class and less able to learn than other students. Children who are undernourished fall ill more than well-nourished children. Thus, they miss more school, learn less from school, and are much more likely than well-nourished children to drop out of school, with its attendant economic consequences.

Nutritional status also plays an important part in the productivity of adults. Numerous studies have shown that improvements in nutritional status, such as eliminating iron deficiency anemia, can improve worker productivity by 5–15 percent.[35] The contribution of nutrition to maintaining good health also has important economic returns. It helps people to avoid disease and the costs associated with treating disease. These points are well illustrated by the policy and program brief on Guatemala later in the chapter.

Moreover, through its impact on health, nutritional status also has an important bearing on life expectancy. Infants and children who are better nourished live longer than those who are poorly nourished, and they also can contribute to the economy for longer. Adults who are properly nourished get sick less and for shorter periods, live longer, and work more years than adults who are not well nourished. Thus, they, too, can make more contributions to the economy than people who are not well nourished.

A look at social and economic history also speaks to the importance of nutrition to economic development. Studies that have been done of the economic development of England showed that improvements in nutritional status of adults in England in the late 19th century were important to improving the stature and strength of workers, their health, and their economic outputs.[36] Other studies have shown that there is a correlation between height and wages. Rubber tappers in Indonesia significantly improved the amount of rubber they could tap when their anemia was treated with iron supplements, and road construction workers in Kenya were 4–12.5 percent more productive after getting calorie supplements.[37] Female mill workers in China increased their production efficiency by 17 percent after being given iron supplements for 12 weeks.[38] A major review of nutrition by the World Bank noted that reducing micronutrient deficiencies in China and India could increase their GDP by $2.5 billion per year.[20]

POLICY AND PROGRAM BRIEFS

Three policy and program briefs follow. The first describes the impressive efforts that Nepal has undertaken to address micronutrient deficiencies, despite being a very poor country. The second discusses an effort in Kenya to launch a flour fortification effort in an exceptionally short period of time, despite many years of not having done so previously. The third brief illustrates the long-term impact of nutrition supplementation. It reviews the findings of a study on Guatemala that examined the long-term impact of improved nutrition on the stature, intellectual abilities, and wages of adults.

Nepal Addresses Micronutrient Deficiencies

Many Nepali families lack the income needed to consistently buy nutrient-rich foods. Many families also lack the knowledge of a healthy diet needed to ensure their children are well nourished. These issues have resulted in high rates of undernutrition and micronutrient deficiencies, particularly in women and children.[39]

In the 1990s, for example, more than half of the under-5 children in Nepal were stunted.[39,40] In addition, nearly 75 percent of pregnant women and over half of all children were anemic. The coverage of nutritional programs was low. Many pregnant women did not receive iron and folic acid supplements,[39] and there was little fortification of food.

More recently, however, Nepal has become a leader in addressing micronutrient deficiencies. To address anemia, the government initiated the National Anemia Control Strategy and Iron Intensification Program in 2003, with support from WHO, UNICEF, and the Micronutrient Initiative. This program provides iron supplements for pregnant women distributed by female community health volunteers, in addition to deworming services, maternal care, and fortified foods. A monitoring system was established to identify pregnant women as soon as possible, and to ensure that women fully participate in the recommended services.

In addition, the United States Agency for International Development (USAID) and the Ministry of Health collaborated to integrate zinc into the national diarrhea management plan. In 2006, only 0.4 percent of caregivers provided zinc during any bout of diarrhea in the previous 2 weeks. To increase the use of both oral rehydration therapy (ORT) and zinc when treating diarrheal disease, USAID is supporting training for private sector healthcare providers. In addition, efforts are underway to increase the availability of zinc in the private sector. Linked with these efforts, public and private sector programs to increase the use of zinc now reach 65 percent of the population.[40] The Micronutrient Initiative is also helping the government to improve popular knowledge and awareness about zinc through local radio advertising, the delivery of zinc in the public and private sectors, the monitoring and reporting system for zinc usage, and the zinc supply chain.[41]

Vitamin A tablets are being distributed to children twice a year to help enhance children's immunity, prevent night blindness, and reduce morbidity and mortality from measles, pneumonia, and diarrhea. The Micronutrient Initiative is also helping the government to pilot a vitamin A supplementation program for newborns.[41]

Community health worker volunteers (CHWV), usually women who live in the community, play an important role in implementing these programs. They administer the needed supplements in their communities, recording the children or women who receive the supplements. Additionally, the CHWVs spend time educating parents, particularly women, on nutrition topics such as the importance of eating nutrient-rich foods and micronutrient supplements, good hygiene habits, and breastfeeding.[42] NGOs have played an important role in addressing issues related to micronutrient deficiencies by helping to train CHWVs to perform the tasks mentioned above.[42]

The collaborative efforts of the government, NGOs, community volunteers, and Nepal's development partners have led to a number of successes. Over 80 percent of pregnant women are receiving iron and folic acid supplements, and anemia has dropped 35 percent among these women. The usage of zinc has increased from less than 1 percent in 2005 to nearly 16 percent in 2008, with 85 percent of users correctly taking zinc and oral rehydration salts together, and 67 percent correctly taking zinc for the recommended 10 full days.[42] Currently, there is 95 percent coverage of vitamin A supplementation among children.[39] Linked to these efforts on micronutrient supplementation, among other programs, Nepal saw a decrease in mortality of children under the age of 5 from 142 per 1000 in 1990 to 51 per 1000 in 2009.[41]

Nepal has demonstrated that it is possible for a country with limited finances to carry out cost-effective programs to address micronutrient deficiencies with substantial results. This has been achieved in Nepal largely through strong political support, the use of community health worker volunteers, effective spread of knowledge about the importance of micronutrients, and careful program supervision and monitoring. It has also been assisted by close collaboration with a number of Nepal's development partners.

Rapid Results Initiative for Food Fortification in Kenya

For many years, African countries have fortified salt with iodine and have even made salt fortification a requirement. However, progress on food fortification in the Africa region has been relatively slow and there are no requirements in the region for the fortification of other foods. This is despite the substantial nutritional gaps in Africa that could be addressed at least partly through fortification.[43]

Until recently, Kenya was among the countries that had successfully fortified salt but had not fortified other staple foods. The failure to move on fortification stemmed at least partly from difficulty in getting the public and private sectors to work together on fortification. In order for fortification to succeed, these parties must collaborate, because both play an important role in food fortification. The public sector is responsible for food safety. The private sector is responsible for producing and selling the fortified foods.[44]

The Kenyan National Food Fortification Alliance (KNFFA) was established to mobilize food companies and government organizations to fortify foods.[44] Initially, the process proved to be slow and little progress was made. Food companies felt that the government would not create and monitor food standards and the government felt that food companies would not willingly fortify foods.

To help overcome these barriers, the KNFFA leadership decided to collaborate with the Micronutrient Initiative (MI) and the Rapid Results Institute (RRI) to produce a fortified food in 100 days or less. The MI is a nonprofit organization based in Canada that is the leading global agency focusing exclusively on addressing micronutrient deficiencies, particularly in poor women and children in low-income countries. The RRI is a nonprofit organization that focuses on helping countries achieve rapid and sustainable results in key areas of health, education, water supply, and related social investments.

In order to move ahead on a fortification program, the stakeholders were brought together to address concerns surrounding food fortification, such as quality standards and standard enforcement, and to invite participation in the project. Second, a training meeting was held for stakeholders, such as food companies and government organizations. During this time, goals were set: in 130 days, a fortified food certification process would be developed and three brands of edible oils would be fortified with vitamin A.[43,44]

Through this effort, Kenya was able to meet its goal and achieve in a very short amount of time what it had not been able to do at all previously. By the end of the 130 days, three brands of oil, or 15 percent of the edible oil market, met international standards for vitamin A fortification in edible oils. Additionally, fortification standards, a fortification certification process, and a fortification logo, which can be put on a product to show that it meets standards, were developed.[44] The Kenya Bureau of Standards monitors food fortification standards and the Ministry of Health now regulates the certification process.[44] As a result of the initiative, there has been increased collaboration and trust between the public and private sectors, laying the foundation for future fortification of additional staple foods.

Childhood Nutrition Supplementation and Adult Productivity in Guatemala

A number of countries have undertaken efforts to provide supplementary food to undernourished children. Some of those programs, such as the Tamil Nadu Nutrition Project, have been evaluated carefully. However, very rarely has anyone followed for more than two decades the children who participated in a supplementary feeding program in order to gauge long-term program impact in adulthood. One such study was done for a program in Guatemala, as described in this section.

In four Guatemalan villages between March 1, 1969, and February 28, 1977, the Institute of Nutrition of Central America and Panama (INCAP) initiated the first phase of a study on nutrition supplementation and child development among 2392 children who were under the age of 7. Researchers randomly assigned one of two treatments to each of the children. In two villages, children were offered a dietary supplement called "atole" that provided protein and energy. This supplement consisted of dry skim milk, Incaparina (a protein mixture), and sugar. In the other two villages, children were offered a supplement called "fresco." Unlike atole, fresco did not provide fat or protein and offered only minimal energy. Both supplements were equally fortified with micronutrients before being distributed twice daily from a central location in each village.[45]

The study followed the cohort of children over time and compared the effects of the nutritional supplement on schooling, adult intellectual functioning, child birthweight, and individual productivity. As part of this effort, between 2002 and 2004—25 years after the nutrition supplementation ended—researchers, in collaboration with Emory University, surveyed 1448 of those who participated in the original study as children.[45] In order to measure literacy and reading comprehension, the InterAmerican Series Test was used. The Raven Progressive Matrices Test was utilized to determine cognitive development.

Children who had received the supplement of protein and energy, atole, scored higher on both tests as adults than those who received fresco. Among men, there was no significant relationship between the type of supplement taken and the amount of school completed. However, women who received atole completed 1.2 more years of school than the other women.[8] Overall, after controlling for the number of years of school completed, it was found that receiving the atole supplement was positively related for both men and women to higher adult intellectual functioning.[45]

Researchers also examined the relationship between economic productivity of individuals, measured through their wages, and which of the supplements was given in the INCAP nutrition intervention. Boys who were under the age of 3 when they first received atole experienced a 46 percent increase in hourly wages as adults, compared to the boys who received fresco in the original study. There was no significant increase in economic productivity in women who received one supplement, compared to the other group.[46]

However, a girl's involvement in the INCAP intervention positively affected her offspring. Compared to those who received fresco, women who had received atole as children were found to have babies, especially sons, with a higher birthweight, a larger head circumference, and a greater height at birth. Additionally, their offspring had greater height-for-age and weight-for-age.[47]

Overall, this study has helped to shed light on the value of nutritional supplementation among children. The protein and energy–based atole nutritional supplement resulted in higher literacy rates and cognitive development among men and women, higher employment wages for men, and offspring with a higher birthweight. This study further supports the premise that some forms of food supplementation in the early years of life can impact the remaining years of life in substantial and positive ways.

CASE STUDIES

In fact, there are a number of investments in improving nutrition status on a large scale that have made a significant difference to the communities in which they took place. One of the best known is the Tamil Nadu Nutrition Project in India. China has also made considerable progress in the last 10 years in controlling iodine deficiency.

Tamil Nadu State, India[48]

Background

The Tamil Nadu Integrated Nutrition Project in India is one of the most important efforts ever undertaken to improve nutritional status on a large scale. This project began in 1980 in the South Indian state of Tamil Nadu. It aimed at improving the nutritional status of poor women and children in the rural areas of the state through a set of well-focused interventions.

These specific goals were set for several reasons. First, the levels of malnutrition in poor women and children in Tamil Nadu were very high at the time the project was conceived. Second, malnutrition persisted despite considerable investments that had already been undertaken to improve nutrition status. Third, studies that had been done on those investments showed that they were not working as planned and were not cost-effective. Rather, the children who needed assistance most were not getting it. In addition, food that was given to children at feeding centers that was meant to be supplementary to their regular diet often replaced their regular food or was taken home and consumed by family members other than the intended children. The form of the food supplement was also difficult for children to eat. Moreover, little attention had been paid to nutrition education for families or to health investments that could complement the investments made in nutrition.

The project design was based on the idea that much of the malnutrition present in Tamil Nadu was because of inappropriate child care practices, rather than just a lack of money to buy food. Thus, the project focused considerable attention on nutrition education and efforts to improve care and feeding practices for young children. In addition, because deficits at an early age often produce irreversible damage to children's physical and mental development, project interventions focused on pregnant and lactating women and on children younger than 3 years of age.

The Intervention

In line with this approach, the project included a package of services that were delivered by health and nutrition workers that consisted of nutrition education, primary health care, supplementary on-site feeding for children who were not growing properly, vitamin A supplementation, periodic deworming, education of mothers for managing childhood diarrhea, and the supplementary feeding of a small number of women.

An important innovation of the project was that it used growth monitoring of the children as a device for mobilizing community action. Groups of mothers met regularly to weigh their young children. They then plotted their weight-for-age on a growth chart. Together with the community nutrition worker, they identified which children were not growing properly. A related innovation of great importance was that supplementary feeding was targeted only to the children identified as faltering. In addition, children received food supplements only while they were not growing well. This was done in conjunction with nutrition education for mothers. The intent of this approach was that short-term feeding, combined with better child care practices, could return the child to normal growth. This was a major change compared with previous practice in which supplementary feeding was more universal and longer term.

Impact

The nutrition interventions of the project were largely implemented as planned, but the health efforts were not fully implemented. Nonetheless, through careful evaluation the project was shown to have significantly reduced the levels of malnutrition of the targeted children. These improvements also continued over a substantial time, suggesting that the gains of the project were sustainable. The project was also more cost-effective than other investments that had tried to achieve similar aims in India.

Lessons Learned

This project was pioneering and revealed some very important lessons, including:

- Growth monitoring, coupled with short-term supplementary feeding of children who are faltering, can be a cost-effective way of improving nutritional status.
- More universal and longer-term feeding of children is not necessary to achieve improvements in nutrition.
- Women can be organized to participate actively in growth monitoring efforts.
- Nutrition education can have a permanent and sustainable impact on child care and child feeding practices, even in the absence of other interventions.

The Challenge of Iodine Deficiency Disease in China

Background

China bears the heaviest burden of iodine deficiency in the world. In 1995, 20 percent of children ages 8 to 10 showed signs of goiter. Overall, some 400 million people in China were estimated to be at risk of iodine deficiency disorders, constituting 40 percent of the global total. Fortunately, iodine deficiency can be simply remedied by adding iodine to salt, a cheap and universally consumed food. Implementing this in a relatively poor and vast country like China, however, is far from simple.

The Intervention

Scientific evidence linking iodine deficiency to mental impairment was seen by the Chinese government as a threat to its one-child-per-family policy, and so the government strengthened its resolve to tackle this widespread health risk. In 1993, China launched the National Iodine Deficiency Disorders Elimination Program, with technical and financial assistance from the donor-funded Iodine Deficiency Disorders Control Project. The public needed to be made aware of the risk of iodine deficiency, especially in regions where goiter was so common that it was regarded as normal. A nationwide public education campaign was launched, using posters on buses, newspaper editorials, and television documentaries to inform consumers and persuade them to switch to iodized salt. Provincial governors ensured that government education efforts reached even the most remote villages. The supply of iodized salt was increased by building 112 new salt iodation factories and enhancing capacity at 55 existing ones. Bulk packaging systems were installed to complement 147 new retail packaging centers, with packaging designed to help consumers easily recognize iodized salt. The sale of non-iodized salt was banned, and technological assistance was provided to salt producers to adopt iodation. Salt quality was monitored, both at production, where the amount of iodine added needs to be just right, and in distribution and sales, because iodine in salt dissipates easily, reducing the shelf life of iodized salt. China's nationally controlled network of production and distribution made licensing and enforcement of legislation easier.

The Impact

By 1999, iodized salt was reaching 94 percent of the country, compared to 80 percent in 1995. The quality of iodized salt also improved markedly. As a result, iodine deficiency was reduced dramatically, and goiter rates for children ages 8 to 10 fell from 20.4 percent in 1995 to 8.8 percent in 1999.[49]

Costs and Benefits

Fortifying salt with iodine costs about 2 to 7 cents per kilogram, or less than 5 percent of the retail price of salt in most countries. The Chinese government invested approximately $152 million in the program, recovering some of this cost by raising the price of iodized salt. The World Bank, one of several donors, deemed the project extremely cost-effective.

Lessons Learned

China's success in reducing iodine deficiency offers valuable lessons for future efforts to reduce other micronutrient deficiencies such as iron and vitamin A through fortification. The government made a firm and long-standing commitment to tackle the problem and brought about administrative, legal, technical, and sociocultural changes that were needed to do so. Donor coordination was strong and effective and was managed by the Chinese government and the donors themselves, and the major players offered mutual support across all activities. The financing strategy was clearly defined from the start. The salt industry seized the opportunity of the investment in eliminating iodine deficiency to restructure and modernize the industry, gaining a firmer commercial footing and positioning itself to compete in the international market, given its cost advantages.

China's iodation program continues, with special targeting of resources on areas where the consumption of iodized salt is particularly low, usually in poor and remote mountainous regions where residents see iodized salt as too costly, especially when salt can be obtained cheaply from local salt hills, dried lakes, or the sea. Research will be needed to determine the best way to ensure iodine intake in these areas—through price subsidies, iodation of well or irrigation water, or even iodine capsules or injections, in the case of nomadic peoples. Through a variety of approaches, China is fast approaching the day when iodine deficiency will be unknown throughout its population. A more detailed review of this case is available in *Case Studies in Global Health: Millions Saved*.

ADDRESSING FUTURE NUTRITION CHALLENGES

The world has made some progress in the last several decades in addressing key nutrition problems. Nonetheless, as we have seen, the overall state of the world's nutrition still faces numerous and serious gaps. This is especially so in South Asia and sub-Saharan Africa. At the present rate of progress in addressing those gaps, the world will not meet the MDGs that relate to nutrition. What steps will have to be taken to speed the world's progress on nutrition? These are discussed briefly below.

It has already been noted that knowledge and behaviors are important determinants of what foods people eat, how they cook them, and how they consume them. Studies have shown that people can improve what they eat, how they cook, and how they eat their food by improvements in knowledge, even in the absence of improvements in income.[50] Nutrition education needs to be spread much more widely and in more appropriate ways to promote appropriate breastfeeding and complementary feeding and to help people eat better and more nutritious foods.

Growth monitoring and promotion programs, like that in Tamil Nadu, as well as others that were carried out in Honduras, Indonesia, and Madagascar, can also be important to improving nutrition outcomes at low cost. It is especially important that these programs be community-based. In addition, mothers who participate in these programs need to understand the importance of child growth and how they can carry out improved feeding and caring practices, such as exclusive breastfeeding, appropriate introduction of complementary foods, and the management of diarrhea. To succeed, growth monitoring and promotion programs must be coupled with programs for behavior change communication.[51]

The two-way relationship between infection, disease, and nutrition status has been noted. Many infections and diseases reduce one's ability to eat or ability to absorb food. At the same time, poor nutritional status reduces immunity to disease. To set the foundation for improvements in the nutritional status of poor people in low- and middle-income countries, especially poor infants, children, and women, it is very important to improve the control of parasitic infections such as hookworm and to control diarrheal diseases, malaria, and measles. Of course, doing this will also demand renewed efforts at health education; more effective basic health services, such as immunization; and improvements in water supply and sanitation.

There will be some people who will simply not eat enough food or enough of the right foods, largely because of income gaps. These problems are also the result of, or are compounded by, natural disaster and conflict. Under these circumstances, it may be necessary that people receive food supplements like a high protein, high calorie "ready to use therapeutic food." Alternatively, some people may receive vouchers for food, such as "food stamps," which are cash transfers that can be used only to buy certain health and nutrition services, or the right to buy certain foods at reduced prices. Conditional cash transfer programs, as discussed in Chapters 5 and 6, are also being used to promote better nutrition, and "smart cards" are increasingly taking the place of food stamps or transfers of cash.

Vitamin and mineral supplementation is widespread in the world, is not expensive, and is often used as a way of improving the micronutrient status of large numbers of people, especially infants, children, and pregnant and lactating mothers. These can be given in capsules or syrups. Vitamin A should be given twice per year and should be integrated with child survival and other health services to minimize the cost of distribution.[52] In the last decade, vitamin A has been given orally to infants and children during national polio immunization days in many countries. These efforts can be expanded. At the same time, additional and carefully monitored efforts can be made to provide iron and folate to pregnant women. Unfortunately, these efforts have not worked as well as planned and need to be carefully reviewed and refined to enhance both coverage of supplementation and the extent to which women take the pills they do get.

Food fortification is practiced in many countries for a number of micronutrients. In fact, fortification in the industrialized countries has contributed greatly to the disappearance of several deficiencies. The fortification of salt with iodine is a very widespread practice and is very inexpensive, as we have seen in the China case noted earlier. About two thirds of the world now consumes iodized salt, and the impact of fortification of salt could be further expanded through its double fortification with iron, as well as iodine. In addition, many different food products can be fortified. The key to effective fortification is to find a food product that is very widely consumed, for which there are no technical impediments to fortification, and for which fortification is inexpensive.[53] Thus, increasingly one can see flour, cooking oil, margarine, soy sauce, and other products fortified, as well as salt. Multiple vitamin and mineral supplements are also being manufactured, which can be sprinkled on children's food to fortify it. Fortification can cost as little as 3 to 5 cents per person reached per year.[54] Clearly, fortification is a good way to harness the resources of commercial marketing networks to enhance the health of the population. Given the difficulties of iron supplementation, it may be that the most effective way of reducing iron deficiency in women is to operate an effective program of fortification for iron and folic acid.

Efforts are also underway for bio-fortification. The aim of this work is to use technologies to improve the nutritional content of foods, such as rice, yams, or other vegetables.

If the world is to do better in nutrition, it will also have to take a number of policy steps. First, policy makers who work both globally and on individual countries need to understand the exceptional importance of nutrition to good health and human productivity and act accordingly. More than 35 percent of the child deaths globally are associated with nutritional causes. In addition, low cost, highly effective solutions are available to deal with a number of critical nutrition issues, but they are not being implemented sufficiently. Thus, much greater attention needs to be paid by all concerned parties to nutrition as an underlying health issue. Nutrition does not fit neatly into governmental bureaucracies because it touches many government units, such as agriculture, health, and education. Governments will also need to think creatively about how to ensure that there are government units accountable and responsible for promoting enhanced approaches to nutrition.

Improving government policy and action on nutrition will also require a good understanding of the nature of the nutrition problem in different settings. Nutritional concerns will vary considerably by income group, gender, and ethnicity, and solutions to these problems will need to be carefully tailored to local circumstances. In addition, governments need to work more effectively with the food industry to improve the way in which foods are fortified. Legal and financial arrangements need to be made in many countries so that more fortification can take place and the demand for fortified foods will be increased, as noted in the policy brief on Kenya. We have also seen the power in Tamil Nadu, for example, of focusing efforts on community-based action, in which affected people are involved in the design, implementation, and oversight of nutrition activities.

Although there is much knowledge of "what works" in nutrition, there are also other areas in which additional knowledge could fill important gaps. The world needs to continue gathering scientific knowledge about how key nutrition issues can be addressed. It would be very valuable to the world's nutrition status and health if more easy to make, nutritious, and inexpensive food supplements were available; if better formulas were available for some of the vitamin and mineral supplements that could be given less frequently, very cheaply, and without side effects; and, if additional cost-effective ways were found for fortifying foods.

Lastly, it is important for all societies to make the health and nutritional well-being of their citizens a national priority. One way to do this would be to create partnerships of civil society, government, and the private sector that can work together to identify nutrition issues, plan on how they can best be addressed, and then collaborate with each other and with communities to implement solutions to these problems.

MAIN MESSAGES

Nutritional status is a major determinant of health status. It has an important bearing on the health of pregnant women and on pregnancy outcomes for both mothers and children. It is a major determinant of the birthweight of children, how children grow, and the extent to which their cognitive functions develop properly. Nutrition status is also closely linked with the strength of one's immune system and one's ability to stay healthy.

In addition, nutritional status has an important bearing on people's capacity to learn and on their productivity. Nutritional deficits can seriously hamper the ability of children to attend school, concentrate while they are there, and learn effectively. Numerous studies have shown that workers who are anemic produce less than workers who do not suffer from iron deficiency anemia.

From the global health perspective, the most important nutritional concerns are breastfeeding practices, whether or not people get enough of the right foods to have sufficient energy and protein, and the extent to which people have a sufficient intake of vitamin A, iodine, iron, and zinc. The importance of these nutrients and micronutrients varies with the place of people in their life cycle, with needs differing for adolescents, pregnant and lactating women, infants, children, adults, and older adults.

More than 1 billion people in the world today suffer from energy and protein malnutrition and deficiencies in key micronutrients. These problems often stem from people's lack of income to purchase enough food or food of appropriate quality. However, these problems also relate to culture, customs, and eating behaviors. Malnutrition disproportionately affects poor people, marginalized people, and females.

Energy and protein malnutrition is associated with low birthweight, being underweight, failing to grow properly, and a weakening of immunity. Vitamin A deficiency is well known for its impact on vision, but is also closely associated with general immunity and child growth. The lack of iron is the primary cause of iron deficiency anemia, which leads to weakness and fatigue; however, it is also associated with maternal morbidity and mortality, poor and stunted growth in children, and poor mental development in children. The lack of iodine causes thyroid problems, goiter, and important deficits in mental abilities. Iodine is also essential for proper child growth. The lack of zinc is associated with general immunity, the growth of children, and the development of children's cognitive and motor abilities. About 35 percent of the child deaths in the world today are associated with undernutrition.

There are cost-effective solutions to the most important nutritional concerns. People can wash their hands more frequently with soap to reduce the rate of infections and diarrhea that take such terrible tolls on nutritional status. Efforts can be enhanced to promote exclusive breastfeeding for 6 months, followed by the appropriate introduction of hygieni-cally prepared complementary feeding. Food supplements can be given to those people who are not getting enough pro-tein and energy. Nutritional supplements can be provided for vitamin A and iron. Salt can be fortified with iodine. Zinc can be given along with oral rehydration to reduce the severity of diarrheal disease. Families can also learn, even in the absence of income gains, to improve what they eat. These actions will be most successful if they are tied to approaches that are taken by communities.

It is also critical to remember that the "window of oppor-tunity" for ensuring that children are well-nourished and develop properly is a small one. It begins at conception and lasts until the children are about 2 years of age. Damage done to the child's development in this period is largely irreversible.

The most critical interventions, therefore, are to:

- Ensure that pregnant women are well-nourished and have sufficient amounts of needed micronutrients
- Promote exclusive breastfeeding for all children until they are 6 months of age
- Encourage the provision of appropriate complemen-tary foods for infants beginning at 6 months of age
- Support effective programs in supplementation and fortification, based on nutritional needs at the local level and embed them in community-based approaches
- Fight infection and illness through better hygiene, improved water and sanitation, and appropriate food and health behaviors
- Focus on South Asia and sub-Saharan Africa

These can be achieved by taking some of the following steps in the short, medium, and longer run:

Short-run
- Initiate community-based growth monitoring and promotion
- Carry out supplementation with vitamin A and iron
- Provide zinc for the management of diarrhea
- Very selectively provide therapeutic food

Medium-run
- Consolidate community-based growth monitoring and promotion
- Implement food supplementation through programs such as vouchers, smart cards, and conditional cash transfers
- Fortify locally appropriate foods with needed micro-nutrients, including completing the agenda on the fortification of salt with iodine

Long-run
- Improve the education of women and take other appropriate measures to enhance the social standing of women in society
- Use technologies to improve the nutritional content of foods[51]

Study Questions

1. What is the importance of nutrition to the MDGs?

2. What are "stunting" and "wasting"?

3. What are some of the direct and indirect causes of undernutrition?

4. What are the links between nutrition and health?

5. How are growth charts used to gauge nutrition status?

6. What are the most important micronutrient deficiencies and what health problems do they cause?

7. Why is anemia a special risk in pregnancy?

8. Why is exclusive breastfeeding for the first 6 months so important?

9. What parts of the world have the worst nutritional problems?

10. What are the links between nutrition and economic development?

REFERENCES

1. Ezzati M, Vander Hoorn S, Lopez AD, et al. Comparative quantification of mortality and burden of disease attributable to selected risk factors. In: Lopez AD, Mathers CD, Ezzati M, Jamison DT, Murray CJL, eds. *Global Burden of Disease and Risk Factors*. New York: Oxford University Press; 2006:251.

2. UNICEF. *Progress for Children: Achieving the MDGs with Equity*. New York: UNICEF; September 2010.

3. Black RE, Allen LH, Bhutta ZA, et al. Maternal and child undernutrition: global and regional exposures and health consequences. *Lancet*. 2008;371(9608):243-260.

4. UNICEF and The Micronutrient Initiative. *Vitamin and Mineral Deficiency: A Global Progress Report*. Ottawa: The Micronutrient Initiative; 2004.

5. UNICEF. *State of the World's Children: Focus of Nutrition*. New York: Oxford University Press; 1998:23-25.

6. UNICEF. Progress for Children. A Report Card on Nutrition, Number 4, May 2006. Available at: http://www.unicef.org/progressforchildren/2006n4. Accessed May 8, 2011.

7. Caulfield LE, Richard SA, Rivera JA, Musgrove P, Black RE. Stunting, wasting, and micronutrient disorders. In: Jamison DT, Breman JG, Measham AR, et al., eds. *Disease Control Priorities in Developing Countries*. 2nd ed. New York: Oxford University Press and The World Bank; 2006:552.

8. Victora CG, Adair L, Fall C, et al. Maternal and child undernutrition: consequences for adult health and human capital. *Lancet*. 2008;371(9609):340-357.

9. GP Notebook: Xerophthalmia. Available at: http://www.gpnotebook.co.uk/cache/664403984.htm. Accessed July 5, 2006.

10. Government of Australia. Iodine Explained. Available at: http://www.betterhealth.vic.gov.au/BHCV2/bhcarticles.nsf/pages/Iodine_explained?open. Accessed June 27, 2006.

11. Caulfield LE, Richard SA, Rivera JA, Musgrove P, Black RE. Stunting, wasting, and micronutrient disorders. In: Jamison DT, Breman JG, Measham AR, et al., eds. *Disease Control Priorities in Developing Countries*. 2nd ed. New York: Oxford University Press; 2006:554.

12. World Bank. *Repositioning Nutrition as Central to Development*. Washington, DC: The World Bank; 2006:23.

13. Mercer LP, Wests Jr. KP. Nutrient Information: Iodine. Available at: http://nutrition.org/nutinfo/content/iodi.shtml. Accessed July 14, 2004.

14. Hunt J. Nutrient Information: Iron. Available at: http://nutrition.org/nutinfo/content/iron2.shtml. Accessed July 14, 2004.

15. Cousins RJ. Nutrient Information: Zinc. Available at: http://jn.nutrition.org/nutinfo. Accessed July 29, 2006.

16. Brown KH, Wuehler SE. *The Micronutrient Initiative*. Ottawa: The Micronutrient Initiative; 2000:7.

17. Ohio State University. Ohio State University Extension Fact Sheet: Nutritional Needs of Pregnancy. Available at: http://ohioline.osu.edu/mobfact/0001.html. Accessed June 28, 2006.

18. Black RE, Morris SS, Bryce J. Where and why are 10 million children dying every year? *Lancet*. 2003;361(9376):2226-2234.

19. International Food Policy Research Institute. The Life Cycle of Malnutrition. Available at: http://www.ifpri.org/pubs/books/ar1999/08-13LC.pdf. Accessed July 4, 2006.

20. The World Bank. *Repositioning Nutrition as Central to Development*. Washington, DC: The World Bank; 2006.

21. National Osteoporosis Foundation. Fast Facts. Available at: http://www.nof.org/osteoporosis/diseasefacts.htm. Accessed June 28, 2006.

22. UNICEF. Nutrition: What Are the Challenges? Available at: http://www.unicef.org/nutrition/index_challenges.html. Accessed June 28, 2006.

23. Food and Agriculture Organization. *The State of Food Insecurity in the World*. Rome: Food and Agriculture Organization; 2004:5.

24. UNICEF. *State of the World's Children: Focus of Nutrition*. New York: Oxford University Press; 1998:109.

25. India National Family Health Survey. National Family Health Survey, 2005–2006: Fact Sheets. Available at: http://www.nfhsindia.org/factsheet.html. Accessed January 8, 2011.

26. Lopez AD, Mathers CD, Murray CJL. The burden of disease and mortality by condition: data, methods, and results for 2001. In: Lopez AD, Mathers CD, Ezzati M, Jamison DT, Murray CJL, eds. *Global Burden of Disease and Risk Factors*. New York: Oxford University Press; 2006:126.

27. Lopez AD, Mathers CD, Murray CJL. The burden of disease and mortality by condition: data, methods, and results for 2001. In: Lopez AD, Mathers CD, Ezzati M, Jamison DT, Murray CJL, eds. *Global Burden of Disease and Risk Factors*. New York: Oxford University Press and The World Bank; 2006:180.

28. UNICEF and World Health Organization. *Low Birth Weight: Country, Regional, and Global Estimates*. New York: UNICEF; 2004.

29. UNICEF and Micronutrient Initiative. *Vitamin and Mineral Deficiency: A Global Progress Report*. Ottawa: The Micronutrient Initiative, 2004.

30. Caulfield LE, Richard SA, Rivera JA, Musgrove P, Black RE. Stunting, wasting, and micronutrient disorders. In: Jamison DT, Breman JG, Measham AR, et al., eds. *Disease Control Priorities in Developing Countries*. 2nd ed. New York: Oxford University Press; 2006:553.

31. World Health Organization. World Health Organization Sets Out to Eliminate Iodine Deficiency Disorder. Available at: http://www.who.int/inf-pr-1999/en/pr99-wha17.html. Accessed July 15, 2006.

32. Mason JB, Lofti M, Dalmiya N, Sethuraman K, Deitchler M. *The Micronutrient Report*. Ottawa: Micronutrient Initiative; 2001.

33. Lopez AD, Mathers CD, Murray CJL. The burden of disease and mortality by condition: data, methods, and results for 2001. In: Lopez AD, Mathers CD, Ezzati M, Jamison DT, Murray CJL, eds. *Global Burden of Disease and Risk Factors*. New York: Oxford University Press; 2006:180-184.

34. de Benoist B, McLean E, Egli I, Cogswell M, eds. *Worldwide Prevalance of Anaemia 1993–2005: WHO Global Database on Anaemia*. Geneva: World Health Organization; 2008.

35. Hunt JM. Reversing productivity losses from iron deficiency: the economic case. *J Nutr*. 2002;132(Suppl 4):794S-801S.

36. Fogel R. *New Sources and New Techniques for the Study of Secular Trends in Nutritional Status, Health, Mortality, and the Process of Aging*. Cambridge, MA: National Bureau of Economic Research; 1991.

37. Wolgemuth JC, Latham MC, Hall A, Chesher A, Crompton DW. Worker productivity and the nutritional status of Kenyan road construction laborers. *Am J Clin Nutr*. 1982;36(1):68-78.

38. Li R, Chen X, Yan H, Deurenberg P, Garby L, Hautvast JG. Functional consequences of iron supplementation in iron-deficient female cotton mill workers in Beijing, China. *Am J Clin Nutr*. 1994;59(4):908-913.

39. Basnet AS, Mathema P. Micronutrient Supplementation Brings New Hope for Children in Nepal. Available at: http://www.unicef.org/infobycountry/nepal_56023.html. Accessed January 10, 2011.

40. Micronutrient Initiative. Investing in the Future: A United Call to Action on Vitamin and Mineral Deficiencies Global Report 2009. Available at: http://www.unitedcalltoaction.org/documents/Investing_in_the_future.pdf. Accessed January 10, 2011.

41. Micronutrient Initiative. Nepal. Available at: http://www.micronutrient.org/english/view.asp?x=605. Accessed January 10, 2011.

42. UNICEF. Getting to the Roots: Mobilizing Community Volunteers to Combat Vitamin A Deficiency Disorders in Nepal. Available at: http://www.mostproject.org/CHVs/gettingattherootscomplete.pdf. Accessed January 10, 2011.

43. Micronutrient Initiative. Accelerating Food Fortification: A Rapid Results Initiative in Kenya. Available at: http://www.rapidresults.org/evaluations/kenya.php?top=504. Accessed January 2, 2011.

44. Micronutrient Initiative. Getting Things Done: Using an Innovative Management Approach to Facilitate Food Fortification in Kenya. Available at: http://www.fortaf.org/files/knffa_case_study_1.pdf. Accessed January 4, 2011.

45. Stein AH, Wang M, DiGirolamo A, et al. Nutritional supplementation in early childhood, schooling, and intellectual functioning in adulthood: a prospective study in Guatemala. *Arch Pediatr Adolesc Med.* 2008;162(7):612-618.

46. Hoddinott J, Maluccio JA, Behrman JR, Flores R, Martorell R. Effect of a nutrition intervention during early childhood on economic productivity in Guatemalan adults. *Lancet.* 2008;371(9610):411-416.

47. Behrman JR, Calderon MC, Preston SH, Hoddinott J, Martorell R, Stein AD. Nutritional supplementation in girls influences the growth of their children: prospective study in Guatemala. *Am J Clin Nutr.* 2009;90:1372-1379.

48. The World Bank. *Impact Evaluation Report: Tamil Nadu Integrated Nutrition Project.* Washington, DC: The World Bank; 1994.

49. Goh, CC. Combating iodine deficiency: lessons from China, Indonesia, and Madagascar. *Food Nutr Bull.* 2002;23(3):280-291.

50. Griffiths M, Dicken K, Favin M. *Promoting the Growth of Children: What Works: Rationale and Guidance for Programs.* Washington, DC: Human Development Department and the World Bank; 1996.

51. Levinson FJ, Bassett L. *Malnutrition Is Still a Major Contributor to Child Deaths.* Washington, DC: PRB; 2008.

52. World Bank. *Repositioning Nutrition as Central to Development.* Washington, DC: The World Bank; 2006:72.

53. Lofti M, Merx R, Naber P, Van der Heuvel P. *Micronutrient Fortification of Foods: Current Prospectus, Research and Opportunities.* Ottawa: International Agriculture Centre; 1996.

54. The World Bank. *Repositioning Nutrition as Central to Development.* Washington, DC: The World Bank; 2006:132-135.

Women's Health

VIGNETTES

Suneeta was pregnant with her first child. She lived in northern India where many families prefer to have sons rather than daughters, especially for their first-born child. Eager to have a son, Suneeta's husband took her to get a sonogram to determine the sex of the baby. When they learned the baby would be a girl, they decided that Suneeta should abort the fetus and try again to get pregnant, in hopes of having a boy.

Sarah lived in rural Pakistan and was pregnant with her second child. When she went into labor, Sarah called for the traditional birth attendant, as most women did in her town. As Sarah's labor continued, she and the birth attendant realized that the labor was complicated. Sarah needed to go to a hospital to deliver the baby. In this part of Pakistan, however, women could not be taken to hospitals without their husband's permission. Sarah's husband was working in another

city and was not available to give such permission. Several hours later, Sarah and the baby died at Sarah's home.

Carmen lived in a slum in Guatemala City, Guatemala. She was not married but became pregnant after relations with a man she had met several months before. In her culture, to become pregnant without being married was a source of great shame to a woman's family. Fearing the reaction of her family to her pregnancy, Carmen decided to get an abortion. Although abortions are illegal in Guatemala, except to save the life of the mother,[1] they are performed there by both licensed physicians and unlicensed medical practitioners. Sarah could not afford the fee charged by a physician and went instead to an unlicensed abortionist. Carmen's abortion was not performed properly; she bled profusely as a result of the procedure, and she died before she could be taken to a hospital.

Elizabeth was a 15-year-old girl in Cape Town, South Africa. She was a good student but came from a poor family and was always short of the money she needed to pay for school supplies, uniforms, and books. John had been eyeing Elizabeth for some time. He was 25 years old, had a good job, and was always interested in spending time with the young ladies at Elizabeth's school. At the start of the second semester, when Elizabeth was trying to get together the money for school, John convinced her to sleep with him in exchange for a small amount of money. Elizabeth had heard about HIV, but John convinced her that he was healthy and there was no need to use a condom. About a year later, Elizabeth fell ill, was given an HIV test, and turned out to be HIV-positive.

THE IMPORTANCE OF WOMEN'S HEATH

The vignettes above suggest several reasons why women's health issues must be given a prominent place in this book and in the global health agenda:

- Being born female is dangerous to your health, especially in low- and middle-income countries.
- In many societies women are subjected to discrimination and very proscribed roles, both of which can be harmful to their health.

TABLE 9-1 Key Links Between Women's Health and the MDGs

Goal 1: Eradicate Poverty and Hunger
Link: Poor health and nutritional status of women is both a cause and an effect of poverty. Enhancing the nutritional status of women will improve both their health and the health of their babies, with many attendant beneficial consequences for both.

Goal 2: Achieve Universal Primary Education
Link: Improving the health of females will enhance their enrollment in, attendance at, and performance in schools. Improving the educational attainments of females will lead to improvements in their health and the health of their children.

Goal 3: Promote Gender Equality and Empower Women
Link: Improvements in equity and empowerment will lead to better education for females, more income-earning opportunities for them, and less violence against them, all of which will improve their health status.

Goal 4: Reduce Child Mortality
Link: An important share of child mortality is linked with poor health and nutritional status of the mother. Improving the health and nutritional status of the mother is the starting point for reducing the share of children born with low birth weight, a major contributor to child morbidity and mortality.

Goal 5: Improve Maternal Health
Link: This is directly connected to the health of women.

Goal 6: Combat HIV/AIDS, Malaria, and Other Diseases
Link: The share of the total number of HIV-affected people who are women is growing worldwide, and HIV/AIDS is a major cause of illness, disability, and death for women. Combating HIV/AIDS would have a major impact on the health of females and, as a result, on their families as well.

Source: Adapted from United Nations. Millennium Development Goals. Available at: http://www.un.org/millenniumgoals/goals. Accessed July 11, 2006.

- Women face a number of unique health problems by virtue of their sex and their place in society.
- There are often important and unjustifiable differentials in the health of men and women.
- Morbidity, disability, and premature death of women can have enormous social and economic consequences on the affected women, on their families, and on society more broadly.
- Many investments in the health of women would result, at relatively low cost, in substantial numbers of deaths and DALYs averted.
- Improving the education and health of women and their place in society is one of the most powerful and cost-effective approaches that can be taken to promote social and economic development.

In addition, the health of women is intimately linked with the MDGs.[2] Table 9-1 indicates how six of the eight goals have a powerful relationship to women's health.

This chapter aims to give the reader a sense of the following:

- The key challenges facing women in low- and middle-income countries that relate to reproductive health and violence against women
- Which women are most affected by these problems
- The key risk factors for these issues
- The social and economic consequences of health problems for women
- What can be done to address these problems in as cost-effective a manner as possible

The chapter includes a number of policy and program briefs and case studies that illustrate some of its main points. The chapter concludes with comments on the key challenges for improving the health of women in low- and middle-income countries in the future. Other aspects of health that relate in particular ways to women are covered elsewhere in the book.

KEY DEFINITIONS

As one reviews the most important health issues that affect women worldwide, a number of terms will be used repeatedly. The most important of these are shown in Table 9-2.

THE DETERMINANTS OF WOMEN'S HEALTH

The determinants of a woman's health relate to both sex and gender. "Sex is biological."[3] It has to do with being born a female. "Gender is cultural."[3] Gender has to do with societal norms about the roles of women and their social position relative to men.[4] Some health issues are primarily

TABLE 9-2 Selected Definitions in Women's Health

Abortion—The premature expulsion or loss of embryo, which may be induced or spontaneous.

Cesarian delivery (section)—The surgical delivery of a fetus through abdominal incision.

Eclampsia—A serious, life-threatening condition in late pregnancy in which very high blood pressure can cause a woman to have seizures.

Family planning—The conscious effort of couples to regulate the number and spacing of births through artificial and natural methods of contraception.

Female genital cutting (female genital mutilation)—Traditional practices that are all related to the cutting of the female genital organs.

Gestational diabetes—Diabetes that develops during pregnancy because of improper regulation of blood sugar.

Hemorrhage (related to pregnancy)—Significant and uncontrolled loss of blood, either internally or externally from the body. Antepartum (prenatal) hemorrhage occurs after the 20th week of gestation but before delivery of the baby. Postpartum hemorrhage is the loss of 500 ml or more of blood from the genital tract after delivery of the baby. Primary postpartum hemorrhage occurs in the first 24 hours after delivery.

Maternal death—The death of a woman while pregnant, during delivery, or within 42 days of delivery.

Obstetric fistula—An injury in the birth canal that allows leakage from the bladder or rectum into the vagina, leaving a woman permanently incontinent.

Preeclampsia (previously called toxemia)—A condition characterized by pregnancy-induced high blood pressure, protein in the urine, and swelling (edema) due to fluid retention.

Sepsis—A serious medical condition caused by a severe infection, leading to a systemic inflammatory response.

Sex-selective abortion—The practice of aborting a fetus after a determination that the fetus is an undesired sex, typically female.

Source: Data from University of Kentucky HealthCare. Glossary Index. Available at: http://www.ukhealthcare.uky.edu/content/content.asp?pageid= P00527. Accessed April 15, 2007; University of New South Wales. UNSW Embryology Glossary Index. Available at: http://embryology.med.unsw.edu.au/ Notes/Index/index.htm. Accessed April 15, 2007; The White Ribbon Alliance. Glossary. Available at: http://www.whiteribbonalliance.org/Resources/ default.cfm?a0=Glossary. Accessed April 15, 2007; Wikipedia. Sepsis. Available at: http://en.wikipedia.org/wiki/Sepsis. Accessed April 15, 2007.

determined by biology, such as the fact that women alone get ovarian cancer. Other women's health issues are determined mostly by social factors, such as sex-selective abortion of female fetuses. Most women's health issues, however, are determined by a combination of biological and social determinants, such as the case of Sarah in the opening vignettes, who died in childbirth for a number of biological and social reasons that interacted. Further comments are given now on the biological and social determinants of women's health.

Biological Determinants

Women face a number of unique biological risks. One is iron deficiency anemia related to menstruation. Other risks are associated with pregnancy, including complications of the pregnancy itself, diseases that may be aggravated by pregnancy, and the effects of some unhealthy lifestyles, such as smoking, on pregnancy.[5] During pregnancy, there are a number of conditions, for example, that can cause women to become ill or to die, including hypertensive disorders of pregnancy. In addition, a woman can be left with a number of permanent disabilities related to pregnancy, including uterine prolapse and obstetric fistula. Women can also die of preeclampsia or eclampsia. It is hemorrhage, however, that is the leading cause of maternal mortality. The conditions that can exacerbate pregnancy-related health risks include malaria, hepatitis, tuberculosis, malnutrition, and obesity, as well as certain mental health issues, such as depression. Unsafe abortions lead to significant morbidity and mortality for women. In terms of the effects of lifestyles on pregnancy, it is clear that certain occupations and the use of alcohol, tobacco, and drugs are especially important to avoid during pregnancy.

Women are also biologically more susceptible to some sexually transmitted infections than men are, including to the

HIV virus.[6] This relates to the fact that women have a greater mucosal area that is exposed during sexual relations than men have. There are also certain health conditions specific to women for biological reasons, such as uterine cancer or ovarian cancer, as mentioned above. There are other health conditions in which women have a disproportionate share of the burden of disease, such as breast cancer. As women age, they also have a higher rate of heart disease than men have, although it is diagnosed far less frequently.[4]

Social Determinants

The social determinants of women's health are also very important, especially in societies that favor males. These social determinants relate predominantly to gender norms, which assign different roles and values to males and females, usually to the disadvantage of females. In many societies, women's inferior status leads to social, health, and economic problems for women that men do not face.

The social determinants of health begin even before women are born. In some societies where male preference is very strong, such as in India and in China, some families determine the sex of their unborn children with the use of sonograms and then abort females, especially for the birth of their first child.[7–9] This was the case for Suneeta in one of the opening vignettes.

Female infants are often breastfed less than boys of the same age and then fed less complementary food when they become toddlers.[10] In addition, young girls in many societies are also fed less than their male siblings. Older women in some cultures feed men first and then eat only the portions that are remaining. Others eat less nutritious food than the men in their family eat. Poor nutrition, often stemming partly from social causes, makes women more susceptible to illness. It also contributes to stunting and small pelvic size, which are hazards to the health of pregnant women and to their offspring.

There are a number of critical social issues that relate to women's sexual experiences. The low social status of women in many societies is linked to the physical and sexual abuse of women. Furthermore, male dominance means that women often have only a limited choice about when to have sexual relations, with whom, how to have them, and whether or not to use protection. As a result, women are often forced to have sex, often at young ages, and often without a condom or other contraceptives. For these social reasons, women face heightened risks of becoming pregnant, of having repeated pregnancies at close intervals, and of getting sexually transmitted diseases, including HIV/AIDS. In addition, rape is common in many settings, especially in areas of conflict.

A dowry is the gifts that a bride's family gives to the family of a groom, and among the worst forms of violence against women is "dowry death." The data on mortality for young women in India suggest that there are a disproportionate number of young married women who suffer burns, which are often alleged to occur when women are cooking. It appears, however, that some of these deaths are not accidental. Rather, the husband's family sometimes perpetrates the burning of the young women when they are not satisfied with the dowry that she has brought to her marriage.[11]

High levels of depression also appear to be related to the low status position of women in different societies and the expectations that those societies have of them. There is also widespread reporting in many societies of general gynecologic discomfort without physical explanation, which may be related to the stresses on the lives of many women.[12]

Especially in low-income populations, there are many households that are headed by females who are divorced, separated, or widowed, or by women whose husbands are working elsewhere. These households tend to be among the poorest people. These women also tend to be among the least well-educated people in a community and low income and limited education mitigate severely against the health of such women. In addition, divorced or widowed women face severe discrimination in a number of cultures.

The roles that women play in different cultures can also pose important hazards to their health. In many societies, for example, women cook indoors on open fires without adequate ventilation, as discussed in Chapter 7. This is strongly associated with respiratory problems and asthma for such women and for their children.

Poverty, lack of or low levels of education, and low social status of women in many societies seriously constrain the access of women to health services. In addition, girls and women who need health services often do not take advantage of such services in a timely way. There are numerous instances, for example, in which women cannot use health services without the permission of a husband or male relative or without having a male relative take them to the health services. In some settings, even when women need emergency care, such as during complications of pregnancy, social constraints prevent them from seeking such care and inhibit their husbands from taking them for treatment, as well, as reflected in the vignette about Sarah.

THE BURDEN OF HEALTH CONDITIONS FOR FEMALES

Having looked at the biological and social determinants of health for women, we can now look at some of the key health issues that females face, their prevalence, and the critical risk factors for those health conditions. This part of the chapter will examine selected women's health issues through their life cycle. In particular, it will focus on sex-selective abortion, female genital cutting, sexually transmitted infections, violence against women, and complications of pregnancy. It will comment on nutrition only briefly, because nutrition is largely covered in Chapter 8.

Sex-Selective Abortion

How common is sex-selective abortion worldwide? How many unborn children are affected? Sex-selective abortion appears to be a phenomenon that is more prevalent in India and China than in any other country in the world.[13] A number of studies have been done of this phenomenon and "one study suggested that close to one million female fetuses were aborted in India in the last 20 years."[14]

An important consequence of sex-selective abortion is the skewed ratios of males to females in a number of countries. Naturally, one would expect that there would be about 105 females born for every 100 males. However, in China today, there are about 120 males born for every 100 females, with similar male-to-female ratios in Taiwan, Singapore, and parts of India. South Korea also has 10 percent more male births than female births.[15]

There is considerable evidence worldwide that both family size and preferences for males go down as income and education rise. In the case of the countries cited above, however, this has not been the case. Rather, as incomes and education have risen, and as technology has become more available, some families have used their income, knowledge, and access to technology—ultrasound in this case—to express their preference for males by engaging in sex-selective abortion. Punjab State, for example, is the wealthiest state in India. Yet, it has the most skewed ratio in India of males to females. The one-child policy in China has exacerbated male preference in that country.

Female Genital Cutting

Female genital cutting (FGC) is also known as female genital mutilation and female circumcision. WHO has grouped FGC into four types, generally varying from excision of the prepuce, the fold of skin surrounding the clitoris, to excision of part or all of the external genitalia and the stitching and narrowing of the vaginal opening. There are also a variety of related practices, including pricking of the genitalia or using chemicals to narrow the vaginal opening.[16]

Female genital cutting is generally carried out on girls 4 to 14 years of age by traditional practitioners, although it is sometimes carried out on infants. The cutting is done with razor blades, knives, or glass. It is estimated that between 100 million and 140 million women worldwide have had genital cutting performed on them. Estimates also suggest that as many as 3 million girls in sub-Saharan Africa and in Egypt have such cutting performed on them each year.[16] In some countries, such as Egypt, FGC is practically universal among women who are 15 to 49 years old. However, there are other countries in Africa in which only a small share of the women have had FGC, such as Niger.[16] The practice appears to be diminishing almost everywhere, with fewer younger girls being cut than their mothers. FGC is very closely related to ethnicity. The higher the level of education of the mother, the lower the level of FGC of the daughter.

When FGC is done initially, it can result in terrible pain or shock. It is also associated with infection and blood poisoning, because the instruments used for FGC are not always clean, as well as with acute hemorrhage. Over the longer term, it can lead to the retention of urine, infertility, and obstructed labor. Studies have also shown that those who have been cut with the more severe forms of FGC are more likely than others to have postpartum hemorrhage, cesarean section, and long stays in hospital. In addition, the babies of such women are more likely than other babies to need resuscitation when they are born, to be stillborn, or to die a neonatal death.[17] If infection and hemorrhage linked to the act of FGC are not addressed in a timely and appropriate manner, FGC can also lead to death.[16]

Sexually Transmitted Infections

Chapter 11, which is on infectious diseases, discusses HIV/AIDS and its relationship with other sexually transmitted infections (STIs). This chapter highlights the facts that women are more biologically susceptible to sexually transmitted infections because of more exposed mucosal surfaces, because they often show no symptoms of those diseases, and because their roles in society make them less likely to get treated for sexually transmitted infections than men.

Sexually transmitted infections that are not treated in a timely and appropriate manner can have a number of long-lasting effects on the health of women. These include pelvic inflammatory disease, chronic pain, ovarian abscesses, ectopic pregnancies, and infertility.[18] When pregnant women cannot get STIs treated in appropriate and timely ways it can lead to fetal wastage, stillbirths, low birthweight babies, eye and lung damage in their babies, and congenital abnormalities.[18] Human papilloma virus is associated with cervical cancer,[18] and the complications of syphilis can lead to death.[19] Chlamydia bears special mention because it is nine times more prevalent in women than in men.[20] Chlamydia is very prevalent in low-income countries and is associated with chronic conjunctivitis, reproductive tract infections, genital ulcer disease, and infertility.[20]

The data on the burden of STIs, other than HIV, is incomplete. However, based on key studies about chlamydia, gonorrhea, and syphilis, it appears that about 176,000 people worldwide died in 2001 from STIs in low- and middle-income countries[21] and about 0.6 percent of the global burden of disease in those countries in 2001 was from STIs.[22] Sub-Saharan Africa faces a disproportionately high share of morbidity and mortality from STIs. In fact, about half of all the DALYs lost from STIs were in that region.[22]

From the limited studies available, the prevalence of chlamydia, gonorrhea, and syphilis appears to vary widely. Studies done in China showed that rates of chlamydia ranged from 1–24 percent.[23] Studies done in other parts of Asia indicated that the prevalence of syphilis ranged from almost negligible to about 15 percent.[23] Studies done in sub-Saharan Africa have shown ranges for chlamydia from 2–30 percent, for gonorrhea from 2–32 percent, and for syphilis from almost negligible to 23 percent.[24]

Worldwide, it is the group aged 15 to 44 in whom we find the largest burden of STIs, and within that group, women have a larger share of disease than men have. About 1.9 percent of the total DALYs lost in this group to women were lost to STIs.[22] About 0.5 percent of the total DALYs lost to men in this age group were lost to these infections.[22]

Young people are at special risk of STIs, because they are often forced to have sex, their sexual relations are often unplanned, and they may not have the power or skills to use a condom.[17]

The risk factors for a woman getting an STI are well known and include young age when engaging in sexual relations, often because of child marriage, especially in Asia and sub-Saharan Africa; multiple sexual partners; sex with high risk partners, including partners considerably older than the woman; and inability to use a condom. The use of alcohol and drugs is also associated with unprotected sex, as is unequal power between the woman and the man who are engaging in sexual relations.

Violence and Sexual Abuse Against Women

Violence and sexual abuse against women occur with remarkable frequency throughout the world. Violence is usually episodic, it is often not reported, and it is often associated with sexual abuse.[25] "Sexual abuse can include rape, sexual assault, sexual molestation, sexual harassment, and incest."[26] It is very hard to get reliable data on violence and sexual abuse against women; however, UNAIDS suggests that 10–50 percent of women worldwide have been abused physically by an intimate partner at least once in their lives.[27] Another study on intimate partner violence indicated that

"one third of women have been beaten, coerced into sex, or subjected to extreme emotional abuse."[28] Other data suggest that between 20–60 percent of women report having been beaten by their partners.[29] A study about forced sex done in a number of countries concluded that "between 20–50% of adolescent girls aged 10–25 report their first sexual encounter was forced."[27] In addition, there have been a number of conflicts in which rape has been used systematically, as a "tool of war."[30]

Violence and abuse against women have a number of negative consequences for the health of women. These include injuries, unwanted pregnancies, STIs, depression, and sometimes permanent disability or death.[31] The risk factors for whether or not a woman will suffer violence can be complicated, are often a result of many factors, and are not well documented. However, it appears that such violence is associated with factors such as young age of the male partner, a history of violence of the male partner, low socioeconomic status of the male and female involved, proximity to drugs or alcohol, social isolation, and gender inequality. The likelihood of violence is heightened in conflict and post-conflict situations.[32]

Maternal Morbidity and Mortality

The most commonly used estimates suggest that there are about 530,000 maternal deaths per year in the world, meaning deaths that occur during pregnancy, during childbirth, or until 42 days after the baby is born.[33] This is equal to about 400 maternal deaths for every 100,000 live births.[34] Birth is the time of greatest risk for the mother and the baby; recent estimates are that 42 percent of maternal deaths happen during birth or the first day after birth.[35] Between 50 and 71 percent of maternal deaths occur in the postpartum period, with most of those occurring in the first week after birth.[31] Of the estimated 530,000 annual maternal deaths, it is thought that about 70,000, or 13 percent, were due to unsafe abortions.[36]

An important study was published in 2009 that made a revised set of estimates of maternal mortality, based on data collected from 1980 to 2008. This study suggested there were about 342,000 maternal deaths annually, rather than 530,000. It also suggested that the maternal mortality ratio had declined by an average of 1.3 percent globally from 1980 to 2008. It further noted that the rate of decline had been as high as 8.8 percent annually in the Maldives, but that the maternal mortality ratio had increased in a number of countries, including Zimbabwe, where it had done so at an annual rate of 5.5 percent. The study estimated that over 50 percent of all maternal deaths in the world occur in only six countries—India, Nigeria, Pakistan, Afghanistan, Ethiopia, and the Democratic Republic of the Congo. Finally, it suggested that about 15 percent of the maternal deaths over this period were associated with HIV/AIDS.[37]

There are both indirect and direct causes of maternal death. About 20 percent of maternal deaths are from indirect causes, meaning diseases that complicate pregnancy or that are complicated by pregnancy. These include malaria, anemia, HIV/AIDS, and cardiovascular disease.[34] The importance of these problems depends on the presence of these diseases in different communities and how effective the health system is in responding to them. About 80 percent of maternal deaths stem from direct causes, including hemorrhage, infection, eclampsia, and obstructed labor. Figure 9-1 indicates the major causes of maternal death and the share of maternal deaths worldwide that are associated with them.

The ratio of maternal deaths to the number of live births varies considerably across regions. The highest maternal mortality ratios are in sub-Saharan Africa, where there are 940 maternal deaths per 100,000 live births.[38] The lowest maternal mortality ratios are in Western Europe, where only about 5 women die of maternal causes per 100,000 live births.[39] Table 9-3 shows the maternal mortality ratio by region and the lifetime chance of maternal death based on data from 2000.

The risk of maternal death is a stark reflection of the disparities in the health status between different countries and within those countries. A woman in Western Europe has only a 1 in 10,000 chance of dying a maternal death. In some of the poorest countries of sub-Saharan Africa, however, a woman has a 1 in 16 lifetime chance of dying a maternal death. This means that a woman in some countries in sub-Saharan Africa faces 250 times the risk of dying a maternal death as does a woman in the high-income countries.

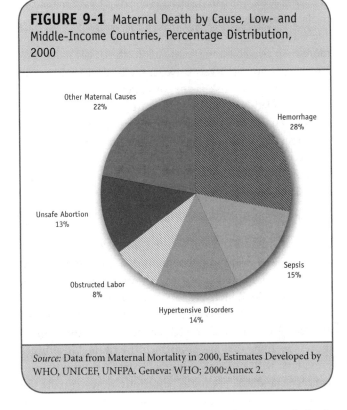

FIGURE 9-1 Maternal Death by Cause, Low- and Middle-Income Countries, Percentage Distribution, 2000

Source: Data from Maternal Mortality in 2000, Estimates Developed by WHO, UNICEF, UNFPA. Geneva: WHO; 2000:Annex 2.

There are a number of risk factors for maternal death. Among the first are the nutritional status and general health status of the mother. There is also a very strong correlation between maternal death and the level of education and income of the mother. Clearly, well-educated women with comfortable incomes do not suffer many maternal deaths; uneducated and poor women do. Maternal death also varies with ethnicity and location, with rural women being at

TABLE 9-3 Maternal Mortality Ratio and Lifetime Risk of Dying a Maternal Death, by Region, 2000

Region	Maternal Mortality Ratio	Lifetime Risk of Dying a Maternal Death (1 in X)
Central & Eastern Europe and Central Asia	64	770
East Asia & Pacific	110	360
Latin America & the Caribbean	190	160
Middle East & North Africa	220	100
South Asia	560	43
Sub-Saharan Africa	940	16
High-Income Countries	13	4000

Source: Adapted with permission from Graham WJ, Cairns J, Bhattacharya S, Bullough CHW, Quayyum Z, Rogo K. Maternal and perinatal conditions. In: Jamison DT, Breman JG, Measham AR, et al., eds. *Disease Control Priorities in Developing Countries.* 2nd ed. Washington, DC and New York: The World Bank and Oxford University Press; 2006.

greater risk than urban dwellers. The risk of maternal death is also associated, among other things, with childbirth by adolescents,[40] women having their first child,[41] women having more than five children,[41] and childbirth at ages older than 35 years.[42] Short intervals between the births of subsequent children are also a risk factor for maternal death. Having a birth attended by a skilled healthcare provider and having access to emergency obstetric care are important to successful outcomes of pregnancy. In addition, consumption of alcohol, tobacco, and drugs during pregnancy can also be harmful to both mother and child. Malaria and HIV also pose substantial risks to pregnancy outcomes.

Unsafe Abortion

Many pregnancies are not wanted. Based on an extensive study of unsafe abortion done by WHO, it is estimated that there are 211 million pregnancies worldwide each year, of which about 46 million end in induced abortion.[31]

One critical issue concerning abortion is whether they are "safe" or "unsafe." WHO defines "safe" abortion as those abortions that are performed "by trained healthcare providers, with proper equipment, correct technique, and sanitary standards." "Unsafe" abortions are essentially the opposite of that definition—performed by an untrained provider, with inappropriate equipment, poor technique, and unhygienic conditions.[31] It is thought that only about 60 percent of the abortions that are carried out every year worldwide are safe.[31]

Fewer than 1 woman per 100,000 who have a safe abortion will die as a result of the abortion. The mortality rate for unsafe abortions, however, is at least 100 times greater, although it varies by country, from about 100 per 100,000 such abortions to about 600 per 100,000. It is estimated that about 70,000 women in the world die every year from unsafe abortions. This would be equal to about 13 percent of the total maternal deaths that occur annually worldwide, using the most common estimates of maternal death.[43,44]

Figure 9-2 shows the extent to which unsafe abortions take place in different regions of the world. The age of those having an unsafe abortion also varies by region. About 60 percent of the unsafe abortions in Africa take place among women younger than 25 years of age, compared to about 30 percent for women this age in Asia. In Latin America and the Caribbean, about half of the unsafe abortions are carried out on women 20 to 29 years of age.[45]

Obstetric Fistula

An obstetric fistula is a condition in which a hole opens up in a woman between the bladder and the vagina or between the rectum and the vagina. It is usually the result of prolonged or failed childbirth. As a consequence, urine or feces leak through the vagina. As discussed later in this chapter in the case study on fistula repair in Tanzania, obstetric fistula can have severe social and economic consequences, since women with fistula are often terribly stigmatized or abandoned.[46]

It is difficult to get good estimates of the number of women who suffer from obstetric fistula every year. Studies suggest that for every 100,000 births, between 50 and 80 women in sub-Saharan Africa, North Africa, and West and South Asia, and about 30 women in Latin America and China suffer a fistula.[47] At these rates, about 50,000 to 100,000 women each year will suffer a fistula.[48] It is thought that about 2 million women worldwide are living with fistula.[48]

The risk factors for fistula are those that are linked with an obstructed delivery, which is the precipitating factor for a fistula. These include undernutrition, young age at first birth, and having had multiple births. In addition, female genital cutting and some traditional practices that damage the birth canal can also cause prolonged labor and lead to fistula. Fistula can also result from trauma, such as rape or sexual violence. The lack of access to emergency obstetric care and the failure to make use of such care, if available, also contribute to the prevalence of fistula.[48]

DIFFERENCES BETWEEN THE HEALTH OF MEN AND WOMEN

Much of the attention paid to the health of women over the last several decades has focused on reproductive health and on "women as child bearers." More recently, however, greater focus has been put on females in all of their roles and on the extent to which gender discrimination negatively impacts their overall health. Although still somewhat limited, increasing amounts of information are available on the health of females compared to the health of males.[49] Overall, women have a higher life expectancy at birth than men. On average, women in low-income countries live 1 year longer than men and women in high-income countries live, on average, 7 years longer than men.[49]

However, an analysis of the extent to which females suffer a burden of disease greater than males identified 19 conditions that disproportionately affect females. Some of these relate to conditions that are specific to women, such as maternal conditions and cancers that overwhelmingly affect females. Some of these conditions are associated with the fact that females live longer than males, such as Alzheimer's disease, osteoarthritis, cerebrovascular and cardiovascular disease, and age-related vision disorders. In fact, it has been estimated that females lose 80 percent more DALYs from

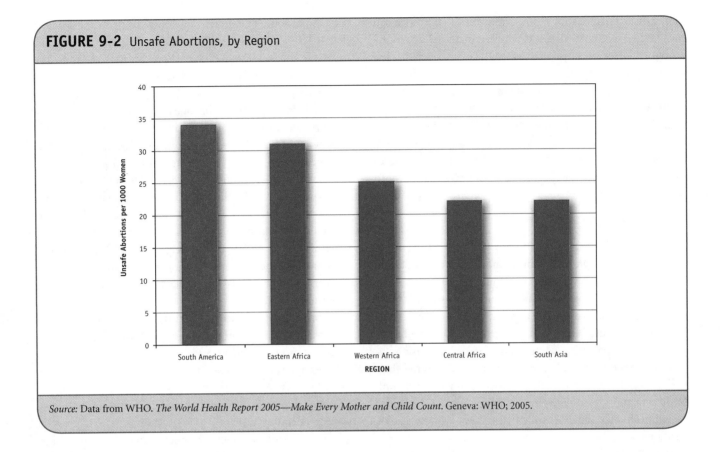

FIGURE 9-2 Unsafe Abortions, by Region

Source: Data from WHO. *The World Health Report 2005—Make Every Mother and Child Count.* Geneva: WHO; 2005.

Alzheimer's disease, more than 60 percent more DALYs from osteoarthritis and age-related vision disorders, and more than 40 percent more DALYs from cerebrovascular and cardiovascular disease than men. Females also lose more than 50 percent more DALYs than males from depression and almost three times more DALYs than men from migraine headaches. As noted earlier, a condition affecting females that appears to be driven solely by discrimination is the excess burden of disease that women in South Asia suffer from fires and burns. In South Asia, females lose more than 250 percent more DALYs from fire and burns than males lose.[50] In fact, South Asia is the region of the world in which females are the least healthy compared to males.

THE COSTS AND CONSEQUENCES OF WOMEN'S HEALTH PROBLEMS

Women's health issues have enormous social costs. Violence against girls and women tends to isolate them socially. When a woman dies in childbirth, the social impacts are enormous. In most societies, women are the primary caregivers for children; therefore, when a mother dies, the death usually has a profound impact on the health of her children, with young children often dying thereafter. The social costs of some problems are particularly high. For example, women who have obstetric fistula are often socially isolated from their community.

As will be discussed in Chapter 11, women are stigmatized for a variety of communicable diseases as well, such as TB, HIV, and some of the neglected tropical diseases. There are also exceptional economic costs related to women's health conditions, and these are not often given the attention they deserve. The economic costs of nutritional issues have already been examined. The costs of violence against women, especially in low-income countries, have not been studied carefully but they are substantial. A study in Chile, for example, suggested that the costs of domestic violence were equal to 2 percent of Chile's GDP. A similar study in Nicaragua indicated that such violence cost 1.6 percent of GDP. A review of intimate partner violence in the United States indicated that it led to 2 million injuries in a year and costs of about $6 billion.[51]

The economic costs of maternal health conditions are also high but not well documented. They also often fail to take account of morbidity associated with maternal health and not just mortality. These morbidities can seriously constrain women's productivity both in the home and outside the home.

They can also significantly reduce the income that women can earn. When a woman dies a premature maternal death, the economic losses are substantial, given the many years that the woman could have engaged in care of her family, work inside and outside the home, and the damage that will likely be done to the future prospects for economic well-being and economic contributions of any children who survive her. Illness associated with maternal conditions seriously constrains women's productivity and reduces the income they can contribute to their family. Similarly, depression in women is also likely to have high economic costs.

POLICY AND PROGAM BRIEFS

Two policy and program briefs follow. The first examines the work of a nonprofit organization, Tostan, that works in community-based development in a number of countries in Africa and that has had some important successes in helping communities abandon FGC. The work of Tostan is especially interesting because it is so embedded in the notion of educating and empowering communities to make decisions as communities that can enhance their rights and improve their well-being. The second brief reviews the progress of Tamil Nadu state in India in reducing maternal mortality. This brief is significant, like the case study that follows it on Sri Lanka, because many countries have made only modest progress over the last 20 years in reducing maternal mortality and have not been able to put into place what has been learned elsewhere.

Addressing Female Genital Cutting in Senegal[52]

Tostan is a U.S.-based nongovernmental organization dedicated to community-led development in Africa. For two decades, Tostan has offered participatory, nonformal education about human rights and responsibilities to adults and adolescents in its Africa programs. In so doing, Tostan has sought to empower individuals and communities to initiate community dialogue and work to establish social change within their communities. Participatory education is intended to allow participants to have an active voice in the educational process, as they engage in group discussions that aim to foster collective learning.

As a central part of its work, Tostan developed and uses the Community Empowerment Program (CEP), a 30-month education program that consists of two parts: the *Kobi* and the *Aawde*. The Kobi, meaning "to prepare the field for planting," begins with sessions on democracy, human rights, and problem solving, and later covers health topics including hygiene, vaccinations, mental and physical development, the reproductive process, HIV/AIDS, STIs, and the risks involved in practices such as female genital cutting (FGC) and child/

forced marriage. The Aawde, meaning "to plant the seed," is devoted to economic empowerment: helping participants draw on financial resources to have greater access to the local economy and choice in occupation, a freedom not traditionally given to individuals. Economic empowerment is achieved through literacy lessons and training in managing small projects. In addition, participants learn to use SMS text messaging on mobile phones to practice their literacy skills.

A keystone of the Tostan program is "organized diffusion," whereby participants directly involved in the CEP share their knowledge with others. Participants "adopt" others with whom they share their newfound knowledge, while participating in the education program. Participants often choose spouses, friends, relatives, or neighbors as their adoptees. This process empowers participants to be both learners and teachers, as they discuss and reflect together on significant community issues.

Tostan conducts classes in local languages and draws on local traditions, including songs and oral stories. By engaging new themes in customary ways, it is hoped that participants will become confident, energized learners, who will begin to identify practices that affirm human rights, as well as other practices they wish to reinforce and harmful practices they want to abandon.

Tostan works with all members of the community in its education program: men, women, children, and religious and local leaders. By educating women and girls, the Tostan program facilitates their involvement in community planning and dialogue. In addition, Tostan believes that it would be impossible to create effective, sustainable change in a community without working with all community members and stakeholders.

Tostan and FGC

Tostan has never been an "anti-FGC organization." Rather, Tostan is a community education organization that works with communities to encourage learning about both human rights and the corresponding responsibilities that result from those rights. For example, communities discuss how having the right to be free from all forms of violence relates to the corresponding responsibility to protect others from violence. This has contributed to the cessation of spousal abuse in many households and communities.

Through participation in the CEP, communities independently decided to abandon FGC. Because this was not part of its founding mission, Tostan was reluctant initially to become involved in it. However, the educational programs inspired participants to create a community-wide dialogue about FGC.

After the first village declared its abandonment of FGC, a local religious leader and participant in the Tostan program, Demba Diawara, approached Tostan and explained that to truly abandon FGC, a single village's declaration was insufficient. He explained that FGC was considered a prerequisite for marriage and that girls who had not undergone the practice could not get married, which would lead to a life of economic uncertainty and social exclusion. Moreover, because communities frequently marry within their own community, it was clear that individual communities could not exclusively abandon FGC. Rather, the decision to abandon FGC in a significant number of communities within a social network would be necessary for abandonment to be both successful and sustainable. As a result, Tostan strategically chooses communities with which to work on FGC, focusing on interlinking social networks and connections to facilitate the spread of education and social change.

FGC is a social norm: an expected behavior that binds people together culturally. It is perpetuated by many actors within a social group and as such, it is impossible to hold any one person or one group responsible for its perpetuation. Tostan's educational approach encourages dialogue and deliberation about the assumptions and beliefs that hold social norms in place within communities. Such public deliberation has led to a shift in social norms and group expectations as thousands of communities have organized to abandon FGC.

Tostan's mission has not been to eradicate FGC, or even ask that villages do so. Rather, its mission is concerned with educating participants about human rights and responsibilities so that they may become empowered to be leaders within their communities. What's more, Tostan believes that in order to achieve lasting changes, communities must decide for themselves what is best for community members. Therefore, Tostan utilizes a holistic educational approach—one that addresses many different topics and issues faced within communities. This approach emphasizes within each community the practices that promote improved rights and well-being, and provides the tools and forums to discuss what changes the community itself would like to see.

Program Impact

Tostan has worked at the grassroots level with thousands of communities in many African countries, including Senegal, Guinea, The Gambia, Mauritania, Somalia, Djibouti, Guinea Bissau, Burkina Faso, and Mali, learning from participants about their priorities, values, and hopes for the future. This deep knowledge of local conditions is a prerequisite for developing innovative strategies that are context-sensitive and responsive to villagers' lives and experiences. Because Tostan's pedagogical methods encourage lively participation and reflection, the organization receives constant participant feedback and is able to adapt quickly to changing circumstances. Tostan tries to foster a relationship of mutual empowerment between staff and participating communities, aiming to ensure that each gains confidence and strength through discussion, with each responsive to and learning from the other.

Tostan conducts internal reviews to assess its impact in the many areas the CEP addresses. This is typically done with reference to three types of communities: those with which it works directly, those that participate in CEP awareness-raising or declaration activities, and those that receive no intervention from Tostan. This approach allows for Tostan to better understand the interaction of social networks and their role in reshaping social norms through intercommunity discussion and debate. Tostan has found that villages with which it is either directly or indirectly involved have experienced a significant reduction in the rate of FGC following the completion of the CEP.

In addition to internal evaluations, organizations such as UNICEF and Macro International assessed the impact of Tostan's CEP in 2008.[53] As of June 2010, and since the first Tostan-supported public declaration for the abandonment of FGC in 1997, 4203 communities in Senegal, 364 in Guinea, 23 in Burkina Faso, 44 in The Gambia, and 36 in Somalia have abandoned the practice. The long-term impact evaluation done by UNICEF and Macro International confirmed that the practice of FGC was reduced by 77 percent in the zones where Tostan had been active.

Tostan seeks to continuously evaluate its performance through internal and external assessments, as well as considering the invaluable feedback of CEP participants.[54] By maintaining a focus on human rights and responsibilities education, Tostan hopes to continue to support sustainable social change in a number of African countries.

Reducing Maternal Mortality in Tamil Nadu, India

The south Indian state of Tamil Nadu has made major improvements in the last 30 years in reducing maternal mortality. The experience in addressing maternal mortality in Tamil Nadu provides valuable lessons for other Indians states and for countries other than India about how to improve maternal health.

Although total fertility and maternal mortality have been lower in Tamil Nadu than in most Indian states for some time, the state government in the early 1980s still found them unacceptable. In 1980, for example, the maternal mortality ratio was 450 per 100,000 live births,[55] about where Ghana is today.[56]

Despite an extensive family planning and reproductive health program in Tamil Nadu (the Family Welfare Program), an estimated 13 percent of families in the state still lacked access to family planning services as late as 1998–1999. In addition, as you read about earlier, there is considerable sex-selective abortion in India; some of this is unsafe, and this, too, contributed to maternal mortality.[1] Moreover, in Tamil Nadu, as elsewhere, poor, rural, and young women suffer the greatest burden of maternal mortality. In addition, the state in the early 1980s was very rural, had high levels of poverty, and there was still substantial marriage and childbearing at a young age.[55]

The "three delays" have also been major contributors to maternal mortality in Tamil Nadu, despite its progress in improving maternal health services. The delay in seeking appropriate obstetric care, which leads to late or no diagnosis, accounted for 40 percent of maternal deaths, even as late as 2004. The delay in transport to an appropriate facility in case of emergency was associated with 37 percent of maternal deaths in 2004. The delay in receiving emergency obstetric care at a referral facility accounted for 23 percent of maternal deaths in 2004.[55]

The government of Tamil Nadu responded to high rates of maternal and infant mortality by revamping its healthcare system in the 1980s to pay more attention to maternal and newborn health. With the object of making pregnancies safer and ensuring newborn survival, the initiatives have improved maternal health in a relatively short amount of time.

The strategy of the Tamil Nadu state government has included three components and seeks to combat the "three delays." First, the policies aim to prevent and terminate unwanted pregnancies. A second objective is to provide greater access to obstetric care at the primary level, which would improve access to high-quality antenatal care, routine obstetric care, facility deliveries, and stabilization of emergencies before referral. Third, the policies seek to provide access to emergency obstetric care at the first referral level.[55]

To prevent unwanted pregnancies, the government increased accessibility and demand for family planning. In addition, the government increased the availability of safe abortion facilities in government-sponsored clinics. In conjunction with increased education, more economic development, and changing social norms, the total fertility rate in Tamil Nadu decreased to 1.7 in 2005.[55]

The state government addressed the delay in seeking appropriate care by improving the quality and accessibility of obstetric care at the primary level. Three staff nurses, who are also trained birth attendants, each work one 8-hour shift a day to ensure that care is available 24 hours a day. The nurses conduct antenatal check-ups, attend deliveries, care for sick newborns, and arrange timely referrals if further care is necessary. Over 96 percent of mothers completed at least three antenatal visits during their last pregnancies in 2005–2006. Accessible obstetric care has led to greater early registration of pregnancies and follow-up visits, causing earlier detection of pregnancy complications and the arrangement of life-saving referrals.[55]

The delay in transport to receive care has been significantly reduced through the introduction of an ambulance service. Vehicles are provided by the government and the service is managed by a local NGO. Poor pregnant women ride the ambulance free of charge, and wealthier patients are required to pay. Ninety-eight percent of deliveries took place in institutions in 2007–2008, compared to 67 percent in 1993–1994.[55]

Availability and access to emergency obstetric care has been improved through the creation of 62 Comprehensive Emergency Obstetric (CEmOC) and Newborn Care Centres. With an obstetrician and pediatrician on staff at all times and an anesthetist on-call, these facilities provide all essential emergency obstetric and newborn care services 24 hours a day. There is an operating theater, laboratory, and blood bank. The CEmOC and Newborn Care Centres are located within an hour of any point, and 86 percent of women reported they could reach one within half an hour or less in 2004–2005. Additionally, 83 percent of women said they received services within half an hour, showing that the delay of receiving treatment has been reduced. Access to emergency facilities is reducing maternal and newborn mortality, reflected by, among other things, the fact that 19 percent of deliveries were caesarean sections.[55]

As it has taken the above steps to improve health services, the government has continued to promote education. Women are getting pregnant less frequently and later in life due to greater use of family planning.[55] In addition, there are fewer early marriages, greater awareness of family planning and nutrition as a whole, and improved literacy.[55] As these changes have occurred, Tamil Nadu was able to reduce the maternal mortality ratio from 450 in 1980 to 90 in 2005.

The government of Tamil Nadu has pursued policies to improve maternal health, despite changes in the political party that has governed the state. The state has also tried to carefully monitor the investments it has made in strengthening primary and emergency health services, ensuring a more dedicated workforce, promoting the availability of essential drugs, and improving community engagement with health centers through outreach programs.[55]

Challenges remain, however, to sustaining the improvements Tamil Nadu has made in maternal health. These include reducing the high incidence of stillborns, closing regional disparities in maternal and neonatal mortality, further expanding access to emergency care facilities, and targeting urban health issues.[55]

CASE STUDIES

There has been some progress in a number of countries in dealing with the critical health issues discussed previously. The next section of this chapter examines three cases about efforts to address health conditions among women and promote family planning. The first deals with the reduction of maternal deaths in Sri Lanka, the second concerns efforts to encourage family planning in Bangladesh, and the third is about a program to deal with obstetric fistula in Tanzania. The Sri Lanka and Bangladesh cases are well-documented success stories. The case about Tanzania concerns a promising effort to help women with fistula.

Maternal Mortality in Sri Lanka[57]

Background

Sri Lanka has had an impressive history of public-sector commitment to education and health, even when its income per capita was low. Today, the female literacy rate in Sri Lanka is more than double the South Asian average, and free health services have been available in rural areas since the 1930s.[57] Another unusual strength of Sri Lanka is that it has a good civil registration system that has recorded maternal deaths since about 1900.[58]

Interventions

Sri Lanka has taken a number of steps to reduce maternal deaths. First, Sri Lanka improved access to health services. Starting in the 1930s, Sri Lanka established health facilities throughout the country that were staffed by medical officers. In addition, Sri Lanka expanded secondary and tertiary facilities in the 1950s and around the same time established a working ambulance service.

Second, as early as the 1940s, Sri Lanka introduced policies to expand the number of midwives, who were the front line workers dealing with pregnant women and childbirth. The focus on midwifery and on promoting easy access to higher-level health services in Sri Lanka has contributed to a wide acceptance by women and their families of giving birth with the assistance of a trained midwife at home or in the hospital. Midwives in Sri Lanka today serve a population of 3000 to 5000 people and they provide an invaluable link between the local community and the health system.

Another step that Sri Lanka took to reduce maternal deaths was to make use of its civil registration data to identify what areas of the country had the most significant problems with maternal mortality. On this basis, the government was able to target its efforts to especially vulnerable groups, including women who were isolated both physically and socially, such as on distant tea estates. The government coupled these efforts with continuous activities, starting in the 1960s, to ensure that the quality of maternal health services was always appropriate. The lessons learned from individual maternal deaths, for example, were disseminated throughout the health system so that the quality of services could be improved and errors in dealing with obstetric problems could be reduced.

At the same time, the government made considerable progress in other health areas. This included efforts to improve health by improving sanitation and by measures to combat malaria and hookworm. These actions also contributed to improved health and lowered maternal mortality rates.

Impact

As a result of these efforts, Sri Lanka has halved maternal deaths every 6 to 12 years since 1935. This has meant a decline in the maternal mortality ratio from between 500 and 600 maternal deaths per 100,000 live births in 1950 to 60 per 100,000 more recently.[59] Skilled medical practitioners now attend 97 percent of the births in Sri Lanka, compared with 30 percent in 1940.

One very important point to note about Sri Lanka is that it has achieved better health outcomes than many countries that have higher per capita incomes and spend more on health than Sri Lanka. In India, for example, the maternal mortality ratio is more than 400 per 100,000 live births, and spending on health constitutes over 5 percent of the GNP. In Sri Lanka, however, the ratio of maternal deaths to live births is less than one quarter of that for India, even though the country spends only 3 percent of its GNP on health. Low-cost, but dedicated and well-trained health personnel, including midwives, helped make the expansion of access to health care in Sri Lanka affordable.

Lessons

Sri Lanka's success in reducing maternal deaths can be attributed to widespread access to maternal health care, including emergency obstetric care, built upon a strong health system that provides free services to the entire population.

The professionalism and broad use of midwives, the systematic use of health information to identify problems and guide decision making, and targeted quality improvements for vulnerable groups were also ingredients for success. Sri Lanka's tradition of public-sector commitment to human development created conditions where gains were reinforced by good education, an emphasis on gender equity, the promotion of family planning, and a coordinated network of health services. Although factors such as the introduction of antibiotics and national efforts against malaria helped lower maternal mortality rates, it was the step-by-step actions of the government rather than better living conditions alone that led to most of the improvements in maternal health. Sri Lanka's success offers important lessons for other low- and middle-income countries that have unacceptably high levels of maternal deaths. Detailed information on this case is available in *Case Studies in Global Health: Millions Saved.*

Reducing Fertility in Bangladesh

Background

Despite the existence of several family planning methods, more than 150 million women in developing countries who wish to limit or space childbearing do not use contraception. In Bangladesh, where more than half the women are illiterate and cultural traditions favor large families, each woman had, on average, almost seven children in the mid-1970s, thereby jeopardizing her health and that of her children. For a country with the world's highest population density where almost 80 percent of the people live in poverty, it became clear that lowering population growth would be very important.

The Intervention

In 1975, the government of Bangladesh launched a program to reduce the national birth rate. The program had four components. First, young, married women were trained as outreach workers to visit women at home and offer information and contraceptive services. The number of these family welfare assistants (FWAs) eventually exceeded 40,000. Their outreach surpassed all expectations, with virtually all Bangladeshi women having been contacted at least once by an FWA, including many women isolated by cultural practices, geographical location, or poor transportation. The second element of the program was the provision of a wide range of family planning methods through a well-managed distribution system. The third component was the establishment of thousands of family planning clinics in rural areas to which outreach workers could refer clients for long-term

family planning methods such as sterilization. The fourth element was the information, education, and communication (IEC) campaign. The IEC program successfully tailored its message to achieve different aims, such as persuading men to talk to their wives about contraception, and winning social acceptance for FWAs by creating a story about a compelling soap opera heroine who eventually becomes an FWA. In fact, the IEC campaign's remarkable success has inspired similar mass media initiatives in other countries such as Kenya, Tanzania, and Brazil.[60]

The government's program evolved substantially over time, benefiting greatly from the existence of the Matlab Health Research Center that has operated for over 35 years as a site for large-scale research on the operation of health, nutrition, and family planning programs. Within villages in the Matlab area, researchers have tested various approaches to the delivery of health services. Matlab evaluations have shaped maternal and child health programs both in Bangladesh and throughout the developing world.

The Impact

The program resulted in virtually all women in Bangladesh becoming aware of family planning options. Contraceptive use increased from 8 percent in the mid-1970s to its current level of about 50 percent, and fertility declined from 6.3 births per woman in the early 1970s to about 3.3 in the mid-1990s.[61] Although other factors such as increased education and employment opportunities for women also increased demand for contraception, the family planning program has been shown to have had an independent effect on attitudes and behaviors.[62]

Costs and Benefits

The program is estimated to have cost about $100 million to $150 million per year, with more than half the funding coming from the United States Agency for International Development (USAID), the United Nations Development Program (UNDP), the World Bank, and other agencies. Efforts are under way to increase program efficiency. The most expensive program component is that of FWAs, who were once critical to program success but are now valued by clients more as a convenience than as an essential source of information.[63] Research suggests that the most cost-effective strategy for the continued promotion of family planning is a fixed site approach that provides health and family planning services from clinics, complemented with targeted outreach to hard-to-reach clients.[64] However, some of those involved in women's health believe that "doorstep delivery" by FWAs would continue to be cost-effective if the FWAs delivered not only family planning, but also other messages on sexual and reproductive health, such as safe motherhood, STIs, and HIV/AIDS. They also note the benefits of the FWAs as role models for women's status in rural areas. [26]

Lessons Learned

The success of the program can be attributed to four factors. The first was political commitment on the part of Bangladesh and the international agencies involved. The second was the broad use of FWAs, who carried the program's message into almost every home, however isolated. The third was the excellent use of mass media strategies to target audiences and change behavior. The fourth was the research and data provided by the Matlab Center that helped to constantly identify problems and improve the program. Although the program is far from perfect and the optimal outreach strategy is yet to be identified, Bangladesh is one of the few low-income countries to have reduced fertility rapidly without resorting to coercive measures. More detailed information on this case is available in *Case Studies in Global Health: Millions Saved.*

Fistula in Tanzania

Background

The emotional and physical side effects of obstetric fistulas stem largely from the fact that urine or feces leak from the fistula of affected women and cause them to be shunned by others. As a result of a fistula, women lose their babies, suffer constant pain or discomfort created by the unrelenting moisture from the leak, and are often deserted by their husbands and communities. Moreover, the women become socially isolated, lose the ability to sustain normal lives, and become economically dependent on others. To make matters worse, many communities view fistulas as a curse and hide the women away, rather than realizing that it is a medical condition. Decreasing the prevalence of obstetric fistulas is challenging, because it requires altering cultural practices on the one hand and strengthening very weak healthcare systems on the other. [65]

To assist in addressing the problem of fistula, the Bill & Melinda Gates Foundation [66] provided funding in 2002 to the United Nations Population Fund (UNFPA) and two NGOs, EngenderHealth and the Women's Dignity Project, to create the Obstetric Fistula Partnership. In conjunction with this funding, in 2003 UNFPA initiated the Global Campaign to End Fistula. The aim of the partnership and campaign, among other things, was to prevent obstetric fistu-las by strengthening emergency obstetric care, to enhance the capacity of the health system to deal with the large number of women who already have a fistula, and to help through advocacy to promote greater attention to and resources for dealing with maternal health. [65]

Surgery for uncomplicated cases of fistula is about 90 percent effective. Surgery for complicated cases of fistula is about 60 percent effective. [66] Most women with a fistula are unaware of any opportunities for repairing their fistula or of getting support to help them return to normal lives.

The Intervention

The Women's Dignity Project (WDP), called *Utu Mwanamke* in Swahili, is a program operated by a Tanzanian NGO that is dedicated to "addressing fistula and advocating for the health rights of the poor, within a human rights framework." [67] The WDP is a partner of the UNFPA's Campaign to End Fistula. It is estimated that more than 1000 new cases of fistula occur every year in Tanzania. [68]

The WDP carries out activities in four areas: participatory research, organizational strengthening, policy and advocacy work, and the funding of fistula repairs. The research work of the WDP began in 2001, with a survey of the magnitude of the fistula problem in Tanzania and of the resources available to help address the problem. This has been followed by other community-based surveys. In addition, the WDP has worked with the Ministry of Health in Tanzania to establish a national referral system for fistulas and to train healthcare workers in how to deal with fistula. The WDP has also advocated to help make the community, the government, and Tanzania's development partners more aware of the fistula problem and to allocate additional resources to address it. Moreover, the WDP has provided funds to five hospitals to support the health services needed to deal with fistulas more effectively. [69]

In carrying out those efforts, the WDP has:

- Identified women with fistula through community-based efforts and arranged transport for them to a hospital at which they could have surgery. [70]
- Published a booklet to raise awareness about fistulas that is based on the life stories of seven women who are affected by this condition. [71]
- Worked with a number of other NGOs, such as the African Medical and Relief Foundation (AMREF), [72] to raise additional money for fistula efforts. AMREF, for example, now contributes $100 to hospitals for each fistula repair they carry out.

- Collaborated with some NGOs, such as Engender-Health, to identify and address the risk factors for fistula.[65]

The Impact

The impact of the WDP efforts has not been studied scientifically or documented extensively and independently. However, it does appear that the activities described have led to an increase in the number of women who are getting fistulas repaired and who can, therefore, return to productive and healthy lives. The work of the WDP is also strengthening the capacity within Tanzania to continue dealing with fistulas more effectively in the future, through work at the community level in identifying the problem, training health providers, and helping to increase financial resources.

Costs and Benefits

According to the UNFPA, the average cost of treating fistula is $300.[73] This includes the reconstructive surgery, postoperation stay at the hospital or clinic, and rehabilitation. There are no data on the economic returns to fistula repair in Tanzania. However, one should expect that a woman with a successful fistula repair could return to a productive life that she could not have without that surgery. In addition, of course, there would be large social benefits to the surgery, because the woman whose fistula is repaired can also overcome the social ostracism that she faced earlier and can return to a more normal social life with her family and community.

Lessons Learned

The WDP's program in Tanzania suggests some promising approaches to dealing with difficult global health issues. First, it appears that combining a global effort such as the Campaign to End Fistula with a local effort, such as the work of the WDP, can set a valuable foundation for addressing some global health problems. Second, careful advocacy efforts with the right stakeholders in a country, such as local communities, key government agencies, and selected development partners, can help to build both awareness and support for trying to address health problems. Third, the initial successes of the WDP seem to stem from its efforts to embed its work at the community level and to involve the community in helping to identify problems and then act to improve them. Finally, carefully trying to build capacity through training and financial support can both provide immediate benefits and set the basis for programs to be sustained in the longer run.

ADDRESSING FUTURE CHALLENGES

The health of females in low-income countries is a powerful reflection of biological susceptibility and gender norms that assign certain roles, restrictions, and values to females, compared to males. It also reflects the fact that the health systems in many countries have profound gender gaps and cannot or do not serve effectively the health needs of females. In this light, making major improvements in the future in the health of females in low- and middle-income countries will require attention to an array of social and public health measures.

One future challenge will be to improve the nutritional status of females, because it is poor nutrition in utero and from infancy that can later lead to women becoming stunted, not reaching their full biological potential, and experiencing a variety of health conditions. Measures to address nutritional concerns more effectively are discussed in Chapter 8.

Another challenge that is central to the long-term improvement in the health of females is access to education. The empowerment of females socially is strongly associated with their level of education. Empowerment will improve the status of females and reduce the extent to which discrimination against them hurts their health. In addition, education improves access to important health information that can make a difference in women's and children's health. As you read in Chapter 3, the education of females is among the most powerful contributors to overall development as well.

Major changes must also be made in the perception that communities have of female roles and the health of females. This will require significant efforts at the level of communities and populations as a whole to put greater value on women's health. This will help to reduce the abortion of female fetuses and to ensure that women in obstructed labor do not die because they lack appropriate and timely medical attention.

A continuing challenge will also be to put greater emphasis on the health of females as people, rather than as just "women who give birth." This would encourage policy makers to take a number of steps that are essential to improving the health of females globally, including gaining a better understanding of the health conditions affecting females and what can be done about them, and making the health of females central to all health efforts. In addition, in many cultures, females are constrained in dealing with male medical workers so it is also very important to train more female health workers and to deploy them appropriately to the places where they are most needed.

The next section comments on further measures that can be taken to deal with some of the particular health problems discussed previously, such as female genital cutting, sexually transmitted infections, violence against women, and other reproductive health issues, including maternal mortality, unsafe abortion, and fistula.

Female Genital Cutting

The policy and program brief on Tostan reflects the importance of ensuring that efforts that promote change need to be specifically tailored to local practices and to local beliefs. Linking these efforts with other measures that promote female empowerment, female education, and female control over economic resources will also be needed. FGC is intimately linked with deep-seated local beliefs and traditions that vary with location, ethnicity, education, and income. Only by taking account of these underlying issues will one be able to address FGC.[16]

Violence Against Women

We have already discussed the extent to which violence against women is usually a result of a complex set of factors and the interactions among them. Although there is increasing evidence on the factors linked to violence against women, there is little evidence about what works to reduce such violence and what are the most cost-effective approaches to doing so, especially in low- and middle-income countries.

Some studies have shown that protecting women against violence through legislation, as has been done in the United States and some other high-income countries, can have important positive effects in some settings. Shelters for abused women can also be used to reduce violence against them. Ensuring that the police, judges, and healthcare personnel are trained to deal with violence against women in more sensitive and more effective ways has also been useful. It also appears that many nongovernmental organizations can deal with violence against women as effectively and at lower cost than some government services can do.[74]

In the end, however, it is a combination of measures adapted to local circumstances that can best address the combination of factors that put women at risk of violence. Some of the most important of these measures are noted in Table 9-4. The Tostan experience also speaks to community-based efforts to reduce violence against women.

Sexually Transmitted Infections

Sexually transmitted infections are important not only because of the morbidity and mortality associated with them, particularly among women in sub-Saharan Africa, but also because they increase the chance of getting HIV/AIDS.

TABLE 9-4 Selected Measures to Reduce Intimate Partner Violence

Prevention and education campaigns to increase awareness of intimate partner violence and change cultural norms about violence against women
Treatment for those who engage in intimate partner violence
Programs to strengthen ties to family and jobs
Couples counseling
Shelters and crisis centers for battered women
Mandatory arrest for offenders

Source: Adapted with permission from Rosenberg ML, Butchart A, Mercy J, Narasimhan V, Waters H, Marshall MS. Interpersonal violence. In: Jamison DT, Breman JG, Measham AR, et al., eds. *Disease Control Priorities in Developing Countries.* 2nd ed. Washington, DC and New York: The World Bank and Oxford University Press; 2006:755-770.

It is critical, therefore, that the burden of these diseases be addressed. Some comments follow about addressing three of the most common STIs among women: syphilis, gonorrhea, and chlamydia.

The goals of any program for reducing these sexually transmitted infections have to be to reduce infection, reduce the complications of infections, and reduce the spread of STIs to infants when they are born.[75] It is much more cost-effective to prevent these diseases and to treat them before they lead to complications than it is to treat them later. Achieving these goals requires that young women initiate their first sexual relations at later ages; be able to refuse unwanted sex, even from their husbands; have relations with fewer partners; use condoms; and have any STIs diagnosed early and treated properly.

Meeting these aims will also require that young people get "the information and skills for making good decisions"; have access to "a range of health services that help them to act on those decisions"; and "live within a social, legal, and regulatory framework that supports health behaviors and protects young people from harm. . . ."[76]

The successes in reducing STIs to date have focused on a common set of health system interventions and capacities. First, the health system must have an ability to carry out surveillance of STIs. Second, there needs to be a health education program, targeted to those people most at risk of infection. Third, appropriately trained health workers need to be able to provide proper treatment of infection. Fourth, a system of partner notification must be in place so that the partners of the infected individuals can also be tested and treated, if necessary. Finally, there must be an effective program for access to health services, including condom use, generally referred to as "condom promotion."[77]

Sweden made important strides in reducing chlamydia. Sweden offered free diagnosis, coupled with a major health education campaign in schools, partner notification, and condom promotion. Linked to this, Sweden was able to reduce the prevalence of gonorrhea by 15 times and cut the prevalence of chlamydia by one half over a 15-year period. Zambia also made good progress in reducing the burden of sexually transmitted infections by expanding the number of STI clinics, improving the training of health educators and clinicians, and expanding health education.[77] South Africa's "Love Life" initiative focuses on improving the sexual health of adolescents ages 12 to 17 years. Some reviews of this program suggest that it is associated with "better understanding of health risks, delayed debut of sexual relations, fewer partners, more assertive behavior regarding condom use, and better communication with parents about sex."[78]

Maternal Mortality

We have already seen that more than 500,000 women die each year of maternal causes, and that 70,000 die as a result of unsafe abortion, according to the most commonly used estimates. There is also considerable morbidity related to pregnancy. The fact that childbirth itself is such a risk in some settings is usually a result of the "three delays": a delay in identifying complications and seeking care, a delay in transporting the woman to a hospital, and a delay in providing appropriate emergency obstetric care in the hospital. There is also considerable disability, illness, and death related to unsafe abortion.

Unsafe Abortion

Most of the disability, morbidity, and mortality associated with abortion is the result of unsafe abortion, mostly in low- and middle-income countries in which abortion is legally restricted. To address the effects of unsafe abortion, it is essential that the health system in these settings be able to provide hygienic and appropriate postabortion care at the lowest level of the health system possible. This means that they must be able to deal effectively with sepsis, hemorrhage, and shock. This may require a hospital stay, antibiotics, the ability to perform anesthesia, and the ability to transfuse blood. The most cost-effective manner in which to deal with incomplete abortion will be to perform vacuum aspiration, rather than to depend on the more surgical dilation and curettage approach. Prevention of unsafe abortion is also important, including universal access to family planning and services, including after abortion.[79]

In countries in which abortion laws are more liberal, it is essential that services be widely available so that women do not turn to unsafe abortion providers. Women also need to know that legal abortion is available. In addition, it is critical that legal abortions be safe and hygienic and that services also be available to deal with any postabortion complications. In these cases, including countries in eastern Europe and Japan in which abortion is a common method of family planning, it is also important that counseling be available about choices of family planning methods.[80]

Family Planning

"Family planning saves lives" is the name of a long-standing publication and a phrase of considerable importance.[81] Indeed, because pregnancy and abortion are such important risks for disability, illness, and death, one way to avoid these problems is to reduce unwanted pregnancy through the promotion and widespread availability of family planning. In fact, it has been suggested that in countries with high rates of maternal mortality, as much as one third of the maternal deaths could be avoided through an effective family planning program.[79] The importance of family planning is highlighted by the fact that many women in the world today would like to delay or avoid pregnancy or space their births, but they do not have the access to family planning needed to do this. Studies done in sub-Saharan Africa, for example, suggest that 20 percent of the women in the region who would like to avoid pregnancy do not have access to family planning.

There are permanent methods of family planning that include sterilization of either males or females, although only about 8 percent of the total number of sterilizations worldwide are among men.[82] There are also long-term methods of family planning, including intrauterine devices and implants. Short-term methods include contraceptive pills, injectables, and barrier methods, including condoms or diaphragms. In addition, exclusive breastfeeding for at least 6 months—before the mother's menstrual period returns—acts as a natural contraception. There are also methods for natural family planning that focus on periodic abstinence.

A number of countries have made important progress in promoting the use of family planning, including Bangladesh, Brazil, Colombia, Korea, and Vietnam. The experience from these countries suggests that an effective family planning program has to include information, education, and communication to promote informed choices by families about family planning; the need for a good selection of family planning technologies; the use of many points of service in both the public and private sector; services that are free or inexpensive enough for the poor to afford them; and health workers who are trained to work on family planning with knowledge and sensitivity, especially female health workers for women who are reluctant to see male health workers.[84] There is considerable evidence that *social marketing* is an effective tool for promoting family planning, as well. Social marketing refers to the use of commercial marketing techniques to sell health-related measures, such as family planning.

Family planning is a cost-effective investment in reducing maternal death, but it is not clear which approach to family planning programs is more cost-effective than other approaches. The high rate of maternal death in sub-Saharan Africa and South Asia suggest that these are the two regions in which family planning would be most cost-effective to reduce maternal morbidity, disability, and mortality.[44] In addition, total fertility remains very high in many parts of sub-Saharan Africa and some parts of South Asia. It continues to be accompanied, as well, by young age of marriage and first birth and closely spaced births.

Complications of Pregnancy

The risks of complications of pregnancy increase when the general health of the mother is not good. Thus, the nutritional status of the mother is very important. In addition, malaria is very dangerous for pregnant women, especially in sub-Saharan Africa.

Some of the conditions that affect pregnancy outcomes can be identified during prenatal care. However, although it is important for pregnant women to get regular medical exams during their pregnancy—and WHO recommends four such visits—some complications of pregnancy cannot be foreseen during those checks-ups. Thus, it is also critical to ensure that births are attended by a skilled healthcare provider who can handle the complications of pregnancy and who can refer the pregnant woman to a facility where these complications can be addressed appropriately. In addition, it is important that communities have transportation to get women to emergency obstetric care urgently when they have complications of pregnancy and that health services be able to address the most important complications to a sufficiently high level of quality.

Studies show that there are several cost-effective packages of services that can reduce maternal death due to complications of pregnancy. The basic package of essential obstetric services that all countries should have is shown in Table 9-5. Countries that have more financial resources may wish to also provide some additional services that can address food, multivitamin supplements, malaria prophylaxis, the ability to deal with complicated deliveries of an HIV-positive mother, and arrangements for caring for a high-risk infant,[84] which are also shown on Table 9-5. As countries carry out these services, they are increasingly encouraged to make them part of a "continuum of care" that addresses maternal, newborn, and child health as a coherent package.

Of course, it is critical that appropriate services of sufficient quality be available. However, it is also essential that there be a demand for such services from the people who need them. This is especially important in places where there are substantial barriers to overcoming the first and second

---

TABLE 9-5 Basic Care Packages for Pregnancy at the Primary Level

Routine Prenatal Care

Clinical examination

Obstetric and gynecological examination

Urine test

Laboratory tests: hemoglobin, blood type and rhesus status, syphilis and other symptomatic testing for sexually transmitted diseases

Advice on emergencies, delivery, lactation, and contraception

Education

Iron and folic acid supplementation

Tetanus toxoid immunization

Screening and treatment for syphilis

Delivery Care

Clean delivery technique, clean cord cutting, clean delivery of baby and placenta

Active management of the third stage of labor

Episiotomy in appropriate cases

Recognition and first-line management of delivery complications

Intravenous fluid

Intravenous uterotonics, if bleeding occurs

Partograph

Essential newborn care

Intravenous antibiotics

Source: Adapted with permission from Graham WJ, Cairns J, Bhattacharya S, Bullough CHW, Quayyum Z, Rogo K. Maternal and perinatal conditions. In: Jamison DT, Breman JG, Measham AR, et al., eds. *Disease Control Priorities in Developing Countries,* 2nd ed. Washington, DC and New York: The World Bank and Oxford University Press; 2006:515.

delays of identifying a problem with the delivery and transporting the woman to a place where she can get emergency obstetric care. As discussed in Chapter 5 on health systems, a number of countries have initiated conditional cash transfer schemes to encourage all women to have births in hospitals. These schemes are meant to overcome the social and economic constraints to hospital deliveries. Parts of India, for example, are implementing conditional cash transfer programs that offer a payment to the person attending the birth for bringing the women to the hospital for delivery and offer the family a payment for coming for a hospital-based delivery. As also noted in Chapter 5, such schemes for increasing demand for hospital-based delivery could be coupled with other incentive programs to improve the amount and quality of the supply of emergency obstetric services.

MAIN MESSAGES

As discussed by a well-known scholar and practitioner of women's health, "being born female is dangerous to your health."[12] Some of the health conditions that women face are biologically determined. Others are socially determined. Some result from the interplay between biological and social determinants of health. The inferior social status of women in many cultures, however, is reflected in certain health conditions that women face and in some of the differentials that favor men between the health of men and the health of women.

As one looks globally at the health of women, especially poor women in low- and middle-income countries, one notes the importance of several key health issues. One is nutrition. Another is sex-selective abortion. A third is discriminatory healthcare practices toward young girls that cause these girls to suffer higher rates of mortality before age 5 than boys. Sexually transmitted infections are an important cause of DALYs lost for women in the reproductive age group, especially in sub-Saharan Africa. Female genital cutting is also a practice that is widespread, especially in parts of Africa, and it is associated with important morbidity and disability for women. Violence against women is also an important cause of ill health for women.

Illness, disability, and death from maternal causes are also unnecessarily high. More than 500,000 women die each year of maternal causes, of which about 70,000 are due to unsafe abortions. Complicated labor that is not properly attended can also lead to problems, such as fistula, from which an estimated 2 million women suffer worldwide.

The risk of maternal morbidity, disability, and mortality is increased by having a stunted mother, young age at marriage, young age at first birth, having more than five children, and having closely spaced pregnancies. The lack of access to family planning and the demand for it is at the foundation of some of these problems. This is particularly the case in some places in South Asia and much of sub-Saharan Africa, where total fertility remains high and the coverage of family planning remains low. Increasing the uptake of family planning to delay the age at first birth, increase birth intervals, and reduce the number of births per woman would save lives, especially in low- and middle-income countries with weak emergency obstetric care.

The costs of women's health problems are very substantial. In many societies, women are the primary caregivers to children, and when the health of the mother suffers, there is often a negative effect on the health of the children, as well. In addition, women play important economic roles in many families and the morbidity, disability, and mortality associated with particular problems of women's health have substantial economic implications.

There are countries, such as Sri Lanka, that have been able to improve the health of women at relatively low levels of expenditure by making wise choices about investments in health and education. These included increasing female education, providing widespread access to midwives, and ensuring adequate backup for the midwives at hospitals.

Improving the health of women in the future will require that health systems provide a cost-effective package of services, including nutrition, family planning, prenatal care, deliveries attended by skilled healthcare providers, emergency transportation of women who are having complicated labors, and emergency obstetric services at a hospital. A number of countries are now undertaking a variety of efforts, including incentive programs, to try to increase the demand for such services and the supply of these services at an appropriate level of quality. In the long run, it will be important to change the gender roles that favor males, promote the education and empowerment of females, promote their prospects for earning income, and educate communities to better understand the health conditions that females face and the measures that can be taken to address them. These measures could help, among other things, to reduce sex-selective abortion, female infanticide, and violence against women, and avoid the "three delays" that are associated with maternal morbidity, disability, and mortality.

Study Questions

1. Why can it be said that "being born female is dangerous to your health"?

2. Why should we pay particular attention to the health of females?

3. In what ways do gender issues affect the health of females?

4. What are some of the key differences in the burden of disease between males and females?

5. What are the sources of those differences?

6. What are the "three delays" and why are they important?

7. What steps do countries need to take to deal with the complications of unsafe abortions?

8. What measures might be taken to reduce intimate partner violence?

9. How could one reduce the risk to women of sexually transmitted infections?

10. What are some of the most cost-effective investments that should be made to improve the health of women in low-income countries?

REFERENCES

1. Prada E, Restler E, Sten C, et al. *Abortion and Postabortion Care in Guatemala: A Report from Health Care Professionals and Health Facilities.* Occasional Report. New York: Guttmacher Institute; 2005:No. 18. Available at: http://www.alanguttmacher.org/pubs/2005/12/30/or18.pdf. Accessed June 24, 2006.

2. UN Millennium Development Goals. Available at: http://www.un.org/millenniumgoals. Accessed March 15, 2006.

3. Murphy EM. Being born female is dangerous for your health. *Am Psychol.* 2003;58(3):1.

4. Buvinic M, Medici A, Fernandez E, Torres AC. Gender differentials in health. In: Jamison DT, Breman JG, Measham AR, et al., eds. *Disease Control Priorities in Developing Countries.* 2nd ed. New York: Oxford University Press; 2006:195-210.

5. WHO. *The World Health Report 2005: Make Every Mother and Child Count.* Geneva: World Health Organization; 2005.

6. Quinn TC, Overbaugh J. HIV/AIDS in women: an expanding epidemic. *Science.* 2005;308(5728):1582-1583.

7. Sex-selective Abortion and Infanticide. Available at: http://en.wikipedia.org/wiki/Sex-selective_abortion. Accessed June 10, 2006.

8. Abeykoon ATPL. Sex preference in South Asia: Sri Lanka an outlier. *Asia-Pacific Popu J.* 1995;10(3):5-16.

9. Gu B, Roy K. Sex ratio at birth in China, with reference to other areas in East Asia: what we know. *Asia-Pacific Popu J.* 1995;10(3):17-42.

10. Tinker A. *A New Agenda for Women's Health and Nutrition.* Washington, DC: The World Bank; 1994:15-17.

11. Rov K. *Encyclopaedia Against Women & Dowry Death in India.* New Delhi: Anmol Publications; 1999.

12. Murphy EM. Being born female is dangerous for your health. *Am Psychol.* 2003;58(3):205.

13. Case Study: Female Infanticide. Available at: http://www.gendercide.org/case_infanticide.html. Accessed June 10, 2006.

14. Jha P, Kumar R, Vasa P, Dhingra N, Thiruchelvam D, Moineddin R. Low female-to-male sex ratio of children born in India: national survey of 1.1 million households. *Lancet.* 2006;367(9506):211-218.

15. Walker M. The geopolitics of sexual frustration. *Foreign Policy.* 2006;153:60.

16. UNICEF. *Female Genital Mutilation/Cutting, A Statistical Exploration 2005.* New York: UNICEF; 2005.

17. Glasier A, Gulmezoglu AM, Schmid GP, Moreno CG, Look PFV. Sexual and reproductive health: a matter of life and death. *Lancet.* 2006;368:1595-1607.

18. Rowley J, Berkley S. Sexually transmitted diseases. In: Murray CJL, Lopez AD, eds. *Health Dimensions of Sex and Reproduction.* Geneva: World Health Organization; 1998:21.

19. Rowley J, Berkley S. Sexually transmitted diseases. In: Murray CJL, Lopez AD, eds. *Health Dimensions of Sex and Reproduction.* Geneva: World Health Organization; 1998:68-72.

20. Buvinic M, Medici A, Fernandez E, Torres AC. Gender differentials in health. In: Jamison DT, Breman JG, Measham AR, et al., eds. *Disease Control Priorities in Developing Countries.* 2nd ed. New York: Oxford University Press; 2006:203.

21. Lopez AD, Mathers CD, Murray CJL. The burden of disease and mortality by condition: data, methods, and results for 2001. In: Lopez AD, Mathers CD, Ezzati M, Jamison DT, Murray CJL, eds. *Global Burden of Disease and Risk Factors.* New York: Oxford University Press; 2006:174.

22. Lopez AD, Mathers CD, Murray CJL. The burden of disease and mortality by condition: data, methods, and results for 2001. In: Lopez AD, Mathers CD, Ezzati M, Jamison DT, Murray CJL, eds. *Global Burden of Disease and Risk Factors.* New York: Oxford University Press; 2006:228-229.

23. Rowley J, Berkley S. Sexually transmitted diseases. In: Murray CJL, Lopez AD, eds. *Health Dimensions of Sex and Reproduction.* Geneva: World Health Organization; 1998:41.

24. Rowley J, Berkley S. Sexually transmitted diseases. In: Murray CJL, Lopez AD, eds. *Health Dimensions of Sex and Reproduction.* Geneva: World Health Organization; 1998:42-46.

25. Tinker A. *A New Agenda for Women's Health and Nutrition.* Washington, DC: The World Bank; 1994.

26. Personal communication with Adrienne Germain, March 2007.

27. UNAIDS. Violence Against Women and AIDS. Available at: http://data.unaids.org/GCWA/GCWA_BG_Violence_en.pdf. Accessed February 28, 2006.

28. Heise L, Moore K, Toubiz N. *Sexual Coercion and Reproductive Health.* New York: Population Council; 1995.

29. *World Development Report 1993.* New York: Oxford University Press; 1993.

30. Amnesty International. Rape as a Tool of War. Fact Sheets. Available at: http://www.amnestyusa.org/stopviolence/factsheets/rapeinwartime.html. Accessed June 10, 2006.

31. WHO. *World Health Report 2005.* Geneva: World Health Organization; 2005.

32. Rosenberg ML, Butchart A, Mercy J, Narasimhan V, Waters H, Marshall MS. Interpersonal violence. In: Jamison DT, Breman JG, Measham AR, et al., eds. *Disease Control Priorities in Developing Countries.* 2nd ed. New York: Oxford University Press; 2006:759.

33. Last JM. *A Dictionary of Epidemiology.* 4th ed. New York: Oxford University Press; 2001:110.

34. WHO. *The World Health Report 2005: Make Every Mother and Child Count.* Geneva: World Health Organization; 2005:61-77.

35. Lawn JE, Lee AC, Kinney M, et al. Two million intrapartum-related stillbirths and neonatal deaths: where, why, and what can be done? *Int J Gynecol Obstet.* 2009;107:S5-S19.

36. WHO. *The World Health Report 2005: Make Every Mother and Child Count.* Geneva: World Health Organization; 2005:4.

37. Hogan MC, Naghavi M, Anh SY, et al. Maternal mortality for 181 countries, 1980 to 2008, a systematic analysis of progress towards Millennium Development Goal 5. *Lancet.* 2010;375(9726):1609-1623.

38. Graham WJ, Cairns J, Bhattacharya S, Bullough CHW, Quayyum Z, Rogo K. Maternal and perinatal conditions. In: Jamison DT, Breman JG, Measham AR, et al., eds. *Disease Control Priorities in Developing Countries.* 2nd ed. New York: Oxford University Press; 2006:506.

39. Herz BK, Measham AR. *The Safe Motherhood Initiative: Proposals for Action.* Washington, DC: The World Bank; 1987.

40. Tinker A. *A New Agenda for Women's Health and Nutrition.* Washington, DC: The World Bank; 1994:10.

41. AbouZahr C. Antepartum and postpartum hemorrhage. In: Murray CJL, Lopez AD, eds. *Health Dimensions of Sex and Reproduction: The Global Burden of Sexually Transmitted Diseases, HIV, Maternal Conditions, Perinatal Disorders, and Congenital Anomalies.* Cambridge, MA: Harvard School of Public Health; 1998:169.

42. AbouZahr C. Antepartum and postpartum hemorrhage. In: Murray CJL, Lopez AD, eds. *Health Dimensions of Sex and Reproduction: The Global Burden of Sexually Transmitted Diseases, HIV, Maternal Conditions, Perinatal Disorders, and Congenital Anomalies.* Cambridge, MA: Harvard School of Public Health; 1998:170.

43. Levine R, Langer A, Birdsall N, Matheny G, Wright M, Bayer A. Contraception. In: Jamison DT, Breman JG, Measham AR, et al., eds. *Disease Control Priorities in Developing Countries.* 2nd ed. New York: Oxford University Press; 2006:1075-1090.

44. The World Bank. *Priorities in Health.* Washington, DC: The World Bank; 2006.

45. WHO. *The World Health Report 2005: Make Every Mother and Child Count.* Geneva: World Health Organization; 2005:41-58.

46. Royal College of Midwives. *Obstetric Fistula: A Silent Tragedy.* London: The Royal College of Midwives Trust; 2010.

47. AbouZahr C. Prolonged and obstructed labor. In: Murray CJL, Lopez AD, eds. *Health Dimensions of Sex and Reproduction: The Global Burden of Sexually Transmitted Diseases, HIV, Maternal Conditions, Perinatal Disorders, and Congenital Anomalies.* Cambridge, MA: Harvard School of Public Health; 1998:243-266.

48. Obstetric Fistula as a Catalyst: Exploring Approaches for Safe Motherhood. Atlanta, GA. Paper presented at: Fistula as a Catalyst Meeting; 2005.

49. Buvinic M, Medici A, Fernandez E, Torres AC. Gender differentials in health. In: Jamison DT, Breman JG, Measham AR, et al., eds. *Disease Control Priorities in Developing Countries.* 2nd ed. New York: Oxford University Press; 2006:197.

50. Buvinic M, Medici A, Fernandez E, Torres AC. Gender differentials in health. In: Jamison DT, Breman JG, Measham AR, et al., eds. *Disease Control Priorities in Developing Countries.* 2nd ed. New York: Oxford University Press; 2006:201.

51. Rosenberg ML, Butchart A, Mercy J, Narasimhan V, Waters H, Marshall MS. Interpersonal violence. In: Jamison DT, Breman JG, Measham AR, et al., eds. *Disease Control Priorities in Developing Countries.* 2nd ed. New York: Oxford University Press; 2006:755-770.

52. This case study is based on a draft case study that was provided by Tostan. More information about Tostan can be found at their website, http://www.tostan.org.

53. UNICEF. Long-Term Evaluation of the Tostan Programme in Senegal: Kolda, Thies and Fatick Regions. New York: UNICEF; 2008.

54. Diop N, Moreau A, Benga H. *Evaluation of the Long-Term Impact of the Tostan Programme on the Abandonment of FGM-C and Early Marriage: Results from a Qualitative Study in Senegal.* New York: Population Council; 2008.

55. World Health Organization. Safer Pregnancy in Tamil Nadu: From Vision to Reality. 2009. Available at: http://whqlibdoc.who.int/searo/2009/9789290223566.pdf. Accessed August 22, 2010.

56. World Health Organization. Global Health Observatory. Available at: http://apps.who.int/ghodata. Accessed August 29, 2010.

57. This case study is largely based on Pathmathan I, Lijestrand J, Martins JM. et al. *Investing in Maternal Health: Learning from Malaysia and Sri Lanka.* Washington, DC: The World Bank; 2003.

58. Wickramasuriya GAW. Maternal mortality and morbidity in Ceylon. *Ceylon Branch British Med Assn.* 1939;36(2):79-106.

59. United Nations. *Human Development Report.* New York, NY: United Nations; 2003.

60. Manoff R. Getting your message out with social marketing. *Am J Tropical Med Hygiene.* 1997;57(3):260-265.

61. Mitra SN, Al-Sabir A, Cross AR, Jamil K. *Bangladesh Demographic and Health Survey 1996–1997.* Dhaka: National Institute for Population Research and Training; 1997.

62. Khuda B-e, Roy NC, Rahman DM. Family planning and fertility in Bangladesh. *Asia-Pacific Pop J.* 2000;15(1):41-54.

63. Janowitz B, Holtman M, Johnson L, Trottier D. The importance of field workers in Bangladesh's family planning programme. *Asia-Pacific Pop J.* 1999;14(2): 23-36.

64. Routh, S, Barkat-e-Khuda. An economic appraisal of alternative strategies for the delivery of MCH-FP services in urban Dhaka, Bangladesh. *Int J Health Plann Manage.* 2000;15(2):115-132.

65. The Obstetric Fistula Partnership—Working in Niger, Sudan, Tanzania and Uganda. Available at: http://www.engenderhealth.org/ia/swh/mcfpartnership.html. Accessed June 10, 2006.

66. Bill & Melinda Gates Foundation. Available at: http://www.gatesfoundation.org/default.htm. Accessed June 9, 2006.

67. Women's Dignity. Welcome to Women's Dignity Project. Available at: http://www.womensdignity.org. Accessed June 9, 2006.

68. Women's Dignity. WDP in the News: Local Press on WDP. Available at: http://www.womensdignity.org/wdp_localpress.asp#1. Accessed June 9, 2006.

69. Women's Dignity. Program Highlights: Funds for Fistula Repairs. Available at: http://www.womensdignity.org/highlights_fff.asp. Accessed June 9, 2006.

70. Women's Dignity. Program Highlights: Participatory Research. Available at: http://www.womensdignity.org/highlights_pr.asp. Accessed June 9, 2006.

71. Mwanamke U. Faces of Dignity: Seven Stories of Girls and Women with Fistula. Available at: http://www.womensdignity.org/Face_of_Dignity.pdf. Accessed June 9, 2006.

72. African Medical and Relief Foundation. Available at: http://www.amref.org. Accessed June 9, 2006.

73. The Campaign to End Fistula. Available at: http://www.endfistula.org. Accessed June 9, 2006.

74. Rosenberg ML, Butchart A, Mercy J, Narasimhan V, Waters H, Marshall MS. Interpersonal violence. In: Jamison DT, Breman JG, Measham AR, et al., eds. *Disease Control Priorities in Developing Countries.* 2nd ed. New York: Oxford University Press; 2006:761.

75. Rowley J, Berkley S. Sexually transmitted diseases. In: Murray CJL, Lopez AD, eds. *Health Dimensions of Sex and Reproduction.* Geneva: World Health Organization; 1998:95-99.

76. Providing interventions. In: Jamison DT, Breman JG, Measham AR, et al., eds. *Priorities in Health.* New York: Oxford University Press; 2006:153.

77. Rowley J, Berkley S. Sexually transmitted diseases. In: Murray CJL, Lopez AD, eds. *Health Dimensions of Sex and Reproduction.* Geneva: World Health Organization; 1998.

78. Providing interventions. In: Jamison DT, Breman JG, Measham AR, et al., eds. *Priorities in Health.* New York: Oxford University Press; 2006:154.

79. Tinker A. *A New Agenda for Women's Health and Nutrition.* Washington, DC: The World Bank; 1994:31.

80. Tinker A. *A New Agenda for Women's Health and Nutrition.* Washington, DC: The World Bank; 1994:32-33.

81. Smith R, Ashford L, Gribble J, Clifton D. *Family Planning Saves Lives.* 4th ed. Washington, DC: PRB; 2009.

82. Jamison DT. Maternal and perinatal conditions. In: Jamison DT, Breman JG, Measham AR, et al., eds. *Disease Control Priorities in Developing Countries.* 2nd ed. New York: Oxford University Press; 2006:499-529.

83. Tinker A. *A New Agenda for Women's Health and Nutrition.* Washington, DC: The World Bank; 1994:29-30.

84. Graham WJ, Cairns J, Bhattacharya S, Bullough CHW, Quayyum Z, Rogo K. Maternal and perinatal conditions. In: Jamison DT, Breman JG, Measham AR, et al., eds. *Disease Control Priorities in Developing Countries.* 2nd ed. Washington, DC: Oxford University Press and The World Bank; 2006:515-516.

CHAPTER 10

Child Health

By the end of this chapter the reader will be able to:

- Understand the most important causes of child illness and death around the world
- Discuss the importance of neonatal death in overall child deaths
- Understand why some children survive and others die
- Describe the most cost-effective child health interventions
- Describe some examples of successful child health initiatives
- Discuss some of the challenges of further enhancing the health of children

VIGNETTES

Nassiba was born in a remote part of Tajikistan. At 3 years of age, she became very ill with measles. She died before her parents could get her to a health center. Nassiba was never registered when she was born because the registration center was far away from where her family lived. In addition, her parents could not afford to pay the registration fee. When Nassiba died, her death was not recorded either. According to the national records, she never existed.

Esther was born in Cape Town, South Africa, several years ago. Esther's mother was HIV-positive. Esther's family depended on the public health system for care but at the time that system did not offer drug therapy to stop transmission of HIV from mother to child. Esther's mother breastfed her for most of the first 6 months, but not exclusively. A few months ago, Esther showed signs of HIV disease.

Tirtha was born in the far west of Nepal and was the fourth child in her family. She was 7 months old and was eating some baby foods, as well as breastfeeding. One day Tirtha became feverish and developed persistent diarrhea. Her mother was not sure if she should continue to feed the baby or if that would make the diarrhea worse. She wanted to take Tirtha to the health center but it was 4 hours away by foot so she decided to see how Tirtha was feeling the next day. The next morning Tirtha was dead from dehydration.

Juan was born in the highlands of Bolivia to an indigenous family. The family did what they could to keep the new baby warm but it was very cold in the mountains. Several days after birth, Juan began to breathe heavily. The family called the community health worker for assistance. The health worker treated Juan for pneumonia with an antibiotic that she had just learned to use as part of a new program for "saving newborn lives." She also gave the family advice about taking care of their new baby. The last baby born to the family had died of pneumonia but Juan survived.

THE IMPORTANCE OF CHILD HEALTH

There are a number of reasons why the health of young children deserves its own chapter in a book on global health. First, it has recently been estimated that about 8.8 million children under 5 years of age die in the world each year. This is equal to more than 24,000 children under 5 who die *each day*.[1] The second reason to pay special attention to child health is that so many of these deaths are preventable. It has been estimated, for example, that more than half of child deaths each year could be avoided through known, simple, and low-cost interventions.[2] Third, children have a special place in the global health agenda because they are so vulnerable. The measures needed to ensure that they are born healthier, breastfed properly, immunized on schedule, and raised in safe and hygienic conditions, for example, can only be taken by others who care for them. Their vulnerability also raises important ethical issues about the responsibility of adults to ensure the health and survival of children.

Child health is also closely linked with poverty. If children had access to safer water and better sanitation, then many of them would not succumb to diarrhea. If their families had more education, especially their mothers, then families would be better equipped to ensure that their children were better cared for. If families had more income, then they would have greater access to health, education, and other social services that would also serve children well.

The health of children is also of particular concern because insufficient progress has been made in some parts of the world in enhancing child health. This has been especially true in parts of sub-Saharan Africa, where the direct and indirect costs of HIV/AIDS and malaria have taken a significant toll on the health of children. This is also the case in some parts of South Asia, where poor nutritional status is at the root of so much ill health for children under 5 years.

TABLE 10-1 Key Links Between Child Health and the MDGs

Goal 1: Eradicate Extreme Hunger and Poverty
   Link: More than 50% of child deaths worldwide are associated with malnutrition.
Goal 2: Achieve Universal Primary Education
   Link: Enrollment, attendance, and performance of children in schools is closely linked with their health.
Goal 3: Promote Gender Equality and Empower Women
   Link: Empowering women will enhance their health, their education, and their ability to raise more healthy children.
Goal 4: Reduce Child Mortality
   Link: This is directly related to child health.
Goal 5: Improve Maternal Health
   Link: Maternal health is a major predictor of the birthweight of a child and the child's subsequent health and survival prospects.
Goal 6: Combat HIV/AIDS, Malaria, and Other Diseases
   Link: HIV/AIDS and malaria are major killers of young children.
Goal 7: Ensure Environmental Sustainability
   Link: An important share of childhood illness and death are related to unsafe water and poor sanitation. Indoor air pollution is also very detrimental to the health of children.

Source: Adapted from United Nations. Millennium Development Goals. Available at: http://www.un.org/millenniumgoals/goals. Accessed July 11, 2006.

For all these reasons, children are featured prominently in the MDGs, as noted in Table 10-1.

This chapter will highlight the most important issues concerning the health of children in low- and middle-income countries. It will review the burden of disease for children, with important comments on the first month of life. It will review the risk factors for illness and death that occur in children under 5 years. The chapter will illustrate key concepts in a number of program and policy briefs and case studies. It will then examine measures that can be taken to reduce the burden of disease in young children. The chapter will conclude with a review of some of the key challenges to further improving the health of children in low- and middle-income countries.

Nutritional factors, often combined with disease, are a major cause of ill health and death in children; however, nutrition was largely covered in Chapter 8. Children also suffer an important burden of morbidity and mortality as a result of conflict. Civil strife and other emergencies will be reviewed in Chapter 14. This chapter will largely cover several of the most important causes of illness and death in children: causes related to the deaths of neonates, diarrhea, pneumonia, measles, and malaria. It will also comment briefly on worms, which will also be covered in greater detail in the next chapter. HIV/AIDS is also largely covered in the next chapter.

KEY TERMS

In Chapter 2, you were introduced to some of the key indicators used in measuring and analyzing global health issues. Those terms, which will be used extensively in this chapter, included neonatal mortality rate, infant mortality rate, and under-5 child mortality rate.

In this chapter, we will continuously speak of four different phases of the lives of young children:

Perinatal—referring to the first week of life
Neonatal—referring to the first month of life
Infant—referring to the first year of life
Under-5—referring to children 0 to 4 years old

In addition, you will read about some of the most important causes of disease, disability, and death in children under 5 years, as shown in Table 10-2.

NOTE ON DATA

The data in this chapter that refer to causes of death and the total numbers of deaths are taken from a study published in 2010 on the causes of child mortality.[1] The Child Health Epidemiology Reference Group of WHO and UNICEF car-

TABLE 10-2 Selected Terms Relating to Causes of Child Illness and Death

Asphyxia—A condition of severely deficient oxygen supply.

Diahhrea—A condition characterized by frequent and watery bowel movements.

Hookworm—A parasite that lives in the intestines of its host, which may be a mammal such as a dog, cat, or human. Two species of hookworm commonly infect humans, *Ancylostoma duodenale* and *Necator americanus*.

Malaria—A disease of humans caused by blood parasites of the species *Plasmodium falciparum, vivax, ovale,* or *malariae* and transmitted by anopheline mosquitoes.

Pertussis—A highly contagious bacterial disease that is one of the leading causes of vaccine-preventable death.

Pneumonia—An inflammation, usually caused by infection, involving the alveoli of the lungs.

Polio—An infectious disease caused by poliovirus that can lead to paralysis.

Sepsis—A serious medical condition caused by a severe infection, leading to a systematic inflammatory response.

Tetanus—A bacterial infection usually contracted through a puncture wound with an unclean object. Neonates acquire tetanus when their birth cord is contaminated, often when cut with an unsterile object.

Source: Data from Birley MH. PEEM Guidelines 2—Guidelines for Forecasting the Vector-Borne Disease Implications of Water Resources Development. Available at: http://www.who.int/docstore/water_sanitation_health/Documents/PEEM2/english/peem2chap4.htm. Accessed April 14, 2007; Doctors Without Borders. Glossary. Available at: http://www.doctorswithoutborders.org/education/bol/Glossary.htm. Accessed April 14, 2007; Wikipedia. Asphyxia. Available at: http://en.wikipedia.org/wiki/Asphyxia. Accessed April 14, 2007; Wikipedia. Hookworm. Available at: http://en.wikipedia.org/wiki/Hookworm. Accessed April 14, 2007; Wikipedia. Pneumonia. Available at: http://en.wikipedia.org/wiki/Pneumonia. Accessed April 14, 2007; Wikipedia. Sepsis. Available at: http://en.wikipedia.org/wiki/Sepsis. Accessed April 14, 2007.

ried out that study. Readers should be aware, however, of another study published in 2010 that also examined the number of maternal and child deaths worldwide, which was already referenced in Chapter 9 on women's health.[2] That study concluded that there are about 10 percent fewer deaths of under-5 children in the world than the Reference Group concluded. The data on infant and child mortality rates by World Bank region that are used in this chapter are taken from the World Bank. The data on neonatal mortality rates are not collected regularly and come from earlier WHO data. A limited amount of data comes from other sources. The reader is reminded that the data on child health given in Chapter 2 are from the 2001 global burden of disease study and were used because they are the latest update by World Bank region of a consistent set of data on the burden of disease. This chapter does not contain data from the WHO 2008 update on the burden of disease.

THE BURDEN OF CHILDHOOD ILLNESS

Children Under 5 Years

As noted earlier, about 8.8 million deaths of children under 5 years of age occur worldwide annually. About 99 percent of them are in low- and middle-income countries. Almost half of these deaths occur in only 5 large countries: India, Nigeria, Democratic Republic of the Congo, Pakistan, and China.[1]

About 41 percent of the under-5 child deaths occurred among neonates, children less than 28 days old. Moreover, about half of the children who die in the first 28 days, die in the first day of life.[3]

Neonatal and infant mortality rates vary dramatically both across and within countries. For ease of reference, Figure 10-1 repeats the figure given in Chapter 2 on the neonatal mortality rate by WHO region.

Neonatal mortality rates are highest in the Africa, Southeast Asia, and Eastern Mediterranean regions, with the high level in the Eastern Mediterranean region, largely reflecting that Pakistan is in that region. Neonatal mortality rates varied in 2004 by four times between the best-off WHO region and the worst-off WHO region, with Europe having a rate of 10 neonatal deaths per 1000 live births and Africa having a rate of 40 per 1000. Within the low- and middle-income countries, of course, the poorest, least well educated, most rural, and most marginalized families would face rates of neonatal mortality dramatically higher than the average.

Infant and under-5 child mortality rates are shown together by World Bank region in Figure 10-2. This figure also reflects enormous differences within regions.

For both infant and under-5 mortality, sub-Saharan Africa and South Asia have the highest rates by far. The infant mortality rate in sub-Saharan Africa is about 17 times higher

FIGURE 10-1 Neonatal Mortality Rate, by WHO Region, 2004

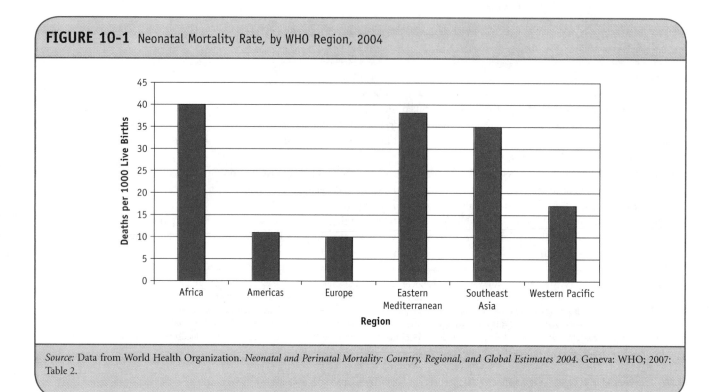

Source: Data from World Health Organization. *Neonatal and Perinatal Mortality: Country, Regional, and Global Estimates 2004.* Geneva: WHO; 2007: Table 2.

FIGURE 10-2 Infant and Under-5 Mortality Rates, by World Bank Region, 2008

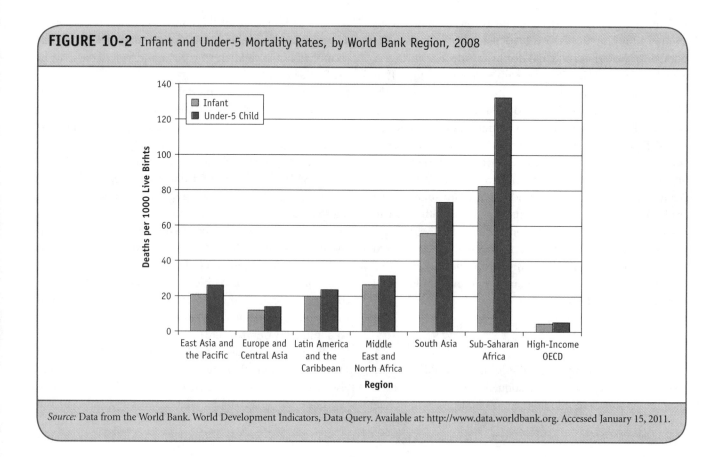

Source: Data from the World Bank. World Development Indicators, Data Query. Available at: http://www.data.worldbank.org. Accessed January 15, 2011.

than the rate in high-income countries. The rate of under-5 child mortality in sub-Saharan Africa is about 25 times that in high-income countries.

As you would expect, the rates of infant and child mortality vary with income, education, and location. In sub-Saharan Africa, children from the lowest income quintile have almost two times the risk of dying before they are 5 as do children in the highest income quintile. In East Asia and the Pacific, South Asia, and the Middle East and North Africa regions, the poorer quintile children are almost three times as likely to die before they are 5 as are those in the highest income quintile.

The differences by rural or urban location are less severe but still important. Rural populations in Latin America and the Caribbean are about 1.7 times more likely to die before their fifth birthday, while those in South Asia are 1.5 times as likely, and those in sub-Saharan Africa are about 1.4 times as likely to die.[4]

For all low- and middle-income countries, under-5 children of mothers with no primary education are about twice as likely to die before they are 5 as are children of mothers with a secondary education or higher. In most regions, other than South Asia, boys are more likely to die before they are 5 than girls. In the East Asia and the Pacific region, however, boys and girls are equally likely to die before they are 5. These data suggest that in India and China girls are still more likely to die under 5 than boys are.[4]

Globally, the leading causes of death for children under 5 years of age are shown in Figure 10-3.

Pneumonia and diarrhea are the leading causes of death of under-5 children, with pneumonia causing 18 percent of deaths and diarrhea 15 percent. This is followed

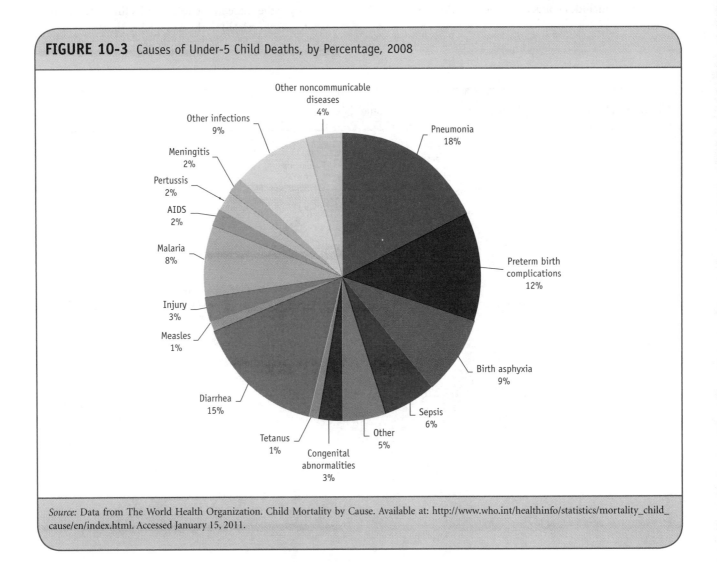

FIGURE 10-3 Causes of Under-5 Child Deaths, by Percentage, 2008

Source: Data from The World Health Organization. Child Mortality by Cause. Available at: http://www.who.int/healthinfo/statistics/mortality_child_cause/en/index.html. Accessed January 15, 2011.

by the complications of preterm birth, at 12 percent. "Other infections" besides those named on the table, birth asphyxia, malaria, and sepsis are the only other causes that make up more than 5 percent of the total.

It is especially important, however, to divide under-5 deaths into those that occur in the first 28 days, among neonates, and those that occur between then and the end of the child's fourth year. When looking at neonatal deaths in Figure 10-4, we can see that preterm complications make up almost 30 percent of the total, asphyxia about 22 percent, sepsis 15 percent, "other" 12 percent, and pneumonia about 10 percent.

As shown in Figure 10-5, the five leading causes of under-5 deaths in the *post*neonatal period are pneumonia and diarrhea at about 24 percent each, "other infections" than those named at about 15 percent, malaria at about 14 percent, and "other noncommunicable diseases," which includes congenital abnormalities, at about 7 percent.

The leading causes of under-5 child death also vary considerably by region. Table 10-3 shows the 10 leading causes of death for children under 5 for three WHO regions: Africa, the Americas, and Southeast Asia.

The table suggests a number of points:

- Pneumonia is the leading cause of death in Southeast Asia, the second leading cause in Africa, and the third leading cause in the Americas.
- Diarrhea remains important in all regions and is the leading cause in Africa, the second leading cause in Southeast Asia, but not among the five leading causes of death in the Americas, although it still accounts for 7 percent of the deaths.
- Malaria is the third leading killer of children under 5 in Africa but not a significant killer in the other regions.
- Generally, the wealthier the region becomes, the larger the share in the total deaths that is represented by causes related to the neonatal period.

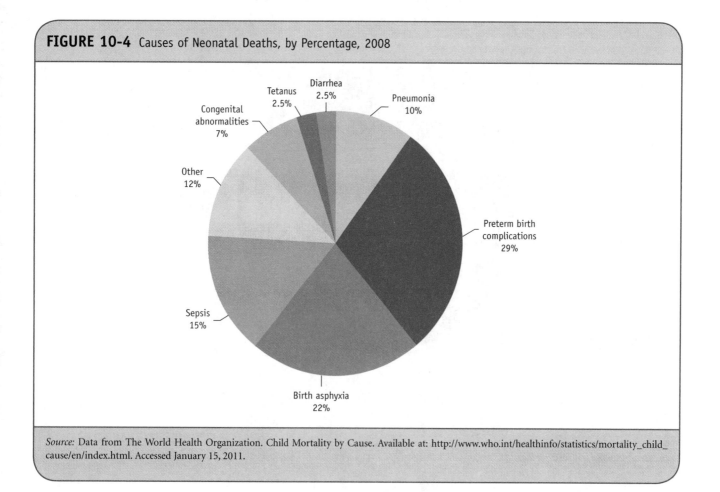

FIGURE 10-4 Causes of Neonatal Deaths, by Percentage, 2008

Source: Data from The World Health Organization. Child Mortality by Cause. Available at: http://www.who.int/healthinfo/statistics/mortality_child_cause/en/index.html. Accessed January 15, 2011.

FIGURE 10-5 Causes of Postneonatal Deaths in Children Under 5, by Percentage, 2008

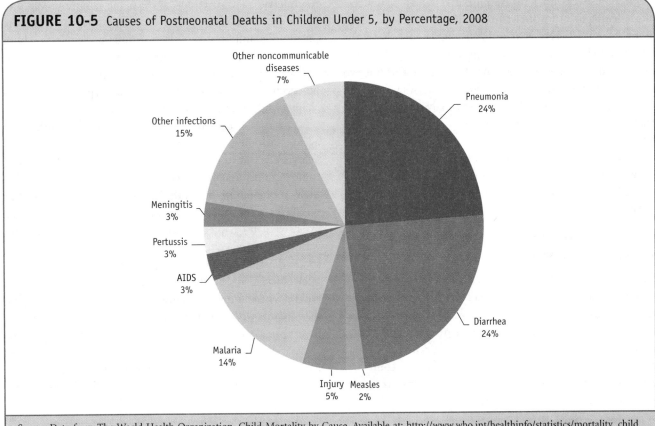

Source: Data from The World Health Organization. Child Mortality by Cause. Available at: http://www.who.int/healthinfo/statistics/mortality_child_cause/en/index.html. Accessed January 15, 2011.

TABLE 10-3 Leading Causes of Under-5 Child Death for Selected WHO Regions, by Percentage, 2008

Africa		The Americas		Southeast Asia	
Diarrhea	19	Preterm birth	18	Pneumonia	21
Pneumonia	18	Other noncommunicable diseases	14	Diarrhea	14
Malaria	16	Pneumonia	12	Preterm birth	14
Other infections	9	Other infections	12	Birth asphyxia	11
Preterm birth	8	Congenital abnormalities	9	Other	9
Birth asphyxia	8	Diarrhea	7	Sepsis	7
Sepsis	5	Birth asphyxia	7	Other noncommunicable diseases	4
HIV/AIDS	4	Other	7	Injury	4
Other noncommunicable diseases	2	Injury	6	Pertussis	4
Pertussis*	2	Sepsis	5	Measles	3

Source: Data from Black RE, Cousens S, Johnson HL, et al. Global, regional, and national causes of child mortality in 2008: a systematic analysis. *Lancet.* 2010;375:1969-1987.

*Note: For the Africa region, injuries and meningitis also comprise 2 percent of the causes of under-5 deaths.

It is also essential to examine the trends in under-5 mortality. Figure 10-6 shows the decline in under-5 mortality by region between 1990 and 2008; Table 10-4 shows the rate of decline. Although all regions have had a decline over this period, the rate of decline has been slowest in the two regions with the highest rates of under-5 deaths, sub-Saharan Africa and South Asia. We would normally expect to see a relatively slower decline in countries such as those in Latin America and the Caribbean and East Asia and the Pacific that had relatively lower rates of under-5 child death in 1990. However, they were still able to further reduce their rates of under-5 child mortality faster than either sub-Saharan Africa or South Asia.

Additional Comments on Selected Causes of Morbidity and Mortality

Acute respiratory infections are very common causes of sickness and death in children younger than 5 years of age in low- and middle-income countries where children average three to six acute respiratory infections per year. These cases are more severe and cause higher rates of death in low- and middle-income countries than in high-income countries. The most common acute respiratory infections are upper respiratory tract infections, such as the common cold and ear infections. The common lower respiratory infections are pneumonia and bronchiolitis. Pneumonia is caused by both bacteria and viruses. The most common forms of bacterial pneumonia are caused by *Streptococcus pneumoniae* (pneumococcus) and *Haemophilus influenzae,* type b (Hib).[5] This chapter will generally speak only of "pneumonia."

Diarrhea is caused by a number of different infectious agents, including bacteria, viruses, protozoa, and helminths.[6] Diarrhea is transmitted by what is known as the "fecal-oral" route of transmission, from the stool of one individual, eventually to the mouth of another. This is generally the result of unsafe water, poor sanitation, and poor hygiene, as discussed extensively in Chapter 7. Dehydration, loss of nutrition and wasting, or damage to the intestines are all consequences of severe diarrhea.[7] Rapid diarrhea due to dehydration can be fatal quickly. In one study, infants with persistent diarrhea and severe malnutrition were at 17 times greater risk of dying than infants with mild malnutrition.[7] Children younger than 5 years in developing countries have around three to four cases of diarrhea per year, with infants 6 to 11 months of age having almost twice as many cases. As noted earlier, this is the age during which they usually stop exclusive breastfeed-

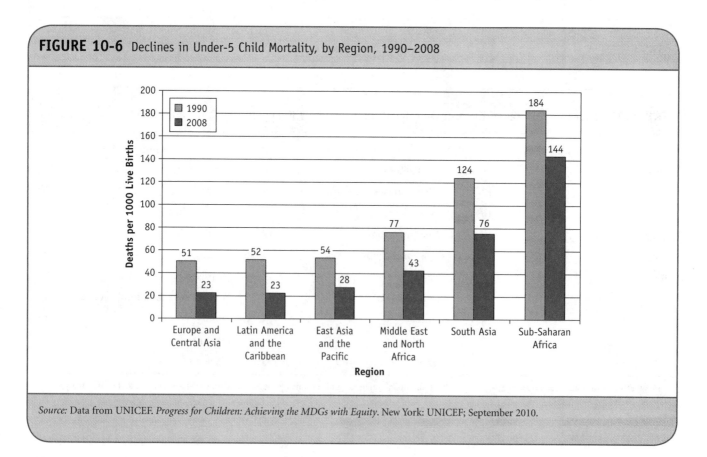

FIGURE 10-6 Declines in Under-5 Child Mortality, by Region, 1990–2008

Source: Data from UNICEF. *Progress for Children: Achieving the MDGs with Equity.* New York: UNICEF; September 2010.

TABLE 10-4 Percent Decline in Under-5 Child Mortality, by Region, 1990–2008

Region	Percent Decline
Europe and Central Asia	55%
Latin America and the Caribbean	56%
East Asia and the Pacific	48%
Middle East and North Africa	44%
South Asia	39%
Sub-Saharan Africa	22%

Source: Data from UNICEF. *Progress for Children: Achieving the MDGs with Equity.* New York: UNICEF; September 2010.

ing and are at most risk of being exposed to unsafe water and foods.[7]

Malaria has an enormous impact on the morbidity and mortality of young children in direct and indirect ways. Almost 750,000 children younger than 5 years are estimated to die yearly from malaria.[1] In addition, the morbidity associated with malaria in young children is staggering. It is estimated that a child in sub-Saharan Africa is likely to have a case of malaria every 40 days.[8] Moreover, the most severe form of malaria, cerebral malaria, has a case fatality rate of close to 20 percent, meaning that 20 percent of the children who get the disease die from it. Beyond the direct consequences of malaria on children are the indirect consequences on them. Malaria is associated with premature birth and intrauterine growth retardation, which are linked with low birthweight and reduced chances of survival.[8]

HIV/AIDS will be discussed at considerable length in Chapter 11, which is on communicable diseases. However, it should be noted here that one route of transmission of HIV is from mother to child. This can take place either during birth or through breastfeeding. The number of HIV-infected children in the world has grown, particularly in sub-Saharan Africa. In Botswana, for example, 37 percent of pregnant women are estimated to be infected with HIV,[9] and child mortality increased from 58 deaths per 1000 births in 1990 to 116 deaths per 1000 births in 2004, with the increase reflecting the problem of HIV/AIDS.[10] As you will read about in Chapter 11, however, a number of countries have made important progress in reducing maternal-to-child transmission of HIV.

Measles is an acute respiratory infection that can lead to complications including pneumonia, diarrhea, encepha-litis, and blindness. Children who are younger than 5 years and either vitamin A deficient or HIV infected are more vulnerable to measles complications and are more at risk of death than other children their age. Recent studies in sub-Saharan Africa suggest that between 0.5 and 10 percent of the children who get measles will die from it. The role of vaccination in preventing measles and other diseases will be discussed later in the chapter. However, it is interesting to note that, in the absence of vaccination, almost 100 percent of a population will get measles.[11]

Chapter 11 will discuss soil-transmitted helminth infections, and in that chapter you will have an additional opportunity to think about the importance of worms to child health. However, it is important to understand now that it is estimated that 2 billion people worldwide suffer from helminth infections. About 300 million suffer severe morbidity from these infections, especially iron deficiency anemia, and these worms are also associated with impaired physical and mental development in childhood. The burden of several species of worms is highest in children around 6 or 7 years of age.[12] Few children die directly from these worms; however, the DALYs lost to these worms in children who are 5 to 14 years old are higher than those lost by this age group from almost any other single cause.[13]

Additional Comments on Neonatal Mortality

There has been some progress in reducing the deaths of children younger than 5 years, as discussed earlier. However, there has been little progress in reducing the neonatal death rate, except from neonatal tetanus.[14] Of the 8.8 million children under 5 years who die annually, about 41 percent, or 3.6 million, of them actually die in the first month of life. Approximately 99 percent of those 4 million children live in low- and middle-income countries.[15]

If the world is to further reduce child death rates, then it will have to reduce neonatal death rates. If the world is to do that, it will have to focus more precisely on when child deaths take place, where they take place, and why they occur. About 75 percent or 2.7 million of the deaths that take place in the first month of life actually take place in the first week of life. In addition, about 25 percent of the neonatal deaths take place in the first 24 hours of life.[14,16] Clearly, every day that a child lives increases the likelihood that he or she will stay alive. This may help to explain why children in a number of cultures are not named until after their first month of life. It may also help to explain why so many births are not registered with civil authorities, as was the case for Nassiba in the vignette that opened this chapter.

In thinking about neonatal deaths, just as in thinking about the deaths of all infants and children under 5 years, we must remember the relationship between the health of the mother and the health of the baby. Between 60 and 80 percent of neonatal deaths occur in low birthweight babies. This generally reflects the poor health and nutritional status of the mother, including her being undernourished or having malaria, for example.[17] We also need to remember that an enormous number of child lives could be saved if the gap in child deaths between the richest and poorest segments of society were narrowed.

RISK FACTORS FOR NEONATAL, INFANT, AND CHILD DEATHS

Why do so many children still die and so many others become disabled at such young ages? As mentioned earlier, poverty contributes to poor health and is a major underlying cause of morbidity and mortality among children. Where there is poverty, there is often inadequate nutrition. Where there is poverty, there is less access to safe water and sanitation, health services, and education. All of these are important determinants of child health.

In addition, you already know that there is very strong correlation between family income and the likelihood that a neonate, an infant, or a child will survive. You also know that there is a similar correlation between the health and the educational status of the mother and the prospects that a child will survive birth and the first 5 years of life. Nutritional status, malaria, and HIV are also powerful determinants of the weight the baby will have at birth and of his or her chances for survival.

The Millennium Report 2006, in commenting on progress toward the Millennium Development Goal of reducing child morbidity and mortality, revealed that higher household income and education for mothers doubles child survival rates. In families where the mother had no education or only primary education, child mortality averaged 157 deaths per 1000 live births, whereas in families where the mother had secondary education or higher, mortality rates were close to 50 percent less, at 82 per 1000 live births.[18]

Related to both income and the educational status of the family is the fact that the survival of a newborn is also closely linked with whether the birth is in an appropriate healthcare setting and is attended by a trained healthcare provider.[19] A baby's chances of survival increase greatly when the baby is born in a setting that can deal with obstetric emergencies. The chances of survival also increase if the delivery is attended by a skilled birth attendant who can resuscitate babies who need it and can help to counsel families about keeping babies warm and initiating breastfeeding early. The child's chances of survival also increase if the family has

access to appropriate antibiotic treatment for pneumonia if it arises. Evidence also suggests that appropriate interventions at the antenatal stage, birth stage, and postnatal period can improve neonatal survival.[14]

The burden of diarrheal disease on child health makes clear that unsafe water and poor sanitation are major risk factors for child health. We have seen how the risk of unsafe hygiene increases greatly as the child begins to eat complementary foods and is no longer exclusively breastfed. We have also seen that better educated families have more awareness about health risks as well as safe behaviors that can improve their children's health and chances of survival.

Chapter 8 reviewed nutrition in detail and made clear the extent to which undernutrition is a risk factor for child morbidity and mortality. However, it is worth reminding ourselves of the profound impact of nutritional status, indirectly, through the mother, and directly, on the health and survival prospects of neonates, infants, and children younger than 5 years.

- "Infants aged 0–5 months who are not breastfed have seven-fold increased risks of death from diarrhea and pneumonia, respectively, compared to infants who are exclusively breastfed."[20]
- ". . . 35% of all child deaths are due to the effect of underweight status on diarrhea, pneumonia, measles, and malaria and relative risks of maternal body mass index for fetal growth retardation and its risks for selected neonatal causes of death."[20]
- "In children with vitamin A deficiency, the risk of dying from diarrhea, measles, and malaria is increased by 20 to 24%. Likewise, zinc deficiency increases the risk of mortality from diarrhea, pneumonia, and malaria by 13 to 21%."[20]

The impact of wars and conflicts on health is covered in Chapter 14. Wars and conflicts take a significant toll on children and are regrettable risk factors for child morbidity and mortality, particularly in sub-Saharan Africa. UNICEF estimates that in a "typical" 5-year war, under-5 mortality increases 13 percent.[21] In addition, the highest rates of neonatal death occur in conflict-ridden countries or countries just emerging from conflict, such as Liberia and Sierra Leone.[22]

THE COSTS AND CONSEQUENCES OF CHILD MORBIDITY AND MORTALITY

One cannot measure "direct losses in productivity" that relate immediately to the morbidity and mortality of young children from the causes discussed in this chapter. There are, however, enormous costs and consequences to these illnesses. Some of them are short-term and relate to the family. Others are medium- or longer-term and relate to the child directly.

First, the direct and indirect costs of caring for a sick child can be very high. As noted earlier in this chapter, the average child in Africa is infected with malaria every 40 days. In addition, the average child in low- and middle-income countries will get three to six bouts per year of acute respiratory infection, and two to three cases of diarrhea. In this light, it is not surprising that families spend considerable parts of their limited financial resources on buying medical care for a sick child.[7] Moreover, caregivers devote special attention to the child who is ill, which prevents them from engaging in their normal income-earning activities.

Second, the medium- and long-term consequences of some childhood illnesses can be very high. The consequences of undernutrition and micronutrient deficiency were explored at length in Chapter 8. Problems associated with prematurity, low birthweight, intrauterine growth retardation, and congenital abnormalities can lead to permanent disability and the related costs to families and to society that are associated with it. A study on diarrheal disease in Brazil concluded that intelligence test scores were "25 to 65 percent lower in children with an earlier history of persistent diarrhea."[23] The complications of measles can lead to encephalitis and blindness, as indicated earlier. By causing anemia, growth retardation, and the retardation of mental development, helminthic infections reduce children's enrollment, attendance, and performance in school and have consequences for later productivity.[24]

Finally, there are a range of social costs and consequences associated with childhood illness and death. Many poor families in low-income countries, knowing the odds are high that their newborn will die, have very high fertility to "compensate" for these deaths. In other words, in the hope of ensuring that the number of children they want will survive, they have more children than they would have otherwise.

POLICY AND PROGRAM BRIEFS

Four policy and program briefs follow. The first examines "kangaroo mother care" as a low-cost, low-tech way in which families can help to care for low birthweight babies who are otherwise stable and healthy. The same brief examines efforts to develop low-cost, low-tech incubators for babies who are low birthweight but for whom kangaroo mother care is unlikely to be effective. The second and third briefs examine efforts to develop and then disseminate pneumococcal and rotavirus vaccines in low- and middle-income countries. The last brief discusses Calcutta Kids. This is a small NGO that was started by an American not long after he finished university, and that aims to improve the health of mothers and children in a slum in Kolkata, India.

Caring for Underweight Babies in Low Resource Settings

Two of the best indicators of infant health and survival are birthweight and period of gestation at delivery. Low birthweight is defined as less than 2500 grams,[25] and a preterm delivery is a live birth before 37 weeks of completed gestation.[26] For a variety of social, economic, and nutritional reasons, women in poor and marginalized communities are more likely to have low birthweight and premature babies than are other women.[27] This is especially important, because complications of low birthweight or prematurity are one of the three leading causes of death of the almost 4 million newborn babies that die each year.[28]

A major cause of neonatal morbidity and mortality in low birthweight and premature infants is hypothermia, defined as body temperature below 36.5 degrees Celsius (97.7 degrees Fahrenheit). This stems from heat loss, to which babies are more susceptible than adults. Preventing heat loss in neonates, especially those who are low birthweight and preterm, is crucial to saving infant lives in low-income countries.[29] Kangaroo mother care and the use of neonatal incubators, detailed in the following sections, are two methods of preventing heat loss and caring for underweight babies. Each approach can be effective, depending on the circumstances.

Kangaroo Mother Care for Low Birthweight Babies in Indonesia

Low birthweight and premature babies remain a persistent problem in Indonesia. According to the Indonesian Hospitals Association, about 30 to 40 percent of all babies born each year are premature.[30]

Conventional neonatal care for low birthweight babies generally involves keeping the infant in an incubator to regulate temperature and air quality. However, there are insufficient incubator services for such infants. Moreover, infant care in an incubator in Indonesia costs about the equivalent of $42 per day,[30] which is more than Indonesia's most marginalized families, who are most at risk for low birthweight and prematurity, can afford to pay.

Although the smallest preterm infants may need prolonged and intensive medical care, kangaroo mother care (KMC) is increasingly proposed as an alternative to conventional neonatal care for premature and low birthweight infants in low- and middle-income countries.[31]

KMC involves skin-to-skin contact between a mother and her newborn, frequent and exclusive or nearly exclusive breastfeeding, and early discharge from the hospital.[31] KMC is a natural and free way to care for infants that has numerous benefits for low birthweight and premature babies. KMC can meet a baby's needs for warmth, breastfeeding, stimulation, safety, and affection.[27] First, the baby, wearing only a diaper, is kept warm through contact with the mother's skin. Second, the skin-to-skin contact between the mother and baby enhances their psychological bond, which improves health and development. Third, the baby can nurse "on-demand," which helps low birthweight babies to gain weight, among other benefits, such as protection from infection.[30] KMC should be continued at least until the baby's health is stable and the baby weighs 1.8 kilograms (4 pounds).[30] KMC can be started at a health facility and continued at home, with proper follow-up and support.[27]

In the case of a baby who is healthy, despite being preterm or low birthweight, KMC could represent a best option for survival in resource-poor communities with limited access to incubators and limited means to pay for such services.[27]

Low Cost Neonatal Incubators in Indonesia

Unfortunately, KMC can only be used effectively when low birthweight or preterm babies are "stable," meaning they are healthy and do not have any underlying health conditions. In addition, and more obviously, KMC is useless if the mother has died during childbirth, or is severely ill.[32]

For newborns in such critical health or without a mother who can engage in KMC, the use of incubators is essential for regulating body temperature. Incubators work in concert with other care for newborns, helping them reach a healthy enough state that they can participate in KMC, which doesn't require any technology.[32]

The incubators produced in high-income countries are often too expensive and hard to maintain in low-income settings. In addition, better-off countries sometimes donate incubators to healthcare facilities in low-income countries. However, if the incubator has mechanical difficulties and does not work properly, healthcare settings in low-income countries often lack the technical expertise and parts necessary to fix them.

To overcome these constraints, the Center for Integration of Medical and Innovative Technology (CIMIT) has invested in the development of an incubator that addresses the challenges faced in low-resource settings.[29] CIMIT is a consortium of Harvard University teaching hospitals, the Massachusetts Institute of Technology, Boston University, and Draper Laboratories, among others.

The incubator developed by CIMIT is designed to provide highly functional and sustainable technology even in low-income countries. The incubator is built with all of its replaceable parts from a Toyota 4Runner, a car that is commonly used in such countries. The availability and accessibility of parts for these cars lowers barriers to building and repairing the incubators. In addition, there are already personnel with expertise in handling these car parts who could, therefore, maintain and repair the incubators.

The incubator is also designed to accommodate the conditions of healthcare facilities in low-income countries, made possible through observations by designers in hospitals in Bangladesh, India, Indonesia, and Nepal, as well as Boston's leading hospitals. However, the design takes account of inputs not only from engineers, but also from end-users in low- and middle-income settings, including healthcare practitioners and family members of sick newborns. The incubator, for example, is designed so that two women can carry it up and down stairs, to account for the fact that healthcare facilities often have broken elevators, or none at all. The incubator also includes a built-in mechanism to retain heat in the case of power outage.

Thus far, three incubator prototypes have been developed. Evaluation of their use has shown that it will be important to carefully assess how many people need to be trained in different settings to operate the incubators and then to develop appropriate training plans for them.

The developers of the incubators are now seeking funding to develop two additional prototypes, which will allow them to develop a production model. As they seek to develop this model, they will have to address, however, a number of remaining design, regulatory, and business issues.

The demand for facility-based deliveries is rising in low-income countries. The demand for working incubators in order to save the lives of newborns in critical conditions will rise with this increase. Low-cost, effective incubators for use in low-income countries could be cost-effective and life-saving investments and an effective complement to kangaroo mother care.

The Pneumococcal Vaccine

Pneumonia is the leading cause of death of children in developing countries. More than 1.6 million children die from pneumonia each year. Yet only half of these children receive appropriate medical care. Pneumococcus, the bacterium that causes pneumonia, is responsible for about half of these deaths and also causes sepsis, meningitis, and otitis media (middle ear infections). In low- and middle-income countries, children under 5 years of age present the highest risk for infection. Pneumonia is associated with 18 percent of all deaths of children under 5 globally, with the highest number of deaths occurring in Africa and Asia.[1] In addition, pneumococcus is the most common bacterial disease among HIV-positive children. Vaccines are a basic and essential component in the global fight against pneumococcal diseases.[33]

Several challenges are associated with the development and use of pneumococcal vaccines. Current vaccines for pneumococcus are effective, but only cover a few of more than 90 serotypes. In addition, these vaccines are extremely expensive and difficult to manufacture. Due to their high cost, the vaccines are unaffordable for many low- and middle-income countries and do not reach the children who need them most. More than 98 percent of pneumonia deaths occur in low- and middle-income countries. Out of the low-income countries, only Rwanda and Gambia have been able to successfully integrate the pneumococcal vaccine into their immunization programs.[34]

A second challenge concerns the widespread use of antibiotics to treat pneumonia and other related diseases. Although antibiotics are an effective form of treatment, in principle, drug-resistant strains of pneumococcus are becoming more common. This makes the development and global dissemination of an effective vaccine even more important, because drug resistance increases the difficulty and costs associated with treating pneumonia.[33]

To address these issues, organizations such as the Program for Appropriate Technology in Health (PATH) and the Global Alliance for Vaccines and Immunisation (GAVI) are working to secure sustainable financing and pricing for pneumococcal vaccines so that more countries are able to immunize a greater number of children at a lower cost. Accomplishing this goal requires a multipronged approach that engages developing countries, the international community, and pharmaceutical manufacturers. Rapid distribution of the vaccine requires a commitment on the part of developing countries to introduce the vaccine, international donors to finance it, and manufacturers to produce the necessary number of doses. New vaccines that are more affordable and therefore provide broader coverage are also needed.[33]

Pneumococcal conjugate vaccines are clinically proven to be safe and effective in both developed and developing countries. In 2000, the U.S. pharmaceutical company Wyeth launched Prevnar, a seven-serotype conjugate vaccine that was subsequently licensed in over 75 countries. Synflorix and Prevnar 13 Valent, two additional pediatric vaccines, provide broader protection against 10 and 13 serotypes, respectively.

In clinical trials, these latter two vaccines were shown to provide 80 percent protection against pneumococcal diseases, with fewer regional disparities than Prevnar. PATH is currently formulating common protein vaccines that will provide protection against more than 90 pneumococcus serotypes. Additionally, it has collaborated with other organizations to develop an inactive whole-cell vaccine, composed of suspensions of dead bacteria, that could be extremely effective and affordable. PATH also supports the development of new conjugate vaccines that are more affordable and contain serotypes common in developing countries.[35]

In the countries where they have been tested, pneumococcal conjugate vaccines have had positive effects on morbidity and mortality. Thirty million children globally have been safely and effectively vaccinated with the seven-valent vaccine. In a clinical trial in the Gambia, 7.4 deaths were prevented for every 1000 children vaccinated. The conjugate vaccine was also extremely effective in preventing pneumococcal disease in children with HIV living in areas with endemic malaria. Hospitalization was reduced by 15 percent as a result of the vaccine, and the costs for caring for disabled survivors decreased substantially as well. Meningitis was prevented in over 85 percent of cases and otitis media occurrence was reduced by 20 percent. Due to the absence of disease, vaccinated children were able to attend school more often than unvaccinated children and, therefore, had better educational outcomes.[34]

Despite promising scientific advances and an increased commitment to address pneumonia in low- and middle-income countries, a number of barriers remain in the dissemination of pneumococcal vaccines. After a vaccine is proven safe and effective, it has generally taken 15 to 20 years for it to be widely distributed among poor populations in low- and middle-income countries. This cycle is triggered by a limited initial supply of the vaccine, which leads to higher prices and an uncertain demand. Uncertain demand leads to low capacity investment in the manufacturing cycle, which eventually leads to delays in distribution of the vaccine. To break this cycle, GAVI has funded the Pneumococcal Accelerated Development and Introduction Plan (pneumo-ADIP), which works to speed up the introduction of a vaccine in low- and middle-income countries after it is proven safe and effective. Without this program, developing countries might have limited access to the vaccine for another 5 to 10 years.[36] Through innovative programs and partnerships, effective planning, and sufficient financing, it is estimated that pneumoADIP will help to prevent 3.6 million deaths from pneumococcal diseases by 2025.[37]

Financing the vaccine is a second major challenge. GAVI estimates that $2.6 billion in additional funding is needed to manufacture new vaccines for pneumonia and rotavirus, one of the leading causes of diarrhea, and provide them to the countries that are most in need. GAVI is already working to provide a level of financial sustainability through the creation of country-owned programs and fixed pricing on pneumococcal vaccines. Countries eligible for GAVI funding can currently access the vaccine at the price of $7 a dose, compared to $70 a dose in the U.S. market. With support from WHO and UNICEF, GAVI plans to introduce new and existing pneumococcal vaccines in more than 40 low- and middle-income countries by 2015. This achievement will help to assuage concerns voiced by developing countries concerning the high price tag of new vaccines.[36] A policy and program brief elaborating on the financing of vaccines is included in Chapter 15.

The Rotavirus Vaccine

Diarrhea is the second largest of killer of children in low-income countries after pneumonia. Nearly 1.3 million children die from diarrhea each year.[1] Rotavirus, one of the most common and deadliest forms of diarrhea, accounts for more than one third of these deaths and 2 million hospitalizations per year. Although nearly every child in the world will contract rotavirus before the age of 5, 85 percent of the related deaths occur in low-income countries in Africa and Asia. Due to the severity of the disease, common methods for preventing diarrhea are not sufficient to stop the spread of rotavirus. The introduction and widespread dissemination of vaccines are the best hope for preventing the spread of the disease and decreasing childhood mortality associated with rotavirus.[38]

Although two rotavirus vaccines are available, they are not yet widely used in low-income countries. Both PATH, a U.S.-based NGO, and the Global Alliance for Vaccines and Immunisation (GAVI) are working to maximize the availability of Merck's RotaTeq and GlaskoSmithKline's RotaRix in low- and middle-income countries, by making them more affordable, as discussed further in Chapter 16. Among low- and middle-income countries, Brazil, El Salvador, Mexico, Panama, and Venezuela have introduced RotaRix, and RotaTeq is now available in Nicaragua. In clinical trials, RotaRix and RotaTeq reduced all cases of rotavirus by 76 percent and 73 percent, respectively, and were safe.[39] Based on significant reductions in morbidity and mortality resulting from the introduction of these vaccines, WHO now recommends that all infants be vaccinated for rotavirus.[40]

In the countries where it has been introduced, the rotavirus vaccine has had a large public health impact. During clinical trials in Africa and Asia, vaccination resulted in a 50 percent reduction of rotavirus incidence among children vaccinated during their first year of life. In another study, 2000 infants were vaccinated in Bangladesh and Vietnam. After 2 years of follow-up, it was estimated that the vaccine reduced rotavirus cases by 48.3 percent, compared to what would have been the case without vaccination.[38]

These clinical trials demonstrate that tens of thousands of lives could be saved in these regions alone if the vaccines were widely available. Similar conclusions were drawn from a clinical trial conducted in Mexico. In 2009, 3 years after RotaRix was introduced, mortality associated with rotavirus dropped in Mexico by 65 percent in children less than 2 years of age. In addition, there was a substantial reduction in hospitalization and the costs related to treatment and care. Shortly after RotaTeq became available in Nicaragua, there was a 60 percent decrease in rotavirus incidence and a 50 percent decrease in hospitalizations. The vaccine is likely to benefit unvaccinated children as well, through the reduction of circulating infections.[38]

PATH is working with others to encourage the development of additional rotavirus vaccines. The availability of new vaccines would create greater market competition, which should lower the price of existing vaccines and increase the likelihood that they will reach children in low-income countries.

In this light, PATH has developed a shared technology platform. This database provides information on methodologies, technology, material, and training for new rotavirus vaccine manufacturers. In addition, PATH is currently collaborating with Bharat Biotech International Ltd. (BBIL) and Shantha Biotechnics Ltd. based in India and China, respectively, to develop safe and affordable rotavirus vaccines that have proven efficacy in low- and middle-income countries. In clinical trials, vaccines from both companies were demonstrated to be safe, well-tolerated, and noninterfering with other vaccines.[41] PATH is also assisting the Children's Research Institute in Australia with clinical trials for a third candidate.

There are, however, a number of constraints to the successful development and use of newer rotavirus vaccines in low- and middle-income countries. First, any vaccine has to be effective against a number of rotavirus serotypes if it is to be effective in low- and middle-income countries.[42] Second, rotavirus vaccines are extremely expensive and have not been produced in the quantities needed to satisfy country demand. Even if countries are willing to introduce the vaccine, it is often very difficult to obtain the necessary number of doses at an affordable price. Third, new vaccines must have minimal risk of harmful side effects. The first rotavirus vaccine, Rotashield, had an elevated risk of intussusception—the reverse telescoping of one part of the intestine to the other—and was withdrawn from the market.[43]

In addition, a number of other challenges must be addressed if rotavirus vaccines are to be integrated into the immunization programs of all low- and middle-income countries. First, there must be sufficient financing for the vaccines. GAVI has already launched a campaign to urge donors to provide funding to support introduction of rotavirus vaccines.[44] Through this campaign, it hopes to introduce the rotavirus vaccines in 44 low-income countries by 2015. To achieve this goal, manufacturers must also be willing to produce the vaccines in the quantities demanded. Although current levels of production are sufficient, demand will quickly outstrip the supply as more countries begin to introduce the vaccine over the next 10 to 15 years. Second, the introduction of new and existing vaccines in low- and middle-income countries must be incorporated into a broader rotavirus prevention strategy. This strategy should also encompass a set of interventions to prevent many of the causes of diarrheal transmission, such as access to clean water, improved hygiene and sanitation, increased availability of oral rehydration solution, and vitamin A and zinc supplementation.[38] Measures the international community is taking to enhance vaccine supply and help make vaccines more affordable are discussed further in Chapter 16.

Calcutta Kids

Calcutta Kids is a nonprofit organization located in Howrah, India. This is an area adjacent to the city of Kolkata. Calcutta Kids was founded in 2004 by a young American named Noah Levinson, not long after he finished his university studies. The organization's underlying goal is to prevent childhood illness.[45] It seeks to achieve this goal by "initiating community-based programs that advance the promotion and delivery of good health care, medical advocacy, and health education."[46]

The main program of Calcutta Kids is its Maternal and Young Child Health Initiative (MYCHI), which was started in late 2005. The goal of the MYCHI is to "increase health during pregnancy, reduce maternal mortality, improve birth weights, and ensure healthy brain and immune system development."[45]

Community health workers (CHWs), local women who are trained and hired by Calcutta Kids, are instrumental in trying to accomplish these goals. CHWs visit homes of newly married couples and pregnant women starting in the prenatal period, continuing until the child is 3 years old. The CHW tries to ensure that the mother receives proper prenatal care and educates her about the necessity of such care, birth spacing, proper nutrition, including use of iron tablets, getting plenty of rest, and other common pregnancy-related problems.[47] In addition, Calcutta Kids provides pregnant women with three prenatal checkups with a doctor, tetanus shots, and iron-folate tablets.[48]

In addition to education on maternal health, pregnant women are also counseled by CHWs about crucial practices for improving child health, including breastfeeding, oral rehydration therapy, and immunization. CHWs also visit homes to make sure children have received immunizations and micronutrient supplementation.[47]

To aid in its goal of reducing maternal mortality, Calcutta Kids was subsidizing until recently 75 percent of the costs for delivery of "high-risk" pregnancies in a nearby healthcare facility. CHWs play a role in identifying women that qualify for this care.[48] The subsidy was meant to encourage women at high risk to give birth in hospitals, even if they are poor and even if they have no tradition of having a hospital delivery. The subsidy has now been dropped, since a new government program includes incentives for hospital-based delivery.

With the goal of improving nutritional status and maintaining healthy weight for children under 3, the organization's Growth Monitoring Promotion program is integral to the MYCHI. Children under 3 are weighed at a camp each month and monitored for healthy weight increase. If a child is underweight, parents are counseled on proper nutrition. The children who are severely undernourished are invited to a daily lunch of rice, milk, and banana.[49] There is also a graduation ceremony at the end of the maternal and child health camps, where the mothers are applauded for their efforts and invited to speak in front of the group. These mothers are used as "positive deviants" and help prove to other community members that Calcutta Kids advice is effective.

To promote health education, Calcutta Kids hosts community meetings during which CHWs discuss a certain health topic with a group of women living in the slums. Past topics have included diarrheal disease, worm infestation, acute respiratory infections, skin disease, infant and child care, self-care, contraceptive use and management, and hygiene practices.[50]

Calcutta Kids also sponsors a weekly health camp in the community center in the Fakir Bagan Slum of Kolkata, the same area where most home visits are conducted. The health camp offers subsidized health care for pregnant women and children under 3 who cannot afford to pay for private care. Between 40 to 60 patients are seen by the doctor each week.[51] In addition, a doctor and CHW complete follow-up visits in patients' homes to ensure that treatment regimens are completed. Practices for preventing future illness are also discussed with patients.[48] Between 2002 and 2004, over 7000 medical examinations were conducted in the weekly health camp.[45]

Calcutta Kids is expanding its work to combat child undernutrition by establishing the Calcutta Kids Diarrhea Treatment Center, funded by a $40,000 grant from the World Bank in the fall of 2009, which Calcutta Kids received as a prize in the Development Marketplace competition. In addition to providing diarrheal disease treatment to young children by CHWs, the center will also counsel mothers on prevention and curing practices for diarrheal disease.[52]

Calcutta Kids also recently created a health insurance scheme for the slum dwellers currently using its healthcare services. After working with groups in the local community to devise a feasible insurance plan, over 1000 individuals were insured by late 2009. Challenges to introducing insurance plans remain, however, including families' inability to pay for premiums.[52] Some concerns about the costs of insurance have recently been alleviated by allowing families to pay their insurance premiums monthly, instead of all at once, and as part of their cell phone bills, since even among the poor, cell phone usage is now high.

Calcutta Kids' emphasis on prevention through home visits to women in the pre- and postnatal period has shown some successes. The birthweight of babies born to women who received counseling from Calcutta Kids increased from an average of 1.8 kilograms (4 pounds) in 2005 to an average of 2.8 kilograms (6.2 pounds) in 2008. Additionally, nearly 80 percent of babies born in 2007 were not considered low birthweight because they were all above 2.5 kilograms (5.5 pounds).[45]

Calcutta Kids is funded primarily by donations from private individuals.[53] In 2009, the organization introduced the Health Efforts Assure Life (HEAL) initiative in which individuals can donate $250 to sponsor Calcutta Kids' services to a specific pregnant mother and her child.[54] Calcutta Kids has also received some grants from foundations, such as the one it received from the Wasyl Kotys Memorial Fund to support the mobile clinics.[51]

CASE STUDIES

Some of the important progress made so far in reducing the burden of disease in children has been associated with the control of diarrheal disease, supplementing children with vitamin A, and the spread of immunization programs. The following three cases look at successful examples in each of these areas that were affordable, effective, and had a substantial impact on reducing morbidity and mortality in young children. You can read about each of these cases in greater detail in *Case Studies in Global Health: Millions Saved*. The case on diarrheal disease in Egypt complements the case on diarrhea in Bangladesh that was featured in Chapter 5. The case on vitamin A in Nepal complements the brief or micronutrients in Nepal that was included in Chapter 8.

Preventing Diarrheal Deaths in Egypt

Background

About 20 percent of child deaths worldwide are due to complications from diarrheal disease, mostly among children younger than 2 years old. Bacteria, protozoa, and viruses cause diarrhea, which can quickly become deadly as the body expels electrolytes and water and becomes dehydrated. Intravenous infusions can help rehydrate patients in hospitals, and some drugs can help stop the diarrhea. However, these infusions are relatively costly, invasive, and difficult to carry out in many low-income environments.

In the 1960s, oral rehydration therapy (ORT) was developed in Bangladesh and India. As discussed earlier, ORT is a simple solution of water, sugar, and salt that was found to be as effective in stopping dehydration as expensive intravenous therapy. In 1970, it was invaluable in saving lives of many of the millions of refugees camped along the Bangladesh and India borders when cholera struck during a war between Bangladesh and Pakistan. In 1972, the World Health Organization declared ORT the world's standard treatment for diarrhea.

Intervention

In the 1970s in Egypt, infant mortality was as high as 100 per 1000 live births. Diarrheal disease caused at least half of all infant deaths in Egypt in 1977 when ORT was introduced into clinics and pharmacies. Initially there was little take-up of the newly available intervention. However, it was realized that physicians and mothers could play a key role in promoting the program, and they were trained to effectively use ORT. The use of ORT rose dramatically, and in pilot areas where training was conducted, diarrhea-related mortality declined by 45 percent.[55]

Based on the impact demonstrated in the pilot areas, a nationwide campaign was launched. In 1981, the National Control of Diarrheal Disease Project (NCDDP) was established in partnership with the private sector, professional societies, and international organizations such as WHO and UNICEF. The program had four components. First, there was product design and branding. ORT packets were distributed in a size that Egyptian mothers considered suitable for a child's drink. Second, production and distribution of an uninterrupted supply of ORT by public and private entities was subsidized by UNICEF and NCDDP. The public sector received ORT through a network of distribution centers, including the private homes of community leaders in remote rural areas. Third, private sector distributors were given incentives to sell ORT rather than antidiarrheal drugs. Lastly, thousands of health workers were trained to teach mothers about ORT, and a national media campaign took advantage of the new TV service to expand access to knowledge about ORT. By 1984, the use of ORT to manage cases of child diarrhea had reached 60 percent.[56]

Impact

Between 1982 and 1987, overall infant mortality dropped by 36 percent and child mortality dropped by 43 percent. Diarrhea mortality fell by 82 percent among infants and by 62 percent among children during the same period. Challenges remained, however, despite the success: private physicians were slow to convert to ORT and a large number of antidiarrheal drugs continued to be sold.[55,56]

Costs and Benefits

The average cost per child treated with ORT was estimated at only $6. The cost per death averted was between $100 and $200. The program cost a total of $43 million, of which $17 million came from Egypt and $26 million came from USAID. UNICEF and WHO provided technical support to the program.[56]

Lessons Learned

Research was the key to the success of Egypt's diarrhea control program. Anthropological and market research about cultural practices and consumer preferences shaped the communication program, product design, and branding. Epidemiological and clinical research led to the appropriate composition of the ORT product. It also contributed to a better understanding of risk factors and kept the medical community engaged in the issue of ORT. Data from ongoing project evaluation and from independent, external evaluations were used continuously to guide decision making. Different approaches were regularly piloted and the program was flexible and open to change as new, effective strategies were identified to ensure continued success of the program.

Reducing Child Mortality in Nepal Through Vitamin A

Background

As discussed in Chapter 8, vitamin A deficiency is a leading determinant of child mortality in low- and middle-income countries. Vitamin A deficiency compromises the immune systems of nearly 40 percent of the developing world's children and leads to the deaths of approximately 1 million young children each year. Additionally, it contributes to 16 percent of the global burden of disease caused by malaria, 18 percent of the global burden of diarrheal disease, and a significant proportion of the acute respiratory infections and measles.[57]

Vitamin A deficiency has been especially important in Nepal, with 2–13 percent of preschool-aged children experiencing xerophthalmia, a form of blindness. Economic and geographic barriers help to explain this high prevalence rate. First, difficult terrain makes it hard to grow or access the types of food that supply vitamin A. Second, 38 percent of the Nepali population lives in absolute poverty, many of whom are socially excluded lower caste families who frequently lack the means to pay for nutritious foods.

Intervention

Prior to the late 1980s, it was widely held that micronutrient deficiencies were a result of diarrhea and other infant illnesses, rather than a cause of them. Yet, as early as the 1970s, Alfred Sommer noticed in conjunction with studies in Indonesia that vitamin A deficiency appeared to be linked with child death. A later randomized controlled trial conducted in Nepal by Keith West and Alfred Sommer indicated that periodic vitamin A delivery could reduce mortality in children ages 6 to 60 months by as much as 30 percent.[58]

In light of these research findings and Nepal's excessive infant mortality rate, the Nepalese Ministry of Health initiated a plan of action on vitamin A in 1992. The Ministry worked closely with other government agencies and NGOs to develop a pilot program to deliver vitamin A capsules throughout Nepal. A technical assistance group was created to assist the health ministry in running the program. His Majesty, the King of Nepal, also demonstrated long-term commitment to this effort by incorporating Nepal's National Vitamin A Program into the Ten Year National Program of Action.

This program aimed to reduce child morbidity and mortality by prophylactic supplementation of high dose vitamin A capsules to children 6 to 60 months of age, twice each year;

the treatment of xerophthalmia, severe malnutrition, and prolonged diarrhea; and the promotion of behavior change to increase dietary intake of vitamin A and promote exclusive breastfeeding for the first 6 months of a baby's life.

The action plan on vitamin A focused on expanding the intervention in phases as Nepal's administrative capacity for the program was strengthened. The program was expanded to 32 priority districts at a rate of 8 districts per year over 4 years. From 1993 to 2001, the program was brought to Nepal's remaining 43 districts. Children and new mothers in districts where the National Vitamin A Program was not yet established received one dose of vitamin A as part of national immunization campaigns. Once the National Vitamin A Program was operating in their district, the children received vitamin A supplementation twice a year.

Nepal's public health system faced severe problems at the time the vitamin A program was developed, from low utilization rates by people who had no confidence in the system to absenteeism by health workers. Consequently, the vitamin A intervention was revised to build upon and improve the existing networks of female community health volunteers (FCHVs) who helped deliver primary health care and family planning services to the villages of Nepal. Before the intervention, there were 24,000 FCHVs throughout 58 districts. However, many were not respected in their communities and had little incentive to remain committed to volunteering. The leader of the program's technical assistance group, Ram Shrestha, changed the way FCHVs were viewed by communities and themselves by focusing on notions of "Respect, Recognition, and Opportunity." Shrestha challenged deeply rooted gender biases by giving women responsibilities valued by their families and communities and the opportunity to make a difference.

A few years later, the number of FCHVs had more than doubled to 49,000 strong, and they were able to reach 3.7 million children twice a year with vitamin A capsules. By directly administering the capsules, the FCHVs served as a critical bridge between the public health sector and the community. Families were urged to bring their children to the distribution site, and many government sectors began to integrate messages about the importance of vitamin A into their programs.

Impact

An evaluation of the program indicated that under-5 mortality decreased by almost 48 deaths per 1000 births, on average. Higher literacy rates among women, improved weight and nutritional status of children, and better vaccination rates were also associated with success. About 134,000 deaths were averted between mid-1995 and mid-2000 as a result of Nepal's Vitamin A Program.[59] Although it took nearly 8 years to achieve nationwide distribution, program coverage never dropped below 90 percent in districts, once they were covered.

Costs and Benefits

Compared to other micronutrient supplement programs, which can cost up to about $5 per child,[60] the vitamin A supplement program in Nepal was a relatively inexpensive approach to ease the burden of a national problem. The cost of the program per child covered was approximately $0.81 to $1.09 for a child receiving one capsule and $0.68 to $1.65 for a child receiving two capsules of vitamin A.[61] Additionally, given the 7500 lives saved annually, the expanded program in 2000 was estimated to cost $345 per death averted or $11 to $12 per DALY averted.[62]

Lessons Learned

The success of Nepal's vitamin A supplementation program demonstrates how a technical innovation, when paired with an equally innovative operational plan, can result in a major population impact. Rather than trying to restructure the health system to accommodate the vitamin A program, Shrestha adapted the vitamin A program to the preexisting network of FCHVs and then refined it in a way that it could be successful. This approach also reinforced a multi-sectoral effort by involving the government, NGOs, and communities. Other key factors associated with this successful effort were partnership building, regular monitoring of quality, straightforward and effective public messages, and clarity of objectives and operational strategy. These lessons are all the more important given that this successful effort took place in a very poor country with extremely weak governance and poor administrative capacity.

Eliminating Polio in Latin America and the Caribbean

Background

Poliomyelitis is caused by the intestinal poliovirus, which enters through the nose or mouth and multiplies in the lymph nodes. Within days, an otherwise healthy person can become paralyzed for life or possibly not survive the disease. In 1952, Dr. Jonas Salk discovered the inactivated polio vaccine. Mass immunizations between 1955 and 1961 led to a 90 percent drop in infections in the Western Hemisphere.[63] Ten years later, in 1962, Dr. Albert Sabin developed an oral polio vaccine that cost less, was easier to administer, and reduced the multiplication of the virus in the intestine.

The new oral polio vaccine became part of a package of six childhood vaccines included in an Expanded Program on Immunization (EPI) launched by WHO in 1977. Latin America adopted the Expanded Program on Immunization in 1977, and the coverage of oral polio vaccine reached 80 percent within just 7 years. Between 1975 and 1981, the incidence of polio was nearly halved and the number of countries reporting polio cases dropped from 19 to 11.[64]

Intervention

Encouraged by the remarkable progress against polio, the Pan American Health Organization (PAHO) launched a program to eradicate polio from Latin America and the Caribbean. Many international organizations joined together in the program and regional and country-level Inter-Agency Coordinating Committees were established to oversee the program. Thousands of health workers, managers, and technicians were trained to implement the strategy for the eradication of polio, which included reaching every child with oral polio vaccination, identification of new polio cases, and aggressive control of any outbreaks. If polio was to be eradicated, then the campaign against it would build on the lessons learned from the smallpox eradication campaign.[65]

Impact

The last case of polio in the Latin America and the Caribbean region was reported in Peru in 1991. Polio reemerged briefly in the year 2000 when 20 vaccine-associated cases were reported in Haiti and the Dominican Republic, but no cases have been reported since the year 2000.

Costs and Benefits

The polio campaign cost $120 million in its first 5 years—$74 million from national sources and $46 million from international donors—and $10 million annually from donor sources thereafter. Taking into account the costs of treating polio and its disabling consequences, the investment paid for itself in only 15 years.[66] The program also generated vast improvements in the region's health infrastructure, and it advanced overall goals for immunization.

Lessons learned

The success of eliminating polio from Latin America and the Caribbean in only 6 years was a result of exemplary political commitment, interagency and regional coordination, and tremendous social and community mobilization. The reemergence of polio in the year 2000 alerted the region to the need for continued vaccination and surveillance. The success in Latin America and the Caribbean prompted a global effort to eradicate polio that was launched in 1998.[67]

The Global Polio Eradication Initiative is an international partnership spearheaded by national governments, WHO, Rotary International, the U.S. Centers for Disease Control and Prevention, and UNICEF. The importance of building trust with local leaders and working closely with communities that was learned in the polio efforts in the Americas is one of many lessons that is being put to good use in the global polio eradication initiative.

ADDRESSING KEY CHALLENGES IN CHILD HEALTH

As noted earlier, there has been some important progress in the last 20 years in reducing morbidity and mortality of children younger than 5 years. Despite this progress, the challenges to meeting the MDG on child health and to improving the health of children in low- and middle-income countries remain substantial. First, the progress that has been made has largely been in reducing the rate of death of children between 1 and 5 years. By contrast, very little progress has been made in reducing the death rate of neonates.[14,15] In fact, about 40 percent of the children younger than 5 years who die are now in their first 28 days of life. Second, progress in reducing child deaths has remained insufficient in the two regions with the highest rate of such deaths—sub-Saharan Africa and South Asia.

In addition, many interventions that are known to be low cost and effective at reducing morbidity and mortality in young children are not being implemented where they are needed most. A large number of births in low-income countries take place without the help of a skilled birth attendant who can assist the mother and, for example, resuscitate the baby if needed. Many families still do not use ORT when their child gets diarrhea. Too often, the pneumonia that kills young children is not diagnosed or treated in a timely way. Insecticide-treated bed nets, which are known to reduce the transmission of malaria, are still not as widely used as they should be. There are also major gaps in the early diagnosis and appropriate treatment of malaria in children.

The experience of high-income countries in reducing neonatal deaths shows that a large proportion of neonatal deaths in the low- and middle-income countries can be avoided with simple technologies that could be effectively implemented in low-income settings.[19] In fact, almost two thirds of the child deaths that occur every year could be prevented by the effective implementation of measures such as these, that are both low cost and effective.[68]

What can be done to increase the uptake of these approaches, especially in South Asia and sub-Saharan Africa? What can be done to decrease as quickly as possible the rate of neonatal deaths, again, largely in these two regions? Can measures be taken that will help children from low-income families with little education die as rarely as children from better-off and better-educated families?[69] The following section examines some of what has been learned about cost-effective interventions to prevent child deaths and how these efforts can be scaled up more rapidly. Some of the comments will be organized around the life cycle. Others will be organized by type of intervention. Additional comments will be made about how such interventions might be put into place most rapidly and effectively.

Critical Child Health Interventions

The Mother and Mother-to-Be

As you have read repeatedly, an extremely important factor in determining the health of the newborn and young child is the health and nutritional status of the mother. The chapters on nutrition and on women's health have commented at length on measures that can be taken to ensure that women are getting enough calories and that they are not deficient in key micronutrients. However, it is also very important to pregnancy outcomes that pregnant women not suffer from malaria. Rather, they should be treated appropriately for malaria, as will be discussed in detail in the next chapter.

The importance of delaying marriage and first birth, as a way to promote healthier pregnancies and births, has also been noted. Birth spacing and reducing total fertility would also encourage healthier mothers and babies.

You have also read about the importance of having a skilled attendant at delivery. Proper monitoring of labor and the fetus can improve pregnancy and birth outcomes. In addition, if the labor is complicated, then access to emergency obstetric care can reduce risks to both mother and child. Preventing infection is also important to the mother and child. Ensuring that the mother is vaccinated against tetanus is also critical to the prospects for child survival.[70] Early postnatal visits can also reduce neonatal deaths.[14]

A substantial number of pregnant women are infected with HIV in parts of Central and Southern Africa in particular, as will also be discussed further in the next chapter. If an HIV-infected mother does not breastfeed, then there is a 15–30 percent chance that her child will contract HIV. If the mother breastfeeds her baby for an extended period of time, then the risk of her child becoming infected with HIV increases to 30–45 percent.

Measures to prevent HIV infection among women and mothers-to-be are the most cost-effective ways to ensure that HIV is not transmitted from mothers to their children. However, if a mother is HIV infected, then providing drug therapy to prevent transmission can also be cost-effective.[71] It is critical for countries to continue making progress in the reduction of maternal-to-child transmission, as also discussed further in Chapter 11.

The Newborn

As discussed earlier, most child deaths in the first month of life will be from the complications of prematurity, asphyxia, or sepsis. Prematurity, infection, and asphyxia are also the leading causes of death in the first week of life and infections are the leading cause of death in the 3 weeks after that.[17] A number of cost-effective measures can be taken to address these problems. They focus on: essential newborn care for all newborns, extra care for small babies, and emergency care, and are summarized in Table 10-5.[72] Low-income countries do not need to adopt expensive, high-technology solutions to immediately reduce their neonatal death rates.

In terms of essential care of newborns, skilled attendance at delivery is crucial to save both newborn lives and the lives of mothers. It is imperative for the health of the baby, for example, that the delivery attendant cut the umbilical cord in a hygienic manner and practice other infection controls. In addition, the baby needs to be kept warm and not bathed for the first 24 hours. The attendant should also be trained and have the equipment needed to resuscitate the baby if necessary, and efforts are underway for that to be done in the simplest possible way in low-income settings. Attendance at delivery is also an appropriate time for a trained practitioner to counsel the family about exclusive breastfeeding and about how to know the danger signs for threats to the baby's health that require immediate attention, such as pneumonia.[72]

Some babies need extra care. If the baby is born prematurely or of low birthweight, then it is especially important that the baby be kept warm, fed properly, and that any complications that arise be managed quickly and appropriately. In high-income countries, of course, premature babies would be kept in an incubator. This option, however, rarely exists for the children of poor families in low-income countries, as noted in the policy and program brief on the care of low birthweight babies. However, a study done in India[73] showed that the neonatal mortality rate among babies born between 35 and 37 weeks, or moderately premature babies, was reduced by 87 percent by the provision of special "sleeping bags" to keep the baby warm, coupled with the promotion of breastfeeding and early treatment of infections. Another effort at keeping premature and low birthweight babies warm is "kangaroo mother care," as also discussed earlier in a brief.

Despite these efforts, some babies will become infected and will require emergency care. The question of providing antibiotics to neonates who have infections is a challenging one in many settings. In many places, only physicians are legally allowed to prescribe antibiotics. Yet, physicians may not be accessible, particularly in rural and impoverished settings that will have the highest rates of neonatal mortality. There is some evidence that community health workers can be trained to safely give antibiotics to neonates who have infections that are life threatening.[73,74]

Managing Diarrhea in Infants and Young Children

The second leading killer of infants and young children in low- and middle-income countries is diarrhea. Such deaths are almost completely unnecessary. As you know, there are many reasons why exclusive breastfeeding until children are 6 months of age is so important, and one of them is to avoid diarrhea in settings that are not hygienic. As children move to complementary foods, a number of measures can be taken to reduce their risk of diarrheal disease. The first, of course, is to engage in better personal hygiene and more hygienic food preparation. Second, complementary foods that are fortified can help children meet their requirements for micronutrients.[75] Third, ensuring that children are immunized against measles can help to reduce deaths from diarrhea. It has been estimated, in fact, that measles immunization could eliminate 6–26 percent of diarrheal deaths of children younger than 5 years.[76] As discussed in Chapter 7, improving water supply and sanitation can be very important to reducing diarrhea in children. Unfortunately, the infrastructure to do so can be very expensive, and health benefits flow mostly when communities adopt safer water and sanitation systems, rather than just having them adopted by individual families.[70]

When young children do get diarrhea that is not of the types that require antibiotics, two very cost-effective measures that can be taken to manage the diarrhea. First is the use at home of ORT, as modeled in the cases on Bangladesh and Egypt about which you read earlier. Second is supplementation with zinc, because such supplements have been shown to reduce the duration and severity of diarrhea, as discussed in Chapter 8 on nutrition.[1]

Immunization

In 1974, WHO launched the Expanded Program on Immunization (EPI), which promoted worldwide a package of six basic vaccines for children. "Vaccination against childhood communicable diseases through the Expanded Program on

TABLE 10-5 Essential Interventions for Newborn Care

Essential Newborn Care

Early and exclusive breastfeeding

Warmth provision and avoidance of bathing during first 24 hours

Infection control, including cord care and hygiene

Postpartum vitamin A provided to mothers

Eye antimicrobial to prevent ophthalmia, inflammation of the eye, or conjunctiva

Information and counseling for home care and emergency preparedness

Extra Care for Small Babies

Extra attention to warmth, feeding support, and early identification and management of complications

Kangaroo mother care

Vitamin K injection

Emergency Care

Providing supportive care for severe infections, neonatal encephalopathy (brain disease), severe jaundice or bleeding, and neonatal tetanus

Source: Adapted with permission from Lawn JE, Zupan J, Begkoyian G, Knippenberg R. Newborn survival. In: Jamison DT, Breman JG, Measham A, et al., eds. *Disease Control Priorities in Developing Countries.* 2nd ed. Washington, DC and New York: The World Bank and Oxford University Press; 2006:537.

Immunization is one of the most cost-effective public health interventions available."[77] The "basic" vaccines in immunization programs in low- and middle-income countries include those against diphtheria, pertussis, tetanus, polio, tuberculosis, and measles. There is a standard schedule for giving these immunizations.

There has been significant progress in immunization. It is estimated that in 2001, in the absence of the vaccinations that were carried out, deaths from measles would have risen by 60 percent, deaths from tetanus by about 70 percent, deaths from pertussis by almost 80 percent, and deaths from diphtheria by more than 90 percent.[78] Moreover, since that time there has been continuing progress in improving vaccine coverage and reducing the number of cases of measles and tetanus, and further progress has been made in trying to eradicate polio.

Nonetheless, despite the enormous importance of immunization and the attention paid to it, there are still significant gaps in coverage for even the basic vaccines, particularly in the third immunization for diphtheria, pertussis, and tetanus

(DTP3) and for the measles vaccine. In 2009, for example, coverage of the DTP3 vaccine in the Africa region of WHO was 71 percent and of the measles vaccine was 69 percent. The corresponding rates for the Southeast Asia region were 73 percent for DTP3 and 76 percent for measles.[79]

Moreover, the rates of coverage in some countries continued to lag substantially. In Nigeria, for example, coverage of DTP3 in 2009 was only 42 percent and measles vaccine was only 41 percent. It was 66 percent for DTP3 and 71 percent for measles in India that same year. There are also enormous disparities in immunization coverage within some countries. Coverage rates among the poorest, most rural, least educated, and most marginalized communities for countries in South Asia and sub-Saharan Africa, in particular, are significantly lower than the average rates for those countries.[79]

Over the last decade, as discussed in two of the policy and program briefs, there have been efforts to encourage the use within low- and middle-income countries of three vaccines in addition to the six "basic vaccines": hepatitis B, *Haemophilus influenza* type b (Hib), and most recently rotavirus. There has been good progress in the uptake of the hepatitis B vaccine. Most regions are covering more than 70 percent of the eligible population with that vaccine, except the Southeast Asia region of WHO, in which vaccine coverage was recently only 41 percent. However, the uptake of Hib vaccine has been considerably lower, with little coverage in the Mediterranean and North Africa region of WHO and almost no coverage in the Southeast Asia region.[79]

In 1999, to speed the coverage of vaccines and the dissemination of new vaccines, the international community established the Global Alliance for Vaccines and Immunisation (GAVI). GAVI is examined further in Chapter 15. In recent years, the international community has taken a number of other steps to try to speed the development of safe, effective, and affordable vaccines to meet the health needs of low- and middle-income countries, as also discussed in the policy briefs on the pneumococcal and rotavirus vaccines. Some of those measures are discussed further in Chapters 15 and 16, Cooperation in Global Health and Science and Technology for Global Health.

Community-Based Approaches to Improving Child Health

As you have seen throughout the book, many of the measures that are needed to reduce the burden of illness and death in neonates, infants, and young children have to do with appropriate knowledge and behavior of individuals and families. You have also read that studies that have been done in a number of places show that home- and community-based

approaches to improving health behaviors and providing basic health services with the help of trained members of the community can lead to significant gains in health. In Chapter 5, you read about how a very large share of all primary healthcare services are delivered in Bangladesh by a community-based NGO called BRAC.

The role of the family and community is key to newborn health. Community awareness and the engagement of women's groups have been highly effective in improving the health and survival of newborns. In one project in rural Bolivia, the involvement of local women's groups in raising awareness of maternal, fetal, and neonatal issues led to increased use of prenatal and postnatal health services, more traditional birth assistants at childbirth, and an overall 62 percent reduction of perinatal mortality. In another study in rural Nepal, working with local women's groups was key to motivating increased hygiene and health-seeking behavior, which contributed to a 30 percent reduction in neonatal mortality.[80]

In fact, a family and community-based approach to promoting hygiene, including handwashing and umbilical cord care, keeping the newborn warm, and exclusively breastfeeding, are all important home measures that could lead to an estimated 10–40 percent reduction in neonatal mortality. Home-based supplementary feeding, using a dropper or a cup, is another important measure to ensure the survival of low birthweight babies, who account for 60–80 percent of neonatal deaths.[80]

Table 10-6 is a summary of measures that families can take, even in low-income communities, to protect the health of their young children. You can see in the table the extent to which families, if they had better knowledge of good health practices and community support to engage in them, could promote important reductions in child morbidity and mortality. Low-income people in developing countries are not going to have any quick increase in formal education, income, or social and political voice. Thus, it will be very important to take community-based approaches to help families improve their knowledge and practice of good health behaviors.

Integrated Management of Childhood Illness

The need for working closely with communities has emerged again in recent efforts worldwide to encourage a more integrated approach to health services for sick children. In many low- and middle-income countries, as discussed in Chapter 5 on health systems, a number of health programs have been organized as somewhat separate programs, sometimes called "vertical," that are not well linked with other parts of health services. It is quite common, for example, for the vaccination program to operate with limited connections to other parts of the health services. The same has tended to be true of family planning services, as well as services for a variety of other programs.[81]

Given the multiple factors that lead to child illness and, in some cases, death, however, it is widely agreed that no single child intervention is adequate to ensure a child's health. It is also agreed that, given the interrelated factors that affect a child's health and survival, an integrated approach to managing illness is important for newborns, infants, and older children.

Integrated management of childhood illnesses, called IMCI, is an approach that recognizes the importance of looking at the "whole" child and not treating one symptom or providing one intervention without looking at other possible needs. It also recognizes that care is needed at the level of overall health system, local health center, and family and community. The IMCI approach focuses on training health workers and caretakers at all levels, but pays special attention to home and community-based care, which is increasingly acknowledged as being able to contribute to significant reduction of childhood deaths at minimal cost.

A number of evaluations of IMCI efforts have taken place and reveal that health workers trained in IMCI programs provide higher quality of care than workers trained in other programs. A review of IMCI experience in Tanzania showed that better care could be provided at lower cost than in non-IMCI areas, because better care led to fewer hospitalizations of children. Overall, however, it appears that if IMCI is to meet its promise, then it will have to be carried out in a way that is more closely linked with the communities where it is being done and in a way that ensures that families engage in the practices noted in Table 10-6.[82]

There is widespread agreement about what interventions are needed to improve child health. The key challenge to gaining such improvements, however, is not what to do, but how to do it and how to engage communities in ensuring that needed interventions happen. There are countries, such as Sri Lanka, Cuba, and China, and states within countries, such as Kerala, in which there is widespread knowledge of appropriate health and hygiene behaviors, appropriate nutrition practices, the home management of illness, and when to seek care from health services. In Bangladesh, as you read, there has been widespread adoption of ORT, despite the low educational and income status of a large share of the population. Families and communities are the key to rapid uptake of critical measures to improve child health, and a central issue in global health today is to learn from experience about how large scale change

---

TABLE 10-6 12 Key Family Health Practices

Communities need to be strengthened and families supported to improve child survival, growth, and development. Evidence suggests that families should:

- Breastfeed infants exclusively for at least 6 months. (Mothers found to be HIV-positive require counselling about possible alternatives to breastfeeding.)
- Feed children complementary foods starting at about 6 months of age, while continuing to breastfeed up to 2 years or longer.
- Ensure that children receive adequate amounts of micronutrients (vitamin A and iron in particular), either in their diet or through supplementation.
- Dispose of feces, including children's feces, safely, and wash hands after defecation, before preparing meals, and before feeding children.
- Complete a full course of immunizations (BCG, DPT, OPV, and measles) for children before their first birthday.
- Protect children in malaria-endemic areas by ensuring that they sleep under insecticide-treated bed nets.
- Promote mental and social development by responding to a child's needs through talking, playing, and providing a stimulating environment.
- Feed and offer more fluids, including breast milk, when children are sick.
- Give sick children appropriate home treatment for infections.
- Recognize when sick children need treatment outside the home and seek care from appropriate providers.
- Follow health worker's advice about treatment, follow-up, and referral.
- Ensure that every pregnant woman has adequate antenatal care, including at least four antenatal visits with an appropriate healthcare provider, and the recommended doses of the tetanus toxoid vaccination. The mother also needs support from her family and community in seeking care at the time of delivery and during the postpartum and lactation period.

Source: Adapted with permission from World Health Organization. Family and Community Practices that Promote Child Survival, Growth and Development: A Review of the Evidence. Geneva: World Health Organization; 2004.

in health and child-caring behaviors can be promoted as quickly, effectively, and efficiently, as possible.

MAIN MESSAGES

Approximately 8.8 million children around the world die each year before they reach their fifth birthday. About 3.6 million, or 41 percent, die in their first 4 weeks of life. Almost 50 percent of the under-5 deaths happen in only five countries—India, Nigeria, the Democratic Republic of Congo, Pakistan and China.

As we learned in the vignettes that opened the chapter, the chances of survival for a newborn, an infant, and a young child are vastly different across different settings. The discrepancies within an individual country can be as wide as differences between countries. High-income countries have, on average, about 6 deaths per 1000 live births for children younger than 5 years, whereas low- and middle-income countries have, on average, 72 deaths per 1000 live births in that same age group. In the poorest and most conflict-ridden countries, the under-5 child mortality rate can be as high as 200 deaths per 1000 live births.[4]

Pneumonia is the biggest killer of children who are younger than 5 years. Almost one fifth, or 1.6 million of the 8.8 million under-5 children who die each year, die of pneumonia. The second most important cause of illness and death among children is diarrheal disease. In Africa, malaria kills almost as many under-5 children each year as pneumonia and diarrhea.

Poverty is a significant underlying factor of morbidity and mortality among children. Where there is poverty, there is often inadequate nutrition and inadequate access to safe water, sanitation, health services, or education. Drinking or eating food prepared with unsafe water, lack of water for hygiene, and inadequate access to sanitation together contribute more than 1 million child deaths annually.[83]

Although a large part of the population can be reached through the health system in many countries, marginalized groups may not have access to health care for social, economic, or geographic reasons. Some children, like Tirtha in one of the opening vignettes, live too far away for their mothers to be able to take them to a health center. In other cases, families may not be far from a health center, but they may not understand that they need to take their child to one. In addition, they may not have enough money for transportation there or for any fees at the health center. For cultural reasons, a woman may not be allowed to go to a health center alone, and must often wait for her husband's permission or for her husband to accompany her.

Most illness and death among young children is due to multiple illnesses or, more often, malnutrition combined with disease. It is important to ensure that children have the right combination of preventive and curative interventions. In the first 6 months of life, exclusive breastfeeding is crucial because there are important antibodies in a mother's breast milk. Appropriate and hygienically prepared complementary feeding, a full course of immunization, insecticide-treated bed nets for malaria prevention, and ORT for children with diarrhea are the most basic and cost-effective child health interventions available. The basic package of vaccines include vaccines against six major diseases including diphtheria, whooping cough (pertussis), tetanus, polio, tuberculosis, and measles. Vaccines for hepatitis B, *Haemophilus influenza* type b, and rotavirus are increasingly also being used in low- and middle-income countries. Safe water and sanitation are also keys to good health. However, relatively low-cost community-based approaches to improving them have not received sufficient attention in many settings, as discussed in Chapter 7.

There is widespread agreement about the interventions needed to enhance child health. The key challenge facing the global health community is not determining what to do. Rather, it is helping families and communities quickly get the information and the means that they need to engage in safer and more appropriate health behaviors on a large scale, in coordination with what will hopefully be enhanced health services, and improvements in water and sanitation.

Study Questions

1. What are the most important causes of child death globally?

2. How do causes of death differ for neonates, infants, and children younger than 5 years?

3. Why are there different levels of child illness and death in different parts of the same country?

4. What is the link between nutrition and child health?

5. How does the health of young children in low-income countries vary with the income of the family?

6. How does the health of young children in low-income countries vary with the mother's level of education?

7. What is the importance to neonatal health of having a skilled birth attendant at delivery?

8. What are some of the most cost-effective interventions for saving the lives of newborns?

9. What are some of the most cost-effective interventions for saving the lives of children younger than 5 years?

10. What measures can families take, even in the absence of additional income or health services, to keep their children healthy?

REFERENCES

1. Black RE, Cousens S, Johnson HL, et al. Global, regional, and national causes of child mortality in 2008: a systematic analysis. *Lancet.* 2010;375(9730):1969-1987.

2. Hogan MC, Naghavi M, Anh SY, et al. Maternal mortality for 181 countries, 1980 to 2008, a systematic analysis of progress towards Millennium Development Goal 5. *Lancet.* 2010;375(9726):1609-1623.

3. Lawn J, Kerber K, Enweronu-Laryea C, Bateman OM. Newborn survival in low-resource settings—are we delivering? *BJOG.* 2009;116(Suppl s1):49-59.

4. UNICEF. *Progress for Children: Achieving the MDGs with Equity.* New York: UNICEF; September 2010.

5. Simoes EAF, Cherian T, Chow J, Shahid-Salles S, Laxminarayan R, John TJ. Acute respiratory infections in children. In: Jamison DT, Breman JG, Measham AR, et al., eds. *Disease Control Priorities in Developing Countries.* 2nd ed. New York: Oxford University Press; 2006:483-484.

6. Keusch GF, Fontaine O, Bhargava A, et al. Diarrheal diseases. In: Jamison DT, Breman JG, Measham AR, et al., eds. *Disease Control Priorities in Developing Countries.* 2nd ed. New York: Oxford University Press; 2006:371.

7. Keusch GF, Fontaine O, Bhargava A, et al. Diarrheal diseases. In: Jamison DT, Breman JG, Measham AR, et al., eds. *Disease Control Priorities in Developing Countries.* 2nd ed. New York: Oxford University Press; 2006:372.

8. Breman JG, Mills A, Snow RW, et al. Conquering malaria. In: Jamison DT, Breman JG, Measham AR, et al., eds. *Disease Control Priorities in Developing Countries.* 2nd ed. New York: Oxford University Press; 2006:418.

9. Centers for Disease Control and Prevention. The Emergency Plan in Botswana. CDC Global AIDS Program. Available at: www.cdc.gov.nchstp/od/gap/countries/Botswana.htm. Accessed July 26, 2006.

10. United Nations. Millennium Development Goals Indicators. Children Under Five Mortality Rate Per 1,000 Live Births. Available at: http://millenniumindicators.un.org/unsd/mdg/SeriesDetail.aspx?srid=561&crid=. Accessed July 26, 2006.

11. Brenzel L, Wolfson LJ, Fox-Rushby J, Miller M, Halsey NA. Vaccine-preventable diseases. In: Jamison DT, Breman JG, Measham AR, et al., eds. *Disease Control Priorities in Developing Countries.* 2nd ed. New York: Oxford University Press; 2006:396-397.

12. Hotez PJ, Bundy DAP, Beegle K, et al. Helminth infections: soil-transmitted helminth infections and schistosomiasis. In: Jamison DT, Breman JG, Measham AR, et al., eds. *Disease Control Priorities in Developing Countries.* 2nd ed. New York: Oxford University Press; 2006:467-482.

13. Lopez AD, Mathers CD, Murray CJL. The burden of disease and mortality by condition: data, methods, and results for 2001. In: Lopez AD, Mathers CD, Ezzati M, Jamison DT, Murray CJL, eds. *Global Burden of Disease and Risk Factors.* New York: Oxford University Press; 2006:180-185.

14. Lawn JE, Cousens S, Zupan J. 4 million neonatal deaths: when? Where? Why? *Lancet.* 2005;365(9462):891-900.

15. Lawn JE, Zupan J, Begkoyian G, Knippenberg R. Newborn survival. In: Jamison DT, Breman JG, Measham AR, et al., eds. *Disease Control Priorities in Developing Countries.* 2nd ed. New York: Oxford University Press; 2006:531.

16. Lawn JE, Zupan J, Begkoyian G, Knippenberg R. Newborn survival. In: Jamison DT, Breman JG, Measham AR, et al., eds. *Disease Control Priorities in Developing Countries.* 2nd ed. New York: Oxford University Press; 2006:532.

17. Lawn JE, Zupan J, Begkoyian G, Knippenberg R. Newborn survival. In: Jamison DT, Breman JG, Measham AR, et al., eds. *Disease Control Priorities in Developing Countries.* 2nd ed. New York: Oxford University Press; 2006:534.

18. United Nations. *The Millennium Development Goals Report 2006.* New York: United Nations; 2006.

19. Darmstadt GL, Bhutta ZA, Cousens S, Adam T, Walker N, de Bernis L. Evidence-based, cost-effective interventions: how many newborn babies can we save? *Lancet.* 2005;365(9463):977-988.

20. Black RE, Morris SS, Bryce J. Where and why are 10 million children dying every year? *Lancet.* 2003;361(9376):2227.

21. UNICEF. *State of the World's Children 2005.* UNICEF; 2005.

22. Lawn JE, Zupan J, Begkoyian G, Knippenberg R. Newborn survival. In: Jamison DT, Breman JG, Measham AR, et al., eds. *Disease Control Priorities in Developing Countries.* 2nd ed. New York: Oxford University Press; 2006:533.

23. Keusch GF, Fontaine O, Bhargava A, et al. Diarrheal diseases. In: Jamison DT, Breman JG, Measham AR, et al., eds. *Disease Control Priorities in Developing Countries.* 2nd ed. New York: Oxford University Press; 2006:375.

24. Hotez PJ, Bundy DAP, Beegle K, et al. Helminth infections: soil-transmitted helminth infections and schistosomiasis. In: Jamison DT, Breman JG, Measham AR, et al., eds. *Disease Control Priorities in Developing Countries.* 2nd ed. New York: Oxford University Press; 2006:467.

25. Kramer M. Determinants of low birth weight: methodological assessment and meta-analysis. *Bull World Health Org.* 1987;6(5):663-737.

26. Goldenberg R, Rouse D. Prevention of premature birth. *New Engl J Med.* 1998;339(5):313-320.

27. The World Health Organization. Kangaroo Mother Care: A Practical Guide. Available at: http://books.google.com/books?id=cTDRwoUvTnoC&printsec=frontcover&cd=1&source=gbs_ViewAPI#v=onepage&q&f=false. Accessed April 23, 2011.

28. Lawn JE, Cousens S, Zupen J. 4 million neonatal deaths: when? Where? Why? *Lancet.* 2005;365(9462):891-900.

29. Olson K, Caldwell A. Designing an early stage prototype using readily available material for a neonatal incubator for poor settings. *Conf Proc IEEE Eng Med Biol Soc.* 2010;2010:1100-1103.

30. Osman, N. "Kangaroo" Incubation Urged for Indonesia's Premature Babies. *Jakarta Globe.* October 13, 2009. Available at: http://www.thejakartaglobe.com/national/kangaroo-incubation-urged-for-indonesias-premature-babies/335372. Accessed April 23, 2011.

31. Conde-Agudelo A, Diaz-Rossello JL, Belizan JM. Kangaroo Mother Care to Reduce Morbidity and Mortality in Low Birthweight Infants (Review). The Cochrane Collaboration. 2007. Available at: http://apps.who.int/rhl/reviews/CD002771.pdf. Accessed April 23, 2011.

32. Kambarami RA, Chidede O, Kowo DT. Kangaroo care versus incubator care in the management of well preterm infants—a pilot study. *Ann Trop Paediatr.* 1998;18(2):81-86.

33. PATH. About Pneumonia and Pneumococcus. Available at: http://www.path.org/projects/pneumococcal_protein_vaccine_project_about_pneumonia.php. Accessed April 23, 2011.

34. World Bank. Levine O, Sow S. The Pneumococcus Challenge. Presented at the Second Meeting of the AMC Technical Working Group on 9 November 2006. Available at: http://siteresources.worldbank.org/INTVACCINES/Resources/382924-1160177658934/Nov2006PneumoDiseaseVaccineLevineSow.ppt. Accessed April 23, 2011.

35. PATH. Pneumococcal Vaccine Project: Projects and Partners. Available at: http://www.path.org/projects/pneumococcal_protein_vaccine_project_partners.php. Accessed April 23, 2011.

36. GAVI. The Challenge of Providing Access to Pneumococcal Vaccine for Children Worldwide. Available at: http://www.ifpma.org/fileadmin/templates/GHR/2010/pdfs/6_Jon_Pearman_GAVI_28Apr10.pdf. Accessed April 23, 2011.

37. GAVI. GAVI's PneumoADIP and Outlook for Affordable, Sustainable Supply and Accelerated Introduction. Presented on 11 November 2005. Available at: http://www.netspear.org/downloads/3rd%20network%20conference%20presentations/Day%20one/GAVI's%20PneumoADIP%20&%20outlook%20for%20affordable%20sustainable%20suppl.PPT. Accessed April 23, 2011.

38. GAVI. New Evidence on Rotavirus Vaccines in Asia Demonstrates Significant Protection Against the Most Common Deadly Form of Childhood Diarrhea. Available at: http://www.gavialliance.org/media_centre/press_releases/2010_08_06_path_rotavirus_pr.php. Accessed April 23, 2011.

39. Barclay L. Rotarix or RotaTeq Vaccination May Be Effective, Safe in Childhood. *Medscape.* 17 May 2010. Available at: http://www.medscape.org/viewarticle/721886. Accessed April 23, 2011.

40. World Health Organization. Statement on Rotarix and Rotateq Vaccines and Intussusception. 22 September 2010. Available at: http://www.who.int/vaccine_safety/topics/rotavirus/rotarix_and_rotateq/intussusception_sep2010/en/index.html. Accessed April 23, 2011.

41. PATH. Developing New Vaccines Against Rotavirus. Available at: http://www.path.org/vaccineresources/files/ARVACTechnicalFactSheet.pdf. Accessed April 23, 2011.

42. World Health Organization. Fact Sheet: Development of New Vaccines. Available at: http://www.whqlibdoc.who.int/fact_sheet/2005/FS_289.pdf. Accessed April 23, 2011.

43. U.S. Centers for Disease Control and Prevention. Rotashield and Intussusception. 2004. Available at: http://www.rotavirusvaccine.org/documents/RotaShield_Fact_Sheet_CDC.pdf. Accessed April 23, 2011.

44. GAVI. GAVI's Accelerated Vaccine Introduction Initiative. Available at: http://www.gavialliance.org/resources/17_AVI_ENG_2p_web__2_.pdf Accessed April 23, 2011.

45. Calcutta Kids. Genesis. Available at: http://www.calcuttakids.org/gens.html. Accessed August 12, 2010.

46. Calcutta Kids [homepage]. Available at: http://www.calcuttakids.org/index.html. Accessed August 12, 2010.

47. Calcutta Kids. Maternal and Young Child Health Initiative. Available at: http://www.calcuttakids.org/mychi.html. Accessed August 16, 2010.

48. Calcutta Kids. Home Visits. Available at: http://www.calcuttakids.org/hmv.html. Accessed August 16, 2010.

49. Calcutta Kids. Growth Monitoring Promotion. Available at: http://www.calcuttakids.org/gmp.html. Accessed August 16, 2010.

50. Calcutta Kids. Community Meetings. Available at: http://www.calcuttakids.org/c_met.html. Accessed August 16, 2010.

51. Calcutta Kids. Calcutta Kids Weekly Health Camp. Available at: http://www.calcuttakids.org/whc.html. Accessed August 16, 2010.

52. Calcutta Kids. Fall 2009. Available at: www.calcuttakids.org/pdf/Fall_2009.pdf. Accessed August 16, 2010.

53. Calcutta Kids. FAQ. Available at: http://www.calcuttakids.org/faq.html. Accessed August 16, 2010.

54. HEAL: A Calcutta Kids Program. HEAL for Children. Available at: http://calcuttakids.org/heal/heal_for_children.html. Accessed August 16, 2010.

55. el-Rafie M, Hassouna WA, Hirschhorn N, et al. Effect of diarrheal disease control on infant and childhood mortality in Egypt: report from the National Control of Diarrheal Diseases Project. *Lancet.* 1990;335(8685):334-338.

56. John Snow, Inc. *Taming a Child Killer: The Egyptian National Control of Diarrheal Diseases Project.* Washington, DC: John Snow, Inc.; 1995.

57. World Health Organization. *The World Health Report 2002: Reducing Risks, Promoting Health Lives.* Geneva: World Health Organization; 2002.

58. West KP, Jr., Pokhrel RP, Katz J, et al. Efficacy of vitamin A in reducing preschool child mortality in Nepal. *Lancet.* 1991;338(8759):67-71.

59. Rutstein SO, Govindasamy P. *The Mortality Effects of Nepal's Vitamin A Distribution Program.* Calverton, MD: ORC Macro; 2002.

60. Caulfield LE, Richard SA, Rivera JA, Musgrove P, Black RE. Stunting, wasting, and micronutrient disorders. In: Jamison DT, Breman JG, Measham AR, et al., eds. *Disease Control Priorities in Developing Countries.* 2nd ed. New York: Oxford University Press; 2006:551-568.

61. Fiedler JL. *The Nepal National Vitamin A Program: A Program Review and Cost Analysis.* Bethesda, MD: Partnerships for Health Reform Project. Abt Associates; 1997.

62. Fiedler JL. The Nepal National Vitamin A Program: prototype to emulate or donor enclave? *Health Policy Plan.* 2000;15(2):145-156.

63. Henderson DA, de Quadros CA, Andrus J, Olive J-M, Guerra de Macedo C. Polio eradication from the western hemisphere. *Annu Rev Publ Health.* 1992;13:239-252.

64. de Cuadros CA. Polio. *Encyclopedia of Microbiology 3*; 3000:762-772.

65. Gawande A. The mop-up: Eradicating polio from the planet. *The New Yorker.* January 12, 2004:34-40.

66. Musgrove P. Is the eradication of polio in the western hemisphere economically justified? *Bull Pan Am Sanitary Bureau.* 1988;22(1).

67. Global Polio Eradication Initiative. Afghanistan, Egypt, India, Niger, Nigeria, and Pakistan, Progress Report. Available at: www.polioeradication.org/content/publication/2003progress.pdf. Accessed August 10, 2004.

68. Black RE, Morris SS, Bryce J. Where and why are 10 million children dying every year? *Lancet.* 2003;361(9376):2226.

69. Victora CG, Wagstaff A, Schellenberg JA, Gwatkin D, Claeson M, Habicht JP. Applying an equity lens to child health and mortality: more of the same is not enough. *Lancet.* 2003;362(9379):233.

70. Lawn JE, Zupan J, Begkoyian G, Knippenberg R. Newborn survival. In: Jamison DT, Breman JG, Measham AR, et al., eds. *Disease Control Priorities in Developing Countries.* 2nd ed. New York: Oxford University Press; 2006:536-538.

71. Bertozzi S, Padian NS, Wegbreit J, et al. HIV/AIDS prevention and treatment. In: Jamison DT, Breman JG, Measham A, et al., eds. *Disease Control Priorities in Developing Countries.* New York: Oxford University Press; 2006:345-346.

72. Lawn JE, Zupan J, Begkoyian G, Knippenberg R. Newborn survival. In: Jamison DT, Breman JG, Measham AR, et al., eds. *Disease Control Priorities in Developing Countries.* 2nd ed. New York: Oxford University Press; 2006:535-543.

73. Bang AT, Bang RA, Baitule SB, Reddy MH, Deshmukh MD. Effect of home-based neonatal care and management of sepsis on neonatal mortality: field trial in rural India. *Lancet.* 1999;354(9194):1955-1961.

74. Lawn JE, Zupan J, Begkoyian G, Knippenberg R. Newborn survival. In: Jamison DT, Breman JG, Measham AR, et al., eds. *Disease Control Priorities in Developing Countries.* 2nd ed. New York: Oxford University Press; 2006:541.

75. Keusch GF, Fontaine O, Bhargava A, et al. Diarrheal diseases. In: Jamison DT, Breman JG, Measham AR, et al., eds. *Disease Control Priorities in Developing Countries.* 2nd ed. New York: Oxford University Press; 2006:376.

76. Keusch GF, Fontaine O, Bhargava A, et al. Diarrheal diseases. In: Jamison DT, Breman JG, Measham AR, et al., eds. *Disease Control Priorities in Developing Countries.* 2nd ed. New York: Oxford University Press; 2006:377.

77. Brenzel L, Wolfson LJ, Fox-Rushby J, Miller M, Halsey NA. Vaccine-preventable diseases. In: Jamison DT, Breman JG, Measham AR, et al., eds. *Disease Control Priorities in Developing Countries.* 2nd ed. New York: Oxford University Press; 2006:389.

78. Brenzel L, Wolfson LJ, Fox-Rushby J, Miller M, Halsey NA. Vaccine-preventable diseases. In: Jamison DT, Breman JG, Measham AR, et al., eds. *Disease Control Priorities in Developing Countries.* 2nd ed. New York: Oxford University Press; 2006:398.

79. WHO. WHO Vaccine-Preventable Diseases: Monitoring System, 2010 Global Summary. Available at: http://whqlibdoc.who.int/hq/2010/WHO_IVB_2010_eng.pdf. Accessed January 15, 2011.

80. Lawn JE, Zupan J, Begkoyian G, Knippenberg R. Newborn survival. In: Jamison DT, Breman JG, Measham AR, et al., eds. *Disease Control Priorities in Developing Countries.* 2nd ed. New York: Oxford University Press; 2006:531-549.

81. Victora CG, Adam T, Bryce J, Evans DB. Integrated management of the sick child. In: Jamison DT, Breman JG, Measham AR, et al., eds. *Disease Control Priorities in Developing Countries.* 2nd ed. New York: Oxford University Press; 2006:1177.

82. Victora CG, Adam T, Bryce J, Evans DB. Integrated management of the sick child. In: Jamison DT, Breman JG, Measham AR, et al., eds. *Disease Control Priorities in Developing Countries.* 2nd ed. New York: Oxford University Press; 2006:1177-1192.

83. Black RE, Morris SS, Bryce J. Where and why are 10 million children dying every year? *Lancet.* 2003;361(9376):2228.

Communicable Diseases

VIGNETTES

Henrietta was a 35-year-old Kenyan mother of four who lived in Mombassa. Over the last 4 months, Henrietta was barely able to digest her food, had frequent bouts of diarrhea, and had been losing weight. She worried about having HIV. Henrietta went to a local clinic where she was tested and found to be HIV-positive. She had been infected by her husband, who was a truck driver.

Maria was 33 years old and lived in the mountains of Peru. For some time, she had not been feeling well. She often had a fever, was coughing a lot, and had night sweats. Maria had tuberculosis (TB) earlier and worried that this might be TB again. Maria was correct. In fact, this time she had drug-resistant TB, which would be difficult and expensive to cure. When Maria was sick the first time, she took most of her drugs. However, because she felt much better after the first 2 months of drugs, she did not take the rest of them.

Wole was 4 years old and lived in southwestern Nigeria. He had flu-like symptoms, a fever, and a headache. His mother suspected he might have malaria but decided she would see if he got better before taking him to the doctor. In another few days, however, Wole was much sicker and weaker. He was also dizzy and, shortly thereafter, lapsed into a coma. His mother then rushed him to the local health center but he died within a few hours. Unfortunately, Wole had the most virulent form of malaria.

Sanjay was 18 months old and lived in Lucknow, India. His mother was a day laborer and his father was a rickshaw driver. They lived in a hut in a large slum with little access to water and no sanitation. Sanjay was below the normal height and weight for his age and looked only 12 months old. Over the past year, Sanjay had four bouts of severe diarrhea.

THE IMPORTANCE OF COMMUNICABLE DISEASES

Communicable diseases are immensely important to the global burden of disease, and in 2001 accounted for about 40 percent of the disease burden in low- and middle-income countries.[1] Each year, HIV/AIDS kills about 1.8 million, TB kills about 1.7 million, diarrhea kills 1.5 million, and malaria kills 1 million.[2–5] Parasitic infections also account for an enormous burden of disease and disability. In addition, the world faces important threats from emerging and re-emerging infectious diseases and from antimicrobial resistance.

Communicable diseases are the most important burden of disease in sub-Saharan Africa. They are also especially important in South Asia. These diseases disproportionately affect the poor. Better-off people have the knowledge and income to protect themselves from diseases spread by unsafe water. They do not live in the crowded circumstances that can spread TB, and they also protect themselves as much as possible against malaria. In addition, they immunize their children against vaccine-preventable diseases at rates that are much higher than poor people do.

Communicable diseases are also of enormous economic consequence. These diseases constrain the physical and mental development of infants and young children and reduce their future economic prospects. The impacts of HIV, TB, malaria, and the neglected tropical diseases on adult productivity are also exceptionally large. In addition, the direct and indirect costs of treatment for the infected person are often a substantial share of their income, causing them to borrow money or sell their already limited assets, and forcing them to sink into poverty. High rates of communicable diseases are also impediments to the investment needed to spur economic growth. The appearance of an emerging infectious disease or the re-emergence of a disease can cause billions of dollars in lost income for individuals, communities, and countries.

Much of the burden of communicable diseases is unnecessary because many of these diseases can easily be prevented or treated. Vaccines are an extremely cost-effective way to prevent a number of communicable diseases in children. The safe use of water can reduce the burden of diarrhea and certain parasitic diseases. There are inexpensive, safe, and effective treatments for TB, malaria, and many parasitic infections. Unfortunately, these technologies are not sufficiently used in low- and middle-income countries, especially by the poor. In addition, the more rational use of antibiotics could reduce the development of antimicrobial resistance.

Given their importance and their impact on the poor, the communicable diseases are of immense relevance to the MDGs, as noted in Table 11-1.

This chapter will introduce the reader to some of the major communicable diseases and the burden of morbidity, disability, and mortality associated with them in low- and middle-income countries. It will also outline how selected communicable diseases can be controlled. The chapter will then present a number of briefs and case studies on efforts to address communicable diseases. The chapter will conclude by reviewing some of the remaining challenges the world faces in the control of these diseases. This chapter will focus on emerging and re-emerging infectious diseases and antimicrobial resistance, HIV/AIDS, TB, malaria, and a set of parasitic and bacterial infections often referred to as "neglected tropical diseases." It will discuss diarrheal disease in a manner complementary to the discussion in Chapter 10 on child health. The chapter will not comment on bio-terrorism, nor

TABLE 11-1 Key Links Between Communicable Diseases and the MDGs

Goal 1: Eradicate Extreme Hunger and Poverty
Communicable diseases are associated with high rates of morbidity and mortality. Communicable diseases can be part of a cycle of disease and malnutrition. In addition, communicable diseases reduce one's ability to work, thereby decreasing productivity and family income. In addition, illness causes people to spend an important share of their income on health care.

Goal 2: Achieve Universal Primary Education
Enrollment, attendance, and performance of children in schools is closely linked with health status. Communicable diseases are the leading cause of illness among the poor in sub-Saharan Africa and South Asia.

Goal 4: Reduce Child Mortality
The leading causes of death among children in the developing world are respiratory infections, diarrheal diseases, HIV/AIDS, and malaria.

Goal 5: Improve Maternal Health
Malaria can cause anemia and mortality in pregnant women and is a major cause of poor maternal outcomes. HIV also has deleterious effects on pregnancy.

Goal 6: Combat HIV/AIDS, Malaria, and Other Diseases
Reducing the burden of communicable diseases is at the core of meeting this development goal.

Goal 8: Develop a Global Partnership for Development
The most important communicable diseases are being addressed through public–private partnerships or through product-development partnerships, such as Roll Back Malaria; Stop TB; The Global Fund to Fight AIDS, TB, and Malaria; The Global Polio Eradication Program; The Global Alliance for TB Drug Development; The Malaria Vaccine Initiative; and The International Partnership on Microbicides.

Source: Adapted from United Nations. Millennium Development Goals. Available at: http://www.un.org/millenniumgoals/goals. Accessed July 11, 2006.

will it add to the discussion of pneumonia that was included in Chapter 10.

This chapter is only introductory. Communicable diseases are a very important topic about which an exceptional amount of material has been written. Those interested in gaining a deeper understanding of these diseases are encouraged to read some of the materials cited in this chapter.

KEY TERMS, DEFINITIONS, AND CONCEPTS

As you begin to explore communicable diseases in greater detail, there are a number of terms and concepts with which you should be familiar. These are defined in Table 11-2. It is also important to recall that a communicable disease is a disease that is transmitted from an animal to another animal, an animal to a human, a human to another human, or a human to an animal. Transmission can be direct, such as through respiratory means, or indirect through a vector, such as a mosquito in the case of malaria. Most people use the term *communicable disease* in a manner that is synonymous with *infectious disease*. However, others prefer to speak separately about diseases caused by infectious agents, such as TB, and those caused by parasites, such as hookworm. This chapter will consistently use the term *communicable disease* to refer to both infectious and parasitic diseases.

As we examine the basic concepts concerning communicable diseases, it is also important to know how such diseases can be spread. This is shown in the following list, which includes examples of diseases spread in each manner:

- *Foodborne:* Salmonella, *E. coli, Entamoeba histolitica*
- *Waterborne:* Cholera, rotavirus
- *Sexual or bloodborne:* Hepatitis, HIV
- *Vectorborne:* Malaria, onchocerciasis
- *Inhalation:* Tuberculosis, influenza, meningitis
- *Nontraumatic contact:* Anthrax
- *Traumatic contact:* Rabies

In addition, it is critical to understand the ways in which communicable diseases can be controlled. These are noted in the following list, also with examples of relevant diseases:

- *Vaccination:* Smallpox, polio, measles, pediatric tuberculosis, diphtheria, pertussis, tetanus, hepatitis B, yellow fever, meningitis, influenza
- *Mass chemotherapy:* Onchocerciasis, hookworm, lymphatic filariasis
- *Vector control:* Malaria, dengue, yellow fever, onchocerciasis, West Nile virus
- *Improved water, sanitation, hygiene:* Diarrheal diseases
- *Improved care seeking, disease recognition:* Maternal health, neonatal health, diarrheal disease, respiratory disease
- *Case management (treatment) and improved caregiving:* Diarrheal disease, acute respiratory illness
- *Case surveillance, reporting, and containment:* Avian influenza, meningitis, cholera
- *Behavioral change:* HIV, sexually transmitted infections

TABLE 11-2 Communicable Disease Definitions

- **Case**—An individual with a particular disease.
- **Case fatality rate**—The proportion of persons with a particular condition (cases) who die from that condition.
- **Control (disease control)**—Reducing the incidence and prevalence of a disease to an acceptable level.
- **Elimination (of disease)**—Reducing the incidence of a disease in a specific area to zero.
- **Emerging infectious disease**—A newly discovered disease.
- **Eradication (of disease)**—Termination of all cases of a disease and its transmission and the complete elimination of the disease-causing agent.
- **Parasite**—An organism that lives in or on another organism and takes its nourishment from that organism.
- **Re-emerging infectious disease**—An existing disease that has increased in incidence or has taken on new forms.

Source: Adapted from Centers for Disease Control and Prevention. Reproductive Health Glossary. Available at: http://www.cdc.gov/reproductivehealth/Data_Stats/Glossary.htm. Accessed April 15, 2007; Dowdle, WR. The Principles of Disease Elimination and Eradication. Available at: http://www.cdc.gov/mmwr/preview/mmwrhtml/su48a7.htm. Accessed December 27, 2010.

A final concept of exceptional importance when discussing communicable diseases is the concept of *drug resistance*. This refers to the extent to which infectious and parasitic agents develop an ability to resist drug treatment.

NOTE ON THE USE OF DATA IN THIS CHAPTER

As you review this chapter, it is important to note the manner in which data are presented. As discussed in Chapter 1, data on the burden of disease are taken from a consistent set of 2001 data, which were part of a study of the global burden of disease. These burden of disease data are used throughout the book. However, the most recent data that are available from reliable sources are used when discussing individual diseases and conditions and the neglected tropical diseases as a group.

THE BURDEN OF COMMUNICABLE DISEASES

Communicable diseases account for about 36 percent of total deaths and about 40 percent of total DALYs lost annually in low- and middle-income countries.[1] Table 11-3 summarizes the major causes of death from communicable diseases for the world and in low- and middle-income countries.

TABLE 11-3 Leading Causes of Death from Selected Communicable Diseases, 2001, by Number of Deaths in Thousands

Condition	World	Low- and Middle-Income
Lower Respiratory Conditions	3753	3408
HIV/AIDS	2574	2552
Diarrheal Diseases	1783	1777
Tuberculosis	1606	1590
Malaria	1208	1207
Measles	763	762

Source: Data with permission from Lopez AD, Mathers CD, Ezzati M, Jamison DT, Murray CJL. Measuring the global burden of disease and risk factors 1990–2001. In: Lopez AD, Mathers CD, Ezzati M, Jamison DT, Murray CJL, eds. *Global Burden of Disease and Risk Factors.* Washington, DC and New York: The World Bank and Oxford University Press; 2006:8.

The relative importance of communicable diseases, compared to noncommunicable diseases and injuries, varies considerably by region. Figure 11-1 indicates the share of the total deaths by region that is represented by communicable diseases. Figure 11-1 further highlights the fact that South Asia and sub-Saharan Africa have the highest burden of deaths from communicable diseases, relative to other causes of death. Communicable diseases are the largest cause of death only in sub-Saharan Africa.

The relative importance of specific communicable diseases to the burden of disease also varies by region. HIV/AIDS is of exceptional importance in sub-Saharan Africa, as is malaria. The "neglected" diseases are also much more important in sub-Saharan Africa than in any other region.

The burden of specific communicable diseases varies by age group. Diarrheal disease, malaria, lower respiratory infections, and measles are most important for young children. HIV/AIDS and TB are most important for people who are 15 to 59 years old, although there is also a substantial TB burden for people older than that. In Table 11-4, one can see the leading causes of deaths from communicable diseases in low- and middle-income countries, by broad age group.

FIGURE 11-1 Deaths from Selected Infectious and Parasitic Diseases, as Percent of Total Deaths, by Region 2001 (Includes Infectious and Parasitic Infections and Lower Respiratory Infections)

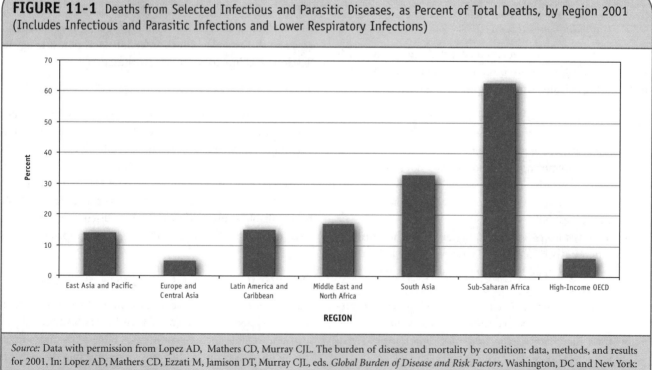

Source: Data with permission from Lopez AD, Mathers CD, Murray CJL. The burden of disease and mortality by condition: data, methods, and results for 2001. In: Lopez AD, Mathers CD, Ezzati M, Jamison DT, Murray CJL, eds. *Global Burden of Disease and Risk Factors.* Washington, DC and New York: The World Bank and Oxford University Press; 2006:126-179.

TABLE 11-4 Leading Causes of Death in Low- and Middle-Income Countries by Broad Age Group, 2001, as Percentage of Total Deaths

Aged 0–14		Aged 15–59	
Cause	Percent of Total Deaths	Cause	Percent of Total Deaths
Perinatal conditions	20.7	HIV/AIDS	14.1
Lower respiratory infections	17.0	Ischemic heart disease	8.1
Diarrheal diseases	13.4	Tuberculosis	7.1
Malaria	9.2	Road traffic accidents	5.0
Measles	6.2	Cerebrovascular disease	4.9
HIV/AIDS	3.7	Self-inflicted injuries	4.0
Congenital anomalies	3.7	Violence	3.1
Whooping cough	2.5	Lower respiratory infections	2.3
Tetanus	1.9	Cirrhosis of the liver	2.2
Road traffic accidents	1.5	Chronic obstructive pulmonary disease	2.2

Source: Data with permission from Lopez AD, Mathers CD, Murray CJL. The burden of disease and mortality by condition: data, methods, and results for 2001. In: Lopez AD, Mathers CD, Ezzati M, Jamison DT, Murray CJL, eds. *Global Burden of Disease and Risk Factors.* Washington, DC and New York: The World Bank and Oxford University Press; 2006:70-71.

There are relatively small differences in the distribution of deaths from communicable diseases between males and females in low- and middle-income countries. However, it is consistently the case that TB affects males more than females.

It is also true that the HIV/AIDS epidemic is being increasingly feminized and that HIV/AIDS is now a more important cause of death for women than it is for men. These facts are illustrated in Table 11-5.

TABLE 11-5 Leading Causes of Death by Sex, Low- and Middle-Income Countries, 2001, as Percentage of Total Deaths

Males		Females	
Cause	Percentage of Total Deaths	Cause	Percentage of Total Deaths
Ischemic heart disease	11.8	Ischemic heart disease	11.8
Cerebrovascular disease	8.5	Cerebrovascular disease	10.7
Lower respiratory infections	6.7	Lower respiratory infections	7.4
Perinatal conditions	5.4	HIV/AIDS	5.2
HIV/AIDS	5.4	Chronic obstructive pulmonary disease	5.1
Chronic obstructive pulmonary disease	4.7	Perinatal conditions	4.9
Tuberculosis	4.1	Diarrheal diseases	3.7
Diarrheal diseases	3.6	Malaria	2.8
Road traffic accidents	3.1	Tuberculosis	2.4
Malaria	2.3	Diabetes Mellitus	1.8

Source: Data with permission from Lopez AD, Mathers CD, Murray CJL. The burden of disease and mortality by condition: data, methods, and results for 2001. In: Lopez AD, Mathers CD, Ezzati M, Jamison DT, Murray CJL, eds. *Global Burden of Disease and Risk Factors.* Washington, DC and New York: The World Bank and Oxford University Press; 2006:70.

THE COSTS AND CONSEQUENCES OF COMMUNICABLE DISEASES

The economic and social costs of the enormous burden of communicable diseases are very high. First, these diseases constrain the health and development of infants and children, often by having an impact on their schooling and on their productivity as adult workers. Second, stigma and discrimination against people with HIV, those with TB, and those with a variety of other debilitating communicable diseases, such as leprosy and lymphatic filariasis, are strong and pervasive. Third, adults who suffer from the diseases discussed in this chapter suffer substantial losses in productivity and income. Fourth, families spend considerable sums of money trying to treat these illnesses. Fifth, high rates of infectious diseases in any country reduce investments in that country's development. Finally, as noted earlier, emerging and re-emerging infectious diseases can have enormous economic consequences, far in excess of their impact on health.

THE LEADING BURDENS OF COMMUNICABLE DISEASES

The sections that follow examine emerging and re-emerging infectious diseases and antimicrobial resistance, HIV/AIDS, TB, malaria, and neglected tropical diseases. The chapter reviews the nature and magnitude of each of these causes, as well as who is affected by them, their risk factors, their social and economic consequences, and what can be done to address these problems in cost-effective ways. The chapter also discusses future challenges in addressing the most important communicable diseases.

Emerging and Re-emerging Infectious Diseases and Antimicrobial Resistance

The Burden of Emerging and Re-emerging Infectious Diseases

Throughout human history, new diseases have appeared periodically, sometimes wreaking substantial damage. The first recorded epidemic of the bubonic plague, for example, was in the 6th century. More recently, new diseases have emerged, such as the Ebola virus in 1976, HIV in the 1980s, severe acute respiratory syndrome (SARS) in the 1990s, and H5N1 influenza, commonly called "bird flu," which first appeared in humans in 2003. These new diseases are referred to as *emerging infectious diseases*.[6,7] Some examples of emerging infectious diseases are shown in Table 11-6.

Even as new diseases have emerged, some existing diseases have spread more widely in areas in which they had already been present, have spread to places in which they had not appeared before, or have taken on new forms. These diseases are referred to as *re-emerging infectious diseases*.[6,7] In recent years, there have been outbreaks of a number of re-emerging infectious diseases, including West Nile virus in the Western Hemisphere; dengue fever, which spread from South America to the Caribbean and into the United States; and cholera in South America. Some examples of re-emerging infectious diseases are given in Table 11-7.

Resistant forms of disease can emerge or re-emerge when bacteria, parasites, and viruses are altered through mutation, natural selection, or the exchange of genetic material among strains and species.[8] The development of resistance is a natural phenomenon; however, it can be sped up by human action, as discussed further later in this chapter. It can also develop and spread faster than would otherwise be the case because of human inaction—the failure to address it in timely and effective ways. It took only a few years after penicillin was introduced, for example, before strains of bacteria that were susceptible to penicillin had become resistant to it. The drug of choice for malaria for many years, chloroquine, can no longer be used in most places, because the malaria there is resistant to it. Table 11-8 shows when a sample of resistant strains of bacteria, viruses, and parasites were first detected.

Emerging and re-emerging infectious diseases are exceptional examples of critical global health issues. They can arise anywhere and at any time. They can spread, sometimes rapidly, within and across countries. Different countries, with the help of various international organizations and networks, have to work together in technically sound ways, and sometimes urgently, if the problem of these diseases is to be addressed effectively.

In fact, the threat of emerging and re-emerging infectious diseases is continuous and has been called "a perpetual challenge."[6] One study examined 335 "events" related to emerging and re-emerging infectious diseases that had occurred between 1940 and 2004.[9] This analysis revealed that about 60 percent of these events were related to zoonoses—the spread of infection from animals to humans. The study also indicated that most of those events came from wildlife and that wildlife were related to an increasing share of emerging and re-emerging infections over time. About 23 percent were related to vectorborne diseases, which are spread by arthropods, such as mosquitoes, ticks, or fleas. The Global Outbreak Alert and Response Network (GOARN) verified

TABLE 11-6 Selected Examples of Emerging Infectious Diseases

Year of Outbreak	Disease	Place	Source
1967	Marburg	Germany and Yugoslavia	Centers for Disease Control and Prevention. Known Cases and Outbreaks of Marburg Hemorrhagic Fever, in Chronological Order. Available at: http://www.cdc.gov/ncidod/dvrd/spb/mnpages/dispages/marburg/marburgtable.htm. Accessed August 31, 2010.
1976	Ebola	Zaire (Democratic Republic of Congo)	Centers for Disease Control and Prevention. Known Cases and Outbreaks of Ebola Hemorrhagic Fever, in Chronological Order. Available at: http://www.cdc.gov/ncidod/dvrd/spb/mnpages/dispages/ebola/ebolatable.htm. Accessed August 31, 2010.
1993	Cryptosporidiosis	Milwaukee, United States	MacKenzie W, Hoxie N, Proctor M, et al. A massive outbreak in Milwaukee of cryptosporidium infection transmitted through the public water supply. *New Eng J Med*. 2004;331:161-197.
1993	Hantavirus	New Mexico, Arizona, Colorado, and Utah, United States	Centers for Disease Control and Prevention. Tracking a Mystery Disease: Highlights of the Discovery of Hantavirus Pulmonary Syndrome. Available at: http://www.cdc.gov/ncidod/diseases/hanta/hps/noframes/history.htm. Accessed August 31, 2010.
1996	Variant Creutzfeldt-Jakob disease (vCJD; mad cow disease)	United Kingdom	Centers for Disease Control and Prevention. Fact Sheet: vCJD (Variant Creutzfeldt-Jakob Disease). Available at: http://www.cdc.gov/ncidod/dvrd/vcjd/factsheet_nvcjd.htm. Accessed August 31, 2010.
1997	H5N1 (avian influenza)	Hong Kong, China	World Health Organization. Avian Influenza ("Bird Flu"). Available at: http://www.who.int/mediacentre/factsheets/avian_influenza/en/#history. Accessed August 31, 2010.
1999	Nipah virus	Malaysia and Singapore	Centers for Disease Control and Prevention. Hendra Virus Disease and Nipah Virus Encephalitis. Available at: http://www.cdc.gov/ncidod/dvrd/spb/mnpages/dispages/nipah.htm. Accessed August 31, 2010.
2002	SARS	China	Centers for Disease Control and Prevention. Frequently Asked Questions About SARS. Available at: http://www.cdc.gov/ncidod/sars/faq.htm. Accessed August 31, 2010.

578 outbreaks in 132 countries that occurred just between 1998 and 2001.[10]

The problem of drug resistance is also substantial. About 4 percent of the tuberculosis in the world is multidrug resistant and not susceptible to at least two of the standard TB drugs.[4] There is also resistance to all of the drugs that treat malaria. A study in Uganda showed that 100 percent of the samples of *Shigella*, a bacterium that causes diarrhea, were resistant to a drug that had been commonly used to treat it.[11] In addition, methicillin-resistant *Staphylococcus aureus*, commonly known as MRSA, which used to be of concern mainly in hospital settings, has now spread to the community in many countries.

The U.S. Institute of Medicine (IOM) carried out important assessments of emerging and re-emerging infectious diseases in 1992 and 2003.[12] The IOM highlighted the most

TABLE 11-7 Selected Examples of Re-emerging Infectious Diseases

Year of Outbreak	Disease	Place	Source
1994	Plague	India	Centers for Disease Control and Prevention. International Notes Update: Human Plague—India, 1994. Available at: http://www.cdc.gov/mmwr/preview/mmwrhtml/00032992.htm. Accessed August 31, 2010.
1997	Cholera	Peru	World Health Organization. 1998—Cholera in Peru. Available at: http://www.who.int/csr/don/1998_02_25/en/index.html. Accessed August 31, 2010.
1998	Rift Valley fever	Ethiopia	Food and Agriculture Organization of the United Nations. Flare-up of Rift Valley Fever in the Horn of Africa. Available at: http://www.fao.org/newsroom/en/news/2007/1000473/index.html. Accessed August 31, 2010.
2003	Human monkeypox	Texas, United States	Centers for Disease Control and Prevention. Monkeypox: Questions and Answers. Available at: http://www.cdc.gov/ncidod/monkeypox/qa.htm. Accessed August 31, 2010.
2009	Dengue	Florida, United States	Centers for Disease Control and Prevention. Locally Acquired Dengue—Key West, Florida, 2009–2010. Available at: http://www.cdc.gov/mmwr/preview/mmwrhtml/mm5919a1.htm. Accessed August 31, 2010.

important factors that contribute to the emergence and re-emergence of infectious diseases, which are summarized in Table 11-9.

It is clear that change in many of these factors and change in their relationship with one another have been linked to the emergence and re-emergence of infectious diseases. Change in the environment and land use, for example, can have a major impact on disease emergence. This could include the well-known example of Lyme disease in the suburban United States, as housing has pushed up against deer populations and deer ticks have spread Lyme disease to humans. The emergence of Ebola virus as populations have pushed up against tropical rain forests also shows the potential impact of environmental change on the emergence of disease. The increasing amounts of travel and commerce in food and other goods also have the potential to spread infectious diseases more rapidly than ever. Improvements in technology may yield many benefits. Yet, they might also create the conditions for the emergence of disease, such as Legionnaire's disease in the cooling towers of air conditioners.[13]

The factors that contribute to the development of drug resistance are well known. They include:

- The increasing use of drugs
- Poor prescribing and dispensing practices
- Inappropriate use of the drugs by prescribers, dispensers, and patients
- Failure of patients to take appropriate doses of drugs

- The use of poor quality or counterfeit drugs that do not contain the appropriate level of therapeutic ingredients
- Too much use of antibiotics in agriculture, cattle and poultry raising, and fish farming
- Weak health systems, with poor laboratory capacity to diagnose disease and test for drug susceptibility[14,15]

Some of the factors that might contribute to the more rapid spread of resistant forms of disease include:

- Weak infection control in healthcare settings
- Poor sanitation and hygiene
- A lack of surveillance, leading to late detection of the disease[14,16,17]

It is important to highlight that weaknesses in public health measures or breakdowns in public health services can also contribute in a number of ways to the emergence and re-emergence of infectious diseases, including the development and spread of drug resistance. From the end of World War II until the advent of HIV, for example, there was an increasing sense in high-income countries that "infectious diseases had been conquered."[18] As a consequence, many countries scaled back their attention to such diseases, including TB. This reduction of attention to TB was associated with a resurgence of TB and drug-resistant TB in a number of settings, such as in New York City in the late 1980s.[18]

TABLE 11-8 Selected Examples of Drug Resistance, by Disease

Disease	Resistant Drug	Place	Description	Source
HIV	Any first-line drug	New York City, New York, United States	Primary resistance was 24.1% in 2003–2004.	Nugent R, Back E, Beith A. Center for Global Development. The Race Against Drug Resistance. 2010 June 14. Available at: http://www.cgdev.org/content/publications/detail/1424207. Accessed August 31, 2010.
		United Kingdom	Primary resistance was 19.2% in 2003.	Nugent et al.
Malaria	Chloroquine	Iran	Median failure rate in the presence of *Plasmodium falciparum* was 72.5% in 1996–2004.	Nugent et al.
		Ecuador	Median failure rate in the presence of *P. falciparum* was 85.4% in 1996–2004.	Nugent et al.
	Sulfadoxine-pyrimethamine	Philippines	Median failure rate in the presence of *P. falciparum* was 42.6% in 1996–2004.	Nugent et al.
		Myanmar	Median failure rate in the presence of *P. falciparum* was 27.8% in 1996–2004.	Nugent et al.
Multidrug-resistant tuberculosis (MDR-TB)	At least isoniazid and rifampicin	New York City, New York, United States	In this outbreak in the early 1990s, 1 in 10 cases of TB was MDR-TB.	Global Alliance for TB Drug Development. Drug-Resistant TB. Available at: http://www.tballiance.org/why/mdr-tb.php. Accessed August 31, 2010.
		Russia	16.3% of TB cases in Russia were MDR-TB in 2007–2008.	World Health Organization. Multidrug and Extensively Drug-Resistant TB (M/XDR-TB): 2010 Global Report on Surveillance and Response. Available at: http://www.who.int/tb/features_archive/world_tb_day_2010/en/index.html. Accessed April 29, 2011.
Methicillin-resistant *Staphylococcus aureus* (MRSA)	Beta-lactams (methicillin and other common antibiotics such as oxacillin, penicillin, and amoxicillin)	Colombia	Over 50% of *S. aureus*–infected individuals carried resistant strains in 2006.	Nugent et al.
		Japan	Over 50% of *S. aureus*–infected individuals carried resistant strains in 2006.	Nugent et al.
Pneumonia	Penicillin	Israel, Poland, Romania, Spain	Over 25% of *S. pneumoniae* isolates were resistant in 2002.	Nugent et al.
		France	Over 53% of *S. pneumoniae* isolates were resistant in 2002.	Nugent et al.
	Erythromycin	Vietnam	92% rate of resistance in 2001.	Nugent et al.
		Taiwan	86% rate of resistance in 2001.	Nugent et al.

TABLE 11-9 Key Factors Contributing to the Emergence and Re-emergence of Infectious Diseases

Microbial adaption and change
Human susceptibility to infection
Climate and weather
Changing ecosystems
Economic development and land use
Human demographics and behavior
Technology and industry
International travel and commerce
Breakdown of public health measures
Poverty and social inequality
War and famine
Lack of political will
Intent to harm

Source: Data from Smolinski MI, Hamburg MA, Lederberg J, eds. *Microbial Threats to Health.* Washington, DC: The National Academies Press; 2003:4-7.

TABLE 11-10 Selected Examples of the Economic Costs of Emerging and Re-emerging Infectious Diseases

Disease	Country	Year(s)	Cost
Cholera epidemic	Peru	1991	$771 million
Plague	India	1994	$1.7 billion
"Mad cow" disease	United Kingdom	1990–1998	$30 billion
Anthrax	United States	2001	$1 billion
SARS	Asia	2003	$30 billion

Source: Data from World Health Organization. *Infectious Diseases Across Borders: The International Health Regulations.* Geneva: WHO; 2007.

The Consequences of Emerging and Re-emerging Infectious Diseases

The costs of emerging and re-emerging diseases have varied considerably, but have sometimes been enormous, as shown in Table 11-10. In each of these cases, there were direct costs of caring for people who were affected, such as the costs of hospitalization. In addition, there were very large indirect costs. The 1991 cholera epidemic in Peru, for example, led to a major decline in people's social activities and their normal expenditures and had a major impact on the local economy. It also led to a substantial decline in tourism in a country in which this sector plays a major role. The plague in India in 1994 led to a major short-term decline in trade and commerce between India and the rest of the world. The U.K. government had to kill livestock to eliminate the possibility of mad cow disease and to convince a world that would not eat beef from the United Kingdom that this beef would be safe in the future. SARS led to a worldwide fear of a pandemic and to major reductions in trade, travel, and commerce between parts of Asia and the rest of the world. SARS also had an impact on the economy of Canada, after travelers received a warning from WHO about the risk of SARS in that country.[7]

It is important to note that these costs are not in proportion to deaths from these events. Between 1990 and 1998, for example, only 41 people died in the United Kingdom of mad cow disease.[7] Although SARS generated great fears, only 774 deaths were caused by this disease.[19] The costs of these "events" appear to be related to the fear of possible spread, rather than the actual morbidity and mortality caused by the disease.

The costs and consequences of drug resistance are also very high. The average cost of treating a case of drug-resistant TB is about 175 times the cost of treating a case that is susceptible to first-line drugs.[14] The cost of curing a patient of malaria with artemisinin-based combination therapy (ACT) is about 100 times the cost of curing a patient with chloroquine.[14] The cost of treating someone for certain infections with amoxicillin/clavulanic acid can be 25 to 60 times more expensive than treating them with penicillin. In addition, people are sicker longer and sometimes die as health providers try to find drugs to which these diseases are susceptible. Moreover, the use of some drugs actually encourages the development of resistance to other drugs, making it harder to treat some conditions.[14]

Addressing Emerging and Re-emerging Infectious Diseases

In some respects, the development of emerging and re-emerging infectious diseases, including antimicrobial resistance, is inevitable, given that it partially arises as a result of natural processes. On the other hand, we do have control over some of the factors that help to drive the development of these diseases. In principle, for example, population pressure on the environment could be reduced and land use planning could limit destruction of animal habitats. In practice, however, these approaches will require substantial change in the way in which people live and will not occur unless incentives are in place and reasonable alternatives exist. There are also many ways we can more appropriately use drugs, including decreasing use when drugs are not needed.[9,20]

Thus, even as people work both within and across countries to change some of the structural factors that drive the emergence and re-emergence of infectious diseases, they can take more immediate actions to reduce these threats and the threat of antimicrobial resistance. Because of their nature, some measures to address emerging and re-emerging infectious diseases will have to be taken within nations and others will require international action.

The foundation for strengthening the capacity to address emerging and re-emerging infectious diseases has to focus on "highly sensitive national surveillance systems, public health laboratories that can rapidly detect outbreaks caused by emerging and re-emerging infections, and mechanisms that permit timely containment."[7] This must also be coupled with the willingness of countries to share information about disease outbreaks in a timely manner with other countries. There is also a need for global coordination of these efforts.

Disease surveillance is based on GOARN. It was established in 2000 and is a network of existing disease surveillance networks.[21] Those who participate in it include an array of technical institutions, networks, and organizations that can contribute information to the global network, such as UN agencies, the International Federation of Red Cross and Red Crescent Societies, and Doctors Without Borders. WHO coordinates the network, building on the resources of its participants.

WHO published an updated version of the International Health Rules (IHR) in 2005.[21] The IHR lay out a framework that is intended to guide national and global efforts at strengthening surveillance capacity and the national and global capacity to respond to outbreaks. They make provisions for generating and reviewing information about disease outbreaks from a variety of sources, including both officials from countries and nonstate actors. This approach is meant to broaden the potential sources of information about outbreaks and overcome risks that would be posed by states that do not want to share information in a timely manner about disease outbreaks within their own country.

National action and global cooperation on disease surveillance and response were tested during an outbreak of H1N1 "swine flu" in Mexico in 2009, which was thought to pose a serious risk of becoming a global pandemic. In this case, the Mexican government did report the outbreak to WHO in a timely manner, there was a rapid global response coordinated by WHO, and a vaccine was developed quickly against this virus. Later, when a pandemic did not come about, there was some criticism of WHO for exaggerating the risks that this outbreak posed.[22] However, it appears that the response of Mexico in this case was considerably more helpful to the world than the long delay that China had in notifying the world about its SARS outbreak in 2003.

In many ways, however, there has been much less progress in addressing the particular issues that affect the development of drug resistance. There has been some progress in addressing resistance on a disease-by-disease basis, such as efforts to better diagnose, track, and treat drug-resistant TB or drug-resistant malaria. There have also been countries, particularly in Europe, that have sought to reduce the use of antibiotics. Nonetheless, the world has continued to fail to establish a well-coordinated mechanism that can work across countries and diseases to address, in a coherent and effective manner, the factors that drive the development of drug resistance.[14] Some believe that this failure is a critical one that places the world at grave risk of additional threats from resistant forms of disease and a real risk of running out of antibiotics and other drugs that can effectively address such diseases.

Over the last few years, however, a Drug Resistance Working Group has convened under the auspices of the Center for Global Development in Washington, D.C. It recently made a number of recommendations about how the world might move against drug resistance more forcefully. These are shown in Table 11-11.

Future Challenges

An important question concerns the extent to which diseases are emerging and re-emerging more rapidly than before, given the pace of changes in our environment and the increasing globalization of travel, trade, and transport. A detailed analysis of this question concluded that between 1940 and 2004, the number of occurrences of emerging and re-emerging infectious diseases did increase over time and peaked in the 1980s, probably in association with the spread of HIV.[6,9] In addition, when considering measures to address emerging and re-emerging infectious diseases, it is critical to remember that, for diseases that spread from human to human, there may only be a limited window for action after an outbreak begins if a pandemic is to be averted.[7] There is also a growing concern about the potential impact of the global economic crisis on the ability or willingness of governments to fund critical public health services. This is despite the fact that the potential economic consequences of possible disease outbreaks should make them more willing, rather than less

TABLE 11-11 Key Recommendations from the Center for Global Development Drug Resistance Working Group on Addressing Drug Resistance

- Improve surveillance by collecting and sharing resistance information across networks of laboratories.
- Establish an expert technical working group to develop, maintain, and monitor global standards for post-marketing drug quality and ensure that publicly funded drug procurement requires adherence to this standard.
- Create a new partnership of associations of medicine providers, regulators, and others involved in the drug supply chain to promote quality-assured provision of drugs, with accreditation of suppliers and better information to consumers.
- Strengthen national drug regulatory authorities in low- and middle-income countries.
- Catalyze research and development of resistance-fighting technologies by creating a web-based marketplace for the sharing of research in this area.

Source: Adapted from Nugent R, Beck E, Beith A. *The Race Against Drug Resistance.* Washington, DC: Center for Global Development; 2010.

willing, to address such threats during times that are already economically distressed.

Indeed, the factors that contribute to the emergence and re-emergence of infectious diseases are becoming more prominent in some places. Infectious disease specialists predict that in the face of rapidly evolving and adapting pathogens, continued population growth, popular encroachment into areas with forests and wildlife, and climate change, new diseases will now emerge and others will re-emerge at an increasing pace.

In addition, these tendencies will be made worse by poverty, environmental degradation, war, or the failure to properly address these diseases in public health terms. Public health specialists also believe that the world must be vigilant about the possibility that a major pandemic could arise from a newly emerging or re-emerging infectious disease. This could be the case, for example, with H5N1 influenza if that virus developed the ability to spread more efficiently from human to human.[9,18,20]

The development of drug resistance is also accelerating and spreading to places where it has not been prominent before.[15] This stems partly from the growing use of drugs in

low- and middle-income countries, as some of them have witnessed significant economic growth and increasing levels of education. It also reflects, however, that this increasing use is taking place in environments in which the other drivers of resistance have not yet been managed effectively.[14]

Of course, once drug-resistant forms of bacteria, viruses, or parasites do develop, they can spread more easily than ever, given the extent to which people travel, for example.[17] In addition, the behaviors in which people engage can also have an important bearing on the spread of resistant forms of microbes, such as people's failure to adhere to drug regimens or their use of poor quality drugs.

The problem of drug resistance is also compounded by the limited number of new anti-infective drugs that are under development and the speed with which even new drugs become subject to resistance.[14] In addition, there has been insufficient research and development for drugs to combat some of the most important burdens of disease for the poor in low- and middle-income countries, including those for which there is increasing resistance. The existing TB drugs, for example, are 50 years old and there is increasing resistance to them.

HIV/AIDS

The Burden of HIV/AIDS

Rarely has a single pathogen had a greater impact on the human condition than HIV. No cure exists for it. Although effective drugs are available to keep HIV/AIDS under control, drug regimens require careful adherence and have significant side effects.

Some of the basic facts about HIV/AIDS are presented in Table 11-12. HIV is a virus that can be spread through:

- Unprotected sex
- Mother-to-child transmission, during birth or through breastfeeding
- Blood, including by transfusion, needle sharing, or accidental needle stick
- Transplantation of infected tissue or organs

Being an uncircumcised male increases the risk of acquiring HIV. Females are also at greater biological and social risk than males of being infected with HIV, as discussed in Chapter 9. Having a sexually transmitted disease also increases the risk of HIV infection.

The efficiency with which the virus is transmitted varies. The virus is spread most efficiently from exposure to infected blood products and through the sharing of infected needles. There is a 90 percent probability of being infected from a transfusion of blood from an HIV-positive person.[23]

The efficiency of transmission is also relatively high from sharing needles with an HIV-infected person. Sexual transmission depends on the type of sexual act and whether the HIV-positive person is male or female. Male-to-female transmission is higher than female-to-male transmission. The risk of unprotected receptive anal intercourse is about 30 times greater than it is for receptive or insertive vaginal intercourse.[23]

HIV attacks the human immune system. The time from becoming infected until one is diagnosed with AIDS can vary from as little as 1 year to as many as about 15 years; however, without treatment for HIV, about half of those infected will be diagnosed with AIDS in 10 years. Infectiousness is high during the initial period of infection and also increases as the immune system weakens and in the presence of other sexually transmitted infections.[24]

As the immune system of an HIV-positive person deteriorates, that person will suffer from a variety of what are called opportunistic infections, because they take advantage of the person's compromised immunity. As their HIV disease reaches a fairly advanced state, for example, HIV-positive people who are not on antiretroviral therapy may fall ill with TB, herpes infections, a variety of cancers, and an array of significant communicable diseases such as toxoplasmosis and cryptococcal meningitis.[25]

The main routes of transmission of HIV vary by location. In the first phases of the epidemic in high-income countries and in Brazil, HIV was largely spread through unprotected sex among men who have sex with men. In sub-Saharan Africa, the disease has been spread overwhelmingly through unprotected sex between men and women, especially among those engaging in "high-risk behaviors," such as sex workers and their clients and men engaging in sex with multiple female partners. In China, the epidemic was centered originally in a group of people who received transfusions from blood that had been infected with the blood of HIV-positive people. From there, it spread largely through sex between men and women but also through injecting drug use. In Russia and much of the former Soviet Union, the epidemic is being driven by injecting drug users who are HIV-positive and who share needles. The epidemic is spreading from them to other groups largely through unprotected sex.

HIV/AIDS epidemics are categorized as either a *concentrated epidemic*, in which less than 1 percent of the population of adults is HIV positive, or a *generalized epidemic*, in which more than 5 percent of the adult population is infected. When HIV first appears in a population, it is generally concentrated in the most at risk populations (MARPs), such as sex workers, men who have sex with men, and injecting drug users. If

TABLE 11-12 HIV/AIDS Basic Facts: 2009
Number of people living with HIV/AIDS: 33.3 million
Number of new HIV infections: 2.6 million
Number of AIDS deaths: 1.8 million
Prevalence among adults: 0.1% in East Asia to 5.0% in sub-Saharan Africa
Distribution of infection by sex: 15.9 million women and 14.9 million men
Children under 15 with HIV: 2.5 million
Number of HIV-positive people being treated with antiretroviral therapy: 5.2 million

Source: Data from UNAIDS. UNAIDS Outlook Report 2010. Available at: http://data.unaids.org/pub/Outlook/2010/20100713_outlook_report_web_en.pdf. Accessed December 21, 2010; UNAIDS. UNAIDS Report on the Global AIDS Epidemic 2010. Available at: http://www.unaids.org/globalreport/Global_report.htm. Accessed December 21, 2010.

the virus is controlled in these groups, then the spread to the general population can be limited. A generalized epidemic means that HIV/AIDS has spread to the general population, transmission is widespread, and prevalence is high. South Africa and Zimbabwe, for example, have generalized epidemics. Cambodia has a concentrated epidemic.

It is estimated that about 33.3 million people worldwide are now infected with the HIV virus, and in the year 2009 about 1.8 million people died of HIV.[2] It is also estimated that about 2.6 million people were newly infected with HIV in 2009.[2] The prevalence of HIV varies considerably by region and by country. The prevalence rate of HIV by country is shown in Figure 11-2.

The highest rates of prevalence of HIV/AIDS are in Central and Southern Africa. Relatively high rates of HIV/AIDS are also found in several other African countries and in parts of the Caribbean. With about 22.5 million infections, sub-Saharan Africa has about 68 percent of the total number of infections in the world and about 72 percent of the AIDS-related deaths.[2]

New HIV infections occur predominantly in people ages 15 to 24.[26] They also occur among infants due to maternal-to-child transmission. In the high-income countries, efforts have been made to address maternal-to-child transmission, and there are almost no such cases any longer. In the highest prevalence countries, maternal-to-child transmission continues, although important progress in reducing it is occurring there as well.

FIGURE 11-2 HIV Prevalence by Country, 2009

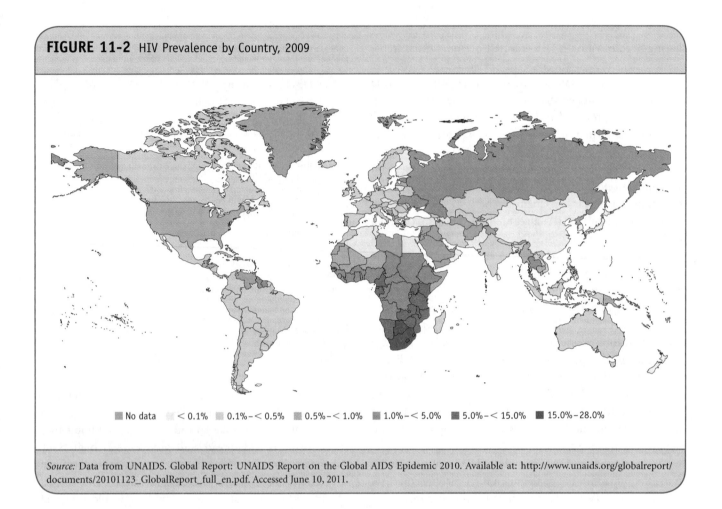

No data   < 0.1%   0.1%–< 0.5%   0.5%–< 1.0%   1.0%–< 5.0%   5.0%–< 15.0%   15.0%–28.0%

Source: Data from UNAIDS. Global Report: UNAIDS Report on the Global AIDS Epidemic 2010. Available at: http://www.unaids.org/globalreport/documents/20101123_GlobalReport_full_en.pdf. Accessed June 10, 2011.

The number of new HIV infections peaked globally in 1999. Between 1999 and 2009, global incidence declined by 19 percent. It also declined by 25 percent in 33 countries, of which 5 were in sub-Saharan Africa. Nonetheless, between 2001 and 2009, 7 countries, 5 in Eastern Europe and Central Asia, had increases in incidence of more than 25 percent. In 2009, there were still 2.6 million new infections, of which 2.2 million were in adults and the remainder in children less than 15 years of age.[2]

The Costs and Consequences of HIV/AIDS

HIV/AIDS has enormous social and economic consequences, especially in high prevalence countries in sub-Saharan Africa, which go beyond its impact on morbidity and mortality. HIV/AIDS affects family cohesion, business, trade, labor, the armed forces, agricultural production, education systems, governance, public services, and even national security.

In the absence of treatment, the person infected with HIV will eventually become sicker, progress to full-blown AIDS, and suffer from a variety of opportunistic infections,

as noted previously. As this happens, the person becomes less able to work, loses part or all of his or her income, and becomes dependent on others for care. The caretaker may also lose his or her income.

This cycle has caused enormous economic losses to individuals and their families, especially in sub-Saharan Africa. A study done in Tanzania, for example, indicated that men with AIDS lost an average of 297 days of work over an 18-month period, and women lost an average of 429 days of work over that same period, which implies that these women were essentially unable to attend to any of their normal tasks.[27] A study in Thailand showed that families that suffered from AIDS lost an average of 48 percent of their income as a result of their illness.[28]

Another important consequence of HIV/AIDS is the creation of an exceptional number of orphans. When speaking of HIV/AIDS, an orphan is defined as an individual 15 years old or younger who has lost one or both parents to the disease. It is thought that there may now be as many as 25 million HIV/AIDS orphans.[2] Despite efforts by many families to care for their relatives, many orphans do not have anyone with whom to live and may resort to living on the street, where they are at risk of falling into commercial sex or crime.

HIV/AIDS is a highly stigmatized condition, as are a number of other communicable diseases. HIV/AIDS, however, has a special stigma because people in many societies believe that people acquire HIV/AIDS because they engage in behaviors that society does not sanction, such as men having sex with men, commercial sex work, or injecting drug use. Understanding the notion of stigma and discrimination against people with HIV is central to understanding the HIV/AIDS epidemic.

In fact, stigmatization of HIV in many societies has led to an unwillingness to allow people with HIV to attend schools or be employed, get health care, live in certain places, or even live with their families. Stigma has also been a major constraint to people's getting tested or treated for HIV. It has also complicated prevention efforts in some settings by driving underground some of the very people it is important to reach, such as sex workers and injecting drug users.

For the poorest countries, the direct cost of AIDS treatment is very expensive compared to per capita income and per capita health expenditure, even at the reduced prices for those drugs that have been agreed upon globally. In fact, the cost of providing drugs and related laboratory and clinical services costs are generally at least $300 per patient, per year. Yet, many of the lowest-income countries that are providing AIDS drugs to people living with HIV/AIDS spend less than about $30 per person per year on health. It will be difficult for low-income countries with high HIV prevalence to support the treatment of a large share of people living with HIV/AIDS without considerable and sustained external assistance. This question is explored later in this chapter in the policy and program brief on the long-term costs and financing of HIV/AIDS.

The increasing attention paid to HIV has been positive in many ways. However, another cost of HIV/AIDS is the extent to which attention to it diverts human and financial resources away from other health priorities, such as child health or the neglected diseases. Striking an effective and equitable balance between HIV/AIDS and other public health priorities is a challenge for many countries.

Many studies of the impact of HIV/AIDS have been used to help convince governments that failure to address HIV early could result in lower economic growth of their country. Overall, the studies suggest that HIV/AIDS will have a large impact on the economic growth of high-prevalence countries in Africa, largely because it tends to strike people in their most productive years.[27] The higher the prevalence and the more families that use their savings to help pay for the costs of illness, the more likely HIV will have a negative impact on the growth of per capita income.[29]

Addressing the Burden of HIV/AIDS

Despite considerable and increasing efforts, there is not yet either a preventive or therapeutic vaccine for HIV/AIDS. In the absence of such a vaccine, halting the spread of HIV will have to focus on the prevention of new infections. Yet, despite 25 years of efforts to prevent HIV, there is little rigorous evidence about the most cost-effective approaches to prevention. Nonetheless, some evidence is emerging, as discussed in this section.

The few successful prevention efforts that have occurred, such as in Cambodia, Thailand, and Uganda, have consistently been associated with a number of factors related to strong political leadership and commitment, and open communications, including:

- Sustained political leadership at the highest levels
- Involvement of a broad range of civil society efforts to address HIV/AIDS, including opinion leaders and religious leaders
- Broad-based programs to change social norms in the population
- Open communication about HIV/AIDS and related sexual matters
- Programs to reduce stigma and discrimination[30]

In addition, we also know that to be successful, prevention efforts need to include:

- Good epidemic surveillance
- Information, education, and communication
- Voluntary counseling and testing
- Condom promotion
- Screening and treatment for sexually transmitted infections
- Prevention of mother-to-child transmission through avoiding pregnancy and antiretroviral treatment
- Interventions that target populations that transmit the virus from high-risk to low-risk populations
- Prevention of bloodborne transmission through blood safety, harm reduction for injecting drug users, and universal precautions in healthcare settings.[23]

Some additional comments on prevention efforts follow.

First, the approach to prevention will need to vary with the nature of the epidemic. In low-level and concentrated epidemics, the focus can be on changing the behaviors of those who engage in high-risk behaviors. The approach to prevention in a more generalized epidemic, however, will need to be broader.[23] Unfortunately, many countries have failed to align their investments in addressing HIV/AIDS with the nature of their epidemics. In Asia, for example, 90 percent of the funds spent on youth are spent on low-risk youth, who make up only 5 percent of the new infections.[2]

Second, there is an increasing understanding that prevention efforts have to include a combination of approaches, with different weight given to different activities, depending on the nature of the epidemic. These efforts will have to combine education and behavior change; bio-medical approaches, such as circumcision and drug therapy; and structural approaches, including measures such as improving income-earning opportunities and food security to reduce the risk of women engaging in transactional sex.

Education and behavior change efforts must focus on increasing correct knowledge of HIV, increasing the demand for HIV testing, later sexual debut, fewer sexual partners, and correct and consistent condom usage when engaging in high-risk sex. These activities are especially important in the most at-risk populations, including sex workers and their clients, and men who have sex with men.

A case study on Thailand is presented later in the chapter; it illustrates one of the most successful prevention efforts to date, which was based on a 100 percent condom use campaign. One of the policy and program briefs at the end of the chapter discusses the costs and financing of HIV/AIDS prevention in Cambodia, which has also had one of the most successful HIV/AIDS prevention programs. This was also based on a well-focused set of interventions, addressing the most at-risk populations, and involving these populations in program design and monitoring. Moreover, it also included a 100 percent condom use program.

These behavior change interventions need to be accompanied by efforts at "harm reduction" for injecting drug users. These are efforts to encourage the use of clean needles among injecting drug users, through needle exchange programs. They also include opioid substitution therapy, to try to wean addicts off heroin.

There has also been increasing attention paid to trying to stem maternal-to-child transmission of HIV. The most cost-effective measure to reduce maternal-to-child transmission of HIV is to avoid unwanted pregnancies of HIV-positive women through contraception. Providing antiretroviral therapy to pregnant women infected with HIV is also cost-effective because this may prevent about one third of the women from having a baby who is HIV-positive. If a woman is going to breastfeed her baby, the baby is less likely to be HIV-positive if the mother exclusively breastfeeds for 6 months and then introduces complementary foods to mix with the breast milk for the next 6 months.[31]

There is evidence that circumcised males are 40–60 percent less likely to be infected with HIV than uncircumcised males.[32] A number of adult circumcision efforts are now underway as a component of HIV/AIDS prevention activities. It will be important to learn from these experiences about the most cost-effective approaches to adult circumcision in different settings.

There is widespread agreement that ensuring that the blood supply is safe and free of the HIV virus, among other things, is cost-effective and must be a high priority in all settings.

There has been substantial progress in low- and middle-income countries in placing HIV-infected people on antiretroviral therapy. It is estimated that about 36 percent of those in need of treatment in these settings are receiving it.[2] In addition, about 1.2 million people were put onto therapy for the first time in 2009, bringing the total under therapy to about 5.2 million.[2] A number of countries, such as Botswana, Cambodia, Cuba, and Rwanda, have placed more than 80 percent of eligible people on treatment.

WHO has recently revised its guidelines on antiretroviral therapy and now calls for HIV-infected people to be placed on therapy when their CD4 cell count (a measure of immunity) is 350, rather than waiting until it drops to 200, as had earlier been the case. This will make more people eligible for treatment.

Once patients are under treatment, it is exceptionally important that they take all of their drugs exactly as prescribed in order to avoid developing resistance and to stay as healthy as possible. If the drugs are discontinued because of interrupted supply, poor compliance by the patient, or poor performance of the health system, resistance may develop and the patient may require more expensive second-line drugs. Drug-resistant strains of HIV also pose risks to others, who can become infected with them directly from others and then face difficulties finding effective drug regimens for their strain of HIV.

Overall, effective HIV/AIDS therapy depends on individuals accessing counseling and testing, a definitive HIV test, a clinical diagnosis of the patient, a laboratory assessment of the individual's immune status with a CD4 cell count, patient adherence to their drug regimen, sound patient nutrition, and sound and continuous monitoring and evaluation of the patient.

Critical Challenges in HIV/AIDS

A number of critical challenges constrain the fight against HIV/AIDS. First has been the difficulty of finding a vaccine for HIV. Given the fact that there are about 2.6 million new infections a year, it is important to continue the search for a vaccine. The search for a safe and effective microbicide, which has recently seen some promising results, must also continue.

Second, although globally there has been a reduction in HIV incidence, the number of new infections suggests that it is essential that greater attention be paid to the prevention of infection. More countries need to focus on prevention, with the political leadership and commitment that has been linked to the HIV "success stories" to date. We also need to learn more about the most cost-effective approaches to prevention in different settings. As long as pregnant women continue to be infected, it is important to continue to scale up prevention of maternal-to-child transmission. Greater attention must also be paid to prevention among the most stigmatized groups, including men who have sex with men and injecting drug users.

The efforts to make treatment universal for those who are eligible will continue. However, they will confront weak health systems and a lack of trained health workers as they expand further. Addressing the needs for treatment will require increasing attention to counseling and testing and understanding the most cost-effective approaches to treatment in different settings. There also needs to be a shift to the new eligibility criteria and increasing attention to therapy for children. Financing treatment, especially in low-income, high-prevalence countries in which there continues to be a substantial number of new infections, will be very difficult and require sustained external support for many years.

Improving the management of TB and HIV co-infection will also be essential. This is discussed further in the section on TB that follows.

Tuberculosis

The Burden of Tuberculosis

Some of the basic facts concerning TB are noted in Table 11-13. In 2009, there were about 14 million people worldwide with active TB disease and about 9.4 million new cases of active TB disease.[4]

Tuberculosis is caused by the bacteria *Mycobacterium tuberculosis*, and it is spread through aerosol droplets. People breathe in the TB bacteria from other infected people. Tuberculosis can affect all organs of the body, but 80 percent of cases infect the lungs.

Not everyone infected with TB becomes sick with it. Rather, the TB remains latent in the bodies of about 90 percent of those infected and they do not have active TB disease.

People with latent TB do not spread TB to others. About 2 billion people in the world are infected with TB but do not have active TB disease.

The nature of latent TB is extremely important, especially in an age of HIV, because latent TB can become active when people's immune systems become weak. This could occur because of immune-suppressing drugs or because of illness such as some cancers, diabetes, or HIV. Thus, the large pool of people in the world with latent TB infection have a very significant risk of developing active TB infection if they become infected with HIV.

An untreated person with active pulmonary TB can infect 10 to 15 people annually. If left untreated, about one third of those with active TB will die, one third will self-cure, and one third will remain infectious to others. Pulmonary TB can be spread from person to person, but people with TB in other organs generally do not spread TB. Active TB is characterized by a persistent cough for more than 3 weeks, decreased appetite, general weakness, and profuse night sweats.

In terms of the extent to which people can spread pulmonary TB, there are two forms of TB disease. One is called smear positive and the other is called smear negative. The recommended means for diagnosing TB in low- and middle-income settings is through a microscopic examination of smears of sputum from a person suspected of having TB. Smear-positive TB cases are those in which the presence of TB bacteria is confirmed by microscopic examination. They are the most contagious, and in resource-poor settings, they

---

TABLE 11-13 TB Basic Facts: 2009

Number of people living with TB: 14 million
Number of new TB cases: 9.4 million
Number of TB deaths: 1.7 million
Estimated number of new multi-drug resistant TB cases, among notified patients: 250,000
Global distribution of prevalence: 35% of cases in South-East Asia, 30% in Africa, and 20% in the Western Pacific Region; half of all new cases in Bangladesh, China, India, Indonesia, Pakistan, and the Philippines
Target of the Global Plan to Stop TB: halve 1990 prevalence by 2015

Source: Data from WHO. The Global Plan to Stop TB 2011-2015. Available at: http://www.stoptb.org/assets/documents/global/plan/TB_GlobalPlanToStopTB2011-2015.pdf. Accessed December 22, 2010; WHO. Global Tuberculosis Control 2010. Available at: http://whqlibdoc.who.int/publications/2010/9789241564069_eng.pdf. Accessed December 22, 2010.

have received priority for treatment, but this is beginning to change.[33]

The TB–HIV interface is a very important public health issue in terms of TB transmission and morbidity and mortality for both TB and HIV. The *lifetime* risk of developing active TB for a person who is *not* infected with HIV is 10 percent. If a person is HIV-positive, however, the *annual* risk of developing active TB is 10 percent; thus, after 8 years, the HIV-positive individual has an 80 percent chance of developing active TB. HIV/AIDS is also associated with a higher proportion of TB that is not pulmonary, compared to TB in people who are not HIV-positive. In addition, TB in HIV-positive people is often very difficult to diagnose.

There are about 9 million new cases of TB each year and about half are sputum-smear-positive.[4] Africa has the highest estimated incidence with 340 new cases per 100,000 population, but the most populous countries of Asia, such as Bangladesh, China, India, Indonesia, Pakistan, and the Philippines, annually comprise half of the total number of new cases in the world.[4,33] Men are more frequently infected with TB than are women, possibly because of reporting, but also because of exposure and, perhaps, susceptibility. Nonetheless, TB is also a leading killer of women, with about 700,000 female deaths attributed to TB annually.[34]

In the 2001 study of the global burden of disease, TB was the eighth most important cause of death worldwide.[4] It also accounted for 36 million DALYs, which was 2.3 percent of the world's total. Seventy-five percent of the TB infections and deaths occur in the most productive age group—those who are 15 to 54 years old.[33]

Incidence rates are falling in four of the six WHO regions, but they are stable in the Southeast Asian region of WHO. Three of the six regions—the Americas, the Eastern Mediterranean Region, and the Western Pacific region—will halve their 1990 TB prevalence rates by 2015, but the other regions will fail to meet this global target.[35]

The main risk factors for TB are exposure to a person infected with TB, living in crowded circumstances, undernutrition, HIV, inadequate health care, and other conditions that weaken the immune system. Smoking, alcohol consumption, and diabetes are also risk factors for TB. Tuberculosis is overwhelmingly a disease of the poor because it is they who have the most exposure to all of these risk factors.

There has been an increase in TB infections that are resistant to one or more TB drugs. These forms of TB are called drug-resistant TB, multidrug-resistant TB (MDR-TB), and extensively drug-resistant TB (XDR-TB). About 4 percent of the TB cases that were detected worldwide in 2009 were estimated to be multidrug resistant.[35] An underlying

cause for the development of resistant forms of TB is the failure to complete TB treatment, as was the case for Maria in one of the opening vignettes. However, it is also possible to be infected with drug-resistant TB directly from another person. Drug-resistant strains are found in many countries and are difficult and expensive to treat. Drug resistance is especially important in countries in which TB programs are weak or have fallen into disarray, as in many of the very poor countries, Russia, and in countries with high rates of HIV. In 2006, a number of cases of XDR-TB were found in South Africa among HIV patients, and 52 of 53 patients died within 25 days, despite being on HIV treatment. This caused considerable alarm in the public health community.[36]

The Costs and Consequences of TB

The cost of TB to families, communities, and countries is very high, given the large number of people who are sick with TB, the relatively long course of the illness, and the losses people face when they do have TB. A study of TB in India suggested that those sick with TB lost about 3 months of wages, spent an amount equal to about one quarter of national income per capita on care and treatment, and took on debts to pay for this care that were equal to about 10 percent of per capita income.[37] A similar study in Bangladesh indicated that those sick with TB lost 4 months of wages.[38] A Thai study showed that TB patients spent more than 15 percent of their annual wages on TB, 12 percent of them took out bank loans to help make up for the costs of their illness, and 16 percent sold part of their property to finance the costs of dealing with their illness.[39]

There are also significant social costs associated with TB. Because of the stigma associated with TB, females who get infected are often shunned by their families. In one Indian study, 15 percent of the women with TB faced familial rejection.[40] In another Indian study, 8 percent faced rejection.[37]

A study of the macroeconomic impact of TB suggested that the economic growth of a country is inversely correlated with the rate of TB. Every increase of 10 percent in the incidence of TB was associated with lower annual economic growth of 0.2–0.4 percent.[41] A study of the economic costs of TB in the Philippines indicated that the annual economic loss due to morbidity and premature mortality from TB was equal to almost $150 million. In addition, the cost to the Philippines of treating all of the expected cases of TB would be between $8 million and $29 million.[42]

Addressing the Burden of TB

There is a vaccine for TB called BCG that is a standard part of the Expanded Program of Immunization for Children. The vaccine reduces severe TB in children, but because children are not important transmitters of TB, the vaccine has little impact on the overall incidence or prevalence of TB.[43] Rather, the control of TB depends on effective treatment of active tuberculosis. In many respects, implementing a poor TB program is worse than not having a TB program at all because a poor TB program can give rise to drug-resistant TB.

The treatment strategy for TB is called DOTS: Directly Observed Therapy, Short-Course. DOTS consists of a 6-month regimen that normally includes four drugs—isoniazid, rifampin, pyrazinamide, and ethambutol—for the first 2 months, and then isoniazid and rifampin for the following 4 months. DOTS is just what it says—a relatively short course of therapy directly observed by a local care provider or community member, compared to the longer course that had previously been given without such observation.

The DOTS strategy has five essential components:

- Sustained political commitment to a national TB program
- Access to quality-assured sputum smears and microscopy
- Standardized regimens of short-course chemotherapy under direct observation
- Regular uninterrupted supply of quality-assured anti-TB drugs
- Monitoring and evaluation for program supervision[33]

Once an active case of TB is identified, appropriate drugs are required in adequate supply for 6 months. Patient compliance with the TB regimen is required for effective therapy, and direct observation is meant to ensure appropriate treatment for the entire course. Healthcare workers, NGO staff, and community volunteers and leaders, such as teachers, religious leaders, and other community members, provide observation. They are sometimes the holders of the medicine, as well as the persons who observe TB patients taking their medicines.

Treating active TB with DOTS is very cost-effective and ranges from $5 to $50 per DALY averted in most regions.[43] The cost of treating a TB case, in fact, can be as low as $100 in a number of low-income countries, such as India and Myanmar. BCG is cost-effective in reducing severe cases of childhood TB in high prevalence settings. Treating multidrug-resistant TB is also relatively cost-effective.

The Management of TB/HIV Co-infection

As noted in the section on HIV/AIDS, TB is an opportunistic infection of HIV. As the immune system of an HIV-positive person declines, TB is one of the diseases that can develop. This is especially so in populations where many people have latent TB. In addition, TB is the leading cause of death of adults who are HIV-positive and not on antiretroviral therapy.

WHO recommends a number of measures to manage TB and HIV co-infection. These include ensuring that all of those who are HIV-positive are tested for TB and all of those with TB are tested for HIV. WHO also recommends immediately putting on antiretroviral therapy anyone who is HIV-positive who has TB. The guidelines also focus on infection control in healthcare settings so that TB does not spread among those who are infected with HIV. There are still substantial gaps in many countries in managing TB/HIV co-infection in conjunction with these guidelines.

Challenges in TB Control

Although there has recently been progress in improving TB diagnostics, one critical challenge in TB is the need to develop more effective vaccines, inexpensive and rapid diagnostics for all forms of TB, and drug therapy that will lessen the duration of treatment and the number of pills that patients have to take. A related challenge is to ensure that new tools, such as new diagnostics, are put into use and scaled up as rapidly as possible.

In some regions there remains the need to diagnose more of those with TB, and in some regions, particularly Eastern Europe and Central Asia, there is a need to cure a larger share of those who are treated. There is an especially large gap in diagnosing MDR-TB, with only about 12 percent of such diagnoses being made now of those who are registered TB patients. Efforts will also need to be made to improve the treatment success for MDR- and XDR-TB patients.

A considerable amount of TB diagnosis and treatment is carried out in the private sector, and often not in acceptable quality ways. Improving TB diagnosis and treatment will require further efforts at linking all providers of TB diagnosis and treatment with national TB control programs. There has been some important progress in this direction, but there remain enormous gaps to fill for public–private partnerships for TB control.

Beyond these points and the need to strengthen the management of TB/HIV co-infection, the Global Plan to Stop TB emphasizes the importance of further linking TB control with the strengthening of health systems. This would include the improvement of laboratory services and infection control and embedding TB control further in enhanced approaches to primary health care. The Plan also highlights the importance of promoting more community-based approaches to information and education about TB and the increased involvement of communities in TB control efforts.

Malaria

The Burden of Malaria

Malaria is caused by parasites in the genus *Plasmodium*, four species of which infect humans: *Plasmodium falciparum*, *Plasmodium vivax*, *Plasmodium ovale*, and *Plasmodium malariae*. These parasite species exist in different proportions in different regions of the world. *Plasmodium falciparum*, for example, dominates in Africa; *Plasmodium vivax* occurs in temperate zones; and *Plasmodium ovale* is found in South Asia and tropical Africa. The disease is spread by the bite of the female *Anopheles* mosquito. Essentially, the mosquito carries the parasite from an infected person to an uninfected person.

Malaria infects 300 to 500 million people annually, kills 1 million people each year, and causes over 40 million DALYs lost annually, which is equal to 2.9 percent of the global total of DALYs.[5,44] Malaria is the ninth leading cause of death in low- and middle-income countries and the fourth leading cause of death among children ages 0 to 14 in those countries. Sub-Saharan African children account for 82 percent of the malaria deaths worldwide. About 11 percent of the childhood deaths worldwide are attributed to malaria.[44] Sub-Saharan Africa and five countries in Asia make up 98 percent of the global burden of malaria.[5]

The most important risk factor for malaria is being bitten by mosquitoes that carry the malaria parasite. This risk varies with the feeding habits of various species of mosquitoes, the climate, and the time of year. Some people have a degree of immunity to malaria from having grown up in malarial zones, and the risks of contracting malaria increase if one does not have such immunity.

Pregnant women are at high risk of giving birth to low birthweight children, and they and their fetuses are at high risk of anemia and death because of malaria. It is estimated that 45 million pregnancies occur annually in malaria-endemic areas of Africa and 23 million occur in high malaria transmission areas. Three to 15 percent of African mothers suffer severe anemia, accounting for 10,000 malaria-related anemia deaths per year. Globally, malaria causes about 30 percent of low birthweight in newborns and between 75,000 and 200,000 infant deaths per year.[45]

The Costs and Consequences of Malaria

The cost of malaria at the family level is substantial because individuals often have malaria up to five times per year. In one study in Ghana, for example, there were 11 cases of malaria per household, per year, on average.[28] These same studies showed that individuals lost one to five work days per episode of malaria, that the indirect cost of dealing with their illness was greater than the direct costs of treatment, and that each episode of malaria probably cost an adult about 2 percent of his annual income.[28] In many African countries, malaria typically accounts for 30 percent or more of outpatient visits and hospital admissions for children under 5 years of age.[46]

It is estimated that $12 billion is lost annually due to malaria in Africa alone.[46] Roll Back Malaria suggests that the economic costs of malaria in countries with a high malaria burden is a loss of about 1.3 percent GDP per year. One study suggested that a 10 percent reduction in malaria was associated with a 0.3 percent increase in economic growth. Clearly, malaria in sub-Saharan Africa is a deterrent to trade, business development, tourism, and foreign investment.[47,48]

Addressing the Burden of Malaria

Despite many years of effort, there is still no vaccine against malaria. However, there is widespread agreement on the key interventions required to "roll back" malaria. These include:

- Prompt treatment of those infected, based on confirmed diagnosis
- Intermittent preventative therapy for pregnant women
- Long-lasting insecticide-treated bed nets for people living in malarial zones
- Indoor residual spraying of the homes of people in malarial zones

Appropriate treatment of malaria is essential to reduce malaria morbidity and mortality. If people with malaria are treated promptly, then mosquitoes that bite them will not carry malaria to another person. Drugs such as chloroquine, fansidar, and mefloquine are being used but face growing levels of drug resistance.

Artemisinin, a relatively new drug for malaria, is now being used in combination with other antimalarial drugs in areas where malaria is resistant to other drugs. Efforts are also underway to get artemisinin into use as soon as possible in all malarial areas, so that the advent of resistance can be delayed. This is discussed in the policy and program brief later in the chapter on the Affordable Medicines Facility—malaria. Treatment with artemisinin plus other antimalarial drugs is referred to as ACT, which stands for artemisinin-based combination therapy. Effective therapy depends on accurate laboratory diagnosis and appropriate case management. In addition, pregnant women are being treated with intermittent preventive therapy from between 18 and 24 weeks of their pregnancy through delivery, to reduce complications and deaths from malaria among this group of people.

The use of long-lasting insecticide-treated bed nets and eliminating mosquito breeding sites represent additional means of malaria control. Bed nets, impregnated with a biologically safe insecticide, are being widely distributed for free and sold by governments, donors, and the private sector. Spraying the inside of homes, or indoor residual spraying, is also to be carried out. Reducing the number of mosquitoes that carry malaria at the community level relies on effective communication and commitment by local leaders, the identification of breeding sites, and the availability of appropriate larvicides and/or tools to drain potential breeding sites. However, reducing the number of mosquitoes, called source reduction, is particularly difficult in Africa because the vector, *Anopheles gambiae*, is ubiquitous and breeds in all types of standing water.

Challenges in Addressing Malaria

The goals of the Global Malaria Action Plan that was developed in 2008 include:[5]

- Reducing global malaria cases from 2000 levels by 50 percent in 2010 and 75 percent in 2015
- Reducing global malaria deaths from 2000 levels by 50 percent in 2010 and to near zero in 2015
- Eliminating malaria in eight countries by 2015, followed by other countries now in a pre-elimination phase

The plan also includes the goal of long-term eradication of malaria, through progressive elimination in different countries.

Achieving these goals will require, first, the scaling up of key interventions for prevention. This includes trying to ensure 100 percent coverage for people at risk with long-lasting insecticide-treated bed nets, indoor residual spraying, and intermittent therapy for pregnant women. Progress in these areas will have to include not only the dissemination of bed nets, but also greater efforts at behavior change, to ensure that families actually use the nets properly when they have them.

There are substantial gaps in the diagnosis and treatment of malaria, with many cases diagnosed without confirming the presence of malaria by microscopy or a rapid diagnostic test. In addition, many of those who suffer from malaria are not given the right medicine or not given medicine in a timely manner, which can result in death. The goal is to treat confirmed cases of malaria with the appropriate medicines within 24 hours of diagnosis.

There has been some progress in the development of a malaria vaccine; however, like for HIV, there is no vaccine yet. A safe, effective, and affordable vaccine could make major inroads against malaria. Better diagnostics could also be helpful. In addition, the continuous development of new drugs to fight malaria is also critical, given the speed with which malaria has developed resistance to other drugs and the limited number of drugs that now work effectively against malaria.

Diarrheal Disease

The Burden of Diarrheal Disease

As briefly discussed in Chapter 10, diarrhea is caused by certain bacteria, viruses, and/or parasites that are transmitted by contaminated water or food through the fecal–oral route, such as *Shigella* sp., *Salmonella* sp., *Cholera vibrio*, rotavirus, and *Escherichia coli*. Diarrheal disease agents can be spread by dirty utensils, dirty hands, or flies. Diarrhea causes severe dehydration and a loss of body water and can kill infants and young children very quickly. Poor recognition of the extent of illness, failed home care, and lack of knowledge about simple therapies increase the severity of diarrhea. Diarrheal diseases can be prevented by access to safe drinking water, improved sanitation, and the carrying out of more hygienic personal behaviors, such as handwashing.

Diarrheal diseases most significantly impact the poor, especially children in developing countries.[49] Poor housing, crowding, lack of safe water and sanitation, cohabitation with domestic animals, lack of refrigeration for food storage, and poor personal and community hygiene all contribute to the transmission of diarrheal disease agents. In addition, poor nutrition contributes to poor immunity and increases the frequency and severity of diarrhea.

Diarrheal disease mortality has decreased significantly in the past 30 years, from an estimated 4.6 million deaths in the 1980s to the 1.5 million estimated today, which is about 20 percent of all childhood deaths.[50,51] The decline is due to improved nutrition of infants, better disease recognition, improved care seeking, and appropriate use of oral rehydration therapy, as discussed in the case studies in Chapters 5 and 10. Nonetheless, the burden of diarrheal disease remains very substantial. Diarrhea is a major cause of death and sickness for children younger than 5 years. Children suffer about 3.2 episodes of diarrhea annually, but rates vary worldwide.[52] It is estimated that each year *Shigella* causes 113 million episodes of bloody diarrhea in children under 5.[49]

Addressing the Burden of Diarrhea

There are five major disease prevention strategies for diarrhea. Perhaps most effective is the promotion of exclusive breastfeeding for 6 months. This is advantageous to the child and mother because the child receives both maternal antibodies and a nutritious and uncontaminated meal. Mothers benefit from an increased birth interval and a healthier child. The second prevention intervention is improved complementary feeding, introduced with breastfeeding after 6 months. The third is rotavirus immunization, which will be increasingly cost-effective as the vaccines are more affordable in low- and middle-income countries. Diarrhea from rotavirus annually kills about 600,000 children under 5 years.[53] The next strategy is increased measles immunizations. Data indicate a clear link between measles immunization and reduced incidence and deaths from diarrhea. If measles coverage is increased, especially in Africa, then the burden of diarrheal disease will decline. The fifth prevention strategy is improving access to safe water supply and sanitation. Clean water and appropriate sanitation will reduce diarrheal disease incidence. Furthermore, handwashing can reduce diarrhea incidence by 3 percent.[54]

Three case management interventions can significantly reduce the severity and mortality of diarrheal disease. The use of oral rehydration therapy (ORT) is the most cost-effective case management intervention, especially if home-made solutions are administered. Although the use of ORT has expanded globally, only about 49 percent of the diarrhea cases worldwide are managed with ORT or home fluids.[49] Second, it is estimated that zinc supplementation during an acute diarrhea episode for 10 to 14 days during and after diarrhea could prevent 300,000 deaths per year.[55] Third, antibiotics can be given for bloody diarrhea, primarily caused by *Shigella* infection. However, delivering this intervention where it is most needed may depend on careful training of nonphysician healthcare personnel because most low-income and many middle-income countries do not have enough physicians living in places where they are most needed.

Neglected Tropical Diseases[56]

The Burden of Neglected Tropical Diseases

More than 1 billion people, about one sixth of the world's population, are infected with one or more of the neglected tropical diseases (NTDs).[57] These 13 diseases, shown in Table 11-14, are the most common afflictions of the world's poorest people.

NTDs have a terrible impact on health, impede child growth and development, harm pregnant women, and often cause long-term debilitating illnesses. They cause an extraordinary amount of ill health, disability, and disfigurement, and are often deadly. As a result, those who suffer from NTDs are frequently shunned by their families and their communities. In addition, people with these diseases are often unable to work productively, leading to enormous economic losses for them, their families, and the nations in which they live.

Despite their significance, relatively little financial support has been provided to address NTDs, compared to the burden of ill health they cause. This is especially regret-table because significant progress has been made to control or eliminate some of the NTDs, including Chagas disease, lymphatic filariasis, onchocerciasis, and leprosy. It is also lamentable because a "rapid-impact package" of four drugs is available that can simultaneously treat the seven most common NTDs for between 40 and 80 cents per person per year.[58] Given the exceptional amount of good health that can be gained in the fight against NTDs for such a small amount of money, an important global challenge is to spread the rapid-impact package as fast as possible to all of the places where it can be of benefit.

The NTDs shown in Table 11-14 are 13 parasitic and bacterial infections that affect approximately 1.4 billion people worldwide. Seven of these diseases are especially important, given the large number of people affected by them. A number of infections related to intestinal worms, which are called *soil-transmitted helminths*, affect an extraordinary number of people. These include roundworm (ascariasis), which affects 807 million people worldwide; whipworm (trichuriasis); and hookworm, each of which affects over 600 million people. The four other most common NTDs are schistosomiasis (snail fever), affecting about 200 million people; lymphatic filariasis (elephantiasis), which affects 120 million people; blinding trachoma, affecting more than 80 million people; and onchocerciasis (river blindness), which affects almost 40 million people.

A number of diseases kill more people than NTDs do. However, some estimates suggest that NTDs result in as many DALYs lost annually as would be lost by malaria,[58] largely because of the extent to which the NTDs make people sick for long periods of time and the manner in which they cause long-lasting disabilities.

Figure 11-3 shows the global distribution of NTDs. Seven different NTDs can be found in a number of countries, mostly in Africa, but also including Brazil and Cambodia. Six of the common NTDs are found in many countries in sub-Saharan Africa and five NTDs can be found in many of the other low- and middle-income countries of Africa, Asia, and Latin America.

NTDs are diseases of poverty, affecting nearly everyone in the "bottom billion" of the world's poorest people. NTDs are especially prevalent in subtropical and tropical climates. Women and children who live in unhygienic environments with limited access to clean water and sanitary methods of waste disposal face the biggest threat of NTDs. Pregnant women also face special risks from some NTDs, as discussed later in this section. People engaged in farming are particularly susceptible to NTDs because of their close contact with soil, which can harbor many of the parasites and worms that

TABLE 11-14 The Major Neglected Tropical Diseases, Ranked by Prevalence

Ascariasis (roundworm)
Trichuriasis
Hookworm infection
Schistosomiasis
Lymphatic filariasis (elephantiasis)
Trachoma
Onchocerciasis (river blindness)
Leishmaniasis
Chagas disease
Leprosy
Human African trypanosomiasis
Dracunculiasis
Buruli ulcer

Source: Data from Hotez PJ, et al. Current concepts: control of neglected tropical diseases. *New Eng J Med.* 2007;357(10):1019.

cause NTDs. People who live in Africa and rely on rivers for drinking and bathing are also more likely to be affected by certain NTDs, such as onchocerciasis. Individuals whose labor or domestic chores are centered on freshwater sources are also more likely to contract NTDs.[59]

In addition, the burden of the "worm" diseases has to do not only with being infected, but also with the number of worms in the body. Children of preschool age have the greatest number of worms. In addition, the prevalence of intestinal worms in many children of school age in the highest burden countries is exceptionally high. It is estimated, for example, that over 75 percent of the school-age children in Rwanda are infected with soil-transmitted helminths.[60]

Without going into too much detail, it is valuable to understand how some of the most common NTDs are transmitted and some of their most important clinical manifestations.

- The *soil-transmitted helminths* have very similar life cycles. Humans ingest the eggs of the worms. The eggs hatch into larvae, which travel to different parts

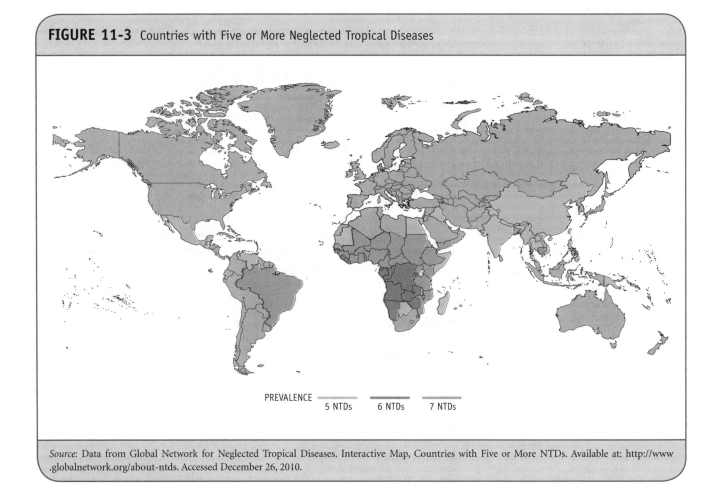

FIGURE 11-3 Countries with Five or More Neglected Tropical Diseases

PREVALENCE
5 NTDs   6 NTDs   7 NTDs

Source: Data from Global Network for Neglected Tropical Diseases. Interactive Map, Countries with Five or More NTDs. Available at: http://www.globalnetwork.org/about-ntds. Accessed December 26, 2010.

of the body, depending on the type of worm. The worms might feed on food from the human host or attach themselves to the intestinal lining and live off the blood of the host. Eggs pass from the human host in feces and can then be picked up by others who will get infected.

- *Schistosomiasis* is caused by a liver fluke. People with schistosomiasis release fluke eggs in their urine or feces. The flukes infect freshwater snails. When humans swim, bathe, or work in water with infected snails, the fluke can penetrate their skin. One form of fluke manifests itself in the intestinal tract and liver and another in the urinary tract; both can cause severe disease.

- The cycle of transmission for *lymphatic filariasis* is very different from that for the helminthic infections. In this case, mosquitoes bite infected humans and pick up the larvae, which develop inside the mosquito and migrate to the insect's mouth. When this mosquito bites a human, it transmits the hatched larvae into the skin. Larvae can survive in the lymphatic system for up to 6 years, and when they die, they cause the severe disfigurement associated with lymphatic filariasis.

- The black fly that causes *onchocerciasis* goes through a similar process. Infected flies carry the larvae from person to person through bites in the skin. These become adult worms, and the females release millions of small larvae into the body.

- *Trachoma* is caused by bacteria that lead to a discharge in the eye. It is transmitted when someone comes in contact with the discharge, usually by touch. However, flies can also spread the disease from person to person.[59]

The Consequences of the Neglected Tropical Diseases

NTDs can have terrible social and economic consequences, as well as a major impact on the health and well-being of those infected. On the clinical side, trachoma, for example, can lead to redness and swelling of the eye, sensitivity to light, corneal scarring, and eventually permanent blindness. Schistosomiasis is associated with painful and/or bloody urination, bloody diarrhea, enlargement of the liver and/or spleen, and liver cancer; it is also the most deadly of the NTDs. Lymphatic filariasis is well known for the horrible swelling it can cause of the limbs and genitals. Onchocerciasis leads to skin problems and can also lead to blindness.

The helminthic infections are generally associated with abdominal pain, loss of appetite, malnutrition, diarrhea, and anemia. In addition, chronic helminthic infection in children can limit the physical and mental development of the child. Pregnant women with hookworm are at high risk of giving birth to low birthweight babies, of having poor milk production, and of birthing babies who fail to thrive. In addition, pregnant women with anemia, commonly caused by hookworm in low-income countries, are three and a half times more likely to die during childbirth than women who are not anemic. This risk is especially significant, because a quarter to a third of pregnant women in sub-Saharan Africa are infected with hookworm.[61] Whipworm also can lead to severe growth retardation in children.

NTDs by themselves not only have enormous effects on individuals, but also worsen the effects of other major infectious diseases or make individuals more susceptible to them. Recent studies have shown that many people have one or more NTDs at the same time as they have HIV or malaria, which worsens the intensity of those diseases. In addition, helminthic infections may serve as important factors in the transmission of HIV/AIDS.[62] Genital schistosomiasis in females may develop into lesions that increase susceptibility to becoming infected with HIV.[63] Neglected tropical diseases are also associated with the onset of some chronic noncommunicable diseases, such as the bladder cancer associated with urinary schistosomiasis.[64]

Social stigma is a major consequence of the NTDs. Many of the NTDs cause disability and disfigurement, resulting in individuals being shunned by their families and their communities. When not treated, for example, leprosy can cause terrible skin lesions that have been stigmatized since biblical times. Few health conditions are as stigmatizing as the swelling of limbs and genitalia that can result from lymphatic filariasis. Individuals who are stigmatized are less likely to leave their homes to seek diagnosis and treatment. Social stigma is particularly demoralizing for young women because they are often left unmarried and unable to work, in settings where the social "value" of a woman has much to do with her marital status.

NTDs also have a major impact on the productivity of individuals and the economic prospects of communities and nations. Children are disproportionately affected by NTDs, and often suffer long-term consequences from them. Hookworm infection in school-age children contributes in some areas to drops in school attendance by greater than 20 percent, and poor school attendance and poor school performance reduce future earnings. In fact, hookworm has been shown to reduce future wage-earning capacity in some affected areas by up to 43 percent.[65]

NTDs adversely affect economic productivity at the individual, family, community, and national levels. NTDs lead to important losses in income that cause some families to sell assets to try to stay financially solvent. In addition, regions severely affected by onchocerciasis often cannot be used effectively for economic activities such as farming, because families that try to live in these areas are at risk of being blinded by the disease. Trachoma alone has been shown to contribute annually to an estimated $2.9 billion loss in productivity worldwide.[66]

Addressing the Neglected Tropical Diseases

Despite the many people still affected by NTDs, considerable progress has been made in the fight against a number of them. Onchocerciasis has been eliminated as a public health problem in 10 countries in West Africa, as discussed in a case study in Chapter 15. Guinea worm is nearing eradication, as a result of a global effort that focused on health education and teaching people to filter their water through finely woven cloth. In fact, the number of Guinea worm cases has fallen from more than 3.5 million in 1986 in 20 countries to fewer than 5000 cases in 6 countries in 2007.[67] Guinea worm is reviewed as a case study in Chapter 3.

In 1997, WHO developed a strategy known as SAFE (surgery, antibiotics, face washing, environmental change) to combat trachoma worldwide. As a result of this program, trachoma prevalence has been reduced globally from 149 million cases in 1997 to 41 million cases in 2008. The program was particularly effective in Morocco, where the SAFE strategy was the first to be tested at the national level. Through the donation of over $72 million worth of drugs by Pfizer to treat trachoma, as well as interventions to improve environmental hygiene, the prevalence of trachoma declined by an extraordinary 99 percent.[68] Trachoma in Morocco is discussed further later in this chapter in one of the case studies.

Lymphatic filariasis has been controlled in China, Thailand, Sri Lanka, Suriname, and the Solomon Islands. This was accomplished by the annual administration of appropriate drugs to all of the people of an affected area, usually by working closely with communities. Two pharmaceutical companies, Merck and Pfizer, have donated drugs for the program against lymphatic filariasis. In its first 8 years alone, the Global Program to Eliminate Lymphatic Filariasis has made significant progress in preventing the disease. An estimated 6.6 million newborns were saved from acquiring lymphatic filariasis during this period and 9.5 million people previously infected with overt manifestations of the disease were protected from developing severe disease.[69]

In addition, a better foundation has been set globally, as well as within some countries, for dealing more effectively and on a broader scale with NTDs. This builds upon work done by a variety of partnerships, including the Global Alliance to Eliminate Lymphatic Filariasis, the African Programme for Onchocerciasis Control, and the Partnership for Parasite Control. The Global Network for Neglected Tropical Diseases, for example, has been established at the Sabin Vaccine Institute to help develop more coherent, effective, and efficient approaches to NTD control. The Global Network is composed of a number of member organizations who deliver treatments on the ground, including the Earth Institute at Columbia University, Helen Keller International, the Global Alliance to Eliminate Lymphatic Filariasis, the International Trachoma Initiative, the Schistosomiasis Control Initiative at Imperial College, and the Task Force for Global Health. The Global Network works to build advocacy, policy, and resource mobilization efforts to support members and local governments in implementing NTD control programs.

Moreover, the Global Network for Neglected Tropical Diseases, with funding from the Bill & Melinda Gates Foundation, has recently developed a regional approach to NTDs that focuses on Africa, Asia, and Latin America. The Global Network will create hubs in each of these regions that will help to coordinate NTD efforts, raise funds for addressing NTDs, and provide technical support to NTD activities. In addition, the Global Network is working with the Inter-American Development Bank and the Pan American Health Organization to create a trust fund for combating NTDs in the Latin America and the Caribbean region. This will support the delivery of about 200 million treatments against NTDs. Funding for NTD control has increased from both the philanthropic sector and bi-lateral development agencies.

The successes against NTDs so far suggest that considerable additional progress can be made, rapidly and at relatively low cost, to combat the exceptional number of cases of NTDs that remain worldwide. However, further progress is likely to require concerted action in a number of areas, including scaling up the rapid-impact package, focusing on deworming, integrating NTD control with other programs, developing new technologies to address NTD control, and moving forward with political will.

It is essential to quickly scale up the rapid-impact package referred to earlier, to address the seven most common NTDs. The package includes a combination of four of six drugs: albendazole or mebendazole, praziquantel, ivermectin or diethylcarbamazine, and azithromycin (see Table 11-15).

Four of the six drugs that are used against the seven most common NTDs are donated by pharmaceutical companies, including GlaxoSmithKline, Johnson & Johnson, Merck, and Pfizer. In sub-Saharan Africa, the projected overall cost of the program is about 40 to 80 U.S. cents per person per year,

TABLE 11-15 NTD Treatment for Selected Endemicity Scenarios

| Medicine Set | Endemicity Scenario | | | | Recommended Combination of Medicines |
	STH	LF	SCH	ONCHO	Medicines
A	✓	✓	✓	✓	ALB + IVM + PZQ
B	✓	✓		✓	ALB + IVM
C	✓	✓	✓		ALB + DEC + PZQ
D	✓	✓			ALB + DEC
E	✓				ALB/MBD

ALB = albendazole; DEC = diethylcarbamazine; IVM = ivermectin; LF = lymphatic filariasis; MBD = mebendazole; ONCHO = onchocerciasis; PZQ = praziquantel; SCH = schistosomiasis; STH = soil-transmitted helminths

Note: The Rapid Impact Package would also include azithromycin to treat trachoma.

Source: Adapted from Weaver, Sankara D. The ABCs of NTDs. Presentation at the USAID Mini-University, September 12, 2008.

which would be a "best buy" in global health, given its low cost and large impact on public health.

Following the lessons of the onchocerciasis program and others, the rapid-impact package can be put in place rapidly with the help of medicine distributors who are chosen from among members of the affected communities. They would be brought into the program through social mobilization activities. These efforts would bring together key actors from the public and private sector in a partnership and would seek to involve affected communities in the design, implementation, and monitoring of the program. This type of community-directed treatment for onchocerciasis with ivermectin has proven particularly successful in rural Africa, where treatment has been extended to nearly 60 million people. In fact, a recent study showed that community-directed interventions are much more effective than conventional delivery approaches, which have less community participation, in combating most communicable diseases in sub-Saharan Africa.[70]

Periodic deworming of young children is also a "best buy" in global health and should be a major focus of attention.[71] Deworming is the single most cost-effective means to improve school attendance. There is also historical evidence that deworming improves children's cognitive skills and their potential to learn and leads to greater literacy and higher productivity among adults.[72] In addition, recent studies have shown that deworming children may significantly reduce the burden of malaria, because children infected with ascariasis are twice as likely to get severe malaria as children who are not infected.[73]

Moreover, there are considerable opportunities, in regions of high prevalence of malaria and HIV, for effectively integrating NTD treatment programs with existing AIDS and malaria control programs. This integration could help such programs to reduce the burden of NTDs and the burden of HIV and malaria, while contributing to improving the cost-effectiveness of all of the programs. This is especially important because hookworm and schistosomiasis often worsen the effects of malaria.[74] The distribution of bed nets and treatment for NTDs such as onchocerciasis and lymphatic filariasis could also help to control malaria. Such a program led to a substantial improvement in the use of bed nets in central Nigeria, where insecticide-treated bed net distribution was combined with mass drug administration for treatment of lymphatic filariasis and onchocerciasis.[75]

Future Challenges

As we look to the longer run, it is also important to invest in the search for new technologies that could help to address NTDs in more effective and efficient ways. With the assistance of the Bill & Melinda Gates Foundation and private donors, work is underway by the Vaccine Development Program at the Sabin Vaccine Institute to develop both hookworm and schistosomiasis vaccines. A safe and effective hookworm vaccine, particularly one that would confer lifelong immunity, would eliminate the need to provide medicine for deworming twice a year to all children living in affected areas, which is a substantial undertaking. The development of a vaccine for schistosomiasis is also being carried out by the Institut Pasteur.

It is also critical to develop new drugs to combat the NTDs. The world is now dependent on only four drugs to address the seven most common NTDs. There is resistance to some of the drugs, and more extensive use of them could lead to additional resistance. Developing drugs that can combat the NTDs more effectively than the present drugs continues to be a goal of considerable importance.[76]

At the same time as countries seek to prevent and treat NTDs through programs of mass drug administration or treatment of specific diseases, they need to work with communities to address the underlying risks for NTDs. For the seven most common NTDs, these risks overwhelmingly relate to the unsanitary living conditions of the poor. It will remain important for people to better understand the importance of good hygiene, to have better access to safe water and sanitary disposal of human waste, and to eliminate worm and parasite breeding sites. In the long run, progress in all of these directions will help to reduce the burden of NTDs and sustain reductions. Unfortunately, however, these developments are not likely to take place quickly. The fastest and most cost-effective route to reducing the burden of NTDs will be to implement as fast as possible the rapid-impact package.

POLICY AND PROGRAM BRIEFS

Three policy and program briefs follow to illustrate some of the key points noted in the chapter. The first concerns a public–private partnership to improve the control of drug-resistant TB. The second introduces readers to a novel international effort that is being piloted to spread the use of artemisinin combination therapy for malaria. The last is a summary of some important new findings concerning the long-term costs of HIV/AIDS and how they might be met both globally and at the level of countries with different burdens of disease and different income levels.

Public–Private Partnerships for Addressing Drug-Resistant Tuberculosis[77]

Eli Lilly is a major pharmaceutical firm. It was founded in 1862 and is based in Indianapolis, Indiana, in the United States. Like a number of major corporations, Lilly has a program of corporate social responsibility (CSR), in which it tries to go beyond its normal corporate activities to be directly helpful to the larger community.

Lilly's flagship CSR program is the Lilly MDR-TB Partnership. This public–private initiative was established in 2003 to confront the deadly global epidemic of MDR-TB. At that time, few global organizations, with the exception of Doctors Without Borders (also known as Médicins Sans Frontières, MSF) and Partners in Health (PIH), recognized the need to treat MDR-TB as a priority. The Partnership, which encompasses global health and relief organizations, academic institutions, and private companies, has adopted a broad-based approach to tackle the complex interwoven medical, social, and economic challenges posed by TB. It mobilizes over 20 global healthcare partners on 5 continents to share resources and knowledge to confront TB and MDR-TB. The partnership is funded to spend $135 million over 9 years.

The Partnership was launched to support WHO's goal of treating 20,000 MDR-TB patients annually by 2010, a goal which was met 3 years early. Lilly first supplied drugs at concessionary prices to MSF, PIH, and WHO. Lilly then embarked on a program to provide knowledge and financial assistance to reputable pharmaceutical manufacturers in China, India, Russia, and South Africa—the countries most severely affected by MDR-TB—so that they might be able to manufacture drugs against MDR-TB in their own countries at a reasonable price.

Understanding that TB cannot be conquered by medicine alone, the Partnership tries to address TB from a number of perspectives. First, for example, the Lilly MDR-TB Partnership has implemented community-level programs in over 80 countries to raise awareness about MDR-TB, increase access to treatment, ensure correct completion of treatment, and empower patients by eliminating the stigma of the disease. These programs include a comprehensive media campaign to try to ensure that TB-related messages reach patients and their families, communities, healthcare workers, and policy makers.

The Partnership also trains healthcare workers to recognize, treat, monitor, and prevent the further spread of MDR-TB. Training materials and courses have been designed to ensure that the knowledge learned is passed on to peers, furthering the quality of patient care. In addition, workplace toolkits and training programs allow companies to adopt policies and procedures to detect TB and properly treat and care for their workers.

The Partnership also undertakes a number of efforts at the global level. It works with policy makers, for example, to raise awareness about the toll that TB takes on the global population and encourage new initiatives to curb the spread of MDR-TB. In addition, Lilly created the Lilly TB Drug Discovery Initiative. This is a not-for-profit partnership that will draw on the global resources of its partners, including medicinal libraries—information on different chemical compounds used in making drugs—donated by Lilly, to pioneer research on the development of new drugs against TB that will require a shorter course of therapy than the existing drugs.

So far, the Lilly MDR-TB Partnership has met a number of its aims, including:

- Training of healthcare practitioners, including thousands of nurses, doctors, and hospital managers, through online courses and in-person workshops. For example, the International Council of Nurses has trained more than 1000 nurses on TB and MDR-TB in more than a dozen countries in their Lilly-supported Training of Trainers program. Each of these nurses has gone on to train other nurses in their workplace, resulting in over 19,000 nurses trained on TB and MDR-TB to date.
- Continued transfer of Lilly drug technologies to seven partners to increase the local supply of drugs at affordable prices.
- Distribution of TB workplace toolkits to help organizations rapidly implement TB control programs to thousands of companies worldwide. Representatives of more than 1500 organizations in India and South Africa have been directly trained on the use of the toolkit.
- Providing valuable input and support into the development and implementation of regional and national TB programs in the four countries hardest hit by MDR-TB (China, India, Russia, and South Africa).

These efforts have produced a number of valuable outcomes to date, including lower death rates, higher cure rates, better adherence to treatment, and increased TB and MDR-TB awareness.

In addition, Lilly believes that its program in MDR-TB has already yielded a number of useful lessons about TB control. This includes the idea that we will not succeed in the fight against TB by tackling only one obstacle. Rather, Lilly believes that success against TB will depend on joint, simultaneous efforts by all organizations involved in the fight—to remove the stigma of TB so patients will seek help; to improve diagnostics at the point of care; to manufacture safe, high-quality medicines administered by trained workers in accessible settings; to support families of TB patients; and to develop new TB treatments.

Affordable Medicines Facility—Malaria

The Affordable Medicines Facility—malaria (AMFm) is a novel arrangement that was created in 2009 to increase access to and ensure affordability of the most effective antimalaria drugs, artemisinin-based combination therapies (ACTs). These are drugs in which the effective substance of artemisinin is combined with another malaria drug in one treatment. The AMFm is hosted and managed by the Global Fund to Fight AIDS, TB, and Malaria.

The AMFm aims to improve access to ACTs by those who need them and to displace the use of older medicines that are no longer effective against malaria or that increase the risk of developing widespread parasitic resistance to artemisinin; this will help to preserve the usefulness of ACTs for future malaria treatment.[78] At present, a number of other drugs for malaria are widely available in public sector clinics, private sector pharmacies, and local retail shops of various types and sizes. They are also inexpensive. However, *Plasmodium falciparum* malaria is already resistant to these drugs in many places and is becoming resistant to them in other places. In addition, artemisinin monotherapy, in which artemisinin is not combined with other drugs, is sold in many places, which can increase the risk of resistance to artemisinin, which is the last line of defence against malaria in many places in which other drugs are no longer effective.

The AMFm seeks to spur the demand for and proper use of ACTs by lowering their price so it is comparable to the price in local markets of chloroquine and sulfadoxine-pyrimethamine. The AMFm also aims to help lower the final price of ACTs to the point where it will be lower than the prices of oral artemisinin monotherapies and will, therefore, drive these drugs out of the market.

The AMFm negotiates with pharmaceutical manufacturers to get the best price possible for ACTs for suppliers with which it is working. However, this price is still quite high compared to the cost of the older drugs or artemisinin monotherapy. Thus, the AMFm shares the wholesale cost of the ACTs with eligible first-line buyers, such as private sector wholesalers, hospitals, and nongovernmental organizations, so that they can sell them to patients at prices that patients can afford.[79] In this way, the AMFm seeks to make ACTs widely available to patients through service providers everywhere, including health clinics in the public sector, NGOs, and the private sector.

Although getting the drugs to patients at affordable prices is necessary, it is not enough, because providers, clinicians, and patients also have to use them rationally. Thus, the AMFm also provides funding for interventions to promote proper use of ACTs in countries already receiving its support. These include training, supervision, and marketing and information campaigns to assist in the safe and effective implementation of the program, as well as additional efforts to reach the more vulnerable populations with this important combination drug.

The AMFm is new and needs to be carefully tested and evaluated before it is refined, expanded, or dropped. Thus, the AMFm is beginning with nine pilot projects from 2010 to 2012 in eight countries: Cambodia, Ghana, Kenya, Madagascar, Niger, Nigeria, Tanzania (mainland and Zanzibar), and Uganda. The intended short-term benefits of the pilots include increased availability, affordability, and market share of ACTs, thus increasing access to ACTs while displacing oral artemisinin monotherapies from the market.[78] The program's principal design challenges include uncertainties about the extent to which middlemen will pass the benefits of price reductions to patients, and the risk that cheap ACTs will be diverted from pilot countries to other countries, and then sold for profit. The solution to the latter is to implement the AMFm in all malaria-endemic countries. The pilots will be carefully and independently evaluated to inform decisions about the future of the AMFm.

Funding for AMFm comes from UNITAID, the Bill & Melinda Gates Foundation, the U.K. Department for International Development (DFID), and the Global Fund. The Roll Back Malaria Partnership coordinates technical support for countries in the AMFm.[78]

The Long-Term Costs and Financing of HIV/AIDS

In 2008, an international consortium of partners, called *aids2031*, was established to examine the future of HIV/AIDS. The consortium was especially interested in understanding the trajectory of the epidemic to 2031—50 years after the virus was discovered—under various scenarios. The idea of taking such a long-term view of the epidemic was that it would allow countries and their partners to better understand how measures they take or fail to take today can impact the course of their epidemic in the long run.

Nine international and multidisciplinary working groups were established to carry out the work of *aids2031*. One of them was charged with examining the long-term costs and financing of HIV/AIDS.[80] This Costs and Financing Working Group was asked to estimate the long-term costs and financing of HIV/AIDS using different scenarios, so that policy makers and stakeholders could make more appropriate policy choices in the short and medium run for addressing their epidemics as effectively and efficiently as possible. The working group was led by the Results for Development Institute, a think tank based in Washington, D.C.

In particular, the Costs and Financing Working Group sought to answer the following questions:

- What would it cost to address the epidemic under various scenarios over the next two decades?

- What factors would be the most important drivers of the costs?
- How can governments, donors, and stakeholders use scarce resources most effectively and efficiently to prevent more infections, keep more people alive, and protect and nurture AIDS orphans?
- How can HIV/AIDS efforts be financed in the future, and in what ways should that financial burden be shared among individuals, their countries, development partners, and private and philanthropic organizations?[78]

The Working Group on Costs and Financing carried out its work on three levels. First, it prepared a global estimate, which looked at costs and financing broadly across a large number of countries. In collaboration with partners in Cambodia and South Africa, the Working Group then examined the long-term costs and financing of HIV/AIDS in greater detail in each of those countries. These case studies sought to apply and validate at the national level the costing, priority setting, and financial mobilization tools that had been developed by *aids2031* through its global work. In addition, it was hoped that the country case studies would provide valuable information for stakeholders in Cambodia and South Africa and provide valuable lessons for other countries, as well.

Global View

The analysis of the estimated global cost of AIDS was led by the Results for Development Institute. The *aids2031* project estimated that globally, between 2009 and 2031, HIV/AIDS will cost between $397 billion and $722 billion, depending on the policy choices that governments and donors adopt.[81] Four different scenarios were considered to estimate this projected cost: current trends, rapid scale-up, hard choices, and structural change.[81]

If the current trends continue, the number of new HIV infections in 2031 drops only slightly to 2.1 million while costing $490 billion. Rapid scale-up would include 80 percent coverage of most interventions, save 7 million lives, avert 14.2 million infections, and cost $722 billion. On the other hand, the hard choices scenario is the most cost-effective approach and focuses on a small number of cost-effective activities, costing $397 billion. The hard choices option is estimated to result in more HIV/AIDS-related deaths than under the rapid scale-up scenario, but would be significantly lower than with the current trends. The structural change option would cost $579 billion and is estimated to have the greatest impact in reducing future spread of the infection, with 1.2 million people newly infected with HIV in 2031.[81]

The Working Group forecasted the availability of funds to fight AIDS. Currently, over half of the funding sources are from domestic expenditures; however, AIDS programs rely heavily on external funding, especially in low-income countries. The Working Group found that middle-income countries with a low burden of HIV/AIDS will eventually be able to take on the costs of their HIV/AIDS response. Middle-income countries with a high burden of HIV/AIDS will be able to address HIV/AIDS over the next 10 years if there is a rapid scale-up, matched by outside funds. However, low-income countries with a high burden of disease will remain dependent on external support to be able to address the high cost of HIV/AIDS.[81]

Cambodia Case Study

The Cambodia case study was led by the Cambodian National Center for HIV/AIDS, Dermatology, and Sexually Transmitted Infections (NCHADS), working in close collaboration with staff from the Ministry of Economy and Finance. Cambodia was selected as an example of a "low-prevalence, low-income" country. In addition, Cambodia was potentially an especially valuable case study because it had made enormous progress against the epidemic, bringing new infections down from about 16,000 a year in 1998 to almost 2000 a year in 2009. However, the financing of its HIV/AIDS program was 90 percent dependent on Cambodia's development partners, and it appeared that these partners would not sustain this level of financing much longer.

The Cambodian study team developed six scenarios to explore the epidemiologic consequences of different policy choices, what each scenario would cost, and how Cambodia's HIV/AIDS program could be financed in the future to maximize desired outcomes at the lowest cost. These scenarios ranged from trying to engage in the best possible level of coverage as fast as possible, the Best Coverage scenario, to a Worst Case scenario, in which Cambodia would not be able to continue even its present levels of coverage of key program activities. They also included a Current Coverage scenario and scenarios in which Cambodia sharply focused on the most at-risk populations, as well as expanded coverage to reduce maternal-to-child transmission of HIV, called the Hard Choice 1 and Hard Choice 2 scenarios.[82] The study team also included a Structural Change scenario to examine how political, social, and economic changes could impact the epidemic and reduce risk for certain populations.

Overall, the analysis indicated that the current HIV/AIDS program in Cambodia is likely to lead to further declines in HIV prevalence and incidence over the next two decades. In fact, all scenarios for HIV incidence, except the Worst Case scenario, have a downward trend. However, even in the Best Coverage scenario, Cambodia would still have 1000 new HIV infections per year. In the Worst Case scenario, in which coverage of interventions falls from current levels, Cambodia could have as many as 3800 new HIV infections per year, which would represent a reversal of the significant gains achieved in Cambodia.

The key findings related to costs are that HIV/AIDS resource requirements will continue to increase over the next two decades. Cumulative financial needs vary between $1.3 billion and $2.2 billion over the next two decades, depending on the path taken by the Cambodian HIV/AIDS program.[82] However, the outcomes from these two choices are not substantially different. Thus, Cambodia will need to focus on getting the best value for money from its HIV/AIDS program by focusing HIV/AIDS investments on those areas that are most cost-effective. This may lead to an approach similar to that of the Hard Choice scenarios, for example, with attention, as well, to key elements in the Structural Change scenario. It will also be valuable for Cambodia to focus on further enhancing the efficiency of its HIV/AIDS program by taking steps such as improving the efficiency of its training and supervision programs, reducing the costs of laboratory supplies and equipment, and increasing the quality of the drug treatment program even as it seeks to reduce costs of drugs.[82]

The Cambodian HIV/AIDS program is very dependent on external financing, and there is substantial risk that such financing will be reduced. Assuming that donor assistance would eventually decline from 90 percent to 50 percent, three scenarios for development assistance were examined: the Optimistic Scenario, gradually reducing funding to 50 percent in 2025; the Moderate Scenario, reducing funding to 50 percent by 2020; and the Pessimistic Scenario, rapidly reducing funding to 50 percent in 2015. The Optimistic Scenario would result in an annual funding gap of $9 million, whereas the Pessimistic Scenario would result in an annual gap of $21 million.[83] Over the longer term, Cambodia should be able to meet the costs of its HIV/AIDS program through increasing fiscal space for HIV/AIDS that will come with economic growth. However, if Cambodia's development partners withdraw financing from the HIV/AIDS program too quickly, Cambodia could face substantial difficulty in making up the deficit in the short term.

South Africa Case Study

South Africa was selected as a case study because of its exceptionally high rate of prevalence of HIV, the large number of new infections annually, the enormous costs associated with treating all of those infected with AIDS, and the need to better understand how those costs would be financed. South Africa, in fact, has the largest number of HIV-infected people of any country, about 5.7 million, and almost half a million new infections per year. South Africa represented a "high-prevalence, middle-income country," the study of which could have lessons for a number of other countries. The South Africa study was conducted by the Centre for Economic Governance and AIDS in Africa (CEGAA), working in close collaboration with the South African Ministry of Health and the South African Ministry of Finance.

The *aids2031*-South Africa project aimed to estimate the influence of political will, available resources, rate of behavioral change, and implementation capacity on the magnitude, nature, costs, and impacts of the national response to HIV/AIDS in South Africa.[83] Three scenarios were developed to explore the financial and epidemiologic consequences of different policy choices: Hard Choices; Narrow NSP (National Strategic Plan), and Expanded NSP.[83]

The analysis showed that the estimated costs from now until 2031 under the Narrow NSP, or the current national approach, are $88 billion, with the number of new infections falling only slightly to 350,000 per year.[83] If the Expanded NSP option is pursued, total costs may rise to $102 billion over the next 20 years, but the number of infections would fall dramatically to 200,000 annually. Under the Hard Choices scenario, only the most cost-effective prevention activities are expanded, decreasing the number of new infections to about 225,000 per year, a scenario whose cumulative costs were estimated at $79 billion.[83] In the coming years, the Hard Choices and Expanded NSP scenarios offer better alternatives to addressing AIDS than the current national strategic plan. The Hard Choices scenario could lower the number of infections at a lower cost, although it would not halve the number of new infections as the more expensive Expanded NSP scenario might.[83]

It will be necessary for South Africa to step up current HIV prevention strategies, carefully manage spending and expansion of antiretroviral therapy, address the impending HIV/AIDS financing gap, and improve cost analysis and monitoring, leading to fewer HIV infections in the future and lower costs to address HIV/AIDS in the next two decades.[83] Stepped up prevention strategies include the widespread implementation of proven effective tools, such as male circumcision, condom promotion, and prevention of mother-to-child transmission. Investment in social change programs that focus on high-risk and vulnerable populations may also result in greater reductions in new HIV infections.[83] The number of ART patients is expected to increase to 2 or 3 million over the next decade. In South Africa, treatment accounts for approximately two thirds of the current HIV/AIDS spending. It will be necessary for South Africa to carefully manage spending related to treatment services, investing in personnel and infrastructure to meet the increased need for treatment. The cost of addressing HIV/AIDS is expected to increase two-fold over the next few years, requiring an effective financial mobilization strategy by the government. It will be necessary to increase domestic financing, while filling in funding gaps with external support sources such as the U.S. President's Emergency Plan for AIDS Relief (PEPFAR) or the Global Fund. In order to assist with the budgeting process, it is recommended that facility- and project-based cost estimates be determined and made available in a database. Cost-effectiveness studies of prevention interventions are needed to pursue the most cost-effective approaches and to inform key policy decisions.[83]

CASE STUDIES

The control of communicable diseases remains challenging. However, important progress has been made against some of these diseases. Given the exceptional importance of communicable diseases in low-income countries, this chapter includes four case studies. One of them examines the efforts of Thailand to address sexually transmitted diseases and HIV/AIDS. Another discusses China's attempt to control TB through DOTS. The last two cases concern NTDs, one on Chagas disease in Latin America and another on trachoma in Morocco. Those interested in more detail on the cases can consult *Case Studies in Global Health: Millions Saved*.[84]

Preventing HIV/AIDS and Sexually Transmitted Infections in Thailand

Background

In Thailand, approximately 1 in every 60 persons is infected with HIV/AIDS and 75,000 children have been orphaned by AIDS.[85,86] Between 1989 and 1990, HIV among sex workers tripled, from 3.1 percent to 9.3 percent, and a year later reached 15 percent. Over the same period, the proportion of male conscripts already infected with HIV when tested upon entry to the army at age 21 rose six-fold, from 0.5 percent in 1989 to 3 percent in 1991.[86]

The Intervention

In 1989, Dr. Wiwat Rojanapithayakorn, director of a regional office for communicable disease control in Thailand's Ratchaburi province, sought to curb AIDS by making sex in brothels safe, going well beyond the government's approach of raising awareness through mass advertising and education campaigns. Knowing that he could only be effective with political support, he sought the cooperation of the provincial governor. The steep rise in AIDS persuaded the governor to acquiesce, even though prostitution is illegal in Thailand and the government's intervention could imply that it tolerated or even condoned it.

A program was launched with one straightforward rule for all brothels in Ratchaburi: no condom, no sex. Until then, brothels had been reluctant to insist that their clients use condoms for fear of losing them to other establishments where condoms were not required. However, with condoms mandatory in all brothels, the competitive disincentive to individual workers and brothels was removed. Health officials, with the help of the police, held meetings with brothel owners and sex workers to provide them with information and free condoms. Men seeking treatment for sexually transmitted infections (STIs) were asked to name the brothel they had last visited, and health officials would then visit the establishment to provide more information. This pilot program had dramatic results, bringing down STIs in Ratchaburi within just a few months.[87] In 1991, the National AIDS Committee, chaired by Prime Minister Anand Panyarachun, adopted this 100 percent condom program at the national level.

The Impact

Condom use in brothels nationwide increased from 14 percent in early 1989 to more than 90 percent by June 1992.[88] An estimated 200,000 new infections were averted between 1993 and 2000. New STI cases fell from 200,000 in 1989 to 15,000 in 2001, while the rate of new HIV infections fell fivefold between 1991 and 1993–1995.[89] Such dramatic results have raised questions about their accuracy, as well as about their real causes, but independent studies have found the program to be genuinely effective.

The program did little to encourage the use of condoms in casual but noncommercial sex. Interventions among injecting drug users also did not expand to the national level, and the prevalence of HIV among this group is now as high as 50 percent.[90]

Costs and Benefits

Total government expenditure on the AIDS program remained steady at approximately $375 million from 1998 to 2001, representing 1.9 percent of the health budget. Of this, 65 percent was spent on treatment and care.

Lessons Learned

The success of the program is due, in part, to the sheer scale and level of organization of the sex industry in Thailand, assisting officials in tracing and co-opting brothel owners.

Thailand also had a good network of STI services within a well-functioning health system, providing treatment and advice, as well as crucial data for decision makers both at the baseline and when the program took effect. Cooperation among health authorities, governors, and the police was critical to success. Strong leadership from the prime minister, backed by significant financial resources, also made swift action possible. Maintaining Thailand's remarkable results in slowing the AIDS epidemic needs continued vigilance. Due to the high cost of treating STIs, the HIV prevention budget declined by two thirds between 1997 and 2004.[91] Although the Thai experience provides no blueprint for other countries with very different starting conditions, it does demonstrate that targeted strategies and political courage can effect change in deeply entrenched behaviors.

Controlling TB in China

Background

Although China established a National Tuberculosis Program in 1981, inadequate financial support hindered its success. In 1991, with $58 million from the World Bank, China embarked on the largest informal experiment in TB control in history: a 10-year Infectious and Endemic Disease Control project in 13 of its 31 mainland provinces.[92] The project adopted the DOTS strategy. Individuals demonstrating TB symptoms were referred to county dispensaries, where they received free diagnosis and treatment. Village doctors were given financial incentives for enrolling patients and completing their treatment. Efforts were also made to strengthen the institutions involved with the establishment of a National Tuberculosis Project Office and a Tuberculosis Control Center. Quarterly reports were submitted by each county to the province, the central government, and the National Tuberculosis Project Office, which strengthened monitoring and quality control.

Impact

China achieved a 95 percent cure rate for new cases within 2 years of adopting DOTS, and a remarkable cure rate of 90 percent for those who had previously undergone unsuccessful treatment.[93] The number of people with TB declined by over 37 percent between 1990 and 2000, and 30,000 TB deaths were prevented each year. More than 1.5 million patients were treated, leading to the elimination of 836,000 cases of pulmonary TB.[94]

Costs and Benefits

The program cost $130 million. The World Bank and WHO estimated that successful treatment was achieved at a cost of less than $100 per person. One healthy life was saved for an estimated $15 to $20, with an economic rate of return of $60 for each dollar invested.[95]

Lessons Learned

The success of China's program can be attributed to strong political commitment, leadership, adequate funding, and a sound technical approach delivered through a relatively strong health system. It was found that DOTS could be scaled up rapidly without sacrificing quality. Free diagnosis and treatment served as an effective incentive for patients, and incentives for doctors to diagnose and complete treatment also worked well. However, the overall rate of case detection proved disappointing, mainly due to the inadequate referral of suspected TB cases from hospitals to TB dispensaries; hospitals charging for services had no incentive to refer patients to dispensaries where services were provided for free.[96] In addition, patients at hospitals often abandoned treatment prematurely. Despite the program's success, TB remains a deadly threat in China, and efforts continue to maintain cure rates, as well as to expand DOTS coverage to the remaining population.

Controlling Chagas Disease in the Southern Cone of South America

Background

Chagas disease, or American trypanosomiasis, was Latin America's most serious parasitic infection in the early 1990s. Endemic in all seven countries of the southern cone, it caused an estimated 16 to 18 million infections and 50,000 deaths each year. In Brazil alone, it was estimated that over a 2-year period the economic costs of the disease were almost $240 million, and that $750 million would have been needed to treat its main health effects.[97]

The Intervention

The disease is named after Carlos Chagas, the Brazilian doctor who first described it in 1909 and subsequently discovered its cause: the parasite *Trypanosoma cruzi*. The parasites are found in the feces of "kissing bugs" that live within house walls in poor, rural areas and emerge at night to suck human blood. The parasites enter the bloodstream when insect bites are rubbed or scratched, or when food is contaminated. They can also enter via infected blood, or be transmitted from mother to fetus.

The first phase of the disease, the acute phase, is marked by fever, malaise, and swelling, and can sometimes be fatal, especially in young children. But most cases enter the second, chronic phase when the parasite damages vital body organs, resulting in heart failure, stomach pain, constipation, and swallowing difficulties that can lead to malnutrition.[98] A third of the cases are fatal.

In the absence of a vaccine or cure, control efforts needed to focus on eliminating the vector and screening the blood supply. Early attempts at control included methods such as dousing house walls with kerosene or scalding water, or enclosing and filling houses with cyanide gas. The introduction of synthetic insecticides offered a more plausible solution, and spraying campaigns began in several countries in the 1950s and 1960s. Brazil launched a national eradication campaign in 1983, involving nationwide spraying and volunteer schemes. Brazil's early success demonstrated the technical feasibility of vector control. However, it also highlighted the need for regional efforts against border-crossing insects, and the need for sustained political commitment.[99]

In 1991 a new control program called INCOSUR (Southern Cone Initiative to Control/Eliminate Chagas) was launched to bolster national resolve and prevent cross-border reinfestations. Led by the Pan American Health Organization (PAHO), the initiative was jointly adopted by Argentina, Bolivia, Brazil, Chile, Paraguay, Uruguay, and later, Peru. The countries financed and managed their own programs but met annually to share operational aims, methods, and achievements. Intercountry technical cooperation agreements fostered the sharing of information among regional scientists and governments, with additional scientific support from a network of researchers in 22 countries. Between 1992 and 2001, more than 2.5 million homes were sprayed. Canisters that release insecticidal fumes when lit were also provided. Houses were improved to eliminate hiding places for insects, adobe walls were replaced with plaster, and metal roofs were constructed. The screening of blood donors for the parasite is now virtually universal in 10 South American countries.[100]

Impact

Incidence in the seven INCOSUR countries fell by an average of 94 percent by 2000. Overall, the number of new cases on the continent fell from 700,000 in 1983 to fewer than 200,000 in 2000.[101] The number of deaths each year from the disease was halved from 45,000 to 22,000. By 2001, disease transmission was halted in Uruguay, Chile, and large parts of Brazil and Paraguay. Surveys indicate an improved sense of well-being, domestic pride, and security. Central America and the Amazon region remain the next major challenges.

Costs and Benefits

Financial resources for INCOSUR, provided by each of the seven countries, have totaled more than $400 million since

1991. The intervention is considered among the most cost-effective interventions in public health, at just $37 per DALY saved in Brazil.[101]

Lessons Learned

Chris Schofield, a researcher at the London School of Hygiene and Tropical Medicine, attributes INCOSUR's success to three factors: it was big and designed to reach a definitive end point; it had a simple, well-proven technical approach; and it gained political continuity from a close coordination between researchers and governments. Alfredo Solari, Uruguay's former minister of health, mentions four elements of success: peer pressure from neighboring countries in an exercise dealing with border-crossing insects; commitment by all participating countries, backed by international organizations like PAHO and WHO; an international technical secretariat at PAHO that verified surveillance, shared information about progress, processed certification requests, and organized annual meetings; and a favorable economic and institutional environment that allowed resources for expensive national health programs. Sustaining the achievements of INCOSUR will require vigilance, because premature curtailment of active surveillance against the disease could lead to disease resurgence.

Controlling Trachoma in Morocco

Background

Trachoma is the second leading cause of blindness, after cataract, and the number one cause of preventable blindness in the world. Although it has been eliminated in North America and Europe, trachoma still afflicts more than 150 million people in 46 countries, especially in hot, dry regions where access to clean water, sanitation, and health care is limited.[102] In Morocco, trachoma was once widespread, but in the 1970s and 1980s, treatment with antibiotics lowered its incidence in urban areas. A 1992 survey found that 5.4 percent of Moroccans still suffered from trachoma, mainly in five rural provinces in the southeast, where 25,000 people showed a serious decline in vision, 625,000 needed treatment for inflammatory trachoma, and 40,000 urgently required surgery.

The Intervention

Caused by the bacterium *Chlamydia trachomatis*, trachoma is highly contagious, spreading mainly among children through direct contact with eye and nose secretions, infected clothing, and fluid-seeking flies. Transmission of the disease is rapid in overcrowded conditions of poor hygiene and poverty. In endemic areas, prevalence rates in children ages 2 to 5 years can reach 90 percent.[103] Women are infected at a rate two to three times that for men because of their close contact with children. Repeated trachoma infections can lead to a painful in-turning of the eyelash, which can cause blindness.

In 1991, Morocco formed the National Blindness Control Program (NBCP) with several international and other agencies to eliminate trachoma by 2005. Between 1997 and 1999, this program implemented a pilot strategy to treat trachoma, developed by the Edna McConnell Clark Foundation, called SAFE (surgery, antibiotics, face washing, and environmental change). SAFE differed from earlier approaches by emphasizing behavioral and environmental change, in addition to medication. Under this four-part strategy, a quick and inexpensive surgery to prevent blindness was provided for large numbers of patients in small towns and villages. Antibiotics were used to treat infection and prevent scarring. Face washing, especially among children, was promoted through an education campaign. Living conditions and community hygiene were improved by constructing latrines, drilling wells, storing dung away from flies, and providing health education.[104]

In the mid-1990s, Pfizer discovered Zithromax, a one-dose cure to replace the 6-week course of tetracycline that had been used for treatment, ensuring a higher compliance rate. Pfizer donated the drug for Morocco, as well as for a number of other countries, through the International Trachoma Initiative (ITI), a private–public partnership that it forged along with the Clark Foundation.

Impact

Between 1999 and 2003, the SAFE strategy led to a 75 percent decline in trachoma in Morocco. Overall, the prevalence of active disease in children under 10 was reduced by 90 percent since 1997.[103,104]

Costs and Benefits

The Moroccan government provided most of the financing for the program. ITI supplemented this with several grants, and UNICEF contributed $225,000. Pfizer's donation of tens of millions of dollars' worth of Zithromax to Morocco and other countries represents one of the largest donations of a patented drug in history.

Lessons Learned

Government commitment to the program was critical to its success, in addition to the array of effective interventions. Four key factors were also listed by ITI: the program was based on solid scientific evidence; it was locally organized and, therefore, responded well to local circumstances; it fit within a broader agenda of health promotion, disease control, and health equity; and treatment was closely linked with prevention and the development of a strong public health infrastructure. ITI and its many partners have helped ensure that Morocco's success with SAFE, like the disease that it has nearly eliminated, is contagious.

FUTURE CHALLENGES TO THE CONTROL OF COMMUNICABLE DISEASES

A number of challenges constrain efforts to address the burden of the most important communicable diseases. Some of these relate to the need for countries to cooperate to combat communicable diseases. Some concern the ability of weak health systems in low- and middle-income countries to tackle communicable disease problems effectively. Others relate to the issues raised by specific diseases.

First, it is imperative to enhance political commitment to the prevention and control of these diseases. You read earlier that sustained political support at the highest levels is essential if progress is to be made against HIV/AIDS, and this is also true for the other leading causes of communicable disease. Countries will only be successful in acting against these diseases if they make them a real priority both politically and financially.

Second, the underlying causes of communicable diseases in low- and middle-income countries relate to poverty, people's lack of empowerment, people's lack of knowledge of appropriate health behaviors, and a lack of access to basic infrastructure such as safe water, sanitation, and health services. These issues will take many years to address in most low-income countries. Ways must be found in the short and medium term to work with communities to overcome some of these constraints, such as through community-based water supply and sanitation schemes and community-based distribution of drugs for neglected diseases.

It is likely that health systems in many low- and middle-income countries will continue to be weak for many years, as well. This suggests that efforts to address communicable diseases will also have to be based on partnerships with a variety of actors. This includes communities, religious groups and other nongovernmental organizations, the private sector, and government. The great successes in the control of infectious diseases to date have all been built upon the foundation of public–private partnerships. The polio eradication effort includes, for example, a remarkable amount of public–private collaboration, as does, for example, the campaign against onchocerciasis. It is especially important that these actors work together in the future

across an array of diseases and health systems issues and not just on individual diseases. Moreover, only by involving private providers of a variety of types can many diseases, such as TB, be addressed, because those providers are already so involved in service delivery.

Strengthening the surveillance of disease at the local, national, and global levels is also fundamental to effective disease control. A competent body of public health professionals needs to be responsible for managing surveillance networks. Appropriate laboratory infrastructure must be an essential part of any improved surveillance efforts. Continuous sharing of surveillance information within and across countries is necessary to prepare for special problems, to know when they arise, and to respond to them effectively.

The lack of adequately trained and appropriately deployed human resources for health will also remain an issue, especially in low-income countries. There will not be enough personnel, the incentives for their performance will be lacking, and the personnel that do exist will largely be available only in the larger cities. Thus, it will be important to have the lowest level of worker possible handle various health services so that scarce higher-level workers can focus on those things they alone can do. In addition, many services can be devolved to community-based workers. This will be an important point, for example, in countries with high HIV/AIDS prevalence but few trained doctors and nurses, as they spread AIDS treatment beyond the largest cities.

Another important issue will be the balance that needs to be struck between prevention and treatment, especially in a world in which there are still 2.6 million new infections per year. This will be especially challenging in the field of HIV/AIDS. There is considerable commitment in the world today to ensuring that all people needing treatment with antiretroviral therapy get it as soon as possible. There are many reasons why this is important. In addition, there is a growing discussion of using widespread HIV testing and early treatment of those found HIV-positive as a way to reduce new infections.

The challenge of financing enhanced efforts in the control of communicable diseases will also be formidable. Without major changes in their spending patterns and rapid economic growth, many low- and middle-income countries will not be able to pay for the stepped-up efforts they need to combat the major communicable diseases. Rather, they will have to depend for some time on financial assistance from the high-income countries and private sector partners. Nonetheless, there is room in many communicable disease control programs to improve efficiency and effectiveness, by focusing on the most cost-effective approaches.

Scientific and technical challenges also remain. There is no effective vaccine for any of the diseases that have been the focus of this chapter, except for rotavirus for some forms of diarrhea. Drug resistance is a constant issue in HIV, a threat in the control of diarrhea and some parasitic infections, and a major issue in the control of TB and malaria. It is imperative that new drugs be developed that can prevent or overcome such resistance.

Another challenge will be the need to develop models in low- and middle-income countries to provide chronic care of people with HIV. Most health service efforts in low-income countries focus on acute care. The treatment of HIV with antiretroviral therapy creates the possibility that people who are HIV-positive can have full and productive lives for many years. However, it also means that countries with very weak health systems that are mostly accustomed to treating acute illnesses will have to develop effective and efficient models for treating some people for many years of their life.

Another important issue is how low-income and resource-poor countries will be able to financially sustain the progress that they do make in AIDS treatment and several other areas related to the prevention and control of communicable diseases. Successful efforts to prevent and control these diseases will reduce prevalence and, ultimately, reduce the demands on the health system. As the prevalence of hookworm declines, for example, countries will be able to spend less money for hookworm treatment programs. However, the demands on health systems for treatment for HIV/AIDS will continue to be great for many years to come. Low- and middle-income countries with high HIV/AIDS prevalence will have to plan carefully how AIDS treatment can be financed in the future. This is especially important because once people start taking antiretroviral therapy, it is imperative that they continue to take it.

Monitoring and evaluation is an essential tool of public health programming. If the world is to make progress against the most important communicable diseases and continue to learn what is most cost-effective in addressing these diseases, then it is important to enhance the quality of monitoring and evaluation of health investments. All activities require a monitoring and evaluation component to track project progress, estimate cost-effectiveness of the effort, and assess the impact of the activities that are being financed.

MAIN MESSAGES

In the 2001 study of the global burden of disease, communicable diseases accounted for about 44 percent of total deaths and 40 percent of DALYs in low- and middle-income countries. Among the communicable diseases, HIV/AIDS and malaria take an enormous toll on sub-Saharan Africa. The

neglected diseases are also a more significant burden of disease in sub-Saharan Africa than in any other region. The toll from communicable diseases is similar for men and women, but the AIDS epidemic is taking an increasing toll on women, and TB generally affects men more than women.

Emerging and re-emerging infectious diseases and antimicrobial resistance represent enormous threats to public health, in all countries. Emerging and re-emerging infectious diseases have the potential to do enormous economic damage to individual countries and the international community, vastly in excess of their direct impact on morbidity and mortality. Enhancing global cooperation on disease surveillance is essential for the effective identification and control of emerging and re-emerging infectious diseases. Substantial efforts will be needed by individual countries and globally to promote more rational use of antibiotics and better quality of antibiotics, if the development of resistant forms of bacteria, viruses, and parasites is at least to be slowed down.

HIV is an especially important burden, but the number of HIV/AIDS cases is declining. About 33.3 million people are now infected with HIV; in 2009 about 1.8 million people died from the disease, and another 2.6 million were infected with it that same year.

The AIDS epidemic is helping to fuel TB. About one third of the world is infected with TB, and there are approximately 9.4 million people in the world with active TB disease. Both HIV/AIDS and TB mostly affect people in their productive years.

Malaria kills about 1 million people a year, mostly young children in Africa. It also causes a huge burden of morbidity because cases of malaria are so common and people may get more than one case a year. Malaria also poses very substantial risks to pregnant women. Diarrhea is an especially important burden of disease for children, as well, and is also responsible for about 1.8 million child deaths a year. A number of parasitic and infectious diseases are often called the neglected tropical diseases, and they pose an exceptional burden of disease, again largely in sub-Saharan Africa and South Asia. The worm *Ascaris*, for example, infects more than 1 billion people worldwide. Trichuris and hookworm infect 800 million and 740 million, respectively.

The economic and social consequences of the communicable diseases are very considerable. Diarrhea and worms can cause children to fail to develop properly, delay their entry into and performance in school, and lessen their productivity as adults. HIV/AIDS, TB, and malaria also greatly affect adult productivity. The direct and indirect costs of these diseases to individuals and families are very high and often cause people to borrow money, sell their limited assets, and fall below the poverty line. There is good evidence that high levels of malaria are an important impediment to economic growth in low-income countries in Africa.

Addressing HIV/AIDS will require redoubled efforts on prevention and continued efforts to learn what can prevent transmission in the most cost-effective ways. There is an increasing understanding that strong political leadership, focusing on the groups most at risk, and addressing the needs of "bridge populations" are parts of successful prevention efforts. Other key parts of prevention are maintaining a clean blood supply, testing and counseling, and condom promotion, in connection with efforts to delay sexual debut and reduce the number of sexual partners. It is also important to stem the transmission of HIV from mother to child. Male circumcision programs are now being expanded. An increasing number of people are being treated for HIV worldwide, and efforts are underway to ensure that all people who need treatment get it.

Although TB incidence and the presentation of TB are being dramatically affected by HIV, the mainstay of efforts to address TB has been DOTS, which stands for Directly Observed Therapy, Short-Course. This is a very cost-effective way of treating TB. Malaria can be addressed through prompt diagnosis and treatment, intermittent treatment of pregnant women, the use of insecticide-treated bed nets, and indoor residual spraying. Proper treatment to avoid the development of resistance is central to efforts in TB, HIV/AIDS, and malaria.

The burden of diarrhea can be reduced through immunization against rotavirus and measles and supplementation with zinc. Oral rehydration therapy is a cost-effective way of managing diarrhea in infants and children. The best approach to diarrhea, of course, would be to try to avoid it through improved hygiene. Better access to safe water and sanitation will help to reduce the burden of some of the parasitic and bacterial infections that make up the neglected diseases. In the short run, however, there is a package of drug therapy that can be integrated with other disease control efforts to reduce the burden of the NTDs in a cost-effective way.

The challenge of addressing the burden of communicable diseases effectively is enormous. They are mostly diseases of poverty that also reflect a lack of access to safe water and sanitation, poor knowledge of appropriate health behaviors, and a lack of health services that are geared to meet the highest priority needs. In addition, several of these diseases are highly stigmatized, efforts to control them must be carried out in countries with weak health systems, and considerably more financing is needed for these efforts than has been available. Nonetheless, there has been major progress in the last 40 years in addressing smallpox, onchocerciasis, Guinea worm, and a number of vaccine-preventable diseases in children. The lessons from those experiences suggest that it is possible, through concerted efforts and partnerships and greatly enhanced disease surveillance efforts, to continue making such progress.

Study Questions

1. What are the most important infectious diseases in terms of deaths in low- and middle-income countries? In terms of DALYs?

2. In what regions will the deaths from HIV/AIDS be most important? In what regions will malaria be most important?

3. What is driving the HIV epidemic in Russia? In sub-Saharan Africa?

4. In sub-Saharan Africa, what would be the most cost-effective measures to try to prevent further transmission of the HIV virus? What approach would you take to prevention in South Asia, and why would it differ from what you would do in sub-Saharan Africa?

5. What groups are especially at risk for malaria? What steps would you take to try to reduce the burden of malaria?

6. What is DOTS? What are the key focuses of this approach? Why has it been more effective than previous approaches to TB control?

7. If relatively few people die as a direct result of parasitic diseases, why are they so important?

8. What are the concerns about drug resistance for malaria and TB? How can resistance be kept to a minimum?

9. Why is it important to develop a vaccine for HIV?

10. What are the drivers of antimicrobial resistance? What measures could a country take to try to reduce the development of resistance?

REFERENCES

1. Lopez AD, Mathers CD, Ezzati M, Jamison DT, Murray CJL. Measuring the global burden of disease and risk factors, 1990–2001. In: Lopez AD, Mathers CD, Ezzati M, Jamison DT, Murray CJL, eds. *Global Burden of Disease and Risk Factors.* New York: Oxford University Press; 2006:8.

2. UNAIDS. UNAIDS Report on the Global AIDS Epidemic. Geneva: UNAIDS; 2010.

3. Centers for Disease Control and Prevention. World Water Day. Available at: http://www.cdc.gov/features/worldwaterday. Accessed December 23, 2010.

4. World Health Organization. *The Global Plan to Stop TB.* Geneva: World Health Organization; 2010.

5. Global Malaria Partnership. GMAP: The Global Malaria Action Plan. Available at: http://www.rbm.who.int/rbmgmap.html. Accessed December 27, 2010.

6. Fauci AS. *2005 Robert H. Ebert Memorial Lecture: Emerging and Re-emerging Infectious Diseases: The Perpetual Challenge.* New York: Milbank Memorial Fund; 2005.

7. Heymann DL. Emerging and re-emerging infectious diseases from plague and cholera to Ebola and AIDS: a potential for international spread that transcends the defences of any single country. *J Contingencies Crisis Manage.* 2005;13(1):29-31.

8. Heymann D. Emerging and re-emerging infections. In: Kirch W, ed. *Encyclopedia of Public Health.* New York: Springer; 2008.

9. Jones KE, Patel NG, Levy MA, et al. Global trends in emerging infectious diseases. *Nature.* February 21, 2008;451:990-993.

10. Heymann DL. The microbial threat in fragile times: balancing known and unknown risks. *Bull World Health Organ.* 2002;80(3):179.

11. Centers for Disease Control and Prevention. Preventing emerging infectious diseases: a strategy for the 21st century. *MMWR Morb Mortal Wkly Rep.* 1998;47(No. RR-15):1-14.

12. National Institutes of Health. *Microbial Evolution and Co-Adaptation: A Tribute to the Life and Scientific Legacies of Joshua Lederberg: Workshop Summary.* Institute of Medicine Forum on Microbial Threats. Washington DC: National Academies Press; 2009.

13. Cohen ML. Changing patterns of infectious diseases. *Nature.* 2000; 406:762-767.

14. Nugent R, Beck E, Beith A. *The Race Against Drug Resistance.* Washington, DC: Center for Global Development; 2010.

15. Okeke IN, Bhutta ZA, Duse AG, et al. Antimicrobial resistance in developing countries. Part I: recent trends and current status. *Lancet Infect Dis.* 2005;5(8):481-493.

16. Okeke IN, Bhutta ZA, Duse AG, et al. Antimicrobial resistance in developing countries. Part II: strategies for containment. *Lancet Infect Dis.* 2005;5(9):568-580.

17. Laxminarayan R, Bhutta ZA, Duse A, et al. Drug resistance. In: Jamison DT, Breman JG, Measham AR, et al., eds. *Disease Control Priorities in Developing Countries.* 2nd ed. Washington, DC: The World Bank; 2006:1031-1051.

18. Snowden FM. Emerging and reemerging diseases: a historical perspective. *Immunol Rev.* 2008;225:9-26.

19. World Health Organization. *April 21, 2004 Concluding Report.* Geneva: World Health Organization; 2004.

20. Morens DM, Folkers GK, Fauci AS. Emerging infections: a perpetual challenge. *Lancet Infect Dis.* 2008;8(11):710-719.

21. World Health Organization. *International Health Regulations.* 2nd ed. Geneva: World Health Organization; 2005.

22. Lynn J. WHO to Review Its Handling of H1N1 Flu Pandemic. *Reuters.* Available at: http://www.reuters.com/article/idUSTRE5BL2ZT20100112. Accessed December 29, 2010.

23. Bertozzi S, Padian NS, Wegbreit J, et al. HIV/AIDS prevention and treatment. In: Jamison DT, Breman JG, Measham AR, et al., eds. *Disease Control Priorities in Developing Countries.* 2nd ed. New York: Oxford University Press; 2006:331-370.

24. Chin J, ed. *Control of Communicable Diseases Manual.* 17th ed. Washington, DC: American Public Health Association; 2000.

25. Bertozzi S, Padian NS, Wegbreit J, et al. HIV/AIDS prevention and treatment. In: Jamison DT, Breman JG, Measham AR, et al., eds. *Disease Control Priorities in Developing Countries.* 2nd ed. New York: Oxford University Press; 2006:353.

26. UNAIDS. 2006 Report on the Global AIDS Epidemic. Available at: http://www.unaids.org/en/media/unaids/contentassets/dataimport/pub/report/2006/2006_gr_en.pdf. Accessed November 15, 2006.

27. Brown LR. The Potential Impact of AIDS on Population and Economic Growth Rates. Available at: http://ideas.repec.org/p/fpr/2020br/43.html. Accessed November 22, 2006.

28. Russell S. The economic burden of illness for households in developing countries: a review of studies focusing on malaria, tuberculosis, and human immunodeficiency virus/acquired immunodeficiency syndrome. *Am J Trop Med Hyg.* 2004;71(2 Suppl):147-155.

29. Ainsworth M, Over M. AIDS and African development. *World Bank Res Observ.* 1994:9(2)203-240.

30. Bertozzi S, Padian NS, Wegbreit J, et al. HIV/AIDS prevention and treatment. In: Jamison DT, Breman JG, Measham AR, et al., eds. *Disease Control Priorities in Developing Countries.* 2nd ed. New York: Oxford University Press; 2006:332.

31. World Health Organization. *Guidelines on HIV and Infant Feeding 2010.* Geneva: World Health Organization; 2010.

32. Centers for Disease Control and Prevention. Male Circumcision and Risk for HIV Transmission: Implications for the United States. Available at: http://www.cdc.gov/hiv/resources/factsheets/circumcision.htm. Accessed March 6, 2007.

33. World Health Organization. Fact Sheet No. 104: Tuberculosis. Available at: http://www.who.int/mediacentre/factsheets/fs104/en. Accessed November 20, 2006.

34. World Health Organization. Tuberculosis and Gender. Available at: http://www.who.int/tb/challenges/gender/en. Accessed December 22, 2010.

35. World Health Organization. *Global Tuberculosis Control 2010.* Geneva: World Health Organization; 2010.

36. Centers for Disease Control and Prevention. Extensively Drug-Resistant Tuberculosis (XDR TB)—Update. Available at: http://www.cdc.gov/tb/topic/drtb/xdrtb.htm. Accessed November 19, 2006.

37. Chand N, Singh T, Khalsa JS, Verma V, Rathore JS. A study of socio-economic impact of tuberculosis on patients and their family. *Chest.* 2004:126(4):832S.

38. Croft RA, Croft RP. Expenditure and loss of income incurred by tuberculosis patients before reaching effective treatment in Bangladesh. *Int J Tuberc Lung Dis.* 1998;2(3):252-254.

39. Kamolratanakul P, Sawert H, Kongsin S, et al. Economic impact of tuberculosis at the household level. *Int J Tuberc Lung Dis.* 1999;3(7):596-602.

40. Rajeswari R, Balasubramanian R, Muniyandi M, Geetharamani S, Thresa X, Venkatesan P. Socio-economic impact of tuberculosis on patients and family in India. *Int J Tuberc Lung Dis.* 1999;3(10):869-877.

41. Grimard F, Harling G. The Impact of Tuberculosis on Economic Growth. Available at: http://neumann.hec.ca/neudc2004/fp/grimard_franque_aout_27.pdf. Accessed November 22, 2006.

42. Peabody JW, Shimkhada R, Tan C, Jr., Luck J. The burden of disease, economic costs and clinical consequences of tuberculosis in the Philippines. *Health Policy Plan.* 2005;20(6):347-353.

43. Dye C, Floyd K. Tuberculosis. In: Jamison DT, Breman JG, Measham AR, et al., eds. *Disease Control Priorities in Developing Countries.* 2nd ed. New York: Oxford University Press; 2006:289-312.

44. Lopez AD, Mathers CD, Murray CJL. The burden of disease and mortality by condition: data, methods, and results for 2001. In: Lopez AD, Mathers CD, Ezzati M, Jamison DT, Murray CJL, eds. *Global Burden of Disease and Risk Factors*. New York: Oxford University Press; 2006:70.

45. Breman JG, Mills A, Snow RW, Mulligan J-A. Conquering malaria. In: Jamison DT, Breman JG, Measham AM, Alleyne G, eds. *Disease Control Priorities in Developing Countries*. 2nd ed. New York: Oxford University Press; 2006:413-432.

46. USAID. The President's Malaria Initiative: Fifth Annual Report to Congress, April 2011. Available at: http://www.fightingmalaria.gov/resources/reports/pmi_annual_report11.pdf. Accessed June 13, 2011.

47. Roll Back Malaria Partnership. Economic Costs of Malaria. Available at: http://www.rbm.who.int/cmc_upload/0/000/015/363/RBMInfosheet_10.htm. Accessed November 22, 2006.

48. Gallup JL, Sachs JD. The economic burden of malaria. *Am J Trop Med Hyg*. 2001;64(1-2 Suppl):85-96.

49. Keusch GT, Fontaine O, Bhargava A, Boschi-Pinto C. Diarrheal diseases. In: Jamison DT, Breman JG, Measham AM, Alleyne G, eds. *Disease Control Priorities in Developing Countries*. 2nd ed. New York: Oxford University Press; 2006:371-388.

50. World Health Organization. Diarrhoeal Disease. Available at: http://www.who.int/mediacentre/factsheets/fs330/en/index.html. Accessed December 23, 2010.

51. World Health Organization/UNICEF. *Diarrhoea: Why Children Are Still Dying and What Can Be Done*. Geneva: World Health Organization; 2009.

52. Parashar UD. Global illness and deaths caused by rotavirus disease in children. *Emer Infect Dis*. 2003;9(5):565-572.

53. Centers for Disease Control and Prevention. Rotavirus. Available at: http://www.cdc.gov/rotavirus/index.html. Accessed October 15, 2006.

54. Huttly SR, Morris SS, Pisani V. Prevention of diarrhoea in young children in developing countries. *Bull World Health Org*. 1997;75:163-174.

55. Black RE. Zinc deficiency, infectious disease, and mortality in the developing world. *J Nutr*. 2003;133(5 Suppl 1):1485S-1489S.

56. This section of the chapter is adapted with permission from PRB, Skolnik, Richard and Ahmed, Ambareen, Ending the Neglect of Neglected Tropical Diseases, February 2010.

57. World Health Organization. Neglected Tropical Diseases. Available at: http://www.who.int/neglected_diseases/en. Accessed December 14, 2009.

58. Musgrove P, Hotez, PJ. Turning neglected tropical diseases into forgotten maladies. *Health Aff*. 2009;28(6):1691-1706.

59. Global Network for Neglected Tropical Diseases, About NTDs. Available at: http://www.globalnetwork.org/about-ntds. Accessed December 14, 2009.

60. The Access Project. Neglected Tropical Diseases Control Program. Available at: http://www.theaccessproject.com/index.php/about/ntd. Accessed December 15, 2009.

61. Brooker S, Hotez PJ, Bundy DAP. Hookworm-related anemia among pregnant women: a systematic review. *Publ Libr Sci Negl Trop Dis*. 2008;2(9):291.

62. Hotez PJ, Brindley PJ, Bethany JM, et al. Helminth infections: the great neglected tropical diseases. *J Clin Invest*. 2008;118(4):1311-1321.

63. Kjetland EF, Ndhlovu PD, Gomo E, et al. Association between genital schistosomiasis and HIV in rural Zimbabwean women. *AIDS*. 2006;20(4):593-600.

64. Hotez PJ, Daar AS. The CNCDs and the NTDs: blurring the lines dividing noncommunicable and communicable chronic diseases. *PLoS Negl Trop Dis*. 2008;2(10):e312.

65. Global Network for Neglected Tropical Diseases. Hookworm. Available at: http://globalnetwork.org/about-ntds/factsheets/hookworm. Accessed December 14, 2009.

66. Global Network for Neglected Tropical Diseases. Trachoma. Available at: http://globalnetwork.org/about-ntds/factsheets/trachoma. Accessed December 14, 2009.

67. The Carter Center. Guinea Worm Eradication Program. Available at: http://www.cartercenter.org/health/guinea_worm/index.html. Accessed December 15, 2009.

68. International Trachoma Initiative. What Is Trachoma?. Available at: http://www.trachoma.org/world's-leading-cause-preventable-blindness. Accessed April 30, 2011.

69. Molyneux DH. 10 years of success in addressing lymphatic filariasis. *Lancet*. 2009;373(9663):529-530.

70. World Health Organization. *Community-Directed Interventions for Major Health Problems in Africa*. Geneva: World Health Organization; 2008.

71. Copenhagen Consensus. Copenhagen Consensus 2008. Available at: http://www.copenhagenconsensus.com/Home.aspx. Accessed December 15, 2009.

72. Deworm the World. The Impact of Deworming on Education. Available at: http://dewormtheworld.org/learn_07.html. Accessed December 15, 2009.

73. Hotez PJ, Molyneux DH, Fenwick A, et al. Incorporating a rapid-impact package for neglected tropical diseases with programs for HIV/AIDS, tuberculosis, and malaria. *PLoS Med*. 2006;3(5):e102. doi:10.1371/journal.pmed.0030102.

74. Hotez PJ, Molyneux DH. Tropical anemia: one of Africa's greatest killers and a rationale for linking malaria and neglected tropical disease control to achieve a common goal. *Publ Libr Sci Negl Trop Dis*. 2008;2(7):e270.

75. Hopkins DR, Eigege A, Miri ES, et al. Lymphatic filariasis elimination and schistosomiasis control in combination with onchocerciasis control in Nigeria. *Am J Trop Med Hyg*. 2002;67(3):266-272.

76. Geraghty J. Expanding the biopharmaceutical industry's involvement in fighting neglected diseases. *Health Aff*. 2009;28(6):1774-1777.

77. The Lilly MDR-TB Partnership. Available at: http://www.lillymdr-tb.com. Accessed August 12, 2010. And personal communications with Karen Van der Westhuizen and Patrizia Carlevaro of the Eli Lilly Corporation.

78. AMFm. Affordable Medicines Facility—malaria (AMFm). Available at: http://www.theglobalfund.org/en/amfm. Accessed August 27, 2010.

79. Friends of the Global Fight. Affordable Medicines Facility for malaria (AMFm). Available at: http://www.theglobalfight.org/view/resources/uploaded/AMFm.pdf. Accessed August 27, 2010.

80. aids2031 Costs and Financing Working Group. *Costs and Choices: Financing the Long-Term Fight Against AIDS*. Washington, DC: Results for Development Institute; 2010.

81. Hecht R, Stover J, Bollinger L, Muhib F, Case K, de Ferrant D. Financing of HIV/AIDS programme scale-up in low-income and middle-income countries, 2009–31. *Lancet*. 2010;376:1254-1260.

82. Saphonn V, Chhorvann C, Sopheab H, Luyna U, Seilava R. *The Long-Run Costs and Financing of HIV/AIDS in Cambodia*. Washington DC: Results for Development Institute; 2010.

83. Guthrie T, Ndlovu N, Muhib F, Hecht R, Case K. *The Long-Run Costs and Financing of HIV/AIDS in South Africa*. Cape Town: Centre for Economic Governance and AIDS in Africa; 2010.

84. Levine R. *Millions Saved*. Washington, DC: Center for Global Development; 2004.

85. UNAIDS. *AIDS Epidemic Update (December)*. Geneva: UNAIDS; 2002.

86. Centers for Disease Control and Prevention. Global AIDS Program, Country Profiles: Thailand. Available at: http://www.cdc.gov/nchsp/od/gap/countries/thailand.htm. Accessed February 6, 2004.

87. UNAIDS. *Evaluation of the 100% Condom Programme in Thailand*. Geneva: UNAIDS, in collaboration with the Ministry of Public Health, Thailand; 2000. Document 00.18E.

88. Rojanapithayakorn W, Hanenberg R. The 100% condom programme in Thailand. *AIDS*. 1996;10(1):1-7.

89. Celentano D, Nelson K, Lyles C, et al. Decreasing incidence of HIV and sexually transmitted diseases among young Thai men: evidence for success of the HIV/AIDS control and prevention program. *AIDS*. 1998;12(5):F29-F36.

90. Chitwarkorn A. HIV/AIDS and sexually transmitted infections in Thailand: lessons learned and future challenges. In: Narain JP, ed. *AIDS in Asia: The Challenge Continues*. New Delhi: Sage; 2004.

91. UNAIDS. *Report on the Global AIDS Epidemic*. Geneva: UNAIDS; 2004.

92. China Tuberculosis Control Collaboration. Results of directly observed short-course chemotherapy in 112,842 Chinese patients with smear-positive tuberculosis. *Lancet*. 1996;347:358-362.

93. World Health Organization Regional Office for the Western Pacific. *DOTS for All: Country Reports*. Geneva: World Health Organization; 2002.

94. Zhao F, Zhao Y, Liu X. Tuberculosis control in China. *Tuberculosis*. 2003;85:15-20.

95. The World Bank. *Implementation Completion Report for the China Infectious Diseases Control Project*. Washington, DC: The World Bank; 2002.

96. Chen X, Zhao F, Duanmu H, Wan L, Wang X, Chin DP. The DOTS strategy in China: results and lessons after 10 years. *Bull World Health Org*. 2002;80(6):430-436.

97. World Health Organization. *Control of Chagas Disease. Report of a WHO Expert Committee*. WHO Technical Report Series: 811. Geneva: World Health Organization; 1991.

98. Centers for Disease Control and Prevention. Fact Sheet: Chagas Disease. Available at: http://www.cdc.gov/parasites/chagas/resources/factsheet.pdf. Accessed April 29, 2011.

99. Dias JCP, Silveira AC, Schofield CJ. The impact of Chagas disease control in Latin America—a review. *Memorias do Instituto Oswaldo Cruz*. 2002;97:603-612.

100. Schmunis GA, Zicker F, Cruz J, Cuchi P. Safety of blood supply for infectious diseases in Latin American countries, 1994–1997. *Am J Trop Med Hygiene*. 2001;65:924-930.

101. Moncayo A. Chagas disease: current epidemiological trends after interruption of vectorial and transfusional transmission in the southern cone countries. *Memorias do Instituto Oswaldo Cruz*. 2003;98(5):577-591.

102. Kumaresan J, Mecaskey J. The global elimination of blinding trachoma: progress and promise. *Am J Trop Med Hygiene*. 2003;69(5 Suppl):S24-S28.

103. Mecaskey J, Knirsch C, Kumaresan J, Cook J. The possibility of eliminating blinding trachoma. *Lancet*. 2003;3:728-734.

104. West S. Blinding trachoma: prevention with the SAFE strategy. *Am J Trop Med Hygiene*. 2003;69(5 Suppl):S18-S23.

CHAPTER 12

Noncommunicable Diseases

LEARNING OBJECTIVES

By the end of this chapter the reader will be able to:

- Describe the most important noncommunicable diseases
- Discuss the importance of these diseases to global health
- Discuss the burden of noncommunicable diseases worldwide
- Outline the costs and consequences of noncommunicable diseases, tobacco use, and excessive drinking of alcohol
- Review measures that can be taken to address the burden of noncommunicable diseases in cost-effective ways
- Describe some successful cases of dealing with noncommunicable diseases

VIGNETTES

Roberto was 45 years old and lived in Bogota, Colombia. He had a government desk job and had been overweight for most of his adult life. Because he lived in the heart of the city, he got little exercise. He had read about increasing rates of diabetes but thought this was largely a disease of people in rich countries. Last year, Roberto started feeling thirsty all the time, had dry mouth, and felt weak after any exertion. He went to his doctor and was diagnosed as having adult onset diabetes.

Shanti was 35 years old and lived in Sri Lanka. She had grown up in a village, had worked hard on her family's small farm, and had been healthy for all of her adult life. She had two children and had not had any problems during either pregnancy. During a recent visit to the local health center, however, the doctor discovered that Shanti had high blood pressure. The doctor talked with Shanti about changing her diet and also prescribed medication for her. The medicine she needed is not expensive, but, unfortunately, Shanti has to take this medicine for the remainder of her life.

Alexei was 47 years old and lived in Moscow, Russia. Alexei had been smoking one pack of cigarettes a day since he was 16 years old. He heard on television and on the radio about the bad effects that cigarettes have on health. Urged by his children to stop smoking, he tried unsuccessfully on several occasions to quit. Over the last few months, Alexei developed a continuous cough and was often short of breath. Alexei had lung cancer.

Lai Ying lived in Guandong Province, China, and was a factory worker. Until recently she had been a happy and healthy young woman. More recently, however, Lai Ying had felt very unhappy. She did not feel like getting out of bed in the morning, did not want to go to work, and had no energy when she was at work. She thought from time to time of death and considered suicide. Lai Ying's family noticed that she was not eating properly and that she was "not herself." However, they thought she was having a difficult time at work or with a boyfriend and that she would soon be fine. After some months of this behavior, Lai Ying committed suicide by taking an overdose of sleeping pills.

THE IMPORTANCE OF NONCOMMUNICABLE DISEASES

Noncommunicable diseases are of immense and growing importance worldwide. In fact, the burden of noncommunicable diseases is greater than the burden of communicable diseases in low- and middle-income countries, as well as in high-income countries. This contradicts the widely held notion that low-income countries do not face a significant burden of noncommunicable disease. Moreover, as discussed in Chapter 2, the burden of noncommunicable diseases will increase in low- and middle-income countries as they develop economically, become more integrated with the global economy, urbanize, and age. WHO estimates that the burden of noncommunicable diseases in sub-Saharan Africa will almost equal by 2020 the burden of group I disorders (communicable, maternal, perinatal, and nutritional).[1] Among the most important of the noncommunicable health conditions that low- and middle-income countries face are cardiovascular disease, diabetes, cancers, and mental disorders.[2]

The risk factors for noncommunicable diseases relate in significant ways to lifestyle, much of which is within people's control. We will discuss, for example, the importance of diet, physical activity, tobacco use, and alcohol abuse to the onset of certain noncommunicable diseases. By engaging in appropriate health behaviors, it is possible for people to considerably reduce the risk of getting heart disease, some cancers, or diabetes.

Some noncommunicable diseases can be prevented at relatively low cost, but these diseases are often very expensive to treat. It is possible, for example, to significantly reduce the chances of getting lung cancer by making a modest investment in smoking cessation therapy and by quitting smoking. By contrast, the cost of treating lung cancer through drugs and surgery is considerably more.

This chapter will focus on noncommunicable diseases. It will pay particular attention to cardiovascular disease, cancer, diabetes, and mental disorders because of their important and growing contribution to the global burden of disease, including in low- and middle-income countries. It will also cover vision and hearing loss, because of the large amount of disability they cause and the extent to which they will become more important causes of disability in the future. Because of the importance of tobacco and alcohol as risk factors for noncommunicable diseases, the chapter will also contain specific sections on these topics.

The chapter will first introduce you to definitions of selected health conditions. It will then examine the burden of noncommunicable diseases and the risk factors for those diseases. Following that, it will comment on some of the most important costs and consequences of these diseases. It will then review what steps can be taken to address the burden of noncommunicable diseases effectively and efficiently, and will discuss several examples of successful efforts to prevent and deal with noncommunicable diseases. The chapter will conclude with comments on some of the future challenges that must be addressed if the burden of noncommunicable diseases is to be reduced.

KEY DEFINITIONS

Communicable diseases are illnesses caused by an infectious agent that spreads from a person or an animal to another person or animal. Noncommunicable diseases are, in many respects, the opposite of communicable diseases. First, they cannot be spread from person to person by an infectious agent, even if they might be associated with one. Second, they tend to last a long time. Third, they can be very disabling, can seriously impair the ability of people to engage in day-to-day activities, and often lead to death if they are not treated appropriately.

The terms *chronic disease* and *degenerative disease* are often used interchangeably with noncommunicable disease. In this book, however, we shall consistently use the term *noncommunicable disease*. The most recent studies of the burden of disease include the following under noncommunicable diseases: malignant neoplasms (cancers); diabetes; endocrine disorders; neuropsychiatric disorders, such as mental disorders, epilepsy, and Alzheimer's disease; and sense organ disorders, such as hearing loss, glaucoma, or cataracts.[2]

You are already familiar with most of the terms used in this chapter; however, a few key terms with which you may be less familiar are defined in Table 12-1.

A NOTE ON DATA

This chapter includes data on both deaths and DALYs for the most important noncommunicable diseases. An important part of the data in the chapter, therefore, is based on the 2001 study of the global burden of disease, because, as noted earlier, that is the most up to date and consistent set of data on the burden of disease by World Bank region. The projections that are referred to come from the 2008 WHO update of the burden of disease, using 2004 data, which was based on WHO regions.

THE BURDEN OF NONCOMMUNICABLE DISEASES

Cardiovascular Disease

Cardiovascular disease (CVD) caused 16.4 million deaths in 2001 and is now the leading cause of death in the world.[1] CVD is the cause of about 30 percent of all deaths worldwide, and it is predicted that by 2020, more than half of all deaths worldwide will be associated with CVD.[1] As noted earlier, it is now the leading cause of death in low- and middle-income countries, as well as in high-income countries. CVD is associated with about 30 percent of all deaths in high-income countries and about 28 percent of deaths in low- and middle-income countries.[1]

The latest estimates suggest that by 2030, ischemic heart disease and cerebrovascular disease combined will be:

- The second leading cause of DALYs lost in low-income countries, behind perinatal conditions but ahead of unipolar depressive disorders
- The largest cause of DALYs lost by a substantial margin in lower-middle-income countries, ahead of unipolar despressive disorders
- The leading cause of DALYs lost in upper-middle-income countries and almost three times more DALYs lost than the next cause of burden, HIV/AIDS
- The leading cause of DALYs lost in high-income countries, with 30 percent more DALYs lost to them than the next leading cause, which is unipolar depressive disorders[3]

CVD is the largest cause of death in all regions, except in sub-Saharan Africa. CVD is the cause of about 58 percent of all deaths in Europe and Central Asia and about 30 percent of all deaths in East Asia and the Pacific, but only about 10 percent of the total deaths in sub-Saharan Africa.[1] CVD rates are higher in Eastern Europe than in Western Europe, although the rates of CVD are falling in some Eastern European countries. The highest rates of CVD are in the former Soviet Union, where they contributed to declines in life expectancy.[1] The rate of prevalence of CVD tends to be higher in urban areas than in rural areas.

About 80 percent of the burden of CVD worldwide is due to three conditions: ischemic heart disease (IHD), stroke, and congestive heart failure.[1] In most regions, IHD is the most important contributor to death due to all cardiovascular diseases. In the Middle East and North Africa, for example, three people die from IHD for every one who dies from stroke. Stroke, however, is the dominant contributor to deaths in both sub-Saharan Africa and China.[4] In India, CVD appears in people at younger ages more than in high-income countries. Whereas in high-income countries only about 22 percent of CVD deaths are in people under 70 years of age, in India, about 50 percent of the CVD deaths occur in people under 70.[5] In fact, given limited access to prevention programs or appropriate treatment, deaths from CVD generally occur earlier in low- and middle-income countries than in high-income countries.

To help get a better understanding of the importance of CVD to the burden of disease, Table 12-2 shows the burden of deaths and DALYs worldwide and by regions that are associated with CVD, compared to some of the other leading causes of death and DALYs lost, including diabetes, cancer, TB, HIV, and malaria.

TABLE 12-1 Key Terms and Definitions

Blood glucose—Blood sugar, the main source of energy for the body.

Cancer—One of a large variety of diseases characterized by uncontrolled growth of cells.

Cardiovascular Disease—A disease of the heart or blood vessels. This term encompasses both ischemic heart disease and stroke.

Cholesterol—A fat-like substance that is made by the body and is found naturally in animal-based foods such as meat, fish, poultry, and eggs.

Diabetes—An illness caused by poor control by the body of blood sugar.

Hypertension—High blood pressure, with a reading of 140/90 or greater.

Ischemic heart disease—A disturbance of the heart function due to inadequate supply of oxygen to the heart muscle.

Stroke—Sudden loss of function of the brain due to clotting or hemorrhaging.

Source: Adapted from: Global Cardiovascular Infobase. Glossary. Available at: http://www.cvdinfobase.ca/cvdbook/En/Glossary.htm. Accessed April 14, 2007; National Institutes of Health. Obesity, Physical Activity, and Weight-Control Glossary. Available at: http://win.niddk.nih.gov/publications/glossary/AthruL.htm. Accessed April 14, 2007.

Diabetes

There are several types of diabetes. The two most common are called type I and type II diabetes. Type I diabetes is "a lifelong condition in which the pancreas stops making insulin. Without insulin, the body is not able to use glucose (blood sugar) for energy. To treat the disease, a person must inject insulin, follow a diet plan, exercise daily, and test blood sugar several times a day."[6] Type I diabetes usually begins before the age of 30. This type of diabetes was previously known as insulin-dependent diabetes mellitus or juvenile diabetes.[6] Type II diabetes was previously known as noninsulin-dependent diabetes mellitus or adult-onset diabetes. Type II diabetes is the most common form of diabetes mellitus, present in about 90–95 percent of all diabetics. People with type II diabetes produce insulin; however, they either do not make enough insulin or their bodies do not efficiently use the insulin they do make.[6]

It is estimated that about 5.1 percent of adults ages 20 to 79 worldwide had diabetes in 2003.[7] The prevalence rate of diabetes among this group was generally higher in

TABLE 12-2 Death and DALYs from Leading Causes, by Region, 2001 as Percentage of Total Deaths and DALYs

Region	CVD	Diabetes	Cancer	TB	HIV	Malaria
East Asia & Pacific						
Deaths	31%	2%	16%	4%	1%	<1%
DALYs	15%	1%	9%	3%	<1%	<1%
Europe & Central Asia						
Deaths	58%	1%	15%	1%	<1%	0%
DALYs	33%	1%	10%	1%	1%	<1%
Latin America & the Caribbean						
Deaths	28%	5%	15%	1%	3%	<1%
DALYs	11%	3%	7%	1%	2%	<1%
Middle East & North Africa						
Deaths	35%	2%	9%	1%	<1%	1%
DALYs	14%	1%	4%	1%	<1%	1%
South Asia						
Deaths	25%	1%	7%	4%	2%	<1%
DALYs	13%	1%	3%	3%	2%	1%
Sub-Saharan Africa						
Deaths	10%	1%	4%	3%	19%	10%
DALYs	4%	<1%	2%	2%	16%	10%

Source: Data with permission from Lopez AD, Mathers CD, Murray CJL. The burden of disease and mortality by condition: data, methods, and results for 2001. In: Lopez AD, Mathers CD, Ezzati M, Jamison DT, Murray CJL, eds. *Global Burden of Disease and Risk Factors.* Washington, DC and New York: The World Bank and Oxford University Press; 2006:126-233.

high-income countries than in low- and middle-income countries. It ranged from a low of 2.4 percent in sub-Saharan Africa to a high of 7.6 percent in Europe and Central Asia.[7] Almost 200 million people worldwide suffered from diabetes in 2003.[7]

Diabetes has a number of important and costly complications. Among the most common are eye problems that can cause blindness, kidney problems, circulatory problems that can result in amputation of the lower extremities, stroke, and coronary heart disease. About two thirds of the people with diabetes have some disability, compared to less than one third of the people without diabetes.[8] For this reason, the DALYs lost from diabetes are far greater than would be suggested just by the prevalence of the disease. In fact, it is estimated that almost 20 million DALYs were lost to diabetes worldwide in 2001, which is a little less than is lost due to maternal conditions and about 50 percent less than is lost due to nutritional deficiencies. The prevalence of diabetes worldwide is increasing at a rapid rate, mostly associated with the rapid increase in the amount of obesity in the world.[9] Some students of global health now refer to diabetes as being an "epidemic." Table 12-3 shows, by country income group, the share of total DALYs that were estimated to have been lost to diabetes in 2004 and the

share that is projected to be lost to diabetes in 2015 and 2030. Between 2004 and 2030, that share is projected to double in low- and upper-middle-income countries, increase by about 60 percent in lower-middle-income countries, and increase by about 30 percent in high-income countries.[3]

The risk factors for type I diabetes are still being studied. However, type I diabetes is associated with a family history of diabetes. In addition, "environmental factors, increased weight and height development, increased maternal age at birth, and exposure to some viral infections" have also been linked to developing type I diabetes.[7] Type II diabetes is also associated with a family history of diabetes. In addition, it is associated with diet and physical inactivity, obesity, insulin resistance, ethnicity, and increasing age.[7,10] In high-income countries, less-educated and lower-income individuals have higher rates of diabetes than better-educated and wealthier people.[11]

Cancer

There are many different types of cancers. Among the most important in terms of the burden of disease worldwide are cancers of the lung, colon, breast, prostate, liver, stomach, and cervix. There are many risk factors for cancer and they vary by

TABLE 12-3 Diabetes Mellitus, Percentage of Total DALYs, by Income Group, 2004 Estimates, 2015 and 2030 Projections

Region	Estimated 2004	Projected 2015	Projected 2030
Low-income countries	0.7%	1.1%	1.4%
Lower-middle-income countries	1.7%	2.4%	2.7%
Upper-middle-income countries	2.1%	3.2%	4.2%
High-income countries	3.0%	3.8%	3.9%

Source: Data from World Health Organization. Global Burden of Disease (GBD). Available at: http://www.who.int/healthinfo/global_burden_disease/en. Accessed September 14, 2010.

the type of cancer. Some cancers are associated with tobacco use, such as lung and esophageal cancers. Other cancers are associated with infectious agents. Liver cancer, for example, is associated with the hepatitis B virus, cervical cancer is associated with the human papillomavirus, and stomach cancer is associated with the bacteria *Helicobacter pylori*. Liver cancer is also associated with schistosomiasis, a parasitic worm that is also called *bilharzia*, which infects more than 200 million people worldwide.[12] There are also numerous environmental and occupational carcinogens, such as asbestos, which was the cause of lung cancer in many roofing workers in the United States, for example.

In 2001, it was estimated that about 7 million people worldwide died of cancer, with about 5 million of those in low- and middle-income countries.[13] At the same time, there were about 10 million new cases of cancer worldwide. The number of deaths caused by different types of cancers varies by region, as shown in Table 12-4, which indicates the first, second, and third leading causes of cancer deaths in each region.

It is clear from the table that lung and breast cancers are two of the five most common types of cancers in both high-income and low- and middle-income countries.

Generally, the higher the income of a country, the more likely it is that the leading forms of cancer deaths will be associated with tobacco use, environmental factors, diet, and lifestyle, whereas there will be a higher preponderance of cancers linked with infectious agents in low-income countries. In high-income countries, for example, lung cancer is

TABLE 12-4 Leading Causes of Cancer Deaths by Region, Number of Deaths in Thousands, 2001

Region	Cancer Type	Deaths	Cancer Type	Deaths	Cancer Type	Deaths
East Asia & Pacific	Stomach	442	Trachea, bronchus, & lungs	387	Liver	373
Europe & Central Asia	Trachea, bronchus, & lungs	165	Stomach	101	Other malignant neoplasms	82
Latin America & the Caribbean	Other malignant neoplasms	82	Stomach	57	Trachea, bronchus, & lungs	55
Middle East & North Africa	Other malignant neoplasms	26	Trachea, bronchus, & lungs	20	Stomach	18
South Asia	Mouth & oropharynx	140	Trachea, bronchus, & lungs	129	Other malignant neoplasms	99
Sub-Saharan Africa	Other malignant neoplasms	55	Liver	46	Prostate	40
High-Income Countries	Trachea, bronchus, & lungs	456	Other malignant neoplasms	257	Colon & rectal	257

Source: Data with permission from Lopez AD, Mathers CD, Murray CJL. The Burden of Disease and Mortality by Condition: Data, Methods, and Results for 2001. In: Lopez AD, Mathers CD, Ezzati M, Jamison DT, Murray CJL, eds. *Global Burden of Disease and Risk Factors.* Washington, DC and New York: The World Bank and Oxford University Press; 2006:126-233.

the predominant cause of cancer deaths and colon and breast cancer are the next most common causes of cancer deaths. East Asia and the Pacific is the only region in which stomach cancers, often linked with infection with *Helicobacter pylori*, are the most common cause of cancer deaths. As you can also see, the leading cause of cancer deaths in sub-Saharan Africa is liver cancer, linked in many cases to infection with the hepatitis B virus. In South Asia, the leading causes of cancer deaths are oral cancers, often associated with the use of betel, a nut that is chewed by many people in the region.[14]

WHO projections suggest that in 2030 cancers will be in the 10 leading causes of DALYs lost only in the high-income countries.[2]

Mental Disorders

As noted earlier, one of the major categories of noncommunicable diseases is neuropsychiatric disorders. This includes a number of neurological disorders, such as epilepsy. It also includes alcohol and drug abuse. Mental disorders are also included in this category. Together, neuropsychiatric disorders are very important to the burden of disease, causing about 10 percent of all DALYs lost in low- and middle-income countries in 2001.[15] Covering a wide range of neuropsychiatric disorders, however, is beyond the scope of this book. This part of the book, therefore, will only cover selected mental disorders.

Four mental disorders contribute the largest share to the burden of mental disorders. These are unipolar depressive disorders, which will be referred to here as depression; schizophrenia; panic disorder; and bipolar affective disorder. These conditions are defined briefly in Table 12-5.

Estimates of the global burden of disease for 2001, indicate that these four most common mental disorders contribute about 5 percent of the total DALYs lost in low- and middle-income countries, about equal to the burden of HIV/AIDS, diseases of vision and hearing, or ischemic heart disease.[16] Depression alone is estimated to be associated with 3.4 percent of the DALYs lost, which would make it the fourth most important burden of any health condition globally.[17,18] One reason for this large burden is the large number of people who suffer mental disorders. Another, however, is that mental disorders start at relatively young ages, they go on for a long time, they are often not "cured," and they, therefore, produce large amounts of disability. There is also some mortality, largely from suicide, that is associated with mental disorders.

There are only limited data on the burden of mental disorders from low- and middle-income countries. Nonetheless, when assessing the burden of these four disorders per million people, it is clear that South Asia has the highest rate of depression among all regions. The rate of depression is fairly consistent across better-off regions, somewhat lower in East Asia and the Pacific, and only about half as high in sub-Saharan Africa as in Europe and Central Asia.[17] The rates of schizophrenia range from about 1600 DALYs per million people in Europe and Central Asia to about 2100 DALYs per million people in East Asia and the Pacific.[17] Bipolar disorder ranges from 1400 DALYs per million people in Europe and Central Asia to 1830 DALYs per million people in the Middle East and North Africa.[17] The range for panic disorders is very narrow, with all regions clustering in the range of 700 to 800 DALYs per million people.[17]

The latest projections of the burden of disease to 2030 by country income group suggest that unipolar depressive disorders will grow in importance in all income groups and be exceptionally important as a share of the total burden of disease in the future. They are projected, for example, to become almost 6 percent of total DALYs in low-income countries and the second leading cause of the burden of disease. They would be over 6 percent in lower-middle-income countries and the highest cause, and about 6 percent in upper-middle-income countries and the third highest cause. The projections also suggest that unipolar depressive disorders will be over 8 percent of the burden of disease in high-income countries in 2030 and would be the leading cause of that burden.[3]

There appear to be both genetic and nongenetic risk factors for mental disorders. It is clear that women suffer from

---

TABLE 12-5 Key Mental Health Terms and Definitions

Bipolar disorder—A serious mood disorder characterized by swings of mania and depression

Depression—A mental state characterized by feelings of sadness, loneliness, despair, low self-esteem, and self-reproach

Panic disorders—An anxiety disorder characterized by attacks of acute intense anxiety

Schizophrenia—A mental illness, the main symptoms of which are hallucinations, delusions, and changes in outlook and personality

Source: Adapted from Ohio Psychological Association. Psychological Glossary. Available at: http://www.ohpsych.org/Public/glossary. htm. Accessed April 14, 2007; The Royal College of Psychiatrists. Diagnoses or Conditions. Available at: http://www.rcpsych.ac.uk/ mentalhealthinformation/definitions/diagnosesorconditions.aspx. Accessed April 14, 2007.

depression more than men, as noted earlier. Early childhood abuse, violence, and poverty may be important environmental risk factors for depression. However, there is still very little definitive evidence on the risk factors for schizophrenia, depression, bipolar disorder, or panic disorders.

Vision and Hearing Loss

Vision Loss[19]

The aging of populations globally and continued improvements in life expectancy will increase the importance of vision and hearing loss as causes of the burden of disease. It will also shift the types of problems that cause disease burden related to visual impairment.

The major reasons for vision loss are refractive disorders, such as near- and farsightedness and astigmatism; cataract; glaucoma; trachoma; and onchocerciasis. Estimates of the burden of disease for 2002 suggested that visual impairment was equal to about 3.3 percent of the total burden of disease globally, with half of all the DALYs lost from visual impairment being due to cataract alone. It was further estimated that about 160 million people worldwide were visually impaired and about 38 million of them were blind.

The main risk factors for visual impairment are poverty, gender, age, and a lack of access to health services. Cigarette smoking is also a risk factor for cataracts and glaucoma. More than 80 percent of the blind are over 50 years of age. Women are disproportionately affected by visual impairment, largely a function of constraints to their accessing appropriate preventive and curative care.

The projections of the burden of disease to 2030 suggest that refractive errors will be the leading cause related to visual impairment in the future. These are projected to be in the top 10 causes of the burden of disease in low-, upper-middle-, and high-income countries in 2030, with between 2.5 percent and 3.5 percent of the total burden of disease.[3]

Hearing Loss[19]

It was estimated that in 2002 about 255 million people globally had hearing loss that was disabling. About 80 percent of them had adult-onset hearing loss and about 20 percent had childhood-onset hearing loss. These groups together represented about 4 percent of the total world population. More males have suffered hearing loss than females, probably a result of exposure to noise.

It was estimated that in 2001 about 1.7 percent of the total burden of disease in low- and middle-income countries was attributable to adult-onset hearing loss. This was almost equal to the burden of cataracts in 2001.[20]

Childhood-onset hearing loss is related to congenital conditions, infection of the ear, or complications of other diseases, such as meningitis. Adult-onset hearing loss is related to exposure to noise and chemicals, as well as to aging. Poverty, poor hygiene, a failure to get vaccinated, and other factors that contribute to children getting infections are also risk factors for hearing loss.

Projections of the burden of disease to 2030 suggest that adult-onset hearing loss will be in the top 10 causes of the burden of disease in all country income groups. It will range from about 2.6 percent of the total burden of disease in low-income countries to just over 4 percent of the total burden of disease in high-income countries.[3]

Tobacco Use

Tobacco is such an important risk factor for cardiovascular disease, cancer, and diabetes that it bears specific mention of its own. It is estimated that about 5 million deaths annually are associated with the use of tobacco, of which about half are in low-income countries.[21] It is also estimated that 1 in 5 males over 30 and 1 in 20 females over 30 who die worldwide, die of tobacco-related deaths.[22] Ultimately, one half to two thirds of those who smoke will die of causes related to tobacco.[21] In addition, half of all tobacco-related deaths occur among people ages 35 to 69.[21] The most common tobacco-related deaths are from CVD; diseases of the respiratory system, such as emphysema; and cancers.

Most tobacco is used through smoking either cigarettes or *bidis*, which are hand-rolled cigarettes used largely in South Asia. It is estimated that about 1.1 billion people smoke worldwide.[23] The rate of prevalence of smoking for all adults varies from 18 percent in sub-Saharan Africa to 35 percent in Europe and Central Asia. In all regions of the world, men smoke more than women do. This is most pronounced in low-income countries, in which a relatively small share of women smoke. Prevalence for men varies from 29 percent in sub-Saharan Africa to 63 percent in East Asia and the Pacific. The rates for women vary from 5 percent in East Asia and the Pacific and the Middle East and North Africa to 24 percent in Latin America and the Caribbean.[21]

The extent to which people take up smoking varies not only by sex, but also by socioeconomic status and level of educational attainment. The higher the socioeconomic status and the higher the level of education, the less likely a person is to smoke. Most people who smoke start when they are teens. In addition, it is important to note that tobacco is physically addictive and once one starts to smoke, it is difficult to stop.[24]

In some countries, such as Canada, Poland, Thailand, the United Kingdom, and the United States, the use of tobacco has been declining. However, usage is increasing among men in low- and middle-income countries and among women in all regions. Unless steps are taken to stop the spread of tobacco use, we are likely to see continued growth in CVD and cancers related to smoking, many of which are avoidable.

Abuse of Alcohol

Alcohol is a major public health problem. About 4 percent of the global burden of disease, in fact, is attributable to alcohol, which is about the same amount as that related to tobacco and hypertension and somewhat more than is attributed to depression.[25]

High-risk drinking is defined as drinking 20 grams or more per day of pure alcohol for a woman and 40 grams a day for a man.[26] This is equal to about one quarter of a bottle of wine for a woman and one half a bottle of wine for a man. High-risk drinking may also be defined to include the total amount that is consumed, the frequency with which it is consumed, and the extent to which one engages in binge drinking.

High-risk drinking has a negative effect on people's health in a number of ways. Among other things, it increases the risks for hypertension, liver damage, pancreatic damage, hormonal problems, and heart disease.[25] In addition, alcohol intoxication is associated with accidents, injuries, accidental death, and a variety of social problems, including the first sexual encounters of teens, unprotected sex, and intimate partner violence. It is also possible to become dependent on alcohol, which has a number of negative psychological and physical consequences. Moreover, fetal alcohol syndrome is associated with low birthweight babies who are at risk of developmental disabilities.

The prevalence of high-risk drinking varies by region. Men in Europe and Central Asia have the highest rates of high-risk drinking: 21.4 percent between ages 45 to 59. People in the Middle East and North Africa have the lowest rates, which are reported to be very low. South Asia also has a very low prevalence of high-risk drinking.[27] The prevalence rate of high-risk drinking also varies by age, with fewer people engaging in high-risk drinking after age 60 than at younger ages. In each region, high-risk drinking is higher among men than women, except in South Asia.[27]

There is very little evidence about the determinants of high-risk drinking, especially in low-income settings. Studies done in high-income countries suggest that lower socioeconomic status and lower educational attainment are risk factors for drinking to the level of intoxication.[28]

THE COSTS AND CONSEQUENCES OF NONCOMMUNICABLE DISEASES, TOBACCO USE, AND ALCOHOL ABUSE

The economic costs of noncommunicable diseases are substantial and are growing, given the increasing burden of cardiovascular disease and diabetes. These costs include the direct costs of treating noncommunicable diseases, which by their nature require many years of treatment. They also include indirect costs that result from lost productivity. These are also very substantial, given that noncommunicable diseases often start at relatively younger ages, often cause substantial disability, and then persist for many years.

In addition, many actors in the global health arena previously carried out their work as if rich countries faced the burden and costs of noncommunicable diseases and poor countries faced only the burden and costs of communicable diseases. However, in light of the increasing amount of noncommunicable diseases, injuries, and accidents in low- and middle-income countries, it is clear that most low-income countries do not have the luxury of facing *either* communicable *or* noncommunicable diseases. Rather, even low-income countries now *simultaneously* face the burden and costs of communicable diseases, noncommunicable diseases, and injuries. Some additional comments follow on the costs and consequences of noncommunicable diseases.

Cardiovascular Disease

Only a small number of studies have been done on the direct and indirect costs of CVD in low- and middle-income countries. A study conducted in South Africa suggested that the direct costs of treating cardiovascular disease were about 25 percent of all healthcare expenditures, which was equal to between 2 and 3 percent of GDP in that country.[29] The indirect costs of cardiovascular disease on the economy are likely to be substantial, given the relatively low age at which such diseases affect people in many countries.

A study conducted in 2007 estimated the economic costs of the burden of noncommunicable diseases in 23 low- and middle-income countries. Noncommunicable diseases in those countries make up about 80 percent of the burden of all deaths from noncommunicable diseases in low- and middle-income countries. This study noted that men in low- and middle-income countries are 56 percent more likely to die at the same age of such causes than men in high-income countries, and women are 86 percent more likely to die at the same age than women in high-income countries of these causes. The study further concluded that these countries would lose $84 billion in economic production between 2006 and 2015 alone, as a result of the large and growing burden of noncommunicable diseases.[30]

Diabetes

It is estimated that the direct costs of treating diabetes vary between 2.5 percent and 15.0 percent of health expenditures in different countries, depending on the prevalence of disease and the extent and costs of treatment available.[7] Given the level of development of different regions, it is likely that the Latin America and the Caribbean region has the highest expenditure on diabetes per capita and sub-Saharan Africa the lowest such expenditures.[7] The indirect costs of diabetes in low- and middle-income countries are probably substantial because many people in those countries are living with diabetes without proper treatment and, therefore, suffer from disability and loss of productivity. The direct and indirect costs of diabetes are likely to grow in all regions as the number of people with diabetes increases, as noted earlier.

Mental Disorders

There are relatively few reliable data on the direct and indirect costs of mental disorders. In addition, the studies that have been done largely refer to high-income countries. Nonetheless, they are indicative of the large and usually unappreciated costs of mental illness in all countries. A study done in the United States estimated that the direct and indirect costs of mental illness were equal to about 2.5 percent of GNP, and a similar study done in Europe estimated that the costs of mental illness there were between 3 and 4 percent of GNP.[31] Studies done in Canada, the United Kingdom, and the United States showed that about half of the total costs of mental illness were direct costs and about half were indirect costs. These indirect costs are so substantial for mental illness that one study done in the United States estimated that almost 60 percent of the productivity losses that come from illness, accidents, or injuries are linked with mental illness.[31] Studies done in the United States and the United Kingdom showed, in addition, that workers suffering from depression lost 40 to 45 days of work in a year as a result of their illness.[31]

Hearing and Vision Loss

Unfortunately, very little information is available about the economic costs of vision and hearing loss, especially in low- and middle-income countries. This is despite the large number of DALYs lost to them now and the growing number that will be lost to them as populations age. The limited information that is available refers mostly to the United States. A study done in 1995, for example, suggested that the economic cost to the United States from vision loss was

almost $40 billion annually, of which about 60 percent was direct costs and 40 percent indirect costs.[32] Another study, published in 2006, estimated that the annual economic loss from major vision disorders in the United States was about $35 billion, of which about $16 billion was direct medical costs, about $11 billion other direct costs, and about $8 billion in productivity losses.[33] A comprehensive review of the existing literature on hearing loss in low- and middle-income countries was recently conducted. It did not indicate either country or global estimates of the economic costs of hearing loss; however, it did indicate some of the costs that would be associated with hearing loss, for which economic costs could be calculated, including:

- Constraints to the formal education of children with hearing loss, with its attendant consequences on their employment and earning prospects
- The number of school days missed by children with disabilities
- The costs of additional medical visits associated with children with disabilities
- The high cost of education for students with hearing loss
- The difficulties of adults with hearing loss in finding and keeping employment
- Income levels for people with hearing loss that can be 45 percent of the levels of people without hearing loss, even in high-income countries[34]

Tobacco Use

Calculating the costs of smoking to an economy can be very complicated.[35] The simplest way to do so is to calculate gross costs, which include all the costs associated with smoking-related diseases. Studies on the costs of smoking have largely focused on the costs of smoking in the high-income countries. These studies suggested that the gross costs of smoking to various high-income economies range from 0.1–1.1 percent of GDP, and that the costs to low- and middle-income countries might be just as high.[35] The prevalence rates of smoking are increasing among women everywhere and among men in low-income countries. We should expect, therefore, that the economic costs of smoking in those countries will increase for some time to come. In fact, it is estimated that 70 million people died of smoking-related causes between 1950 and 2000 and that, if present trends in tobacco use continue, an additional 150 million people will die of smoking-related causes between 2000 and 2025. Of course, the economic costs of this will be enormous. In addition, it is important to note that the economic burden of smoking in the future is likely to have a disproportionate impact on relatively poorer people, in relatively poorer countries, because they smoke at higher rates than do better-off people.[36]

Alcohol Abuse

For the economic costs of alcohol abuse, as for many other issues, there are relatively few data for low- and middle-income countries. Excessive alcohol use, as discussed earlier, is linked with health problems of the drinker. In addition, it is linked with violence and injuries caused by the drinker, such as when driving while intoxicated. When calculating the economic costs of excessive alcohol drinking, therefore, one has to take account of the costs of health care for the user and for others whose injuries or health condition were caused by the user. The indirect costs of excessive alcohol drinking will include the productivity losses not only of the drinker, but also of people hurt by the drinker because of excessive drinking. The limited studies that have been done on the costs of alcohol abuse can only be considered indicative because they did not follow any standard methodology. However, they all reveal substantial costs of alcohol abuse, as a share of GDP:

> Canada: 1.1 percent
> France: 1.4 percent
> Italy: 5.6 percent
> New Zealand: 4.0 percent
> South Africa: 2.0 percent[37]

A 2009 study examined the economic costs attributable to alcohol in four high-income countries and two middle-income countries. The costs were greater than 1 percent of GDP in all countries. The highest costs were found in the United States, at 2.7 percent of GDP, and South Korea, at 3.3 percent of GDP.[38]

ADDRESSING THE BURDEN OF NONCOMMUNICABLE DISEASES

There are also relatively few data available about cost-effective investments to address the burden of noncommunicable diseases, including tobacco and alcohol-related illness, in low- and middle-income countries. However, there is an increasing amount of information about efforts to address these issues in high-income countries and a growing body of information on dealing with these issues in low- and middle-income countries. Although the circumstances in high-income countries may be quite different from those in low- and middle-income countries, the efforts undertaken to date may provide some useful lessons for low- and middle-income countries as they seek to prevent the burden of noncommunicable diseases from growing. In considering how to address noncom-

municable diseases, it is important to note that some interventions can be made at the level of the population, whereas others are based on personal contact with an individual. Because smoking tobacco and excessive alcohol drinking are such important risk factors for cancer, cardiovascular disease, and diabetes, the following section starts with a discussion about measures that can be taken to reduce smoking and excessive alcohol consumption.[39]

Tobacco Use

Evidence suggests a number of steps can be taken to reduce the use of tobacco. Almost all countries tax cigarettes; however, low- and middle-income countries tend to tax cigarettes at lower rates than do high-income countries. Public demand for cigarettes is sensitive to price, and the poorer the country, the more price increases will affect demand. Studies conducted in low- and middle-income countries indicate that a 10 percent increase in cigarette taxes can lead to an 8 percent reduction in the demand for cigarettes. Under these circumstances, taxing cigarettes would be an effective policy for reducing cigarette consumption.[40]

For countries where there is weak government enforcement of laws, it will be more difficult to enforce restrictions on smoking; however, an increasing number of countries are undertaking these measures. Studies suggest that countries that can enforce legal restrictions can reduce the number of cigarettes smoked between 5 and 25 percent and can reduce smoking uptake by about 25 percent.[40] The effectiveness of these actions is likely to be enhanced in settings in which there are also strong social norms against smoking.

There is also evidence from high-income countries that consumption of cigarettes can be reduced by about 6 percent through a total ban on cigarette advertising, which is another step that low- and middle-income countries might consider.[40] Countries should also provide the public with information about the negative effects of smoking tobacco. There is evidence from high-income countries that such efforts led to short-term reduction in cigarette consumption of between 4–9 percent and long-term declines of 15–30 percent.[40]

High-income settings that have had the biggest impact on reducing tobacco consumption have undertaken comprehensive tobacco control programs that generally included efforts to prevent young people from starting smoking, encouraging all smokers to quit smoking, reducing exposure to passive smoking, and eliminating disparities in smoking among different population groups by helping those most at risk to reduce tobacco consumption.[41] It remains critically important to stop people from taking up smoking; however, in order to reduce tobacco-related deaths in the near future, it is essential to reduce consumption among those already smoking. Preventing young people from taking up smoking will only have an impact on tobacco-related deaths in the more distant future.

Abuse of Alcohol

Despite the high burden of disease and economic costs that are related to excessive drinking of alcoholic beverages, very few countries have embarked on coherent efforts to reduce alcohol consumption. Those that have done so generally focused their attention on policy and legislative actions, such as taxation, laws on drunk driving, and restricting alcohol sales to selected places, times, and age limits. Controlled advertising and tightened law enforcement, such as through more widespread breath testing of drivers, have also been imposed. Another successful part of their program was to encourage counseling by healthcare providers through "brief interventions with individual high risk drivers."[42]

Just as is the case for cigarette taxation, increased taxation on alcohol will likely lead to a decrease in the purchase and consumption of alcohol. Whereas in the case of tobacco, increased taxation can lead to the smuggling of untaxed cigarettes, in the case of alcohol, increased taxation can lead to a rise in the consumption of illicit alcohol. This is an issue that countries must take into account when considering raising taxes on alcohol.

In selected high-income countries, studies suggest that reducing the number of hours when alcohol can be sold can lead to a 1.5–3 percent decrease in high-risk drinking and to a 1.5–4 percent decrease in alcohol-related traffic deaths.[43] Government authorities have to assess the extent to which such measures could be implemented effectively, especially in low- and middle-income countries with weak governance, as well as the extent to which such measures might also drive people to seek illicit alcohol.

Bans on alcohol advertising can be put into effect, as discussed for tobacco; however, it appears that such bans have had relatively little effect on the consumption of alcohol.[43] In healthcare settings in a number of countries, efforts have been made to engage high-risk drinkers in brief but specific education and counseling about the risks of excessive drinking. Even when taking relapses into account, it appears that such counseling is effective in reducing excessive consumption by 14–18 percent, compared to no treatment at all.[44] Although this approach might be effective in middle-income countries, it is unlikely to be effective in many low-income countries, given the scarcity of effective health services, the lack of health providers, and the already excessive demands on their weak health systems.

A recent study that was part of a broader major review of alcohol and health suggested that countries should take a "step-wise" approach to reducing alcohol consumption. Such an approach would allow countries to implement an increasing number and level of policies on alcohol as their capacity to legislate and enforce such approaches grew. The paper recommended, at a minimum, that all countries make alcohol more expensive through excise taxes; reduce availability through regulation, licensing, and controlled sales to minors; check sobriety of drivers; and engage in the brief treatment approach noted above. As countries move to the next level of addressing alcohol abuse, they can, for example, ban sales and drinking in public places, regulate discounts on alcohol, and do random breath testing. At the last level, countries could set high minimum prices for alcohol; ban all forms of product marketing and restrict the design of packaging; and provide mandatory treatment for drunk driving, as well as treatment options for alcoholism.[45]

High Blood Pressure, High Cholesterol, and Obesity

The majority of risk associated with cardiovascular disease relates to a combination of high blood pressure, high cholesterol, high body mass index, low intake of fruits and vegetables, physical inactivity, and tobacco and alcohol use. The single most important risk factor for type II diabetes is obesity. This section comments on measures that can be taken to improve diet and to reduce obesity.

To reduce the burden of CVD and diabetes, healthy eating and maintaining a healthy weight is key. Generally, this requires eating more fruits and vegetables and decreasing the intake of salt and foods that are high in saturated fat and trans fats. It also entails limiting the intake of sugar and replacing refined grains with whole grains. People who are overweight generally need to consume fewer calories each day and need to become more active physically.[46]

The lack of regular physical activity, in fact, is associated, among other things, with CVD, stroke, type II diabetes, and colon and breast cancer. Urbanization, motorization, and television-watching all reduce physical activity. Countries can use public policies to try to limit the role of automobiles, promote walking and biking, and design communities in ways that encourage healthy lifestyles. In Singapore and London, for example, taxes are levied on cars that enter the center of the city to reduce the use of vehicles and their attendant traffic and pollution. Many cities promote the use of bicycles and have bicycle lanes, as one can see in a number of European cities such as Amsterdam. Some communities in the United States, for example, have no sidewalks, little public transport, and services that are very spread out, all of which provide an incentive for people to use automobiles to get from place to place, rather than to walk or bike.[46]

One way to promote healthier diets is through population-based "health education." Large-scale education efforts of this type, often through the mass media, have had mixed results because it is difficult to successfully promote the reduction of obesity on a large scale.[47] Generally, mass programs are more effective when they are combined with direct communication with individuals.

Few efforts to undertake population-based education measures have been studied. However, a study on a project to reduce salt intake among men in one part of China found a reduction in both hypertension and obesity after 5 years. In another effort, the government of Mauritius encouraged the population to switch from cooking with palm oil, which is high in saturated fat, to soybean oil, which has less saturated fat. Over a 5-year period, the intake of saturated fat decreased and the total cholesterol levels of the population fell.[48] Regulations and legislation on labeling food products and the reduction of unhealthy ingredients in commercial food products can also contribute to reducing obesity. New York City, for example, banned the use of trans fats in its restaurants.

Studies suggest that if large-scale health education efforts are to succeed in changing what people eat, then it is important that such programs:

- Have a realistic time frame that takes account of the time it takes to change deeply ingrained behaviors
- Be carried out by a respected organization and headed by a competent manager, with clear responsibility
- Encourage different organizations and agencies to work together to maximize the reach of the program and ensure that messages get disseminated in appropriate ways
- Involve the food industry and enhance food labeling[49]

Some countries, such as Brazil and Mexico, simultaneously face substantial burdens of underweight and overweight children and women. It may be politically and socially difficult for countries that face such a double burden to get the support they need to address problems of overweight, because many people believe that obesity is a problem that only affects wealthier people. There are few examples to date of best practices for addressing the two problems simultaneously.

Even as countries undertake the steps noted, they will still need to treat those who already have CVD, or who have some of the key risk factors for CVD, including hypertension. Most low- and some middle-income countries do not have

the level of health system or the financial resources needed to carry out sophisticated medical procedures. In such settings, however, an important reduction in risks and in the burden of disease can be realized through preventive interventions, such as getting people to take an aspirin a day and getting people with high cholesterol and hypertension to take inexpensive medicines to lower blood pressure and cholesterol.

Further Addressing Diabetes

There is no evidence that type I diabetes can be prevented; however, avoiding being overweight is the single most important way to avoid type II diabetes. Although large-scale efforts to reduce obesity have generally not been very successful, a pilot project that used intensive personal counseling to promote weight loss through healthier eating and more physical activity was successfully carried out in China, Finland, Sweden, and the United States. The average weight loss after almost 3 years of participation in this study was about 10 pounds more than in the control group. In addition, the study group had a 58 percent lower rate of type II diabetes than the control group.[11]

Treatment for people with diabetes is needed in all countries. Treating people with type I diabetes with insulin is a cost-effective investment, although difficult to afford or manage in the poorest countries, especially for people living outside of the main cities. For all diabetics, it is cost-effective to control hypertension because the combination of the two diseases can produce major vascular complications. Diabetics are also subject to foot problems from circulation difficulties associated with their diabetes, and appropriate foot care is another cost-effective investment. The cost of not doing this can be ulcers and eventual amputation of the foot.[11] Those countries with greater resources and a health system that can deliver additional interventions can also consider other cost-effective measures for treating diabetes, including vaccination against influenza and pneumococcal infections, diagnosis and treatment of retinal problems associated with diabetes, and treating hypertension with ACE inhibitors to prevent kidney problems from getting worse.[11]

Cancer

Tobacco control is overwhelmingly the first priority for preventing cancer, as noted earlier. Countries can also try to reduce the burden of cancer by addressing infectious agents that are associated with cancers, such as hepatitis B, which is vaccine-preventable; *H. pylori*, which is treatable with antibiotics; and schistosomiasis, which is also treatable with drugs.[50] An increasing number of countries are adding the hepatitis B vaccine to their national immunization programs as noted in Chapter 10. This is especially important in countries where a relatively large share of the population carries hepatitis B. Many countries have schistosomiasis control programs; some of the most successful efforts against schistosomiasis have been undertaken in Egypt and China. *H. pylori* is important in settings like Japan, China, or Colombia where there is a significant amount of stomach cancer linked with this bacteria. In these settings, it might be cost-effective to carry out a screening and treatment program for *H. pylori*.

Mental Disorders

Unfortunately, despite the enormous and growing importance of mental disorders, there is often an inadequate understanding of the importance of mental health, a lack of funds for mental health, a shortage of people who understand mental health issues, and stigma around mental disorders. As a result, there has been little progress in most low-income countries and many middle-income countries in addressing mental disorders.[50]

Given the important burden of disease associated with mental disorders and the low level of development of mental health services in most low-income and many middle-income countries, the World Health Organization recommends that countries take a number of fundamental steps to address mental health issues. These include:

- Having a mental health policy
- Ensuring there is a unit of government responsible for mental health
- Budgeting for mental health programs—including program development, training, drug procurement, and program monitoring
- Training primary healthcare workers in mental health
- Integrating mental health into the primary healthcare program[51]

In addition, a number of public health measures can be taken to address some of the risk factors that are associated with mental disorders. Reducing abuse of women and children can reduce the burden of mental illness among the abused. Curtailing bullying of students in schools can also be important. Improving parenting skills is helpful to the healthy development of children. Appropriate care and counseling for children and adults affected by war, conflict, and other complex emergencies can also reduce the risks of mental illness.

A significant amount of the mental health care in low- and middle-income countries is offered in large psychiatric hospitals that consume an overwhelming share of the mental health budget in those countries. Evidence is growing, however, that for $2–4 per person per year, countries could provide more community-based approaches to care that would offer drug therapy, combined with psychosocial support, for bipolar disorder, depression, and schizophrenia, and drug therapy for panic disorder. The goal would be to integrate such support into routine primary healthcare services, as far as possible.[52,53]

Given the weak state of health systems in most low-income and many middle-income countries and their lack of attention to mental health, accomplishing these aims will require much greater political attention to mental health issues. In addition, it will require measures to get additional funds for mental health and wiser use of them, including for services for the poor.[54]

There have been few mental health success stories in low- and middle-income countries. However, one of the case studies that follows deals with the efforts to improve mental health services in Uganda, a low-income country. There have also been some interesting efforts to provide community-based care for schizophrenia in India. In addition, although Chile is now considered a high-income country, it will be important to follow the progress of mental health services for depression in Chile, which has become a model for a national effort to address depression.[53]

CASE STUDIES

Most efforts to try to reduce the burden of noncommunicable diseases, alcohol abuse, and tobacco use have taken place in high-income countries. However, middle- and low-income countries are beginning to gather evidence about what works most effectively in preventing noncommunicable diseases. The following section examines efforts to reduce tobacco use in Poland. It will be followed by a review of the cataract blindness control program in India. The last case study is about the program to integrate mental health into primary health care in Uganda that was referred to earlier.

The Challenge of Curbing Tobacco Use in Poland

Background

More than three quarters of the world's 1.2 billion smokers live in low- and middle-income countries, where smoking is on the rise.[55] In the late 1970s, Poland had the highest rate of smoking in the world, with the average Pole smoking 3500 cigarettes a year and nearly three quarters of Polish men smoking daily. The impact on the nation's health was staggering. In 1990, the probability of a 15-year-old boy in Poland reaching his 60th birthday was lower than in most countries, including China and India.[56] Lung cancer rates were among the highest in the world. But because tobacco production, run by the state, provided a significant source of revenue, the government did not fully disclose to the population the negative consequences of smoking. The fall of communism further exacerbated smoking because tobacco, the first industry to be privatized, was taken over by powerful multinational corporations who flooded the market with international brands, spent vast sums on advertising, and kept prices so low that cigarettes cost less than a loaf of bread.

The Intervention

As the tobacco epidemic escalated, Poland's scientific community laid the foundation of the antitobacco movement. Research in the 1980s by the Marie Sklodowska-Curie Memorial Cancer Centre and Institute of Oncology contributed to the first Polish report on smoking, highlighting the link between tobacco and the country's alarming rise in cancer. A series of international workshops and scientific conferences in Poland further strengthened these findings. Civil society was experiencing a renewal at the time, with the formation of antitobacco groups such as the Polish Anti-Tobacco Society that began to interact with international bodies, such as WHO and the International Union Against Cancer. In addition, the Health Promotion Foundation was established to lead public efforts on health issues and antitobacco education efforts.

With the fall of the Berlin Wall, the media became free to cover health topics and played an important role in disseminating information, raising awareness about the dangers of smoking, and shaping public opinion. When tobacco control legislation was introduced in 1991, a heated public debate ensued between health advocates and the powerful tobacco lobby, increasingly viewed by the public as a contest between David and Goliath. In 1995, groundbreaking legislation was finally passed, requiring sweeping measures such as large health warnings on cigarette packs and bans on smoking in enclosed workspaces and health centers, on electronic media advertising, and on tobacco sales to minors. A 30 percent increase in taxes levied on cigarettes was subsequently passed in 1999 and 2000, and advertising was completely banned. In parallel, the Health Promotion Foundation also launched extensive health education and consumer awareness efforts. These included an annual "Great Polish Smoke-Out" competition to encourage smokers to quit, with incentives like winning a week-long stay in Rome and a chance to meet the Polish-born Pope John Paul II. Since the first smoke-out in 1991, more than 2.5 million Poles have permanently snuffed out their cigarettes because of the campaign.

The Impact

Cigarette consumption dropped 10 percent between 1990 and 1998, and the number of smokers declined from 14 million in the 1980s to under 10 million by the end of the 1990s. The reduction in smoking led to 10,000 fewer deaths each year, a 30 percent decline in lung cancer among men ages 20 to 44, a nearly 7 percent decline in CVD, and a reduction in infant mortality and low birthweight.[57] Life expectancy in the 1990s increased by 4 years.

Lessons Learned

Poland's experience shows that once smoking is seen for what it is—the leading cause of preventable deaths among adults worldwide—then governments do act. Working in concert with civil society and using state-of-the-art communication strategies, the Polish government succeeded in countering the powerful economic influence of the tobacco industry and inducing major shifts in smoking, an addictive behavior that was also then an ingrained social norm. Poland's sweeping legislative measures came to serve as a model for other countries. The experience of South Africa provides an interesting parallel: once the African National Congress came to power in 1994, the antismoking movement gained a powerful ally in Nelson Mandela and his first health minister, ultimately leading to the passage of strict tobacco control legislation and dramatic price control measures that increased the real value of cigarette taxes by 215 percent. As a result, cigarette consumption fell by more than 30 percent, from 1.9 billion packs in 1991 to 1.3 billion packs in 2002. As a South African researcher noted, "You need the right combination of science, evidence, and politics to succeed. If you have one without the other, you don't see action."[58] For a more detailed discussion of the Polish efforts, see *Case Studies in Global Health: Millions Saved.*

Cataract Blindness Control in India

This chapter has focused on a limited number of the leading causes of deaths and DALYs lost due to noncommunicable diseases. As you would expect, few people die of diseases related to vision disorders; however, the burden of disability of these diseases, especially in low- and middle-income countries in which they are not generally treated in a timely manner, is great. In fact, about 45 million people worldwide are blind and another 135 million people are visually impaired.[59] The total number of DALYs lost from cataracts alone in low- and middle-income countries is almost the same as those lost to nutritional deficiencies, is slightly more than those lost to maternal conditions, and is about 15 percent fewer than the amount lost to TB. It is also just under the number of DALYs lost to road traffic injuries.[60]

Background

About one quarter of the total number of people in the world who are blind live in India, and the case study that follows deals with controlling cataract blindness there.[61] The blindness control program in India has been one of the most extensive such programs in low-income countries for many years. In addition, over the last decade, this program has emerged, in many respects, as a public health "success story." Those wishing to examine this case in greater detail can read further about it in *Case Studies in Global Health: Millions Saved*.

History

Cataracts are the leading cause of blindness in India. About 80 percent of all of the people in India who are blind are blind due to cataracts. In addition, another 10 million people in India are visually impaired due to untreated cataracts.

In the simplest terms, a cataract is a clouding of the lens of the eye. It blurs the image on the retina, producing a visual effect that is like looking through a window that is frosted or fogged with steam. Cataracts form when protein clumps in the lens of the eye. This is associated with age, excessive exposure to sunlight, diabetes, undernutrition, and other risk factors. Cataracts can affect one or both eyes.

Cataracts are treatable through surgery. One form of surgery requires a large incision in the eye and the removal of the lens and lens capsule. This form of surgery (ICCE) is relatively easy to perform and relatively inexpensive; however, it requires that the patient wear thick eyeglasses after surgery, and it has a high rate of complications. Nonetheless, it has been the form of surgery traditionally done in low-income settings. The other form of surgery is more technically sophisticated (ECCE); however, it has a lower rate of complications when done by trained surgeons. In addition, research in India showed that those having ECCE surgery were 2.8 times more likely to have a good outcome than those having ICCE surgery.[62]

Intervention

India's response to the problem of blindness has been impressive in breadth and duration. India's first intervention in 1963 aimed specifically at controlling trachoma, a highly contagious eye infection. By the end of the decade, the government expanded its approach to include all visual impairment. In 1975, the Central Council of Health declared that "one of the basic human rights is the right to see." In 1976, India formed the National Program for the Control of Blindness (NPCB) to expand access to surgical treatment of vision disorders and to increase ophthalmologic services.

India's first international collaboration in eye care was with DANIDA, the Danish International Development Assistance Agency. Until 1989, DANIDA assisted India in funding the improvement and expansion of its cataract blindness control program through the provision of equipment, mobile units, training, and enhancements of monitoring and evaluation. The program focused then on mass ICCE surgeries in camps that were mostly set up in areas with limited health infrastructure. This demonstrated the ability of the government to lead mass screening and treatment camps, even in rural areas. It also generated enormous demand for cataract surgeries, even among the poor and rural. However, the limited amount of time a camp was stationed in a particular location, as well as the nature of field work, meant that postsurgical follow-up was difficult to implement. Consequently, although the efforts succeeded in reaching many people, only about 75 percent of those who got surgery returned to an acceptable level of vision.[63]

In 1994, building on its experience with DANIDA, the Government of India began to collaborate with the World Bank to finance a 7-year Cataract Blindness Control Project. The project focused on seven Indian states that had the highest prevalence of blindness and, in simple terms, it aimed to assist India in moving its cataract blindness control program from a focus on quantity to a focus on quality and outcomes. The aims of the program were to improve surgical outcomes by shifting from ICCE to ECCE, strengthen India's capacity to provide high quality surgery done by competently trained staff, and increase the coverage of the program to areas which had previously been underserved. Much greater attention was paid than before to monitoring the outcomes of surgery.

The program also focused on trying to achieve its aims through enhancing collaboration between the public and the private sectors. Some surgeries were done in public facilities. The government financed other surgeries that were conducted by the private and NGO sectors. In addition, NGOs such as Sight Savers International, Lions Clubs International, and Christoffel Blinden Mission also financially supported eye hospitals, training institutes, and the development of school vision-screening programs and outreach. The Aravind Eye Hospital in Madurai, India, was a world famous leader in eye care and became increasingly involved in training and other assistance to the NPCB.

Impact

Over 15 million cataract operations were performed in connection with the Cataract Blindness Control Project. In addition, ECCE surgeries increased as a share of the total surgeries from between 15 and 65 percent across different states in 1998–1999 to between 44 and 91 percent in 2001–2002.[63] Moreover, by 2001, 92 percent of surgeries occurred in fixed facilities where better outcomes can be expected. Most importantly, surgical outcomes have improved, with the introduction of improved procedures, well-equipped surgical procedures, and trained personnel. The ability to see at an acceptable level after surgery grew from 75 percent in 1994 to 82 percent from 1999 to 2002. The number and quality of surgeries was associated with a decrease in the prevalence of cataract blindness by 26 percent.

Cost Effectiveness

The World Bank–assisted intervention cost $136 million, with close to 90 percent coming from the Bank and the remainder from the government of India. When done correctly and in areas of high prevalence, cataract surgery is among the most highly cost-effective interventions.[64] ECCE surgery is estimated to cost about $60 per DALY averted in the South and East Asia regions. Through the combination of serving those most in need and their educational and awareness raising campaigns, NGOs operating under the project used their financial resources very effectively.

Lessons Learned

The efforts in India demonstrate the benefits of collaboration among different public and private sectors and international institutions. The government of India and its political commitment to the problem in the 1960s was a requirement for success, because it offered a big push to combating cataract blindness. In addition, even though the government's early efforts were not always at the level of quality desired, they provided a baseline for further studies on how the program could be improved and expanded in a high quality manner. Finally, the involvement of the NGOs helped to bring innovative approaches to the project and continually encouraged the government to improve and maintain quality services.

Integrating Mental Health into Primary Care in Uganda

Mental disorders are neglected in most low- and middle-income countries. They are difficult to diagnose and treat, they carry considerable stigma, and low-income countries often lack the skilled personnel and financial resources needed to address mental health issues. Uganda is one of the few low-income countries that has made an effort to tackle the important burden of mental disorders, and the case study that follows describes this effort and some of the outcomes associated with Uganda's move to integrate mental health concerns into its primary healthcare program.

Background

In 1986, Uganda came out of a 5-year civil conflict that had been preceded by 8 years of government led by General Idi Amin, which were characterized by misrule and violence. Although the civil conflict was, for the most part, over in the southern parts of the country, the conflict continued in the north, with abduction of children and terrorizing of the communities carried out by the Lord's Resistance Army. At about the same time, Uganda was increasingly being impacted by the emerging HIV/AIDS epidemic.

According to the 1995 Uganda Burden of Disease study, over 75 percent of life years lost from premature deaths was the result of preventable communicable disorders.[60] However, it was also recognized that there was a simultaneous surge in the occurrence of noncommunicable disorders, such as hypertension, diabetes, cancer, and mental disorders. It was also becoming clearer that HIV/AIDS and the prolonged armed conflict created an increased need for attention to be paid to mental health.

In order to address the increasing burden of mental disorders, the Ministry of Health decided to promote the integration of mental health into primary health care. This involved developing standards and guidelines for the management of eight priority mental disorders for the community, district, and national referral levels of care. This was part of Uganda's efforts to address health care in an effective and efficient manner through the establishment of a minimum healthcare package.

The Intervention

The process of integrating mental health into primary health care was to be implemented through training all healthcare workers to recognize and manage common mental disorders, as well as establishing and strengthening a referral and supportive supervision system. The initiative was outlined in the Uganda Health Sector Strategic Plan 1999 to 2004.[65]

Central-level activities included the creation of a Mental Health Coordinating Committee whose main responsibilities were the development of standards and guidelines for the management of common mental disorders, developing materials for the training of health workers, and developing and participating in the referral and supervision system. Central-level activities also included participation in the creation of a Core Team on Psychosocial Disorders, a group of representatives of two government sectors—the Ministry of Health and the Ministry of Gender, Labor, and Social Development, which was responsible for child protection—and five NGOs working in the field of psychosocial disorders, and UNICEF.

The Core Team carried out an assessment of the psychosocial situation of the conflict-affected population in eight districts of northern Uganda, disseminated the results to the district leaders, and facilitated the affected districts in the development of psychosocial components to be included in District Development Plans. The Core Team developed indicators, as well as a monitoring and evaluation plan, that they then implemented. The Core Team was instrumental in the coordinated safe return and reintegration of abducted children into their communities.

As a result of having mental health in the Health Sector Policy and the Health Sector Strategic Plan, a budget line for mental health was created. Although the allocation to mental health from the government of Uganda was only 0.7 percent of the total health budget, having mental health as a budget item made it easier for other funding agencies to support mental health efforts in Uganda.

The African Development Bank (AfDB) provided a loan to the government for support in the integration of mental health into primary health care. This AfDB-assisted project provided $17.73 million to mental health efforts in Uganda over a 5-year period. Activities include rehabilitation of Butabika National Referral Psychiatric Hospital, down-sizing it from a 900-bed to a 450-bed hospital, as well as the construction of six regional mental health units. The project includes provision of essential mental health medications and support to the training of healthcare workers at all levels of the care system, from training primary healthcare nurses in the recognition and management of common mental disorders, to the training of specialized personnel, such as psychiatrists, psychologists, and psychiatric social workers.[65]

Lessons Learned

It is often thought that mental health is not a priority in low-income countries, or that feasible mental health interventions are not available. This case study, however, demonstrates that mental disorders are of importance in low-income countries, especially those affected by disasters, complex emergencies, and HIV/AIDS. It also demonstrates that countries, even with limited resources, can take measures to considerably improve mental health services.

This case study also suggests that it is possible to design and implement a strategy for dealing with mental disorders that builds on an existing healthcare system. As a result of the investments made, resources for mental health are better allocated in Uganda than before, and funds for mental health have moved from the large psychiatric institution to the regional levels, where services are more accessible to the populations that require them.

Nonetheless, there remain great challenges in trying to provide appropriate mental health services in Uganda. These include the need to strengthen information and public education so the population is aware of what constitutes mental disorders, as well as where help can be sought. A further challenge is likely to be sustainability of the established services. The AfDB project provides the infrastructure and the start-up costs; however, the government of Uganda will have to ensure that recurrent costs for staff, maintenance of equipment and infrastructure, referral and supervision, and other inputs such as drugs are provided for in the long-term.

FUTURE CHALLENGES

The world must face a number of challenges if it is to reduce the burden of noncommunicable diseases in low- and middle-income countries. First, the number of people with new cases of noncommunicable diseases will grow in low- and middle-income countries as a result of the aging of the population, urbanization, globalization, and lifestyle changes. In addition, because noncommunicable diseases are chronic, the number of people with these diseases will also rise. The increasing number of people who will be at risk of and living with chronic diseases in low- and middle-income countries will pose a huge challenge to the health of these countries, to their health systems, and to their national finances.

Related to this, a number of low-income countries will have to deal with the challenge of addressing increasing amounts of noncommunicable disease simultaneously with having to address substantial burdens of communicable diseases. This will severely tax the managerial, technical, and financial capacity of many developing countries. It will also require greater attention by low-income countries to noncommunicable diseases and to improved surveillance of these diseases. Low- and middle-income countries will need to strengthen primary care and integrate the prevention and control of noncommunicable diseases into it.

In addition, it will be important to spread as rapidly as possible to low- and middle-income countries the lessons that the high-income countries have already learned about how to address noncommunicable diseases in cost-effective ways. This body of evidence, especially for low-cost interventions that have a high payback, needs to be disseminated in low- and middle-income countries as rapidly as possible. Ongoing mechanisms need to be established to ensure, as well, that cost-effective diagnostics and drugs continuously get disseminated as early as possible to low- and middle-income countries.

Even as they continue to learn from the experience of the high-income countries, the low- and middle-income countries need to take the measures that are known to prevent noncommunicable diseases. This should include comprehensive approaches to reducing tobacco and alcohol consumption. Even in the face of undernutrition, a number of countries need to promote healthier diets and more physical activity for people who are overweight, as well as policy measures to combat the growing problem of obesity. Some of the low-cost but effective preventive therapy for cardiovascular disease, such as aspirin, can also be promoted. An international panel, in fact, recently outlined specific priority actions for dealing with what it called a crisis of noncommunicable diseases. The panel based the selection of these actions on a number of criteria, including that the actions: would have a solid evidence basis; could lead to a substantial reduction in premature deaths and disability; would be low-cost and cost-effective; and, that they would be politically and financially feasible. On this basis, the panel suggested that countries should immediately begin to take the following actions, in the five priority areas that are noted:

- Tobacco: Accelerate the implementation of the Framework Convention on Tobacco Control
- Salt: Promote greater popular awareness and voluntary action by the food industry to reduce salt consumption
- Obesity, unhealthy diet, and physical inactivity: Promote greater knowledge and take measures on taxes, food labeling, food subsidies, and food marketing to reduce overconsumption and the consumption of unhealthy fats, and to encourage greater consumption of fresh fruits and vegetables and of physical activity
- Harmful alcohol intake: Increase alcohol taxes, ban advertising, and restrict sales
- Cardiovascular disease: Promote the use of proven drugs for high risk individuals[66]

A major goal of public health policy is to try to help people live longer lives that are as healthy as possible. The epidemiologic and demographic changes that are occurring globally suggest this goal can be achieved only if countries take measures now to prevent as much noncommunicable disease as possible. At the same time, countries need to increasingly prepare their health systems to deal with the prevention and treatment of noncommunicable diseases in cost-effective and efficient ways. The failure to address these aims effectively will result in older but unhealthy populations, whose needs for care and cost of care overwhelm the health systems of a number of countries.[67]

MAIN MESSAGES

Noncommunicable diseases now constitute the largest burden of disease worldwide. In all regions of the world, except sub-Saharan Africa, the burden of these diseases is greater than the burden of communicable diseases. Cardiovascular disease is the single largest cause of death worldwide. Diabetes, some forms of cancer, and mental disorders are also major causes of disability and death from noncommunicable diseases. In fact, about 14 percent of the DALYs lost in 2001 were attributable to CVD, about 7 percent to cancer, 1.3 percent to diabetes, and about 5 percent to the four mental disorders discussed earlier.

Moreover, economic development, globalization, urbanization, and aging will encourage the growth of noncommunicable diseases globally. In this light, it is projected that by 2030, even in low-income countries, there will be a major epidemiologic shift toward noncommunicable disease. As this happens, it is projected that diarrhea, malaria, and TB will no longer be in the top 10 causes of DALYs lost in low-income countries. Rather, depression and cardiovascular disease will rise on the list from where they are now, and chronic obstructive pulmonary disease, hearing loss, and refractive errors (vision disorders including nearsightedness, farsightedness, and astigmatism) will make it into the top 10 causes of DALYs lost for such countries. It is also projected that by 2030 no communicable disease will be in the top 10 causes of DALYs lost for middle- or upper-income countries.

The leading risk factors for cardiovascular disease are hypertension, obesity, high cholesterol, and tobacco use. A lack of physical activity contributes to CVD and obesity, and the main risk factor for diabetes is obesity. Some cancers are associated with an infectious agent, such as hepatitis B, *H. pylori*, or the humanpapilloma virus. Other cancers are linked with tobacco use. Little is known about the nongenetic risk factors that are associated with mental disorders.

The costs of noncommunicable diseases and the use of tobacco and alcohol abuse are substantial. They have a considerable impact on people in their productive years of life. In addition, mental disorders and diabetes are associated with very large amounts of disability. The costs of trying to prevent the burden of noncommunicable diseases include efforts to promote "healthier lifestyles," including a healthy diet, maintaining an appropriate weight, and increasing physical activity, while trying to reduce obesity, cigarette consumption, and excessive drinking. The costs of treating noncommunicable diseases can be high, both because of the high cost of some medical treatments for specific episodes of illness and the need to treat some diseases and conditions for many years. Mental disorders, for example, frequently start early in life and often continue throughout a life. Nonetheless, aspirin and some medicines used for hypertension, for example, are highly cost-effective at dealing with CVD, even in low- and middle-income settings.

The single most important step that countries can take to reduce the burden of noncommunicable diseases is to reduce the consumption of tobacco. There is good evidence from high-income and some lower-income countries that taxing cigarettes more heavily, banning smoking from public places, and trying to educate the population about the impact of tobacco on health can all contribute to reducing tobacco consumption.

Reducing the burden of noncommunicable diseases will also require that alcohol-related harm is reduced. In addition, it is critical that obesity be reduced through healthier diets, fewer calories, increased intake of fruits and green leafy vegetables, and more physical activity. Other measures to reduce obesity can be complemented with food labeling legislation and legislation to encourage the use of healthier ingredients in food products. The intake of salt must also be reduced.

Study Questions

1. How important are noncommunicable diseases to the global burden of disease?

2. Why are noncommunicable diseases less important to that burden in sub-Saharan Africa?

3. What are the leading risk factors for cardiovascular disease?

4. What are the most important cancers that affect low-income countries?

5. What are the most important risk factors for cancers?

6. What factors are causing the "epidemic" of diabetes that is occurring worldwide?

7. Why are mental disorders so important to the burden of disease if so few people die of them?

8. What measures have proven effective in reducing the use of tobacco?

9. What lessons of Uganda's approach to mental health concerns are important for other resource-poor countries?

10. What measures have been effective in reducing the abuse of alcohol?

REFERENCES

1. World Health Organization. Global Status Report on Noncommunicable Diseases 2010. Geneva: World Health Organization; 2011.

2. Lopez AD, Mathers CD, Murray CJL. The burden of disease and mortality by condition: data, methods, and results for 2001. In: Lopez AD, Mathers CD, Ezzati M, Jamison DT, Murray CJL, eds. *Global Burden of Disease and Risk Factors*. New York: Oxford University Press; 2006:45-240.

3. World Health Organization. Global Burden of Disease (GBD). Available at: http://www.who.int/healthinfo/global_burden_disease/en/index.html. Accessed October 20, 2010.

4. Gaziano TA, Srinath Reddy K, Paccaud F, Horton S, Chaturvedi V. Cardiovascular disease. In: Jamison DT, Breman JG, Measham AR, et al., eds. *Disease Control Priorities in Developing Countries*. 2nd ed. New York: Oxford University Press; 2006:649-650.

5. Gaziano TA, Srinath Reddy K, Paccaud F, Horton S, Chaturvedi V. Cardiovascular disease. In: Jamison DT, Breman JG, Measham AR, et al., eds. *Disease Control Priorities in Developing Countries*. 2nd ed. New York: Oxford University Press; 2006:650.

6. National Institutes of Health. Obesity, Physical Activity, and Weight-Control Glossary. Available at: http://win.niddk.nih.gov/publications/glossary/MthruZ.htm. Accessed April 15, 2006.

7. International Diabetes Association. *Diabetes Atlas*. 2nd ed. Brussels: International Diabetes Federation; 2003.

8. Ryerson B, Tierney EF, Thompson TJ, et al. Excess physical limitations among adults with diabetes in the U.S. population, 1997–1999. *Diabetes Care*. 2003;26(1):206-210.

9. Mathers C, Stein C, Fat CMF, et al. *Global Burden of Disease 2000: Version 2 Methods and Results*. Geneva: World Health Organization; 2000.

10. Haffner SM. Epidemiology of type 2 diabetes: risk factors. *Diabetes Care*. 1998;21(Suppl 3):C3-6.

11. Venkat Narayan K, Zhang P, Kanaya AM, et al. Diabetes: the pandemic and potential solutions. In: Jamison DT, Breman JG, Measham AR, et al., eds. *Disease Control Priorities in Developing Countries*. 2nd ed. New York: Oxford University Press; 2006:645-662.

12. Centers for Disease Control and Prevention. Fact Sheet—Schistosomiasis. Available at: http://www.cdc.gov/ncidod/dpd/parasites/schistosomiasis/default.htm. Accessed April 20, 2006.

13. Jamison DT, Breman JG, Measham AR, et al., eds. *Priorities in Health*. Washington, DC: TheWorld Bank; 2006.

14. Lopez AD, Mathers CD, Murray CJL. The burden of disease and mortality by condition: data, methods, and results for 2001. In: Lopez AD, Mathers CD, Ezzati M, Jamison DT, Murray CJL, eds. *Global Burden of Disease and Risk Factors*. New York: Oxford University Press; 2006:158.

15. Lopez AD, Mathers CD, Murray CJL. The burden of disease and mortality by condition: data, methods, and results for 2001. In: Lopez AD, Mathers CD, Ezzati M, Jamison DT, Murray CJL, eds. *Global Burden of Disease and Risk Factors*. New York: Oxford University Press; 2006:128.

16. Lopez AD, Mathers CD, Murray CJL. The burden of disease and mortality by condition: data, methods, and results for 2001. In: Lopez AD, Mathers CD, Ezzati M, Jamison DT, Murray CJL, eds. *Global Burden of Disease and Risk Factors*. New York: Oxford University Press; 2006:230.

17. Hyman S, Chisholm D, Kessler R, Patel V, Whiteford H. Mental disorders. In: Jamison DT, Breman JG, Measham AR, et al., eds. *Disease Control Priorities in Developing Countries*. 2nd ed. New York: Oxford University Press; 2006:605-625.

18. Lopez AD, Mathers CD, Murray CJL. The burden of disease and mortality by condition: data, methods, and results for 2001. In: Lopez AD, Mathers CD, Ezzati M, Jamison DT, Murray CJL, eds. *Global Burden of Disease and Risk Factors*. New York: Oxford University Press; 2006:228-233.

19. The comments on vision and hearing loss are based on: Cook J, Frick KD, Baltussen R, et al. Loss of vision and hearing. In: Jamison DT, Breman JG, Measham AR, et al., eds. *Disease Control Priorities in Developing Countries*. Washington, DC: The World Bank; 2006:953-962.

20. Lopez AD, Mathers CD, Ezzati K, Jamison DT, Murray CJL. *Global Burden of Disease and Risk Factors*. Washington, DC: The World Bank; 2006.

21. Jha P, Chaloupka FJ, Moore J, et al. Tobacco addiction. In: Jamison DT, Breman JG, Measham AR, et al., eds. *Disease Control Priorities in Developing Countries*. 2nd ed. New York: Oxford University Press; 2006:870.

22. Jha P, Chaloupka FJ, Moore J, et al. Tobacco addiction. In: Jamison DT, Breman JG, Measham AR, et al., eds. *Disease Control Priorities in Developing Countries*. 2nd ed. New York: Oxford University Press; 2006:869.

23. Jamison DT, Breman JG, Measham AR, et al., eds. *Priorities in Health*. Washington, DC: The World Bank; 2006.

24. Jamison DT, Breman JG, Measham AR, et al., eds. *Priorities in Health*. Washington, DC: The World Bank; 2006.

25. Rehm J, Chisholm D, Room R, Lopez AD. Alcohol. In: Jamison DT, Breman JG, Measham AR, et al., eds. *Disease Control Priorities in Developing Countries*. 2nd ed. New York: Oxford University Press; 2006:887.

26. Rehm J, Chisholm D, Room R, Lopez AD. Alcohol. In: Jamison DT, Breman JG, Measham AR, et al., eds. *Disease Control Priorities in Developing Countries*. 2nd ed. New York: Oxford University Press; 2006:888.

27. Rehm J, Chisholm D, Room R, Lopez AD. Alcohol. In: Jamison DT, Breman JG, Measham AR, et al., eds. *Disease Control Priorities in Developing Countries*. 2nd ed. New York: Oxford University Press; 2006:889.

28. Rehm J, Chisholm D, Room R, Lopez AD. Alcohol. In: Jamison DT, Breman JG, Measham AR, et al., eds. *Disease Control Priorities in Developing Countries*. 2nd ed. New York: Oxford University Press; 2006:890.

29. Rodgers A, Lawes CM, Gaziano TA, Vos T. The growing burden of risk from high blood pressure, cholesterol, and bodyweight. In: Jamison DT, Breman JG, Measham AR, et al., eds. *Disease Control Priorities in Developing Countries*. 2nd ed. New York: Oxford University Press; 2006:854.

30. Abegunde DO, Mathers CD, Adam T, Ortegon M, Strong K. The burden and costs of chronic diseases in low-income and middle-income countries. *Lancet*. 2007;370(9603):1929-1938.

31. World Health Organization. *Investing in Mental Health*. Geneva: World Health Organization; 2003.

32. U.S. National Institutes of Health. Healthy People 2010. Working Paper 28: Vision and Hearing Loss. Available at: http://www.healthypeople.gov/2010/Document/pdf/Volume2/28Vision.pdf. Accessed January 16, 2011.

33. Eein DB, Zhang P, Wirth KE, et al. The economic burden of major adult visual disorders in the United States. *Arch Opthalmol*. 2006;124(12):1754-1760.

34. Tucci DL, Merson MH, Wilson BS. A summary of the literature on global hearing impairment: current status and priorities for action. *Otol Neurotol*. 2010;31(1):31-41.

35. Lightwood J, Collins D, Lapsley H, Novotny TE. Estimating the costs of tobacco use. In: Jha P, Chaloupka FJ, eds. *Tobacco Control in Developing Countries*. London: Oxford University Press; 2000:63-104.

36. Chaloupka FJ, Tauras JA, Grossman M. The economics of addiction. In: Jha P, Chaloupka FJ, eds. *Tobacco Control in Developing Countries*: London: Oxford University Press; 2000:107-130.

37. World Health Organization. *Global Status Report on Alcohol 2004*. Geneva: World Health Organization; 2004.

38. Rehm J, Mathers C, Popova S, Thavorncharoensap M, Teerawattananon Y, Patra J. Global burden of disease and injury and economic cost attributable to alcohol use-disorders. *Lancet*. 2009;373(9682):2223-2233.

39. Jha P, Chaloupka FJ, Moore J, et al. Tobacco addiction. In: Jamison DT, Breman JG, Measham AR, et al., eds. *Disease Control Priorities in Developing Countries*. 2nd ed. New York: Oxford University Press; 2006:869-885.

40. Jha P, Chaloupka FJ, Moore J, et al. Tobacco addiction. In: Jamison DT, Breman JG, Measham AR, et al., eds. *Disease Control Priorities in Developing Countries*. 2nd ed. New York: Oxford University Press; 2006:876.

41. Jha P, Chaloupka FJ, Moore J, et al. Tobacco addiction. In: Jamison

DT, Breman JG, Measham AR, et al., eds. *Disease Control Priorities in Developing Countries.* 2nd ed. New York: Oxford University Press; 2006:881.

42. Jha P, Chaloupka FJ, Moore J, et al. Tobacco addiction. In: Jamison DT, Breman JG, Measham AR, et al., eds. *Disease Control Priorities in Developing Countries.* 2nd ed. New York: Oxford University Press; 2006:893.

43. Rehm J, Chisholm D, Room R, Lopez AD. Alcohol. In: Jamison DT, Breman JG, Measham AR, et al., eds. *Disease Control Priorities in Developing Countries.* 2nd ed. New York: Oxford University Press; 2006:887-906.

44. Rehm J, Chisholm D, Room R, Lopez AD. Alcohol. In: Jamison DT, Breman JG, Measham AR, et al., eds. *Disease Control Priorities in Developing Countries.* 2nd ed. New York: Oxford University Press; 2006:894.

45. Casswell S, Thamarangsi T. Reducing harm from alcohol: a call to action. *Lancet.* 2009;373(9682):2247-2257.

46. Willett WC, Koplan JP, Nugent R, Dusenbury C, Puska P, Gaziano TA. Prevention of chronic disease by means of diet and lifestyle changes. In: Jamison DT, Breman JG, Measham AR, et al., eds. *Disease Control Priorities in Developing Countries.* 2nd ed. New York: Oxford University Press; 2006:833-850.

47. Rodgers A, Lawes CM, Gaziano TA, Vos T. The growing burden of risk from high blood pressure, cholesterol, and bodyweight. In: Jamison DT, Breman JG, Measham AR, et al., eds. *Disease Control Priorities in Developing Countries.* 2nd ed. New York: Oxford University Press; 2006:863.

48. Rodgers A, Lawes CM, Gaziano TA, Vos T. The growing burden of risk from high blood pressure, cholesterol, and bodyweight. In: Jamison DT, Breman JG, Measham AR, et al., eds. *Disease Control Priorities in Developing Countries.* 2nd ed. New York: Oxford University Press; 2006:856.

49. Rodgers A, Lawes CM, Gaziano TA, Vos T. The growing burden of risk from high blood pressure, cholesterol, and bodyweight. In: Jamison DT, Breman JG, Measham AR, et al., eds. *Disease Control Priorities in Developing Countries.* 2nd ed. New York: Oxford University Press; 2006:855-856.

50. Hyman S, Chisholm D, Kessler R, Patel V, Whiteford H. Mental disorders. In: Jamison DT, Breman JG, Measham AR, et al., eds. *Disease Control Priorities in Developing Countries.* 2nd ed. New York: Oxford University Press; 2006:620.

51. World Health Organization. The world health report 2000. Mental health: new understanding, new hope. Geneva: WHO; 2001.

52. Lancet Mental Health Group. Scale up services for mental disorders: a call to action. *Lancet.* 2007;370(9594):1241-1252.

53. Patel V, Araya R, Chatterjee S, et al. Treatment and prevention of mental disorders in low-income and middle-income countries. *Lancet.* 2007;370(9591):991-1005.

54. Saxena S, Thornicroft G, Knapp M, Whitford H. Resources for mental health: scarcity, inequity, and inefficiency. *Lancet.* 2007;370(9590):878-889.

55. Jha P, Chaloupka FJ. The economics of global tobacco control. *BMJ.* 2000;321(7257):358-361.

56. Witold Z. *Evolution of Health in Poland Since 1988.* Warsaw: Marie Sklodowska-Curie Memorial Cancer Center and Institute of Oncology, Department of Epidemiology and Cancer Prevention; 1998.

57. Zatonski W. Democracy and health: tobacco control in Poland. In: de Beyer J, Brigden LW, eds. *Tobacco Control Policy, Strategies, Successes and Setbacks.* Washington, DC: The World Bank and International Development Research Center; 2003:97-119.

58. Malan M, Leaver R. Political change in South Africa: new tobacco control and public health policies. In: de Beyer J, Brigden LW, eds. *Tobacco Control Policy: Strategy, Success, and Setbacks.* Washington, DC: The World Bank and International Development Research Center; 2003.

59. World Health Organization. *Global Initiative for the Prevention of Avoidable Blindness.* Geneva: World Health Organization; 1997. WHO/PBL/97.61.

60. Lopez AD, Mathers CD, Murray CJL. The burden of disease and mortality by condition: data, methods, and results for 2001. In: Lopez AD, Mathers CD, Ezzati M, Jamison DT, Murray CJL, eds. *Global Burden of Disease and Risk Factors.* New York: Oxford University Press and The World Bank; 2006:180-185.

61. Thomas R, Paul P, Rao GN, Muliyil J, Matahai A. Present status of eye care in India. *Surv Ophthalmol* 2005;50(1):85-101.

62. Bachani D, Gupta GK, Murthy G, Jose R. Visual outcomes after cataract surgery and cataract surgical coverage in India. *Int Ophthamol.* 1999;23(1):49-56.

63. The World Bank. *Cataract Blindness Control Project Implementation Completion Report.* Washington, DC: The World Bank; 2002.

64. Javitt J, Venkataswamy G, Sommer A. The economic and social aspect of restoring sight. In: Henkind P, ed. *ACTA: 24th International Congress of Ophthalmology.* New York: JP Lippincott; 1983:1308-1312.

65. Government of Uganda. *Uganda Health Sector Strategic Plan 1999–2004.* Uganda: Government of Uganda; 1999.

66. Beaglehole R, Bonita R, Horton R, et al., for *The Lancet* NCD Action Group and the NCD Alliance. Priority actions for the non-communicable disease crisis. *Lancet.* 2011;377(9775):1438-1447.

67. Adeyi O, Smith O, Robles S. *Public Policy and the Challenge of Chronic Noncommunicable Diseases.* Washington, DC: The World Bank; 2007.

CHAPTER 13

Unintentional Injuries

LEARNING OBJECTIVES

By the end of this chapter the reader will be able to:

- Define the most important types of unintentional injuries
- Describe the burden of disease related to those injuries
- Discuss how that burden varies by age, sex, region, and type of injury
- Outline the costs and consequences of those injuries
- Review measures that can be taken to address key injury issues in cost-effective ways
- Describe some successful cases of preventing unintentional injuries

VIGNETTES

Juan was 25 years old. He was driving his 15-year-old car from Lima, Peru, to a small town in the mountains, where he planned to visit his grandmother. Juan had received only a small amount of driver training. His car was very old, had never been inspected for safety, and had worn tires and poor brakes. The road was very mountainous, did not have good lane markings or signs, and had few safety barriers. As the sun was setting, another car came rapidly around a mountain bend, headed right toward Juan's car. Juan tried to avoid the car but in doing so went off the road. His car slid down the side of the mountain and Juan was killed in the crash.

Mary was 12 years old and lived in a farming community in northern Tanzania. People in her village used fertilizer and pesticide in their agricultural work. They cooked with kerosene stoves. One day, after coming home from school, Mary was thirsty and saw some of her favorite soft drink near the area in which her mother cooked. Mary reached for the drink and began to consume it quickly. As she did so, she realized that her mother was storing in the soft drink bottle the kerosene that she used for cooking. Mary lived far from health services, got very sick that evening, and died of kerosene poisoning before she could get proper medical treatment.

Paitoon was a 70-year-old physician in Bangkok, Thailand. He was still practicing medicine, but was becoming more frail every month. He fancied himself to be a young man and enjoyed fixing things around his house and his office. While standing on a stool in his office one day to repair a broken light, Paitoon fell. Like many people his age who suffer falls, Paitoon broke his hip. Paitoon was hospitalized, had surgery, and could not attend to his patients for several months while he recovered.

Shahnaz was a 26-year-old woman in Lahore, Pakistan. Like almost all lower-income women in Pakistan, Shahnaz spent much of the day doing chores around the house. She lived in a very small house with a tiny cooking area. While preparing dinner one evening, the sleeve of Shahnaz's outfit dipped into the cooking fire. Before her family could help her, all of Shahnaz's clothing was engulfed in flames. Shahnaz died the next day from burns.

THE IMPORTANCE OF UNINTENTIONAL INJURIES

Unintentional injuries are among the single leading causes of death and DALYs lost worldwide. In 2001, about 3.5 million people died of unintentional injuries.[1] This is about the same number of people who died of respiratory infections worldwide. It was more than the number of people who died of HIV/AIDS, diarrheal diseases, and vaccine-preventable diseases of children. It was also more than the number of people who died of maternal and perinatal conditions combined.[2] In addition, unintentional injuries often lead to disability. Thus, while they represent about 6 percent of all deaths worldwide,[2] they represent almost 8 percent of the DALYs lost.[3] Although unintentional injuries are often neglected in global health work, they are, in fact, exceptionally important.

This chapter is about unintentional injuries. It first reviews definitions that are commonly used when discussing unintentional injuries. The chapter then reviews the global burden of disease from these injuries and how that burden varies by type of injury, sex, age, and region of the world. After that, the chapter examines the costs and consequences of unintentional injuries. The chapter concludes by examining measures that can be taken to reduce the burden of unintentional injuries and by reviewing some cases of successful injury prevention efforts.

KEY DEFINITIONS

As we begin this chapter, it is important to define the focus of our attention. For the purposes of this chapter, we can define an *injury* as:

> the result of an act that damages, harms, or hurts; unintentional or intentional damage to the body resulting from acute exposure to thermal, mechanical, electrical, or chemical energy or from the absence of such essentials as heat or oxygen.[4]

Some injuries, such as being shot by someone trying to do you harm, are intentional injuries. Unintentional injuries are "that subset of injuries for which there is no evidence of predetermined intent."[5]

Chapter 14 deals with humanitarian emergencies and civil conflict, but it also will discuss briefly some issues related to intentional injury. This chapter, however, will deal only with unintentional injuries, other than occupational injuries.

In focusing on unintentional injuries, this chapter will deal with:

- Road traffic accidents
- Poisonings
- Falls
- Fires
- Drownings

Because the chapter focuses on the unintentional injuries noted above, it will use the term *injury* to refer to these injuries for the sake of simplicity. Any references to "intentional injuries" will be specified.

THE BURDEN OF UNINTENTIONAL INJURIES

In 2001, about 3.5 million people died of unintentional injuries worldwide, which was about 6 percent of all deaths in the world that year. In terms of DALYs lost, unintentional injuries that year were almost 8 percent of the total.[5] Table 13-1 shows the share of deaths globally that can be attributed to unintentional injuries and how that compares with deaths from a number of other causes.

Although injuries have most commonly been thought of as a problem of high-income countries, more than 90 percent of deaths from unintentional injuries in 2001 were in low- and middle-income countries.[6,7] This is another reminder that low- and middle-income countries simultaneously face the multiple burdens of communicable diseases, noncommunicable diseases, and injuries.

TABLE 13-1 Deaths from Unintentional Injuries, 2001, Compared to Total Deaths from Group I and Group II Diseases

Region	Group I Deaths (% of all deaths)	Group II Deaths (% of all deaths)	Unintentional Injuries (% of all deaths)
East Asia & Pacific	19%	71%	7%
Europe & Central Asia	6%	84%	7%
Latin America & the Caribbean	22%	67%	6%
Middle East & North Africa	24%	65%	9%
South Asia	43%	47%	7%
Sub-Saharan Africa	71%	21%	5%

Note: Group 1 = communicable, maternal, perinatal, and nutritional conditions; Group II = noncommunicable diseases.

Source: Data with permission from Lopez AD, Mathers CD, Murray CJL. The burden of disease and mortality by condition: data, methods, and results for 2001. In: Lopez AD, Mathers CD, Ezzati M, Jamison DT, Murray CJL, eds. *Global Burden of Disease and Risk Factors.* Washington, DC and New York: The World Bank and Oxford University Press; 2006:132-167.

TABLE 13-2 Percentage Distribution of Deaths and DALYs from Unintentional Injuries, Low- and Middle-Income Countries, 2001

	% of Total Deaths from Unintentional Injuries		% of Total DALYs from Unintentional Injuries
Road traffic accidents	33%	Other unintentional injuries	36%
Other unintentional injuries	26%	Road traffic accidents	28%
Drownings	11%	Falls	12%
Falls	10%	Fires	9%
Poisonings	10%	Drownings	8%
Fires	9%	Poisonings	6%

Source: Adapted with permission from Lopez AD, Mathers CD, Murray CJL. The burden of disease and mortality by condition: data, methods, and results for 2001. In: Lopez AD, Mathers CD, Ezzati M, Jamison DT, Murray CJL, eds. *Global Burden of Disease and Risk Factors.* Washington, DC and New York: The World Bank and Oxford University Press; 2006:128-184.

The leading cause of deaths from unintentional injuries in 2001 that were categorized were road traffic injuries. This was followed by drownings, poisonings, falls, and fires. The leading cause of DALYs lost from unintentional injuries was road traffic injuries. This was followed by falls, fires, drownings, and poisonings. The difference in order between deaths and DALYs largely reflects the disability associated with fires and falls.[8] Table 13-2 portrays the percentage distribution for deaths and DALYs of the main categories of unintentional injuries. When considering unintentional injuries, it is important to note the category "other unintentional injuries," which is a very large one. The 2001 study on the global burden of disease defines this as: ". . . injuries due to environmental factors, machinery and electrical equipment, cutting and piercing implements, and various other external causes of unintentional injury."[9]

The percentage of deaths from unintentional injuries in low- and middle-income countries in 2001 was 2.2 percent—twice as high as that in high-income countries. The rate of deaths from unintentional injuries in the low- and middle-income countries was six times that in high-income countries. Males more commonly suffer from unintentional injuries than females, and about two thirds of the deaths from unintentional injuries were among males.[5] In low- and middle-income countries, men were more likely to die than women of all six categories of unintentional injuries, except fires, as shown in Table 13-3.

Men were also almost three times as likely as women to die in road traffic accidents. They were almost twice as likely to die as women in all other categories of unintentional injury, except fires, for which women were almost twice as likely to die as men.[8]

When the leading causes of death globally are examined by age, we note that only HIV/AIDS kills more men ages 30–44 than are killed by unintentional injuries. Only cancer and cardiovascular disease kill more women every year than die from unintentional injury. Table 13-4 gives a breakdown of deaths from unintentional injuries for men compared to women.

Deaths are only part of the injury story. Although the number of deaths is significant, the number of people who suffer disability annually from an injury is much greater than those who actually die from an injury. As an example, a study of fatal and nonfatal injuries in two states in the United States

TABLE 13-3 Death Rates from Unintentional Injuries per 100,000 for Males and Females, Low- and Middle-Income Countries, 2001

	Males	Females
All unintentional injuries	75	41
Drowning	9	4
Falls	8	5
Fires	4	6
Poisonings	7	4
Road traffic accidents	28	11
Other unintentional injuries	19	11

Source: Adapted with permission from Norton R, Hyder AA, Bishai D, Peden M. Unintentional injuries. In: Jamison DT, Breman JG, Measham AR, et al., eds. *Disease Control Priorities in Developing Countries.* 2nd ed. Washington, DC and New York: The World Bank and Oxford University Press; 2006:738.

TABLE 13-4 Distribution of Deaths from Unintentional Injuries, Males and Females in Low- and Middle-Income Countries, 2001 (in Thousands)

	Total Deaths from Unintentional Injuries	
	Males	**Females**
Drownings	252	116
Falls	199	117
Fires	113	187
Poisonings	211	117
Road traffic accidents	781	288
Other unintentional injuries	539	293

Source: Adapted with permission from Lopez AD, Mathers CD, Murray CJL. The burden of disease and mortality by condition: data, methods, and results for 2001. In: Lopez AD, Mathers CD, Ezzati M, Jamison DT, Murray CJL, eds. *Global Burden of Disease and Risk Factors.* Washington, DC and New York: The World Bank and Oxford University Press; 2006:130-131.

reported 13,052 deaths from injury but also identified over 2 million injuries for which medical care was sought over the course of the study.[10] In other words, for every person who died from an injury there were approximately 153 people who were injured seriously enough to seek the help of a health professional. Moreover, this figure does not include those injuries for which people did not seek medical help, whether due to the minor nature of the problem, lack of access to care, or other unknown reasons.

It is apparent that when disability due to injuries is taken into consideration, as well as mortality, the scope of the problem presented by such injuries is magnified. Moreover, these figures likely underestimate the total impact of injuries around the world. The true burden is likely to be much higher than that based on simple reporting of injuries within the developing world. Indeed, some authorities have questioned the reliability of disability data from lower-income settings where mechanisms to accurately collect and report injury data are lacking and where many injured persons do not seek or do not have access to medical care.[11–13]

When we examine data for unintentional injuries by region, we see some variation. Deaths from unintentional injuries as a share of total deaths in sub-Saharan Africa are relatively lower than in any other region, probably a reflection of the very high burden of communicable diseases in sub-Saharan Africa. The share of deaths due to unintentional injuries in the Middle East and North Africa region is much higher than in any other region, largely a reflection of the

high rates of motor vehicle deaths in this region. Table 13-5 shows the share of total deaths by region that is composed of unintentional injuries. Table 13-6 reflects the percentage of total deaths by region that is caused by road traffic accidents.

There is considerable variation in the contribution of road traffic accidents to total deaths in different regions. The lowest rate is in the Europe and Central Asia Region, as anticipated. This largely reflects better-trained drivers, better-engineered and maintained roads, and safer cars than in other regions. The highest rate of deaths for unintentional injuries that are caused by road traffic accidents is in the Middle East and North Africa regions. This probably reflects the extensive use of motor vehicles in this region without sufficient attention to driver education, engineering of roads, automobile safety, or emergency medical services.

The World Health Organization has projected the global burden of disease to 2030, as discussed in Chapter 2. Road traffic accidents were estimated to be 2.2 percent of the total number of deaths in low- and middle-income countries in 2001. However, it is projected that they will be 3.6 percent of the burden in low- and middle-income countries in 2030.[14]

CHILDHOOD INJURY

Discussion thus far has centered primarily on older adolescents and adults. However, children throughout the world sustain an alarming number of injuries with high levels of attendant death and disability. Moreover, estimates place 98 percent of childhood injury deaths in the low- and middle-income countries.[12]

Deaths from unintentional injuries for children ages 0–4 in low- and middle-income countries in 2000 were about 2.7 percent of total deaths. For those 5–14 years of age, these deaths were 3.5 percent of total deaths. With regard to specific injuries, children younger than 5 years account for 25 percent of drowning deaths and 15 percent of fire-related deaths globally.[7] To cast a slightly different perspective on these figures and the disproportionate occurrence of injuries in the young, children ages 0–14 years comprise about 30 percent of the population but account for 50 percent of total injury-related DALYs.[12,15]

RISK FACTORS FOR UNINTENTIONAL INJURIES

Numerous reasons are thought to underlie the high prevalence of injuries in young children in the developing world. A partial list of factors includes developmental immaturity relative to the dangers these children face within their environments, the influence of poverty on families' ability to provide adult supervision and child care, and exposure to workplaces with unsafe, hazardous, and developmentally

TABLE 13-5 Percentage of Total Deaths from Unintentional Injuries, by Region, for Low- and Middle-Income Countries, 2001

Region	Percentage of Total Deaths from Unintentional Injuries
East Asia & Pacific	7%
Europe & Central Asia	7%
Latin America & the Caribbean	6%
Middle East & North Africa	9%
South Asia	7%
Sub-Saharan Africa	5%

Source: Adapted with permission from Lopez AD, Mathers CD, Murray CJL. The burden of disease and mortality by condition: data, methods, and results for 2001. In: Lopez AD, Mathers CD, Ezzati M, Jamison DT, Murray CJL, eds. *Global Burden of Disease and Risk Factors.* Washington, DC and New York: The World Bank and Oxford University Press; 2006:126-127.

TABLE 13-6 Percentage of Total Deaths from Road Traffic Accidents, by Region, Low- and Middle- Income Countries, 2001

Region	Percentage of Total Deaths from Road Traffic Accidents
East Asia & Pacific	3%
Europe & Central Asia	1%
Latin America & the Caribbean	3%
Middle East & North Africa	5%
South Asia	2%
Sub-Saharan Africa	2%

Source: Adapted with permission from Lopez AD, Mathers CD, Murray CJL. The burden of disease and mortality by condition: data, methods, and results for 2001. In: Lopez AD, Mathers CD, Ezzati M, Jamison DT, Murray CJL, eds. *Global Burden of Disease and Risk Factors.* Washington, DC and New York: The World Bank and Oxford University Press; 2006:126-167.

inappropriate machinery.[16–18] In support of this last point, a study in the Philippines found that 60 percent of working children were exposed to unsafe conditions, and 40 percent of these had suffered a serious workplace injury.[19]

It might be assumed that as children grow older, they become less susceptible to injury. However, the reality is that as children grow older and better able to maneuver in their environment, the incidence of injuries does not decrease. More developmentally mature young persons tend to roam more widely within their environments and thus encounter more risks and complex situations, which challenge their reasoning and ability to react. Although the incidence of injury does not vary appreciably, the types of injuries sustained do vary, with important implications for injury prevention programs.

The risk factors for falls for young people in low- and middle-income countries appear to be associated with physical activity and also may vary with socioeconomic status.[20] The risk factors for injury from falls for older people are mostly related to age and overall physical condition.[20]

Low income, poor housing, and living in a crowded area are all risk factors for burns. Rural dwellers also suffer higher rates of burns than urban people. Children are more likely to suffer burns than any other age group. In addition, as discussed before, in South Asia and China, females are more likely to be burned than men.[21]

The risk factors for drowning in low- and middle-income countries are consistent with what we would expect.

Young children are the most likely age group to drown and males are more likely to drown than females. Most drownings occur during normal activities that take place near water. This is unlike in high-income countries where most drownings are associated with recreational activities. Children from poorer and larger families probably drown more frequently than other children.[21]

Studies done on poisoning in low- and middle-income countries have shed some light on risk factors. Poisoning is more likely in young boys than young girls. It also tends to be correlated with using nonstandard containers for poisonous goods and storing them within the reach of young children. Lower-income parents who are unable to supervise their children sufficiently around poisons are also more likely to have their children poisoned than better-off parents.[22]

The risk factors for road traffic injuries in low- and middle-income countries that differentiate them from high-income countries are well known. First is the increasing use of motor vehicles in low- and middle-income countries. In addition, in many countries two-wheeled vehicles, which are especially unsafe, are very common. In addition, most low- and middle-income countries pay insufficient attention to road planning, design, engineering, signage, or traffic management. Third, enforcement of speed limits is lax in many low- and middle-income countries; studies done on road traffic accidents show that about half of all such accidents are associated with excessive speed. It is also true in low- and middle-income countries that vehicles are less safe than in high-income countries, that many vehicles will not have safety belts or airbags, and that infant seats for cars are barely known or used. Motorcycle helmets are also used much less than in high-income countries.[23]

THE COSTS AND CONSEQUENCES OF INJURIES

The costs associated with unintentional injuries worldwide are considerable. The economic burden due to such injury includes direct costs such as medical care, hospitalization, rehabilitation, and funeral fees as well as indirect costs such as lost wages, sick leave from work, disability payments, insurance payouts, and costs associated with family care. These costs may be catastrophic for people within certain socioeconomic strata or those without access to sufficient health insurance. In this case, costs are frequently borne by government or private social services. In all cases, however, injuries represent a significant drain on personal and societal resources. The total costs of injuries in Canada during 1993, for example, were estimated to be $14.3 billion Canadian dollars.[24]

The direct costs due to road traffic injuries alone are estimated at 1–2 percent of the GNP of low- and middle-income countries. The total costs of road traffic injuries globally have been estimated at over $500 billion, with the share borne by the low- and middle-income countries estimated at $65–100 billion. At the regional level, Asia has the highest direct costs attributable to road traffic injuries at $24.5 billion. Africa, the least affected region by cost, still bears a significant burden, with an estimated $3.7 billion annually in total costs.[25,26]

Kenya examined the economic burden due to road traffic injuries and found a rapidly increasing economic burden over a 12-year period from 1984 to 1996. Costs, including health care, administrative expenses, and vehicle and property damage, increased from 1.5 billion Kenyan shillings in 1984 to 3.8 billion shillings in 1991, which was equivalent to 5 percent of GNP. By 1996, injury-related costs had continued to escalate to between 5 and 10 billion Kenyan shillings.[27]

The consequences of unintentional injury are not limited to financial costs. There are significant social consequences for individuals and families that may be associated with such injury. Numerous studies have documented the long-term physical and psychosocial consequences of unintentional injuries. Persisting problems with pain, fatigue, memory, and psychosocial functioning are common in victims of trauma.[28–30] Moreover, these social consequences may be relatively independent of injury severity and reflect the influence of other noninjury variables.[31] Lastly, the psychosocial consequences for families of child injury victims may be significant, with difficulties relating to finances, changes in

work status required to care for injured children, and altered family dynamics.[32]

ADDRESSING KEY INJURY ISSUES

One of the key issues in addressing the burden of injuries is to raise awareness about how to apply rigorous methods of prevention and control to the injury problems. In fact, even among the industrialized countries, the prioritization of injuries as a significant health problem and the application of scientific methods of injury prevention and control are relatively recent phenomena.[12,33] Many public policy makers and public health actors in low- and middle-income countries have failed to appreciate the importance of injuries to the burden of disease or to understand what can be done to prevent unintentional injuries.

In order to design effective prevention and control activities for unintentional injuries, formal surveillance systems are fundamental to obtain reliable information as to numbers and patterns of injury. Although the formal surveillance systems in many high-income countries may be inappropriate to developing country settings, minimal standards for injury morbidity and mortality should be implemented in all countries. In this light, the World Health Organization has published guidelines for collecting, coding, and reporting injury data, which have been specifically developed for use in low-resource settings and do not require the use of technology-intensive data management systems or specialized training.[34,35]

In addition, it will be important to develop local capacity to analyze injury data and design injury prevention and mitigation programs. Injury prevention and control activities from one setting cannot be grafted onto another setting. Rather, planners with an intimate understanding of local knowledge, attitudes, beliefs, and practices are required to design effective interventions for injury prevention in specific settings.

The theoretical foundation of many injury prevention and control efforts is called Haddon's matrix, and it is widely used in efforts to understand and address injury issues. Haddon's matrix models the interaction of host, vector, and environment in an injury event. Moreover, it is dynamic and models the events prior to, during, and after an injury.

The example of road traffic injuries provides a useful learning tool for thinking about injuries using Haddon's matrix and how they can be prevented. The roadway (environment), automobile (vector), and host (human driver and behavior) interact in the moments leading up to a collision, during the collision, and in the moments after the collision.

Measures to prevent unintentional injuries have usually focused on education, enforcement, and engineering in the context of Haddon's matrix. Recent efforts to reduce road traffic injuries have emphasized safer roads, safer vehicles, and safer systems. They have also paid increasing attention to land use and transport planning.[36] Roads can be made safer from the engineering point of view by paying particular attention to building safety into road designs, improving high risk intersections and routes, providing for slow-moving vehicles and pedestrians, improving barriers and median strips, and enhancing lighting. Ghana was able to reduce road traffic injuries by installing speed bumps at selected places, as discussed further later.[37] In countries in which there are many types of vehicles, it would also help to separate those that can travel at high speed from those, like two-wheeled motorized rickshaws, that can only go slowly and that are unsafe in many ways.[38]

Vehicles can be made safer by engineering safety features into them, such as crash protection zones, headrests, seat belts, and daytime running lights. Including daytime running lights on motorcycles in China did reduce injuries.[36] People can be encouraged to use vehicles in safer ways through enforcement of speed limits, reducing the driving of those consuming alcohol, limiting the hours allowed for commercial driving, and enforcing the use of bicycle and motorcycle helmets.[36] Although there is considerable corruption in the police forces of many countries, enforcement of driving laws has helped in a number of settings to reduce road traffic injuries by up to 34 percent.[36] The introduction of mandatory seat belt and child restraint laws has been associated in high-income countries with a reduction in deaths and injuries by 25 percent.[39]

Few low- and middle-income countries have taken measures to deal with poisonings. However, South Africa carried out a program in which child-proof containers were given to families for free. This program was associated with a cost-effective reduction in child poisonings and deaths.[40] It appears that to reduce poisonings in low- and middle-income countries, it is important to educate families to store poisons away from other household goods and out of the reach of children, to store them in appropriate and marked containers, and to enforce rules that prohibit the sale of poisons in unmarked and inappropriate containers.[41]

It is not easy to prevent falls by older people. It appears, however, that steps that have been taken in high-income countries to address such falls have included working with the elderly to improve their balance and modifying their home environment to reduce risks.[39] In low- and many middle-income countries, it may be that the only cost-effective measure that could be taken to reduce falls among the elderly would be to provide community-based education to families about the risks of falls to their elderly relatives and about measures that are appropriate in that cultural context to reducing those risks.

Few efforts at reducing childhood injuries from falls have taken place in a systematic way in low- or middle-income countries. Here, too, it may be that the most reasonable step initially is community-based education of families about the risks of falling and what can be done to reduce those risks. Of course, if schools do have play equipment, it will be valuable to design that equipment in a way that reduces injury if children fall from it. There is also little evidence from developing countries about what might be done in cost-effective ways to reduce drownings. Perhaps on this front, as well, one has to start with community-based information efforts about increased parental and older sibling supervision and with obvious measures, such as covering wells.[42] A community-based pilot program was carried out in Bangladesh to determine if communities would accept door barriers and playpens as means for protecting children from the risk of being around water unsupervised and drowning. Families provided with a playpen were almost 7 times more likely to use it than were the families provided with a door barrier. Further study, however, is needed to determine if such an approach will translate into fewer deaths by drowning of young children.[43] Not unexpectedly, there is also very little data on effective measures to reduce burns in low- and middle-income countries, despite their importance both generally and especially for women. Separate from the special circumstances of "dowry deaths," it appears that, for this, too, community-based efforts at behavior change must be the starting point for improved action.[44]

EMERGENCY MEDICAL SERVICES

In low- and many middle-income countries, unintentional injuries will remain an important component of the burden of disease for some time. In addition, that burden may grow in both absolute and relative importance as some societies witness economic growth and increasing motorization of transport. Thus, even low-income countries should examine investments in low-cost but effective ways of improving emergency medical services in their country.

As discussed in Chapter 9 on women's health, one important measure would be to arrange for emergency transport. This could be in special vehicles made for low-income or rural communities or it could be advance arrangements with the owner of available transport. A bicycle ambulance was established in Malawi for the transport of obstetric emergencies, and turned out to be used more for medical emergencies and dealing with accident victims.[45] In addition, one could train members of the community who frequently come in contact with road accidents, such as truck drivers, in how to provide first aid and transport to accident victims. This was done with some important successes, for example, in Ghana.[46]

Low-income countries could also begin to invest in better training of healthcare personnel who work in emergency services. They could do the same in emergency transport services based in selected locations known to the public, for example, so that the emergency transport could be hailed quickly, even in environments in which most people would not have a telephone.[47]

CASE STUDIES

Two very brief cases are presented below about efforts that countries have undertaken to reduce the burden of morbidity, disability, and death linked with road traffic accidents. The first concerns the use of a mandatory motorcycle helmet law in Taiwan. The second concerns the use of speed bumps in Ghana, which were meant to slow drivers down and thereby reduce accidents. Both appear to have produced substantial gains in health at relatively low cost, as other countries might wish to do, as well.

Motorcycle Helmet Use in Taiwan

Helmet use for moped and motorcycle riders can help to protect them from death and serious injury. Worldwide, head injuries sustained by a rider are the principal cause of death in riders after a road accident. Yet, the risk of injury if a rider wears a helmet is only one third the risk of those who do not wear a helmet. Nevertheless, unless a country has a law requiring helmet use, riders will most likely not use one. In addition, helmet use interventions in developing countries must be "sensitive to local manufacturing capabilities, cost, and comfort for local climates" in order to provide local governments with the means to legislate regulatory laws that are easily enforced in the community.[48]

In Taiwan, more than 60 percent of all motor vehicles registered in the late 1990s were motorcycles. As the number of motorcycles has increased, the incidence of motorcycle road traffic injuries has risen. Moreover, nearly 80 percent of motor vehicle fatalities in Taiwan, most of which involve motorcycle riders, have resulted from serious head injuries.[49]

In 1994, Taipei City began a 6-month pilot program in the use of motorcycle helmets. This resulted in increasing helmet use from 21 percent to 79 percent of motorcycle riders in only 5 months. It also reduced injuries and fatalities by 33 percent and 56 percent, respectively. However, since the intervention was not linked with a mandatory helmet use law, this was a short-lived success that ended soon after it began.[49]

Three years later, Taiwan passed a nationwide law regulating motorcycle helmet use for all riders. In Taipei City, the law was preceded by a 6-month information campaign that was meant to inform residents on the benefits of helmet use. Within 2 months, helmet use was nearly 96 percent nationally, with greater use in Taipei City than in other counties, partly due to greater law enforcement. Furthermore, head injuries decreased by 33 percent and the severity of these injuries also decreased, as indicated by the reduced number of patients with head injuries admitted to intensive care units, as well as those dying or being in a vegetative state following their injury. Linked to the helmet law, head injuries in Taiwan dropped from the fourth to the fifth leading cause of death. Associated with the new law, hospital costs decreased by $3.93 million per month.[49]

As indicated by higher levels of use in Taipei City than in other areas of Taiwan, the passage of a law requiring helmet use is not sufficient to ensure that it will produce the intended benefits. Rather, it is also important that an education campaign be oriented toward getting motorcycle riders to wear their helmets and that the laws requiring helmet use be enforced.

Rumble Strips and Speed Bumps in Ghana

In 2000, speeding contributed to over 50 percent of all motor vehicle accidents in Ghana. In addition, as in other countries, many of those injured as a result of these accidents were pedestrians or passengers in vehicles who had no seat belts or were not using them. Studies in high-income countries demonstrate that reducing speed by 1 km/hr results in a 3 percent reduction in crashes and a higher likelihood of survival if hit by a car. In this light, the government of Ghana decided to put rumble strips and speed bumps at road intersections that had proved to be dangerous.[50]

The Ghanaian authorities first located accident hot spots on the main highway between Accra and Kumasi and installed rumble strips along the highest risk area, the Suhum Junction. In less than a year, this public health measure resulted in a 35 percent decrease in the number of motor vehicle crashes and a 55 percent reduction in related fatalities. The cost of laying rumble strips was $20,900, compared to an estimated $100,000 to redesign lanes or $180,000 to construct a physical division to separate pedestrians from vehicles.[50]

As noted earlier in the chapter, there are other cost-effective measures that countries can take to reduce the burden of road traffic injuries. Nonetheless, it appears that even relatively poor countries, such as Ghana, can avert a considerable toll of injuries, disability, and death from road traffic injuries through the construction of very low-cost speed bumps and rumble strips in selected locations.

FUTURE CHALLENGES

The fact that there is so little data in this chapter that comes from low- and middle-income countries indicates that one important challenge for reducing the burden of unintentional injuries will be to focus additional attention on this topic within these countries. It is too large a source of deaths and disabilities to ignore, even in the face of continuing communicable diseases and a growing burden of noncommunicable diseases.

There is increasing information about what works in cost-effective ways to reduce the burden of injury in high-income countries, and this can serve as a starting point for adapting this learning to other settings. It will be important for selected low- and middle-income countries to carry out pilot schemes in preventing injury, especially from road traffic accidents, and then to expand them more broadly as they learn how to make them work effectively in different settings.

As low- and middle-income countries develop economically and become more motorized, it will be valuable for them to engineer safety into their newer investments in road transportation. Insufficient attention has been paid by many countries to enhancing their people's knowledge of good public health practice. It will be important for them to increase their efforts significantly to provide information and education to the public about key areas of injury prevention. Although governance is weak in many countries, they can already begin to selectively enforce laws concerning road safety that can have a high return with little effort, such as encouraging the use of motorcycle helmets. As governance improves and people have more knowledge of road safety and trust that enforcement of laws will be honest, the government can pay more attention to enforcing other regulations affecting road safety. The challenge of reducing injuries from falls, burns, and drowning will depend almost completely on informing and educating the public in a community-based manner.

MAIN MESSAGES

Unintentional injuries are an important cause of deaths and DALYs lost in all regions of the world. In 2001, about 3.5 million people died of such injuries. In addition, these injuries are major causes of disability, with many people being disabled by injuries, even if they do not die from them. The rate of deaths from unintentional injuries is twice as high in low- and middle-income countries as it is in high-income countries.

The leading cause of both deaths and DALYs lost from unintentional injuries is road traffic accidents. This is followed by deaths from drowning, poisoning, falls, and fires. Men are almost three times as likely to die in road traffic accidents as women. However, women die more frequently in fires than men do. Deaths from road traffic accidents as a share of total deaths is particularly high in the Middle East and North Africa region, compared to other regions. Unintentional injuries are an important source of deaths for young children, who account for 25 percent of drowning deaths and 15 percent of fire-related deaths globally.

The risk factors for road traffic accidents revolve around education, enforcement, and engineering. The risk factors of other leading causes of unintentional injuries relate largely to lower socioeconomic status, inadequate supervision of children, a failure to store poisons safely, and household cooking arrangements that pay insufficient attention to fire hazards in areas that tend to be crowded and hazardous.

Although there have been few studies of the economic costs of unintentional injuries in low- and middle-income countries, estimates of such costs have ranged from 1–2 percent of GNP. The social costs of dealing with the disabilities caused by accidents can also be very high.

There is increasing evidence from high-income countries of measures that can be taken to improve operator safety, build safety into vehicles, make plans for land use and traffic, and enforce key traffic rules. These measures can selectively be implemented in low- and middle-income countries and adapted to their local settings. Reducing the burden of road traffic injuries and other injuries will require enhancing community-based approaches to providing information about how the community can reduce risk factors for such injuries.

Study Questions

1. How important are unintentional injuries to the global burden of disease?

2. What unintentional injuries cause the most deaths?

3. How does the rate of death from road traffic accidents vary by region and why?

4. What are the most important unintentional injuries that affect children?

5. Do men and women suffer from unintentional injuries at the same rates? Why or why not?

6. What are the risk factors for road traffic accidents?

7. What are the risk factors for drownings?

8. What are the key risk factors for burning, and how do they vary by region?

9. What is Haddon's matrix, and how would you apply it to analyze accidents?

10. What are the most cost-effective steps that low- and middle-income countries can take to reduce the burden of road traffic accidents on health?

REFERENCES

1. Lopez AD, Mathers CD, Murray CJL. The burden of disease and mortality by condition: data, methods, and results for 2001. In: Lopez AD, Mathers CD, Ezzati M, Jamison DT, Murray CJL, eds. *Global Burden of Disease and Risk Factors*. New York: Oxford University Press; 2006:130.

2. Lopez AD, Mathers CD, Murray CJL. The burden of disease and mortality by condition: data, methods, and results for 2001. In: Lopez AD, Mathers CD, Ezzati M, Jamison DT, Murray CJL, eds. *Global Burden of Disease and Risk Factors*. New York: Oxford University Press; 2006:126-130.

3. Lopez AD, Mathers CD, Murray CJL. The burden of disease and mortality by condition: data, methods, and results for 2001. In: Lopez AD, Mathers CD, Ezzati M, Jamison DT, Murray CJL, eds. *Global Burden of Disease and Risk Factors*. New York: Oxford University Press; 2006:228-232.

4. National Highway Traffic Safety Administration. Trauma System Agenda for the Future: Glossary. Available at: http://www.nhtsa.dot.gov/people/injury/ems/emstraumasystem03/glossary.htm. Accessed June 23, 2006.

5. Norton R, Hyder AA, Bishai D, Peden M. Unintentional injuries. In: Jamison DT, Breman JG, Measham AR, et al., eds. *Disease Control Priorities in Developing Countries*. 2nd ed. New York: Oxford University Press; 2006:737.

6. Peden M, McGee K, Krug E. *The Injury Chart Book: A Graphical Overview of the Global Burden of Injuries*. Geneva, Switzerland: World Health Organization; 2002.

7. Razzak J, Sasser S, Kellermann A. Injury prevention and other international public health initiatives. *Emerg Med Clin N Am.* 2005;23:85-98.

8. Norton R, Hyder AA, Bishai D, Peden M. Unintentional injuries. In: Jamison DT, Breman JG, Measham AR, et al., eds. *Disease Control Priorities in Developing Countries*. 2nd ed. New York: Oxford University Press; 2006:738.

9. Lopez AD, Mathers CD, Ezzati M, Jamison DT, Murray CJ, eds. *Global Burden of Disease and Risk Factors*. New York: Oxford University Press; 2006.

10. Wadman M, Muelleman R, Coto J, et al. The pyramid of injury: using ecodes to accurately describe the burden of injury. *Ann Emergency Med.* 2003;42:468-478.

11. Bangdiwala S, Anzola-Perez E, Rommer C, et al. The incidence of injuries in young people: I. Methodology and results of a collaborative study in Brazil, Chile, Cuba, and Venezuela. *Int J Epidemiol.* 1990;19:115-124.

12. Bartlett S. The problem of children's injuries in low-income countries: a review. *Health Policy Plan.* 2002;17(1):1-13.

13. Mohan D. Injuries in less industrialized countries: what do we know? *Inj Prev.* 1997;3:241-242.

14. World Health Organization. *The Global Burden of Disease 2004 Update*. Geneva, Switzerland: World Health Organization; 2008.

15. Lopez AD, Mathers CD, Murray CJL. The burden of disease and mortality by condition: data, methods, and results for 2001. In: Lopez AD, Mathers CD, Ezzati M, Jamison DT, Murray CJL, eds. *Global Burden of Disease and Risk Factors*. New York: Oxford University Press; 2006:45-240.

16. Jordan J, Valdez-Lazo F. Education on safety and risk. In: Manciaux M, Romer C, eds. *Accidents in Childhood and Adolescence: The Role of Research*. Geneva: World Health Organization; 1991.

17. Ljungblom B-A, Köhler L. Child development and behavior in traffic. In: Manciaux M, Romer CJ, eds. *Accidents in Childhood and Adolescence: The Role of Research*. Geneva: World Health Organization; 1991.

18. Leflamme L, Diderichsen F. Social differences in traffic injury risk in childhood and youth—a literature review and a research agenda. *Inj Prev.* 2000;6:293-298.

19. International Labour Office. *Child Labour: Targeting the Intolerable*. Geneva: International Labour Office; 1996.

20. Norton R, Hyder AA, Bishai D, Peden M. Unintentional injuries. In: Jamison DT, Breman JG, Measham AR, et al., eds. *Disease Control Priorities in Developing Countries*. 2nd ed. New York: Oxford University Press; 2006:740-741.

21. Norton R, Hyder AA, Bishai D, Peden M. Unintentional injuries. In: Jamison DT, Breman JG, Measham AR, et al., eds. *Disease Control Priorities in Developing Countries*. 2nd ed. New York: Oxford University Press; 2006:741.

22. Norton R, Hyder AA, Bishai D, Peden M. Unintentional injuries. In: Jamison DT, Breman JG, Measham AR, et al., eds. *Disease Control Priorities in Developing Countries*. 2nd ed. New York: Oxford University Press; 2006:740.

23. Norton R, Hyder AA, Bishai D, Peden M. Unintentional injuries. In: Jamison DT, Breman JG, Measham AR, et al., eds. *Disease Control Priorities in Developing Countries*. 2nd ed. New York: Oxford University Press; 2006:739-740.

24. Ministry of Health—Canada. *Economic Burden of Illness in Canada*. Ottawa, Ontario: Canadian Public Health Association; 1993.

25. Hoffman K, Primack A, Keusch G, Hrynkow S. Addressing the growing burden of trauma and injury in low- and middle-income countries. *Am J Public Health.* 2005;95:13-17.

26. Jacobs G, Aaron-Thomas A, Astrop A. *Estimating Global Road Fatalities*. London: Transport Research Laboratory; 2000.

27. Odero W, Meleckidzedeck K, Heda P. Road traffic injuries in Kenya: magnitude, causes and status of intervention. *Inj Control Safe Promot.* 2003;10(1-2):53-61.

28. Depalma J, Fedorka P, Simko L. Quality of life experienced by severely injured trauma survivors. *AACN Clin Issues.* 2003;14(1):54-63.

29. van der Sluis C, Eisma W, Groothoff J, ten Duis H. Long-term physical, psychological and social consequences of severe injuries. *Inj* 1998;29(4):281-285.

30. Landsman I, Baum C, Arnkoff D, et al. The psychosocial consequences of traumatic injury. *Behav Med.* 1990;13(6):561-581.

31. Mayou R, Bryant B. Outcome in consecutive emergency department attenders following a road traffic accident. *Brit J Psychiatry.* 2001;179:528-534.

32. Osberg J, Khan P, Rowe K, Brooke M. Pediatric trauma: impact on work and family finances. *Pediatrics.* 1996;98(5):890-897.

33. Haddon W. The changing approach to epidemiology, prevention, and amelioration of trauma: the transition to approaches etiologically rather than descriptively based. *Inj Prev.* 1999;5:231-235.

34. Holder Y, Peden M, Krug E, et al. *Injury Surveillance Guidelines*. Geneva: World Health Organization; 2001.

35. McGee K, Peden M, Waxweiler R, et al. Injury surveillance. *Inj Control Safe Promot.* 2003;10:105-108.

36. Norton R, Hyder AA, Bishai D, Peden M. Unintentional injuries. In: Jamison DT, Breman JG, Measham AR, et al., eds. *Disease Control Priorities in Developing Countries*. 2nd ed. New York: Oxford University Press; 2006:742-743.

37. Norton R, Hyder AA, Bishai D, Peden M. Unintentional injuries. In: Jamison DT, Breman JG, Measham AR, et al., eds. *Disease Control Priorities in Developing Countries*. 2nd ed. New York: Oxford University Press; 2006:746.

38. Norton R, Hyder AA, Bishai D, Peden M. Unintentional injuries. In: Jamison DT, Breman JG, Measham AR, et al., eds. *Disease Control Priorities in Developing Countries*. 2nd ed. New York: Oxford University Press; 2006:742-750.

39. Norton R, Hyder AA, Bishai D, Peden M. Unintentional injuries. In: Jamison DT, Breman JG, Measham AR, et al., eds. *Disease Control Priorities in Developing Countries*. 2nd ed. New York: Oxford University Press; 2006:744.

40. Krug E, Sharma G, Lozano R. The global burden of injuries. *Am J Public Health.* 2000;90:523-526.

41. Norton R, Hyder AA, Bishai D, Peden M. Unintentional injuries. In: Jamison DT, Breman JG, Measham AR, et al., eds. *Disease Control Priorities in Developing Countries*. 2nd ed. New York: Oxford University Press; 2006:747-748.

42. Norton R, Hyder AA, Bishai D, Peden M. Unintentional injuries. In: Jamison DT, Breman JG, Measham AR, et al., eds. *Disease Control Priorities in Developing Countries*. 2nd ed. New York: Oxford University Press; 2006:745.

43. Callaghan JA, Hyder AA, Blum LS, Arifeen S, Baqui AH. Child supervision practices for drowning prevention in rural Bangladesh: a pilot study of supervision tools. *J Epidemiol Comm Health*. 2010;64:645-647.

44. Norton R, Hyder AA, Bishai D, Peden M. Unintentional injuries. In: Jamison DT, Breman JG, Measham AR, et al., eds. *Disease Control Priorities in Developing Countries*. 2nd ed. New York: Oxford University Press; 2006:744-745.

45. Kobusingye OC, Hyder AA, Bishai D, Hicks ER, Mock C, Joshipura M. Emergency medical systems in low- and middle-income countries: recommendations for action. *Bull World Health Org*. 2005;83(8):626-631.

46. Mock C, Arreola-Risa C, Quansah R. Strengthening care for injured persons in less developed countries: a case study of Ghana and Mexico. *Inj Control Saf Promot*. 2003;10(1-2):45-51.

47. Kobusingye OC, Hyder AA, Bishai D, Joshipura ERH, Mock C. Emergency medical services. In: Jamison DT, Breman JG, Measham AR, et al., eds. *Disease Control Priorities in Developing Countries*. 2nd ed. New York: Oxford University Press; 2006:1265.

48. World Health Organization and The World Bank. World Report on Road Traffic Injury Prevention. Available at: http://www.who.int/world-health-day/2004/infomaterials/world_report/en. Accessed February 25, 2007.

49. Chiu WT, Kuo CY, Hung CC, Chen M. The effect of the Taiwan motorcycle law on head injuries. *Am J Public Health*. 2004;90(5):793-796.

50. Afukaar FK. Speed control in developing countries: issues, challanges and opportunities in reducing road traffic injuries. *Inj Control Saf Promot*. 2003;10(1-2):77-81.

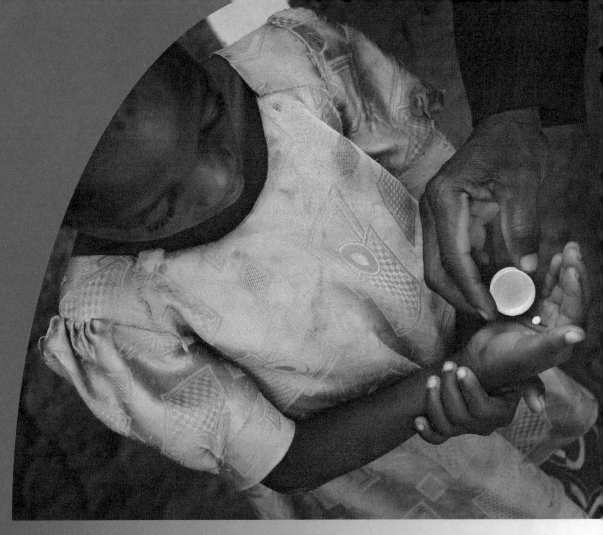

PART **IV**

Working Together to Improve Global Health

CHAPTER 14

Natural Disasters and Complex Humanitarian Emergencies

LEARNING OBJECTIVES

By the end of this chapter the reader will be able to:

- Describe several types of disasters that impact human health
- Discuss the health effects of natural disasters and complex humanitarian emergencies
- Review how those health impacts vary by age, sex, location, and type of disaster
- Describe key measures that can be taken to mitigate the health impacts of natural disasters and complex humanitarian emergencies

VIGNETTES

Javad lived in the Pakistani province of Kashmir when the earthquake hit. All the buildings in his village were destroyed. Hundreds of people in the village were killed, mostly a result of being buried in the rubble. Many other people were badly injured from rubble falling on them. Their injuries were overwhelmingly orthopedic in nature. As the earthquake destroyed the village, it also destroyed wells, a health center, and roads leading to and from the village. Javad feared that many of those injured would soon die.

Samuel was living in the Eastern part of Sierra Leone when the war started. He did all that he could to protect his family, but it was not enough. In the first year of the conflict, as he and his family were getting ready to flee, a band of armed men stormed the village. As Samuel had heard they would do, they used machetes to kill or take limbs off of many village people. They also raped a large number of women. In addition, they kidnapped some of the children in hopes of making them into sex slaves or soldiers.

As the civil war spread in Rwanda, Sarah and her family fled across the border to what was fast becoming a large refugee camp in Zaire, later called the Democratic Republic of Congo. Although the camp workers did what they could to help the refugees, the circumstances at the camp were not good. There was little shelter, water, or food. In addition, a cholera epidemic spread through the camp not long after Sarah's arrival there. It hit the camp especially hard and led to a large number of deaths.

A number of international organizations rushed staff to refugee camps, just across the border from intense fighting. Some of the agencies involved had many years of experience doing such work and had clear guidelines for their staff concerning relief efforts. Other agencies, however, were not so experienced in this work. They brought to the camps medicine that was not appropriate for the health conditions they found and food to which the local people were completely unaccustomed. Although it would have been most efficient if all of the aid agencies worked together, they did not. Many of them had their own way of working and wanted the local government to do it their way.

THE IMPORTANCE OF NATURAL DISASTERS AND COMPLEX EMERGENCIES TO GLOBAL HEALTH

Complex emergencies and natural disasters have a significant impact on global health. They can lead to increased death, illness, and disability and the economic costs of their health impacts can also be very large. Measures can be taken in cost-effective ways, however, to reduce the costs of disasters and conflicts and to address the major health problems that relate to them. These measures would be most effective if those involved in disaster relief would work together according to agreed standards that focus on the most important priorities for action.

This chapter will review the relationships between natural disasters and health and complex humanitarian emergencies (CHEs) and health. The chapter will begin by introducing you to some key concepts and definitions that relate to these topics. The chapter will then review the incidence of natural disasters and CHEs. Following that, the chapter will review their main health impacts. Lastly, the chapter will examine measures that can be taken to prevent and address in cost-effective ways some of their effects on health.

KEY TERMS

Understanding the health impacts of natural disasters and complex humanitarian emergencies requires an introduction to several terms and concepts that are examined briefly here.

A disaster is "any occurrence that causes damage, ecological destruction, loss of human lives, or deterioration of health and health services on a scale sufficient to warrant an extraordinary response from outside the affected com-

---

TABLE 14-1 Selected Natural Disasters, 2007–2009

2007

July: Flooding and monsoon rains killed 660 people and left more than a million homeless in India.

August: An 8.0 magnitude earthquake in Peru killed at least 337 people.

November: Cyclone Sidr, with 100-mile-per-hour winds, killed about 3500 people in Bangladesh.

2008

May: Cyclone Nargis killed 24,000 people in Myanmar.

May: A 7.9 magnitude earthquake hit Western China, killing 67,000 people.

August: Flooding from the Kosi River killed at least 75 people and displaced over 2 million in India.

2009

August: Typhoon Morakat caused mudslides, burying at least 600 people in southern Taiwan.

September: A tsunami, after an 8.0 magnitude earthquake, killed more than 115 in Samoa and American Samoa.

September: A 7.6 magnitude earthquake killed more than 1000 people in Padang, Indonesia.

Source: Data from Infoplease. World Disasters—2007, 2008 and 2009 Disasters. Available at: http://www.infoplease.com/ipa/A0001437.html. Accessed September 28, 2010.

---

munity area."[1] Another way to think of this would be as "an occurrence, either natural or man made, that causes human suffering and creates human needs that victims cannot alleviate without assistance."[1] Some disasters are natural. These include, for example, the results of floods, volcanoes, and earthquakes. Some, however, are man-made, such as the cloud of poisonous gas that rained over the town of Bhopal, India, in 1984, as a result of an industrial accident. Some disasters are rapid-onset, such as an earthquake, whereas others are slow-onset, such as a drought or famine. Although the long-term effects of these natural and man-made disasters can be substantial, they are often characterized by an initial event and then its aftereffects. Some examples of recent natural disasters that caused a significant loss of life are listed in Table 14-1.

In response to the large number of civil conflicts that have taken place, the term *complex emergency* or *complex humanitarian emergency* has been established. A complex emergency can be defined as a "complex, multi-party, intra-state conflict resulting in a humanitarian disaster which might constitute multi-dimensional risks or threats to regional and international security. Frequently within such conflicts, state institutions collapse, law and order break down, banditry and chaos prevail, and portions of the civilian population migrate."[2] CHEs have also been described as: "situations affecting large civilian populations which usually involve a combination of factors, including war or civil strife, food shortages, and population displacement, resulting in significant excess mortality."[3]

Such emergencies include war and civil conflict. They usually affect large numbers of people and often have severe impacts on the availability of food, water, and shelter. Linked to these phenomena and the displacement of people that often go with them, complex humanitarian emergencies usually result in considerable excess mortality, compared to what would be the case without such an emergency.[4] Some examples of complex humanitarian emergencies are listed in Table 14-2.

Complex emergencies create refugees. Under international law, a refugee is a person who is outside his or her country of nationality or habitual residence; has a well-founded fear of persecution because of his or her race, religion, nationality, membership in a particular social group, or political opinion; and is unable or unwilling to avail him- or herself of the protection of that country, or to return there, for fear of persecution. They are a subgroup of the broader category of displaced persons.[5] It is important to note that there are a number of international conventions that define refugees and that accord them rights according to international law, as well. Table 14-3 notes a number of countries with significant refugee populations and the countries they fled. A United Nations Agency, the United Nations High Commissioner for Refugees (UNHCR), is responsible for protecting the rights of refugees.

Some of the people who flee or are forced to migrate during a disaster or complex humanitarian emergency leave their homes but stay in the country in which they were living. These are called internally displaced people (IDP). These are more formally defined as "someone who has been forced to

leave their home for reasons such as religious or political persecution or war, but has not crossed an international border."[6] The term is a subset of the more general *displaced person*. There is no legal definition of an *internally displaced person*, as there is for refugee, but the thumbnail rule is that "if the person in question would be eligible for refugee status if he or she crossed an international border then the IDP label is applicable."[6] Table 14-4 shows selected examples of countries with large numbers of internally displaced persons. It is important to note that the legal status of IDP is not as well defined as that for refugees.[7] It is also important to understand that, unlike the case for refugees, no agency or organization is responsible for IDPs. Rather, their own government is responsible for them, but that government is often part of the problem as to why these people are fleeing.

One of the significant indicators of the health impact of a complex humanitarian emergency is the *crude mortality rate*. This is the proportion of people who die from a population at risk over a specified period of time.[8] For addressing CHEs, the crude mortality rate is generally expressed per 10,000 population, per day. The extent to which diseases might spread in a refugee camp depend partly on the *attack rate* of a disease, which is "the proportion of an exposed population at risk who become infected or develop clinical illness during a defined period of time."[2] Finally, it is important to understand *case fatality rate*, which is "the number of deaths from a specific disease in a given period, per 100 episodes of the disease in the same period."[9]

THE CHARACTERISTICS OF NATURAL DISASTERS

There are several types of natural disasters. Some of these are related to the weather, including droughts, hurricanes, typhoons, cyclones, and heavy rains. Tsunamis, like the one that occurred in 2011, can also cause extreme devastation, injuries, and death. In addition, earthquakes and volcanoes can have important impacts on the health of various communities. Despite the exceptional nature of tsunamis and the deaths associated with them, earthquakes are the natural disasters that generally kill the most people.

It appears that the number of natural disasters is increasing, affecting larger numbers of people, causing more economic losses than earlier, but causing proportionately fewer deaths than before. In addition, the biggest relative impact of natural disasters is in low- and middle-income countries. In fact, more than 90 percent of the deaths from these disasters occur in low- and middle-income countries.[10] The relative impact of natural disasters on the poor, of course, is greater than on the better-off because the share of the poorer people's total assets that are lost in these disasters

---

TABLE 14-2 Selected Complex Humanitarian Emergencies of Importance

Angola: A civil war lasted 27 years and ended in 2002.

Armenia/Azerbaijan: Conflict between the two countries has created almost 250,000 refugees and 600,000 internally displaced people (IDP).

Bosnia and Herzegovina: Between 1992 and 1994, war with various parts of the former Yugoslavia led to more than 100,000 deaths and 1.8 million people displaced.

Burma: Government offensives against a number of ethnic groups have gone on for more than 20 years and produced between 500,000 and 1 million IDP.

The Democratic Republic of Congo: Fighting since the mid-1990s between government forces and rebels has led to more than 2 million displaced people.

Liberia: Civil war from 1990–2004 led to almost 500,000 IDP and more than 125,000 refugees in Guinea alone.

Nepal: Conflict between the government forces and Maoist rebels from 1996–2006 led to 100,000–200,000 IDP.

Rwanda: More than 800,000 people were killed in the 1994 genocide, which also produced more than 2 million refugees who fled to Burundi, what is now the Democratic Republic of Congo, Tanzania, and Uganda.

Sudan: Internal conflicts since the 1980s, including a war with groups in the south and genocide against people in the Darfur region, have displaced 5–6 million people.

Uganda: Rebellion by the Lord's Resistance Army in the north for almost 20 years has led to between 1 and 2 million displaced people.

Zimbabwe: President Mugabe initiated a series of land and political reforms using violent measures, which caused human rights violations, an increase in human trafficking, and 570,000 to 1 million people to be internally displaced.

Source: Data from CIA. The World Fact Book. Available at: https://www.cia.gov/library/publications/the-world-factbook. Accessed September 28, 2010.

TABLE 14-3   Selected Refugee Populations and Source of Refugees, 2006

Country	Number of Refugees	Source Countries
Jordan	1,828,000	Palestinian refugees
Iran	1,040,000	Afghanistan, Iraq
Gaza Strip	990,000	Palestinian refugees
Pakistan	960,000	Afghanistan
West Bank	700,000	Palestinian refugees
Tanzania	597,000	Burundi, Democratic Republic of Congo
Syria	446,000	Palestinian refugees, Iraq
Lebanon	404,000	Palestinian refugees
China	350,000	Vietnam, North Korea
Serbia	275,000	Croatia, Bosnia, and Herzegovina
Uganda	258,000	Sudan, Rwanda, Democratic Republic of Congo
Chad	255,000	Sudan, Central African Republic
Armenia	235,000	Azerbaijan
Kenya	229,000	Somalia, Ethiopia, Sudan
India	157,000	Tibet/China, Sri Lanka, Afghanistan
Zambia	151,000	Angola, Democratic Republic of Congo, Rwanda
Guinea	141,000	Liberia, Sierra Leone, Ivory Coast
Sudan	139,000	Eritrea, Chad, Uganda, Ethiopia
Ethiopia	125,000	Sudan, Somalia, Eritrea
Thailand	121,000	Myanmar (Burma)
Nepal	105,000	Bhutan

Source: Data from CIA. The World Fact Book. Field Listing Refugees and Internally Displaced People. Available at: http://www.cia.gov/cia/publications/factbook/fields/2194.html. Accessed October 8, 2006.

TABLE 14-4 Internally Displaced People: Selected Countries of Importance, 2007

Country	Number of IDP
Sudan	5,300,000–6,200,000
Colombia	1,800,000–3,500,000
Democratic Republic of Congo	1,400,000
Uganda	1,270,000
Turkey	1,000,000–1,200,000
Somalia	1,100,000
Côte d'Ivoire	709,000
India	at least 600,000
Azerbaijan	580,000–690,000
Zimbabwe	570,000

Source: Data from CIA. The World Fact Book. Field Listing Refugees and Internally Displaced People. Available at: https://www.cia.gov/library/publications/the-world-factbook/fields/2194.html. Accessed September 28, 2010.

is greater than that lost by higher-income people. Moreover, the poor are often the most vulnerable to losses from natural disasters because they often live in places at risk from such disasters or have housing that cannot withstand such shocks.[11] As discussed in Chapter 2, climate change could also have an important impact on the number, type, and severity of natural disasters in the future.

Natural disasters can cause significant harm to infrastructure, such as water supply and sewage systems, that are needed for safe water and sanitation, and roads that may be needed to transport people requiring health care. Natural disasters can also damage the health infrastructure itself, such as hospitals, health centers, and health clinics. People can die directly as a result of the natural disaster, such as from falling rubble during an earthquake or drowning during a flood. However, they may also die as an indirect result of the disaster because of epidemics linked to the lack of safe water or sanitation, food, or access to health services.[11] In addition, people affected by the disaster could wind up living in camps, which pose a range of health hazards.

THE CHARACTERISTICS OF COMPLEX EMERGENCIES

Over the 10-year period from 1975 to 1985, there were on average about five complex emergencies per year, according to the International Committee of the Red Cross. However, it is estimated that at the end of the 1990s there were about 40 such emergencies per year in countries in which more than 300 million people live.[7] It is also estimated that in 2001 there were more than 14 million refugees and more than 20 million internally displaced people in the world.[12] Although natural disasters have been associated with considerable death and economic loss, the impact of complex emergencies on health over the last decade has been considerably greater than that of natural disasters.

Complex humanitarian emergencies have a number of features that particularly relate to their health impacts. First, these emergencies often go on for long periods of time. The strife in Sudan, for example, has gone on for more than a decade.[13] In addition, these emergencies are increasingly civil wars, as in Bosnia, Liberia, Sierra Leone, Rwanda, and the Democratic Republic of Congo. As a result of the nature of the conflict, it is quite common that one or more of the groups that are fighting will not allow humanitarian assistance to be provided to other groups. In fact, humanitarian workers have increasingly been the targets of those who are fighting, despite what should be their protected status.

During complex emergencies, combatants often intentionally target civilians, as well, for displacement, injury, and death. Many fighters also engage in systematic abuse of human rights, including torture, sexual abuse, and rape "as a weapon of war," as discussed in Chapter 9. Those same fighters often intentionally destroy health facilities. Given the nature of some of the fighting and its impact on civilians, large numbers of people have been displaced by some of these conflicts, as noted above. Sometimes they choose to flee, but sometimes they are forced to flee.[14]

Unfortunately, these are not the only characteristics of complex humanitarian emergencies. The disruption of society often leads to food shortages. Besides the loss of some health facilities, it is also common that the publicly supported health system may break down entirely, as it did, for example, during the civil war in Liberia. Damage may also be done to water supply and sanitation systems.[15] In El Salvador, for example, the shortage of safe drinking water for the poor was a significant health threat.[13]

It is important to understand that the migration of large numbers of people, some of whom will live in camps, brings with it a number of problems, as well. Migrants carry diseases with them, sometimes into areas that did not previously have that disease. When Ethiopian refugees who were living in Sudan returned home, for example, they brought malaria from Sudan. Diseases can also spread faster among refugee populations than they would normally, given the large number of people living in crowded conditions, often without appropriate hygiene and sanitation. In addition, large numbers of migrants, sometimes suddenly, need care from health systems that were weak before and that may now be almost nonexistent after suffering the effects of civil conflict. Finally, one should note that many factions in civil conflicts use landmines, and their health effects on individuals can be devastating.[13]

THE HEALTH BURDEN OF NATURAL DISASTERS

In the 1990s, about 62,000 people per year died on average during natural disasters. There are very few data available on the morbidity and disability associated with natural disasters. The direct and indirect health effects of natural disasters depend on the type of disaster. Earthquakes can kill many people quickly. In addition, they can cause a substantial number of injuries in a very short period of time. In the longer term, earthquake survivors face increased risks of permanent orthopedic disabilities, mental health problems, and possibly an increase in the rates of heart disease and other chronic disease. The indirect effect of earthquakes on health depends on the severity and location of the earthquake and the extent to which it damages infrastructure and forces people out of their homes.[16]

In the popular imagination, people are thought to die from the lava flows of volcanoes. In fact, this is rarely the case. About 90 percent of the deaths from volcanoes are due to mud and ash or from floods on denuded hillsides affected by the volcano.[17] In addition, volcanoes can harm health by displacing people, rendering water supplies unsafe, and causing mental health problems among the affected population.[17]

Tsunamis take most of their victims immediately by drowning and cause relatively few injuries, compared to the number of deaths.[17] In storms and flooding, most fatalities occur from drowning and few deaths result from trauma or wind-blown objects. These flood-related events generally lead to an increase in diarrheal disease, respiratory infections, and skin diseases. Most of these problems that relate to natural disasters are relatively short-lived, except for drought-related famine. Epidemics do not often spring up as a result of them, except in drought-related famine and when health systems are completely destroyed for long periods of time.

There are few data on the distribution by age and sex of morbidity, disability, and death related to natural disasters. It appears, however, that being very old, very young, or very sick makes one more vulnerable to disasters in which one has to flee for survival. These groups were disproportionately affected by the 1970 tidal wave in Bangladesh and the 2004 tsunami in Asia. Whether men or women suffer the effects of a natural disaster may depend on when and where it occurs and be most related to the kind of work men or women are doing. Women, however, face considerable risks in the aftermath of natural disasters if housing has been harmed and people are living in camps, as will be discussed further later.[11]

THE HEALTH EFFECTS OF COMPLEX HUMANITARIAN EMERGENCIES

The burden of illness, disability, and death related to complex humanitarian emergencies is large and probably underestimated, given the difficulties of collecting such data. Some of the effects of these CHEs are direct. It has been estimated for example, that between 320,000 and 420,000 people are killed each year as a direct result of these CHEs.[7] In addition, it is estimated that between 500,000 and 1 million deaths resulted from trauma during the genocide in Rwanda in 1994.[18] It is thought that about 4–13 percent of the deaths during CHEs in Northern Iraq, Somalia, and the Democratic Republic of Congo were the direct result of trauma.

Other illness, disability, and death, however, come about as an indirect result of the emergencies. These stem from malnutrition, the lack of safe water and sanitation, shortages of food, and breakdowns in health services. They are exacerbated by the crowded and difficult circumstances in which people have to live when they are displaced. One estimate, for example, suggested that almost 1.7 million more people died in a 22-month period of conflict in the Democratic Republic of Congo than would have died in a "normal" 22-month period in that country.[7]

The burden of deaths related to wars is also hard to estimate. One estimate suggests that about 200,000 people died in war in 2001 in low- and middle-income countries. Just over 10 percent of these deaths occurred in the South Asia region. Almost 70 percent of these deaths, however, took place in sub-Saharan Africa.[19] About 6.5 million DALYs were lost in 2001 due to war in low- and middle-income countries. That was about one third as much as was lost due to other forms of violence. It was about two thirds as much as the number of DALYs lost from all sexually transmitted diseases and about the same as those lost due to maternal sepsis or breast cancer.[19] Other estimates suggest that between 1975 and 1989 more than 5 million people died in civil conflicts.[20] In terms of deaths from CHEs, some of the most severely affected

countries in the last two decades have been the Democratic Republic of Congo, Afghanistan, Burundi, and Angola.[7]

The data on the breakdown of deaths by age in CHEs suggest that child mortality rates early in the CHE are two to three times the rates of adults but that they slowly decline to those of the rest of the population. The data on deaths by sex are limited.[21] About 20 percent of the nonfatal injuries in the Bosnian conflict were among children. Almost 50 percent of the deaths in the Democratic Republic of Congo were among women and children younger than 15 years of age.[18] UNICEF estimates that more than 2 million children were killed as a result of war over the last decade.[22] In European conflicts, the overwhelming majority of those who died have been men between 19 and 50 years of age.[18]

Causes of Death in CHEs

In the early stages of dealing with large numbers of displaced people in CHEs, most deaths occur from diarrheal diseases, respiratory infections, measles, or malaria.[18,23] Generally, diarrheal diseases are the most common cause of death in refugee situations. Major epidemics of cholera occurred in refugee camps in Malawi, Nepal, and Bangladesh, among others, and the case fatality rates from cholera have ranged from 3–30 percent in settings such as these. Dysentery, which refers to severe diarrhea caused by an infection in the intestine, has also commonly occurred in such situations over the last 20 years, including in camps in Malawi, Nepal, Bangladesh, and Tanzania. The case fatality rate for dysentery has been highest among the very old and very young, for whom it reaches about 10 percent.[18,23] In one of the most significant humanitarian crises in the last few decades, tens of thousands of Rwandan refugees poured into the Democratic Republic of Congo during the genocide in Rwanda. Between July and August 1994, 90 percent of the deaths among the refugees in Goma, Democratic Republic of Congo, were from cholera spread by the contamination of a lake from which the refugees got their water.[18,23]

Measles has also been a major killer in camps for displaced persons. This is especially significant in populations that are malnourished and have not been immunized against measles. As you learned in Chapter 10, the risk of a child dying of measles is increased substantially if the child is vitamin A deficient, as would be the case for many refugees. Up to 30 percent of the children who get measles in these situations may die from it.[23]

Malaria is also a significant contributor to death in refugee camps. This is especially the case when refugees move from countries in which there is relatively little malaria to places in which it is endemic. The risk of malaria in such cases is highest in sub-Saharan Africa and a few parts of Asia.[23,24] Acute respiratory infections are also major causes of death in refugee camps. This is to be expected because the camps are crowded, housing is inadequate, and refugees could remain in the camps for many years. Although less common than the problems noted previously, there have also been outbreaks of meningitis in some refugee camps in areas in which that disease is prevalent, such as Malawi, Ethiopia, and Burundi. These outbreaks have generally been contained by mass immunization, as it became clear that there was a risk of epidemic.[25] However, an outbreak in Sudan in 1999 led to almost 2400 deaths.[24] Outbreaks of hepatitis E have occurred in Somalia, Ethiopia, and Kenya. These led to high case fatality rates among pregnant women, in particular.[25]

The populations that are affected by CHEs are generally poor and not well nourished, and nutritional issues are always of grave concern during CHEs, when there may also be problems of food scarcity. In addition, the relationship of infection and malnutrition also poses risks to displaced populations. In CHEs in sub-Saharan Africa, the rates of acute protein-energy malnutrition during at least the early period of a CHE have been very high, particularly among young children. Reported rates of such malnutrition varied from around 12 percent among internally displaced Liberians[26] to as high as 80 percent among internally displaced Somalis.[24] In CHEs in Bosnia and Tajikistan, the elderly were the group that was the worst affected by acute protein-energy malnutrition.[24]

The underlying nutritional status of the refugees or internally displaced people is often poor, and micronutrient deficiencies can also be very important in CHEs. Vitamin A deficiency can be very important among these populations, given their low stores of vitamin A; the fact that some of the diseases most prevalent in camps, such as measles, further deplete their stores of vitamin A; and the fact that food rations in camps have historically been deficient in vitamin A. There have also been epidemics of pellagra, which is a deficiency of niacin that causes diarrhea, dermatitis, and mental disorders. One such case affected more than 18,000 Mozambican refugees in Malawi, whose rations in the camp were deficient in niacin. Scurvy, from a lack of vitamin C, has also occurred in a number of settings, such as Ethiopia, Somalia, and Sudan. Iron deficiency anemia has also been a problem in some camps and affects primarily women of childbearing age and young children. It appears that women and children who are in the camps without a male adult are at particular risk of not getting enough food in camps and of

suffering acute protein-energy malnutrition and micronutrient deficiencies.[23]

Violence Against Women in CHEs

As discussed in Chapter 9 on women's health, the security conditions during CHEs put women at considerable risk of sexual violence. Rape may be used as a "weapon of war." In addition, the chaos and economic distresses of conflict situations place women at risk of sexual violence and sometimes force them to "trade" sex for food or money, what people call "survival sex." Such women are often very young.

The data on sexual violence against women during CHEs are not good. Some recent data suggest that the rates of violence against women are very high in these circumstances. A survey carried out in East Timor indicated that 23 percent of the women surveyed after the crisis there reported that they had been sexually assaulted. Fifteen percent of the women in Kosovo who were surveyed reported sexual violence against them during the conflict period. It is estimated that between 50,000 and 64,000 women in Sierra Leone were sexually assaulted during the conflict there, and 25 percent of Azerbaijani women reported sexual violence against them during a 3-month period in 2000.[27]

Mental Health

Those who study CHEs agree that they are associated with a range of social and psychological shocks to affected people due to changes in their way of living, their loss of livelihoods, damaged social networks, and physical and mental harm to them, their families, and their friends. Nonetheless, there is considerable disagreement among those working with CHEs about the validity of defining the impact on people affected by CHEs through the framework of a "Western" medical model of mental health.[28,29]

Some studies have focused on post-traumatic stress disorder (PTSD) and have shown rates of prevalence for PTSD among adults that ranged from 4.6 percent among Burmese refugees in Thailand to 37.2 percent among Cambodian refugees in Thailand. The rate of PTSD is about 1 percent in the population of the United States. Similar studies showed rates of depression in Bosnian refugees of 39 percent, Burmese refugees of almost 42 percent, and Cambodian refugees of almost 68 percent. By comparison, one estimate of the baseline rate of depression in the U.S. population is 6.4 percent.[30]

Other studies have looked at the mental health impacts of CHEs on children and the extent to which they suffer from both post-traumatic stress and depression. The studies that have been done on such populations have been small ones that cannot be used to draw major conclusions on this question. However, they suggest that children who have been through conflict situations do suffer from high rates of both PTSD and depression. A survey of 170 adolescent Cambodian refugees, for example, indicated that almost 27 percent of them suffered from PTSD. A survey of 147 Bosnian children refugees suggested that almost 26 percent of them suffered from depression.[31]

It should be noted, however, that a number of those involved with the mental health impacts of CHEs believe that the stress placed by some on PTSD is not valid. Rather, they believe that although a small minority of those affected may need psychotropic medication, the most important issue is to help people as rapidly as possible to rebuild their lives and their social networks. This requires a variety of forms of social assistance and help in reuniting families, finding families a place to live, rebuilding social networks, and restoring livelihoods.[21,28,29] The Inter-Agency Standing Committee of the WHO has issued guidelines for planning, establishing, and coordinating integrated responses, across sectors, for mental health and psychosocial well-being in emergencies. The core principles of these guidelines are shown in Table 14-5.

ADDRESSING THE HEALTH EFFECTS OF NATURAL DISASTERS

The health effects of rapid-onset natural disasters occur in phases, starting with the immediate impact of the event and then continuing for some time until displaced people can be resettled. It is very important that the health situation be assessed immediately after the disaster has occurred. This assessment will set the basis for the initial relief effort. At the same time, care must begin for those injured in the disaster. Once the immediate trauma cases are taken care of, relief workers and health service providers can turn their attention to other injured people who are in need of early care and treatment. This would include urgent psychological problems. In the earliest stages of the disaster, some important public health functions also need to be carried out, including the establishment of continuous disease surveillance among the affected populations and provision of water, shelter, and food.[17]

Many countries do not have all of the resources needed to cope with the health impacts of the disaster, and they will depend on assistance from other countries to address their health problems. Unfortunately, there have been many instances when such help was poorly coordinated and did not effectively match the conditions on the ground. It has

become clear over time, however, that to be most helpful in addressing the impact of natural disasters, external assistance will have to:

- Include all of the external partners
- Be based on a cooperative relationship among the partners
- Have partners working in ways that are complementary to each other
- Be evidence-based and transparent
- Involve the affected communities[32]

In some respects, it is easier to predict places that are at risk of natural disasters than it is to predict where CHEs will occur. There are certain countries that are vulnerable to earthquakes, volcanoes, hurricanes, typhoons, and flooding during major rains. In this light, much can be done to prepare for natural disasters and to reduce their health impact. Disaster preparedness plans can be formulated to:

- Identify vulnerabilities
- Develop scenarios of what might happen and its likelihood
- Outline the role that different actors will play in the event of an emergency
- Train first responders and managers to deal with such emergencies[33]

It is also possible when constructing water systems and hospitals, for example, to take measures that will make them less vulnerable to damage during natural disasters.

Given the way that the health impacts of natural disasters unfurl, what would be the most cost-effective ways for external partners to help in addressing the disaster? There are at least several lessons that have emerged on this front. First, although many countries send search and rescue teams to assist the victims of natural disasters, the efforts of such teams are not cost-effective. Most people who are freed from the rubble of an earthquake, for example, are saved by people in their own community immediately after the event. By the time foreign search and rescue teams arrive, most victims of falling rubble will already have been saved or will be dead. There may be important humanitarian and foreign policy rationale for external search and rescue teams. However, they will generally save few lives at very high cost per life saved.[34]

It is also common that countries will send field hospitals to disaster areas. The cost of each hospital is about $1 million, and they generally arrive two to five days after the initial event. Unfortunately, by the time they arrive, they are of little value in addressing the most urgent trauma cases. It appears to be more cost-effective to have fewer field hospitals but to have a few that will remain in place for some time, in addition to building some temporary but durable buildings that can also serve as hospitals.[34]

Countries send different kinds of goods to disaster-affected places. Unfortunately, these goods can be inappropriate to the needs of the problem. This has often been the case, for example, for drugs. Better results occur when the impacted country clearly indicates what it needs and other countries send only those goods. Large camps of tents are often established after natural disasters. This is generally also not a cost-effective approach to helping the affected community to rebuild. Providing cash or building materials to affected families allows them to rebuild as quickly as possible, in a manner in line with their cultural preferences. The lack of income, even beyond the cost of rebuilding their home, can be a major impediment to the reconstruction of affected areas. Although it must be managed carefully to avoid abuse, cash assistance to families appears to be a cost-effective way of helping communities rebuild.[34]

ADDRESSING THE HEALTH EFFECTS OF COMPLEX HUMANITARIAN EMERGENCIES

It is difficult to take measures that can prevent complex humanitarian emergencies from occurring and harming human health because these emergencies so often relate to civil conflict. Thus, the key to avoiding such problems lies in the political realm and in the avoidance of conflict, rather than by taking measures that are directly health related. "Primary prevention in such circumstances, therefore, means stopping the violence."[35]

However, if such conflicts continue to occur, are there measures of "secondary prevention" that can be taken to detect health-related problems as early as possible and take actions to mitigate them? To a large extent, the early warning systems that exist for natural disasters do not exist for political disasters. Although some groups do carry out analyses of political vulnerability in countries, corruption, and the risk of political instability, these analyses are not used to prepare contingency plans for civil conflict.

Given the extent of conflict, however, it would be prudent if organizations, countries, and international bodies would cooperatively establish contingency plans for areas of likely conflict. It would also be prudent to stage near such areas the materials needed to address displacement and health problems that would occur if conflict breaks out. This would be similar

---

TABLE 14-5 Guidelines on Mental Health and Psychosocial Support in Emergency Settings

Human Rights and Equity
- The human rights of all affected persons should be protected, with a special focus on at-risk populations.
- Ensure equity and nondiscrimination for the provision of support services to all affected populations.

Participation
- The participation of the affected population in assistance and reconstruction efforts should be promoted.
- This can empower affected populations to make decisions regarding their own care, which subsequently improves program quality, equity, and sustainability.

Do No Harm
- Due to the highly sensitive issues humanitarian workers are faced with, it is imperative to reduce the risk of harm.
- Some recommended techniques are the use of *coordination groups*, the integration of *local knowledge* into interventions, *flexibility* and project *transparency*, *cultural sensitivity*, knowledge of *current research* in emergency response techniques, and an *understanding* of universal human rights, power relations, and participatory approaches.

Building on Available Resources and Capacities
- Utilize existing mental health services by building on local capacities, supporting self-help practices, and fortifying available resources.
- To improve sustainability, the capabilities of government and civil society should be supported, as well as community-level mobilization.

Integrated Support Systems
- Avoid systemic fragmentation by integrating activities and programs into a broader structure (i.e., general health services or community support mechanisms).
- This enables programs to have a more extensive reach, improve sustainability, and reduce stigmatization.

Multi-layered Supports
- In order to access the majority of the affected population four categories of response need to be provided: basic services and security, community and family support, focused nonspecialized support, and specialized services.
- This is organized into a pyramidal system, with all services sharing an equal weight of importance.

Source: Data from Inter-Agency Standing Committee. *IASC Guidelines on Mental Health and Psychosocial Support in Emergency Settings.* Geneva: Inter-Agency Standing Committee; 2007.

to what is done for disaster preparedness in some places, such as those regularly exposed to hurricanes.[36] You read earlier that complex humanitarian emergencies are characterized by:

- Potentially massive displacement of people
- The likelihood that these displaced people will live in camps for some time
- The need in those camps for adequate shelter, safe water, sanitation, and food
- The importance of security in the camps, especially for women
- The need to address early in the crisis the potentially worst health threats, which are malnutrition, diarrhea, measles, pneumonia, and malaria
- The need to avoid other epidemic diseases, such as cholera and meningitis
- The need as one moves away from the emergency phase of a CHE to deal with longer-term mental health issues, primary health care, TB, and some non-communicable diseases

Some of the most important measures that can be taken to address these points are discussed briefly hereafter. As you review these, it is important to keep in mind that the aim of these efforts is to establish a safe and healthy environment, treat urgent health problems and prevent epidemics, and then to address less urgent needs and establish a basis for longer-term health services among the displaced people.[37]

Assessment and Surveillance

As with natural disasters, among the first things that need to be done during the emergency phase of a CHE is to carry out an assessment of the displaced population and establish a system for disease surveillance. Such an assessment would try to immediately gather information on the number of people who are displaced, their age and sex, their ethnic and social backgrounds, and their state of health and nutrition. Although it is difficult to get this information in the chaotic moments of an emergency, it is impossible to rationally plan services for displaced people without this information.

There are a number of health indicators that guide services in CHEs, and a surveillance system needs to be established at the start of the emergency phase of a CHE. Given the difficulties of the emergency, the surveillance system must be simple but still give a robust sense of the health of the affected community. Given the importance of nutrition and the likelihood that a large part of the population will be undernourished, it is essential that the weight for height of all children younger than 5 years of age be checked.[38] It is also important to have surveillance for diseases that cause epidemics among displaced persons, such as measles, cholera, and meningitis.

In general, the daily crude mortality rate is used as an indicator of the health of the affected group; one goal is to keep that rate below 1 death per 10,000 persons in the population per day. Where the daily rate is twice the normal rate, it signifies that a public health emergency is occurring. Say, for example, that the baseline crude mortality rate for sub-Saharan Africa is 0.44/10,000 per day. Thus, if the rate in an affected population were to get to 0.88/10,000 per day, it would signal a public health emergency that would require urgent attention. For children younger than 5 years, the crude mortality rate for sub-Saharan Africa is 1.14/10,000 per day. The goal in a public health emergency, therefore, would be to keep that rate below about 2.0/10,000 per day.[39] Death rates in a large camp are not always easy to get; sometimes people have resorted to innovative ways of getting such data, such as daily reports by grave-diggers.

A Safe and Healthy Environment

It is critical in camps and other situations with large numbers of displaced people that efforts be made to ensure that environmental and personal hygiene are maintained. This will be the key to avoiding the potentially serious effect of diarrheal disease. It is recommended that 15 liters of water per person per day should be provided, people should not have to walk more than 500 meters to a water source, and people should not have to wait more than 15 minutes to get their water when they get to a source. Of the 15 liters per day that are recommended, about 2.5 to 3 liters are considered the minimum essential for drinking and food. Another 2 to 6 liters are needed for personal hygiene, and the remainder is needed for cooking.[40]

Providing appropriate sanitation in situations of displaced people is also very challenging. Ideally, every family would have their own toilet. This, however, is certainly impossible in the acute phase of an emergency. The goal instead is one toilet for every 20 people. These should be segregated by sex to provide the most safety to women. They should not be more than 50 meters from dwellings, but must be carefully situated to avoid contamination of water sources.[40]

Many of the displaced people will be poor people with little education and, often, poor hygiene practices. It is very important in these circumstances that efforts be made to make the community aware of the importance of good hygiene and to see that soap is available to all families and used.

Of course, people will also need shelter. The long-term goal is to help them return as quickly as possible to their homes. In the short term, if possible, the goal is to have families be sheltered temporarily with other families. Nonetheless, it is obvious from the tables shown earlier that many displaced people do end up living in camps, often for very long periods of time. When shelter is needed, the goal is to provide 3.5 square meters of covered area per person, with due attention paid in the construction of the shelter to the safety of women. Whenever possible, local and culturally appropriate building materials should be used. In the short-run, the aim is to get people into covered areas. When the emergency phase has passed, the need to enhance some of the structures can be prioritized.[41]

Food

It is suggested that each adult in a camp should get at least 2100 kilocalories of energy from food per day.[42] Food rations should be distributed by family unit, but special care has to be taken, as noted earlier, to ensure that female-headed households and children without their families get their rations. Vitamin A should be given to all children, and the most severely malnourished children may also need urgent nutrition supplementation.[42]

Disease Control

As suggested earlier, "The primary goals of humanitarian response to disasters are to 1) prevent and reduce excess morbidity and mortality, and 2) promote a return to normalcy."[39] Along these lines, the control of communicable diseases is one of the first priorities in the emergency phase of a disaster, especially a complex humanitarian emergency.

An important priority in the emergency phase of a complex humanitarian emergency is to prevent an epidemic of measles. This starts with vaccinating all children from 6 months to 15 years of age. Another important priority is to ensure that children up to 5 years of age get vitamin A. Systems also need to be put in place so that other epidemics that sometimes occur in these situations, such as meningitis and cholera, can be detected and then urgently addressed. Other priorities will include the proper management of diarrhea in children and the appropriate diagnosis and treatment for malaria, in zones where that is prevalent. Of course, health education and hygiene promotion must take place continuously to try to help families prevent the onset of these diseases in the first place.[39]

Unfortunately, preventing the outbreak of communicable diseases is not the only effort that needs to be taken in the emergency phase of a CHE. Measures need to be in place to handle injuries and trauma, first to stabilize people and then to refer them to where they can receive the addi-tional medical help they need. There will almost certainly be pregnant women among the displaced people, and there will be an immediate need for some reproductive health services. This will generally have to focus on the provision of a minimum package of care that would include safe delivery kits, precautions against the transmission of HIV, and transport and referral in case of complications of pregnancy.[39–44]

The care of noncommunicable diseases will be a lower priority in emergency situations than addressing communicable diseases. However, some psychiatric problems will require urgent attention and will need to be treated as effectively as possible with counseling, the continuation of medicines people were taking, and the provision of new medications, if needed. As the emergency recedes, greater attention can be paid to long-term treatment, counseling, and psychosocial support for dealing with mental health problems and the many disruptions that people have faced in their lives.[30] At that time, one can also turn additional attention to ensuring the appropriate medication of people with other noncommunicable diseases.

POLICY AND PROGRAM BRIEFS

This chapter does not contain any case studies that have been based on careful review of the evidence about specific interventions. However, policy and program briefs follow on four CHEs of importance. One concerns the genocide in Rwanda and the plight of Rwandan refugees in Goma, in what is now the Democratic Republic of Congo. A second concerns a major earthquake that hit Pakistan in 2005. A third brief concerns an earthquake in Haiti in 2010. The comments on Haiti largely follow a chronological account of the work done by Doctors Without Borders in the 6 months following the earthquake. The last case is about the impact of Cyclone Nargis on Myanmar in 2008.

The Genocide in Rwanda

In mid-July 1994, nearly 1 million Rwandan Hutus tried to escape persecution from the newly established government of Rwanda that was led by the Tutsis. The border town of Goma, in what is now the Democratic Republic of Congo, situated in the North Kivu region, became the entry point for the majority of the refugees. Many of them settled around Lake Kivu.[45]

Almost 50,000 people died in the first month after the start of the influx, largely as a result of an epidemic of cholera, which was followed by an epidemic of bacillary dysentery. In the first 17 days of the emergency, the average crude mortality rate of Rwandans was 28.1–44.9 per 10,000 per day, compared to the 0.6 per 10,000 per day in pre-war conditions inside Rwanda. This crude mortality rate is the highest by a considerable margin over the rate found in any previous CHE. In addition, in Goma, diarrheal disease affected young children and adults alike, whereas normally young children are much more severely affected than adults.[45]

Humanitarian assessments began in the first week of August, 3 weeks after the initial flow of refugees. Rapid surveys conducted in the three refugee camps of Katale, Kibumba, and Mugunga indicated that diarrheal disease contributed to 90 percent of deaths; food shortages were prevalent, especially among female-headed households; and acute malnutrition afflicted up to 23 percent of the refugees. In early August, a meningitis epidemic arose.[45]

The circumstances were complicated by the large numbers of people who fled to Goma in such a short period of time. In addition, the lake represented an easy source of water, but one from which disease could be spread. The soil around Goma was very rocky, which made it very difficult to construct an appropriate number of latrines. In addition, Hutu leaders were given control over the distribution of relief, but this did not provide for the equitable distribution of food that was hoped for.[45]

By early August, the response of the international community was beginning to have the desired effect, under the coordination of the United Nations High Commissioner for Refugees (UNHCR). A disease surveillance network was established. An information system was set up for the camps. Five to 10 liters of safe water per day per person was distributed. Measles immunization was carried out, vitamin A supplements were distributed, and disease problems were attacked using standard protocols.[45]

Despite the exceptional efforts made by many people to deal with the crisis, the events in Goma highlighted a number of shortcomings of the response. First, there was a general lack of preparedness for dealing with this type of emergency, despite the well-known political instability of Rwanda. Second, the medical teams on the ground did not have the physical infrastructure or the experience needed for a task of this magnitude. Many of these staff, for example, were not as knowledgeable about oral rehydration as they needed to be, even though this is fundamental to treating diarrheal disease. Third, the work of the military forces that joined the effort was not integrated into the planning of the other work.[45]

Although the Goma crisis was exceptional in many ways, it does suggest a number of lessons for enhancing the response to CHEs in the future. These include the need to:

- Establish early warning systems for CHEs
- Prepare in advance for CHEs

- Strengthen the existing nongovernmental groups with capability to respond to CHEs

The Earthquake in Pakistan

In early October 2005, Pakistan experienced an earthquake measuring 7.6 on the Richter scale. The epicenter was in Kashmir but the earthquake also devastated the North-West Frontier Province (NWFP). Within a matter of minutes, homes and livelihoods were destroyed, leaving over 3 million people homeless and many individuals buried under the rubble or injured by debris.[46]

It is estimated that 76,000 people, many of whom were children, lost their lives either from instantaneous death, such as severe head injury or internal bleeding; rapid death, such as asphyxia due to dust; or delayed death, such as wound infections. An additional 80,000 people were injured.[47] Moreover, 84 percent of the infrastructure in Kashmir, including 65 percent of all previously existing healthcare facilities, failed to withstand the seismic forces and collapsed. Thus, the immediate needs of the population included "winterized shelter, medical care, food and water, and sanitation facilities."[46]

To respond to the earthquake, the government of Pakistan created the Federal Relief Commission (FRC) and the Earthquake Rehabilitation and Reconstruction Authority (ERRA) that offered short- and long-term recovery efforts. Furthermore, a week after the initial earthquake, the government presented a plan for relief that included compensation for survivors. The World Bank, along with the Asian Development Bank, conducted assessments to identify vulnerable groups and areas that might hinder early recovery, such as unsanitary environments. Moreover, the South Asia Earthquake Flash Appeal (SAEFA) was created to receive donations for the recovery effort.

Doctors Without Borders (MSF) was an integral part of the interventions, as it provided emergency relief within a day of the earthquake, given that MSF medical teams were already on the ground in Kashmir. These teams focused initially on hygiene promotion; distributing tents, cookware, and mattresses; and treating the injured. They administered 30,000 measles vaccines and later redirected attention to rebuilding medical infrastructure. In NWFP, MSF created hospitals with beds to house patients, and also developed medical villages that were used to treat the overwhelming number of injured people.[46]

Despite national and international efforts to mobilize an effective response, injured individuals flooded hospitals that were still intact but did not have the personnel or the equipment to respond effectively. Thus, many patients suffered more severe secondary complications due to prolonged waiting for medical treatment, a common occurrence when earthquakes significantly affect the medical system.[46,47]

Furthermore, small, remote villages remained inaccessible because of significant road damage. Given the impending winter, the Pakistani military, MSF, and UN agencies used helicopters to distribute basic relief. In addition, the government pledged the provision of tents. People inside and outside of Pakistan responded very generously with donations to help those affected by the disaster. However, many of the donations did not fit what was most needed.[46]

Several valuable lessons emerge from the efforts of the government and military of Pakistan and Pakistan's foreign partners to assist in the rescue and recovery from the earthquake. First, buildings in rural areas in seismic zones should be built or designed to decrease human injury. Second, governments should analyze existing risks to their ability to rapidly respond to emergencies and prepare emergency plans in advance that take those risks into account. Third, donations of materials and supplies should be managed carefully so that they fit real needs. Lastly, NGO expertise, like that provided by MSF in Pakistan, can be very helpful in addressing natural disasters, particularly if the involved organizations already have a presence in the affected country.[46,47]

Haiti's 2010 Earthquake[48]

In January 2010, Haiti experienced an earthquake that was centered about 15 miles southwest of Port-au-Prince, the capital city, and measured 7.0 on the Richter scale. Given the magnitude of the earthquake, the poor quality of construction in Haiti, and the exceptionally poor living conditions of many people there, the earthquake caused major devastation. In addition, the country's already weak health system, with only a limited number of trained personnel, was ill equipped to handle the overwhelming health needs stemming from the earthquake. Moreover, with 60 percent of existing health facilities destroyed and 10 percent of medical staff either killed or absent from the country, Haiti was in dire need of external assistance to address the health needs of its people.

Doctors Without Borders (MSF) played a key role in the relief effort. The timeliness and scale of its response was strengthened by the fact that it had already been providing health services in Haiti for 19 years prior to the earthquake. MSF's response to the earthquake provides an informative example of the chronology and focus of health efforts after natural disasters in low-income countries. The actions taken by MSF are also a good reflection of how such external assistance moves through different phases, starting with the acute phase of the emergency and then leading over time toward efforts at reconstruction, rehabilitation, and development.

Providing emergency medical services was the first priority for MSF after the earthquake. In order to perform life-saving surgeries and wound care for people injured by the earthquake, MSF created new emergency facilities. These facilities were needed because so many existing ones had been damaged and because there were so many injured survivors. In addition, MSF sent in more surgical supplies and increased the number of personnel on the ground, which reached 3500 at its highest point. An inflatable hospital was even constructed, which provided 100 beds and 3 operating theatres. Creating sanitary conditions suitable for performing surgery was one challenge faced in this stage of the emergency response. In total, MSF provided emergency medical care to over 173,000 patients in the 5 months following the earthquake, performing over 11,000 surgeries. The nature of emergency care for earthquake-related injuries soon shifted with time, from lifesaving, often including amputation of limbs, to treating infected wounds.

Provision of emergency obstetric care was also a priority, which is crucial to saving maternal lives. Because MSF's own maternity hospital was demolished, the organization provided support to the Ministry of Health's maternity hospital by providing personnel and critical medicines. MSF helped to deliver 3752 babies in all its facilities in the first 5 months after the earthquake, spending 4 million Euros on maternal health services during this period.

To address the effects of the disaster on mental health, psychological care was integrated with emergency care for trauma patients. Soon after, outreach programs in communities were initiated, reflecting the importance of mental health care both immediately and later in relief efforts. Group counseling sessions and individual consultations were aimed primarily at reducing the anxiety that comes with losing a loved one, coping with injury and poor living conditions, and the fear of an aftershock. MSF delivered psychological care to over 80,000 Haitians in the first 5 months after the earthquake; even so, provision of mental health care remains a great challenge in Haiti due to the lack of psychiatrists to address short- and long-term psychiatric disorders.

Providing primary health care was also a priority for MSF, which was addressed by setting up additional primary health clinics. In the weeks following the earthquake, 400 to 500 people visited each clinic daily (6 months after the earthquake, about 70 people visited daily). In addition to providing basic check-ups, which allowed MSF to monitor common health problems in the area, primary health clinics enabled MSF to screen for disease epidemics. Services provided included ante- and postnatal care, vaccinations, infection treatment, and referrals to mental health services or a hospital.

The delivery of health services consumed the majority of MSF's efforts in Haiti after the earthquake. However, additional efforts to address the health threats of lack of water, sanitation, and shelter as quickly as possible were also needed. Thus, MSF set up "sanitation areas" in camps surrounding Port-au-Prince, each composed of a latrine, shower, and wash area. In addition to the creation of a waste disposal system, good hygiene was promoted through the distribution of 35,000 "hygiene kits" that included soap, toothpaste, and a toothbrush. As of May 2010, MSF was distributing about 1270 cubic meters of water per day by water trucks, in partnership with other organizations.

At the same time, MSF attempted to improve living conditions for the displaced by distributing tents for shelter and nonfood household items, such as cooking materials and sheets. Almost 27,000 tents were distributed, which are supposed to last about 6 months.

MSF also expanded its mobile clinics, which included bringing care to communities and seeking out patients. Mobile clinics are commonly used by MSF. However, the number of such clinics was not expanded immediately because the organization's personnel were already overburdened by the number of patients coming on their own immediately following the disaster to other MSF supported healthcare facilities.

As it tried to carry out the above work, particularly its immediate response to the earthquake, MSF confronted the challenge of obtaining landing spots for planes carrying urgently needed medical supplies and personnel. With planes often diverted to the neighboring Dominican Republic, supplies had to be brought to their destination by car, which took an additional 36 hours.

By the second month after the disaster, medical needs shifted from emergency care to longer-term care, with an emphasis on recovery and rehabilitation. In addition, hospitals and primary clinics started to treat conditions not inflicted by the earthquake, which amounted to about half of the cases treated by MSF by early June 2010. During this stage of the response, violence-related injuries and pediatric issues were especially common. During this period, hospitals also had to respond more frequently to conditions such as road traffic accidents, burn injuries, sexually transmitted infections, and illnesses such as TB, HIV, and respiratory infections.

By the third month after the earthquake, MSF was able to replace many of its international workers, who had flown to Haiti for emergency relief, with Haitian workers. By June 2010, the ratio of Haitian to international workers had returned to 10 to 1, the standard before the earthquake.

MSF spent about 53 million Euros in Haiti in the first 5 months following the earthquake, with 11 million Euros spent on surgical and postoperative care and 8.5 million Euros spent on providing shelter.

Despite health improvements in Haiti made possible by MSF, the organization will confront some major challenges in the aftermath of the earthquake. First, proper shelter for earthquake victims will remain an issue, because reconstruction is slow and the makeshift tents distributed are starting to deteriorate. Second, MSF is faced with the task of rebuilding medical facilities that were destroyed in the earthquake, in addition to replacing temporary facilities with permanent ones. Third, Haiti is subject to natural disasters, including hurricanes, and a serious hurricane could dramatically complicate the already weak infrastructure in Haiti and create additional health problems.

Myanmar: Cyclone Nargis

In early May 2008, a cyclone swept through the southern coastal region of Myanmar. Submerging entire towns, the cyclone killed over 138,000 people and left hundreds of thousands of survivors homeless. Over 50 townships and 2.4 million people were affected.[49] The Irrawaddy Delta, commonly known as the Rice Bowl of Myanmar and populated mostly by farmers, fishermen, laborers, and traders, experienced the worst destruction of infrastructure, water supplies, homes, fuel, and electricity.[50] The livelihoods of the population were swept away with the cyclone, because the coastline and farmlands were in ruins.

Myanmar did not have the resources to adequately respond to the needs of its people after a disaster of such great scale. The health system, for example, was already weak. Myanmar spends only 2.3 percent of GDP on health per year, or about $43 per capita.[51] In addition, the rural population, which made up 70 percent of the total population, had little to no access to basic health and sanitation services or clean water, even before the cyclone. Myanmar also lacked the healthcare professionals needed to deliver critical healthcare services. Moreover, one out of four people live below the poverty line, and Myanmar already suffered from a high burden of communicable disease, including malaria and tuberculosis.[50]

Myanmar is run by a military regime in which elections have been deemed by international standards to be neither free nor fair. In addition, the government is generally perceived as repressive, nontransparent, and limiting of political freedom. These factors had an important impact on the relief effort, as noted below.

In the aftermath of the cyclone, the need for emergency relief efforts was exacerbated by poor health and living conditions. As in any natural disaster, short-term needs included emergency health care for cyclone-related injuries; basic necessities for survival, such as food, shelter, water, and sanitation services; and provision of mental health services for psychological disorders such as depression and anxiety. In the longer term, Myanmar was tasked with reconstruction of infrastructure for health, shelter, food, and transportation.

For about 3 weeks following the disaster, however, the State Peace and Development Council (SPDC) of the Myanmar government did not allow most foreign aid or supplies into the country. Despite the scale of devastation and the country's lack of adequate resources for relief efforts, the government feared foreign influence and possible unrest from civilians if any international assistance groups intervened. Thus, Myanmar relied on local government and community-based organizations to address the acute phase of disaster relief. Even private initiatives by local citizens were subject to government control through mandatory checkpoints.[49] Unfortunately, Myanmar had less than 10 percent of the staff, capacity to manage logistics, and supplies needed to manage the crisis, according to the World Food Programme.[50] Thus, initial relief efforts could not possibly provide the food, shelter, sanitation, and emergency health care that was needed.

Many countries and humanitarian relief organizations were outraged by the government's blockage of foreign aid to the people in Myanmar who they thought were in need of additional life saving assistance.[49] The Association of South East Asian Nations (ASEAN) protested by rapidly deploying medical teams to serve in Myanmar. Following great pressure from the international community, including a visit from the UN Secretary General Ban Ki-moon, the SPDC finally allowed international aid agencies to enter the country in late May.[49]

To facilitate cooperation between foreign assistance groups and the Myanmar government, the Tripartite Core Group (TCG) was created to coordinate and oversee relief efforts. Made up of ASEAN, the United Nations, and the Government of Myanmar's Ministry of Health, the TCG created a plan for short-term and long-term rebuilding and pledged to look into measures for increasing preparedness and prevention efforts for future cyclones.

Once let into the country, international aid agencies did not escape tight government controls over their relief efforts. Travel restrictions were placed on many aid workers, and they experienced extensive government monitoring. Each foreign team was assigned a specific township in which to work, where activities were coordinated through a local liaison officer to the government. Differing sharply from previous large-scale disaster relief efforts in other countries, this aid structure lessened the possibility that foreign groups could work together in the same geographical area. In addition,

the government restricted communication of information between groups.[49]

Government authorities forced many relief workers to give aid directly to them, according to interviews with cyclone survivors and relief workers in a study conducted by the Johns Hopkins Center for Public Health and Human Rights.[49] According to the same reports, some of the aid was not used as intended. Additionally, foreign aid teams were not allowed to collect data independently.[49]

The same study also confirmed abuses against healthcare workers and cyclone survivors, including land confiscation and forced relocation of survivors. Official assessments conducted by the SPDC have not recognized these occurrences.[49]

With restrictions on communication regarding the disaster throughout the country, the government relied on state-controlled media to disseminate information, which downplayed the extent of the devastation and remaining needs of the people. In effect, the cyclone survivors, and the tragedy of the crisis as a whole, did not receive the attention it deserved within Myanmar.[49]

The types of health conditions treated by foreign relief efforts, once they did arrive in Myanmar, suggest that the delay in international response may have contributed to high rates of early mortality. Instead of deep wound and emergency injuries that would be expected after a cyclone, international relief organizations more commonly treated chronic conditions. For example, one international group that hosted mobile clinics reported that the most common illnesses among adults and children were upper respiratory tract infections and gastritis.[50] The lack of deep wounds and lacerations treated, according to this data, suggests that those people who were severely injured immediately following the cyclone, and who would have required emergency care, most likely did not receive it and lost their lives. The in-country operations lacked the resources to manage the acute phase of emergency response to the scale required.

The mishandling of aid and strict government control of relief efforts prevented aid from reaching many survivors for more than a year after the cyclone. Food, water, and shelter were the most crucial unmet needs 18 months following the cyclone. At that point, an estimated 450,000 people in the Delta still did not have shelter, according to the UN Human Settlements Programme (UN-HABITAT). At the time, food was still in short supply due to the destruction of farmland and farming equipment.[49]

The cyclone in Myanmar raises questions for the international humanitarian assistance community about the appropriate response to emergency situations in which the local government is ill-equipped to address the needs of its people with the necessary quality and scale, yet blocks outside bodies from helping to address these needs. In addition, the cyclone raises questions about the appropriate degree of autonomy for international relief efforts in the presence of a controlling local government that obstructs aid efforts.

FUTURE CHALLENGES IN MEETING THE HEALTH NEEDS OF COMPLEX HUMANITARIAN EMERGENCIES AND NATURAL DISASTERS

A number of critical challenges confront efforts to address the health effects of natural disasters and complex humanitarian emergencies. One such challenge for the future is how to prevent these from having such negative health impacts. It is difficult in resource-poor settings, many of which are poorly governed, to focus attention on the prevention of disasters and their impacts. Nonetheless, through better mitigation measures, such as water control, better building standards, greater education of the community about how to deal with disasters, and having a disaster preparedness plan for which people are trained, it should be possible, even for very poor countries, to reduce deaths from natural disasters. If these steps are coupled with the development of standard approaches for dealing with health issues when they do arise and the forward staging of medicines, equipment, and materials near to disaster-prone areas, it should be possible to reduce deaths from natural disasters, even in very low-income settings. Bangladesh, which is subject to annual flooding, has reduced the annual deaths from such floods, for example, with a series of the previously mentioned measures.[52]

There has been considerable progress among the international community in the establishment of common standards and protocols for responses to disasters. In fact, a code of conduct has been developed for use by the International Red Cross and Red Crescent Societies and NGOs, to guide their work in emergencies. The core principles of this code are shown in Table 14-6. There remains, however, the need to enhance further the coordination of responses. Ideally, the organizations involved in responding to natural disasters and CHEs will:

- Subscribe to a common set of norms, such as the Sphere Project
- Have common protocols for dealing with key issues
- Train their staff to work with those protocols
- Work in close conjunction with the affected communities and local governments[53]

In addition, it is important that responses to disasters focus on cost-effective approaches to the provision of healthcare services in emergencies. We have already seen that search

---

TABLE 14-6 The Code of Conduct: Principles of Conduct for the International Red Cross and Red Crescent Movement and NGOs in Disaster Response Programmes

- The humanitarian imperative comes first.
- Aid is given regardless of the race, creed, or nationality of the recipients and without adverse distinction of any kind. Aid priorities are calculated on the basis of need alone.
- Aid will not be used to further a particular political or religious standpoint.
- We shall endeavor not to act as instruments of government foreign policy.
- We shall respect culture and custom.
- We shall attempt to build disaster response on local capacities.
- Ways shall be found to involve programme beneficiaries in the management of relief aid.
- Relief aid must strive to reduce future vulnerabilities to disaster as well as meeting basic needs.
- We hold ourselves accountable to both those we seek to assist and those from whom we accept resources.
- In our information, publicity, and advertising activities, we shall recognize disaster victims as dignified humans, not hopeless objects.

Source: Adapted from International Federation of Red Cross and Red Crescent Societies. The Code of Conduct. Available at: http://www.ifrc.org/publicat/conduct/code.asp. Accessed October 3, 2010.

---

and rescue assistance from abroad is not cost-effective. The same is true for most field hospitals. Moreover, many agencies have provided health services in emergencies that did not focus on immediate needs and could have waited. Morbidity and mortality can be prevented and reduced more quickly if the agencies involved in disaster relief carefully set priorities for action that would be based on the principle of cost-effectiveness analysis, taking appropriate account of concerns for social justice and equity.[53–55]

The continued refinement of indicators that can be used to measure performance of services in disasters will be helpful to gauging the performance of local and international relief efforts.[54]

MAIN MESSAGES

Natural disasters and complex humanitarian emergencies are important causes of illness, death, and disability. They affect large numbers of people, have a huge economic impact, and their aftereffects can go on for some time. Their biggest relative impact is on the poor, who are generally more vulnerable to the effects of these disasters than are better-off people. Some of these disasters are man-made. Some are slow-onset and some are rapid-onset.

Natural disasters, such as droughts, famines, hurricanes, typhoons, cyclones, and heavy rains have important health impacts. Earthquakes and volcanoes are also natural disasters with large potential effects on health. It appears that the number of natural disasters is increasing but the number of deaths from them is decreasing. More than 90 percent of deaths from natural disasters occur in low- and middle-income countries. Climate change could increase the type and severity of natural disasters.

Some deaths are a direct result of natural disasters. However, the impact of those disasters on water supply and sanitation systems, health services, and availability of food can also, indirectly, lead to many more deaths. There are also special health problems associated with living in camps, which sometimes happen to those who survive natural disasters that displace many people from their homes.

In the late 1990s, there were about 40 CHEs each year. There are probably more than 14 million refugees in the world and more than 20 million internally displaced people. Overall, CHEs are associated with considerably larger health impacts than natural disasters. In addition, they may have an acute phase when large numbers of people flee, and they generally go on for long periods of time.

Complex humanitarian emergencies have increasingly been linked to civil conflict. Like natural disasters, they also have direct and indirect impacts on health. They not only take lives directly through war-related trauma, but also lead to the destruction of infrastructure. The health effects of some of these conflicts have been dramatic, sometimes because civilians have been targeted by combatants. Women are especially vulnerable in CHEs to sexual violence.

In the emergency phase of a CHE, when large numbers of displaced persons are coming into camps, a number of health risks have to be addressed. Among the most important are diarrhea, measles, malaria, and pneumonia. Malnutrition is also of exceptional importance. Cholera epidemics can also arise and kill large numbers of people quickly.

Countries at risk can take a number of measures to mitigate vulnerability to damage from natural disasters. This could include preparing a disaster plan, building seawalls and levees, and requiring, for example, that buildings in earthquake-prone areas be earthquake proof. It might also be cost-effective to strengthen other infrastructure, such as water supply systems, so that they can withstand significant threats.

Addressing the health impacts of a natural disaster requires that the health situation be assessed quickly and that urgent cases be handled immediately. Less urgent problems can be handled in the following days, weeks, and months. Long-term support for those psychologically affected by the disaster will also need to be provided in the medium and long term.

The health situation of a CHE also needs to be assessed quickly and continuously. Early attention in dealing with large numbers of displaced people must focus on the environment, shelter, water, and food. The next step is the prevention of disease outbreaks, and their treatment if they do occur. Particular attention must be paid to malnutrition, measles, pneumonia, and malaria. Some immediate attention will also have to be paid to a minimum package of reproductive health services and the avoidance of HIV. As the acute phase of the emergency subsides, more attention can be paid to TB, overall primary health care, noncommunicable diseases, and longer-term mental health issues.

There has been some important progress in the coordination and standardization of measures to address CHEs and natural disasters. However, there are still gaps in the preparation and training of staff in some organizations. In addition, there has been inadequate attention to the cost-effectiveness of interventions. There is now enough information about the lessons of CHEs and natural disasters that the priority actions that are needed should be clear and organizations active in relief work need to concentrate their efforts on what will prevent the most deaths, disability, and morbidity, at least cost, with due attention to concerns for social justice.

Study Questions

1. How does the annual burden of disease from natural disasters and complex humanitarian emergencies compare with other causes of illness, death, and disability?

2. What is a disaster? A natural disaster? A complex humanitarian emergency?

3. What is an internally displaced person? A refugee? What are the differences between them?

4. What have been some of the most significant natural disasters in the last decade? How many deaths were associated with them? How did people die? How did deaths vary for different types of disasters by age and sex?

5. What countries in sub-Saharan Africa have been the largest sources of displaced people? What countries in sub-Saharan Africa have received the largest numbers of refugees?

6. In the early stages of a complex humanitarian emergency, what are likely to be the most significant health concerns for the refugees? How do those health concerns change over time? Who are the most affected by malnutrition, measles, pneumonia, and cholera?

7. In what ways are women especially vulnerable during complex humanitarian emergencies? What problems do they face as a consequence of these vulnerabilities?

8. What are key steps that can be taken to reduce the vulnerability of certain places to the potential health threats of natural disasters?

9. What are key steps that need to be taken within the first few days of people fleeing to a refugee camp? How do those concerns change over time?

10. How can one try to ensure that relief agencies work together around a common framework and that they focus on the most cost-effective activities?

REFERENCES

1. National Highway Traffic Safety Administration. Glossary. Available at: http://www.nhtsa.dot.gov/people/injury/ems/emstraumasystem03/glossary.htm. Accessed September 29, 2006.

2. ILSI Risk Science Institute. Food Safety Risk Assessment. Available at: http://www.fsra.net/glossary.html. Accessed October 13, 2006.

3. Burkholder BT, Toole MJ. Evolution of complex disasters. *Lancet*. 1995;346:1012-1015.

4. Toole MJ, Waldman RJ. The public health aspects of complex emergencies and refugee situations. *Annu Rev Public Health*. 1997;18:285.

5. Wikipedia. Refugee. Available at: http://en.wikipedia.org/wiki/Refugees. Accessed September 29, 2006.

6. Wikipedia. Internally Displaced Person. Available at: http://en.wikipedia.org/wiki/Internally_displaced_person. Accessed September 29, 2006.

7. Brennan RJ, Nandy R. Complex humanitarian emergencies: a major global health challenge. *Emerg Med (Fremantle)*. 2001;13(2):149.

8. Last JM. *A Dictionary of Epidemiology*. 4th ed. New York: Oxford University Press; 2001:47.

9. The White Ribbon Alliance. Glossary: Case Fatality Rate. Available at: http://www.whiteribbonalliance.org/Resources/default.cfm?a0=Glossary. Accessed November 9, 2006.

10. de Ville de Goyet C, Zapata Marti R, Osorio C. Natural disaster mitigation and relief. In: Jamison DT, Breman JG, Measham AR, et al., eds. *Disease Control Priorities in Developing Countries*. 2nd ed. New York: Oxford University Press; 2006:1148.

11. de Ville de Goyet C, Zapata Marti R, Osorio C. Natural disaster mitigation and relief. In: Jamison DT, Breman JG, Measham AR, et al., eds. *Disease Control Priorities in Developing Countries*. 2nd ed. New York: Oxford University Press; 2006:1149.

12. Brennan RJ, Nandy R. Complex humanitarian emergencies: a major global health challenge. *Emerg Med (Fremantle)*. 2001;13(2):149-150.

13. Hansch S, Burkholder B. When chaos reigns. *Harvard Int Rev*. 1996;18(4):10-14.

14. Brennan RJ, Nandy R. Complex humanitarian emergencies: a major global health challenge. *Emerg Med (Fremantle)*. 2001;13(2):148-149.

15. Toole MJ, Waldman RJ. The public health aspects of complex emergencies and refugee situations. *Annu Rev Public Health*. 1997;18:283-312.

16. de Ville de Goyet C, Zapata Marti R, Osorio C. Natural disaster mitigation and relief. In: Jamison DT, Breman JG, Measham AR, et al., eds. *Disease Control Priorities in Developing Countries*. 2nd ed. New York: Oxford University Press; 2006:1149-1150.

17. de Ville de Goyet C, Zapata Marti R, Osorio C. Natural disaster mitigation and relief. In: Jamison DT, Breman JG, Measham AR, et al., eds. *Disease Control Priorities in Developing Countries*. 2nd ed. New York: Oxford University Press; 2006:1150.

18. Brennan RJ, Nandy R. Complex humanitarian emergencies: a major global health challenge. *Emerg Med (Fremantle)*. 2001;13(2):151.

19. Lopez AD, Mathers CD, Murray CJL. The burden of disease and mortality by condition: data, methods, and results for 2001. In: Lopez AD, Mathers CD, Ezzati M, Jamison DT, Murray CJL, eds. *Global burden of disease and risk factors*. New York: Oxford University Press; 2006:45-240.

20. Zwi AB, Ugalde A. Political violence in the Third World: a public health issue. *Health Policy Plan*. 1991;6:203-217.

21. Personal communication, Waldman RJ to Skolnik R, March 2007.

22. UNICEF. Child Protection from Violence, Exploitation and Abuse. Available at: http://www.unicef.org/protection/index_armedconflict.html. Accessed October 2, 2010.

23. Waldman RJ. Prioritising health care in complex emergencies. *Lancet*. 2001;357(9266):1427-1429.

24. Brennan RJ, Nandy R. Complex humanitarian emergencies: a major global health challenge. *Emerg Med (Fremantle)*. 2001;13(2):152.

25. Toole MJ, Waldman RJ. The public health aspects of complex emergencies and refugee situations. *Annu Rev Public Health*. 1997;18:295.

26. Toole MJ, Waldman RJ. The public health aspects of complex emergencies and refugee situations. *Annu Rev Public Health*. 1997;18:297.

27. Marsh M, Purdin S, Navani S. Addressing sexual violence in humanitarian emergencies. *Global Public Health*. 2006;1(2):138.

28. Ager A. Psychosocial needs in complex emergencies. *Lancet*. 2003;360:43-44.

29. Almedom A, Summerfield D. Mental well-being in settings of complex emergency: an overview. *J Biosocial Sci*. 2004;36:381-388.

30. Mollica RF, Cardozo BL, Osofsky HJ, Raphael B, Ager A, Salama P. Mental health in complex emergencies. *Lancet*. 2004;364(9450):2058-2067.

31. Mollica RF, Cardozo BL, Osofsky HJ, Raphael B, Ager A, Salama P. Mental health in complex emergencies. *Lancet*. 2004;364(9450):2061.

32. de Ville de Goyet C, Zapata Marti R, Osorio C. Natural disaster mitigation and relief. In: Jamison DT, Breman JG, Measham AR, et al., eds. *Disease Control Priorities in Developing Countries*. 2nd ed. New York: Oxford University Press; 2006:1154.

33. de Ville de Goyet C, Zapata Marti R, Osorio C. Natural disaster mitigation and relief. In: Jamison DT, Breman JG, Measham AR, et al., eds. *Disease Control Priorities in Developing Countries*. 2nd ed. New York: Oxford University Press; 2006:1155.

34. de Ville de Goyet C, Zapata Marti R, Osorio C. Natural disaster mitigation and relief. In: Jamison DT, Breman JG, Measham AR, et al., eds. *Disease Control Priorities in Developing Countries*. 2nd ed. New York: Oxford University Press; 2006:1157.

35. Toole MJ, Waldman RJ. The public health aspects of complex emergencies and refugee situations. *Annu Rev Public Health*. 1997;18:300.

36. Toole MJ, Waldman RJ. The public health aspects of complex emergencies and refugee situations. *Annu Rev Public Health*. 1997;18:302.

37. Brennan RJ, Nandy R. Complex humanitarian emergencies: a major global health challenge. *Emerg Med (Fremantle)*. 2001;13(2):153.

38. Toole MJ, Waldman RJ. The public health aspects of complex emergencies and refugee situations. *Annu Rev Public Health*. 1997;18:296.

39. The Sphere Project. Minimum standards in health services. *The Sphere Handbook 2004: Humanitarian Charter and Minimum Standards in Disaster Response*. Geneva: Oxfam Publishing; 2004:249-312.

40. The Sphere Project. Minimum standards in water supply, sanitation, and hygiene promotion. *The Sphere Handbook 2004: Humanitarian Charter and Minimum Standards in Disaster Response*. Geneva: Oxfam Publishing; 2004:51-102.

41. The Sphere Project. Minimum standards in shelter, settlements, and non-food items. *The Sphere Handbook 2004: Humanitarian Charter and Minimum Standards in Disaster Response*. Geneva: Oxfam Publishing; 2004:203-248.

42. UNHCR. Refugee Health. Available at: http://www.unhcr.org/3de68bf424.html. Accessed September 30, 2010.

43. Toole MJ, Waldman RJ. The public health aspects of complex emergencies and refugee situations. *Annu Rev Public Health*. 1997;18:303-304.

44. Krasue SK, Meyers JL, Friedlander E. Improving the availability of emergency obstetric care in conflict-afffected settings. *Global Public Health*. 2006;1(3):229-248.

45. Goma Epidemiology Group. Public health impact of Rwandan refugee crisis: what happened in Goma, Zaire, in July 1994? *Lancet*. 1995;345(8946):339-344.

46. Médicins Sans Frontières. South Asian Earthquake: 6-month Overview of MSF Operations MSF Response to the Disaster. Available at: http://www.doctorswithoutborders.org/news/2006/04–21–2006.cfm. Accessed February 25, 2007.

47. Noji EK. Earthquakes. In: Noji EK, ed. T*he Public Health Consequences of Disasters*. New York: Oxford University Press; 1997.

48. This brief is based on: Doctors Without Borders. Emergency Response After the Haiti Earthquake: Choices, Obstacles, Activities and Finance. 8 July 2010. Available at: http://www.doctorswithoutborders.org/publications/article.cfm?id=4581&cat=special-report. Accessed October 1, 2010.

49. Suwanvanichkij V, Murakami N, Lee C, et al. Community-based assessment of human rights in a complex humanitarian emergency: the Emergency Assistance Teams—Burma and Cyclone Nargis. *Conflict Health*. 2010;4:8.

50. Lateef F. Cyclone Nargis and Myanmar: a wake up call. *J Emergencies Trauma Shock*. 2009;2:106-113.

51. World Health Organization. Myanmar. Available at: http://www.who.int/countries/mmr/en/index.html. Accessed October 13, 2010.

52. ICDDR,B Center for Health and Population Research. Documenting effects of the July–August floods of 2004 and ICDDR,B's response. *Health Sci Bull*. 2004;2(3).

53. The Sphere Project. *The Sphere Handbook 2004: Humanitarian Charter and Minimum Standards in Disaster Response*. Geneva: Oxfam Publishing; 2004.

54. Spiegel P, Sheik M, Gotway-Crawford C, Salama P. Health programmes and policies associated with decreased mortality in displaced people in postemergency phase camps: a retrospective study. *Lancet*. 2002;360(9349):1927-1934.

55. de Ville de Goyet C, Zapata Marti R, Osorio C. Natural disaster mitigation and relief. In: Jamison DT, Breman JG, Measham AR, et al., eds. *Disease Control Priorities in Developing Countries*. 2nd ed. New York: Oxford University Press; 2006:1147-1162.

CHAPTER 15

Working Together to Improve Global Health

LEARNING OBJECTIVES

By the end of this chapter the reader will be able to:

- Discuss the value of cooperation in addressing health problems
- Discuss the most important types of cooperative action in global health
- Describe the major organizational actors in global health and their focuses
- Discuss the rationale for the creation of public–private partnerships for health
- Outline the key challenges to enhancing cooperative action in global health

VIGNETTES

The world came close to eradicating polio in 2004. However, in 2005, polio spread from Northern Nigeria to a number of other African countries, due to a failure to immunize children in Northern Nigeria by some groups. By July 2005, polio cases had moved from Africa to Saudi Arabia and Indonesia, and then began appearing in Angola, which had not had a case of polio since 2001. By September 2005, cases appeared in Somalia, which had also been free of polio for several years.[1] Stopping new cases of polio and preventing it from spreading from one country to another requires a global effort to correctly identify polio cases and then immediately carry out special immunization campaigns.

In 2008, about 11 million people worldwide suffered from tuberculosis, which is one of the leading causes of deaths of adults in the developing world. The number of TB cases worldwide, as noted in Chapter 11, has grown with the spread of HIV, and 23 percent of the deaths of people with AIDS are due to TB.[2] Despite the importance of TB, however, no new drugs for TB have been developed since the 1960s.[3] TB is a disease that largely affects poor people in low- and middle-income countries. These people have little money to spend on drugs and there is minimal economic incentive for pharmaceutical companies to develop new TB drugs. Can actors in global health work together to encourage the development of new drugs for TB and other neglected diseases? What would they have to do to encourage public and private sector investment in such drugs? What would they have to do to ensure investors that if they are able to develop such drugs that there will be a market for them?

Vaccines are among the most cost-effective investments in health. For young children in developing countries, there are six basic vaccines. There are also other vaccines that would be cost-effective in some countries, including the vaccines for hepatitis B and for *Haemophilus influenza* type b. Yet, throughout the 1990s there were important gaps in coverage of the six basic vaccines in the poorest countries. In addition, the rate of coverage was actually going down in some countries.[4] Although the hepatitis B vaccine began to be widely used in developed countries in the 1980s, almost 20 years later it was still rarely used in developing countries. The main reasons behind this failure included limited money for immunization, a lack of the infrastructure needed to carry out effective immunization programs, and a lack of political interest in immunization. In 2000, a number of governments, foundations, and individuals established the Global Alliance for Vaccines and Immunisation (GAVI), the aim of which is to provide financing and technical assistance to dramatically improve vaccine coverage and the spread of new vaccines. So far, GAVI has been involved in enhancing immunization coverage in many low-income countries.[5]

INTRODUCTION

This chapter focuses on how different actors work together to enhance global health. First, it discusses the importance of such cooperation. The chapter then extensively reviews the key organizational actors in global health activities. Third, the chapter examines the roles in cooperation of different types of organizations. The chapter then outlines how the global health agenda is set and how that agenda has evolved historically. The chapter concludes with a number of policy and program briefs, case studies, and an assessment of some of the future challenges to cooperative action in global health.

COOPERATING TO IMPROVE GLOBAL HEALTH[6,7]

There are a number of reasons why different actors cooperate in global health activities and why such cooperation is in everyone's interest. First is the value of cooperating to create consensus around and advocate on behalf of different health causes. Although health is an extremely important issue for both individuals and societies, it does not always receive the political, economic, and financial support that it should. A good example of this is the lack of attention by many countries to nutrition, despite the poor nutritional status of their people. The impact of advocacy efforts is likely to be much greater if numerous actors, across organizations and across countries, work together to promote important health causes. This has been evident in the field of HIV, for example, where AIDS activists worldwide have been able to work together to promote the treatment of people who are HIV-positive with antiretroviral drugs.

The need to share knowledge and to set global standards for health activities are other reasons for cooperation in the global health field. It has become clear from trials of different antimalarial drugs, for example, that some drug regimens for malaria are more effective than others. This knowledge is especially important because some malaria has become resistant to what has been standard treatment. If lessons like this are to be shared globally, then it is important that technical standards be developed and disseminated by an organization that countries believe is technically sound and internationally representative. As you will read later, helping to define and promulgate such standards is one of the main functions of the World Health Organization.

Another important reason for cooperation to achieve global health aims is the fact that many aspects of global health are "global public goods." Thus, it is only through cooperative efforts that the world can ensure that a sufficient amount of these goods are produced and shared. Individual countries, for example, may not have an interest in reducing pollution generated within their borders that causes health problems in adjacent countries, and it is only through collective action that countries will be able to address such problems. A similar issue arises with respect to efforts to reduce the burden of communicable diseases. Individual countries may have little incentive to take the measures needed to effectively address some communicable diseases, despite the fact that the spread of these diseases does not respect national boundaries. Efforts to deal with them, therefore, require cooperative efforts across countries.

The surveillance of disease also has many aspects of a "global public good" and requires cooperation among many actors to be successful. It is important for all countries to work together to monitor the appearance of diseases and to fashion approaches to dealing with them. Surveillance by individual countries, for example, is not sufficient to stem the spread of disease *across* countries. The global effort to address the SARS problem in 2003 is an excellent example of the need for close collaboration among countries on surveillance.[8]

Cooperation to achieve better global health outcomes can also take place to assist in financing health efforts in poorer countries. There are multiple motivations for this aid. In one case, wealthier countries may contribute out of humanitarian concern for the well-being of less fortunate people. Richer countries may also wish to assist in addressing these problems because of "enlightened self-interest." In an age of travel and extensive contacts among people of different countries, governments may be concerned that the health problems of developing countries will endanger their own people if not properly tackled. Many low-income countries, for example, have high burdens of TB but may not have the financial, technical, or institutional resources needed to combat TB effectively. Yet, TB can endanger both their population and that of other countries. Thus, it is in everyone's interest for high-income countries to provide financial and technical assistance to developing countries to deal effectively with diseases such as TB.

KEY ACTORS IN GLOBAL HEALTH

The number of actors in the global health arena has grown exponentially. Some of these are international organizations with a global reach. Others are organizations that work globally but are based in individual countries. Some are public organizations. A number are private and for-profit, while others are private but operate on a not-for-profit basis. Foundations are also actively involved in global health activities. Increasingly, there are also organizations that bring the public and private sectors together to work cooperatively on a global health problem. The next section discusses some of the most important organizations that are broadly involved in global health and examples of how they operate in that field.

There are so many actors in global health that it is necessary to think in terms of the type of organizations they represent and the kind of roles that they play. Table 15-1 lists a sample of the types of organizations involved in global health and selected organizations representing those types. It is important to consider the activities in which these organizations engage. They could, for example, participate in generating and sharing knowledge. They could engage in advocacy.

TABLE 15-1 Selected Organizational Actors in Global Health, by Type of Organization

United Nations Agencies
- UNAIDS
- United Nations Development Program (UNDP)
- United Nations Population Fund (UNFPA)
- United Nations Children's Fund (UNICEF)
- World Health Organization (WHO)

International Health Programs
- Global Alliance for Vaccines and Immunisation
- The Global Fund to Fight AIDS, TB, and Malaria

Multilateral Development Banks
- African Development Bank
- Asian Development Bank
- Inter-American Development Bank
- The World Bank

Bilateral Development Agencies
- Australian Agency for International Development
- Canadian International Development Agency
- Danish International Development Agency
- Department for International Development of the United Kingdom
- Dutch Agency for Development Cooperation
- Norwegian Agency for Development Cooperation
- U.S. Agency for International Development

Foundations
- The Aga Khan Foundation
- The Bill & Melinda Gates Foundation
- The Clinton Foundation
- The Rockefeller Foundation
- The Wellcome Trust

WHO Related Partnerships
- Roll Back Malaria
- Stop TB
- Tropical Disease Research Program

Public–Private Partnerships for Health/Product Development Partnerships
- Aeras
- Global Alliance for TB Drug Development
- International AIDS Vaccine Initiative
- Malaria Vaccine Initiative

National Scientific Organizations
- Canadian Institutes of Health Research
- Institute of Tropical Medicine, Antwerp, Belgium

- National Health and Medical Research Council, Australia
- U.S. National Institutes of Health

Nongovernmental Organizations
- BRAC
- CARE
- Catholic Relief Services
- Doctors Without Borders
- Oxfam
- Partners in Health
- Save the Children

Advocacy Organizations
- Global Health Council
- The ONE Campaign
- RESULTS

Technical Organizations
- International Union Against TB and Lung Disease
- KNCV—The Dutch Tuberculosis Foundation
- U.S. Centers for Disease Control and Prevention

Consulting Firms
- Abt Associates
- FHI
- HLSP
- JSI
- PSI

University-Affiliated Programs
- Department of Global Health and Development, London School of Hygiene and Tropical Medicine
- Global Health Leadership Institute, Yale University
- Harvard Institute for Global Health, Harvard University
- Institute for Health Metrics and Evaluation, University of Washington
- Institute for Global Health and Infectious Diseases, University of North Carolina

Think Tanks
- Center for Global Development
- Results for Development Institute

Human Right Organizations
- Amnesty International
- Human Rights Watch
- Physicians for Human Rights

They might be involved in the setting of technical standards or the provision of technical assistance. In addition, they might provide financing for health efforts. Generally, these organizations work along a continuum, engaging in one or more of the listed activities, but often specializing in only a few of them. When reviewing Table 15-1, readers should also be aware that some of the organizations could be placed into more than one category. The Center for Global Development, for example, does important advocacy work, as well as research on global health policy.

Because of the enormity of the topic, this chapter can only be introductory. It is meant to provide an overview of the main types of actors in global health. It is largely descriptive and outlines the stated aims of the organizations that it covers. This chapter does not look critically at these organizations. Students interested in a more critical view may consult the extensive literature that is available on each of these organizations.[9–12]

Agencies of the United Nations

A number of United Nations (UN) agencies work on health and focus on a specific set of public health concerns. Among the most important are the World Health Organization (WHO), the United Nations Children's Fund (UNICEF), the United Nations Population Fund (UNFPA), and the United Nations Development Program (UNDP). This section will examine the three UN agencies most involved in health: the World Health Organization, the United Nations Children's Fund, and UNAIDS.

The World Health Organization

The World Health Organization (WHO) was established in 1948 and is the United Nations agency that is responsible for health.[13] The headquarters of WHO is located in Geneva, Switzerland, and WHO employs about 8000 people, including experts on many health topics. The World Health Organization has offices located in each region of the world, with special responsibility for work within that geographic area, as shown in Table 15-2. In addition, WHO has 147 country offices.[13]

The objective of WHO is to promote "the attainment by all peoples of the highest possible level of health."[13] In pursuit of this goal, WHO largely focuses its attention on the following:

- Advocacy and consensus building for various health causes, such as HIV and TB.
- Generating and sharing health knowledge across countries, through studies, reports, conferences, and other forums. The publication of the *World Health*

Report on a different topic of global health importance each year is an example of this work.
- Carrying out selected critical public health functions within an international forum, such as the surveillance of epidemics, including influenza, or the outbreak of potentially dangerous diseases, such as Ebola. This also includes, for example, WHO certification of quality standards for the manufacturing of vaccines and pharmaceuticals.
- Setting global standards on key health matters, such as appropriate regimens for drug therapy for leprosy, TB, and HIV.
- Leading the development of international agreements and conventions, such as the Framework Convention on Tobacco Control and the International Health Regulations.
- The provision of technical assistance to its member states, such as helping China to contain the outbreak of SARS or assistance to countries in managing their child vaccine programs.
- Serving as the secretariat of a number of cooperative efforts, such as Stop TB, Roll Back Malaria, and the Tropical Disease Research Program.

WHO is primarily a technical agency that engages in advocacy and the generation and sharing of knowledge. It also plays critical roles in the setting of technical standards and norms. Although WHO does have relatively small country budgets to assist in the financing of selected health projects in low- and middle-income countries, it is not a financing agency. Rather, the work that WHO does both globally and in particular countries is largely financed with assistance from high-income countries.

WHO is governed through its annual World Health Assembly, which sets policy, reviews and approves the bud-

TABLE 15-2 WHO Regional Offices

Regional Office	Location
The Americas	Washington, DC, USA
Europe	Copenhagen, Denmark
North Africa and the Middle East	Alexandria, Egypt
Sub-Saharan Africa	Harare, Zimbabwe
Southeast Asia	Delhi, India
Western Pacific	Manila, Philippines

Source: Data from World Health Organization. About WHO. Available at: http://www.who.int/about/en. Accessed November 3, 2006.

Key Actors in Global Health

get, and appoints the Director-General of the organization. Voting power at the WHO Health Assembly is based on the principle of "one country–one vote." The overall budget of WHO comes from membership subscriptions and from special donations, again, mostly from better-off countries.

WHO has helped lead some of the world's most important cooperative efforts in health, including the "Health for All" program[14] that began with the Declaration of Alma Ata on primary health care. WHO also led the world's smallpox eradication campaign, has played a major role in efforts to expand the coverage of immunization for children in low- and middle-income countries, and is one of the leaders of the world's global polio eradication program. More recently, WHO has been instrumental in helping to address issues of tobacco control. WHO also leads the global surveillance of disease and has played an active role in work on avian flu, H1N1 influenza, SARS, and other new and emerging diseases, such as the Ebola virus. There is an extensive literature on WHO for those who are interested in understanding it in greater detail.

UNICEF

The United Nations Children's Fund was established in 1946 by the UN to respond to the effects of World War II on children in Europe and China. UNICEF is headquartered in New York but has offices in 190 countries.[15] The main function of UNICEF is to enhance the health and well-being of children. In these efforts, UNICEF has been deeply involved in the promotion of family planning, antenatal care, and safe motherhood practices.

UNICEF is involved in a wide range of activities in support of its mission, including advocacy, knowledge generation and knowledge sharing, and the financing of investments in health. In addition, UNICEF works closely with other development partners such as WHO and the World Bank to help raise the health status of poor women and children globally. UNICEF has carried out significant programs in a number of areas. Traditionally, it has been involved in major ways in nutrition and early childhood development issues, in which it is generally considered the world's leader. Immunization and child survival have also been areas of deep UNICEF involvement. In addition, UNICEF has been a major supporter of primary education, especially for poor girls in low- and middle-income countries. More recently, UNICEF has paid particular attention to child protection, child rights, and HIV/AIDS. UNICEF is also deeply involved in emergency relief work.[16] UNICEF has an Executive Board of 36 members who guide all UNICEF work and administration under the leadership of the Executive Director. All of UNICEF's funding is from voluntary contributions. Governments provide

two thirds of funding while 37 National Committees, consisting of private entities and millions of individuals, raise the remaining third. These National Committees are non-governmental organizations (NGOs) that advocate for children, sell UNICEF products, and fundraise through several well-known campaigns, such as "Check out for Children" in grocery stores, "Change for Good" on airplanes, and "Trick or Treat for UNICEF" on Halloween.[17] UNICEF's total expenditure in 2009 was about $3.3 billion.[18]

UNAIDS

In 1996, six agencies joined forces to launch UNAIDS—the Joint United Nations Program on HIV/AIDS. Today, as shown in Table 15-3, there are 10 co-sponsors for UNAIDS.[19] The UNAIDS budget was about $500 million in 2009. Funding was contributed to UNAIDS over that period by 33 governments and the World Bank.[20]

UNAIDS is based in Geneva, Switzerland, has offices in more than 70 countries, and is guided by a Program Coordinating Board that consists of 22 representatives from country governments, its co-sponsors, and 5 NGOs.

UNAIDS is the global agency with primary responsibility for dealing with HIV/AIDS. UNAIDS monitors and evaluates the epidemic and the world's response to it. It also advocates on behalf of the epidemic and engages civil society, the private sector, and development partners in the fight against HIV/AIDS. In addition, UNAIDS generates and shares knowledge, sets standards, and mobilizes resources. UNAIDS focuses its attention on the regions of the world most affected by HIV/AIDS, particularly sub-Saharan Africa.[21]

TABLE 15-3 UNAIDS Co-Sponsors

- International Labor Organization
- Office of the United Nations High Commissioner for Refugees
- UNICEF
- United Nations Development Program
- United Nations Educational, Scientific, and Cultural Organization
- United Nations Population Fund
- United Nations Office on Drugs and Crime
- World Bank
- World Food Program
- World Health Organization

Source: UNAIDS. Available at: http://www.unaids.org/en/AboutUNAIDS/Cosponsors_about/default.asp. Accessed November 3, 2006.

Another important emphasis of the work of UNAIDS is to assist countries in developing and implementing national AIDS plans. Technical experts from UNAIDS also help countries build their technical and institutional capacity and mobilize resources to fight against HIV/AIDS. UNAIDS, for example, assists countries in preparing applications for funding from the Global Fund to Fight AIDS, TB, and Malaria, which is discussed further later.[21]

UNAIDS is engaged in a range of HIV/AIDS activities. First, UNAIDS works with countries to strengthen their surveillance of the epidemic. Second, UNAIDS continues to put an important emphasis on prevention of HIV. Third, UNAIDS is also increasingly involved in efforts to increase the number of HIV-positive people worldwide who are treated with antiretroviral therapy. UNAIDS has a particular concern for the extent to which the epidemic affects females. In addition, UNAIDS cooperates with others in the search for technologies, such as microbicides and vaccines, that might be able to help halt the epidemic.

Multilateral Development Banks

There are a number of development banks that lend or grant money to developing countries and economies in transition to help promote their economic and social development. These banks are owned by all of their member countries and they are referred to as "multilateral." These institutions have some characteristics of real banks; however, these banks do not function to earn money through their lending operations. Rather, their main focus is to serve as a financial intermediary. Essentially, they channel financial resources from more developed countries and their people through bond sales and grants to help finance development activities in low- and middle-income countries and countries that are making the transition to more open, market-based economies. All of these banks are involved in work on health, to some degree, but the ones most involved are the African Development Bank, the Asian Development Bank, the Inter-American Development Bank, and the World Bank.

Among the multilateral development banks, the World Bank is the largest, has the broadest scope of activities, and is the most involved in health.[22] The World Bank is located in Washington, D.C., and is "owned" by 187 member countries. The stated aim of the World Bank is to assist countries in improving the lives of their people and reducing poverty. It seeks to do this by helping them to strengthen the management of their economy and to finance investments in selected areas, including agriculture, transport, private sector development, health, and education. The World Bank lends money at reduced rates to countries with per capita

incomes above a certain point, lends money interest free to the poorest countries, and also provides grants to some countries for special activities that affect the poor, such as HIV/AIDS. Total lending from the World Bank was about $60 billion in 2009. This was a substantial increase from $40 billion the year before, engendered partly by the global economic crisis. The World Bank has about 10,000 staff that work in Washington and in a large number of other country offices.[23,24]

In its health work, the World Bank carries out a wide range of functions. It advocates on behalf of important causes, generates and disseminates information and knowledge about key health issues, provides technical assistance to countries, and finances specific investments in health and related work in nutrition and family planning. The World Bank focuses its health work largely on the links between health and poverty. It pays considerable attention to health financing and the development of health systems. The World Bank has also emphasized investments in nutrition, maternal and child health, HIV/AIDS, malaria, and TB.

The World Bank is also a partner in a number of global health initiatives, including GAVI, Stop TB, Roll Back Malaria, and UNAIDS. In addition, the World Bank has provided financing to other initiatives, such as the International AIDS Vaccine Initiative (IAVI). The World Bank provided about $18 billion for the health sector between 1997 and 2008. World Bank lending for health in 2009 was about $2.9 billion. This was nearly three times more than the previous year, also largely a result of special efforts to help countries deal with the global financial crisis.[25] Until the advent of the Bill & Melinda Gates Foundation and the Global Fund to Fight AIDS, TB, and Malaria, the World Bank was, for many years, the largest provider of development financing for health. Those interested in a more analytical assessment of the World Bank's work both generally and in health can consult extensive literature on those subjects.

Bilateral Agencies

Another set of organizations that are very actively involved in global health are bilateral agencies. These are mostly the development assistance agencies of developed countries that work directly with developing countries to help them enhance the health of their people. Some of the bilateral development agencies that are most involved in the health sector are shown in Table 15-4.

USAID is the development assistance agency of the U.S. federal government. USAID promotes U.S. foreign policy goals by advancing economic and social development all over the world. USAID works with other governments and with universities, businesses, international agencies, and NGOs to support its development assistance efforts. In the health field, USAID engages in a wide variety of activities, including advocacy for global health, the generation and sharing of knowledge, and the financing of health investments.

USAID is headquartered in Washington, D.C., and has regional field offices for sub-Saharan Africa, Asia and the Near East, Latin America and the Caribbean, and Europe and Eurasia. In addition to these geographic bureaus, USAID has functional bureaus for Economic Growth, Agriculture and Trade, Democracy, Conflict Prevention and Humanitarian Assistance, and Global Health. USAID has offices in many countries, especially poorer countries in Africa, Asia, and Latin America.

USAID's Bureau for Global Health aims to improve health services and enhance the health status of poor and disadvantaged people, particularly in poorer countries. USAID focuses its health work on maternal and child health, HIV/AIDS, other communicable diseases, family planning and reproductive health, nutrition, and health systems. For these purposes, USAID provides grants and technical expertise to other governments, NGOs, and the private sector. In supporting the development of health in other countries, USAID collaborates with other development assistance agencies.[26]

In the 1970s and 1980s, USAID helped support research to develop a number of interventions that are key to saving the lives of poor children in poorer countries, including oral rehydration therapy, vitamin A supplementation, and immunizations. USAID has also been very supportive of efforts to address malaria, TB, HIV/AIDS, and, most recently, neglected tropical diseases. Traditionally, USAID has also been very involved in supporting family planning.

Foundations

Global health is an area in which foundations have been involved for almost a century. Many of the largest foundations support health efforts, including, for example, the Ford, Hewlitt, MacArthur, Packard, and Soros Foundations. The Rockefeller Foundation has been among the foundations most involved in global health. The Wellcome Trust has also been engaged in global health activities, primarily through support for scientific research, for more than 70 years. More recently, the UN Foundation was established with a focus on health. The Clinton Foundation and the Bill & Melinda Gates Foundation have become major actors in the global health arena. This section comments briefly on the health work of the Rockefeller and Gates Foundations, and the Wellcome Trust.

TABLE 15-4 Selected Bilateral Development Assistance Agencies Involved in Global Health

Australian Agency for International Development
Canadian International Development Agency
Danish International Development Agency
Department for International Development of the United
    Kingdom
Dutch Agency for Development Cooperation
United States Agency for International Development

The Rockefeller Foundation

The Rockefeller Foundation is based in New York City and has regional offices in San Francisco, California, Bangkok, Thailand, and Nairobi, Kenya. The foundation aims to "enrich and sustain the lives and livelihoods of poor and excluded people throughout the world."[27] In the health field, the foundation seeks to "reduce avoidable unfair differences in the health status of populations."[27]

The Rockefeller Foundation has focused considerable attention on the development of knowledge and technology that can be applied to addressing the conditions that most affect the health of the poor globally. The Rockefeller Foundation was instrumental in establishing the first schools of public health in the United States and was also deeply involved in the development of a vaccine against yellow fever. The Rockefeller Foundation does finance a small number of activities in health every year. However, its strength as an organization is the way in which it uses a relatively small amount of money to invest in the generation of knowledge that can make an important difference to the health of the poor globally.

More recently, the Rockefeller Foundation has focused its attention in the health field in three areas. First, the foundation established the framework for developing partnerships between the public and private sector to meet key health needs that had been neglected. In line with this work, the foundation was instrumental in establishing the first and then a number of additional public–private partnerships for health, including the International AIDS Vaccine Initiative, the International Partnership on Microbicides, and the Global Alliance for TB Drug Development. Second, it has tried to help better understand the problems that HIV/AIDS inflicts on families and how they might deal with those problems. Third, the foundation has helped to "strengthen the production, deployment, and empowerment" of key human resources needed for delivering health services in poor countries.[27]

Most recently, the Rockefeller Foundation has highlighted two global health initiatives. The first aims at strengthening health systems by supporting research on universal coverage and insurance, the training of high-level staff to plan and manage health systems, better linking the private sector to the financing and delivery of health services, and using new technologies to improve health systems. The foundation also aims at strengthening disease surveillance. It hopes to establish disease surveillance networks in Southeast Asia and East and Southern Africa, strengthen the capacity of institutions engaged in surveillance, support the development of better surveillance tools, and ensure that those working on surveillance work across disciplines, including public health, veterinary sciences, and the environment.[28]

The Wellcome Trust

The Wellcome Trust was founded in London in 1936 with the vision of improving human and animal health through research. Its mission is to "support the brightest minds in biomedical research and the medical humanities."[29] It is the second largest charitable foundation in the world, behind the Bill & Melinda Gates Foundation. The trust spends about $1.1 billion annually on charitable projects,[30] compared to about $3 billion spent by the Gates Foundation.[31]

Although a majority of the 3000 independent researchers funded by the Wellcome Trust conduct their work in the United Kingdom, the foundation funds programs in more than 40 countries.[32] Research is conducted either at independent institutions or institutes created by the foundation, and encompasses a wide array of health-related matters, ranging from biomedicine to the ethics of healthcare policy and delivery. The foundation is particularly well known for sequencing one third of the human genome, which has significantly enhanced our understanding of the genes associated with disease. In addition, research funded by the Wellcome Trust has uncovered genetic links to cancer and diabetes, paving the way for future treatments.

Out of the £720.4 million spent between 2008 and 2009 on grants, direct funding for activities, and support,[30] about 15 percent went toward funding research in low- and middle-income countries.[33] Focusing its international initiatives mainly in sub-Saharan Africa, South Asia, and central Europe, the foundation supports research in public health, including communicable and noncommunicable diseases, health services, health systems, and policy. Research in infectious diseases is also supported, specifically neglected tropical

diseases, animal health, and emerging infections. Both clinical and biomedical research is conducted. Malaria receives the most funding of any infectious disease, with £100 million invested over the past 10 years.[33]

The Wellcome Trust has a strong track record in research for antimalarial drugs. In the early 1990s, scientists developed and tested the drug artemisinin in Vietnam and Thailand, which significantly decreased malaria mortality and the incidence of malaria. This drug is now the standard treatment for malaria, when used in combination with other antimalarial drugs.

In addition to funding biomedical research, the Wellcome Trust seeks to improve research facilities and "broaden the base for scientific endeavors" from low-income countries.[34] For example, £28 million was invested from 2008–2009 in the African Institutions Initiative, which funds over 50 scientific institutions in 18 African countries.[30] In addition, £10 million was invested in improving Kenya and Malawi's research and health policy-making institutions, in partnership with the UK Department for International Development and International Development Research Centre, Canada.[35] In doing so, the goal of the Wellcome Trust is to improve the capacity of low-income countries to do research and make informed health policy decisions.[35]

The Bill & Melinda Gates Foundation

The most substantial change in many years in the key actors involved in global health has been the advent of the Bill & Melinda Gates Foundation. The Gates Foundation is based in the United States in Seattle, Washington. The main aims of the foundation in the health field are to help spread known technologies for improving health, such as immunization, to the places where they are most needed. At the same time, the foundation seeks to encourage the development of new technologies that can meet the major health needs of the poor globally. The foundation hopes to meet these aims by "supporting discoveries and inventions essential to solving major global health problems, supporting the development and testing of specific tools and technologies, and helping to ensure that new health interventions and technologies are adopted in the developing world."[36]

The foundation supports programs in three cross-cutting theme areas:

- *Discovery:* Filling gaps in scientific knowledge and developing new technologies
- *Delivery:* Ensuring that proven approaches and technologies get delivered at scale
- *Policy and Advocacy:* Promoting the more effective and efficient use of resources

As it focuses on these thematic areas, the foundation also focuses on a number of specific issues that concern the health of the poor in low- and middle-income countries:

- Nutrition
- Maternal health and family planning
- Neonatal and child health
- Infectious diseases—HIV, TB, malaria, pneumonia, neglected diseases, and diarrheal diseases
- Vaccine-preventable diseases
- Tobacco[37]

The foundation also supports the Grand Challenges in Global Health, which are discussed further in Chapter 16.

In support of these areas, and in addition to the substantial funding that the foundation has provided for scientific discovery, the foundation has been a supporter of an array of organizations, programs, and projects. The foundation has been a major supporter, for example, of public–private partnerships for health since their inception, and has funded, among others, Aeras, IAVI, the Human Hookworm Vaccine Initiative, and the International Partnership on Microbicides. The foundation has provided considerable funding, as well, for reproductive health issues, such as a $60 million grant that it provided to Johns Hopkins University to improve reproductive health globally. More recently, the foundation has supported major efforts in nutrition, with a focus on breast-feeding, micronutrients, and bio-fortification. The foundation was an early supporter of efforts to "save newborn lives," partly through funding to Save the Children. In addition, the Gates Foundation has been a major and continuous financier of GAVI and the Global Fund. The foundation has also financed a major program to address HIV/AIDS in India.[38]

The foundation is now one of the largest providers of financing for global health efforts. At the end of 2009, the Gates Foundation had an endowment of about $33 billion. From its establishment in 1994 until 2009, the foundation provided about $13.2 billion for global health activities. In 2009, the foundation provided about $1.8 billion for global health efforts.[39]

Research Funders

There are a number of organizations whose primary function is to carry out and fund research, some of which focuses on issues in global health. Although it is a foundation, the Wellcome Trust fits into this category. Funding research is also central to the work of the Gates Foundation. The Howard Hughes Medical Research Institute in the United States and the Institut Pasteur in France are also foundations that are deeply involved in medical research. However, many of the

organizations focused on conducting and funding research are supported by national governments. The largest of these is the U.S. National Institutes of Health (NIH). Others include the National Health and Medical Research Council of Australia, the Canadian Institutes of Health Research, the Chinese Academy of Medical Sciences, the South African Medical Council, and the Medical Research Council of the United Kingdom. Some comments follow on the work in global health of the U.S. National Institutes of Health.

The U.S. National Institutes of Health[40]

The National Institutes of Health, part of the U.S. Department of Health and Human Services, is the primary federal agency for conducting and supporting medical research to improve human health. NIH fulfills its mission by performing biomedical and behavioral research in its own laboratories, supporting research conducted by scientists at major academic and research institutions in the United States and around the world, supporting the training of research investigators, and fostering communication of medical and health sciences information.

Research in global health is an integral part of the NIH agenda and one of five priorities for the Institutes. As part of these efforts, NIH has called for increasing its efforts in neglected tropical diseases and in noncommunicable diseases. NIH has also emphasized the need to build local research capacity in low- and middle-income countries.

NIH-funded research, conducted both in the United States and in other countries, has yielded numerous discoveries with global health impact. For example, NIH has supported studies that have aided efforts to thwart HIV/AIDS. These have included research on the effectiveness of male circumcision in the prevention of HIV transmission, simplified HIV combination antiretroviral therapies, and the use of nevirapine for prevention of mother-to-child transmission. During the 2009 H1N1 pandemic, NIH scientists played a crucial role in understanding the epidemiology of the H1N1 virus, which led to recommendations that influenza vaccination be targeted at young-to-middle-age adults. Studies conducted in Tanzania and South Africa demonstrated that unless drug treatment for tuberculosis is properly administered, tuberculosis can evolve rapidly to become resistant to available drugs. Another NIH-funded study conducted in Nigeria identified three genes that contribute to high fatality rates and insensitivity to treatment of breast cancer in African women compared with Caucasian women.

NIH has provided substantial support to scientific institutions in low- and middle-income countries that have emerged as research hubs in their own region. For example, in 1983, NIH began funding GHESKIO, a Haitian nongovernmental organization dedicated to clinical service, research, and training in HIV/AIDS and related diseases. In leading Haiti's response to the HIV/AIDS epidemic, GHESKIO is making significant contributions to the understanding of clinical presentation, epidemiology, and transmission of AIDS in that country, as well as in implementation of evidence-based models of care.

Similarly, NIH has supported the International Centre for Diarrhoeal Disease Research, Bangladesh (ICDDR,B) for more than four decades. ICDDR,B is a pioneer nonprofit organization that conducts research and is credited, among other things, with developing oral rehydration therapy, which has been used to treat millions with diarrheal disease. In addition, the center has trained more than 20,000 researchers over the past 20 years.

Through the NIH Visiting Program, approximately 3800 foreign scientists conduct research and receive research training every year at NIH. The Institutes also support training programs that educate scientists from developing countries to conduct health research relevant to their country, primarily through collaborative programs between research institutions in the United States and abroad.

In fiscal years 2004 and 2005, NIH invested about $600 million in global health research, of which $185 million was invested in low- and middle-income countries.

Those wanting a more critical look at research funding for global health can consult the extensive literature on the conduct and financing of research to address the burden of disease in low- and middle-income countries. There is also a Global Forum for Health Research that pays particular attention to this matter.

Nongovernmental Organizations

There are thousands of NGOs in the world today that have as one of their primary aims the improvement of the health of poor people in low- and middle-income countries. Most of these organizations raise money from private sources or receive grants from governments or global health partnerships that they help to invest in activities that address important health issues, such as improving the availability of clean water, strengthening nutrition and immunization programs, or enhancing programs for the treatment of TB and HIV. Some of the organizations are small and focus their attention on only a limited number of activities. Other organizations are very large, comprehensive in the topics they cover, and global in their reach. Some NGOs are completely secular, whereas others are faith-based. Some of the most important NGOs that operate internationally on health are listed in Table 15-5.

TABLE 15-5 Selected Nongovernmental Organizations Involved in Global Health

BRAC
CARE
Catholic Relief Services
Doctors Without Borders
Oxfam
Partners in Health
Save the Children
World Vision

Some additional comments are provided in the following sections on BRAC, Doctors Without Borders, Oxfam, and Save the Children, which are four of the most important NGOs that work on health globally. These are just a few examples of the hundreds of large NGOs and thousands of small NGOs that are involved in health efforts in low- and middle-income countries.

BRAC

BRAC was founded in Bangladesh in 1972. It is the largest NGO in the world that is involved in international development work, reaching 110 million people through its staff and volunteers.[41] With the mission "to empower people and communities in situations of poverty, illiteracy, disease, and social injustice," BRAC is currently working in several countries in Asia and Africa, including Afghanistan, Bangladesh, Pakistan, Sri Lanka, Liberia, Sierra Leone, Southern Sudan, Tanzania, and Uganda.[42]

BRAC was originally responsible for relief projects for refugees in rural northeastern Bangladesh but eventually turned its focus toward long-term development work. Its most established programs are in Bangladesh; however, the organization launched international initiatives in Asia in 2002 and in Africa in 2006.[43] BRAC works in the areas of "human rights and social empowerment, education and health, economic empowerment and enterprise development, livelihood training, environmental sustainability and disaster preparedness."[44] In all its initiatives, women and children are the priority.

BRAC spent nearly $535 million on its projects in 2008,[45] of which about $30 million was for its health and population programs.[45] The main goals of its health initiatives are to "improve maternal, neonatal and child health and decrease vulnerability to communicable diseases and common ailments."[46] Water and sanitation, family planning, immunization, obstetric care, basic services, and education for nutrition and health are some of the health issues BRAC targets. Additionally, the organization seeks to provide prevention and treatment for tuberculosis, malaria, pneumonia, and other common illnesses.[47]

BRAC seeks to improve the health of women and children in Bangladesh through a variety of approaches. The organization has created birthing centers for women living in slums and initiated programs to promote exclusive breastfeeding and timely introduction of complementary foods.[48] In addition, BRAC works in partnership with the Bangladeshi government to assist with national distribution of vitamin A supplements and information about family planning.[47] Shushasthyas, or health centers, have also been established since 1995, in which patients can receive consultation, basic inpatient services, laboratory tests, and medications. Nine of these health centers have more advanced capabilities, including emergency obstetric and neonatal care, minor surgeries, and other testing procedures.[49] BRAC is particularly well known for its success in decreasing infant mortality in Bangladesh due to diarrheal disease, made possible through its Oral Therapy Extension Programme introduced in 1980 and discussed in Chapter 5.

Trained healthcare workers are the force behind BRAC's malaria and tuberculosis control programs in Bangladesh. These workers cover an area that includes 88.5 million people[41] in 42 districts in Bangladesh.[50] Health workers are trained to provide directly observed therapy for TB and to diagnose malaria through a "rapid diagnostic test" and then administer malaria treatment, as appropriate.[50]

BRAC's health initiatives in other countries include home visits by trained community health workers (CHWs) and community health volunteers (CHVs) who can provide basic health services and education about common illnesses, modeled after the system used in Bangladesh, in which home visitors educated families about diarrheal disease treatment. In Pakistan, CHVs visit households to sell healthcare products covered under insurance. CHVs are trained to diagnose and treat common illnesses, recommend how to get further care, and educate the family about health threats such as malaria, diarrhea, and polio. CHVs also encourage families to use government services available to them. Each CHW oversees 10 CHVs, who are each responsible for 150 homes and visiting 8–10 households each day.[51]

This model has also been adopted for BRAC's initiatives in Africa. In Liberia, 40 CHWs and 197 CHVs were trained in 2009.[52] In Uganda, 240,000 families receive home visits each month, which amounts to contact with over 1.6 million people.[53]

Afghanistan is the second largest of BRAC's programs, reaching 24 million[54] people in 25 out of 34 provinces in 2008.[55] In partnership with the Afghan Ministry of Public Health, BRAC trained health workers, called community health promoters, who are meant to drive the delivery of essential health services to the people through home visits. Drawing upon years of experience with this model of health care and education, BRAC-supported efforts in Afghanistan are reaching over 500,000 families each month. These trained health workers focus primarily on encouraging use of family planning and community health initiatives and providing reproductive health care, malaria control, TB control, and other basic services.[54]

Over 73 percent of BRAC's expenditures on its programs in 2008 were paid for by earnings from its microfinance program, as well as its social enterprises, which create jobs for poor people in local communities and provide production or marketing support for the enterprises of its microfinance clients. BRAC's social enterprises include selling handicrafts, dairy products, agricultural products, and printing supplies, among other goods. Some enterprises produce a commodity that will aid in improving the health of the community, such as iodized salt in Bangladesh. BRAC's enterprises had combined sales of $105 million and a total net surplus of $8.6 million in 2008.[56] Donors contributed to 27 percent of the organization's expenditures in 2008, or $146 million. More than half of all donations were split between the Netherlands Organization for International Development Cooperation and DFID.[45]

Doctors Without Borders

Doctors Without Borders was founded in 1971 and is based in Brussels, Belgium. It is an umbrella organization made up of affiliated groups in 18 countries.[57] The groups located in Belgium, France, Holland, Spain, and Switzerland carry out health work in more than 80 countries. Doctors Without Borders, usually referred to by its French name, Médicins Sans Frontières, or by the abbreviation of that name, MSF, is best known for its work in humanitarian crises. It has often been involved in the provision of health services following natural disasters, such as earthquakes and hurricanes, or those humanitarian emergencies related to war and famine.[58] MSF, for example, assisted Nicaragua after an earthquake, Ethiopia during a famine, and Somalia after a war. MSF has also been extensively engaged in health services for refugees and displaced people. In addition, when health services have been severely weakened due to war or conflict, MSF often helps to provide health services temporarily, while trying to help rebuild health system capacity. One example of this was in Liberia after its civil war.

MSF is also well known for its commitment to political independence, medical ethics, and human rights. Related to this, MSF has increasingly sought to become a voice in international health policy arenas for the disenfranchised. More recently, MSF has also become very involved with prevention, care, and treatment for HIV/AIDS. In this work, MSF has helped to mobilize international support for antiretroviral therapy in poor countries and has become a leader in trying to lower the price of those drugs.[58]

Oxfam

Oxfam International was founded in 1995 as a confederation of 14 member organizations from around the world, with its largest and original office located in Oxford, United Kingdom. Working in nearly 100 countries in partnership with over 3000 local organizations, Oxfam's stated mission is to "overcome poverty and injustice" by providing health, education, and economic opportunities to poor and marginalized groups.[59]

Oxfam supports long-term development programs in local communities, all of which share the goal of improving the rights of the poor, with a specific focus on women. For example, the organization works with local partners in Cuba to create jobs for women and enhance food security by building greenhouses and nurseries where women can work. In addition, women are taught leadership skills so they can take on more powerful positions in the community.[60]

Oxfam provides emergency relief for natural disasters and conflict in over 30 countries, with an emphasis on providing clean water, sanitation, and shelter to reduce death and disease. Improving hygiene and providing food and basic necessities are the organization's primary goals in emergency situations.

Oxfam is also deeply involved in health work. It has a particular interest in HIV/AIDS and works with local partners on prevention and treatment, in addition to combating stigma and discrimination surrounding the disease. Oxfam also advocates on behalf of access to health care. To address this goal, Oxfam supports improvement in public sector health services, largely by seeking to increase the number of healthcare facilities and trained workers, improve quality, and lower costs. An important part of this effort includes advocating with donor governments and drug companies to lower costs and improve quality of medicines delivered to low-income countries. In the past, Oxfam has also invested in water supply and sanitation in poor countries to improve health and in agriculture to enhance food security.

Oxfam also works on the international policy front on issues that affect poor and marginalized populations. One of Oxfam's major goals, for example, is to provide a voice for small producers to fight for trade rules that open markets. In addition, the organization advocates for the rights of indigenous and minority groups by campaigning for equal access to jobs and essential services, reform of discriminatory laws, and expanded opportunities for leadership roles from members of their communities.

Not including management costs, Oxfam spent $771.75 million during 2007–2008 on its development and humanitarian response projects.[60]

Save the Children

Save the Children was established in 1932 in New York City by a group of people who wanted to help meet the needs of poor people in the Appalachian region of the United States who had been hurt by an economic depression. Today, it is part of an international alliance of related organizations and is one of the largest NGOs in the world. One affiliate of Save the Children is based in the United States in Westport, Connecticut. It is actively involved in relief and development work in a number of areas in health. Save the Children focuses its attention on working with poor families and communities to identify their most important health and development needs. It then addresses these needs in ways that seek to contribute to individual and community self-sufficiency.[61]

Save the Children (U.S.) is involved in efforts to improve health in more than 30 countries, focusing on community-based efforts for poor and disadvantaged people. The health work of Save the Children also pays particular attention to the survival and well-being of newborns and children, reproductive health, and HIV/AIDS. "Saving Newborn Lives," as noted earlier, is an initiative of Save the Children that is financed with the assistance of the Bill & Melinda Gates Foundation. This effort tries to identify and disseminate simple approaches to preventing deaths among newborn children.[62] Save the Children is also deeply involved in nutrition through food relief, enhancing agricultural production, and specific investments in nutrition education and food and micronutrient supplementation.

Advocacy Organizations

A number of organizations advocate on behalf of global health issues and financing as a primary or major focus. Generally, these organizations carry out research and policy studies and then use these and evidence generated by others to carry out advocacy activities for key stakeholders, including the public at large, funding agencies, and national legislatures and governments. Many of these organizations are membership organizations, in whole or in part. Some of these organizations may be aligned with a specific issue, such as the many organizations of this type that focus on HIV. This includes for example, the International AIDS Alliance and the AIDS Vaccine Advocacy Coalition. Others may work on a cluster of issues, such as communicable diseases. The Global Network on Neglected Tropical Diseases, as another example, focuses an important part of its work on advocacy but also helps to raise funds to address NTDs and coordinates some NTD efforts. Other advocacy organizations, however, address a broader range of global health topics. Examples of the better-known advocacy organizations that address a range of issues are the ONE Campaign, RESULTS, and the Global Health Council. Additional comments on the Global Network for Neglected Tropical Diseases and the Global Health Council are given in the policy and program briefs section of this chapter.

Think Tanks and Universities

A number of organizations focus at least part of their efforts on generating knowledge about key issues in global health. Among the best-known of these is the Center for Global Development, based in Washington, D.C. The Center has a number of staff that are experts in various global health topics. The Center carries out an extensive research program on global health, publishes widely on global health matters, and hosts and participates in a wide array of seminars to disseminate the information that it has generated. The Results for Development Institute, also in Washington, D.C., is another think tank, and is becoming actively involved in research on policy and program issues in global health. It has recently carried out important work, for example, on the long-term financing of HIV.

As interest in global health has spread and the financing for global health has increased, many universities throughout the world have become more involved in teaching, research, and practice on global health issues. Many universities with a public health school, and even some without, have created "centers" or "institutes" that bring researchers together from different parts of the university to work on global health. Yale University, for example, has a Global Health Leadership Institute under which it organizes many of its activities in global health. Harvard University has the Harvard Institute for Global Health, which is meant to play an important role in enabling Harvard's work on education and research in global health. Many universities also carry out considerable technical assistance for the design, monitoring, and evaluation of global health programs and projects; some universities have established what are essentially consulting firms to engage in this work.

Consulting Firms

A wide array of consulting firms engage in global health work, either as the main focus of their work or as an important part of their activities. Some of these firms are for-profit, such as Abt Associates and HLSP. Others, however, operate on a not-for-profit basis, such as FHI, JSI, and PSI. Some of the firms may have a broad range of expertise and be able to work, for example, on key management, economic, financing, or policy issues, as well as on critical health programs, such as maternal and child health or the control of communicable diseases. Others, however, have a particular area of expertise, such as supply chain management, nutrition, behavior change communication, or social marketing. Countries sometimes hire these firms directly; however, the majority of such services provided to low-income countries will be financed by development assistance agencies such as the World Bank, USAID, or DFID. In fact, a substantial share of the development assistance from some agencies, such as USAID, is channeled through technical assistance from consulting firms. The staff of consulting firms is often quite involved in policy work and in program design, monitoring, and evaluation, especially in low-income countries with limited technical capacity of their own.

Specialized Technical Organizations

A number of specialized governmental and nongovernmental technical organizations are important actors in global health. Perhaps the best known of these is the U.S. Centers for Disease Control and Prevention (CDC), based in Atlanta, Georgia, in the United States. The CDC is part of the U.S. Department of Health and Human Services. The CDC's mission is to:

> collaborate to create the expertise, information, and tools that people and communities need to protect their health—through health promotion, prevention of disease, injury and disability, and preparedness for new health threats."[63]

The CDC is deeply involved in helping the United States and other countries to plan and carry out disease surveillance and control, across a broad range of disease conditions. CDC staff, for example, collaborate with many countries in work on infectious disease control programs, such as those for HIV, TB, and malaria. In addition, CDC staff are often called upon to assist WHO and individual countries to identify disease threats and address them. This could be for outbreaks of dengue, the Ebola virus, the plague, or other diseases of national and international importance. The CDC has a team of field epidemiologists that are at the forefront of such work, and also provides extensive laboratory services to its collaborators. The CDC has also been very involved in technical assistance to build capacity in low- and middle-income countries for improved disease surveillance and control, including the strengthening of laboratories.

Two other specialized technical organizations of importance are both nongovernmental and work on TB. KNCV is the Dutch TB Foundation and is based in The Hague, the capital of the Netherlands.[64] KNCV aims to help address TB both in the Netherlands and in low- and middle-income countries by providing technical assistance in the development and implementation of TB control programs. The International Union Against Tuberculosis and Lung Disease (IUATLD), which is based in Paris, France, is a membership organization that is also deeply involved in TB control efforts.[65] The Union has a number of regional offices and works not only on TB, but also on lung health more broadly. Both KNCV and the Union have staff with high levels of expertise in all aspects of TB control. Both have been deeply involved in helping many countries to address TB more effectively and efficiently and to build national capacity for addressing TB in the future.

Partnerships Related to WHO

Some global health problems affect an exceptional number of people in a large number of countries. The costs of addressing these problems are great and the skills needed to combat them are substantial. Most of the resource-poor countries cannot tackle these problems without aid, and no individual development partner can provide enough assistance to help deal effectively with the scale of these problems. Therefore, a number of organizations have decided to work together to help address some of the most important burdens of disease. Some of the partnerships that have ensued are closely related to WHO, as noted in Table 15-6. Two of the most important such partnerships are Stop TB and Roll Back Malaria.

Stop TB

The Global Partnership to Stop TB was established in 2000. It aims to "eliminate TB as a public health problem, and ultimately, to obtain a world free of TB."[66] Stop TB is composed of a wide array of partners including countries, development agencies, private sector organizations, and NGOs. WHO plays a prominent role in Stop TB, and the secretariat for the partnership is housed at WHO headquarters in Geneva, Switzerland. The primary goals of Stop TB have been to ensure that 70 percent of the people in the world with TB will be diagnosed, that 85 percent of them will be cured, and that by 2015 the burden of TB disease will be cut in half. The

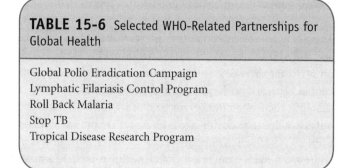

TABLE 15-6 Selected WHO-Related Partnerships for Global Health

Global Polio Eradication Campaign
Lymphatic Filariasis Control Program
Roll Back Malaria
Stop TB
Tropical Disease Research Program

partnership tries to encourage the wider use of effective TB strategies, such as DOTS, including those for dealing with HIV/TB co-infection and drug-resistant TB. It also works to promote the development of new TB diagnostics, drugs, and vaccines. Stop TB engages in advocacy and technical assistance, and helps to mobilize funding for the fight against TB.[66]

Roll Back Malaria

Roll Back Malaria was founded in 1998 by WHO, UNICEF, and the World Bank to advocate for malaria control, to promote the development of better approaches and technologies for malaria containment, and to help finance and spread appropriate malaria control and treatment.[67] The partnership has expanded since then to include a variety of public and private actors in a number of countries. In these activities, they promote appropriate prevention and treatment of malaria. In addition, Roll Back Malaria has established a Malaria Medicines and Supplies Service. This aims to help resource-poor countries better organize and manage the procurement of supplies and medicines needed to manage effective malaria control.[68]

Other Partnerships and Special Programs

In the last decade, global partners have expressed considerable concern over a number of health issues that affect the poor. One has been the need to strengthen immunization programs for children and for pregnant women. Related to this has been a growing interest in trying to more quickly increase the use of several "newer vaccines" that have been used for some time in better-off countries but have only rarely been provided in poorer countries. In addition to this, there has been a growing fear that the pace of progress against HIV, TB, and malaria has been insufficient and that urgent and bold measures need to be taken to move more forcefully against these diseases. To address immunization more effectively, the Global Alliance for Vaccines and Immunisation

(GAVI) was established. The Global Fund to Fight AIDS, TB, and Malaria was established to make more rapid progress against HIV, TB, and malaria.

GAVI

GAVI is a partnership among public and private sector organizations that was established in 2000.[4] The founding partners of GAVI include WHO, UNICEF, and the World Bank. GAVI is based in Geneva, Switzerland. The Bill & Melinda Gates Foundation made a major grant to help establish GAVI and provide for its operations. The main aims of GAVI are to improve the ability of health systems to carry out immunization; raise rates of coverage in low-income countries of key vaccines; promote more rapid uptake of underused vaccines, such as hepatitis B, *Haemophilus influenzae* type b, and yellow fever; speed up the development of other vaccines of importance; and help countries ensure that vaccines are given safely.[69] GAVI has tried to improve global health work through two innovative approaches. The first is to tie its financing to the achievement of goals that are agreed to by the countries that are being helped. The second is to work closely with countries to develop plans to sustain the investments that are being supported. GAVI is an organization that advocates for the importance of immunization, provides technical assistance to countries to enhance their immunization efforts, and finances those efforts.

The Global Fund

The Global Fund to Fight AIDS, TB, and Malaria was also established in 2002 and is based in Geneva, Switzerland.[70] The driving force behind the establishment of the fund was increasing global concern about HIV and a growing recognition among development partners that measures to address the AIDS epidemic had been insufficient. Interest in establishing the Global Fund was also heightened by the growing attention to global health discussed hereafter, and a special concern for the exceptional burden of HIV, TB, and malaria, especially in Africa.[71]

The Global Fund is a partnership of the public and private sectors; WHO, UNAIDS, and the World Bank are also key partners. The Global Fund is governed by a board of directors that represents governments, international organizations, civil society, and communities affected by AIDS, TB, and malaria. The fund is financed by grants that come largely from high-income country governments, but which also come from the private and foundation sector, including the Bill & Melinda Gates Foundation.

The Global Fund is primarily a financing agency, but it also engages in advocacy and policy work for global health

and the three diseases on which it focuses. The main aim of the fund is to finance proposed investments in these diseases, with an emphasis on AIDS and Africa. It has a particular interest in helping to scale up programs for antiretroviral therapy against HIV. The fund has taken innovative approaches to a number of aspects of development assistance for health, including the following:

- It is strictly a financing mechanism and not a technical or implementing agency.
- It seeks to raise funds for investments that will be additional to other funding already available.
- It tries to work on the basis of a national plan that is developed by a group representing diverse national interests, for the use of Global Fund financing.
- It evaluates proposals through an independent review process.
- It tries to operate in a performance-based manner by supporting investments that are meeting their targets and reducing or eliminating support for programs that are not meeting their aims.[70]

To date, the Global Fund has committed $19.3 billion in 144 countries to support large-scale prevention, treatment, and care programs against the three diseases.[72]

Public–Private Partnerships

As interest in global health rose in the mid-1990s, many of the actors in this field increasingly believed that the mechanisms for developing, manufacturing, and distributing new vaccines, drugs, diagnostics, and medical devices needed to alleviate key global health problems were not sufficient. They noted with growing concern, for example, that the vaccine for TB was over 100 years old and that no new TB drugs had been developed for decades. They saw insufficient attention to the development of vaccines against HIV and malaria in both the public and the private sector and fewer firms willing to engage in vaccine development. They also understood that private pharmaceutical firms did not see a profitable market in the development of low-cost diagnostics, vaccines, drugs, or medical devices that could address the major killers of the poor globally. They knew that without changes in the way the market for these products worked that private sector firms would remain on the sidelines.

In the face of these issues, the Rockefeller Foundation encouraged key global health actors to think creatively about how they could spur the more rapid development of products that could attack global health problems in a low-cost but effective way. One idea that emerged from this was the notion of organizations that would combine the strengths of public and private organizations in a common quest for better health. They would also seek broader sources of financing for these health ventures; try to tackle intellectual property issues that constrained the availability of affordable diagnostics, drugs, medical devices, and vaccines in poor countries; and see how they could encourage more private sector involvement in the search for these products. In some respects, they were conceived of as venture capital firms that would have a social goal, rather than a goal that was mostly aimed at maximizing profit. Today, there is a wide array of public–private partnerships for health. The aim of many of these is to develop new products, and these are often called product development partnerships. Some of the most important of such partnerships are noted in Table 15-7. Additional information is provided about the Global Alliance for TB Drug Development, the International AIDS Vaccine Initiative, and the Malaria Vaccine Initiative in the policy and program briefs section of this chapter.

Pharmaceutical Firms

In the last decade, international pharmaceutical firms have also engaged in partnerships to try to improve global health at low cost. This has generally been done in one of three ways. First, some firms donate drugs to global health programs. Novartis, for example, donates leprosy drugs to the Global Alliance to Eliminate Leprosy, and today no country needs to purchase such drugs.[75] Pfizer and the Edna McConnell Clark Foundation work with the International Trachoma Initiative by donating an antibiotic, azithromycin, to its efforts to reduce trachoma-related blindness.[76] Merck donates ivermectin to the Onchocerciasis Control Program, which has been successful in reducing river blindness in Africa.[77] These are only some of the many donation efforts now underway.

TABLE 15-7 Selected Public–Private Partnerships for Public Health

Aeras
Global Alliance for TB Drug Development
Human Hookworm Vaccine Institute
International AIDS Vaccine Initiative
International Partnership on Microbicides
Malaria Vaccine Initiative
Medicines for Malaria Venture

In addition, a number of drug companies, including Abbott, Boehringer Ingelheim, Bristol Myers Squibb, Gilead, GSK, and Merck, have agreed to sell antiretroviral drugs for HIV at greatly discounted prices to developing countries affected by the AIDS epidemic. Some of the drug companies also sponsor programs to address diseases such as HIV in particular countries, such as Merck's support for the national HIV/AIDS control program in Botswana.[78] The Ely Lilly Corporation supports a program that helps to address drug-resistant TB, as discussed in Chapter 11.

The role of the major drug companies in global health is a subject of considerable controversy. There is a serious concern among some members of the global health community, for example, that the approach of the branded drug manufacturers to patents raises the price of drugs beyond what people in low-income countries can afford. Some people also believe that the major manufacturers should be far more generous than they have been in offering their drugs at reduced prices in low- and middle-income countries. Others have expressed concern that these manufacturers have not been open enough in licensing their products to other companies in a way that would reduce their prices in low- and middle-income countries. The role of pharmaceutical firms in global health is very important, complicated, and controversial and goes considerably beyond the scope of this book.

TRENDS IN GLOBAL HEALTH EFFORTS

The notion of cooperating to improve health globally is not a new one. Rather, different countries have realized for more than 100 years that many health problems could not be solved by individual countries and had to be addressed through collective action across countries.

In the ensuing period, in fact, many actors have cooperated in a variety of health activities. This section examines how the themes of those efforts varied over time. The threat of cholera, for example, led to the first international conference on health in 1851.[79] Numerous international conferences on health followed that, and by 1903, the International Commission on Epidemics was created.[80] In 1909, the International Office of Public Hygiene was set up in Paris, and this was followed by the establishment of the League of Nations Health Office in 1920 in Geneva, Switzerland. The International Sanitary Bureau was set up in 1924. The Rockefeller Foundation assisted in financing and providing technical support to the League of Nations Health Office. The early international organizations for health focused their efforts on the surveillance of disease, the provision of global standards for drugs and vaccines, and selected technical advice to countries on key health matters, including medical education.[81]

International efforts in health took a substantial leap forward with the establishment of the United Nations agencies after World War II, including WHO and UNICEF. In the more than 50 years since then there have been a number of areas of focus for international cooperation on health, as noted hereafter.[82–84] Following the establishment of WHO, efforts at international cooperation in health shifted to focus on helping to build capacity for global public health efforts, for health systems development in countries that were newly independent, and in working together to fight disease. Perhaps the greatest single effort at global cooperation in health began in 1966 with the start of the global program to eradicate smallpox. During this period of intensive attention to specific diseases, WHO also led work to combat malaria and other communicable diseases that most affected the poor, such as leprosy,[85] lymphatic filariasis,[86] and onchocerciasis.[87,88]

Historically, another important area of focus for global cooperation has been family planning. Much of the early work on family planning was led by the United States. Over time, the focus on family planning shifted from one that was centered almost exclusively on limiting family size to an approach that centered much more on reproductive health. This shift was encouraged by and reflected in a series of global conferences on family planning, safe motherhood, reproductive health, and women starting in 1974 in Bucharest, Romania.[89] The 1987 conference on women in Nairobi, Kenya, for example, was used to launch the Safe Motherhood Initiative.[84]

In 1978, the world launched a major effort when it enacted the Alma Ata declaration on primary health care, as mentioned earlier. This declaration noted that health was a fundamental human right and that countries had the obligation to ensure that all people had access to appropriate primary health care. The Alma Ata declaration heralded a new global focus on primary health care and on the health needs of the poor. It also led to much greater attention to the needs for health systems that could deliver primary care and to the importance of taking a community-based approach to the health needs of poor people. The Alma Ata Declaration was linked to the world's efforts to achieve what was called globally "Health for all by the Year 2000."[90]

An immense amount of attention has also been paid to "child survival." These efforts focused on what were called the GOBI interventions: growth monitoring, oral rehydration, breastfeeding, and immunization. UNICEF was the leader of this effort. USAID was also instrumentally involved in child survival activities, which ultimately became an important focus of attention for the World Bank, WHO, and a variety of bilateral organizations.[91]

As the world moved into the late 1980s and early 1990s, considerable concern arose that despite more than 30 years of global efforts to improve the health of the poor, the unfinished agenda remained very large. Many of those working on health believed that some of the weaknesses stemmed from an approach to health that was too disjointed and that needed to be better grounded in a more systemic view of health that would focus on trying to improve health services more broadly. This led to considerable work being done on "health sector reform." At the same time, the *1993 World Development Report* of the World Bank articulated the need to take an approach to decision making on health investments that would be grounded in cost-effectiveness analysis.[92] This framework for analysis soon became the foundation for actions of a number of key actors in global health.

At about the same time, much greater attention began to be paid, even in low-income countries, to the role of the private sector in health. Development partners also created new ways of working together cooperatively within individual countries. Increasingly, for example, development partners would cooperate and jointly help countries to develop and finance investments in health. In much of the work done prior to this period, many development partners worked individually with a country, often leading to a lack of coordination across that country's health sector efforts.

Toward the mid-1990s, the global health community began to pay considerably more attention to HIV, as well as to other major killers of the poor in resource-poor countries, including malaria and TB. Particular attention has been paid since then to reducing the cost of AIDS drugs and getting more people treated, raising case finding and cure rates for TB by expanding coverage with DOTS, and strengthening malaria control programs through the use of insecticide-treated bed nets, intermittent treatment of pregnant women, and greater use of artemisinin-based combination therapy. There has also been an enormous increase in cooperation through the many health partnerships that have been formed, as noted earlier in the chapter.

More recently there has been a renewed emphasis on some of the topics noted above, greater interest in others, and considerable attention paid to how countries and their partners work together to enhance health. Driven partly by the Millennium Development Goals, whose targets are for 2015, greater attention is now being paid, for example, to nutrition and maternal health. Considerable effort is being expended to complete polio eradication, which has proven to be more difficult than planned, and attention to measles and the possibility of its eradication is growing. Much greater attention is being paid than previously to the neglected tropical diseases and how they can be addressed in more coherent ways, as discussed in Chapter 11. There is growing concern about drug-resistant TB and the need to ensure that tools exist to diagnose it more rapidly and treat it more effectively. In fact, as discussed in Chapter 16 on science and technology for public health, there is also much greater focus than ever on the development of new diagnostics, drugs, and vaccines that can address the most important burdens of disease of poor people in poor countries. At the same time, substantial efforts are being directed to helping countries to develop more effective and efficient health systems that can provide "universal coverage" of key health services in more effective and efficient ways and afford more financial protection to their people from the costs of health care.

Much attention is also being paid to how development partners and countries can work together to achieve these aims, particularly in low-income countries. Increasing focus has been placed on ensuring that development assistance for health is "harmonized" and "aligned" with development partners working together on a common platform in each country and ensuring that the processes they use follow the processes of the countries with which they are working. There is also an emphasis on how countries can more effectively and efficiently achieve the intended results from their investments in health, through mechanisms such as results-based financing, which was discussed further in Chapter 5 on health systems. Important attention is also being paid to how the investments needed to improve health in low- and middle-income countries, particularly among the poor, can be financed, especially in times of global economic distress. Two initiatives for addressing this issue, UNITAID and Debt2Health, are discussed further in the policy and program briefs section of this chapter.

SETTING THE GLOBAL HEALTH AGENDA

As we think about how different actors cooperate in global health activities and the themes on which they focus, it is important to consider how global health policies get established. This section comments briefly on how the overall global health agenda and the agenda for particular global health topics are set. This is another topic that is quite complicated and often the subject of controversy that readers may wish to explore further.

One important activity in setting global health priorities is the World Health Assembly of the World Health Organization.[93] Once each year, ministers of health of WHO member countries meet in Geneva, Switzerland, to consider important global health matters and resolutions proclaiming their interest in and commitment to addressing key health issues. The World Health Assembly has been the foundation for some of the most important global health efforts undertaken, such as the smallpox eradication campaign.

Some important developments in global health have been encouraged by writings, advocacy efforts, and program activities of WHO, multilateral or bilateral development assistance agencies, and some of the important NGOs involved in health. The *1993 World Development Report* of the World Bank focused on health and was widely read and debated around the world. This document set the basis for the next generation of World Bank–assisted health projects in many countries and for important work done by other development organizations and countries in health, as well. Given the importance of World Bank assistance for health to so many countries, the approaches suggested in the *1993 World Development Report* had a major impact on the world's thinking about health in developing countries.

Movement in the policy agenda for global health can also follow significant investments by development partners. This has clearly been the case, for example, as a result of the substantial funds that the Bill & Melinda Gates Foundation has provided to selected global health activities. As noted earlier, the Gates Foundation has focused considerable attention on improving and disseminating technology for improving the health of the poor, as well as selected investments in key health problems, such as HIV. The investments the Gates Foundation has made, for example, in immunization and in the development of AIDS vaccines has considerably raised the world's attention to these matters and placed them more firmly on the global health agenda.

Popular action, often led by NGOs or other advocates for health, can also influence the setting of the global health agenda. In the late 1990s, for example, Professor Jeff Sachs, then of Harvard University, began to be actively involved in speaking and writing about the importance of health to economic and social development. His work attracted attention to health issues and led to considerable international engagement and action on the health of poor people globally. At about the same time, some important NGOs, such as Doctors Without Borders, became major advocates for AIDS treatment and the reduction of the prices of AIDS drugs. Through their advocacy work and efforts to treat people with antiretroviral drugs, they attracted considerable attention to these topics and had a major impact on the way the world approached them.

Another good example of how an NGO affected the global health agenda is the impact of Partners in Health, an NGO based in the city of Boston, Massachusetts, in the United States, on the global agenda for TB and for HIV.

Largely led by the work of Dr. Paul Farmer and Dr. Jim Kim of Harvard University, Partners in Health tried to develop in Peru and Haiti a model of how one could treat drug-resistant TB and then HIV at an acceptable cost and in a sustainable way. At the time, the prevailing opinion globally was that drugs for these conditions were so expensive that they could not be used in resource-poor settings. The work of Partners in Health helped to shift global efforts toward finding ways to make treatment affordable for all people.[94]

In other respects, one can think of efforts to set the global health agenda as a kind of ongoing meeting around a negotiating table at which important actors in global health are sitting. The organizations most involved in such discussions will generally be WHO, UNICEF, and the World Bank. Selected bilateral development agencies will also participate, such as USAID, the Department for International Development of the UK, and often the Canadian International Development Agency and the Dutch Development Agency, while AusAID plays a unique role in some of Asia in the Pacific. The Global Fund has been increasingly involved in policy discussions, as its portfolio has grown, as has UNAIDS, as AIDS has become more important. The Gates Foundation, the Rockefeller Foundation, and selected NGOs might also participate in setting the agenda. Some other NGOs, such as MSF, may not be present, but through advocacy they do bring their interests to the policy-setting group.

The way in which the agenda is set for specific health topics will be similar to those mentioned previously, but will usually also include actors who have particular interests in the topic at hand. WHO and the World Bank will almost always be involved. The key bilateral agencies will also participate. In addition, the agencies working with the topic under discussion and groups representing people affected by particular conditions increasingly have inputs into these discussions. If TB is being discussed, for example, then the key NGOs working globally with TB will be involved, as will the TB programs from representative countries. If leprosy is being discussed, then the leprosy programs of some countries will be involved, NGOs working in leprosy will be involved, and groups of people affected by leprosy will also be involved.

POLICY AND PROGRAM BRIEFS

This section examines additional examples of the types of global health actors that are discussed in this chapter. These policy and program briefs generally go into greater detail than most of the descriptions in the text.

The first two examples concern organizations that focus an important part of their work on advocacy, although they also engage in other activities. These are the Global Health Council and the Global Network on Neglected Tropical Diseases. The second set of examples explores three public–private partnerships for health: the Global Alliance for TB Drug Development, the International AIDS Vaccine Initiative, and the Malaria Vaccine Initiative. Two examples discuss innovative financing mechanisms for global health, the Debt2Health Initiative and UNITAID. The last brief discusses enhanced approaches to tracking development assistance for global health.

Advocacy Organizations

The Global Health Council[95]

The Global Health Council (GHC) is the world's largest member alliance working on global health issues, with nearly 600 organizational members and 5400 individual members in more than 100 countries. The Council's mission is to promote better health for all by ensuring that all who strive for improvement and equity in global health have the information and resources they need to work effectively. This mission is based on the understanding that the health challenges we face today cannot be surmounted by any single entity. The Global Health Council believes that reducing the burden of disease in the world's poorest countries requires effective cooperation and a unified voice.

The Global Health Council is a U.S.-based, nonprofit organization created in 1972 (as the National Council of International Health until 1998), and today includes a diverse membership of health professionals and organizations, such as nongovernmental organizations, corporations, academic institutions, foundations, faith-based and civil society organizations, and individuals concerned with global health issues. The Council identifies global health problems and reports on them to the general public, legislators, international and U.S. government agencies, academic institutions, and the global health community. Together with members and other partners, the GHC advocates for more global health resources. It also promotes the establishment of policies that are based on the best available evidence and seeks to move resources to where they will produce the most population health gains and save the most lives.

In an increasingly interdependent world, global health dialogue helps to move global health policy in the right direction through collaboration and knowledge-sharing. The Council tries to work with allies and partners that share common messages and goals. For example, the GHC joined with organizations such as the Global Campaign Against Poverty to connect with the broader global community on issues relevant to members of groups of countries known as the G8 and G20. In addition, the Global Health Council engages with

WHO, UNAIDS, the World Bank, and international partnerships, such as Roll Global Health Council Back Malaria and the Partnership for Maternal, Newborn, and Child Health.

The Global Health Council has established an information exchange with members and partners. With the goal of sharing knowledge, experience, ideas, and strategies, this dialogue occurs among program implementers, policy makers, researchers and academicians, health care providers, and other global health experts. It is facilitated through policy roundtables, discussions and presentations on crucial issues, an annual international conference, action alerts to members, an interactive website, member newsletters, *Global Health* magazine and its associated blog, a policy-advocacy-research blog (blog4globalhealth.wordpress.com), Facebook, and Twitter. The Global Health Council is also working with its members in Africa, Asia, Europe, and Latin America to build local capacity for designing and implementing global health programs and advocacy around global health issues.

In addition, the Council produces materials that compile and synthesize the peer-reviewed global health literature, program reviews published by research organizations, and field reports from program implementers and service providers. These materials describe global health facts and figures, highlight trends, and articulate policy priorities and positions.

The Global Network for Neglected Tropical Diseases[96]

The Global Network for Neglected Tropical Diseases is an advocacy and resource mobilization initiative of the Sabin Vaccine Institute dedicated to raising the awareness, political will, and funding necessary to control and eliminate the seven most common neglected tropical diseases (NTDs)—soil-transmitted helminths (hookworm, ascariasis, trichuriasis), onchocerciasis, schistosomiasis, trachoma, and lymphatic filariasis.

The vision of the Global Network is a world free of NTDs where children and families are able to grow, learn, and become productive members of their communities. The organization works with governments, individuals, institutions, and corporations around the world to make this vision a reality.

The Global Network focuses on sustainable, nationally owned, integrated, multidisease efforts that are aligned with or supported by a country's Ministry of Health and WHO. The Global Network also serves as a bridge between multiple stakeholders, including policymakers, philanthropists, foundations, corporations, and individuals interested in investing in NTD control and elimination efforts at the local, national, and international level.

Through a $34 million catalytic grant from the Bill & Melinda Gates Foundation in 2009, the Global Network is working with WHO to develop an innovative global plan to combat NTDs. The goal is to establish transparent and accountable regional funding mechanisms that will promote the scale-up of disease control and elimination efforts specific to the needs of each region.

The Global Network has also partnered with the Inter-American Development Bank (IDB) and the Pan American Health Organization (PAHO) to launch a major effort to fight NTDs plaguing more than 200 million people in Latin America and the Caribbean. This partnership aims to coordinate and support country ownership and capacity building to address the burden of NTDs in the region. Designed to link national governments, national NTD programs, and NGOs, the partnership hopes to harmonize and integrate NTD efforts while taking advantage of the resources in primary healthcare systems and other cross-sectoral efforts.

Working in collaboration with various international partners, the Global Network has supported NTD treatment campaigns in several countries to address the needs of more than 16 million individuals in sub-Saharan Africa alone in 2009.

The Global Network's advocacy efforts, in tandem with the NTD community, have raised significant awareness and support for NTDs globally. As a result, both the U.S. and British governments have made impressive monetary commitments in recent years to control and eliminate NTDs.

The Global Network faces a number of challenges in moving forward, however. First, the 2008 worldwide financial crisis has caused some donors and other stakeholders to reduce their budgets. Second, despite the increasing attention to NTDs, they continue to compete for attention and financing with diseases with higher mortality rates.

Nonetheless, at a cost of approximately 50 cents a treatment in most cases, NTD control is clearly a "best buy" in global health. The Global Network hopes that by providing donors with information about the adverse impact of NTDs on education, health, worker productivity, and economic growth and the benefits of low-cost treatment strategies, support for addressing NTDs in low-cost, highly effective ways will continue to grow.

Public–Private Partnerships for Health

The Global Alliance for TB Drug Development

The Global Alliance for TB Drug Development was created in 2000 with the mission to "accelerate the discovery and development of faster-acting and affordable drugs to fight tuberculosis."[97] It is a partnership among governments, non-governmental organizations, professional organizations, academia, foundations, and pharmaceutical and biotechnology companies that have pledged to work together to accomplish this mission. Spending nearly $30 million in 2009 on its programs, this product development partnership comprises the largest effort in history for TB drug development.[98] Also known as the TB Alliance, the partnership has led to the largest portfolio of TB drug candidates to date. Its main office is located in New York City, and research is conducted in public and private laboratories around the world.

The TB Alliance aims to develop a therapy for TB that will "shorten treatment, be effective against susceptible and resistant strains, be compatible with antiretroviral therapies for those HIV-TB patients currently on such therapies, and improve the treatment of latent infection."[97] In doing so, the partnership hopes to increase cure rates overall by improving patient compliance with treatment and lowering toxic side effects. Long-term goals include developing a treatment that could be administered in less than 2 weeks, significantly shorter than the current 6-month treatment. Developing a drug that could be given once a day orally is another priority.[99] Currently, three drugs are in clinical trials and over 20 projects are under way related to further drug development.[98]

A main concern of the Global Alliance for TB Drug Development is that treatment for TB, once developed, must be widely available and affordable, especially in low-income countries. To accomplish this goal, the partnership works toward patent and marketing arrangements that will allow the drug to be sold at affordable prices in low-income countries. It is also working with drug regulatory authorities to ensure that future drugs will get early approval in the countries in which they are to be sold.[99] In addition, the TB Alliance is collaborating with others to ensure that any future TB drugs can be manufactured at the lowest possible cost.[100]

By the end of 2009, total contributions to the Global Alliance for TB Drug Development amounted to more than $250 million, with the donor base composed of foundations, enterprises, governments, multilateral donors, and individuals. Half of all funding is from the Bill & Melinda Gates Foundation, followed by the U.S. Agency for International Development, contributing 18 percent of funds, and the U.K. Department for International Development, contributing 14 percent. Research and development costs are also funded largely by contributions from its partners who work on drug development.[101]

The International AIDS Vaccine Initiative[102]

The International AIDS Vaccine Initiative (IAVI) is a global, not-for-profit, public–private partnership working to accelerate the development of a vaccine to prevent HIV infection and AIDS. IAVI is dedicated to ensuring a future AIDS vaccine will be available to all who need it at reasonable prices. Founded in 1996, IAVI researches and develops vaccine candidates, conducts policy analyses, and serves as an advocate for AIDS vaccine development generally. IAVI supports a comprehensive response to HIV/AIDS that balances the expansion and strengthening of existing HIV prevention and treatment programs with targeted investments in new AIDS prevention tools. The organization has offices worldwide, in New York, La Jolla (California), London, Amsterdam, New Delhi, Nairobi, and Johannesburg.

IAVI's scientific team, drawn largely from industry, researches and develops AIDS vaccine candidates and engages in clinical studies through partnerships with more than 50 academic, biotechnology, pharmaceutical, and governmental institutions. The organization uses industry-like project-management systems to direct a portfolio of research and development (R&D) projects, prioritizing the most promising products and moving them swiftly through the vaccine development pipeline.

In the last decade, IAVI and its network of partners have translated innovative technologies into 15 vaccine candidates, 7 of which have entered human trials in 11 countries in Asia, Africa, Europe, and North America. The organization conducts translational research at its AIDS Vaccine Design and Development Laboratory in New York City; its Neutralizing Antibody Center at The Scripps Research Institute in La Jolla, California; and its Human Immunology Laboratory at Imperial College London in London, England.

To address major obstacles in AIDS vaccine development, IAVI connects HIV researchers from around the world in two AIDS vaccine consortia. The Neutralizing Antibody Consortium is a network dedicated to discovering and understanding broadly neutralizing antibodies against HIV and using that knowledge in the design of vaccines. The Vectors Consortium pursues novel delivery vehicles—called viral vectors—that are promising for use in HIV vaccines. IAVI also operates the Innovation Fund—a financing mechanism established jointly with the Bill & Melinda Gates Foundation—that identifies and supports nascent technologies from other fields that may advance AIDS vaccine development.

IAVI promotes AIDS vaccine education worldwide, engaging communities in the clinical research process and improving research capacity in low- and middle-income countries, where 95 percent of new HIV infections occur. IAVI works with other organizations to analyze how improved public policies could help to accelerate AIDS vaccine R&D and ensure rapid global access to a future vaccine. IAVI's policy papers document a range of topics, including vaccine R&D expenditures and future spending needs, vaccine demand forecasting, the public health and economic impacts of an AIDS vaccine, and incentives that would increase industry participation in vaccine discovery.

IAVI's advocacy program promotes awareness among political, community, financial, and scientific leaders about the urgent need for an AIDS vaccine.

The Malaria Vaccine Initiative

The Malaria Vaccine Initiative (MVI) was established through a grant from the Bill & Melinda Gates Foundation in 1999. Based in Bethesda, Maryland, inside the nonprofit organization PATH, MVI's mission is "to accelerate the development of malaria vaccines and ensure their availability and accessibility in the developing world."[103]

Like other public–private partnerships, MVI hopes to accomplish its aims by engaging partners in private enterprise, governments, and academia. Today, MVI receives funding not only from the Gates Foundation, but also from the U.S. Agency for International Development, ExxonMobil, and private donors.[104]

By 2025, MVI hopes to spur the development of a vaccine with 80 percent or greater efficacy that lasts up to 4 years without a booster,[105] paying special attention to efficacy in children under 5 and pregnant women.[106] By 2015, the goal of MVI is to develop a vaccine that is 50 percent effective against "severe disease and death," and protects for at least 1 year without a booster.[107]

MVI identifies potential malaria vaccine candidates and oversees the entire development process by establishing product development partnerships with the organization responsible for vaccine development. Hoping to enable the development of a malaria vaccine as quickly as possible, MVI also develops sites for clinical trials and makes sure these trials adhere to international standards.

MVI aims to support at least eight preclinical projects, at least four early clinical projects, and at least one late clinical project at any given time.[106] MVI currently supports 20 different projects in vaccine development,[108] four of which are in clinical development. One project is considered a vaccine candidate and is currently in phase three clinical trials. Developed by GlaxoSmithKline Biologicals, the vaccine is the farthest along in trials that a malaria vaccine has ever come.[107] To speed the development of this vaccine candidate, MVI is

building and overseeing clinical trials in sites in a number of African countries.

In line with the aims of the public–private partnerships for health, MVI also seeks to ensure that there is a demand for an eventual malaria vaccine and that the vaccine will be affordable in low-income countries. With these aims in mind, MVI not only works on product development, but also advocates internationally and within specific countries for the necessity of developing a malaria vaccine and greater funding to do so.[106] MVI also engages in efforts to reduce eventual manufacturing costs and to arrange intellectual property rights so that costs of any vaccine will be as low as possible in low-income countries.

In addition, MVI aims to ensure that countries are prepared to administer a malaria vaccine once developed. Thus, MVI works with countries in which an eventual vaccine is needed to ensure that their regulatory authorities will speedily approve such a vaccine for use in their country. MVI also works with these countries to prepare for use of an eventual vaccine through existing health delivery systems.[109]

In addition, MVI seeks to enable countries to make informed decisions surrounding a vaccine. To accomplish this goal, MVI has developed a framework for decision making about a potential malaria vaccine, which has been adopted by 30 countries.[110] In addition, MVI has helped those African countries currently hosting clinical trials establish institutions for decision making surrounding the vaccine.

MVI faces significant challenges to accomplishing its goal of developing a safe and effective malaria vaccine. First, immunization against the deadliest malaria parasite, *Plasmodium falciparum*, is complex due to the various stages of its life cycle in the human body. Achieving the greatest efficacy for the vaccine may even require targeting multiple stages of the parasite's life cycle.[111] In addition to scientific challenges, MVI is faced with garnering sufficient funding, because available MVI funds trail far behind the estimated $300 to $500 million necessary for the development of one vaccine.[112]

Innovative Financing Mechanisms for Global Health: UNITAID and Debt2Health

Within the past decade, there has been significant growth in international development assistance for health; this financing accounted for about one fifth of all development assistance in 2007. Nonetheless, there remains a substantial gap between the available financing and the estimated financial needs for meeting the MDGs. WHO has estimated that between 2008 and 2015, an additional $251 billion would be necessary to achieve the MDGs in the 49 poorest countries.[113]

Besides being insufficient in amount, conventional development financing for health has a number of shortcomings. First, most countries can only allocate such assistance on a year-to-year basis, which makes it difficult for recipient countries to plan how to use the assistance in the soundest way. Second, this type of assistance may not provide the incentives needed to achieve desired outcomes in the most effective and efficient manner. This relates to the fact that development assistance for health has typically financed health inputs, such as drugs, medical equipment, clinics, training, and technical advice, rather than finance outputs and measureable results on the ground, such as vaccine coverage for childhood diseases or reduction in malaria morbidity from the use of bed nets. There has also been a concern that getting financial assistance from multiple sources can lead to wasteful spending and inefficient duplication of systems for procurement, financial management, and reporting.[113]

In this light, discussion began in 2004 to develop "innovative financing mechanisms" for development assistance in health that could increase the amount of funding available, and be more predictable and stable than traditional development assistance for health. Such discussions have centered on financial mechanisms that include levies on currency transactions, a voluntary rebate by businesses on their value-added taxes for the use of international development, and other kinds of voluntary consumer contributions. Two efforts that have been put into place are UNITAID and a debt swap program called Debt2Health.[113]

UNITAID

In 2006, Brazil, Chile, France, Norway, and the United Kingdom collaborated to develop an international drug purchase facility, called UNITAID. Officially launched in September 2006, UNITAID was established to scale up access to HIV/AIDS, TB, and malaria treatment for people in low-income countries. UNITAID now has the support of 29 countries and of the Bill & Melinda Gates Foundation. UNITAID is housed in WHO and works closely with 10 partner organizations.[114]

UNITAID is largely financed by a new source of funding: a tax on the purchase of airline tickets in donor countries. Thus far, six countries have levied such a tax, and another nation donates to UNITAID part of the tax it levies on jet fuel. UNITAID's business model is based on the idea that this predictable source of financing will allow it to purchase high volumes of diagnostics and drugs for use in low- and middle-income countries, thus encouraging investment in the development of these products and reductions in their prices.[114]

Since 2006, UNITAID has contributed over $1 billion to projects in 94 countries. UNITAID has contributed to the financing of treatment for about 1 million adults and children for HIV. It has also contributed $72 million to address maternal-to-child transmission of HIV. In addition, it has helped to bring down the cost of antiretroviral therapy, supported the procurement of diagnostics, and helped to enhance the quality of drugs being procured. UNITAID has financed drugs to treat about 1.5 million people for TB, the purchase of about 20 million insecticide-treated bed nets, and about 19 million treatments for malaria.[114] In 2010, UNITAID had a budget of about $400 million.

UNITAID has raised substantial funds, and the prospects for such funding in the long term generally appear good. However, air travel is vulnerable to shifting economic conditions, and funding available to UNITAID might not be as much as expected. In addition, especially during the present economic crisis, consumers in donor countries might reject this tax burden.

Debt2Health

The Debt2Health approach was approved by the Board of the Global Fund in 2007. The core element of the Debt2Health model is a three-party agreement among a creditor, a beneficiary country, and the Global Fund. The creditor country will forgive an agreed portion of the beneficiary's debt, provided that such debt is changed into local currency payments for disease control activities approved by the Global Fund.[115]

Thus far, the total amount of debt swapped under the Debt2Health initiative has been 163.6 million Euros.[116] The first creditor, Germany, has agreed to cancel a total of €50 million of debt for Indonesia and also has a Debt2Health agreement with Pakistan. In July 2010, Australia offered an AU$75 million Debt2Health swap for Global Fund programs for TB in Indonesia.[115] In September 2010, Côte d'Ivoire became the first African country to benefit from Debt2Health; Germany agreed to cancel €19 million of debt for investment in Global Fund programs for HIV/AIDS in that country.[116]

The Debt2Health initiative has several advantages. By working through the Global Fund, Debt2Health can keep its transaction costs relatively low. In addition, creditors may gain political capital as supporters of this effort. On the other hand, Debt2Health requires that creditor countries be willing to cancel a substantial amount of debt if the swap is to be an efficient financial transaction.

Tracking Financing for Global Health[117]

As noted throughout the book, there has been dramatic growth in the funding for global health over the last decade. Unfortunately, it has been difficult to track that funding and understand clearly how much money has been spent over time, by whom, and to what it has been allocated. This information is central to policymaking for global health. It is needed to assess the effectiveness and efficiency of such expenditure. It is also critical to understand the relationship between the burden of disease in a country and the amount of development assistance provided to meet that burden.

To enhance the quality of this data, the Institute for Health Metrics and Evaluation prepared a major report entitled *Financing Global Health 2009*. This report focused on tracking development assistance for health over much of the last two decades. The report was based on a study of data from 1990 to 2007 on development assistance for health, government health expenditures, and private health expenditures. The study focused on expenditure on HIV/AIDS, TB, and malaria, as well as how development assistance for health was distributed across countries.

The study found that from 1990 to 2007, development assistance for health increased by about four times, from $5.6 billion to $21.8 billion (measured in real 2007 US$). It also noted that much of this increase was driven by expenditure on HIV/AIDS. Of $13.8 billion of project-financed development assistance for health in 2007, $4.9 billion was directed toward HIV/AIDS, $0.6 billion toward TB, $0.7 billion toward malaria, and $0.9 billion toward health sector support. Although possibly overestimated, technical assistance and drug donations were found to be $8.7 billion in 2007.

Publicly financed aid accounted for two thirds of total development assistance for health from 1990 to 2007. The new public–private initiatives, such as the Global Fund to Fight AIDS, Tuberculosis and Malaria and the Global Alliance for Vaccines and Immunisation, are responsible for the rapid growth of development assistance for health since 2002 and represented a greatly increased share of this expenditure in 2007. By contrast, the share of development assistance coming from multilateral and United Nations organizations declined.

Private philanthropy, largely driven by funding from the Bill & Melinda Gates Foundation, represented about $5.9 billion, or about 27 percent of development assistance for health in 2007. Nongovernmental organizations contributed $5.4 billion, or almost 25 percent of all development assistance for health, an amount almost equal to that of private philanthropy.

Overall, the study generally found that countries with a higher burden of disease and countries that were poorer did receive relatively more development assistance for health. However, it also found that a number of middle-income countries received development assistance for health that was not consistent with either their burden of disease or their economic standing. These countries included Argentina, Colombia, and Iraq. At the same time, it also found that a small number of very poor countries received relatively less development assistance for health than their income level or burden of disease would have warranted.

The Institute for Health Metrics and Evaluation plans to issue an annual report on the financing of global health. The Institute hopes that by doing this, it can enhance the transparency of development assistance for health and establish mechanisms for reporting valid data on that assistance on a more regular and coherent basis.

CASE STUDY

Chapter 1 ended with a case study on smallpox, which is widely regarded as one of the great efforts in global cooperation of any kind, but especially in health. It is fitting that one of the last chapters of the book should include a case study of the successful effort to eliminate onchocerciasis in Africa. This case study complements the one in Chapter 5 that addresses the integrated provision of drugs to treat onchocerciasis and vitamin A deficiency. More detailed information on this case is available in *Case Studies in Global Health: Millions Saved*.

Background

Onchocerciasis, or river blindness, is a pernicious disease afflicting approximately 18 million people worldwide. More than 99 percent of its victims are in sub-Saharan Africa. In the most endemic areas, over a third of the adult population is blind, and infection often approaches 90 percent.[118] In 11 West African countries in 1974, nearly 2.5 million of the area's 30 million inhabitants were infected with onchocerciasis, and approximately 100,000 were blind. The remaining 19 endemic countries in Central and East Africa were home to 60 million people at risk of the disease.

The Intervention

Onchocerciasis is caused by a worm called *Onchocerca volvulus* which enters its human victim through the bite of an infected blackfly. The flies breed in fast-moving waters in fertile riverside regions. Once inside a human, the tiny worm grows to a length of 1 to 2 feet and produces millions of microscopic offspring called microfilarie. The constant movement of the microfilarie through the infected person's skin causes torturous itching, lesions, muscle pain, and, in severe cases, blindness. Fertile land is often abandoned for fear of the disease.

Early efforts to control the disease proved ineffective because blackflies cover long distances and cross national borders, rendering unilateral efforts ineffective. An international conference in Tunisia in 1968 concluded that onchocerciasis could not be controlled without regional collaboration and long-term funding of at least 20 years to break the life cycle of the worm. World Bank President Robert McNamara's tour of drought-stricken West Africa in 1972 served as a catalyst to progress. Moved by seeing communities where nearly all the adults were blind and were led by children, McNamara decided to spearhead an international effort against onchocerciasis.[118]

The Onchocerciasis Control Program (OCP), the World Bank's first large-scale health program, was launched in 1974 in conjunction with WHO, the UN Food and Agriculture Organization (FAO), and UNDP. The program included a significant research budget and set out to eliminate onchocerciasis in 7, and eventually in 11, West African countries.[119] Breeding grounds of blackflies were sprayed with larvicide, and the spraying program was able to persist even through regional conflicts and coups. In the 1980s, a Merck drug called ivermectin was included as a powerful new weapon against the disease, a single dose of which could effectively paralyze the tiny worms for up to a full year.[120] The drug proved popular because it quickly reduced uncomfortable symptoms and provided protection against other parasites. Merck donated ivermectin and Dr. William Foege of the Carter Center managed its distribution.

The African Programme for Onchocerciasis Control (APOC) was established in 1995 as a broad international partnership to control the disease throughout Africa and to carry onchocerciasis control to 19 countries in East and Central Africa. These were countries in which long distances and thick forests made spraying difficult. APOC pioneered a system of community-directed treatment (ComDT) with ivermectin to ensure local participation, reach remote villages, and maintain distribution of the drug after donor funding expired in 2010.[121] ComDT workers are often the only health personnel to reach distant villages, and their access could be used for other health interventions in the future.

The Impact

By 2002, OCP halted transmission of onchocerciasis in 11 West African countries, preventing 600,000 cases of blindness, and protecting 18 million children born in the OCP area from the risk of the disease. About 25 million hectares of arable land—enough to feed an additional 17 million people—is now safe for resettlement.[122] APOC is expanding this success to Central and East Africa, where 40,000 cases of blindness are expected to be prevented each year.

Costs and Benefits

OCP operated with an annual cost of less than $1 per protected person. Total commitments from 22 donors amounted to $560 million. The annual return on investment, due mainly to increased agricultural output, was 20 percent, and it is estimated that $3.7 billion will be generated from improved labor and agricultural productivity.[123] APOC coverage cost even less, at just 11 cents per person. The economic rate of return for the program has been estimated at 17 percent for the years 1996 to 2017, and it is estimated that 27 healthy life days will be added per dollar invested.[124]

Lessons Learned

Success in controlling onchocerciasis could not have been attained without a genuinely shared vision among all partners in the program. Commitment among the African governments was critical to coordinating a regional effort across national borders. Long-term commitments from donors, along with Merck's decision to donate ivermectin indefinitely, were essential elements for the program's sustainability. The participation of a wide range of organizations, such as multilateral institutions, private companies, and local NGOs, allowed for a cost-effective and efficient intervention. The ComDT framework, by emphasizing local ownership and participation, proved a cost-effective and self-sustaining means of delivering drugs to remote populations. The onchocerciasis program proved that effective aid programs, implemented with transparency and accountability, can deliver lasting results.

FUTURE CHALLENGES

There are a number of challenges to effective collaborative action in global health. First, as discussed in the chapter on communicable diseases, the types of health conditions that the world faces may change and new conditions might develop. Smallpox was once a disease of considerable importance, as was polio. Smallpox was eradicated, and there are very few cases of polio in the world today. In recent years, however, there have been outbreaks of new and emerging diseases, such as Ebola, the avian flu, and SARS. It is possible that there will be a major epidemic of influenza and that other new and emerging diseases will appear in the future. The world will have to be ready, through collaborative efforts, to carry out surveillance, prevention, and treatment of those diseases.

Second, it will be very important for development partners to work together to help countries strengthen their health systems, as well as to try to combat individual diseases. If countries are to be able to meet their most important health needs in a sustainable manner in the future, then they must have health systems that work. In most low-income countries, this will require better management, more appropriate forms of organization, sounder systems for key public health functions, better trained staff at all levels, and a consistent manner of providing financing for health system needs, while helping to cover the costs of health care for the very poor. Achieving these aims is not as attractive politically as fighting a specific disease or health problem. Yet, in the long run, a systems approach must be taken to developing health services, and different global health actors will have to work together to achieve this, since they are usually only involved in working with a part of the health system of any country.

Another set of future challenges concerns the need to ensure that actors in global health work together to address the knowledge gaps that prevent sufficient progress against health conditions that cause people to be sick too often and to die prematurely, especially poor people in low-income countries. There will continue to be an important need, for example, for increasing our knowledge of the basic science concerning many diseases, including AIDS, TB, and malaria. It will not be possible to develop preventive vaccines for these diseases or better treatment for them without significant improvements in scientific knowledge. There will also be a need for operational research in global health so that we can learn more about what approaches are effective and efficient. What is the best way, for example, to ensure that people take all of their drugs for HIV or TB? How should a health system in a low- or middle-income country be organized to ensure that it can operate in a cost-efficient way, while paying sufficient attention to the poor? These questions can only be answered through the generation and sharing of knowledge and experience globally, a process dependent upon cooperation and coordination.

The factors that have encouraged the development of public–private partnerships for health will also continue to challenge the global health community. There are many such partnerships now and it will be very important to learn as quickly as possible which aspects of these partnerships encourage product development in effective and efficient ways and which ones do not. It is also necessary to continue to encourage the development of new and innovative approaches to enabling the development of new diagnostics, vaccines, and therapies that can be affordable in low- and middle-income countries. If any of the public–private partnerships are successful in developing new products, then it will be essential that efforts turn to ensuring that they are used quickly where they are most needed.

The financial needs for addressing global health concerns are very considerable and will continue to have a prominent place on the global health agenda. The multilateral development banks, bilateral aid agencies, and special programs such as The Global Fund need continuous financing. In addition, some of the important initiatives that have been started, such as the considerable push for treatment against HIV, cannot be sustained without many years of additional financing by rich countries, foundations, the private sector, and their partners. The amount of money that is spent on global health is much less than is spent on defense globally. Yet, there are still many risks that donors will develop "aid fatigue" and not have the political will necessary to continue financing global health efforts at the level needed.

It will be important that any development financing for health be as effective as possible. Although the topic of development effectiveness is considerably beyond the scope of this book, Table 15-8 summarizes some of the factors most closely associated with the success of development assistance in health.

There are also a number of important challenges to the way that actors in global health cooperate to assist countries in investing in the health sector. In recent years, development assistance agencies have increasingly tried to cooperate closely in their aid work on specific countries. However, there are always tendencies in development agencies to act independently rather than in coordination with other agencies. Although we should expect these tensions to continue, it is important if development assistance in health is to be effective that agencies work increasingly in a cooperative fashion.

Finally, it will be very important that good leadership in the global health field continues. Different agencies will need to work together in ways that address the challenges noted earlier. New groups and organizations need to join the community of global health actors to continue to inspire innovative and efficient methods of addressing and financing global health needs.

MAIN MESSAGES

It is very important that key actors work together to address global health problems because they may have effects that go beyond one country, they may be expensive to deal with, and they may require technical and managerial resources larger than some poorer countries can bring to bear on their own. In addition, it is very important that there be global standards in some health fields, and these standards need to be broadly developed and widely accepted. Good examples of areas in which it is imperative that different actors work together globally would include efforts to carry out disease surveillance, the global fight for polio eradication, and the standards for some disease control programs, such as TB.

There are many actors in global health; among the most actively involved are WHO, UNICEF, UNAIDS, and the World Bank. Most high-income countries have development assistance organizations, such as USAID, AusAID, and DFID, and they often play important roles in global health. The Global Fund and GAVI are also prominent global health actors. A number of foundations are also deeply involved in global health work, and the Bill & Melinda Gates Foundation has become a major actor in global health since the late 1990s. Many NGOs are also very engaged in global health efforts; Doctors Without Borders is among the best known of these. Organizations like this play one of several roles, singly or all together, including advocacy, knowledge generation, technical assistance, or financing.

A relatively new form of organization was created specifically to deal with difficult global health problems, called public–private partnerships for health. These organizations include, among others, the International AIDS Vaccine Initiative and the International Partnership on Microbicides. Essentially, they try to combine the skills and financing of public and private sector organizations, in order to advocate for specific health issues; develop new vaccines, diagnostics, or drugs; and ensure that what they develop will be appropriate to the health needs of poor countries and affordable to them, as well. Some other new organizations, such as GAVI and the Global Fund are established to try to dramatically increase the pace of immunizing children and combating AIDS, TB, and malaria.

TABLE 15-8 Factors Associated with Positive Outcomes in Development Assistance

- Strong leadership in the host government and in the development partner agencies
- Close collaboration among governments, donors, and nongovernmental organizations in the design and implementation of the program
- Household and community participation in the design, implementation, and monitoring of programs
- Simple and flexible technologies and approaches that can be adapted to local conditions and do not require complex skills to operate and maintain
- Approaches that help to strengthen health systems, especially human resources for health
- Consistent, predictable funding

Source: Adapted with permission from Hecht RM, Shah R. Recent trends and innovations in development assistance in health. In: Jamison DT, Breman JG, Measham AR, et al., eds. *Disease Control Priorities in Developing Countries.* 2nd ed. Washington, DC and New York: The World Bank and Oxford University Press, 2006:246.

The global health community is likely to face many challenges that will continue to require collective action by global health actors. Some of the key challenges will include filling key gaps in knowledge and encouraging public and private sector organizations to develop the diagnostics, vaccines, and drugs needed to address the most important global health issues. They will also include the need for organizations to work together to strengthen health systems, to combat individual diseases, and to try to ensure that critical global health needs have adequate financing.

Study Questions

1. What are the most important organizations that work on global health issues?

2. What functions do these organizations play?

3. Why is it important that different actors cooperate to address global health concerns?

4. Name some of the most important successes of cooperative action on global health.

5. What were some of the key factors that led to those successes?

6. What are the lessons of these successes for future global health efforts?

7. What are some of the future challenges that demand continued or strengthened collaboration in global public health?

8. What is a public–private partnership for health, and why might it be valuable?

9. Why is cooperative action needed to address problems like onchocerciasis and Guinea worm?

10. How might the world raise the money needed to further address problems like HIV and the need for drug treatment against AIDS?

REFERENCES

1. UNICEF. Polio Experts Warn of Largest Epidemic in Recent Years, as Polio Hits Darfur: Epidemiologists "Alarmed" by Continuing Spread of Virus—Warn Thousands of Children Could Be Paralyzed Across West and Central Africa. *Joint Press Release.* Available at: http://www.unicef.org/media/media_21872.html. Accessed July 12, 2006.

2. World Health Organization. Tuberculosis and HIV. Available at: http://www.who.int/hiv/topics/tb/en. Accessed October 5, 2010.

3. Global Alliance for TB Drug Development. No R&D in 30 Years. Available at: http://www.tballiance.org/2_3_C_NoRandDin30Years.asp. Accessed July 12, 2006.

4. The GAVI Alliance. GAVI Alliance for Vaccines and Immunization. Available at: http://www.gavialliance.org. Accessed July 5, 2006.

5. The GAVI Alliance. General Principles for Use of GAVI/Vaccine Fund Resources. Available at: http://www.gavialliance.org/General_Information/About_alliance/GAVI/Principles.php. Accessed July 12, 2006.

6. Merson MH, Black RE, Mills AJ. *International Public Health: Diseases, Programs, Systems, and Policies.* Gaithersburg, MD: Aspen Publishers; 2001.

7. Lele U, Ridker R, Upadhyay J. Health System Capacities in Developing Countries and Global Health Initiatives on Communicable Diseases. Available at: http://www.umalele.org/content/view/85/109. Accessed July 12, 2006.

8. Heymann DL, Rodier G. Global surveillance, national surveillance, and SARS. *Emerg Infect Dis.* Feb 2004;10(2):173-175.

9. Walt G. Global cooperation in international public health. In: Merson MH, Black RE, Mills AJ, eds. *International Public Health.* Gaithersburg, Maryland: Aspen Publishers; 2001:667-669.

10. Basch P. *Textbook of International Health.* 2nd ed. New York: Oxford University Press; 2001:486-509.

11. Basch P. *Textbook of International Health.* 2nd ed. New York: Oxford University Press; 2001:42-72.

12. Kickbusch I, Buse K. Global influences and global responses: international health at the turn of the twenty-first century. In: Merson MH, Black RE, Mills AJ, eds. *International Public Health.* Gaithersburg, MD: Aspen Publishers; 2001:701-733.

13. World Health Organization. About WHO. Available at: http://www.who.int/about/en. Accessed October 15, 2010.

14. World Health Organization. Declaration on Occupational Health for All. Available at: http://www.who.int/occupational_health/publications/declaration/en/index.html. Accessed July 12, 2006.

15. UNICEF. The Structure of UNICEF. Available at: http://www.unicef.org/about/structure/index.html. Accessed October 15, 2010.

16. UNICEF. What We Do. Available at: http://www.unicef.org/whatwedo/index.html. Accessed October 15, 2010.

17. UNICEF. Support UNICEF. Available at: http://www.unicef.org/support/14884.html. Accessed October 15, 2010.

18. UNICEF. Annual Report 2009. Available at: http://www.unicef.org/publications/files/UNICEF_Annual_Report_2009_EN_061510.pdf. Accessed October 5, 2010.

19. Joint United Nations Programme on HIV/AIDS. Cosponsors. Available at: http://www.unaids.org/en/Cosponsors/default.asp. Accessed July 12, 2006.

20. UNAIDS. Annual Report 2009. Available at: http://data.unaids.org/pub/Report/2010/2009_annual_report_en.pdf. Accessed October 5, 2010.

21. Joint United Nations Programme on HIV/AIDS. Focus Areas. Available at: http://www.unaids.org/en/Coordination/FocusAreas/default.asp. Accessed July 12, 2006.

22. World Bank. Health, Nutrition, & Population. Available at: http://www.worldbank.org/html/extdr/hnp/hnp.htm. Accessed July 6, 2006.

23. Bretton Woods Project. Bank's $100 Billion Annual Lending Plan. Available at: http://www.brettonwoodsproject.org/art-565290. Accessed October 5, 2010.

24. World Bank. Working for a World Free of Poverty. Available at: http://siteresources.worldbank.org/EXTABOUTUS/Resources/wbgroupbrochure-en.pdf. Accessed July 12, 2006.

25. World Bank. *The World Bank Annual Report 2009.* Washington, DC: The World Bank; 2009.

26. USAID. Health: Overview. Available at: http://www.usaid.gov/our_work/global_health. Accessed July 12, 2006.

27. The Rockefeller Foundation. Available at: http://www.rockfound.org. Accessed July 6, 2006.

28. The Rockefeller Foundation. Global Health. Available at: http://www.rockefellerfoundation.org/who-we-are/our-focus/global-health. Accessed October 12, 2010.

29. Wellcome Trust. 2010–2020 Strategic Plan: Extraordinary Opportunities. 2010. Available at: http://www.wellcome.ac.uk/About-us/Strategy/index.htm. Accessed July 26, 2010.

30. Wellcome Trust. 2009 Annual Report and Financial Statements. 2009. Available at: http://www.wellcome.ac.uk/About-us/Publications/Annual-Report-and-Financial-Statements/index.htm. Accessed July 21, 2010.

31. Bill & Melinda Gates Foundation. Fact Sheet. 2010. Available at: http://www.gatesfoundation.org/about/Pages/foundation-fact-sheet.aspx. Accessed July 26, 2010.

32. Wellcome Trust. 2005–2010 Strategic Plan: Making a Difference. 2005. Available at: http://www.wellcome.ac.uk/About-us/Strategy/Previous/index.htm. Accessed July 21, 2010.

33. Wellcome Trust Malaria. Funding Malaria Research. 2006. Available at: http://malaria.wellcome.ac.uk/node40023.html. Accessed July 21, 2010.

34. Wellcome Trust. International Strategy 2006–2010. Available at: http://www.wellcome.ac.uk/Funding/Biomedical-science/International-funding/WTX032640.htm. Accessed July 21, 2010.

35. Wellcome Trust. Health Research Capacity Strengthening in Kenya and Malawi. Available at: http://www.wellcome.ac.uk/Funding/Biomedical-science/International-funding/Global-health-research/WTDV026103.htm. Accessed July 21, 2010.

36. Bill & Melinda Gates Foundation. Available at: http://www.gatesfoundation.org/default.htm. Accessed June 9, 2006.

37. Bill & Melinda Gates Foundation. Programs and Partnerships. Available at: http://www.gatesfoundation.org/global-health/Pages/overview.aspx. Accessed October 12, 2010.

38. Bill & Melinda Gates Foundation. Grants. Available at: http://www.gatesfoundation.org/grants/Pages/overview.aspx. Accessed October 12, 2010.

39. Bill & Melinda Gates Foundation. 2009 Annual Report. Available at http://www.gatesfoundation.org/annualreport/2009/Pages/overview.aspx. Accessed October 16, 2010.

40. The section on NIH is based on a draft of this section provided by the Fogarty International of Center of NIH and on a series of personal communications with the Fogarty International Center in October 2010.

41. BRAC. For Partners: Financial Information. Available at: http://www.brac.net/content/partners. Accessed August 17, 2010.

42. BRAC. Who We Are: Mission. Available at: http://www.brac.net/content/who-we-are-mission. Accessed August 17, 2010.

43. BRAC. Who We Are: Evolution. Available at: http://www.brac.net/content/who-we-are-evolution. Accessed August 17, 2010.

44. BRAC. What We Do. Available at: http://www.brac.net/content/what-we-do. Accessed August 17, 2010.

45. BRAC. Annual Report 2008. Available at: http://www.brac.net/oldsite/useruploads/files/BRAC%20Annual%20Report%20-%202008.pdf. Accessed August 17, 2010.

46. BRAC. Where We Work: Bangladesh: Health. Available at: http://www.brac.net/content/where-we-work-bangladesh-health. Accessed August 17, 2010.

47. BRAC. Bangladesh: Health: Essential Health Services. Available at: http://www.brac.net/content/bangladesh-health-essential-health-services. Accessed August 17, 2010.

48. BRAC. Bangladesh: Health: Maternal, Newborn, and Child Health and Nutrition. Available at: http://www.brac.net/content/bangladesh-health-maternal-newborn-and-child-health-and-nutrition. Accessed August 17, 2010.

49. BRAC. Bangladesh: Health: Shushasthyas. Available at: http://www.brac.net/content/bangladesh-health-shushasthyas. Accessed August 17, 2010.

50. BRAC. Bangladesh: Health: Communicable Diseases. Available at: http://www.brac.net/content/bangladesh-health-communicable-diseases. Accessed August 17, 2010.

51. BRAC. Pakistan: Health. Available at: http://www.brac.net/content/pakistan-health. Accessed August 17, 2010.

52. BRAC. Where We Work: Liberia: Health. Available at: http://www.brac.net/content/where-we-work-liberia-health. Accessed August 17, 2010.

53. BRAC. Where We Work: Uganda: Health. Available at: http://www.brac.net/content/where-we-work-uganda-health. Accessed August 17, 2010.

54. BRAC. Where We Work: Afghanistan: Health and Water. Available at: http://www.brac.net/content/where-we-work-afghanistan-health-and-water. Accessed August 17, 2010.

55. BRAC. Where We Work: Afghanistan. Available at: http://www.brac.net/content/where-we-work-afganistan. Accessed August 17, 2010.

56. BRAC. Social Enterprises. Available at: http://www.brac.net/content/social-enterprises-0. Accessed August 17, 2010.

57. Doctors Without Borders. Available at: http://www.doctorswithoutborders.org. Accessed July 15, 2006.

58. Doctors Without Borders. About Us. Available at: http://www.doctorswithoutborders.org/aboutus/index.cfm. Accessed July 12, 2006.

59. Oxfam International. About Us: What We Do. 2010. Available at: http://www.oxfam.org/en/about/what. Accessed July 20, 2010.

60. Oxfam International. Annual Report 2008–2009. Available at: http://www.oxfam.org/en/about/annual-reports. Accessed July 20, 2010.

61. Save the Children. Mission and Strategy. Available at: http://www.savethechildren.org/mission/index.asp. Accessed July 12, 2006.

62. Save the Children. Save the Children Receives $60 Million Grant from the Bill & Melinda Gates Foundation to Save Newborn Lives Globally. Available at: http://www.savethechildren.org/news/releases/release_120205.asp. Accessed July 12, 2006.

63. CDC. About CDC Mission and Vision. Available at: http://www.cdc.gov/about/organization/mission.htm. Accessed November 6, 2010.

64. KNCV. KNCV Tuberculosis Foundation—An Overview. Available at: http://www.kncvtbc.nl/Site/Components/SitePageCP/ShowPage.aspx?ItemID=e93456d3-d112-41b4-aac4-973b5b9f7763&SelectedMenuItemID=628a592b-25e8-440b-b04e-6ee3779d13c3. Accessed November 6, 2010.

65. The International Union Against Tuberculosis and Lung Disease. About the Union. Available at: http://www.theunion.org/about-the-union/about-the-union.html. Accessed November 6, 2010.

66. World Health Organization. The Stop TB Department. Available at: http://www.who.int/tb/about/en. Accessed July 12, 2006.

67. Roll Back Malaria Global Partnership. Available at: http://rbm.who.int. Accessed July 15, 2006.

68. Roll Back Malaria Global Partnership. What is MMSS? Available at: http://rbm.who.int/mmss. Accessed July 13, 2006.

69. The GAVI Alliance. Progress and Challenges 2004. Available at: http://www.gavialliance.org/General_Information/About_alliance/pandc2004_index.php. Accessed July 12, 2006.

70. The Global Fund. The Global Fund to Fight AIDS, Tuberculosis, and Malaria. Available at: http://www.theglobalfund.org/en. Accessed July 6, 2006.

71. The Global Fund. The Global Fund to Fight AIDS, Tuberculosis, and Malaria. History of the Fund in Detail. Available at: http://www.theglobalfund.org/en/about/road/history/default.asp. Accessed July 6, 2006.

72. The Global Fund. Available at: http://www.theglobalfund.org/en. Accessed October 14, 2010.

73. International AIDS Vaccine Initiative. About IAVI. Available at: http://www.iavi.org/viewpage.cfm?aid=24. Accessed July 12, 2006.

74. International AIDS Vaccine Initiative. IAVI's Intellectual Property Agreements for AIDS Vaccine Development. Available at: http://www.iavi.org/viewpage.cfm?aid=40. Accessed July 12, 2006.

75. International Federation of Pharmaceutical Manufacturers & Associations. Global Alliance to Eliminate Leprosy. Available at: http://www.ifpma.org/Health/other_infect/health_lep.aspx. Accessed July 12, 2006.

76. National Institutes of Health. A Leading Cause of Blindness May Be Controlled by Simple Course of Oral Antibiotic. Available at: http://www3.niaid.nih.gov/news/newsreleases/1999/trachoma.htm. Accessed July 12, 2006.

77. Benton B. The Onchocerciasis (Riverblindness) Programs: Visionary Partnerships. Available at: http://www.worldbank.org/afr/findings/english/find174.htm. Accessed July 12, 2006.

78. African Comprehensive HIV/AIDS Partnerships. Available at: http://www.achap.org. Accessed July 12, 2006.

79. Basch P. *Textbook of International Health*. 2nd ed. New York: Oxford University Press; 2001:38-39.

80. Basch P. *Textbook of International Health*. 2nd ed. New York: Oxford University Press; 2001:43.

81. Basch P. *Textbook of International Health*. 2nd ed. New York: Oxford University Press; 2001:45.

82. Merson MH, Black RE, Mills AJ. *International Public Health: Diseases, Programs, Systems, and Policies*. Gaithersburg, MD: Aspen Publishers; 2000:667-669.

83. Basch P. *Textbook of International Health*. 2nd ed. New York: Oxford University Press; 2001:47-70.

84. Whaley RF, Hashim TJ. *A Textbook of World Health: A Practical Guide to Global Health Care*. New York: Parthenon; 1994:187-199.

85. World Health Organization. Fact Sheet No 101: Leprosy. Available at: http://www.who.int/mediacentre/factsheets/fs101/en. Accessed July 7, 2006.

86. World Health Organization. Fact Sheet No 102: Lymphatic Filariasis. Available at: http://www.who.int/mediacentre/factsheets/fs102/en. Accessed July 7, 2006.

87. World Health Organization. Onchocerciasis. Available at: http://www.who.int/topics/onchocerciasis/en. Accessed July 7, 2006.

88. Whaley RF, Hashim TJ. *A Textbook of World Health: A Practical Guide to Global Health Care*. New York: Parthenon; 1994:197.

89. Bruce FC. Highlights from the national summit on safe motherhood: investing in the health of women. *Maternal Child Health J.* 2002;6(1):67-69.

90. World Health Organization. Declaration of Alma-Ata. *International Conference on Primary Health Care*. Alma-Ata, USSR: WHO; 1978.

91. Merson MH, Black RE, Mills AJ. *International Public Health: Diseases, Programs, Systems, and Policies*. Gaithersburg, MD: Aspen Publishers; 2000:682.

92. The World Bank. *World Development Report 1993*. New York: The World Bank, Oxford University Press; 1993:25-29.

93. World Health Organization. Fifty-eighth World Health Assembly. Available at: http://www.who.int/mediacentre/events/2005/wha58/en. Accessed July 7, 2006.

94. Kidder T. *Mountains Beyond Mountains*. New York: Random House; 2003.

95. This brief is based on a draft provided by the Global Health Council. Additional information can be found at their website, http://www.globalhealth.org.

96. This brief is based on a draft provided by the Global Network for Neglected Tropical Diseases. Additional information can be found at their website, http://www.globalnetwork.org.

97. The Global Alliance for TB Drug Development. Mission and History. 2010. Available at: http://www.tballiance.org/about/mission.php. Accessed July 26, 2010.

98. The Global Alliance for TB Drug Development. 2009 Annual Report: Accelerating the Pace. 2009. Available at: http://www.tballiance.org/newscenter/publications.php. Accessed July 26, 2010.

99. The Global Alliance for TB Drug Development. TB Drug Portfolio. 2010. Available at: http://www.tballiance.org/new/portfolio.php. Accessed July 26, 2010.

100. The Global Alliance for TB Drug Development. Business Model. 2010. Available at: http://www.tballiance.org/about/business.php. Accessed July 26, 2010.

101. The Global Alliance for TB Drug Development. Donors. 2010. Available at: http://www.tballiance.org/about/donors.php. Accessed July 26, 2010.

102. This brief is based on a draft provided by the International AIDS Vaccine Initiative. Additional information can be found at their website, http://www.iavi.org.

103. PATH Malaria Vaccine Initiative. About Us. 2010. Available at: http://www.malariavaccine.org/about-overview.php. Accessed August 3, 2010.

104. PATH Malaria Vaccine Initiative. Current Status, Future Plans. June 2008. Available at: http://www.malariavaccine.org/publications-presentations.php. Accessed August 3, 2010.

105. PATH Malaria Vaccine Initiative. Frequently Asked Questions About MVI. 2010. Available at: http://www.malariavaccine.org/about-faqs.php. Accessed August 3, 2010.

106. PATH Malaria Vaccine Initiative. What We Do. 2010. Available at: http://www.malariavaccine.org/about-what-we-do.php. Accessed August 3, 2010.

107. PATH Malaria Vaccine Initiative. The State of Global Malaria Vaccine Development. 2010. Available at: http://www.malariavaccine.org/malvac-state-of-vaccine-dev.php. Accessed August 3, 2010.

108. PATH Malaria Vaccine Initiative. Fact Sheet. January 2010. Available at: http://www.malariavaccine.org/factsheets.php. Accessed August 3, 2010.

109. PATH Malaria Vaccine Initiative. Preparing for Vaccines. 2010. Available at: http://www.malariavaccine.org/preparing-overview.php. Accessed August 4, 2010.

110. PATH. An Initiative for Hope: The Malaria Vaccine Initiative Works to Accelerate Vaccine Development. 2010. Available at: http://www.path.org/projects/mvi.php. Accessed August 4, 2010.

111. PATH Malaria Vaccine Initiative. Accelerating Progress Toward Malaria Vaccines. 2007. Available at: http://www.malariavaccine.org/files/080212_MVI_portfolio_bro_mvilogo_000.pdf. Accessed August 11, 2010.

112. Malaria Vaccine Initiative. Malaria Vaccine R&D: The Case for Greater Resources. 2003. Available at: http://www.malariavaccine.org/files/Two-page-funding.pdf. Accessed August 12, 2010.

113. Hecht R, Palriwala A, Rao A. Innovative Financing for Global Health: A Moment for Expanded U.S. Engagement? A Report of the CSIS Global Health Policy Center. Available at: http://csis.org/files/publication/100316_Hecht_InnovativeFinancing_Web.pdf. Accessed October 7, 2010.

114. UNITAID. Innovative Financing for Health: Increasing Access and Affordability of Medicines Through Market Impact. Available at: http://www.unitaid.eu/images/Factsheets/unitaid_brochure_july_en.pdf. Accessed October 8, 2010.

115. The Global Fund to Fight AIDS, Tuberculosis and Malaria. Innovative Financing of the Global Fund: Debt2Health. Available at: http://www.theglobalfund.org/documents/publications/other/D2H/Debt2Health.pdf. Accessed October 7, 2010.

116. The Global Health Fund to Fight AIDS, Tuberculosis and Malaria. Fourth Debt2Health Agreement Signed Between Germany, Côte d'Ivoire and the Global Fund in Abidjan, 16 September 2010. Available at: http://www.theglobalfund.org/en/innovativefinancing/stories/?story=story201009. Accessed October 7, 2010.

117. This brief is based on: Institute for Health Metrics and Evaluation. Financing Global Health 2009: Tracking Development Assistance for Health. Available at: http://www.healthmetricsandevaluation.org/publications/policy-report/financing-global-health-2009-tracking-development-assistance-health. Accessed May 5, 2011.

118. Benton B, Bump J, Seketeli A, Liese B. Partnership and promise: evolution of the African river blindness campaigns. *Ann Trop Med Parasitol.* 2002;96(suppl 1):S5-S14.

119. Laolu A. Victory over river blindness. *Africa Recovery.* 2003;17(1):6.

120. Merck. The Story of Mectizan. Available at: http://www.merck.com/about/cr/mectizan. Accessed August 6, 2004.

121. Amazigo U, Brieger W, Katabarwa M, et al. The challenges of community-directed treatment with ivermectin (CDTI) within the African Programme for Onchocerciasis Control (APOC). *Ann Trop Med Parasitol.* 2002;96(1):S41-S58.

122. The World Bank. Defeating Onchocerciasis in Africa. Available at: http://www.worldbank.org/operations/licus/defeatingoncho.pdf. Accessed October 1, 2003.

123. Hopkins D, Richards F. Visionary campaign: eliminating river blindness. *Med Health Ann.* 1997:8-23.

124. Benton B. Economic impact of onchocerciasis control through the African Programme for Onchocerciasis Control: an overview. *Ann Trop Med Parasitol.* 1998;92(suppl 1):S33-S39.

CHAPTER 16

Science, Technology, and Global Health

By the end of this chapter the reader will be able to:

- Articulate the needs for diagnostics, vaccines, and drugs to address high-burden diseases that affect the poor in low- and middle-income countries
- Assess the extent to which existing products meet those needs
- Note the potential of science and technology to develop new products to address high-burden diseases
- State some of the key constraints to investments in such products
- Indicate mechanisms to overcome these constraints and encourage the development and uptake of new diagnostics, vaccines, and drugs
- Outline the lessons for future efforts of selected cases of new product development

VIGNETTES

Juan lived in the highlands of Peru. He had tuberculosis. He was being treated at a local TB clinic. He had to take four drugs for the first 2 months of his treatment and two drugs for 4 months after that. Juan felt better within weeks of starting his drugs and struggled to take the remaining pills because there were so many to take and he had to take them for so long.

Wezi lives in South Africa, where about 16.9 percent of the adults are HIV positive.[1] Despite intensifying efforts to reduce the spread of new HIV infections in South Africa, the number of these infections is still growing. In fact, the latest estimates suggest there were just under 500,000 new infections in 2009[2] and that about 5.7 million people in South Africa are now living with HIV.[1] Many people believe that

stemming transmission of HIV in countries like South Africa will depend on the discovery of a safe, effective, and affordable HIV vaccine.

Mei-Ling was 4 years old and lived in the west of China. Like so many children in her region, Mei-Ling was infected with hookworms. The community had a deworming program, and every 6 months Mei-Ling was given medicine to get rid of the worms. This medicine was generally safe and effective. However, it had to be given twice a year and there was some indication that the hookworms were becoming resistant to it.

David was 7 years old and lived in the eastern part of Kenya. He had a high fever and chills and his mother took him to the local health clinic. The nurse there examined David, decided he had malaria, and prescribed antimalarial medicine. This was the third time in a year that David had malaria. A safe, effective, and affordable malaria vaccine would have prevented him from getting malaria, being sick so often, missing so much school, and spending so much money on medical care.

INTRODUCTION

Scientific and technological progress has contributed substantially to improvements in human health. Such progress has included, for example, vaccines for a number of potential killers; a variety of drugs, such as penicillin; and safer and more effective family planning devices.

In fact, some scientific and technological discoveries have been of exceptional importance to public health. The discovery of the smallpox vaccine led to the first important efforts at vaccination, and ultimately to the eradication of smallpox.

Jonas Salk's discovery of the polio vaccine began to eliminate the scourge of polio from many societies, and this work was advanced further by Albert Sabin's work on the oral polio vaccine. It is difficult to imagine living in a world without antibiotics, but they only emerged just before World War II.

The enhancement of medical devices has also had an important impact on public health. The invention of the bifurcated needle, as you read earlier, was instrumental in enhancing the effectiveness of the smallpox eradication campaign. The intraocular lens for cataracts has provided a very low-cost tool for improving visual acuity, as you read about in Chapter 12.

The purpose of this chapter is to examine how science and technology could assist in speeding up the development and dissemination of new products that could address the largest burdens of disease in low- and middle-income countries. First, the chapter will examine the characteristics that such products need to possess if they are to have the desired impact. Next, the chapter will review the extent to which some existing diagnostics, vaccines, and drugs have those traits. The chapter will then discuss the potential of science and technology to develop products in selected areas of importance and review the constraints to product development. Lastly, the chapter will examine mechanisms to assist in overcoming those constraints, partly by reviewing a number of policy and program briefs and two case studies as examples of efforts at the development and dissemination of new products.

As you read this chapter, it is very important that you keep several things in mind. First, you should remember, as noted continuously in the book, that very substantial gains in health could be obtained from the effective implementation of existing technologies. There are, for example, a number of low-cost but highly effective interventions that are well-known but not widely enough used, including:

- Reducing maternal disability and deaths by better identification of complications, speedy transport to the hospital, and appropriate emergency obstetric care
- Reducing neonatal deaths by training birth attendants in resuscitation and the provision of antibiotics and by keeping the baby warm
- Reducing young child deaths by expanding coverage with the six basic antigens
- Reducing infant morbidity and mortality by promoting exclusive breastfeeding for 6 months
- Reducing morbidity and mortality from TB by expanding case finding and cure rates using DOTS as the approach to treatment

In addition, we must remember that better hygiene practices do not require the development of any new products and could substantially improve health.

As you read this chapter, it is also important to keep in mind that the development of new products will not be a "quick fix." Rather, while supporting the continued search for scientific and technical progress, it is critical to continue to focus on the underlying sources of ill health in low- and middle-income countries. These include poverty, the lack of education, the lack of political interest in the health of the poor, and the place of some minority groups and women in society. Enhancement in basic infrastructure, water, and sanitation will also be critical in many settings to sustainable improvements in health.[3]

Finally, you should note that this chapter focuses on a narrow range of the scientific and technological matters that concern global health. It looks largely at new product development, the constraints to it, and what might be done to speed up the process. It does not examine research or operational research. Nor does it focus on the dissemination of existing technologies, some of which is covered elsewhere in the book.

THE NEED FOR NEW PRODUCTS

As we think about the characteristics of diagnostics, drugs, vaccines, and medical devices that could most effectively and efficiently address the critical health problems of low- and middle-income countries, we need to keep several points in mind. First, the most important target groups for these products are poor people. Their financial resources are limited and the countries in which they live, particularly low-income countries, spend very little on health. Second, the quality of care in many countries is low and injection safety is often poor. Third, many low- and middle-income countries have health systems that are poorly organized and cannot effectively manage logistics. Transport and storage of goods is weak and electricity for keeping goods cool is often limited, as well.

In this light, what would be some of the ideal characteristics of diagnostics, drugs, vaccines, and medical delivery devices intended to help address the most critical burdens of disease in low- and middle-income countries? The most important of these characteristics are shown in Table 16-1.

As you can see in the table, it is important that diagnostics be specific, sensitive, easy to use, and noninvasive. Ideally, diagnostic tests could be done quickly by relatively untrained workers and would rapidly produce easy-to-read results, as well. They would also be easy to transport, heat stable, inexpensive and not require refrigeration.

Much the same would be true for the "ideal" drugs. These drugs would be safe, effective, and inexpensive. They could also be used for many years without becoming susceptible to resistance. In addition, the number of pills that patients would have to take would be limited and they would not have to take them for very long.

Vaccines to meet the most important health needs in low- and middle-income countries would also be safe, effective, and inexpensive. They would be easy to transport and store, would be heat stable, and would not require refrigeration. The ideal vaccines would be an inexpensive combination of many antigens, and only one dose would confer lifelong immunity against a number of diseases.

The present state of key products does not meet the ideals noted above. Presently, for example, a child receiving full coverage of the six basic antigens would require five contacts with the health system to get all of these vaccines.[4] Could vaccines be developed that combine required antigens in such a way that only a few contacts would be needed between the health system and patients?

You read earlier about the cultural preference in many societies for injections, despite problems with injection safety. Could vaccines be delivered in noninvasive ways, such as sprays, air injectors, and skin patches, that would be safe, effective, heat stable, easy to transport, and not very costly?

There is a vaccine for tuberculosis and drugs that are effective against tuberculosis, as well. However, the effectiveness of the TB vaccine against adult pulmonary TB is "variable."[5] In addition, the drugs that are used to treat TB require a large pill burden, and TB bacteria are increasingly becoming resistant to some of them.[6] What is needed to develop new drugs for TB that could make treatment shorter and easier? Is it possible to develop a safe and effective TB vaccine?

Artemisinin-based combination therapy is effective against malaria that is resistant to chloroquine, although resistance to artemisinin is already growing. However, the cost per treatment with this drug, even at globally negotiated prices, is about $1 for the treatment of a child and about $2 for the treatment of an adult.[7] This is about 15 times the cost per treatment with chloroquine.[8] In addition, while the search for a malaria vaccine has gone on for many years, there is still no approved vaccine for malaria. What would it take to develop additional low-cost and highly effective malaria drugs? What can encourage the development of a safe and effective malaria vaccine?

TABLE 16-1 Some Ideal Characteristics of Diagnostics, Vaccines, Drugs, and Delivery Devices

Diagnostics: Affordable; specific and sensitive; provide quick and easy-to-interpret results; easy to store and transport; heat stable

Vaccines: Affordable; safe and effective; require few doses; confer lifelong immunity; easy to transport and store; heat stable

Drugs: Affordable; safe and effective; not easy for pathogens to become resistant to; require small doses over a limited period; easy to store and transport; heat stable

Delivery devices: Affordable; safe and effective; not invasive; easy to transport and store; heat stable

Drugs for HIV can control the virus for most people but cannot cure them. In addition, people develop resistance to those drugs, and some of them have serious side effects. Moreover, there is still no preventive or therapeutic vaccine for HIV. How can the world encourage the development of safer and more effective AIDS drugs, an HIV vaccine, and mechanisms by which women could protect themselves better from the risk of HIV, such as microbicides?

The scientific and technological gaps indicated above also apply to some of the "other neglected diseases." Despite the ubiquity of hookworm, there is no vaccine for hookworm, the drug has to be administered regularly, and resistance to the drug is increasing. Can a vaccine be developed for hookworm and some of the other parasitic diseases?

THE POTENTIAL OF SCIENCE AND TECHNOLOGY

Scientific progress has led to a number of areas in which science could be harnessed to address some of the gaps noted in the previous section and to improve human health. Four such areas of science, as examples, are noted in this section.

Sequencing the genomes of important pathogens will help scientists understand better why those pathogens cause disease, how they develop resistance, and what drugs can best fight them, while reducing the onset of resistance. The genomes have now been sequenced for more than 100 microbial species.[9] The speed with which the SARS virus was sequenced is an indication of the speed with which this can be done, if sufficient priority is given to this work.[10] The sequencing of the mosquito genome may allow scientists to engineer mosquitoes so that they cannot carry malaria and other diseases, such as lymphatic filariasis.[11]

Improvements in information technology, chemistry, and robotics, as well as in genetic and molecular epidemiology, will also facilitate the development of new and better drugs. These tools will allow scientists to understand better the nature of disease. They will also enable scientists to more quickly try different chemical compounds to address those pathogens.[9]

In addition, a number of technologies exist that can assist in the design and manufacture of new and improved vaccines.[9] The use of recombinant DNA technology, for example, helped an Indian vaccine company to reduce the cost of hepatitis B vaccine from about $8 to 50 cents.[11] DNA technology should also be very helpful to the development of drugs.[11]

Genetic modification of plants is a controversial subject because, among other things, there are concerns over the environmental and health risks associated with them. Yet, it is possible to engineer plants that can carry higher levels of certain nutrients, such as vitamin A, while being very resistant to disease.[12] In addition, plants can be modified genetically so that they can produce "edible vaccines." The most advanced such work is for a vaccine for hepatitis B, but work is underway for other vaccines, as well.[12]

In fact, there is an increasing understanding of the promise of science and technology for improving global health. In one study, the views of 28 experts were sought about the "major biotechnologies that can help improve health in developing countries in the next 5 to 10 years."[13] In particular, these scientists were polled about the extent to which technologies would:

- Improve health
- Be affordable and appropriate to the circumstances of developing countries
- Address the most pressing health needs
- Be developed in the next 5 to 10 years
- Advance knowledge
- Have important indirect benefits[13]

They were also asked how they would use science and technology to achieve these aims. As the highest priority, these scientists would use biotechnology to develop new diagnostics, vaccines, and drugs, in that order. They would use technology to improve the environment, including water and sanitation. The scientists also put a high premium on the development of products that can help empower women to protect themselves against sexually transmitted diseases, including HIV, such as microbicides.[13]

The Grand Challenges in Global Health is a grants scheme that aims at financing discoveries that address these important concerns. The scheme was launched in 2003 by the Bill & Melinda Gates Foundation, in conjunction with the Canadian Institute for Health Research, the Foundation for the U.S. National Institutes of Health, and the Wellcome Trust. By 2005, the Grand Challenges program had awarded more than $400 million in 43 grants. The specific goals of this program and the challenges it seeks to address are shown in Table 16-2. In 2008, the Bill & Melinda Gates Foundation launched a related initiative, Grand Challenges Explorations, which provides $100 million in financing for what are planned to be bold and unconventional ideas for tackling the needs for new tools to address the burden of disease among the poor in low- and middle-income countries. This program has already awarded grants to 340 researchers.[14,15]

A number of projects that have been funded aim to improve vaccines. One of the projects, for example, seeks to develop a vaccine that can prevent pertussis with a single dose, instead of the three doses needed now. Another project will try to develop a vaccine against pneumococcus that can be given in a single dose, instead of the four doses for the present vaccine. Several projects will try to make vaccines more heat stable. Others aim to create vaccine delivery systems that can be eaten, inhaled, or sprayed into the nose. Several projects relate to the development of a malaria vaccine. Others concern efforts to develop strategies for genetically engineering mosquitoes so they will be unable to spread the dengue virus.[15]

Several of the projects that were funded will try to use genetic engineering to biofortify plants, such as making bananas contain more usable vitamin A, vitamin E, and iron in Uganda, where bananas are a staple food. Similar work would be done on rice with vitamins A and E, iron, zinc, and improved protein quality. Additional projects would focus on the science relating to the development of drugs for addressing latent TB and vaccines for the human papillomavirus.[15] Table 16-3 lists a small number of examples of the newer grants.

CONSTRAINTS TO APPLYING SCIENCE AND TECHNOLOGY TO GLOBAL HEALTH PROBLEMS

Given the strengths of existing scientific knowledge, why is it that some of the products that could make an important difference to the health of the poor globally have not been developed? Beyond the inherent scientific difficulties in some of these efforts, such as the development of HIV and malaria vaccines, there are several common constraints to the development of desired products. First, much of the research and

TABLE 16-2 Goals and Related Challenges of the Grand Challenges in Global Health

Improve Vaccines
- Create effective single dose vaccines that can be used soon after birth.
- Prepare vaccines that do not require refrigeration.
- Develop needle-free delivery systems.

Create New Vaccines
- Devise reliable tests in model systems to evaluate live attenuated vaccines.
- Solve how to design antigens for effective, protective immunity.
- Learn which immunological responses provide protective immunity.

Control Insect Vectors
- Develop a genetic strategy to deplete or incapacitate a disease-transmitting insect population.
- Develop a chemical strategy to deplete or incapacitate a disease-transmitting insect population.

Improve Nutrition
- Create a full range of optimal, bioavailable nutrients in a single staple plant species.

Limit Drug Resistance
- Discover drugs and delivery systems that minimize the likelihood of drug-resistant micro-organisms.

Cure Infection
- Create therapies that can cure latent infection.
- Create immunological methods that can cure chronic infections.

Measure Health Status
- Develop technologies that permit quantitative assessment of population health status.
- Develop technologies that allow assessment of multiple conditions and pathogens at point-of-care.

Source: Adapted from Grand Challenges in Global Health. Goals. Available at: http://www.grandchallenges.org/Pages/BrowseByGoal.aspx. Accessed September 28, 2010.

TABLE 16-3 Selected Examples by Goal of Grand Challenge Awards

Improve Vaccines
- Needle-free delivery of stable, respirable powder vaccine
- Comprehensive studies of HIV resistance in highly exposed uninfected women

Create New Vaccines
- Malaria transmission blocking vaccine
- Improve mucosal immune responses to oral typhoid vaccine

Control Insect Vectors
- Single-dose vaccines for newborns with a long-lasting immune response
- Thermostable vaccines with improved stability at nonrefrigerated temperatures

Improve Nutrition
- Vitamin A–secreting probiotics to stimulate healthy immunity in the GI tract
- Deworming as intervention against secondary diseases

Limit Drug Resistance
- Strategies to disable rapid increases in mutations of malaria parasites
- Combating antibiotic resistance in tuberculosis

Cure Infection
- Preseason elimination of malaria infections
- Malaria detection using earth's magnetic field

Measure Health Status
- TB Rapid Test (TBRT) Project
- Simple early breath diagnosis of pneumococcal pneumonia

Source: Adapted from Grand Challenges in Global Health. Grants Map. Available at: http://www.grandchallenges.org/Pages/GrantLocations.aspx. Accessed September 28, 2010.

development on new diagnostics, vaccines, drugs, and delivery devices is carried out in the for-profit sector, and that sector has historically believed it could not make a sufficient return from products oriented toward low- and middle-income countries. These firms see the market for their goods in low- and middle-income countries as a small one. They also doubt the ability of low-income individuals to pay prices for their products that would give them a sufficient return on

their capital. In addition, they doubt that governments in low-income countries could afford their products. As evidence of this, for example, they point to the slow uptake in developing countries of the vaccines against *Haemophilus influenzae* type b (Hib) and hepatitis B.

Moreover, the costs of research and development on new products can be very high, some suggesting as high as $800 million, to bring a new drug from research to market. Given these costs, profit-making firms will invariably want to use their capital to develop, for example, a potential "blockbuster" drug against high cholesterol that can be sold in

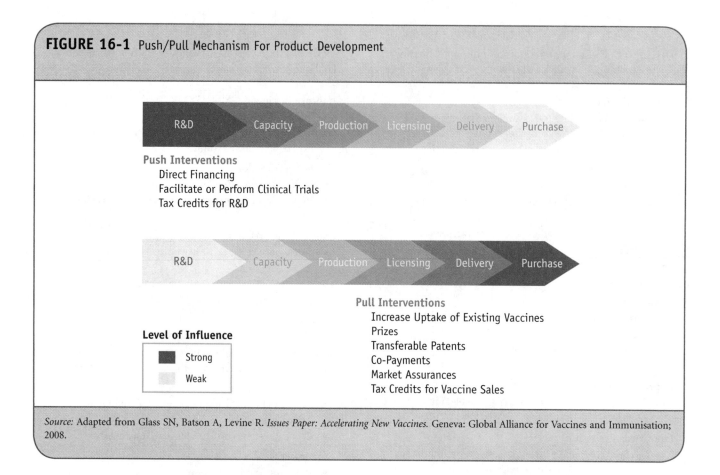

FIGURE 16-1 Push/Pull Mechanism For Product Development

R&D → Capacity → Production → Licensing → Delivery → Purchase

Push Interventions
Direct Financing
Facilitate or Perform Clinical Trials
Tax Credits for R&D

R&D → Capacity → Production → Licensing → Delivery → Purchase

Pull Interventions
Increase Uptake of Existing Vaccines
Prizes
Transferable Patents
Co-Payments
Market Assurances
Tax Credits for Vaccine Sales

Level of Influence
Strong
Weak

Source: Adapted from Glass SN, Batson A, Levine R. *Issues Paper: Accelerating New Vaccines.* Geneva: Global Alliance for Vaccines and Immunisation; 2008.

high-income countries, rather than develop a drug for low-income countries on which the firm believes it will not be able to recoup its investment.[16]

In addition, vaccine markets have some particular constraints to entry. Vaccine development requires a considerable amount of upstream investment, the cost of developing vaccine candidates is very high, and governmental regulations may also reduce the prospects that firms can make sufficient profit from vaccines to attract them to this market. In addition, the number of firms engaged in vaccine production worldwide is small and production capacity is limited. Developing vaccines for low- and middle-income countries is also complicated by the fact that there is an increasing divergence between the vaccines used in the immunization programs of low- and middle-income countries and the vaccines used in high-income countries. This relates primarily to the relatively expensive combination vaccines that are increasingly used in high-income countries. Moreover, pharmaceutical companies can generally earn a higher return on money invested in the development of drugs than money invested in developing vaccines.[17]

Another constraint to greater focus on the health conditions of low- and middle-income countries until recently has been insufficient attention to them by some of the major national research institutions. The basic research that is conducted at places like the U.S. National Institutes of Health often sets a foundation for product development later by the for-profit manufacturers. The greater the attention that national research institutes in high-income countries pay to high-burden problems of developing countries, the greater the likelihood that new products for them will eventually be developed.

Some of the above constraints are reflected in the extent to which drugs have been developed to address diseases that most affect poor people in low- and middle-income countries. A study of drugs that were approved for marketing showed that between 1975 and 1999, for example, 1393 new chemicals were approved but only about 3 percent were relevant to infectious and parasitic diseases that are the most significant burdens of disease in low-income countries. The same study looked at the number of new drugs approved for every million DALYs lost and found that two to three times more drugs were produced for every million DALYs lost to diseases of high-income countries, rather than diseases of low- and middle-income countries.[18] Over the same period, only about 1 percent of the drugs approved concerned the neglected tropical diseases and only about 0.2 percent concerned TB.[18]

A study of 20 major pharmaceutical manufacturers found that several of the firms spent less than 1 percent of their research and development budget the previous fiscal year on TB, malaria, African trypanosomiasis, Chagas' disease, and leishmaniasis. Only malaria appears to be an area of infectious diseases that is attracting any substantial investment from pharmaceutical manufacturers. Yet, the amount of investment by drug companies in asthma drugs was about 20 times the amount they invested in malaria drugs.

Moreover, about 90 percent of expenditure on research and development on health is oriented toward the diseases of the developed world and only about 10 percent toward the diseases of the developing world. The Global Forum for Health Research called this the "10/90 gap."[19,20]

ENHANCING NEW PRODUCT DEVELOPMENT

We have seen that gaps in the development of diagnostics, drugs, vaccines, and medical devices that can serve the needs of low- and middle-income countries reflect failures of the market. In general, the public sector tries to reduce its risks by waiting for such products to be developed by the private sector. However, the private sector generally believes that it is too risky to produce products that are expensive to develop and for which an adequate return on investment cannot be assured. Is it possible to change the market for these products? Can one reduce the cost of product research and development to the point where the private for-profit sector might be interested in such products? What other steps can be taken to speed product development?

Push Mechanisms

A number of steps could encourage a larger share of research and development to focus on the needs of low- and middle-income countries. Some of these are shown in Figure 16-1, which depicts push and pull mechanisms and where in the product development cycle they have the most impact.

One type of effort is called "push mechanisms." These refer to mechanisms meant to encourage product development by helping to "reduce the risks and costs of investments."[17] Push mechanisms could include:

- Direct financing: Government financing or carrying out of research activities needed to develop a product.

- Performing or facilitating clinical trials: This could include government measures to make it easier to carry out clinical trials for the product and to help with the ethical issues involved in such trials.
- Tax credits for research and development: Governments can lower the cost to firms of research and development by giving them credits against their taxes for certain investments.[17]

These push mechanisms operate on the early stages of product development. Such mechanisms have been used successfully before. In addition, they can reduce risk and thereby encourage investment in product development. The disadvantage of push mechanisms, however, is that there is no guarantee that they will produce a product. Even if a product is developed, it may not be the best one, and product developers will then not produce what might have been better candidates. Furthermore, when the money is spent on push mechanisms it is gone whether or not a product has been developed.[17]

Some of the direct financing and facilitation of clinical trials could be done through programs like the U.S. National Institutes of Health or similar institutes in other countries. Additional money could also be channeled, for example, to the Special Program for Research and Training in Tropical Diseases that is sponsored by WHO, the United Nations Development Program, and the World Bank.[21] Some of the financing of the Bill & Melinda Gates Foundation, like that for the Grand Challenges, is meant to push new product development.

In conjunction with these efforts, it is important to strengthen the links between researchers in low- and middle-income countries and high-income counties. The links can also be enhanced between researchers in low- and middle-income countries. The aim of these efforts would be to attract more research money to institutions within the developing countries that are engaged in research and development on the most important burdens of disease in such countries. A number of low- and middle-income countries, especially India, China, Brazil, South Africa, Mexico, Indonesia, and Cuba, have the ability to carry out basic research and to develop products that emanate from that research.[22]

It is also important to comment on some aspects of governmental regulation of pharmaceutical and vaccine development. Regulation is necessary, but it is also an important part of the costs of research and development. By arranging to speed drug approvals and harmonize approval processes across countries, the costs of research and development can be reduced to provide some incentives to manufacturers. Granting fast track approval for generic AIDS drugs, for example, *has* encouraged the development of such drugs.[18]

Pull Mechanisms

A number of mechanisms are intended to help "assure a future return in the event that a product is produced." These are called pull mechanisms.[17,19] Some of the most important pull mechanisms include:

- Increasing the uptake of existing vaccines: Using public funds to increase the use of vaccines that have not been taken up sufficiently, such as the vaccines for Hib and hepatitis B.
- Prizes: Offering monetary rewards to those firms that develop desired products.
- Transferable patents: In exchange for the development of the desired product, providing the manufacturer with the right to extend a patent on another one of their products or patents in markets in high-income countries.
- Co-payments: Governments can provide the manufacturer with a payment for every product sold.
- Market assurances: The public sector can promise to buy the products if they are produced.
- Tax credits for vaccine sales: Governments can offer tax credits for products that are sold.[17]

From the point of view of the public sector, pull mechanisms have the advantage of providing funds only when desired products have been developed. However, governments and the private sector have to agree early on what such arrangements would be for any product, and neither party might be satisfied with these arrangements when products do emerge.[17] There has been little experience until recently with financing mechanisms that are meant to exert a pull on new product development and use, but the Advance Market Commitments and the International Finance Facility for Immunisation are now in place and are discussed later in the chapter.

A mechanism that has been used for vaccines for some time and more recently for AIDS drugs is called *tiered pricing*. This is an arrangement by which a firm charges different prices in different markets. The idea behind tiered pricing is that a firm can charge enough to make a profit in high-income markets to offset the fact that the products will not make a profit in low- and middle-income markets. The profits from one market could cross-subsidize the sales at reduced prices in other markets. This is being practiced now

for some drugs for which there is a global market. However, tiered pricing is not likely to work effectively for products that are needed exclusively in low- and middle-income countries because the basis for cross-subsidizing will not exist.[18] Efforts are now being proposed to develop tiered pricing mechanisms for products as soon as they are available, rather than wait until many years after their development, as has been the case until now.[23]

In addition, as discussed in Chapter 15, considerable hope is being put into the role that public–private partnerships can play in encouraging the development of the diagnostics, drugs, vaccines, and medical devices that could have a significant impact on the health of the poor in low- and middle-income countries. As indicated earlier, many of these efforts are organized around the search for new products for particular diseases, such as HIV, TB, and malaria. These public–private partnerships are also referred to as product development partnerships (PDP) and are organized on a not-for-profit basis. They aim to attract private, public, and philanthropic funds to invest in needed research and development, tapping the strengths of the private sector in product development as they do so. There are now PDPs for a large number of vaccines and drugs, including, for example, TB and malaria. A brief is given later in this chapter on the development of TB vaccines.

Meeting product development goals will probably require a combination of the above efforts. First, they can start with a greater focus by research institutions in high-income countries on the problems of low- and middle-income countries. They can also promote greater networking of research institutions in low- and middle-income countries. This can help encourage product development, with other push mechanisms. At the same time, it will be important to change the market and perceptions of the market for needed products through pull mechanisms that can ensure that money will be available for products if they are developed. Third, the public and private sectors can collaborate with each other, bringing complementary skills and financing to the partnership. Over the next several years, evidence should emerge that will allow one to evaluate the effectiveness of PDPs and the push and pull mechanisms that are discussed above.

POLICY AND PROGRAM BRIEFS

This section contains four briefs that highlight some of the different approaches to harnessing science and technology to enhance new product development and use. The first concerns the development and use of vaccine vial monitors, which enable the quality of vaccines to be assured and for vaccine wastage to be reduced. The second discusses a PDP, Aeras, that aims to spur the development of more effective TB vaccines. The third and fourth concern financing mechanisms that are intended to provide a pull on new product development and diffusion, the Advance Market Commitments (AMC) and the International Finance Facility for Immunisation (IFFIm).

Vaccine Vial Monitors

Vaccines are extremely sensitive to temperature; a change of even a few degrees can spoil them. Yet, these vaccines are at constant risk of spoiling[24] as they are transported in low- and middle-income countries that often lack the infrastructure needed to ensure they stay at a safe temperature.

Previously, when the vaccines reached their final destination, there was no way of knowing if they had spoiled along their journey. This put health providers in a risky predicament. They could administer the vaccines that might be spoiled and, thereby, risk that they would not be effective. Alternatively, they could err on the side of caution and discard the vaccines, thereby wasting an expensive investment. Clearly, uncertainty about a vaccine's viability drains resources in low-income settings and could lead to spread of disease.

The uncertainty about a vaccine's viability is now greatly reduced thanks to a small sticker applied to the vial that indicates whether the vaccine has been exposed to excessive heat or cold and is spoiled. A square on the sticker, known as a vaccine vial monitor (VVM), darkens continuously in the presence of temperature change. If the square's color is equal to or darker than the outer circle on the sticker, then the vaccine is spoiled. VVMs can be applied to the vial label, cap, or neck.

The initial concept of a temperature exposure indicator for vaccine vials was first devised by WHO in 1979, but the actual product was not commercially available until 1996 from the Temptime Corporation. By 2004, VVMs had become a labeling requirement for all vaccines purchased through UNICEF and GAVI. A number of stakeholders played key roles throughout the development and advancement of VVMs, including WHO, PATH, USAID, GAVI, UNICEF, and the U.S. Centers for Disease Control and Prevention.

The application of this technology makes immunization programs more effective and efficient. Instant indication of a vaccine's viability through a VVM leads to minimizing distribution costs and also increasing flexibility of delivery programs. PATH has estimated that $5 million per year could be saved on the costs of vaccines by using VVMs.

Temptime is the only current producer of VVMs. No other suppliers have been successful in developing a competitive product, despite technical assistance from WHO and PATH. Even though Temptime's principal patents have expired, technology transfer to other companies is not being pursued due to Temptime's manufacturing expertise and its ability to meet global demand.

A major obstacle in ensuring widespread use of VVMs has been convincing vaccine distributors and procurers to supply vaccines with VVMs. These vaccines cost a small amount more than vaccines without VVMs, and manufacturers are concerned that even a minimal price increase discourages the use of VVMs in low-resource settings. The requirement of VVMs on the labels of all vaccines distributed by UNICEF and GAVI has helped to overcome this hurdle.

Nonetheless, achieving widespread and consistent use of VVMs by all vaccine distributors will continue to be a challenge. VVMs are not currently available on most vaccines produced and sold in low-income countries through the domestic market, except in India, Indonesia, and Pakistan. Even though WHO and UNICEF have released statements calling for VVMs to be a requirement, achieving this standard will require greater coordination with national governments, donors, and NGOs.

VVMs exemplify how advances in science and technology, although they may not seem very complicated, can help make health programs more cost-effective. With the support of key players in vaccine distribution, this new technology has been taken from an idea to a reality in low-resource settings.

Aeras

The Aeras Global TB Vaccine Foundation was founded in 2003. Aeras's mission is to develop safer, more effective and affordable new vaccine regimens that will prevent tuberculosis—including drug-resistant TB—in all age groups, including people living with HIV/AIDS.[25]

Aeras is one of the most fully integrated of the PDPs and undertakes the full spectrum of vaccine development—vaccine construction, preclinical research, manufacturing, and clinical development. Like other PDPs, the key to Aeras's mission is ensuring the availability of new vaccines for all who need them. Aeras seeks to accomplish this through agreements with its vaccine development partners that emphasize affordability and access for poor people in low-income countries of any eventual TB vaccine that might be developed.

Based in Rockville, Maryland, in the United States, and with an office in Cape Town, South Africa, Aeras employs 140 staff members from 30 different countries. Aeras's operations resemble those of biotech companies, with in-house vaccine discovery laboratories, immunology, clinical trial coordination, data management, and state-of-the-art manufacturing capabilities. Its partners are spread across four continents and include academia, other research institutions, multilateral organizations, industry, foundations, governments, patient groups, and advocates. Aeras also works closely with other PDPs focused on new TB drugs and diagnostics to advocate for research and development.

Aeras's key accomplishments to date include the establishment of a network of partner clinical trial sites in endemic countries, advancing several vaccine candidates into clinical trials, and the development of backup vaccine candidates. Aeras is sponsoring clinical trials in Africa, Europe, India, and the United States of four candidate vaccines originated by external partners. Two of those candidates have advanced to the proof-of-concept stage—a phase of development intended to demonstrate that the proposed approach is feasible. A fifth candidate, invented by Aeras, entered trials in 2010. In addition, Aeras is undertaking epidemiology studies in Cambodia in preparation for possible future trials there. A new vaccine is unlikely to appear before 2020 at the earliest.

One of Aeras's main goals is to modernize the existing TB vaccine, known as BCG, which was invented in 1921. BCG is widely used, but has had little impact on the growing TB epidemic because it is unreliable at preventing pulmonary TB infection, which accounts for most of the TB disease burden worldwide, and does not appear to protect against latent TB. In addition, it is not recommended for use in infants infected with HIV. To address these challenges, Aeras scientists have developed an improved BCG vaccine that has the potential to help the immune system respond better to the vaccine. This newly developed BCG, or the current BCG, would be used in combination with a different booster vaccine, such as one of the four candidates that are in clinical development. It is intended that this combination would not only enhance the protection afforded by the BCG vaccine, but also extend protection over a longer period of time.

One of the biggest challenges facing Aeras and other PDPs is mobilizing the resources to fund their work, particularly as they start larger and more expensive later-stage clinical trials, which are aimed at testing whether the vaccine is effective. Scientific hurdles include the lack of measurable signs that a person is protected against infection after immunization and the lack of models for testing the vaccine on animals, which can save time and money in vaccine development. These are also barriers to the development of HIV and malaria vaccines. Aeras has also been faced with unpredictable events that slow down timelines, such as political unrest at one trial site.

Collaboration is key to accomplishing Aeras's mission. Like all PDPs, Aeras's work is made possible through the involvement of partners in developing and high-income countries, in industry and the nonprofit sector, and among researchers, government officials, donors, politicians, and volunteers.

Aeras has received funding from the Bill & Melinda Gates Foundation; the governments of Denmark, the Netherlands, the United Kingdom, and the United States; the Research Council of Norway; and the State of Maryland in the United States.

Advance Market Commitments

Advance Market Commitments (AMC) is a financing mechanism that aims to encourage investment in the development and manufacturing of vaccines that can be sold at affordable prices in low-income countries. The AMC was devised in 2005 and further refined during 2006–2009. It started in 2009 and is housed at the GAVI.[26]

The need for a financing mechanism such as the AMC is based on the problem discussed earlier—the unwillingness of vaccine manufacturers to invest in "newer" vaccines that meet the needs of low-income countries because the manufacturers believe that the market for such vaccines will not be profitable. The high risk and high cost of such an investment ultimately leave suppliers with little incentive to produce. What's more, even if a manufacturer did find reason to supply vaccines, these vaccines would be unaffordable for people in low-income countries at the prices at which they would have to be sold for the manufacturers to make a profit on them.

The AMC can best be thought of as a fund that will make financing available to vaccine manufacturers under certain circumstances they agree to with the AMC management. To erase uncertainties about the market for vaccines and provide an incentive to vaccine manufacturers to produce the needed quantities of the desired vaccines, a pool of money from donors guarantees that the manufacturer will receive a set price per dose produced, provided that the manufacturers will supply a predetermined quantity of vaccines for a certain amount of time at the agreed price.

In addition, manufacturers participating in the scheme must meet certain technical criteria for vaccine quality and safety predetermined by the World Health Organization. The AMC ensures that no single supplier receives all of the funding for a particular vaccine, thereby avoiding the possibility of a monopoly and problems of supply if a sole manufacturer could not meet its production commitments.

The first AMC pilot program for a vaccine against pneumococcal disease was adopted by a group of core donors including Italy, the United Kingdom, Canada, Norway, and the Gates Foundation in 2007, and became fully operational in 2009. The decision to invest in a pneumococcal vaccine for the pilot program was made by a diverse group of experts in epidemiology and vaccine manufacturing. The AMC is projected to save over 7 million lives by 2030 at $33 per DALY. GAVI has pledged to contribute $1.3 billion through 2015, with the hope of making the vaccine available to nearly 60 countries in this time.[27]

In exchange for incentives offered by guaranteed purchase and financing, manufacturers who participate in the AMC must sell the vaccine at or below a predetermined price of $7 a dose, to ensure that the vaccine is affordable in low-income countries. The AMC will cover half of this price—$3.50 a dose—and the balance of $3.50 will be paid by GAVI and the participating country as part of its normal "co-financing share." The AMC will eventually discontinue its subsidy to the manufacturer, at which point the manufacturer must continue to sell the vaccine at or below the predetermined, affordable "tail" price of $3.50. This preset price is a more than 90 percent discount on the current price of the vaccine in high-income countries.[27,28]

Setting an appropriate price for the pneumococcal vaccine and subsidy for manufacturers was a major challenge in devising the pilot program. This is largely due to suppliers keeping information about manufacturing costs confidential. To overcome this obstacle, outside consultants helped to assess the cost of manufacturing. The fact that the two main multinational suppliers of the pneumococcal vaccine and several emerging suppliers from India all expressed interest in participating in the AMC suggests that they find the AMC price and the tail price to be reasonably remunerative. Assessing a fair price for vaccines funded by the AMC will continue to be a challenge for this financing mechanism.

The large number of donor and technical organizations that worked together with GAVI and developing country partners to develop the AMC and launch the pilot is a testimony to the widespread interest in this innovative mechanism. In addition to the donors mentioned earlier, who committed $1.5 billion to the AMC, the World Bank is providing its financial services, WHO is responsible for technical matters related to the AMC, and UNICEF is leading vaccine procurement efforts.[28]

International Finance Facility for Immunisation

The International Finance Facility for Immunisation (IFFIm) is a financing mechanism that seeks "to rapidly accelerate the availability and predictability of funds for immunization." IFFIm funds are used by the GAVI Alliance to accomplish its mission of "reducing the number of vaccine-preventable deaths and illnesses among children under 5."[29] IFFIm was originally launched in 2006 as a charity by the government of the United Kingdom but now includes France, Italy, the Netherlands, Norway, South Africa, Spain, and Sweden.

The IFFIm was created to address the lack of secure funding for immunization in low-income countries. Another issue the IFFIm seeks to address is that donors usually provide financing on a year-to-year basis, making it hard for recipient governments to plan their budgets for programs that receive assistance, such as immunization programs. The IFFIm is meant to help ensure longer term and more predictable financing for vaccine programs.

To ensure a reliable stream of funding for GAVI, donor countries pledge a certain amount of money to be paid to GAVI over about 20 years. IFFIm then sells bonds to raise this money in the capital markets of high-income countries. This makes the money available immediately, without having to wait for year-to-year-financing from donor governments. The donor countries repay the bonds over time, based on their initial pledges. The fact that the IFFIm is backed by the promises of these countries allows it to maintain a good credit rating and to sell bonds at rates that are acceptable to the donor countries that have to honor the bonds.

GAVI is using IFFIm funds to purchase and deliver vaccines in 72 countries, in addition to working with health services to strengthen immunization programs. With funding from the IFFIm, GAVI has introduced pentavalent vaccines in 57 countries; these immunize against diphtheria, pertussis, tetanus, hepatitis B, and Hib in a single vaccine.[30] The IFFIm has enabled GAVI to double its spending, amounting to $1.2 billion between 2006 and 2009. Over 4 million children have been immunized with the additional money raised to date from IFFIm funds.[30]

With secure funding, GAVI hopes to deliver reliable aid to countries for the long term, enabling these countries to plan and implement immunization programs more effectively. In addition, having more secure and longer term funding allows GAVI to purchase vaccines in bulk, at lower prices than would otherwise be possible. Thus, the IFFIm hopes to enable the purchase of more vaccines with the same amount of money.

The IFFIm had generated more than $2 billion by September 2009, and is projected to raise $4 billion by 2015. Over

20 years, 500 million children are projected to receive immunization with the $5.3 billion pledged by donor countries.[29]

CASE STUDIES

Two case studies follow. The first concerns the effort to develop a vaccine for hookworm. It centers on a public–private product development partnership that is being funded by the Bill & Melinda Gates Foundation. This is especially significant, given the burden of disease from hookworm, the fact that treatment has to be repeated every 6 months, and the fact there is no vaccine at the moment for any of the neglected tropical diseases. The second case concerns efforts to spread the use of relatively new vaccines for Hib and hepatitis B in Chile and The Gambia. This case also highlights the measures that can be taken to speed the uptake of both existing and new vaccines.

The Human Hookworm Vaccine Initiative

Background

As discussed in Chapter 11, the neglected tropical diseases (NTDs) are a group of chronic disabling and poverty promoting conditions that affect the world's poorest people in rural and peri-urban communities of low-income countries. They include, among other diseases, helminth infections such as ascariasis, hookworm, trichuriasis, schistosomiasis, dracunculiasis (guinea worm), lymphatic filariasis (elephantiasis), and onchocerciasis (river blindness). The NTDs cause human suffering and impede economic development either because of their disfiguring properties or through their impact on child health and development, maternal health and pregnancy outcomes, and worker productivity. The combined disease burden of the NTDs is equivalent to that of HIV/AIDS, malaria, or tuberculosis, and their economic impact results in the loss of tens of billions of dollars annually.[31]

Despite their enormous health and economic importance, there has been little interest in developing new drugs or vaccines for the NTDs. A major reason for this situation is the absence of any commercial market for products related to these diseases, because they affect almost exclusively the world's 3 billion people who live on less than $2 per day.[32] As a result, many of the drugs in use for the NTDs were first developed during the early or middle parts of the 20th century.

Similarly, there are no licensed vaccines available for the NTDs even though there have been significant basic research efforts related to their development over the last 20 years. If preventive or therapeutic vaccines could be developed, then they would represent a generation of "antipoverty vaccines," which could serve as powerful new tools in achieving the Millennium Development Goals.

Human hookworm infection is an example of an NTD that would benefit from the development of a vaccine. Hookworm affects an estimated 600 million people, almost all of them impoverished individuals living in sub-Saharan Africa, Southeast Asia, and tropical regions of the Americas. The infection is caused by nematode parasites that attach to the inside of the intestine and ingest host blood. When individuals are infected with large numbers of hookworms, the blood loss is sufficient to cause iron-deficiency anemia and protein malnutrition. This is especially a problem for young children and pregnant women.

There are inexpensive drugs available to treat human hookworm infection. The two major drugs for hookworm are the benzimidazoles—albendazole and mebendazole—which are typically administered as single doses to school-age and preschool children in mass drug administration (MDA) programs, sometimes referred to as "deworming" programs. However, deworming does not prevent hookworm re-infection, which can occur within 4–12 months following treatment in areas of high transmission. Moreover, there is evidence that the efficacy of drugs against hookworm diminishes with increasing use and there is concern that the hookworm parasites may develop resistance to them. Single-dose mebendazole is no longer considered an effective drug for hookworm, for example. These concerns have prompted interest in developing complementary or alternative approaches to controlling the infection through vaccination.

The Intervention

The Human Hookworm Vaccine Initiative (HHVI) was established at the Sabin Vaccine Institute in Washington, D.C. in 2000 with funding from the Bill & Melinda Gates Foundation. The HHVI is a PDP composed of a network of laboratories and clinical trial sites, with program management, quality assurance, regulatory affairs, and clinical development and oversight units based at the Sabin Vaccine Institute. There are two different vaccine antigens currently under development, each building on well-established academic research and development efforts based at The George Washington University (Washington, D.C.) and James Cook University (Cairns, Australia). It is proposed that the two vaccine antigens eventually will be combined into a single human hookworm vaccine.

Critical to the success of the HHVI is the concept that it is possible to develop and test vaccines in nonprofit and academic settings. This requires the purchase and operation of special equipment and the recruitment of scientists with industrial manufacturing experience, as well as experts in quality control, quality assurance, and documentation. The process development and quality control facilities for the HHVI are located at The George Washington University, located near the Sabin Vaccine Institute.

Process development and manufacture of one of the two candidate hookworm antigens—*Na*-GST-1—has been completed and a series of trials to test the safety and immune response in individuals living in Brazil will be started in 2011. This will be done in collaboration with Fundação Oswaldo Cruz (FIOCRUZ), a Brazilian governmental organization that combines research and public health activities. Process development and manufacture of the second hookworm vaccine antigen is underway, with clinical trials scheduled to begin in 2012.

Impact

To ensure that any safe and effective vaccine that is developed will be distributed to the people who need it, the HHVI is working with public sector vaccine manufacturers in countries where hookworm infection is endemic. The HHVI is currently working with FIOCRUZ, as well as the nonprofit and state-owned Instituto Butantan in São Paulo, Brazil, to ultimately ensure a supply of locally made and affordable hookworm vaccine.

Another component of the HHVI's global access plan is to develop strategies for administering the vaccine in settings where deworming is currently practiced. For most low- and middle-income countries, deworming is conducted in schools or on child health days because children, on average, harbor the greatest numbers of intestinal worms. A human hookworm vaccine will likely be administered following deworming in a strategy of vaccine-linked chemotherapy. Analyses have been conducted that support the cost-effectiveness of combining hookworm vaccination with deworming over deworming alone, mostly due to the additional reduction in morbidity and the reduced frequency of deworming that would be afforded by vaccination.

Lessons Learned

Several important and useful lessons have been learned so far from the HHVI experience, including:

- It is feasible to produce and test vaccines in the nonprofit sector through product development partnerships.
- Partnering with an "innovative developing country," like Brazil, represents a new strategy for developing, testing, and distributing neglected disease products.

- Achieving these goals requires strong program management for structuring the partnership, maintaining timelines, and achieving milestones.
- There are important advantages to cooperating with scientifically capable developing countries for both manufacture and clinical testing of new products, and looking to these countries as a means to initiate global access for NTD vaccines.
- There is a need to consider novel healthcare delivery systems, such as schools, to ensure that the products that will be delivered will be accessible to the populations who need them the most.

Preventing Hib Disease in Chile and The Gambia

Background

Although the microbe *Haemophilus influenzae* type b (Hib) causes 450,000 deaths worldwide each year, it has avoided the notoriety of other major killers. Hib disease occurs in many invasive forms such as meningitis, pneumonia, and bacteremia. Hib meningitis is particularly lethal, killing 20–40 percent of the children who get it, and leaving many survivors with lasting impairments such as deafness or intellectual and developmental disability.[33] Children under the age of 5 are most susceptible to Hib disease—particularly when they are between 6 and 11 months—and 23 per 100,000 develop Hib meningitis every year. Infection and fatality rates are highest in sub-Saharan Africa.

Many low- and middle-income countries have not been able to afford Hib vaccines, available since the late 1980s, unlike industrialized nations where Hib has been dramatically reduced. However, the successful experience of two very different countries—Chile and The Gambia—has persuaded other developing countries to introduce the vaccine. In Chile, a study in the late 1980s revealed the extent of Hib meningitis in Santiago: 32 per 100,000 among infants up to 5 months and 63 per 100,000 among infants ages 6 to 11 months.[34,35] The disease was fatal for 16 percent of Hib cases. In The Gambia, surveillance of hospitals in the western region in the 1990s showed that more than 200 children per 100,000 had Hib meningitis each year.[36]

The Intervention

Chile is a middle-income country with largely modern infrastructure, where 95 percent of infants receive routine vaccines. Nonetheless, Hib vaccines were not previously included because of their cost. Research done in the 1980s, however, showing the prevalence of Hib disease, persuaded the government to launch a program to further explore the efficacy of the vaccine. Hib immunization was provided at

36 health centers and their results compared with other centers where no Hib inoculations were provided. The vaccine, donated by Aventis Pasteur, was injected along with the usual DTP antigens in the same syringe. The dramatic results of this study convinced the government to include Hib in the routine immunization program, starting in 1996.

The Gambia is among the world's poorest countries, with a far less developed infrastructure than Chile. Although immunization coverage of 85 percent is higher than in many parts of Africa,[33] infant mortality in The Gambia remains high. However, once the government recognized the severity of the Hib problem through the 1990s survey, it began a large, controlled trial of the Hib vaccine in 1993. Here too, Aventis Pasteur donated the vaccine, and WHO, UNICEF, USAID, and other organizations supported the program. The government improved its vaccine cold chain with the use of solar power, decentralizing vaccine storage and healthcare management to improve supply. As in Chile, the results were impressive, and in 1997, a 5-year program of immunization and surveillance was launched in the western region.

The Impact

Among children at Chile's health centers who received the vaccine, Hib meningitis was reduced by 91 percent, and pneumonia and other forms of Hib disease by 80 percent, compared to the children in the DTP-only centers.[37] In The Gambia, the 5-year program yielded equally remarkable results. Within the first year, the number of children developing Hib meningitis dropped almost tenfold, from 200 per 100,000 to 21 per 100,000. In the last 2 years of the study, there were only two cases.[33]

Costs and Benefits

The government of Chile paid $3.39 million for the combined DTP-Hib vaccine, which is 23 percent of the total immunization budget. The price per Hib dose has declined from $15 in 1996 to an average today close to $3.50,[38] and the government saves an estimated $78 for every case of Hib prevented. In The Gambia, the 5-year program was made possible by Aventis Pasteur's donation of Hib vaccines. Financial support from the Vaccine Fund and GAVI helped sustain the program through 2008.

Lessons Learned

The governments of Chile and The Gambia both found ways of overcoming the obstacle of cost, which remains the main impediment to adoption of the vaccine by other countries. The success of the program in The Gambia demonstrated the effectiveness of the vaccine in a country where the health system is severely underfunded at every level. Other developing countries have since adopted the Hib vaccine, often with the help of GAVI or the Pan American Health Organziation (PAHO).

However, it is not yet known whether some other low- and middle-income countries, where Hib is a major problem, will introduce the vaccine. The answer depends in part on how and whether financing is made available, and on how expensive the vaccine will be over the medium term. The effects on regions without the vaccine are still undocumented, and it remains to be seen whether the positive experiences now being consolidated in Latin America and the Caribbean, and parts of Africa, will be shared elsewhere. Another unknown element lies in the spread of antibiotic-resistant strains of the Hib microbe, complicating treatment of the disease in the future.

MAIN MESSAGES

Science and technology have the potential to make major contributions to the development of diagnostics, vaccines, drugs, and medical devices that can help address the highest burdens of disease in low- and middle-income countries. Progress in scientific areas like the sequencing of genes, information technology, chemistry, robotics, and biotechnology can help, for example, to engineer mosquitoes that will not carry disease, discover new drugs much more rapidly than before, and develop less expensive and more effective vaccines.

In a more "ideal" world, diagnostics, vaccines, drugs, and medical devices would be appropriate to the needs of the health conditions that cause the largest burden of disease in low- and middle-income countries. They would also be appropriate to the ability of countries to manage their health systems. If these were the case, they would be affordable by low-income patients and countries that are unable to spend much on health. They would also be heat stable, not require refrigeration, and be easy to store and transport. The number of pills needed to cure a disease would be few and require a short course of therapy. Ideal vaccines would be a combination of many of the vaccines that exist today, so that children would need fewer vaccinations to be "fully covered." Given the risks of injections being unsafe, the delivery devices for vaccines would increasingly rely on noninvasive means, such as nasal sprays, skin patches, or perhaps, vaccines that are edible.

Unfortunately, the needed advances are unlikely to come about on their own. This is largely a reflection of the fact that the for-profit sector has historically been a major developer of diagnostics, vaccines, and drugs but does not believe that the market for these products in low- and middle-income countries is sufficient to give it an adequate return on its investment. In addition, the public sector is risk averse and would prefer to purchase a product developed by the private sector rather than to try to develop these products itself. The failure of the market is reflected, as an example, in the very small number of drugs that have been developed over the last 20 years to address the main burdens of disease among the poor in low- and middle-income countries. Moreover, vaccine development is constrained by the need for substantial investments, limited capacity in an industry with a very small number of producers, and an increasing divergence between the vaccines used in high-income countries and those used in low- and middle-income countries.

Overcoming these market failures and encouraging the development of the desired products will probably require a series of measures. Some of these can be push mechanisms that are meant to lower the cost of research and development for the private sector. These could include, for example, direct financing by government of research, the facilitation by government of clinical trials, or governments offering tax credits for research and development. Push mechanisms do lower the cost of research and development, but they provide no certainty that the desired product will be produced.

Another set of efforts could focus on pull mechanisms, which are intended to help assure a satisfactory return to investors in the event that a product is produced. These mechanisms could include funding mechanisms to increase the uptake of existing vaccines, prizes, transferable patents, co-payments, market assurances, and tax credits for vaccine sales. Pull mechanisms have the advantage of providing funding only when the desired product is available. However, they have the disadvantage of having to be negotiated far in advance of product availability, and parties may not be satisfied with the terms of their agreement at the time in the future when the products are available.

A mechanism already in use for vaccines and for AIDS drugs is tiered pricing. This is an arrangement in which products are sold at different prices in different markets, with the principle being that the price of sales in developed country markets will help defray the low cost of the products in developing country markets. However, these arrangements have generally been put in place only when products were established; efforts are now underway to try to put them in place at the early stages of a product's life.

Considerable hope for new product development is being placed in public–private product development partnerships, such as Aeras, the International AIDS Vaccine Initiative, the Global Alliance for TB Drug Development, and the Medicines for Malaria Venture. The aim of these ventures is to bring the strengths of the public and private sector together in complementary ways that can spur the development of new products. The chapter suggests in its policy and program briefs and in case studies on hookworm vaccine, and the dissemination of Hib and hepatitis B vaccines in Chile and The Gambia, some steps that can be taken both to develop products that are needed and to see that they are widely used once they are developed.

Study Questions

1. What are some of the "ideal" properties that diagnostics, vaccines, and drugs should have to be most appropriate to the health and health system needs of low- and middle-income countries?

2. To what extent do some of the available vaccines for the six basic antigens and the vaccination schedule for them meet the "ideal"?

3. What health conditions and risk factors deserve additional attention from science and technology? Why have you chosen those conditions and risk factors?

4. What are some of the specific gaps in diagnostics, drugs, vaccines, and other medical equipment that could most improve global health if filled?

5. What have been some of the major constraints to the development of drugs and vaccines that could better meet health needs in low- and middle-income countries?

6. What steps can be taken to overcome those constraints? What are the roles in this of publicly supported research? What are the roles of public–private partnerships for health?

7. Why does only 10 percent of all research expenditure worldwide focus on the diseases that most affect the poor in the developing world? What is the 10/90 research gap?

8. What "push" and "pull" mechanisms could most help to encourage the development of new diagnostics, drugs, and vaccines?

9. What lessons does the case study on hookworm suggest for the discovery of other drugs and vaccines?

10. If you were the Bill & Melinda Gates Foundation, how would you spend money on research and development of new products for global health? Why?

REFERENCES

1. UNAIDS. 09 AIDS Epidemic Update. Available at: http://data.unaids.org:80/pub/Report/2009/JC1700_Epi_Update_2009_en.pdf. Accessed September 28, 2010.

2. UNAIDS. Republic of South Africa: Country Progress Report on the Declaration of Commitment on HIV/AIDS. Available at: http://data.unaids.org/pub/Report/2010/southafrica_2010_country_progress_report_en.pdf. Accessed September 28, 2010.

3. Birn AE. Gates's grandest challenge: transcending technology as public health ideology. *Lancet.* 2005;366(9484):514-519.

4. UNICEF. Facts for Life. Available at: http://www.unicef.org/ffl/pdf/factsforlife-en-part7.pdf. Accessed October 27, 2006.

5. Centers for Disease Control and Prevention. BCG Vaccine. Available at: http://www.cdc.gov/nchstp/tb/pubs/tbfactsheets/250120.htm. Accessed October 27, 2006.

6. Global Alliance for TB Drug Development. New TB Drugs Urgently Needed to Replace Treatment from the 1960s. Second Gates Grant to TB Alliance Quadruples Initial Support. Available at: http://www.tballiance.org/gates.asp. Accessed October 27, 2006.

7. Roll Back Malaria. 2009 Counting Malaria Out. Available at: http://www.rollbackmalaria.org/partnership/wg/wg_advocacy/docs/RBM.SEC.2009.COM.2.pdf. Accessed September 28, 2010.

8. Roll Back Malaria. Facts on ACTs (Artemisinin-based Combination Therapies): January 2006 Update. Available at: http://www.rbm.who.int/malariacmc_upload/0/000/015/364/RBMInfosheet_9.htm. Accessed April 13, 2007.

9. Fauci AS. Infectious diseases: considerations for the 21st century. *Clin Infect Dis.* 2001;32(5):675-685.

10. World Health Organization. Genomics and World Health: A Report of the Advisory Committee on Health Research. Available at: http://whqlibdoc.who.int/hq/2002/a74580.pdf. Accessed October 27, 2006.

11. Weatherall D, Greenwood B, Chee HL, Wasi P. Science and technology for disease control: past, present, and future. In: Jamison DT, Breman JG, Measham AR, et al., eds. *Disease Control Priorities in Developing Countries.* 2nd ed. New York: Oxford University Press; 2006:127.

12. Weatherall D, Greenwood B, Chee HL, Wasi P. Science and technology for disease control: past, present, and future. In: Jamison DT, Breman JG, Measham AR, et al., eds. *Disease Control Priorities in Developing Countries.* 2nd ed. New York: Oxford University Press; 2006:132.

13. Daar AS, Thorsteinsdottir H, Martin DK, Smith AC, Nast S, Singer PA. Top ten biotechnologies for improving health in developing countries. *Nat Genet.* 2002;32(2):229-232.

14. Grand Challenges in Global Health. About the Grand Challenges. 2010. Available at: http://www.grandchallenges.org/about/Pages/Overview.aspx. Accessed September 25, 2010.

15. The Bill & Melinda Gates Foundation. Grand Challenges in Global Health Initiative Selects 43 Groundbreaking Research Projects for More Than $436 Million in Funding. Available at: http://www.gatesfoundation.org/GlobalHealth/BreakthroughScience/GrandChallenges/Announcements/Announce-031016.htm. Accessed October 14, 2006.

16. Mahmoud A, Danzon PM, Barton JH, Mugerwa RD. Product development priorities. In: Jamison DT, Breman JG, Measham AR, et al., eds. *Disease Control Priorities in Developing Countries.* 2nd ed. New York: Oxford University Press; 2006:141.

17. Glass SN, Batson A, Levine R. *Issues Paper: Accelerating New Vaccines.* Geneva: Global Alliance for Vaccines and Immunisation; 2006.

18. Trouiller P, Torreele E, Olliaro P, et al. Drugs for neglected diseases: a failure of the market and a public health failure? *Trop Med Int Health.* 2001;6(11):945-951.

19. Bloom BR, Michaud CM, LaMontagne JR, Simonsen L. Priorities for global research and development interventions. In: Jamison DT, Breman JG, Measham AR, et al., eds. *Disease Control Priorities in Developing Countries.* 2nd ed. New York: Oxford University Press; 2006:106.

20. Global Forum for Health Research. Available at: http://www.globalforumhealth.org/Site/000__Home.php. Accessed October 27, 2006.

21. Reich MR. The global drug gap. *Science.* 2000;287(5460):1979-1981.

22. Morel CM, Acharya T, Broun D, et al. Health innovation networks to help developing countries address neglected diseases. *Science.* 2005;309(5733):401-404.

23. Batson A, Glass SN, Levine R. *Differential Pricing of Vaccines, Draft Report.* Geneva: Global Alliance for Vaccines and Immunisation; 2006.

24. Baker P. Vaccine vial monitors: Small labels with an immense impact. In: *Case Studies for Global Health: Building Relationships. Sharing Knowledge.* Deerfield, IL: Alliance for Case Studies for Global Health; 2009.

25. Aeras. Mission. Available at: http://www.aeras.org/about/mission.php. Accessed August 27, 2010.

26. Kher U. A marriage of divergent interests: partnership in making of the world's first advance market commitment. In *Case Studies for Global Health: Building Relationships. Sharing Knowledge.* Deerfield, IL: Alliance for Case Studies for Global Health; 2009.

27. GAVI Alliance. Advance Market Commitments (AMCs). Available at: http://www.gavialliance.org/vision/in_financing/amcs. Accessed May 6, 2011.

28. Advance Market Commitments. The Pneumococcal Vaccine: Ready to Save Lives. Available at: http://www.vaccineamc.org/pneu_amc.html. Accessed September 18, 2010.

29. IFFIm. Available at: http://www.iff-immunisation.org. Accessed September 21, 2010.

30. International Finance Facility for Immunisation (IFFIm). Bringing Together Capital Market Investors and Children in the World's Poorest Countries. Both Benefit. Available at: www.iff-immunisation.org/pdfs/Iffim_booklet_EN.pdf. Accessed September 24, 2010.

31. Hotez, PJ. Control of neglected tropical diseases. *New Engl J Med.* 2007;357:1018-1027.

32. Hotez, PJ. *Forgotten People, Forgotten Diseases: The Neglected Diseases and Their Impact on Global Health and Development.* Washington, DC: ASM Press; 2008.

33. Adegbola R, Usen SO, Weber MW, et al. *Haemophilus influenzae* type b meningitis in The Gambia after introduction of a conjugate vaccine. *Lancet.* 1999;354(9184):1091-1092.

34. Ferreccio C, Ortiz E, Astriza L, Rivera C, Clemens J, Levine MM. A population-based retrospective assessment of the disease burden resulting from invasive *Haemophilis influenzae* in infants and young children in Santiago, Chile. *Pediatr Infect Dis J.* 1990;9(7):488-494.

35. Lagos R, Levine OS, Avendano A, Horwitz I, Levine MM. The introduction of routine *Haemophilus influenzae* type b conjugate vaccine in Chile: a framework for evaluating new vaccines in newly industrializing countries. *Pediatr Infect Dis J.* 1998;17(9 suppl):S139-S148.

36. Mulholland K, Hilton S, Adegbola R, et al. Randomised trial of *Haemophilus influenzae* type b tetanus protein conjugate for prevention of pneumonia and meningitis in Gambian infants. *Lancet.* 1997;349:1191-1197.

37. Lagos R, Horwitz I, Toro J, Martin O, Bustamente P. Large scale post-licensure, selective vaccination of Chilean infants with PRP-T conjugate vaccine: practicality and effectiveness in preventing *Haemophilus influenzae* type b infections. *Ped Infect Dis J.* 1996;15:216-222.

38. The Hib Initiative. Vaccine Supply and Finance. Available at: http://www.hibaction.org/vaccine.php. Accessed May 6, 2011.

CHAPTER 17

Working in Global Health

LEARNING OBJECTIVES

By the end of this chapter the reader will be able to:

- Understand the wide variety of professional opportunities available in the global health field
- Appreciate the skills, knowledge, and experience required to take advantage of those opportunities
- Understand some of the many different routes to a career in global health
- Be familiar with key resources for information about careers in global health
- Articulate career goals in the global health field, as appropriate to your own interests

VIGNETTES

Edith was among the best students in her schools in Kenya and she had a strong desire to become a scientist. After finishing secondary school and university in her home country, Edith won a fellowship to study HIV in graduate school in the United States. Edith's scientific research has focused on people who have contracted HIV but do not develop AIDS. Edith is now back in Kenya and working at a research institute in Nairobi. She focuses much of her work on "nonprogressors," in close collaboration with the International AIDS Vaccine Initiative.[1] The findings from these efforts could be instrumental to the eventual development of an HIV vaccine. Edith remains excited by her research efforts, even in the face of immense scientific challenges.

John is a Canadian civil engineer who works with the development of community-based water supply in poor countries. As a secondary school student, John already knew that he wanted to use engineering to provide poor people with better water and sanitation. He was inspired to pursue such a career by videos he saw in social studies class about the terrible impact on health of a lack of safe water. During his engineering studies, John spent three summers working in Africa with Engineers Without Borders.[2] John learned much in those summers about applying engineering techniques in poor communities. John also learned the importance of working closely with communities in the development and operation of water and sanitation schemes. Through his work as an engineer, John is making important contributions to health.

Vivian is a Filipina. She studied English at the University of the Philippines and then began to work as a journalist for a Manila newspaper. During more than a decade in journalism, Vivian became increasingly familiar with the poor health circumstances of many Filipinos and how they often relate to a lack of knowledge of good health behaviors. As she approached her 35th birthday, Vivian decided to leave journalism and apply her knowledge of that field and communications to working in health. Today, Vivian is the Director of Communications of an NGO that focuses on community-based approaches to improving the health of the poor.

Joseph is a graduate of the U.S. Military Academy, a former U.S. Army Ranger, and the former head of logistics for Doctors Without Borders (MSF) in Africa.[3] Joseph grew up in a family with a strong sense of social justice and considered for some time how he might help poor people in low-income countries. When he finished his time in the Army, Joseph looked for jobs with NGOs working in Africa, to see if he could bring to them some of the organizational and management skills that he had learned in the Army. Logistics management is of great importance to everyone working in health, and this was an area in which Joseph had considerable expertise. This knowledge served him well as he worked with Doctors Without Borders in the Democratic Republic of the Congo, Liberia, Sierra Leone, and Somalia. Because these were countries in conflict or that had recently been in conflict, Joseph's knowledge of how to manage programs in conflict zones and negotiate with groups in conflict was also very helpful.

INTRODUCTION

Interest in global health has been growing worldwide. As described earlier, there has been an enormous increase over the last decade in financing for global health, the number of public–private partnerships that address global health issues, and the number of students at all levels who are studying global health. With this expansion of global health activities and studies has come a growing interest in careers in global health.

The purpose of this chapter is to introduce you to those careers; the knowledge, skills, and experience you need to work in global health; and how you can acquire the background you need to become a global health professional. Consistent with the rest of the book, this chapter primarily focuses on careers related to "the unfinished agenda"—the health issues that confront poor people in poor countries. The chapter is not meant to be a complete guide to job hunting in global health; rather, it is intended to help you understand whether this is a field in which you would like to work and, if so, how you might pursue such interests. The chapter largely provides the type of information needed by university students who have minimal global health experience.

As you read this chapter, it is important to keep two critical points in mind:

- There are a wide variety of ways to work in global health.
- There is a large number of professions that can serve global health needs.

These points may seem trite. However, many people do not understand them and believe that only those people trained in the health professions can work in the field of global health. Of course, you can work in global health as a physician, nurse, or public health graduate; however, you do not need to be trained as a health professional to work in global health. For example, there is also an enormous need for people in global health who understand communications, ecology, economics, engineering, finance, health systems management, law, logistics management, and water and sanitation.

OPPORTUNITIES IN GLOBAL HEALTH

As you begin to explore careers in global health, it is valuable to consider such work opportunities from two different perspectives. The first is the kinds of organizations with which you can work. The second is the types of skills and professions that can best meet the needs of these organizations.

NGOs That Engage in Global Health Work

Many people want to work with nongovernmental organizations (NGOs) that are engaged in health in low- and middle-income countries. As discussed in Chapter 15, some of these are local NGOs, such as the Self-Employed Women's Association of India and the Population Foundation of India. Others are international NGOs, such as Oxfam, CARE, and Save the Children. The largest of these organizations support a wide variety of activities, including the delivery of health services and strengthening health systems. They may also engage in research, policy, and advocacy activities.

The largest NGOs tend to recruit people with substantial experience and high-level skills for their fieldwork in low- and middle-income countries. However, at their headquarters, these organizations generally have a broader range of positions, and they recruit staff with a variety of skill sets to carry out this work. These positions range from entry-level program assistants, who coordinate and track program information, to senior technical positions. The latter may include physicians, often with an advanced degree in an area of public health, such as epidemiology. These NGOs also recruit nurses, but usually only those with advanced degrees in public health, as well as experience working in public health in low- or middle-income countries.

In addition, many large NGOs hire public health graduates at the masters and doctoral level. These public health professionals have expertise in some of the key global health issues that were previously described in the book, such as maternal and child health, family planning, nutrition, communicable diseases, and health systems development. Most large NGOs will also employ a range of social scientists, including economists and anthropologists. Their staff may also include people with knowledge of behavior change education or information, education, and communication. Technical staff are usually involved in research, policy, or advocacy work, or in the design, implementation, and monitoring of health programs.

Organizations Involved in the Delivery of Humanitarian Services

A number of organizations, many of which are NGOs, are involved in the delivery of clinical services in low- and middle-income countries, especially related to complex emergencies or other humanitarian efforts. Such organizations would include, for example, Doctors Without Borders or the International Rescue Corps.[4] They may also provide services as part of shorter-term "medical missions," as in the work of Sightsavers[5] or Operation Smile.[6] In addition, the largest of these organizations are also involved with research, policy, and advocacy work. Many of the people engaged in these organizations are trained in medicine, nursing, and pharmacy; however, these organizations also have staff members who may be trained, for example, in finance or logistics management to support their clinical work, or economics, policy, and communications to support their other efforts. For their humanitarian work overseas, these organizations tend to hire relatively few junior staff that lack clinical training.

Bilateral Organizations and Government Agencies

The leading bilateral aid organizations, such as AusAID, the Canadian International Development Agency (CIDA), the U.K. Department for International Development (DFID), or USAID, also support important health programs in low- and middle-income countries. The profiles of staff members recruited by these organizations are similar to those of the largest NGOs. However, the bilaterals may include more people with training in economics and finance on their technical staff than most of the NGOs. In addition, the NGOs tend to focus on a relatively narrow range of technical areas, whereas the bilaterals may be involved in a wide range of health activities and require staff with skills in all of those areas. For example, the largest bilateral organizations may simultaneously work on health systems strengthening, maternal and child health, and infectious diseases, among other things. The staff who work with these organizations may be engaged in advocacy, research, or policy activities. They also work on the design, implementation, and evaluation of health programs in developing countries.

Multilateral Organizations and UN Agencies

The multilateral organizations and United Nations (UN) agencies that work on health tend to hire very seasoned professionals for their technical work. Most of these staff are recruited mid-career, after they have already had distinguished careers in their fields. However, many of these organizations also have programs for "junior professionals" or "young professionals." The junior professionals are generally recent graduates of a first degree or an advanced degree program. Other programs, like the World Bank's Young Professional program, select people who have advanced degrees, outstanding academic and professional records, and substantial experience, compared to most people their age.[7] In addition, these organizations recruit some relatively recent graduates of both first degree and advanced programs to work as program assistants and research assistants.

Multilateral organizations and UN agencies are also involved in a broad range of health sector activities and need professionals with skills in all of these areas. Similar to the work of the bilateral organizations, this generally includes research, policy, and advocacy, as well as program design, implementation, and evaluation. These organizations, however, often place more emphasis on health systems activities, and the work of economists and finance specialists than do other organizations working in global health. The World Health Organization, of course, is the most "technical" of these organizations, and a large share of its staff are trained as physicians.

Public–Private Partnerships for Health

As discussed in Chapters 15 and 16, the number of public–private partnerships for health has grown substantially. These organizations tend to be highly technical in nature and employ professionals with high-level technical skills. Because the organizations work in science, research, policy, and health services delivery, they recruit staff members with skills in each of these areas. However, their employment needs are frequently determined by new product development efforts, such as for a TB vaccine or a microbicide that could stem the transmission of HIV. In such cases, the organizations hire professionals with the knowledge and skills needed for these specific projects and for the policy, regulatory, and communications efforts needed to support them.

Consulting Firms

The consulting firms that work on global health also work in a wide variety of health efforts, including research and policy analysis, as well as program development, implementation, and evaluation. To carry out this work, the consulting firms generally require the same skill sets as the bilateral and multilateral organizations. This includes high-level technical expertise from a select number of domains in which the firm wants to specialize. However, they may also recruit younger staff to serve as research assistants, program assistants, and other entry-level positions.

Foundations

In general, the foundations that work in global health have a relatively small number of employees who tend to be very highly trained in their field. However, they often couple these staff with a small number of junior staff. The largest foundations that work in global health, such as the Bill & Melinda Gates Foundation, are generally staffed in a manner similar to the largest bilateral and multilateral organizations.

Academia

A large number of universities throughout the world are involved in education, training, research, and practice in global health. Universities and their associated research programs are generally staffed by faculty that have doctoral-level degrees in a discipline or degrees in law or medicine, frequently in conjunction with a public health degree. These faculty are in a wide variety of academic departments, most often including anthropology, economics, medicine, political science, public health, and sociology.

Many universities now have global health institutes or global health centers that coordinate and bring together faculty research and practice from across different parts of the university. These centers and institutes are often the university organizations that receive grants or contracts for global health projects and recruit people for work in university-affiliated global health activities. These efforts often engage a range of professionals, as well as more junior research assistants and program assistants. Of course, many universities prefer to hire their own students and graduates for such programs.

Policy and Advocacy Organizations

Policy-oriented organizations, such as think tanks, generally focus on research and analysis on key policy matters and on trying to set the intellectual agenda for moving forward on key global health issues. They tend to recruit highly skilled staff, and often quite seasoned staff, for their technical work. They usually recruit some junior staff to support their overall work, as well.

Advocacy organizations, which focus on raising awareness and funding for key global health issues, tend to recruit relatively young individuals who have some background in health, communications, and/or advocacy. These organizations are looking less for technical expertise and more for people with a deep sense of commitment to their work, the ability to strategize about how to influence policymakers, and exceptional ability to speak and write well on policy matters. Advocacy organizations do recruit for professional-level posi-

tions and may hire those with only a first degree, as well as those with advanced degrees, in areas related to their work.

YOUR FUTURE IN GLOBAL HEALTH

Now that you have a better understanding of the broad range of jobs in organizations that work in global health, it is time to establish a framework within which you can consider a possible career in global health. It is also important to provide a basic overview of how you can pursue such a career.

As you begin to think about your professional interests and a possible career in global health, it might be useful to ask yourself the following question: "Ten years from now, what impact do I hope to have had on the global health field?" Thinking about this question will help you focus on what you would like to do *and* the impact you would like to make from doing it.

If you are new to the global health field, it may be difficult to know the different types of global health work in which you could engage. You are probably familiar with some of the clinical work that health professionals, such as physicians, engage in to improve global health. However, you may have had little exposure to the work done by other professions. You may never have heard of work like Vivian's on health communications, Joseph's logistics work with Doctors Without Borders, or Edith's use of science to help develop new diagnostics, drugs, or vaccines that could improve the health of the poor in low- and middle-income countries.

Therefore, as you begin to develop your interest in a global health career, it is very important to:

- Become familiar with the types of opportunities there are for working in global health
- Understand the background needed for the type of career you may wish to pursue and how much of that background you already possess
- Establish a plan to gain the knowledge, skills, and experience you still need for such a career, in a manner consistent with your other personal and professional interests and obligations
- Identify people who can serve as "role models" to help you understand global health professions and how you can pursue them

More is said about each of these topics in the following sections.

What You Need to Know to Work in Global Health

In many respects, careers in global health are just like other careers. Both require a certain type of background to obtain a job and to carry it out effectively. In global health, as in other fields, certain specific types of knowledge, skills, and experience are usually necessary to gain employment and to grow in the field professionally. For example, if you think broadly about work in low- and middle-income countries, these would include:

- A good understanding of key political, social, and economic issues in the development of low- and middle-income countries, as well as how these issues might be addressed
- An appreciation for and an understanding of different cultures
- Knowledge of one or more languages commonly used in low- and middle-income countries
- Experience living and working in low- and middle-income countries, ideally close to the grassroots level
- Technical skills that can be used to help address global health issues
- An outstanding ability to write and speak simply and clearly for a wide range of audiences

Developing Your Knowledge, Skills, and Experience

Once you have outlined the knowledge, skills, and experience you are likely to need to pursue your global health career, it is important to assess your progress in each of these areas. You can then determine the gap between where you are and where you need to be. This assessment can serve as the foundation upon which you decide how best to fill that gap. Some of the ways of enhancing your readiness for a career in global health are noted in the following sections.

University Studies

The first step to set the foundation for your future career in global health is to get a good education in the field you want to pursue, if that is already defined. As noted earlier, it could be engineering. It could be anthropology. It could be economics. Whatever field you choose, it is important to master the material and take advantage of every opportunity to link your studies with the field of global health. For an engineering student, this could be a focus on water and sanitation. For an economics student, this could be a focus on the relationship between health and development. For an anthropology student, this could be a focus on medical anthropology.

As you pursue your first or later degrees, it is also important that you engage in the study of development. You do not need to become a development economist; however, you do need to have a good understanding and appreciation of the key issues in development, how they play out in low- and middle-income countries, and how those countries might

address them. In addition, it is crucial to understand the many links, in both directions, between health and education and health and development.

It is also essential to master as much as you can of English, Spanish, and French. Several other languages can also be very useful for work on health and development, including Portuguese and some languages commonly used in low-income countries, such as Swahili. It is important to note that the more languages in which you can work efficiently and effectively, the greater the opportunities will be for you in the global health field. The inverse is also important; a lack of knowledge of languages other than your own can be a major obstacle to gaining employment in the global health field.

In the end, the best way to learn about other cultures and languages is to live and work with other culture groups. However, until you can do that, it is essential that you take advantage of opportunities to study other cultures, languages, and development.

Internships and Work-Study

One excellent way to build the foundation for a career in global health while you are still a student is to engage in *internships* or *work-study* opportunities in the global health field. By undertaking a variety of internships throughout your studies, you can learn about numerous aspects of global health. This can also help you understand which parts of the global health field are most interesting to you and best suit your strengths. For example, with good planning and some luck, you might be able to work at different times for an NGO that works on health and human rights, another that focuses on the health of women and children, a third that emphasizes TB, and a fourth that is an advocacy organization. Alternatively, if you develop a specific interest at an early stage in your studies, such as HIV/AIDS, you could use your internships to gain a better understanding of the many aspects of HIV/AIDS work.

Most universities provide considerable information on how to find internships. This information may be available in a career office, on a university job or internship website, or through other forms of communication such as mass informational emails and print brochures. Other ways that students obtain internships include searching for advertisements on specialized websites, word of mouth from student to student, or asking for internships directly from specific organizations of interest to them.

Of course, finding an internship is easiest if you attend a university in a location with a tradition of internships and a wide array of internship opportunities, such as Washington, D.C., in the United States or London, in the United Kingdom.

If you study somewhere with ongoing global health efforts, you should have opportunities to learn about various aspects of global health throughout the course of your studies.

On the other hand, if you attend a university in a location with few such global health opportunities, you can still prepare yourself for global health work by pursuing internships in areas of domestic health that focus on marginalized populations, such as lower-income or immigrant communities. People in these communities face many of the same challenges that the poor face in low- and middle-income countries, and much can be learned from working with them.

Study Abroad

Another way you can build a foundation for work in global health is by studying for a semester or two in a low- or middle-income country. An increasing number of opportunities exist to study in low-income countries, such as Kenya, Senegal, or Uganda, as well as middle-income countries, such as Brazil, China, or South Africa. In addition, some of these programs specifically focus on health and provide students with opportunities to engage in independent research on health topics of their choice. Moreover, many study abroad programs have *home stays*, in which students live with a local family. These opportunities can be transformational and extremely enlightening for university students. The chance to live, even for a short time, with a family in a low- or middle-income country is a unique and invaluable experience.

Students in the International Honors Program visit a number of countries and may choose to focus some of their study program on health.[8] Other programs highlight health issues in a single country. The SIT program in Mali, for example, focuses on "health, gender, and community empowerment."[9] In the SIT Study Abroad program called "Switzerland: Global Health and Development Policy," students spend a semester in Geneva, Switzerland, studying global health issues from a policy perspective.[10] Geneva, of course, is especially well suited for such a program, because it is home to the World Health Organization (WHO), the Global Alliance for Vaccines and Immunisation (GAVI), and the Global Fund.

Work Abroad During Vacation

Another outstanding way to develop a foundation for a career in global health is to work on health in a low- or middle-income country during your university vacations. Some students do this over relatively short breaks, such as the winter break or spring break in the United States. However, others undertake such an experience during their long vacation, which is the summer break in the United States.

You can arrange such a work experience abroad in multiple ways. One possibility is to arrange the work through personal contacts. In many countries, university students are a diverse group, and a student may be able to spend time in the home country of a classmate, working, for example, with a health-oriented NGO. Another way to work in low- or middle-income countries over school vacations is to participate in a variety of programs that are arranged by organizations and firms, such as:

- *Cross-Cultural Solutions:* For 15 years, Cross Cultural Solutions has sent students of any age to volunteer or intern in one of 12 countries in Africa, Asia, Latin America, and Eastern Europe in the fields of education, health, and social service. Trips last anywhere from 1 to 12 weeks.[11]
- *Visions in Action:* Also known as Africa Development Corps, Visions in Action has sent students for over 20 years to work on development projects in South Africa, Uganda, Liberia, and Tanzania on issues of health, food security, and education. In health specifically, most projects in which students participate are related to combating HIV/AIDS. Most programs last anywhere from 6 to 12 months.[12]
- *Global Service Corps:* Located at SUNY Albany (State University of New York at Albany), Global Service Corps has sent students to intern in Cambodia, Tanzania, and Thailand for nearly 20 years. Internships are related to health care, education, and other community development projects and last anywhere from one week to indefinitely. Academic credit can be obtained for the internship.[13]

Unfortunately, one generally has to pay for opportunities such as these. However, many students have found them worthwhile.

Many universities and student groups sponsor short humanitarian visits to low- and middle-income countries during breaks. The visiting groups may help provide needed health services or may engage in broader aspects of community development, such as home building or the installation of water and sanitation systems.

Some universities also have travel fellowships that support student-led research during the university breaks. Although these fellowships tend to be highly competitive, they represent an excellent opportunity for students to explore research topics in another country. For example, a student at Yale University recently used such a fellowship to do research on sex trafficking in Mumbai, India. A George Washington University student used a travel fellowship during her winter break to conduct interviews in Mexico on the impact of the *Oportunidades* program on reducing maternal mortality among poor women. This research was part of an honors thesis she did during the final year of her Bachelor of Science degree program.

Postgraduate Work Overseas

Although it is very valuable to engage in global health efforts during your university studies, there are also opportunities to gain global health experience after completing your first degree. There are a small number of travel fellowships that can support such activities. These fellowships are sometimes offered by foundations, such as the Luce Foundation Fellowship in the United States.[14] Some universities also have their own fellowship programs for recent graduates. The United States also has a Fulbright scholars program that supports research and teaching in other countries.[15] There are also a large number of teaching fellowships that can help one live and work in a low- or middle-income country. Upon arriving in-country for such teaching fellowships, teachers can find health activities to engage in during their stay, as well. It is possible to conduct valuable global health research or practice through each of these fellowships.

Another popular way of gaining work experience in low- and middle-income countries is through a national overseas volunteer program, such as the U.S. Peace Corps[16] or the British Voluntary Service Overseas.[17] Although one is not guaranteed to work in health, even if one is trained in that area, many volunteers do work in health or a related field. However, even if volunteers do not work specifically on health issues, they can still gain excellent exposure to critical issues in development that will be valuable throughout their global health career. In addition, organizations like the Peace Corps have strong alumni networks that can be an excellent resource during job searches. Moreover, many employers place a premium on recruiting ex-volunteers because they believe that such people have personal traits that will make them especially productive employees.

Graduate Studies

An important question after completing your first degree is whether you should pursue graduate studies, and if so, in what field. The main point worth reiterating here is that you can work in global health and serve the needs of marginalized people in many ways and with many academic backgrounds. The second point worth reiterating is that no matter what field of study you pursue, it is crucial that you bring high-level professional skills to your future work in global health. A third point is that your future field of graduate study could be different from the field of your first degree. A person who studied science can do graduate work in economics or public policy. In North American educational systems, one could study film or English for the first degree and still attend medical school later, provided one also met the prerequisites for that field.

Indeed, many people who work in global health both clinically and on policy and program issues are trained as physicians. Many of these people also have graduate degrees in public health. Some of them do global health work that is highly technical and requires clinical training. For example, there are physicians who work abroad clinically through organizations like Doctors Without Borders or the International Rescue Committee. However, many, if not most, of the physicians who work in global health have stopped practicing clinical medicine and now focus on public health work, instead. This is the case, for example, for most physicians who work on TB control with the Global Partnership to Stop TB or on HIV/AIDS control with UNAIDS.

Clearly, if you want to work in global health, there is still considerable merit in studying medicine. Indeed, physicians have led many of the most important contributions to global health. For example, Donald "D.A." Henderson, who has an MD and an MPH, led WHO's Smallpox Eradication Program. In addition, William Foege, who also has an MD and an MPH, made substantial contributions to smallpox eradication efforts, directed the U.S. Centers for Disease Control and Prevention (CDC), and has been instrumental in efforts to control neglected tropical diseases. Of course, many of the above comments can also be said of other health professionals, such as nurses, pharmacists, or dentists. It also appears that there will be increasing roles in global health for veterinarians who understand and are trained in public health.

Economists have also made important contributions to global health. They have generally focused their attention on the costs and financing of health systems, the provision of financial protection to the poor, and how to ensure value for money from health investments. Some economists have made major contributions to research and practice on global health. For example, Dean Jamison, who holds a doctorate in economics, was the main author on a number of global health reports that had a major impact on how low- and middle-income countries invest in health. Rachel Nugent, who has a PhD in economics, was the Deputy Director of Global Health for the Center for Global Development and has done pioneering work on antimicrobial resistance. Ramanan Laxminarayan, who also has a PhD in economics, has conducted important research on cost-effectiveness analysis that is widely used in the global health field. Abdo

Yazbeck, another PhD in economics and who is featured in one of the profiles in the next chapter, has done seminal work on poverty and health.

As noted throughout the text, global health issues are inextricably linked with culture. Thus, you might want to study medical anthropology, focusing on selected issues in global health. This might include, for example, the cultural issues that relate to women's health or nutrition. Many people do not know that Paul Farmer and Jim Kim, who have been so involved with the NGO Partners in Health, are both physicians with PhDs in anthropology.

Many people who work in global health have pursued graduate degrees in international affairs or development studies and built strengths in particular areas of global health around those studies. Similarly, many others have gotten advanced degrees in public policy, focusing their work on development, human resources development, or global health issues. There is a risk that degrees in development studies or public policy may leave one without in-depth expertise in any one discipline. They also leave one without a specific professional title. Yet, many employers appreciate the way that graduates of these programs are trained in policy analysis, development, economics, and finance. Keith Hansen, for example, who heads the health program for Latin America at the World Bank, is a graduate of the Woodrow Wilson School at Princeton University, a public policy school. He also has a law degree. His colleague at the World Bank, Tim Johnston, who heads the World Bank's health work in Cambodia, is also a Woodrow Wilson School graduate. Many of the staff of organizations that engage in policy and advocacy work are graduates of public policy programs.

It was noted earlier that many students interested in global health have never thought of pursuing an advanced degree in business and may even see business as something contrary to global health. Yet, nothing prevents a business school graduate from devoting his or her life to applying those business skills to work on public health issues. For example, Pape Gaye, who is profiled in Chapter 18, heads an important nonprofit consulting firm that works on global health. One of the ways that he prepared for this was by obtaining an advanced degree in business. In addition, many people who studied marketing are involved in social marketing for health.

Studying engineering to an advanced level can provide one with an excellent basis for work on global health. For example, designing roads to enhance safety and improve access to social services would have a major impact on health in many countries. Moreover, strengthening water and sanitation systems could make a substantial impact

on the burden of disease. Yet, most people do not consider engineering when imagining a career in global health. John Briscoe, who is now on the faculty of the Harvard Schools of Engineering, Public Health and Government, is an engineer who has made major contributions to work on water supply and sanitation.

As you know, a substantial share of the burden of disease is linked with under- or overnutrition. A number of graduate programs, like those at Tufts University and Cornell University, have excellent education programs in nutrition at both the masters and the PhD level. Proper nutrition is fundamental for the well-being of young children; consistent with this, many UNICEF staff members have obtained a PhD in nutrition.

Those with a strong interest in health and human rights might want to study law or even philosophy. A number of law programs have concentrations in human rights issues, and many staff members who work on health at organizations such as Amnesty International and Human Rights Watch have law degrees. Those who have studied law might also be in the forefront of work on intellectual property issues and trade matters that affect health, such as access to affordable medicines in developing countries. Surprising to some people, many of the most distinguished writers on ethical issues in health have a background in philosophy. For example, Norman Daniels, the author of *Just Health*, which focuses on social justice and health, is a philosopher.

Many people still fail to consider the important role that journalists, film makers, and others in media and communications can have in enhancing interest in global health and efforts to improve it. Despite the apparent decline in newspapers in some countries, a number of newspapers continue to have reporters who regularly write on global health issues. For example, Laurie Garrett, now at the Council on Foreign Relations, is a journalist who became interested in global health and wrote several widely read books on public health issues. Documentary films on global health issues, such as *Rx for Survival*,[18] as well as popular films, such as *While the Band Played On* or *Philadelphia*, can have a major impact on popular perceptions of key health issues. Many organizations that are involved in global health are now active users of social media, such as Facebook.

This list of areas for possible graduate study could include many more fields, such as those related to mental health, which is also an enormous burden of disease. Although the above comments are only illustrative, they highlight the importance of considering graduate studies as you complete your first degree. At this time, it is also crucial to get a sense of the field of study you wish to pursue, knowing that you do not need to compromise your interests in order to work in global health. By contrast, there are many academic paths that can prepare one for a career in global health.

SELECTED ADDITIONAL RESOURCES IN CAREERS IN GLOBAL HEALTH

In this chapter you have been exposed to a framework for thinking about careers in global health. If you are still interested in considering a career in global health, you may want to pursue some additional information on this topic.

Somewhat surprisingly, given the growth of interest in careers in global health, there are still only a limited number of resources available to help guide those interested in pursuing such a career. These include:

- *Caring for the World: A Guidebook to Global Health Opportunities*[19]
- *Finding Work in Global Health: A practical guide for jobseekers or anyone who wants to make the world a healthier place*[20]

Another book that might be helpful, although it's not specific to just global health, is *Idealist Guide to Nonprofit Careers for First-Time Job Seekers.*[21]

In addition, the Global Health Education Consortium has a module on Global Health: Career Options & Specialization.[22] This is oriented largely toward physicians in training or physicians, but is still valuable for students studying for their first degree.

There are also a number of websites that list job postings in global health or fields related to global health and development, including the following:

- The Global Health Council, which was highlighted earlier, operates a clearinghouse for global health careers that is available to those seeking a position in global health, as well as, for a fee, those recruiting people to work in this field.[23]
- The International Jobs Center is an online weekly of international jobs.
- Idealist.org is an "interactive site where people and organizations can exchange resources and ideas, locate opportunities and supporters, and take steps toward building a world where all people can lead free and dignified lives."[24] This website has a number of resources related to jobs in the nonprofit field.
- Zebra Jobs is a resource for jobs in Africa.[25]

- Eldis is a clearinghouse of information on development that has a jobs listing on its website.[26]
- The U.S. government operates a website with information about U.S. government jobs in global health and some related positions.[27]
- The U.S. Centers for Disease Control and Prevention has a website that focuses on its jobs overseas.[28]
- The Public Health Employment Connection is a job clearinghouse operated by the Rollins School of Public Health at Emory University.[29]
- Public Health Career Mart is a website of the American Public Health Association that focuses on jobs for public health professionals.[30]

MAIN MESSAGES

Global health is a growing field and there are many opportunities to work in it. There are positions, for example, in NGOs, bilateral and multilateral aid organizations, and consulting. Although there are a variety of jobs in the global health field for those trained in the health professions, there are also many opportunities for those trained in other areas, including anthropology, communication, economics, engineering, and logistics management.

If you are considering a career in global health, it is valuable to get a sense of the range of such careers that are available. You will then want to understand better the skills, knowledge, and experience this type of career would entail, your own background, and how you might fill any gaps you have in terms of the required background for such positions. Most jobs in global health will require a good understanding of economic development; an appreciation of other cultures; an ability to write and speak well, both in English and in other languages; and skills in at least one of the areas important to global health. They often require experience living and working in low- and middle-income countries, as well.

If you want to pursue a career in global health, it would be valuable to get your first degree in an area related to the one in which you want to work. It is also important to build on that with internships, fellowships, and other opportunities to live and work abroad. Many different graduate programs can build on your studies and experiences and further prepare you for a career in global health. There are many routes to becoming involved in global health. It is always valuable to learn from the career paths of those already involved in the field and mentors with whom one can work directly.

Study Questions

1. What are some of the organizations most involved in global health work?

2. What types of staff carry out their health activities?

3. What types of knowledge and experience are generally essential to working in global health?

4. How can university students get a better understanding of life in low- and middle-income countries?

5. What role might an economist, anthropologist, engineer, or public policy specialist play in global health?

6. What are some of the careers in global health that might be open to physicians?

REFERENCES

1. International AIDS Vaccine Initiative. Available at: http://www.iavi. org/Pages/home.aspx. Accessed August 16, 2010.

2. Engineers Without Borders—International. Available at: http:// www.ewb-international.org. Accessed August 16, 2010.

3. Doctors Without Borders. Available at: http://www.doctorswithout borders.org. Accessed August 16, 2010.

4. International Rescue Corps. Available at: http://www.intrescue.org. Accessed August 16, 2010.

5. Sightsavers. Available at: http://www.sightsavers.org/default.html. Accessed August 16, 2010.

6. Operation Smile. Available at: http://www.operationsmile.org. Accessed August 16, 2010.

7. The World Bank. Young Professionals Program. Available at: http:// web.worldbank.org/WBSITE/EXTERNAL/EXTHRJOBS/0,,contentMDK:20 519630~menuPK:64262363~pagePK:64262408~piPK:64262191~theSitePK: 1058433~isCURL:Y,00.html. Accessed August 16, 2010.

8. International Honors Program. Available at: http://www.ihp.edu. Accessed August 16, 2010.

9. SIT Study Abroad. Mali: Health, Gender, and Community Empowerment. Available at: http://www.sit.edu/studyabroad/ssa_mlr.cfm. Accessed August 16, 2010.

10. SIT Study Abroad. Switzerland: Global Health and Development Policy. Available at: http://www.sit.edu/studyabroad/ssa_szh.cfm. Accessed August 16, 2010.

11. Cross-Cultural Solutions. Available at: http://www.crosscultural solutions.org. Accessed August 16, 2010.

12. Visions in Action. Available at: http://www.visionsinaction.org. Accessed August 16, 2010.

13. Global Service Corps. Available at: http://www.globalservicecorps. org/site. Accessed August 16, 2010.

14. Henry Luce Foundation. Luce Scholars. Available at: http://www. hluce.org/lsprogram.aspx. Accessed August 16, 2010.

15. Institute of International Education. Fulbright Program. Available at: http://www.iie.org/en/Fulbright. Accessed August 16, 2010.

16. Peace Corps. Available at: http://www.peacecorps.gov. Accessed August 16, 2010.

17. Volunteer Service Overseas. Available at: http://www.vso.org.uk. Accessed August 16, 2010.

18. PBS. Rx for Survival: A Global Health Challenge. Available at: http:// www.pbs.org/wgbh/rxforsurvival. Accessed August 16, 2010.

19. Drain P, Huffman S, Pirtle S, Chan K. Caring for the World: A Guidebook to Global Health Opportunities. Toronto: University of Toronto Press; 2009.

20. Ohmans P, Osborn G. Finding Work in Global Health: A Practical Guide for Jobseekers or Anyone Who Wants to Make the World a Healthier Place. Saint Paul: Health Advocates Press; 2005.

21. Busse M. Idealist Guide to Nonprofit Careers for First-Time Job Seekers. Action Without Borders; 2008. Available at http://www.idealist.org/ en/career/guide/firsttime/index.html. Accessed September 3, 2010.

22. Global Health Education Consortium. Global Health: Career Options & Specialization. Available at: http://globalhealtheducation.org/ resources/Pages/GlobalHealthCareer.aspx#top. Accessed June 25, 2010.

23. Global Health Council. Global Health Career Network. Available at: http://careers.globalhealth.org. Accessed May 13, 2010.

24. Idealist.Org. Available at: http://idealist.org. Accessed February 21, 2010.

25. Society for International Development. Zebra Jobs. Available at: http://www.zebrajobs.com. Accessed July 24, 2010.

26. Eldis. Available at: http://www.eldis.org. Accessed January 12, 2010.

27. U.S. Department of Health and Human Services. Global Health.gov. Available at: http://www.globalhealth.gov. Accessed September 3, 2010.

28. Centers for Disease Control and Prevention. Global Health—Jobs Overseas. Available at: http://www.cdc.gov/globalhealth/employment.htm. Accessed May 2, 2010.

29. Emory University Rollins School of Public Health. Public Health Employment Connection. Available at: http://cfusion.sph.emory.edu/PHEC/ phec.cfm. Accessed March 10, 2010.

30. American Public Health Association. Public Health Career Mart. Available at: http://www.apha.org/about/careers. Accessed July 30, 2010.

CHAPTER 18

Profiles of Global Health Actors

LEARNING OBJECTIVES

By the end of this chapter the reader will be able to:

- Articulate a range of global health careers
- Understand the array of people involved in global health
- Appreciate the factors that have inspired people to work in global health and the diverse ways they entered the field
- Identify the types of mentors one might find in global health
- Outline some key lessons of experience from global health work

VIGNETTES

Sarah is an HIV-positive woman from Kenya. She founded and heads an NGO in Nairobi that provides support services to other HIV-positive women. Her organization helps them find centers where they can be tested for the virus and get treatment if they are infected. The organization also provides social support for women, to help them overcome the stigma of the disease. In addition, it helps them link with potential employers, so the women can have a source of independent income. Sarah was inspired to establish this NGO by a group of HIV-positive women who helped her when she was diagnosed with HIV. Sarah is now an inspiration to many other people.

John is a Canadian physician who also has a doctorate in public health and tropical medicine. He was trained at outstanding institutions in Canada, the United States, and the United Kingdom. John originally planned to work clinically; however, after taking a 1-month rotation during medical school in Malawi, John decided that he should focus on helping to meet the health needs of poor people in poor countries. He therefore took every opportunity during medical school, residency, and graduate studies to become especially knowledgeable about newborn health. Today, John manages a Center for Global Health at a major U.S. hospital. He spends 3 months each year helping to train health personnel in low-income countries about simple, low-cost ways of saving newborn lives.

Graciella is a Bolivian anthropologist and the Director for Social Development at a multilateral development bank. Graciella completed her first degree in Bolivia and then earned a doctorate in cultural anthropology in the United States. Graciella's doctoral thesis focused on how to build safe motherhood practices in low-income countries on the basis of local birthing practices. Graciella worked for the Ministry of Social Development in Bolivia on the health of indigenous people and then joined a Brazilian consulting firm that worked on international development projects. After 5 years, Graciella joined a nonprofit consulting firm in the United States, focusing largely on health projects serving minority people in different parts of the world. Graciella brought to that work increasing attention to cultural issues. She is now one of the most experienced anthropologists working in development assistance for health.

Joe is an American who has worked in development and health since graduation from university. Between his first and second years in university, Joe spent 3 months working with a small NGO in Mumbai, India, that served the health needs of a large slum. That experience convinced Joe that he should work in development. He majored in international affairs at his university, with a concentration in global health. However, even as he finished at his university, Joe was keen to further enhance his understanding of low- and middle-income countries. Thus, he applied to the U.S. Peace Corps, which gave him a position in Malawi as a community health educator. After two challenging but enlightening years in Malawi, Joe returned to the United States for graduate studies, with a focus on development. Today, Joe is the director of a large project for maternal and child health in Africa.

INTRODUCTION

A common problem when university students think about possible careers is a lack of information about jobs in different fields. Often, they are not familiar enough with specific areas to know if they would be of long-term professional interest. In addition, university students often do not know enough people who work in these fields to learn firsthand from them about the content, challenges, and rewards of the professional's work. As you consider careers in global health, it is essential to explore a variety of global health areas through a combination of coursework, internships, jobs, and research, as suggested earlier. Throughout your experiences in global health, it is also crucial to learn as much as you can from the people with whom you work:

- What inspired them to get involved in global health?
- What knowledge, skills, and experience did they seek to become a global health professional?
- Who were the role models for their global health career?
- Who have been their mentors in this field?
- What are the most important lessons they have learned about having an impact on global health?

The remainder of this chapter provides profiles of 13 people who have made important contributions to the global health field. It also includes their responses to the preceding questions. Those who are profiled come from diverse backgrounds and nationalities and have become involved in global health in different ways. Some people have contributed largely locally, by working with community-based organizations in their own country. Some have contributed through work on a national scale. Others have had a global impact through research, practice, and roles at key global institutions.

The profiles that follow are meant to inspire you, as well as inform you. Each person featured has a compelling life story that has influenced their interest in global health and in serving the disadvantaged. Many of the people highlighted here engaged in one or more transformational experiences at some stage of their life, which helped lead them into the global health arena. Of course, there are tens of thousands of

people like those profiled in this chapter who make exceptional contributions daily to enhancing the health of the poor. The people discussed in the following sections have been selected for profiling because, individually and collectively, their stories provide enlightenment and inspiration to those interested in global health.

The profiles have been compiled largely from interviews and personal communications. Thus, there are no endnotes for this chapter. Readers who are interested in learning more about those who are discussed in this chapter will easily be able to find additional information on all of them.

One of the challenges of presenting these profiles has been the order in which to put them. Should they be in order of length of experience? Region of the world from which they come? The level of position they have attained? In the end, it was decided to arrange the profiles alphabetically. This is meant to encourage the reader to look at each profile individually, without trying to discern the "position" of the person being profiled, compared to any of the other people whose stories are told here.

JOANNE CARTER

Joanne Carter is a specialist on global poverty issues, to which she has devoted most of her life. She started her career as a veterinarian, but has worked with RESULTS Education Fund (REF), a grassroots health and poverty alleviation advocacy organization, for the last 18 years. Joanne is an internationally recognized leader of advocacy efforts to support TB, HIV/AIDS, and child survival programs, as well as microfinance. Joanne also plays major roles in a number of international forums. Her career path provides an example of the different routes people take to become involved in global health.

Joanne grew up in Brooklyn, New York, in the United States. Joanne's parents imbued her with a strong sense of social justice and the need to be engaged in making the world a fairer and better place. From an early age, therefore, Joanne had a substantial interest in politics and social causes. She also had a great interest in science.

Joanne received a BS in Biology from the State University of New York at Albany, setting what she thought might be the foundation for a career as a veterinarian or researcher. However, still pulled by her social and policy interests, Joanne spent the 2 years immediately following her first degree as a participant in the VISTA program—Volunteers in Service to America. As part of this work, Joanne was engaged in helping to improve access to health services in poor communities outside of Charleston, South Carolina.

Joanne followed her VISTA service by doing coursework and research toward a master's degree program in reproductive physiology, hoping to set an even stronger foundation for veterinary school. Joanne then enrolled in veterinary school and received a Doctor of Veterinary Medicine (DVM) from the New York State College of Veterinary Medicine at Cornell University. During her studies at Cornell, Joanne was actively involved with a group of faculty and students who were interested in the international and public health aspects of veterinary medicine, and she had the opportunity to spend one summer at an agricultural college in Orissa, India.

Joanne was a practicing veterinarian in the United States from 1987 to 1992. Shortly after starting this work, she took the opportunity to explore her international interests and spent 3 months visiting veterinary training institutions in Africa. Deciding she could have more impact on the root causes of poverty and hunger through changing U.S. policies and priorities rather than practicing as a veterinarian overseas, Joanne returned to New York City and began to explore ways to contribute her personal time.

In 1988, Joanne began volunteering with RESULTS and REF in New York City. She started as a volunteer coordinator of advocacy efforts for the RESULTS chapter in New York City, and her responsibilities grew to include supporting chapters across the Northeast. Joanne carried out this volunteer work, even as she continued her veterinary practice.

In 1992, pulled by the opportunity to work in these areas full time, despite her continuing appreciation for her work as a veterinarian, Joanne became an employee of RESULTS. She initially served at RESULTS as Legislative Director out of its headquarters in Washington, D.C. In this capacity, Joanne worked with key Congressional allies, U.S. government agencies and members of the executive branch, partner organizations, technical agencies, and international campaigns to combat the diseases of poverty, improve access to education, create economic opportunity for the poor, and reform World Bank and International Monetary Fund policies to best meet the needs of the poor.

Joanne was appointed Associate Executive Director of RESULTS and REF in 2007. Joanne is currently the Executive Director of REF, a position she assumed in 2008. In addition, Joanne plays a number of other important roles, including as a board member for the Global Fund to Fight AIDS, TB and Malaria, representing the Developed Country NGO delegation. She is also a founding board member of Global Action for Children. In 2005, she was the first Chair of the Advocacy, Communications, and Social Mobilization Working Group of the Global Stop TB Partnership.

Joanne is especially proud of the work she and RESULTS have done, with others, to highlight TB as a major public health and poverty issue, build a network of partners together around TB, help focus attention on the links between TB and HIV, and dramatically increase the funding for TB. Joanne feels that these efforts were necessary to overcome the perception in many rich countries that TB was a disease of the past, and to reverse the chronic neglect stemming from the fact that TB is largely a disease that affects poor people. Joanne is also extremely gratified by the role she and her organization have played in helping to establish and support the Global Fund to Fight AIDS, TB and Malaria, which was created from the ground up in 2002 and has since mobilized tens of billions of dollars for health in low- and middle-income countries.

Joanne offers the following advice to university students interested in pursuing a career in global health:

- In advocacy and in public health, it is essential to look at where you want to be in the future and then be bold and brave enough to lay out a plan to get there. Work for transformational rather than incremental change.
- Remember that "Hope is not a feeling—it's a decision." We can generate that hope by envisaging what is possible and working with allies to make it happen. As you do this, keep in mind stories of leaders like Jim Grant, the former UNICEF director who helped launch and drive the "child survival revolution." Grant was told during a briefing on progress in immunization in El Salvador that targets were not being met due to the civil war then raging. Rather than accepting this, Grant replied, "Then stop the war." Indeed, both sides agreed to "Days of Tranquility" so that national immunization campaigns could continue unmolested.
- Work as much as you can with people who give you energy, rather than those who drain it away. Draw as much energy as you can from a network of allies who share your vision and will help you retain that vision in the face of naysayers.
- Follow your passion, even if you start by volunteering in that field. Doors will open.
- Work as much as you can with mentors. Much of what you will learn in life will come from them.

PAPE GAYE

Pape Gaye is the President and Chief Executive Officer of IntraHealth International, Inc. and a well-respected leader in global health. Pape, however, came to this work through a somewhat improbable route. In fact, his story also reflects the many different ways in which people get involved in global health and the many academic backgrounds they bring to it.

Pape is Senegalese. He was born in Dakar, the capital of Senegal. Pape did his primary and secondary schooling and began his university studies in Senegal. Pape's worldview began to open when he befriended a U.S. Peace Corps volunteer who was living in his neighborhood while Pape was in secondary school. Pape met other volunteers and learned of the work they were doing in settings that were often poor, rural, and lacking in basic services. Pape was inspired by the commitment and dedication that these outsiders showed to helping to improve his own country.

This connection to the U.S. Peace Corps program was transformational for Pape in many other ways, as well. While he was still in secondary school, Pape began to work for the Peace Corps, training their volunteers to speak Wolof and French. In 1971, Pape made his first trip outside of Senegal when he traveled to Benin with the Peace Corps to help train volunteers there. In addition, Pape married one of the volunteers he met in Senegal. Pape's growing experiences with the Peace Corps set the foundation for and sparked a growing interest in development and in bridging gaps across cultures.

Political turmoil in the universities in Senegal made it difficult for Pape to complete his university studies there, so in 1975, Pape moved to the United States to finish university. Although he wanted to build on his language skills, Pape initially thought after going to the United States that he would work in a large U.S. corporation. With this in mind, Pape received his BA in Business Economics and Linguistics from the University of California at Santa Barbara in 1980. Still aiming for a job in the corporate sector, Pape continued his education at the University of California at Los Angeles and received an MBA in Human Resources Management and International Business Management in 1982.

While en route to a job interview for a corporate position, however, Pape decided that his attachment to work in Africa remained strong and that he should return to work there. He immediately withdrew from the interview process and took a position for a year as a management consultant for the Peace Corps Regional Training Resource Office in Togo. In 1984, building on his proficient language skills and passion for cross-cultural understanding, he moved back to the United States and took an assignment with the International Olympic Committee working as a trainer in language services for the Los Angeles Olympic Organizing Committee. In 1985, Pape undertook his first global health assignment as a training consultant for the U.S. Centers for Disease Control and Prevention working on the Combatting Childhood Communicable Diseases program.

Having built a reputation as a leader in the intersecting fields of global health and training, Pape was approached by IntraHealth (then International Training in Health, INTRAH) to establish a regional office in West and Central Africa. From 1986 to 2003, Pape was IntraHealth's Regional Director for West, Central and Northern Africa and served in Abidjan, Lome, and Dakar. In this role he worked to help countries develop their capacity to train reproductive, maternal, and child health providers. He also developed training programs for clinical and public healthcare workers in project countries.

In 2003, Pape moved to IntraHealth headquarters in Chapel Hill, North Carolina, to serve as Senior Vice President. Since 2004, Pape has been the Chief Executive Officer of IntraHealth, which now has almost 20 offices and over 500 employees around the world. IntraHealth, originally based out of the University of North Carolina School of Medicine, is now a nonprofit organization that works to build local capacity to deliver health care that is both accessible and sustainable.

Pape is most proud of the work that he carried out building a robust and meaningful program for IntraHealth in Africa, despite the challenges of working in low-resource environments with weak governance structures and unstable leadership. In addition, he found substantial challenges in trying to help countries enhance their health work in environments in which their health efforts were often too focused on medical approaches and not sufficiently based on the needs or circumstances of local communities.

When asked what advice he has for university students interested in careers in global health, Pape highlighted the following:

- It is essential to bring a global perspective and a deep appreciation of local cultures to work on health and development.
- There is much to learn. You have to be open to learning at all times if you are to keep up with the field, be effective, and know when to seek help from other people.
- The world has changed considerably and all parties have much to learn from each other. The world must therefore move to a new way of engaging in partnership between richer and poorer countries in which more knowledge and experience is shared in all directions.

DAVID HEYMANN

In 2004, U.S. epidemiologist Dr. David Heymann received the American Public Health Association Award for Excellence and was named to the U.S. Institute of Medicine for his contributions to reducing the global burden of infectious diseases. These honors recognized David's important contributions to improving global health.

David always wanted to be a physician, thinking this was the best way he could serve other people. He received his first degree from Pennsylvania State University and then completed medical studies at Wake Forest University.

Just after completing medical studies, David joined the U.S. Public Health Service. As part of this work, David served 1 year on an icebreaker in Antarctica. He served a second year as a family medicine physician in a U.S. Coast Guard Clinic in California. David had taken a rotation during medical school with Project Hope in Tunisia and, as he considered his professional interests, David decided that the public health work in which he engaged in Tunisia was a better fit for him than clinical medicine.

Thus, after his work with the U.S. Public Health Service, David decided to pursue a public health degree with a specialty in tropical medicine. He had a number of friends who had done such studies at the London School of Hygiene and Tropical Medicine, and decided to pursue a 2-year diploma in Tropical Medicine and Hygiene there.

As David was finishing up his program in London, Dr. Donald A. Henderson, who was then the Director of the WHO Smallpox Eradication Programme and is widely recognized as a "giant" in public health, spoke to David's class and requested students to help with smallpox eradication. David traveled that summer to India with Dr. Henderson and then worked as a medical epidemiologist in smallpox eradication for 2 years. Like many other prominent actors in public health over the last several decades, David's work with smallpox was an exceptionally formative experience. David learned many lessons from this program, including the power of public health work and the importance of building country capacity to locally lead and carry out such work.

After completing his work with the Smallpox Eradication Programme, David returned to the United States and joined the Epidemic Intelligence Service of the U.S. Centers for Disease Control and Prevention. He completed 2 years of practical epidemiology training and during this training traveled to Africa, where he worked for the first time on a disease outbreak outside of the United States, which turned out to be the first outbreak of Ebola virus.

David continued to work for the CDC for about 25 years as a medical epidemiologist, mainly on international assignments to Africa and Asia. David's work at the CDC focused on strengthening the surveillance and control of infectious diseases in developing countries, including field research that tested concepts that were just being developed by WHO for the Expanded Programme on Immunization; investigation of outbreaks of hemorrhagic fevers and human monkeypox in West and Central Africa; and applying research to develop methodologies to monitor certain types of antimalarial resistance. During David's work with CDC, he was based in Cameroon, Malawi, and Switzerland. He also spent substantial periods of time in the Democratic Republic of the Congo, Côte d'Ivoire, Burkina Faso, and Thailand.

In 1989, David moved to the World Health Organization in Geneva, where he served in a number of key positions. From 1989 to 1995, David was Chief of Research Activities for the WHO Global Programme on AIDS. In October 1995, he became the Director of the WHO Programme on Emerging and Other Communicable Diseases. From July 1998 to July 2003, he was the Executive Director of the WHO Communicable Diseases Cluster. He then became the head of the Polio Eradication Initiative, and WHO's Assistant Director-General for Health Security and Environment, where he worked on communicable disease issues, food safety, and the health effects of climate change.

While serving at WHO, David was instrumental in strengthening the fight against infectious diseases, establishing the STOP TB partnership and leading the world's efforts to combat the outbreak of SARS in 2002 and 2003. During this period David also authored numerous articles, reports, and chapters within textbooks, making important contributions to global health literature. David especially appreciated the opportunities he had at WHO to help motivate countries to effectively address key issues in infectious diseases.

David is currently the Chairman of the Board of the Health Protection Agency of the United Kingdom, Head and Senior Fellow of the Centre for Global Health Security at Chatham House, and a professor at the London School of Hygiene and Tropical Medicine.

When asked what advice he would give to students interested in a career in global health, David offered four key suggestions:

- Get field experience. You need to have an understanding of low-, middle-, and high-income countries to engage in global health work. You must have a deep understanding of low- and middle-income countries if you are to serve their needs effectively.
- Plan your career in 5-year intervals. Look at where you want to be in 5 years and what you need to do to get there. Once you get there, then you can move on to the next steps.
- Keep yourself affiliated, if possible, with an outstanding public health organization, even if you are

working on assignment for another organization. This will help provide you with the support you need to carry out your work effectively, such as technical assistance and laboratory services. This will also give you a place to return to after you have finished an overseas experience and an organization in which you can continue to develop your career.

- Always make yourself available to new opportunities. Much of this depends on being in the right place at the right time, but if you remain open and available, you will create opportunities for yourself and develop a network to open doors for further opportunities.

JERKER LILJESTRAND

Jerker Liljestrand is a Swedish obstetrician-gynecologist (OB/GYN) who has been at the forefront of efforts to improve reproductive and maternal and child health in low- and middle-income countries. He is one of only a handful of OB/GYNs from high-income countries that have devoted their lives to improving the reproductive health of poor women in poor communities. Jerker's background in both clinical medicine and public health has brought an invaluable perspective to the field of global reproductive health.

Jerker grew up in a family of doctors, which cultivated an interest in health and medicine at a very young age. He attended medical school at Lund University, and completed residencies in OB/GYN, surgery, and anesthesiology at Västervik Hospital in Sweden. During medical school, he became curious about health in low- and middle-income countries and made a concerted effort to meet people working in the global health field.

Jerker worked as a clinical OB/GYN for approximately 20 years. During this time, he spent 2 years as Head of the Department of OB/GYN at Beira Central Hospital in Mozambique, simultaneously training midwives; 10 years as Head of Reproductive Health for the Blekinge Country Council in Sweden; and 13 years involved with midwifery training at Kalmar Nursing College, also in Sweden. Throughout these experiences, Jerker paid increasing amounts of attention to the social issues that contribute to poor maternal and child health outcomes.

In 1985, Jerker received his PhD in OB/GYN at Uppsala University. He conducted his dissertation research in Mozambique on area-based studies of maternal health, focusing on the relationship between pregnancy outcomes and risk factors such as anemia, syphilis, nutrition, and socioeconomic factors. During this period, Jerker was also involved in a variety of other public health activities, including teaching perinatal health in Hanoi, Vietnam; starting an HIV/AIDS campaign in Mozambique; and rolling out a sexual education program in a province of Sweden.

From 1994 to 1996, Jerker was Director of the Blekinge International School of Public Health in Sweden. He then spent 3 years as Chief of Maternal-Newborn Health at WHO headquarters in Geneva, Switzerland. From 2000 to 2002, Jerker was Reproductive Health Advisor at the World Bank, in Washington, D.C.

Jerker returned to Sweden from 2002 to 2007 and helped develop the Department of Community Medicine at Lund University, which focuses on global health. Jerker also began to play a key role in the International Federation of Gynecology and Obstetrics (FIGO). He was Treasurer of FIGO from 2003 to 2009 and Chair of the FIGO Safe Motherhood Committee from 2003 to 2006. In 2006, he became Program Manager for an Advanced Training Program in Sexual and Reproductive Health and Rights for midwives and OB/GYNs in low-income countries, based at Lund University in Sweden and sponsored by the Swedish International Development Agency (SIDA).

Jerker's work with the SIDA training program eventually led him to Cambodia, where he now lives and works. He is currently Team Leader for maternal, newborn, and child health with the Better Health Services Project.

Jerker is most proud of his work training midwives in many low- and middle-income countries. He also considers one of his most meaningful experiences to be the development of WHO's book entitled *Managing Complications in Pregnancy and Childbirth*, which he spearheaded.

When asked what advice he would give to university students studying global health, Jerker responded:

- Get a reasonable field experience early in your professional life; don't wait until you are very senior in a high-income country. Go as a volunteer, with an NGO, through the Peace Corps, or something similar; you will learn a lot and get invaluable experience and friendships that will carry you through life. Good people are needed in global health, at all ages and from all directions. Getting some solid understanding early on helps you understand key issues from the beginning, and may well influence your life path.
- The world has changed very dramatically in the last 50 years, mostly with very significant improvements in areas such as infant mortality, life expectancy, and poverty reduction. With this in mind, don't despair. If we work well, learning from global mistakes, we can expect more successes ahead. Let us work hard on this; the options are otherwise not great for our grandchildren.

- Get into teaching, you will learn a lot!
- Sexual and reproductive health, in many ways, is a key to development—from gender issues and women's development issues, to helping people achieve their fertility desires, to the excitement of birthing care.

ELAINE MURPHY

Elaine Murphy has made major contributions to global health work, especially in areas related to the well-being of women in low- and middle-income countries. Indeed, a paper that Elaine wrote was the inspiration for the women's health chapter of this book. Yet, Elaine's path to working in global health has not been a traditional one, beginning with a liberal arts undergraduate degree, a master's degree in a special program for writers (with a book of poetry as her thesis), and a doctorate in human development. Her career does reflect again, however, that people from many backgrounds can work effectively in global health.

Teaching and learning have inspired Elaine throughout her life. Elaine found that by working with a variety of people and organizations—through the preparation of briefing papers, articles in peer-reviewed journals, book chapters, academic and training curricula, and presentations at professional meetings—she could help to seize policymakers' and funders' attention and commitment to important areas of public health. In addition, volunteer work on the environment and population eventually led Elaine to focus more attention on global issues, including reproductive health and gender equity. She considered reproductive health and gender equity especially important because global concern about population often seemed to overlook the situation of individual women in developing countries and what motivates the attitudes and behavior of such women.

In 1962, Elaine received a BA from Marquette University with majors in English and French and a minor in Education. She then received an MA in Writing from Johns Hopkins University in 1965. Elaine continued her studies at the University of Maryland and received a PhD in Human Development Psychology in 1978.

From 1964 to 1968, Elaine was a high school teacher and counselor in Wisconsin, Minnesota, and Maryland. She then spent a year as a researcher on a project studying learning styles and creativity with the Montgomery County Public Schools in Rockville, Maryland.

Elaine's volunteer work on population and the environment came to the attention of the Population Institute and she was invited to apply for a fellowship. In 1974, Elaine became a fellow in the Population Institute in Washington, D.C., where she developed an interdisciplinary college course on population and reproductive health. Once the University of Maryland agreed to offer the course Elaine had developed, the Population Institute recommended her to the director of the NGO Zero Population Growth, who was looking for someone to lead a new program that would educate teachers in the United States about population. Beginning in 1975, she led this program for 3 years and then left to become the population education director at the Population Reference Bureau (PRB), a demographic think tank in Washington D.C.

From 1978 to 1983, Elaine was the Director of Population Education at PRB. She organized training workshops and produced training materials on population and the environment for university and high school teachers and students. In addition, she helped initiate PRB's international population education work. Having become an active fixture of the community working on population and reproductive health, Elaine moved to the U.S. Agency for International Development (USAID), where she worked from 1983 to 1985. She designed, monitored, and evaluated large-scale family planning communication and training projects for their Office of Population. From 1985 to 1991, Elaine returned to PRB, where she was Director of International Programs. While at PRB she directed a project to communicate population and reproductive health research findings to policymakers in low- and middle-income countries.

Elaine then joined the Program for Appropriate Technology in Health (PATH) in Washington, D.C., and worked on several international programs from 1991 to 2002. She developed and directed the Women's Reproductive Health Initiative (WRHI), a policy project to promote women's reproductive health from a gender and human rights perspective. This program aimed to build a bridge between public health issues and human rights concerns. For example, WRHI highlighted the trafficking of girls and women as a public health issue, not only a human rights violation. At the same time, the project stressed that maternal mortality, although clearly a public health issue, is also a human rights issue.

WRHI disseminated research findings via publications and presentations on the scope of such problems and identified successful programs that address them. WRHI joined other organizations to stress the importance of recognizing and addressing gender inequity, particularly in developing countries. This work, along with the efforts of many others, helped to spur action among policymakers and major donors. The landmark 1994 UN Conference on Population and Development was dedicated to these issues for the first time. In addition, continued, concerted advocacy was responsible for the Millennium Development Goals' inclusion of women's equality, reproductive health, and maternal mortality issues.

From 2002 to 2006, Elaine was a Professor of Global Health and a Senior Associate in the Center for Global Health at the George Washington University School of Public Health and Health Services.

Elaine is currently a Visiting Scholar at PRB and a global health consultant for a variety of organizations, including Georgetown University's Institute for Reproductive Health, the Academy for Educational Development's Communication for Change Project, and the World Bank Institute's training program in reproductive health. Her work with PRB includes giving seminars, mentoring staff, and writing educational materials about population and reproductive health and related projects. In addition, she is chair of the board of the Willows Foundation, a family planning and reproductive health organization that implements programs in Turkey, Ghana, and Pakistan. She is also a board member of Options for Youth, a teen pregnancy prevention program in Chicago.

When asked what advice she would give university students interested in careers in global health, Elaine offered the following:

- Doing volunteer work in the area of one's concern is not only a good thing to do, but also can be the springboard to an exciting career.
- Of course, just getting the job of your dreams is not enough. One must perform well in the job and bring passion and creativity to it.
- Do not be afraid to "color outside the lines." Having initiative can lead to applying for the funds that will permit your organization to develop expertise in an exciting new area.
- When you rise to a position of leadership within an organization, foster the talent of those whom you supervise. Don't be one of those supervisors who feels threatened by the skills of your staff. Remember the line from the hairdresser Vidal Sassoon: "If you look good, I look good."

POONAM MUTTREJA

Poonam Muttreja is an Indian woman who has been a pioneer in peace promotion, poverty eradication, and women's health efforts in India and elsewhere for many years.

Growing up in New Delhi, India, Poonam was exposed at a young age to poverty, to the poor position of women in Indian society, and to the discrimination often shown to poor and lower caste people in India. Poonam vividly remembers

some of the people to whom she was exposed at a young age, whose stories have been an inspiration to her working for social justice ever since. First, was the woman who was living on less than $1 a day equivalent, who could not send her children to even a free government school because the cost of transportation, uniforms, and books was more than she could afford. Poonam also remembers the person who cleaned toilets in the homes of middle-class people and who was not allowed to touch anything in their homes because the work he did was "unclean" and because he was from the lower castes.

Moved by these experiences, Poonam began to seek ways to help those in need, even as she entered university. She helped, for example, to organize lower caste leather workers into a cooperative, so that they could sell their goods at a better price. She then helped to set up markets in New Delhi so that other poor workers could improve their ability to sell their goods at fair prices. Inspired by Gandhi, Poonam spent much time during this period visiting poor villages in India, always asking if she could stay in the home of the poorest persons, so that she could gain a better understanding of their lives and how she could be helpful to the poor.

Poonam built on her early activities with poor workers and became a "social entrepreneur" who helped to found, develop, and then pass on a number of nongovernmental organizations of importance. These organizations were oriented toward poverty issues and the development, often through fellowships, of talented people from outside the elite who could become agents of social change and innovation.

From 1979 to 1981, for example, Poonam was the first Executive Director of the Ashoka Foundation in New Delhi. Poonam co-founded Dastkar—Delhi in 1981, a nonprofit organization that promotes economic opportunities for craftspeople. She then served 2 years as its Executive Director. In 1983, Poonam founded the Society for Rural, Urban, and Tribal Initiative (SRUTI) in New Delhi. This nonprofit organization provides fellowships to less-known social activists in India. As founding Director, she established the office and implemented a fellowship program. In 1984, Poonam was the founding Secretary of Nagarik Ekta Manch (Citizen's Unity Forum) in New Delhi. This was established after the 1984 communal riots in Delhi following the assassination of Prime Minister Indira Gandhi. The organization was instrumental in promoting peace and mobilizing volunteers for relief and rehabilitation activities.

In 1986, Poonam moved to the United States, largely following her husband who was to attend graduate school there. From 1986 to 1991, Poonam was the Program Director for the Coolidge Center for Environmental Leadership in

Massachusetts. In that role, Poonam developed training programs on the environment, poverty, and gender for mid-career professionals from low- and middle-income countries. From 1987 to 1988, Poonam was a Chairperson for the Harvard–MIT Women in Development Group. In this capacity, Poonam organized programs and seminars on gender issues in developing countries. In 1991, Poonam received a master's degree in Public Administration from Harvard University's Kennedy School of Government.

While still in the United States, Poonam was also invited to teach at two American colleges. She served first as a Visiting Professor and Packard Fellow in the Peace and Global Studies Program at Earlham College in the state of Indiana, where she taught a course on international development and offered a faculty seminar series on poverty in low- and middle-income countries. In the spring of 1992, Poonam taught a course on social action, international development, and poverty alleviation at Hampshire College in the state of Massachusetts.

Poonam then returned to India. From 1993 to 1994, she was the Advisor to the Representative of the UN Development Program. Poonam then served 15 years as the Country Director for the MacArthur Foundation in India. In 1994, she established the India office for the Foundation, which develops and oversees the Foundation's grants for programs related to population and reproductive health in India.

Poonam is most proud of the work she did while at the MacArthur Foundation to help build a group of civil society leaders in women's reproductive health who were drawn from outside the establishment. She is also pleased that her work has contributed to moving many Indian stakeholders to a broader and more rights-based approach to reproductive health than would otherwise be the case.

Poonam offers a number of lessons for those who would like to work in health and development:

- Get a sense of people's real needs. Get a sense, as well, of what really works and does not work in addressing those needs.
- Guide your decisions on the basis of the life of the poor. Close your eyes and think constantly about how the problem you are trying to address really looks to the poor.
- You have to work at every level, all the time, to address the issues of poverty and ill health. You have to do this in coalition with partners, to whom you must be open. Collective action is better than individual action.
- You must be able to learn from others at all times. You need to doubt the wisdom of your work and test

it against people more knowledgeable than you. You also need to learn from failures. Keep an open mind, open eyes, and an open heart at all times.

ALBERTINA NYATSI

Albertina Nyatsi has been instrumental in empowering Swazi women living with HIV/AIDS to improve their quality of life. In 2004, she helped start a support group for HIV-positive women, which has since grown into the organization Positive Women Together in Action (Positive Women Together). Her devotion to improving communication and open discussion about HIV remains crucial in the effort to curb the further spread of HIV in Swaziland.

Swaziland has the highest HIV prevalence in the world; 26.1 percent of adults are HIV-positive, and women are disproportionately impacted. Yet, pervasive stigma prevents open communication and education on HIV/AIDS prevention, diagnosis, and treatment options. To make matters more difficult, Swaziland faces an exceptionally burdensome TB epidemic.

Through her work with Positive Women Together, Albertina strives to counter prejudice and empower HIV-positive women, so they can lead normal and fulfilling lives. As an HIV-positive Swazi woman, Albertina understands the fears, concerns, and social forces that influence the behaviors of women in Swaziland.

Albertina has a life story that is both touching and compelling. Albertina was diagnosed with HIV after becoming sick with TB at age 25. She likely was infected with TB because HIV had compromised her immune system. Shortly after her diagnosis with HIV, Albertina, hoping to get information about HIV, joined a support group called Swaziland AIDS Support Organization. This was the first support group of people living with HIV in Swaziland and was composed of both men and women. Albertina found the group quite helpful. Because the members were HIV-positive, they understood what she was going though and could offer advice on how to deal with the challenges associated with HIV. In addition, they did not stigmatize her, as so many others had done.

At the time she was diagnosed with HIV, Albertina taught seventh grade home economics and all subjects in Grade 3 at a school called Zinyane primary school in northern Swaziland. Wanting to be honest about her health and why she had been absent, Albertina told the school's head teacher that she had been diagnosed with HIV. Two weeks later, he told Albertina to go home and terminated her teaching contract. He gave no explanation, but Albertina believes that she lost the job because she was HIV-positive. She soon was placed at a different primary school, and the teachers at that school were much more supportive. During this period, Albertina also became the mother to her six nieces and nephews when two of her sisters died at young ages of TB.

Albertina has personally experienced, and is deeply troubled by, the challenges that HIV-positive women face each day in Swaziland. Albertina seeks to unite Swazi women through Positive Women Together in Action, so they can work collaboratively to teach women of their rights and provide them with information and tools to improve their own lives.

Positive Women Together is a nonprofit, nonpolitical organization that involves 210 Swazi women living with HIV. Positive Women Together provides a range of services, including pre- and posttesting counseling, treatment for HIV and TB, and adherence counseling for those on TB and HIV medications. They also provide educational materials, advocacy, assistance with income generation, and life skills education for children infected with and affected by HIV.

As Positive Women Together develops, Albertina hopes the organization can become a comprehensive network of support for HIV-positive women in Swaziland, incorporating services that fulfill an even wider variety of the needs of these women.

Swazi women have very little social or political voice, and life for an HIV-positive woman in Swaziland is exceptionally challenging. Keeping this in mind, Albertina believes there are several lessons that those interested in working on global health must understand:

- Women must be proactive and learn to stand up for themselves, although these qualities are not always welcome in many societies. Throughout your work, focus on women. Enable women to care for themselves. Invest in women and you can improve the lives of children, families, and entire communities.
- To improve their health, women must have access to information on how to take care of themselves. Women must also have access to services for effective prevention, diagnosis, and treatment of diseases such as HIV/AIDS, TB, and cancers that affect women.
- Encourage women in low- and middle-income countries to work in health. There is great need for strong young women devoted to improving women's health. Especially in countries where women do not have equal opportunity with men, it is crucial that women come together to support one another and create new opportunities for themselves and their daughters.
- Relieve the burden of caring for others from women and girls and encourage and assist them to study further.

- Work to stop abuse of women and girls.
- Involve women and girls in the development of policies, decision making, and leadership.

CAROL NYIRENDA

Carol Nyirenda is a health activist. Carol sits on the Board of Directors of the Global Fund to Fight AIDS, TB, and Malaria, where she represents people affected by the diseases. She also represents affected communities on the board of Stop TB and earlier played the same role for UNITAID. Carol is actively involved in a Task Force of the Treatment Action Group, serves as a TB Media Champion for Stop TB, and works on advocacy for global health with the international grassroots NGO RESULTS.

Carol was motivated to become a health activist through two sets of experiences. Following her studies, Carol was employed by the Association of Federations of Women in Business, where she focused on trying to improve economic opportunities for women to engage in business in Zambia. This set the foundation for Carol's efforts as a gender activist.

Carol was also moved to engage in health work, with a special focus on women, when she learned she was HIV-positive. In 2002, Carol developed a cancer on her leg, called Kaposi's sarcoma. She also developed TB. Although both illnesses are associated with HIV, Carol waited 6 months after her diagnosis with TB to get a test for HIV, because she was afraid of testing HIV-positive. When she was tested, it turned out Carol did have HIV.

In the face of her diagnosis, Carol suffered from both "self-stigma" and the stigma of others. In response, she moved from Zambia's capital to another Zambian city, to get away from people who knew she was HIV-positive and who, because of her HIV status, stopped shopping at a food store she had been operating.

Later, however, Carol moved back to Lusaka, the capital, and joined a support group for HIV-positive people. She also began to be involved in work with the support group, including helping the group to raise funds from international organizations. In 2006, in conjunction with these activities, Carol won a fellowship to participate in the International AIDS Conference in Toronto. This exposed Carol to the international side of advocacy work on HIV. It also gave others a chance to meet Carol, who a number of organizations soon began to ask for help in their own work.

Carol says that parts of her work with the UNITAID Board of Directors have been especially rewarding, because she has influenced the board to be concerned not only with drugs, but also with diagnostics. She is also very excited by the opportunities she has to advocate in Zambia for HIV treatment, for better TB diagnosis and treatment, and for the health of women. Carol says that the prominence she has gained working internationally has raised her stature as a health activist in Zambia and allowed her to accomplish more than might otherwise be possible. On the other hand, Carol has sometimes been frustrated by her inability to have greater influence as a community representative on some national and international health initiatives because some are still finding it difficult to fully appreciate and embrace the meaningful engagement of civil society organizations at these decision-making levels.

Carol has three lessons for those considering a career in global health:

- It is essential to have real passion for this work.
- One must also have patience if you work in global health. There are many actors and lots of politics involved in global health, and even if you want to help take a great leap forward, you might only be able to help take some small steps forward instead.
- Work in global health requires considerable dedication, lots of reading, lots of collaboration with other stakeholders, and lots of time.

ELLYN OGDEN

In January 2009, Ellyn Ogden was awarded the Heroism Award of the U.S. Agency for International Development (USAID) for her tireless efforts, sometimes in areas of conflict, to help eradicate polio. This important work in global health was the natural outgrowth of experiences Ellyn had at earlier stages of her life and valuable lessons she had learned over almost 30 years of international development efforts.

As a young woman, growing up in the United States, Ellyn developed a strong interest in doing something to make the world a better place for the poor. Initially, Ellyn thought she should become a doctor. Thanks to a secondary school teacher who told her about the Peace Corps, Ellyn aimed initially to become a Peace Corps doctor who would provide medical care to the poor in low-income countries. Ellyn smiles today when talking about this, because at the time she had only limited knowledge of the Peace Corps, of different kinds of public health work, and of international health problems.

During her first 2 years in university, Ellyn's interest in public health grew and she transferred to Tulane University, in order to take advantage of its well-known programs in international affairs and public health. Her studies at Tulane further strengthened Ellyn's desire to make a career in public health and to study for an advanced degree in public health, which she completed at Tulane in 1984.

Ellyn also gained valuable experience working in the United States while a student in various hospital settings such as nursing assistant, laboratory phlebotomist, cardiac care aide, and clinical research assistant. Following interests she had entertained since childhood, Ellyn did join the Peace Corps and from 1987–1988 she served as an Infectious Disease Control officer in Papua New Guinea. This was her first international work experience. Ellyn worked in Kavieng, the capitol of the island province of New Ireland, with a population of 80,000 people and very limited medical services. Papua New Guinea was very poor at the time, and Ellyn focused her public health efforts on TB, malaria, leprosy, and sexually transmitted diseases. She paid special attention in her work to women, who were often neglected by public health and medical programs.

Following her stay in Papua New Guinea, Ellyn worked with companies in Washington, D.C., that helped to implement health projects financed by USAID. In one of these positions, Ellyn led an evaluation of the child survival activities that had been financed by USAID during a period when this was the focus of important international efforts. Ellyn learned a great deal from this experience about the importance of evaluation, the need for it to be independent, and the value of using the knowledge gained in evaluation to enhance the quality of the programs being reviewed.

Ellyn moved to USAID in 1993, first serving as a Child Survival Fellow for the Latin America and the Caribbean Region and from 1997 to the present, heading up USAID's work on polio eradication. Despite the setbacks in the world's efforts to eradicate polio by 2000, Ellyn remains committed to trying to achieve eradication in the shortest possible time. In her work on polio, Ellyn has helped to negotiate "days of tranquility" in the Eastern Democratic Republic of Congo (DRC), so that warring factions would stop fighting and allow children to be immunized. In Nigeria, Ellyn worked with local leaders to help overcome fears they had of the polio vaccine, which had led to many children not being immunized. With others, she has worked very hard to help India, Afghanistan, and Pakistan immunize all of their children so that polio transmission could be stopped there, as well.

When asked to point out critical lessons from her own experience for today's students of global health, Ellyn offered the following:

- Work on the basis of evidence and be courageous in using evidence to help do things in better ways. Do not accept things as they are if they are not working well. Be gracious to everyone, but don't be afraid to use your evidence to prove people wrong and to highlight more effective and efficient ways of achieving key goals.

- Develop a broad perspective and an ability to work across disciplines. You never know what skills you will need in the future.
- Develop an ability to "flash forward." Imagine how issues will develop in the future and how they might be addressed in that light. Related to this, learn to "envision failure" and what can be done to avoid failure of your efforts over time.
- Understand how business gets done in different places. One cannot succeed in global health without a deep understanding of the cultural context within which you are working.
- Know your audience. It is imperative to know what motivates people in different places, to see how the world looks through their eyes, and to be able to communicate with them in terms they understand.
- Create and seize opportunities to advance your mission. Be alert to the possibilities for positive change.

DAN AND LINDSAY PALAZUELOS

Dan and Lindsay Palazuelos are a married couple who have devoted their lives to improving the health and well-being of marginalized groups in both the United States and Latin America. Dan is a physician who splits his time between clinical medicine and global health work with the NGO Partners in Health (PIH) in Mexico and Guatemala. Lindsay is a development expert, also working with PIH in Mexico and Guatemala.

Dan and Lindsay aspire to listen carefully to the people with whom they work, collaborate closely with others, and show compassion at all times. They recognize the importance, both to their personal and professional aims, of their relationships with the communities with which they are engaged. For this reason, they spend 6 months of each year in Mexico and Guatemala and 6 months in the United States. They collaborate closely in Mexico with the PIH partner organization EAPSEC and in Guatemala with the partner organization ETESC.

Dan and Lindsay work as a husband–wife team in the field of global health equity. Their personal relationship comes first, but they simultaneously support and inspire one another professionally. This may involve helping each other write grant applications one day, and the next day reflecting together on the range of emotions that are part of working in poor communities.

Dan did not always plan to study medicine. He initially thought he would be a filmmaker, poet, photographer, or other type of "starving artist," as he puts it. In 1999, he received a BA in English and American Literature from Brown University as a part of their Program in Liberal Medical Education. This program allowed Dan to study the humanities, while guaranteeing him a spot in Brown Medical School, contingent on his maintaining a certain grade point average and meeting certain science requirements. During this time, Dan spent a year at Oxford University in England studying English poetry. In the end, he believes that studying the arts led him to a career in medicine and taught him invaluable skills such as patience, flexibility, humor, and an appreciation of the role culture plays in people's lives.

Dan continued his studies at Brown University Medical School and received his MD in 2004. He completed his residency in Internal Medicine at the Brigham and Women's Hospital (BWH) in Boston, Massachusetts, with a focus on health care for the poor and marginalized. In 2009, he received an MPH with a concentration in Clinical Effectiveness at the Harvard School of Public Health.

Between his third and fourth years of medical school, Dan spent a year doing independent research in Mexico. Throughout the year, much of which he spent in public hospitals, he interviewed patients on their views of health, dying, and end of life care. This experience opened his eyes to the pervasive inequities in health, as well as the complex relationship among culture, race, class, and health care.

Dan is currently a physician at BWH and an Instructor at Harvard Medical School, teaching in the Department of Global Health and Social Medicine. He is also Clinical Director of the Partners in Health projects in Guatemala and Mexico. In this role, he works with rural communities on program development, provision of care, and training of community health promoters, among other things. Dan still finds each patient encounter meaningful, feeling both pride and humility as he works in close personal ways with other people.

Lindsay's interest in global health and development began in high school after reading about the parasitic infection schistosomiasis. She was appalled by the enormous number of people it affected, especially considering that she had never heard of the disease. From this point on, Lindsay was drawn to international issues and pursued a variety of internships and volunteer experiences with community-based organizations that aimed at addressing such issues. Two of these organizations were the Austin Entrepreneurs Foundation in Texas, and Dorcas Place, a language learning resource center in Rhode Island. In 2005, Lindsay received a BA in International Development from Brown University. During her studies, Lindsay spent a summer in rural Ecuador working in community development with indigenous communities.

After graduating, Lindsay worked with a community-based AIDS prevention organization and volunteered with PIH in Boston. Her volunteer work with PIH expanded, and she eventually took on her current position as Project Coordinator for their programs in Mexico and Guatemala. She works with community health workers to improve access to primary care in marginalized villages. In this role, she seeks to connect grassroots efforts with the ideas and resources of PIH.

Dan has several suggestions for those interested in a career in global health:

- Learn from each patient. Patients can teach you their context. Understanding the social and cultural context will allow you to best meet people's needs. Healthcare providers who ignore their patients because they are too busy, do so at their peril.
- Remember that you are only a part of the solution. Progress depends on a number of different actors.
- Always keep reading, from pop culture to the *New England Journal of Medicine*. To do more, you must always learn more.
- Remember that people must always be at the center of what you are doing. Big ideals, such as justice and equity, must guide us; however, the world is much more complex than being guided by a sole ideal will allow for. "Many people, for love of a concept, make terrible decisions that end up hurting many others."

Lindsay also has several suggestions for students interested in global health and development:

- Assume that you do not know the answers. When working in developing countries, you will encounter new things that you do not understand. It will be tempting to ascribe your own explanations to them. Instead, talk to people and ask open-ended questions so that you may start to truly understand what you are seeing.
- You must earn people's trust. The poor may expect powerful people and institutions to make their lives harder. For example, police may harass rather than protect them. You must prove that you will be different. Keep your word, despite how challenging it may be. If you say you will raise funds or return in a week, you must follow through.

- Work to make your job obsolete. Developing countries are full of optimistic, energetic, and talented people just like you. Use your skills, perspective, and connections to help them become successful.
- Think in terms of decades. Progress takes time and perseverance. If immediate solutions existed, they would have already been put in place. Meaningful change results from incremental, creative, collaborative efforts.

DAVID PETERS

David Peters is an Associate Professor at the Johns Hopkins University Bloomberg School of Public Health. David has devoted all of his professional life to service to the poor and disadvantaged.

David is a Canadian. He was born in Winnipeg, Manitoba, and did his primary and secondary schooling in Winnipeg, as well. David's parents had a strong commitment to social justice, a concern for the poor globally, and were involved in the work of the Mennonite Central Committee (MCC). Their church supported development projects in poor countries, and David and his family knew people affiliated with the church who worked on these projects. From a young age, David saw the overseas development work that MCC was carrying out as a model for work he should do in public health and development.

With this in mind, David sought to engage in medical studies in Canada and then public health studies overseas, because Canada did not have a public health school at the time. David studied Chemistry and Religious Studies in college, receiving a BSc from the University of Manitoba in Winnipeg, where he also went to medical school. He spent half a year in medical school in Nepal and remote parts of Canada. David received his MD in 1986. David then did a 1-year medical internship at McGill University in Montreal, Quebec, that exposed him to a number of different medical fields. He also spent a month during his internship in Nepal.

In 1987 and 1988, David pursued a variety of clinical experiences as a physician in Canada, including work on The Pas, Grand Rapids, and Moose Lake Indian Reserves, and at a nursing home that was also on an Indian reservation. Looking back at those years, David says the experience was inspiring in some regards but humbling in others. On the one hand, David worked with people he considers heroes who devoted themselves to trying to enhance the health of native people. On the other hand, he realized that even good clinical care could not help people overcome the many social problems from which they suffered and that often were at the base of their medical problems, such as poor diets, alcoholism, substance abuse, and domestic violence. In addition, he found it difficult to overcome generations of institutionalized prejudice and poorly performing social programs. Most importantly, David says he learned that real change will only come in the long run when people are empowered to take charge of their own destinies.

After his work in Canada, and with a constant eye on a career in public health, David carried out a residency in General Preventive Medicine at the Johns Hopkins University School of Public Health (JHSPH) in Baltimore, Maryland, in the United States between 1988 and 1991. David was especially interested in doing a residency and graduate work in public health at either Johns Hopkins or the London School of Hygiene and Tropical Medicine, because these were the premiere places at the time for work on health and development.

While completing his residency, David continued his studies at the JHSPH, receiving a Masters of Public Health degree in 1989 and a Doctor of Public Health degree in 1993. David's research for his doctoral dissertation focused on trying to understand how Sri Lankan children could have such high rates of survival when they suffered from relatively high rates of being born underweight. David found answers to this question in the high level of female education in Sri Lanka, the focus of the health system on safe birthing practices, and the emphasis the health system placed on the care of newborns. Related to these and good breastfeeding practices, Sri Lankan children who were born underweight often had "catch-up growth" that kept them on the path to proper child development.

When David finished his studies, he joined the World Bank and served as a Senior Public Health Specialist for the Africa and South Asia Regions from 1993 to 2001. He carried out this work from postings in Washington, D.C., and New Delhi, India. During this time, he was also an Associate in the Department of International Health at the JHSPH, and joined as a full-time faculty member in 2002.

From 2006 to 2008, David served as the Senior Public Health Specialist for the Human Development Network at the World Bank. In this position, David managed the Bank's efforts at assisting low- and middle-income countries in strengthening their capacity for health system reform and management, in an attempt to improve the delivery of health services and health outcomes, especially for the poor. During these years, David split his time between the Johns Hopkins University School of Public Health and the World Bank.

David left the World Bank in 2008 and is currently working at the JHSPH, where he is the Director of the Health Systems Program and Associate Chair in the Department of International Health. In this position, David oversees faculty, staff, and students involved in teaching, research, and service in the field of health systems development in low- and middle-income countries. Much of his work aims to find ways to make health systems work for the poor, such as providing financial protection, engaging the poor in policy processes, and developing new ways to deliver and regulate health care.

David has found most gratifying the efforts he undertook in a postconflict situation in Sierra Leone to help the country rebuild its health system. He is also pleased with the activities he carried out to help Ghana create a sectorwide approach to health. This included bringing together in a coherent manner the many development partners with which Ghana had been working in fragmented ways that were often at cross-purposes. David is very excited by the work he is now doing with the Future Health Systems Consortium, which is an unusual multidisciplinary effort across a number of universities to reduce poverty through innovative health and livelihood activities, such as working with informal health providers in Bangladesh, providing health insurance for the poor in China, and testing innovations in health services in Afghanistan, Uganda, and India.

David has also found work in health and development to be challenging. Some of the most important challenges he has faced include the difficulty of ensuring that effective technical interventions can be implemented successfully and in a sustained way in low-income countries. He has also found challenging the "relentless attention that one has to pay to keeping people moving in the same direction," because many institutions do not take a sufficiently long-term view of their work.

David offers the following advice for university students interested in careers in global health:

- Be humble and keep learning. There is always more to learn.
- Take every chance you can find to create positive outcomes for the poor. There is always a chance to innovate, even under the most difficult circumstances, such as in fragile states or states that are emerging from conflict.
- Keep your goals in mind at all times. Think systematically about how vulnerable people experience life and how their lives can be changed for the better. Do not look so much at the way things have always been done, or to rely on formal organizations. Rather, look increasingly to neglected, new, or different ways in which you might be able to encourage the achievement of better health for the poor.

OUK VONG VATHINY

Ouk Vong Vathiny is a Cambodian physician who is head of the Reproductive Health Association of Cambodia (RHAC) and has been at the forefront of efforts to improve reproductive health for the most vulnerable women in Cambodia. Vathiny has carried out this work despite incredible challenges in her personal and professional lives.

Vathiny has always been interested in helping women and children. As a child, her family helped support a number of orphanages, and she dreamed of one day running an orphanage herself. Vathiny was also inspired by family members who were doctors, and eventually became more interested in health.

In 1974, Vathiny began to study medicine at Faculty of Medicine in Phnom Penh, the capital of Cambodia, with the goal of improving the health of women and children. As with all Cambodian people and students, Vathiny's studies were interrupted when the Khmer Rouge, followers of the Communist Party of Kampuchea, took control of Cambodia in 1975. The Khmer Rouge controlled the country until 1979, evacuated the cities, and forced the population to work in the countryside. They also committed genocide. Like many other Cambodians during this period, Vathiny and her family endured almost 4 years of very difficult labor and starvation in the countryside, and a number of Vathiny's family members perished.

Upon returning to Phnom Penh in 1979, Vathiny and her fellow medical students spent about a year reestablishing the medical faculty and the Ministry of Health before continuing their studies. In 1986, Vathiny finally received her MD, 6 years later than she had initially planned.

From 1986 to 1989, Vathiny was Chief of the Infectious Disease Ward of the Phnom Penh Municipal Hospital. After 3 years, she switched her focus to obstetrics and gynecology and soon became the Head of Maternal Health within the Maternal and Child Health Department of the Phnom Penh Municipality. She worked in this capacity until 1994 and was responsible for overall staff training and for more specialized training in sexually transmitted diseases and HIV/AIDS counseling. She also organized mobile health teams in surrounding semi-urban areas and supervised 47 medical staff.

At the same time, Vathiny was also Director of the Toul Kork Dike Community Clinic, where she provided health services for sex workers from the local red light district at the Dike Community Clinic and Toul Kork Dispensary. HIV had begun to spread among certain populations engaging in high-risk behaviors, including sex workers. Because the government was doing little to address this public health challenge,

Vathiny and a British colleague started outreach activities for sex workers, and from there developed the clinic.

Although the new clinic was acclaimed by a number of organizations, the Phnom Penh governor tried to ban sex work and closed the brothels around the clinic, leading to the spread of sex workers all over the city. Vathiny decided to move from the public to the NGO sector. From 1994 to 1997, she worked with Family Planning International Assistance (FPIA), initially as a clinic physician and later as Deputy Director/Project Director. Her responsibilities with FPIA grew, and as FPIA transited into a national NGO, she became the Executive Director of the RHAC. She was thus a co-founder of RHAC in 1996.

RHAC currently has about 670 employees and 20,000 volunteers. The organization runs 18 reproductive health clinics and conducts a variety of community-based and outreach programs, especially for high-risk groups such as sex workers, men who have sex with men, and youth in schools and in the community. In addition, RHAC supports approximately a third of the government health centers in Cambodia.

Even as Vathiny has carried out this work, she has continually sought to improve her knowledge and skills. In 1998, she received a graduate certificate in Managing Health Programs in Developing Countries from the Harvard School of Public Health in the United States. In 2002, she received an MBA in Health, Population, and Nutrition in Developing Countries at the University of Keele in the United Kingdom. In 2007, she received a Diploma in Sexual and Reproductive Health and Rights from Lund University in Sweden.

Vathiny is most proud of the work that she and others did during the early 1990s to help control the initial spread of HIV/AIDS in Cambodia. Their approach focused directly on the source of the epidemic. They created programs to help sex workers protect themselves, sometimes even risking their own lives as they did so. For example, they developed the government clinic for sex workers, despite government opposition, and they were threatened at gunpoint by some brothel owners on more than one occasion.

Vathiny offers the following advice for university students interested in global health:

- Focus on vulnerable populations within your field of interest. If you do not help them, who else will?
- Look for role models—women and men—who have both compassion and knowledge.
- Always remember the relationships among health, nutrition, hunger, poverty reduction, and development. Society needs to address all these links. We are all responsible for the well-being of our society.

- Some things must be changed, such as stigmas, taboos, and violations of people's rights. We must fight for these changes.
- We hope for a world with equity in health care and well-being. In this endeavor, we must especially focus on women and children. Women are the backbone of society. Perhaps it is a dream, but if everyone is involved, it may come true.

ABDO YAZBECK

Abdo Yazbeck is a health economist. He has spent much of his professional life developing innovative strategies for health sector reform to reduce health inequality in low- and middle-income countries.

Abdo always admired those who possess both a social conscience and a diligent work ethic. He remembers being particularly inspired by Mother Teresa's work in Kolkota, India. However, his interest in health and development originated from his experiences growing up during a time of civil conflict.

Abdo was born in Beirut, Lebanon. The Lebanese Civil War began in 1974, when he was 12 years old, and continued long after he left Lebanon to attend graduate school in the United States. Because of the war, Abdo spent part of his early teenage years in Cairo, Egypt, where he first saw extreme poverty and inequality. He recalls seeing very poor children beg for money and depend on scavenging through trash dumps to survive.

When he returned to Lebanon, Abdo volunteered at the American University Hospital in Beirut and helped distribute food to Palestinian refugees in the area. Through these experiences, he learned that there are ways to improve the health of the poor and marginalized without being a physician.

In 1984, Abdo received a BA in economics from the American University of Beirut. He then moved to the United States for graduate studies in economics at Rice University in Houston, Texas. He received an MA in economics in 1988 and a PhD in economics in 1991. His dissertation research focused on health, labor, and applied microeconomics.

While studying in Texas, Abdo conducted research on aging and the relationship between labor choices and health outcomes, funded by the National Institute on Aging. He then began exploring racial and socioeconomic inequality in health, which sparked his lifelong professional focus on health inequality.

In 1987, Abdo participated in a Population, Health, and Nutrition summer internship at the World Bank. He analyzed data related to family size, children's education, and family labor supply. Abdo was inspired to pursue a career in economic development and poverty reduction by what he saw as the high level of motivation and dedication of the employees at the World Bank.

In the early 1990s, after 2 years lecturing in the Department of Economics at Texas A&M University, Abdo began to solidify his work as a health economist. In 1992, he worked as a Health Economist for the World Bank, helping to prepare background papers for the 1993 World Development Report, which became an extremely important work globally. From 1993 to 1996, Abdo worked with the consulting firm Abt Associates as a Health Economist and Research Manager. In this capacity, he helped develop training programs and provided technical assistance for a variety of health projects in low- and middle-income countries.

Abdo rejoined the World Bank in 1996. From then to 2002, Abdo was a Senior Health Economist for the South Asia Human Development Unit. Abdo's work on South Asia focused on supporting health sector projects and analysis in Bangladesh, India, the Maldives, and Sri Lanka. The work emphasized using economic tools to analyze the health sector and design health policies. He also provided technical and operational assistance to countries with which he was working. From 2002 to 2008, he was Program Manager and Lead Health Economist for the Health and AIDS Program in the World Bank Institute, a kind of "World Bank university." In this role, he helped develop training programs related to health sector reform, health financing, health inequality, and HIV/AIDS, among other things. Some of the more important publications in which Abdo participated include the World Bank's *World Development Report 1993: Investing in Health*, *Reaching the Poor with Health Nutrition and Population Services* (2005), and *Attacking Inequality in Health* (2009).

Since 2008, Abdo has been a Health Sector Manager for Europe and Central Asia at the World Bank. In this position, he manages World Bank efforts to strengthen the health sectors of project countries in three main areas: the creation of effective core public health functions; work toward equitable, efficient, and high quality health services; and the integration of the health sector into overall development.

Abdo is most proud of his efforts that have focused on health inequality in low- and middle-income countries. At the time that he and others started this work, inequality was seen as the poverty of low-income countries compared to higher-income countries. It was generally assumed that all people in poor countries were poor. There was insufficient attention to inequality within countries. Abdo worked with the Reaching the Poor Program to build knowledge of inequality in health outcomes and access to health services, in addition to developing ways to address these issues.

When asked what advice he would offer to current university students interested in global health, Abdo offered the following points:

- Global health and development work is both immensely rewarding and incredibly frustrating. "This will require hard work, persistence, and the ability to manage failures and keep your bearing."
- Gain skills in a specific field, such as public health, medicine, economics, finance, business, or law. This will allow you to more effectively improve global health.
- "Advocacy is a wonderful thing if it is based on evidence and not just emotions. Advocacy without knowledge is potentially destructive and wasteful."

MAIN MESSAGES

A diverse set of people work in a wide array of global health activities. Many of these people became interested in global health at a young age and oriented their studies and professional experiences around their interest in global health. Others, however, came to global health at a later stage in their career. Many of the people you read about in this chapter had "transformative experiences" that set the foundation for their global health efforts. Some of these were by design, such as those who sought early in their professional life to work in a low-income country. Some others were encouraged to become active in global health by the people with whom they studied or worked, or by falling ill themselves. Some were moved by living in areas of political crisis or among marginalized people.

A number of themes emerge consistently from these profiles:

- Focus on the disadvantaged, the poor, and the marginalized. Social justice and fairness are central to work on global health.
- Be open to learning.
- Seek mentors from whom you can learn.
- Learn from all with whom you work.
- Develop role models, after whom you may want to model parts of your own work.
- Think big. Don't accept things the way they are. Ask instead what it will take to make your vision a reality.
- Work with others in coalitions and alliances. The power of many is greater than the power of one.
- If possible, find a platform from which you can engage in global health efforts, that you can make a home, and to which you can return regularly.

Study Questions

1. What common themes do you see in the lives of the people in the profiles?

2. What different professions are well suited to working in global health?

3. What skills are most valuable in global health work?

4. What personal traits lend themselves well to a career in global health?

Glossary

Abortion	Premature expulsion or loss of embryo, which may be induced or spontaneous
Anemia	Low level of hemoglobin in the blood
Asphyxsia	A condition of severely deficient supply of oxygen to the body
Body mass index	Body weight in kilograms divided by height in meters squared
Cardiovascular disease	A disease of the heart or blood vessels
Case fatality rate	The proportion of cases of a specified condition that is fatal within a specified period of time
Cataract	A clouding of the lens of the eye
Cesarean delivery (section)	The delivery of a fetus by surgical incision through the abdominal wall and uterus
Communicable diseases	Illnesses that are caused by a particular infectious agent and that spread directly or indirectly from people to people, from animals to animals, from animals to people, or from people to animals
Control	Reduction of disease incidence, prevalence, morbidity, or mortality to a locally acceptable level
Cost-effectiveness analysis	In health, a tool for comparing the relative cost of two or more investments with the amount of health that can be purchased with those investments
Culture	A set of rules or standards shared by members of a society, which when acted upon by the members, produce behavior that falls within a range of variation that members consider proper and acceptable
Demographic transition	The shift from high fertility and high mortality to low fertility and low mortality
Diabetes	Medical illness caused by too little insulin or poor response to insulin
Diarrhea	A condition in which the sufferer has frequent and watery or loose bowel movements
Disability	The temporary or long-term reduction in a person's capacity to function

Disability adjusted life year	A composite measure of premature deaths and losses due to illnesses and disabilities in a population
Drug resistance	The extent to which infectious and parasitic agents develop an ability to resist drug treatment
Eclampsia	A serious, life-threatening condition in late pregnancy in which very high blood pressure can cause a woman to have seizures
Elimination	Reduction of case transmission to a predetermined very low level
Epidemiologic transition	A shift in the pattern of disease from largely communicable diseases to noncommunicable diseases
Eradication	Termination of all transmission of infection by extermination of the infectious agent through surveillance or containment
Family planning	The conscious effort of couples to regulate the number and spacing of births through artificial and natural methods of contraception; connotes conception control to avoid pregnancy and abortion, but also includes efforts of couples to induce pregnancy
Female genital mutilation (also called female circumcision and female genital cutting)	A collective term for various traditional practices that are all related to the cutting of the female genital organs; four different forms and grades are usually distinguished
Gestational diabetes	Diabetes that develops during pregnancy because of improper regulation of blood sugar; it usually goes away after delivery, but can increase the woman's risk of developing type II diabetes later
Global health	Health problems, issues, and concerns that transcend national boundaries and may best be addressed by cooperative actions
Gross domestic product	The total market value of all the goods and services produced within a country during a specified period of time
Gross national product	A measure of the incomes of residents of a country, including income they receive from abroad but subtracting similar payments made to those abroad
Health-adjusted life expectancy	A composite health indicator that measures the equivalent number of years in full health that a newborn can expect to live, based on current rates of ill health and mortality
Health system	The combination of resources, organization, and management that culminate in the delivery of health services to the population
Hemorrhage (related to pregnancy)	Significant and uncontrolled loss of blood, either internally or externally from the body. Antepartum (prenatal) hemorrhage occurs after the 20th week of gestation but before delivery of the baby; postpartum hemorrhage is the loss of 500 ml or more of blood from the genital tract after delivery of the baby; primary postpartum hemorrhage occurs in the first 24 hours after delivery
Hookworm	A parasite that lives in the small intestine of its host, which may be a mammal such as a dog, cat, or human
Hypertension	High blood pressure
Incidence rate	The rate at which new cases of a disease occur in a population

Infant mortality rate	The number of deaths of infants under age 1 per 1000 live births in a given year
Injury	The result of an act that damages, harms, or hurts; unintentional or intentional damage to the body resulting from acute exposure to thermal, mechanical, electrical, or chemical energy or from the absence of such essentials as heat or oxygen
Life expectancy at birth	The average number of years a newborn baby could expect to live if current mortality trends were to continue for the rest of the newborn's life
Low birthweight	Birthweight less than 2500 grams
Malaria	A disease of humans caused by blood parasites of the species *Plasmodium falciparum*, *vivax*, *ovale*, or *malariae* and transmitted by anopheline mosquitoes
Maternal death	The death of a woman while pregnant, during delivery, or within 42 days of delivery, irrespective of the duration and the site of pregnancy; the cause of death is always related to or aggravated by the pregnancy or its management; does not include accidental or incidental causes
Maternal mortality ratio	The number of women who die as a result of pregnancy and childbirth complications per 100,000 live births in a given year
Measles	A highly communicable disease characterized by fever, general malaise, sneezing, nasal congestion, a brassy cough, conjunctivitis, and an eruption over the entire body, caused by the rubeola virus
Morbidity	Illness
Mortality	Death
Neonatal mortality rate	Number of deaths to infants under 28 days of age in a given year per 1000 live births in that year
Neonatal tetanus	A bacterial infection usually contracted by a puncture wound with a dirty object
Noncommunicable disease	Illnesses that are not spread by any infectious agent
Nongovernmental organization	A nonprofit group or association organized outside of institutionalized political structures to realize particular social objectives, such as environmental protection, or serve particular constituencies, such as indigenous peoples
Obesity	Excessive body fat content
Obstetric fistula	An injury in the birth canal that allows leakage from the bladder or rectum into the vagina, leaving a woman permanently incontinent, often leading to isolation and exclusion from the family and community
Overweight	Excess weight relative to height
Parasite	An animal or vegetable organism that lives on or in another and derives its nourishment therefrom
Pneumonia	An inflammation, usually caused by infection, involving the alveoli of the lungs
Poliomyelitis (polio)	Infantile paralysis, a viral paralytic disease

Preeclampsia (previously called toxemia)	A hypertensive disorder of pregnancy said to exist when a pregnant woman with gestational hypertension develops proteinuria. Originally, edema was considered part of the syndrome of preeclampsia, but presently the former two symptoms are sufficient for a diagnosis of preeclampsia
Prevalence	The number of people suffering from a certain condition over a specific time period; *prevalence rate* is the share of the population, which is being measured, who have the condition
Public health	The science and art of preventing disease; prolonging life; and promoting physical health and mental health and efficiency through organized community efforts toward a sanitary environment, control of community infections, education in hygiene, and the development of social machinery to ensure capacity in the community to maintain health
Push mechanism	Interventions that assure a future return in the event that a product is produced
Pull mechanism	Interventions that reduce the risks and costs of investments
Risk factor	An aspect or personal behavior or lifestyle, an environmental exposure, or an inborn or inherited characteristic that, on the basis of epidemiologic evidence, is known to be associated with health-related conditions
Sepsis	Infection in the blood
Sex-selective abortion	The practice of aborting a fetus after a determination, usually by ultrasound but also rarely by amniocentesis or another procedure, that the fetus is an undesired sex, typically female
Sexually transmitted infections (STIs)	Diseases, also known as sexually transmitted diseases (STDs), that are commonly transmitted between partners through some form of sexual activity, most commonly vaginal intercourse, oral sex, or anal sex
Society	A group of people who occupy a specific locality and share the same cultural traditions
Stroke	Temporary or permanent loss of the blood supply to the brain
Stunting	Failure to reach linear growth potential because of inadequate nutrition or poor health; two z-scores below the international reference
Under-5 child mortality rate	The annual number of deaths in children under 5 years, expressed as a rate per 1000 live births, averaged over the previous 5 years
Undernutrition	Low weight-for-age; two z-scores below the international reference for weight-for-age
Unintentional injury	That subset of injuries for which there is no evidence of predetermined intent
Uterine prolapse	A condition in which the uterus protrudes into, and sometimes out of, the vagina
Wasting	Weight, measured in kilograms, divided by height in meters squared that is two z-scores below the international reference

Index